Treatises on the Trinity

Edited by Anthony Uyl

Devoted Publishing

Woodstock, Ontario, Canada 2018

Treatises on the Trinity
Edited by Anthony Uyl

By:
Anicius Manlius Torquatus Severinus Boethius(480-524)
Jonathan Edwards (1703-1758)
John Owen (1616-1683)

What kind of philosophies do you have?
Let us know!

Contact us at: devotedpub@hotmail.com
Visit our shop on Facebook: Devoted Publishing

Published in Woodstock, Ontario, Canada 2018.

For bulk educational rates, please contact us at the above email address.

ISBN: 978-1-77356-230-8

Table of Contents

The Trinity is One God Not Three Gods
By Boethius

A Treatise by Anicius Manlius Severinus Boethius Most Honourable, of the Illustrious Order of Ex-Consuls, Patrician to His Father-in-Law, Quintus Aurelius Memmius Symmachus Most Honourable, of the Illustrious Order of Ex-Consuls, Patrician

NOTE ON THE TEXT

IN preparing the text of the Consolatio I have used the apparatus in Peiper's edition (Teubner, 1871), since his reports, as I know in the case of the Tegernseensis, are generally accurate and complete; I have depended also on my own collations or excerpts from various of the important manuscripts, nearly all of which I have at least examined, and I have also followed, not always but usually, the opinions of Engelbrecht in his admirable article, Die Consolatio Philosophiae des Boethius in the Sitzungsberichte of the Vienna Academy, cxliv. (1902) 1-60. The present text, then, has been constructed from only part of the material with which an editor should reckon, though the reader may at least assume that every reading in the text has, unless otherwise stated, the authority of some manuscript of the ninth or tenth century; in certain orthographical details, evidence from the text of the Opuscula Sacra has been used without special mention of this fact. We look to August Engelbrecht for the first critical edition of the Consolatio at, we hope, no distant date.

The text of the Opuscula Sacra is based on my own collations of all the important manuscripts of these works. An edition with complete apparatus criticis will be ready before long for the Vienna corpis Scriptorum Ecclesiasticorum Latinorum. The history of the text of the Opuscula Sacra, as I shall attempt to show elsewhere, is intimately connected with that of the Consolatio.

E. K. R.

INTRODUCTION

ANICIUS MANLIUS SEVERINUS BOETHIUS, of the famous Praenestine family of the Anicii, was born about 480 A.D. in Rome. His father was an ex-consul; he himself was consul under Theodoric the Ostrogoth in 510, and his two sons, children of a great granddaughter of the renowned Q. Aurelius Symmachus, were joint consuls in 522. His public career was splendid and honourable, as befitted a man of his race, attainments, and character. But he fell under the displeasure of Theodoric, and was charged with conspiring to deliver Rome from his rule, and with corresponding treasonably to this end with Justin, Emperor of the East. He was thrown into prison at Pavia, where he wrote the Consolation of Philosophy, and he was as brutally put to death in 524. His brief and busy life was marked by great literary achievement. His learning was vast, his industry untiring, his object unattainable--nothing less than the transmission to his countrymen of all the works of Plato and Aristotle, and the reconciliation of their apparently divergent views. To form the idea was a silent judgment on the learning of his day; to realize it was more than one man could accomplish; but Boethius accomplished much. He translated the E of Porphyry, and the whole of Aristotle's Organon. He wrote a double commentary on the E, and commentaries on the Categories and the De Interpretatione of Aristotle, and on the Topica of Cicero. He also composed original treatises on the categorical and hypothetical syllogism, on Division and on Topical Differences. He adapted the arithmetic of Nicomachus, and his textbook on music, founded on various Greek authorities, was in use at Oxford and Cambridge until modern times. His five theological Tractates are here, together with the Consolation of Philosophy to speak for themselves.

Boethius was the last of the Roman philosophers and the first of the scholastic theologians. The present volume serves to prove the truth of both these assertions.

The Consolation of Philosophy is indeed, as Gibbon called it, "a golden volume, not unworthy of the leisure of Plato or of Tully." To belittle its originality and sincerity, as is sometimes done, with view to saving the Christianity of the writer, is to misunderstand his mind and his method. The Consolatio is not, as has been maintained, a mere patchwork of translations from Aristotle and the Neoplatonists. Rather it is the supreme essay of one who throughout his life had found his highest solace in the dry light of reason. His chief source of refreshment, in the dungeon to which his beloved library had not accompanied him, was a memory well stocked with the poetry and thought of former days. The development of the argument is anything but Neoplatonic; it is all his own.

And if the Consolation of Philosophy admits Boethius to the company of Cicero or even of Plato, the theological Tractates mark him as the forerunner of St. Thomas. It was the habit of a former generation to regard Boethius as an eclectic, the transmitter of a distorted Aristotelianism, a pagan, or at best a luke-warm Christian, who at the end cast off the faith which he had worn in times of peace, and wrapped himself in the philosophic cloak which properly belonged to him. The authenticity of the Tractates was freely denied. We know better now. The discovery by Alfred Holder, and the illuminating discussion by Hermann Usener, [1] of a fragment of Cassiodorus are sufficient confirmation of the manuscript tradition, apart from the work of scholars who have sought to justify that tradition from internal evidence. In that fragment Cassiodorus definitely ascribes to his friend Boethius "a book on the Trinity, some dogmatic chapters, and a book against Nestorius." [2] Boethius was without doubt a Christian, a Doctor and perhaps a martyr. Nor is it necessary to think that, when in prison, he put away his faith. If it is asked why the Consolation of Philosophy contains no conscious or direct reference to the doctrines which are traced in the Tractates with so sure a hand, and is, at most, not out of harmony with Christianity, the answer is simple. In the Consolation he is writing philosophy; in the Tractates he is writing theology. He observes what Pascal calls the orders of things. Philosophy belongs to one order, theology to another. They have different objects. The object of philosophy is to understand and explain the nature of the world around us; the object of theology is to understand and explain doctrines delivered by divine revelation. The scholastics recognized the distinction, [3] and the corresponding difference in the function of Faith and Reason. Their final aim was to co-ordinate the two but this was not possible before the thirteenth century. Meanwhile Boethius helps to prepare the way. In the Consolation he gives Reason her range and suffers her, unaided, to vindicate the ways of Providence. In the Tractates Reason is called in to give to the claims of Faith the support which it does not really lack.[4] Reason, however, has still a right to be heard. The distinction between fides and ratio is proclaimed in the first two Tractates . In the second especially it is drawn with a clearness worthy of St. Thomas himself; and there is, of course the implication that the higher authority resides with fides. But the treatment is philosophical and extremely bold. Boethius comes back to the question of the substantiality of the divine Persons which he has discussed in Tr. I. from a fresh point of view. Once more he decides that the Persons are predicated relatively; even Trinity, he concludes, is not predicated substantially of deity. Does this square with catholic doctrine? It is possible to hear a note of challenge in his words to John the Deacon, fidem si poterit rationemque coniunge. Philosophy states the problem in unequivocal terms. Theology is required to say whether they commend themselves.

One object of the scholastics, anterior to the final con-ordination of the two sciences, was to harmonize and codify all the answers to all the questions that philosophy raises. The ambition of Boethius was not so soaring, but it was sufficiently bold. He set out, first to translate, and then to reconcile, Plato and Aristotle; to go behind all the other systems, even the latest and the most in vogue, back to the two great masters, and to show that they have the truth, and are in substantial accord. So St. Thomas himself, if he cannot reconcile the teaching of Plato and Aristotle, at least desires to correct the one by the other, to discover what truth is common to both, and to show its correspondence with Christian doctrine. It is reasonable to conjecture that Boethius, if he had lived, might have attempted something of the kind. Were he alive today, he might feel more in tune with the best of the pagans than with most contemporary philosophic thought.

In yet one more respect Boethius belongs to the company of the schoolmen. He not only put into circulation many precious philosophical notions, served as channel through which various works of Aristotle passed into the schools, and handed down to them a definite Aristotelian method for approaching the problem of faith; he also supplied material for that classification of the various sciences which is an essential accompaniment of every philosophical movement, and of which the Middle Ages felt the value.[5] The uniform distribution into natural sciences, mathematics and theology which he recommends may be traced in the work of various teachers up to the thirteenth century, when it is finally accepted and defended by St. Thomas in his commentary on the De Trinitate.

A seventeenth-century translation of the consolatio Philosophiae is here presented with such alterations as are demanded by a better text, and the requirements of modern scholarship. There was, indeed not much to do, for the rendering is most exact. This in a translation of that date is not a little remarkable. We look for fine English and poetry in an Elizabethan; but we do not often get from him such loyalty to the original as is here displayed. Of the author "I. T." nothing is known. He may have been John Thorie, a Fleming born in London in 1568, and a B.A. of Christ Church, 1586. Thorie "was a person well skilled in certain tongues, and a noted poet of his times " (Wood, Athenae Oxon ed. Bliss, i. 624), but his known translations are apparently all from the Spanish.

Our translator dedicates his "Five books on Philosophical Comfort" to the Dowager Countes of Dorset, widow of Thomas Sackville, who was part author of A Mirror for Magistrates and Gorboduc and who, we learn from I. T.'s preface, meditated similar work. I. T. does not unduly flatter h patroness, and he tells her plainly that she will not understand the philosophy of the book, though the theological and practical parts may be within her scope.

The Opuscucla Sacra have never before, to our knowledge, been translated. In reading and rendering them we have been greatly helped by two mediaeval commentaries: one by John the Scot (edited by E. K. Rand in Traube's Quellen und Untersuchungen, vol. i. Pt. 2, Munich, 1906); the other by Gilbert de la Porree (printed in Migne, P.L. lxiv. We also desire to record our indebtedness in many points of scholarship and philosophy to Mr. E. Thomas of Emmanuel College.

H.F.V.

E.K.R.

Footnotes:

1. Anecdoton Holderi, Leipzig, 1877.

2. Scripsil librum de sancta trinitate et capita quaedam dogmatica et librum contra Nestorium. On the question of the genuineness of Tr. IV. De fide catholica see note ad loc.

3. Cp. H. de Wulf, Histoire de la Philosophie medieval (Louvain and Paris 1915), p. 332.

4. See below, De Trin. vi. ad fin.

5. Cp. L. Baur, Gundissalinus: de divisione, Munster, 1905.

Main Treatise

I HAVE long pondered this problem with such mind as I have and all the light that God has lent me. Now, having set it forth in logical order and cast it into literary form, I venture to submit it to your judgment, for which I care as much as for the results of my own research. You will readily understand what I feel whenever I try to write down what I think if you consider the difficulty of the topic and the fact that I discuss it only with the few--I may say with no one but yourself. It is indeed no desire for fame or empty popular applause that prompts my pen; if there be any external reward, we may not look for more warmth in the Verdict than the subject itself arouses. For, a part from yourself, wherever I turn my eyes, they fall on either the apathy of the dullard or the jealousy of the shrewd, and a man who casts his thoughts before the common herd--I will not say to consider but to trample under foot, would seem to bring discredit on the study of divinity. So I purposely use brevity and wrap up the ideas I draw from the deep questionings of philosophy in new and unaccustomed words which speak only to you and to myself, that is, if you deign to look at them. The rest of the world I simply disregard: they cannot understand, and therefore do not deserve to read. We should not of course press our inquiry further than man's wit and reason are allowed to climb the height of heavenly knowledge. [6] In all the liberal arts some limit is set beyond which reason may not reach. Medicine, for instance, does not always bring health to the sick, though the doctor will not be to blame if he has left nothing undone which he ought to do. So with the other arts. In the present case the very difficulty of the quest claims a lenient judgment. You must however examine whether the seeds sown in my mind by St. Augustine's writings [7] have borne fruit. And now let us begin our inquiry.

I.

There are many who claim as theirs the dignity of the Christian religion; but that form of faith is valid and only valid which, both on account of the universal character of the rules and doctrines affirming its authority, and because the worship in which they are expressed has spread throughout the world, is called catholic or universal. The belief of this religion concerning the Unity of the Trinity is as follows: the Father is God, the Son is God, the Holy Spirit is God. Therefore Father, Son, and Holy Spirit are one God, not three Gods. The cause of this union is absence of difference: [8] difference cannot be avoided by those who add to or take from the Unity, as for instance the Arians, who, by graduating the Trinity according to merit, break it up and convert it to Plurality. For the essence of plurality is otherness; apart from otherness plurality is unintelligible. In fact, the difference between three or more things lies in genus or species or number. Difference is the necessary correlative of sameness. Sameness is predicated in three ways: By genus; e.g. a man and a horse, because of their common genus, animal. By species; e.g. Cato and

Cicero, because of their common species, man. By number; e.g. Tully and Cicero, because they are one and the same man. Similarly, difference is expressed by genus, species, and number. Now numerical difference is caused by variety of accidents; three men differ neither by genus nor species but by their accidents, for if we mentally remove from them all other accidents, [9] still each one occupies a different place which cannot possibly be regarded as the same for each, since two bodies cannot occupy the same place, and place is an accident. Wherefore it is because men are plural by their accidents that they are plural in number.

II.

We will now begin a careful consideration of each several point, as far as they can be grasped and understood; for it has been wisely said, [10] in my opinion, that it is a scholar's duty to study the real nature of anything before he formulates his belief about it.

Speculative Science may be divided into three kinds: [11] Physics, Mathematics, and Theology. Physics deals with motion and is not abstract or separable (i.e.); for it is concerned with the forms of bodies together with their constituent matter, which forms cannot be separated in reality from their bodies. [12] As the bodies are in motion--the earth, for instance, tending downwards, and fire tending upwards, form takes on the movement of the particular thing to which it is annexed.

Mathematics does not deal with motion and is not abstract, for it investigates forms of bodies apart from matter, and therefore apart from movement, which forms, however, being connected with matter cannot be really separated from bodies.

Theology does not deal with motion and is abstract and separable, for time Divine Substance is without either matter or motion. In Physics, then, we are bound to use scientific, in Mathematics, systematical, in Theology, intellectual concepts; and in Theology we will not let ourselves be diverted to play with imaginations, but will simply apprehend that Form which is pure form and no image, which is very Being and the source of Being For everything owes its being to Form. Thus a statue is not a statue on account of the brass which is its matter, but on account of the form whereby the likeness of a living thing is impressed upon it: the brass itself is not brass because of the earth which is its matter, but because of its form. Likewise earth is not earth by reason of unqualified matter, [13] but by reason of dryness and weight, which are forms. So nothing is said to be because it has matter, but because it has a distinctive form. But the Divine Substance is Form without matter, and is therefore One, and is its own essence. But other things are not simply their own essences, for each thing has its being from the things of which it is composed, that is, from its parts. It is This and That, i.e. it is the totality of its parts in conjunction; it is not This or That taken apart. Earthly man, for instance, since he consists of soul and body, is soul and body, not soul or body, separately; therefore he is not his own essence. That on the other hand which does not consist of This and That, but only of This, is really its own essence, and is altogether beautiful and stable because it is not grounded in any alien element. Wherefore that is truly One in which is no number, in which nothing is present except its own essence. Nor can it become the substrate of anything, for it is pure Form, and pure Forms cannot be substrates. [14] For if humanity, like other forms, is a substrate for accidents, it does not receive accidents through the fact that it exists, but through the fact that matter is subjected to it. Humanity appears indeed to appropriate the accident which in reality belongs to the matter underlying the conception Humanity. But Form which, is without matter cannot be a substrate, and cannot have its essence in matter, else it would not be form but a reflexion. For from those forms which are outside matter come the forms which are in matter and produce bodies. We misname the entities that reside in bodies when we call them forms; they are mere images; they only resemble those forms which are not incorporate in matter. In Him, then, is no difference, no plurality arising out of difference, no multiplicity arising out of accidents, and accordingly no number.

III.

Now God differs from God in no respect for there cannot lie divine essences distinguished either by accidents or by substantial differences belonging to a substrate. But where there is no difference, there is no sort of plurality and accordingly no number; here, therefore, is unity alone. For whereas we say God thrice when we name the Father, Son, and Holy Spirit, these three unities do not produce a plurality of number in their own essences, if we think of what we count instead of what we count with. For in the case of abstract number a repetition of single items does produce plurality; but in the case of concrete number the repetition and plural use of single items does not by any means produce numerical difference in the objects counted. There are as a fact two kinds of number. There is the number with which we count (abstract) and the number inherent in the things counted (concrete). "One" is a thing--the thing counted. Unity is that by which oneness is denoted. Again " two "belongs to the class of things as men or stones; but not so duality; duality is merely that whereby two men or two stones are denoted; and so on. Therefore a repetition of unities [15] produces plurality when it is a question of abstract, but not when it is a question of concrete things, as, for example, if I say of one and the same thing, "one sword, one brand, one blade." [16] It is easy to see that each of these names denotes a sword; I am not numbering unities but simply repeating one thing, and in saying "sword, brand, blade," I reiterate the one thing and do not enumerate several different things any more than I produce three suns instead of merely mentioning one thing thrice when I say "Sun, Sun, Sun."

So then if God be predicated thrice of Father, Sun, and Holy Spirit, the threefold predication does not result in plural number. The risk of that, as has been said, attends only on those who distinguish Them according to merit. But Catholic Christians, allowing no difference of merit in God, assuming Him to be Pure Form and believing Him to he nothing else than His own essence, rightly regard the statement "the Father is God, the Son is God the Holy Spirit is God, and this Trinity is one God," not as an enumeration of different things but as a reiteration of one and the same thing, like the statement, "blade and brand are one sword" or "sun, sun, and sun are one sun."

Let this be enough for the present to establish my meaning and to show that not every repetition of units produces number and plurality. Still in saying "Father, Son, and Holy Spirit," we are not using Synonymous terms. "Brand

and blade " are the same and identical, but

"Father, Son, and Holy Spirit" though the same, are not identical. This point deserves a moment's consideration. When they ask, "Is the Father the same as the Son?" Catholics answer "No." "Is the One the same as the Other?" The answer is in the negative. There is not, therefore, complete indifference between Them; and so number does come in--number which we explained was the result of diversity of substrates. We will briefly debate this point when, we have done examining how particular predicates can be applied to God.

IV.

There are in all ten categories which can be universally predicated of things, namely, Substance, Quality, Quantity, Relation, Place, Time, Condition, Situation, Activity, Passivity. Their meaning is determined by the contingent subject; for some of them denote real substantive attributes of created things, others belong to the class of accidental attributes. But when these categories are applied to God they change their meaning entirely. Relation, for instance, cannot be predicated at all of God; for substance in Him is not really substantial but super-substantial. So with quality and the other possible attributes, of which we must add examples for the sake of clearness.

When we say God, we seem to denote a substance; but it is a substance that is supersubstantial. When we say of Him, "He is just," we mention a quality, not an accidental quality--rather a substantial and, in fact, a supersubstantial quality. [17] For God is not one thing because He is, and another thing because He is just; with Him to be just and to be God are one and the same. So when we say, "He is great or the greatest, we seem to predicate quantity, but it is a quantity similar to this substance which we have declared to be supersubstantial; for with Him to be great and to be God are all one. Again, concerning His Form, we have already shown that He is Form, and truly One without Plurality. The categories we have mentioned are such that they give to the thing to which they are applied the character which they express; in created things they express divided being, in God, conjoined and united being--in the following manner. When we name a substance, as man or God, it seems as though that of which the predication is made were itself substance, as man or God is substance. But there is a difference: since man is not simply and entirely man, and therefore is not substance after all. For what man is he owes to other things which are not man. But God is simply and entirely God, for He is nothing else than what He is, and therefore is, through simple existence, God. Again we apply just, a quality, as though it were that of which it is predicated; that is, if we say "a just man or just God," we assert that man or God is just. But there is a difference, for man is one thing, and a just man is another thing. But God is justice itself. So a man or God is said to be great, and it would appear that man is substantially great or that God is substantially great. But man is merely great; God is greatness.

The remaining categories are not predicable of God nor yet of created things. [18] For place is predicated of man or of God--a man is in the market-place; God is everywhere--but in neither case is the predicate identical with the object of predication. To say "A man is in the market" is quite a different thing from saying "he is white or long," or, so to speak, encompassed and determined by some property which enables him to be described in terms of his substance;

this predicate of place simply declares how far his substance is given a particular setting amid other things.

It is otherwise, of course, with God. "He is everywhere" does not mean that He is in every place, for He cannot be in any place at all--but that every place is present to Him for Him to occupy, although He Himself can be received by no place, and therefore He cannot anywhere be in a place, since He is everywhere but in no place. It is the same with the category of time, as, "A man came yesterday; God is ever." Here again the predicate of "coming yesterday" denotes not something substantial, but something happening in terms of time. But the expression "God is ever" denotes a single Present, summing up His continual presence in all the past, in all the present --however that term be used--and in all the future. Philosophers say that "ever" may be applied to the life of the heavens and other immortal bodies. But as applied to God it has a different meaning. He is ever, because "ever" is with Him a term of present time, and there is this great difference between "now," which is our present, and the divine present. Our present connotes changing time and sempiternity; God's present, unmoved, and immoveable, connotes eternity. Add semper to eternity and you get the constant, incessant and thereby perpetual course of our present time, that is to say, sempiternity. [19]

It is just the same with the categories of condition and activity. For example, we say "A man runs, clothed," "God rules, possessing all things." Here again nothing substantial is asserted of either subject; in fact all the categories we have hitherto named arise from what lies outside substance, and all of them, so to speak, refer to something other than substance. The difference between the categories is easily seen by an example. Thus, the terms "man" and "God" refer to the substance in virtue of which the subject is--man or God. The term "just " refers to the quality in virtue of which the subject is something, viz. just; the term "great" to the quantity in virtue of which He is something, viz, great. No other category save substance, quality, and quantity refer to the substance of the subject. If I say of one "he is in the market" or "everywhere," I am applying the category of place, which is not a category of the substance, like "just" in virtue of justice. So if I say, "he runs, He rules, he is now, He is ever," I make reference to activity or time--if indeed God's "ever" can be described as time--but not to a category of substance, like "great" in virtue of greatness.

Finally, we must not look for the categories of situation and passivity in God, for they simply are not to be found in Him.

Have I now made clear the difference between the categories? Some denote the reality of a thing; others its accidental circumstances; the former declare that a thing is something; the latter say nothing about its being anything, but simply attach to it, so to speak, something external. Those categories which describe a thing in terms of its substance may be called substantial categories; when they apply to things as subjects they are called accidents. In reference to God, who is not a subject at all, it is only possible to employ the category of substance.

V.

Let us now consider the category of relation, to which all the foregoing remarks have been preliminary; for qualities which obviously arise from the association of another term do not appear to predicate anything concerning the substance of a subject. For instance, master and slave [20] are relative terms; let us see whether either of them are predicates of substance. If you suppress the term slave, [21] you simultaneously suppress the term master. On the other hand, though you suppress the term whiteness, you do not suppress some white thing,[22] though, of course, if the particular whiteness inhere as an accident in the thing, the thing disappears as soon as you suppress the accidental quality whiteness. But in the case of master, if you suppress the term slave, the term master disappears. But slave is not an accidental quality of master, as whiteness is of a white thing; it denotes the power which the master has over the slave. Now since the power goes when the slave is removed, it is plain that power is no accident to the substance of master, but is an adventitious augmentation arising from the possession of slaves.

It cannot therefore be affirmed that a category of relation increases, decreases, or alters in any way the substance of the thing to which it is applied. The category of relation, then, has nothing to do with the substance of the subject; it simply denotes a condition of relativity, and that not necessarily to something else, but sometimes to the subject itself. For suppose a man standing. If I go up to him on my right and stand beside him, he will be left, in relation to me, not because he is left in himself, but because I have come up to him on my right. Again, if I come up to him on my left, he becomes right in relation to me, not because he is right in himself, as he may be white or long, but because he is right in virtue of my approach. What he is depends entirely on me, and not in the least on the essence of his being.

Accordingly those predicates which do not denote the essential property of a thing cannot alter, change or disturb its nature in any way. Wherefore if Father and Son are predicates of relation, and, as we have said, have no other difference but that of relation, and if relation is not asserted of its subject as though it were time subject itself and its substantial quality, it will effect no real difference in its subject, but, in a phrase which aims at interpreting what we can hardly understand, a difference of persons. For it is a canon of absolute truth that distinctions in incorporeal things are established by differences and not by spatial separation. It cannot be said that God became Father by the addition to His substance of some accident; for he never began to be Father, since the begetting of the Son belongs to His very substance; however, time predicate father, as such, is relative. And if we bear in mind all the propositions made God in the previous discussion, we shall admit that God the Son proceeded from God the Father, and the Holy Ghost from both, and that They cannot possibly be spatially different, since They are incorporeal. But since the Father is God, the Son is God, and the Holy Spirit is God, and since there are in God no points of difference distinguishing Him from God, He differs from none of the Others. But where there are no differences there is no plurality; where is no plurality there is Unity. Again, nothing but God can be begotten of God, and lastly, in concrete enumerations the repetition of units does not produce plurality. Thus the Unity of the Three is suitably established.

VI.

But since no relation can be affirmed of one subject alone, inasmuch as a predicate wanting relation is a predicate of substance, the manifoldness of the category of relation, Trinity is secured through the category of relation, and the Unity is maintained through the fact that there is no difference of substance, or operation, or generally of any substantial predicate. So then, the divine substance preserves the Unity, the divine relations bring about the Trinity. Hence only terms belonging to relation may be applied singly to Each. For the Father is not the same as the Son, nor is either of Them the same as the Holy Spirit. Yet Father, Son, and Holy Spirit are each the same God, the same in justice, in goodness, in greatness, and in everything that can he predicated of substance. One must not forget that predicates of relativity do not always involve relation to something other than the subject, as slave involves master, where the two terms are different. For equals are equal, like are like, identicals are identical, each with other, and the relation of Father to Son, and of both to Holy Spirit is a relation of identicals. A relation of this kind is not to be found in created things, but that is because of the difference which we know attaches to transient objects. We must not in speaking of God let imagination lead us astray; we must let the Faculty of pure Knowledge lift us up and teach us to know all things as far as they may be known. [23]

I have now finished the investigation which I proposed. The exactness of my reasoning awaits the standard of your judgment; your authority will pronounce whether I have seen a straight path to the goal. If, God helping me, I have furnished some support in argument to an article which stands by itself on the firm foundation of Faith, I shall render joyous praise for the finished work to Him from whom the invitation comes. But if human nature has failed to reach beyond its limits, whatever is lost through my infirmity must be made good by my intention.

Footnotes:

6. Cf. The discussion of human ratio and divine intellegetia in Cons. v. pr. 4 and 5.

7. e.g. Aug. De Trin.

8. The terms differentia, numerus, species, are used expertly, as would be expected of the author of the In Isag. Porph. Commenta. See S. Brandt's edition of that work (in the Vienna Corpus, 1906), s.v. differencia, etc.

.9. This method of mental abstraction is employed more elaborately in Tr. iii. (vide infra, p. 44) and in Cons. v. pr. 4, where the notion of divine foreknowledge is abstracted in imagination.

10. By Cicero (Tusc. v. 7. 19).

11. Cf. the similar division of philosophy in Isag. Porph. ed. Brandt, pp 7 ff.

12. Sb. Though they may be separated in thought.

13. of Aristotle. Cf. (Alexander Aphrod. De Anima, 17. 17); (id. De anima libri mantissa, 124. 77).

14. This is Realism. Cf. "Sed si rerum ueritatem atque integritatem perpendas, non est dubium quin uere sint. Nam cum res omnes quae uere sunt sine his quinque (i.e. genus species differentia propria accidentia) esse non possint, has ipsas quinque res uere intellectas esse non dubites".

Isag. In Porph. ed. pr. i. (M. P.L. lxiv. Col. 19, Brandt, pp. 26 ff.). The two passages show that Boethius is definitly commited to the Realistic position, although in his Comment. In Porphyr. A se translatum he holds the scales between Plato and Aristotle, "quorum diiudicare sententias aptum esse non duxi" (cp. Haureau, Hist. De la philosophie scolastique, i. 120). As a fact in the Comment. in Porph. he merely postpones the question, which in the De Trin. he settles, Boethius was ridiculed in the Middle Ages for his caution.

15. e.g. if I say "one, one, one," I enounce three unities.

16. The same words are used to illustrate the same matter in the Comment. in Arist. 2nd ed. (Meiser) 56. 12.

17. Gilbert de la Porree in his commentary on the De Trin. Makes Boethius's meaning clear. "Quad igitur in illo substantiam nominamus, non est subiectionis ratione quod dicitur, sed ultra omnem quae accidentibus est subiecta substantiam est essentia, absque omnibus quae possunt accidere solitaria omnino" (Migne, P.L. lxiv. 1283). Cf. Aug. De Trin.

vii. 10.

18. i.e. according to their substance.

19. The doctrine is Augustine's, cf. De Ciu. Dei, xi. 6, xii. 16; but Boethius's use of sempiternitas, as well as his word-building, seem to be peculiar to himself. Claudianus Mamertus, speaking of applying the categories to God, uses sempiternitas as Boethius uses aeternitas. Cf. De Statu Animae i. 19. Apuleius seems to use both terms interchangeably, e.g. Asclep. 29-31. On Boethius's distinction between time and eternity see Cons. v. pr. 6, and Rand, Der dem B. zugeschr. Trakt. De fide, pp. 425 ff, and Brandt in Theol. Littzg., 1902, p. 147.

20. Dominus and seruus are similarly used as illustration, In Cat. (Migne, P.L. lxiv. 217).

21. i.e. which is external to the master.

22. i.e. which is external to the whitened thing.

23. Cf. Cons. v. pr. 4 and 5, especially in pr. 5 the passage "quare in illius summae intellegentiae acumen si possumus erigamur."

An Unpublished Essay on the Trinity
By Jonathan Edwards (1703-1758)

It is common when speaking of the Divine happiness to say that God is infinitely happy in the enjoyment of Himself, in perfectly beholding and infinitely loving, and rejoicing in, His own essence and perfection, and accordingly it must be supposed that God perpetually and eternally has a most perfect idea of Himself, as it were an exact image and representation of Himself ever before Him and in actual view, and from hence arises a most pure and perfect act or energy in the Godhead, which is the Divine love, complacence and joy. The knowledge or view which God has of Himself must necessarily be conceived to be something distinct from His mere direct existence. There must be something that answers to our reflection. The reflection as we reflect on our own minds carries something of imperfection in it. However, if God beholds Himself so as thence to have delight and joy in Himself He must become his own object. There must be a duplicity. There is God and the idea of God, if it be proper to call a conception of that that is purely spiritual an idea.

If a man could have an absolutely perfect idea of all that passed in his mind, all the series of ideas and exercises in every respect perfect as to order, degree, circumstance and for any particular space of time past, suppose the last hour, he would really to all intents and purpose be over again what he was that last hour. And if it were possible for a man by reflection perfectly to contemplate all that is in his own mind in an hour, as it is and at the same time that it is there in its first and direct existence; if a man, that is, had a perfect reflex or contemplative idea of every thought at the same moment or moments that that thought was and of every exercise at and during the same time that that exercise was, and so through a whole hour, a man would really be two during that time, he would be indeed double, he would be twice at once. The idea he has of himself would be himself again.

Note, by having a reflex or contemplative idea of what passes in our own minds I don't mean consciousness only. There is a great difference between a man's having a view of himself, reflex or contemplative idea of himself so as to delight in his own beauty or excellency, and a mere direct consciousness. Or if we mean by consciousness of what is in our own minds anything besides the mere simple existence in our minds of what is there, it is nothing but a power by reflection to view or contemplate what passes.

Therefore as God with perfect clearness, fullness and strength, understands Himself, views His own essence (in which there is no distinction of substance and act but which is wholly substance and wholly act), that idea which God hath of Himself is absolutely Himself. This representation of the Divine nature and essence is the Divine nature and essence again: so that by God's thinking of the Deity must certainly be generated. Hereby there is another person begotten, there is another Infinite Eternal Almighty and most holy and the same God, the very same Divine nature.

And this Person is the second person in the Trinity, the Only Begotten and dearly Beloved Son of God; He is the eternal, necessary, perfect, substantial and personal idea which God hath of Himself; and that it is so seems to me to be abundantly confirmed by the Word of God.

Nothing can more agree with the account the Scripture gives us of the Son of God, His being in the form of God and His express and perfect image and representation: (II Cor. 4:4) "Lest the light of the glorious Gospel of Christ Who is the image of God should shine unto them." (Phil. 2:6) "Who being in the form of God." (Col. 1:15) "Who is the image of the invisible God." (Heb. 1:3) "Who being the brightness of His glory and the express image of His person."

Christ is called the face of God (Exod. 33:14): the word [A.V. presence] in the original signifies face, looks, form or appearance. Now what can be so properly and fitly called so with respect to God as God's own perfect idea of Himself whereby He has every moment a view of His own essence: this idea is that "face of God" which God sees as a man sees his own face in a looking glass. 'Tis of such form or appearance whereby God eternally appears to Himself. The root that the original word comes from signifies to look upon or behold: now what is that which God looks upon or beholds in so eminent a manner as He doth on His own idea or that perfect image of Himself which He has in view. This is what is eminently in God's presence and is therefore called the angel of God's presence or face (Isa. 63:9). But that the Son of God is God's own eternal and perfect idea is a thing we have yet much more expressly revealed in God's Word. First, in that Christ is called "the wisdom of God." If we are taught in the Scripture that Christ is the same with God's wisdom or knowledge, then it teaches us that He is the same with God's perfect and eternal idea. They are the same as we have already observed and I suppose none will deny. But Christ is said to be the wisdom of God (I Cor. 1:24, Luke 11:49, compare with Matt. 23:34); and how much doth Christ speak in Proverbs under the name of Wisdom especially in the 8th chapter.

The Godhead being thus begotten by God's loving an idea of Himself and shewing forth in a distinct subsistence or person in that idea, there proceeds a most pure act, and an infinitely holy and sacred energy arises between the Father and Son in mutually loving and delighting in each other, for their love and joy is mutual, (Prov. 8:30) "I was daily His delight rejoicing always before Him." This is the eternal and most perfect and essential act of the Divine nature, wherein the Godhead acts to an infinite degree and in the most perfect manner possible. The Deity becomes all act, the Divine essence itself flows out and is as it were breathed forth in love and joy. So that the Godhead therein stands forth in yet another manner of subsistence, and there proceeds the third Person in the Trinity, the Holy Spirit, viz., the Deity in act, for there is no other act but the act of the will.

We may learn by the Word of God that the Godhead or the Divine nature and essence does subsist in love. (I John 4:8) "He that loveth not knoweth not God; for God is love." In the context of which place I think it is plainly intimated to us that the Holy Spirit is that Love, as in the 12th and 13th verses. "If we love one another, God dwelleth in us, and His love is perfected in us; hereby know we that we dwell in Him ... because He hath given us of His Spirit." 'Tis the same argument in both verses. In the 12th verse the apostle argues that if we have love dwelling in us we have God dwelling in us, and in the 13th verse He clears the force of the argument by this that love is God's Spirit. Seeing we have God's Spirit dwelling in us, we have God dwelling in [in us], supposing it as a thing granted and allowed that God's Spirit is God. 'Tis evident also by this that God's dwelling in us and His love or the love that He hath exerciseth, being in us, are the same thing. The same is intimated in the same manner in the last verse of the foregoing chapter. The apostle was, in the foregoing verses, speaking of love as a sure sign of sincerity and our acceptance with God, beginning with the 18th verse, and he sums up the argument thus in the last verse, "and hereby do we know that He abideth in us by the Spirit that He hath given us."

The Scripture seems in many places to speak of love in Christians as if it were the same with the Spirit of God in them, or at least as the prime and most natural breathing and acting of the Spirit in the soul. (Phil. 2:1) "If there be therefore any consolation in Christ, any comfort of love, any fellowship of the Spirit, if any bowels of mercies, fulfil ye my joy that ye be likeminded, having the same love, being of one accord, of one mind." (II Cor. 6:6) "By kindness, by the Holy Ghost, by love unfeigned." (Romans 15:30) "Now I beseech you, brethren, for the Lord Jesus Christ's sake, and for the love of the Spirit." (Col. 1:8) "Who declared unto us your love in the Spirit." (Rom. 5:5) "Having the love of God shed abroad in our hearts by the Holy Ghost which is given to us." (Gal. 5:13-16) "Use not liberty for an occasion to the flesh, but by love serve one another. For all the law is fulfilled in one word, even in this: Thou shalt love thy neighbour as thyself. But if ye bite and devour one another, take heed that ye be not consumed one of another. This I say then, Walk in the Spirit, and ye shall not fulfill the lusts of the flesh." The Apostle argues that Christian liberty does not make way for fulfilling the lusts of the flesh in biting and devouring one another and the like, because a principle of love which was the fulfilling of the law would prevent it, and in the 16th verse he asserts the same thing in other words: "This I say then walk in the Spirit and ye shall not fulfill the lusts of the flesh."

The third and last office of the Holy Spirit is to comfort and delight the souls of God's people, and thus one of His names is the Comforter, and thus we have the phrase of "joy in the Holy Ghost." (I Thess. 1:6) "Having received the Word in much affliction with joy of the Holy Ghost." (Rom. 14: 17) "The kingdom of God is ... righteousness, and peace, and joy in the Holy Ghost." (Acts 9:31) "Walking in the fear of the Lord and in the comfort of the Holy Ghost." But how well doth this agree with the Holy Ghost being God's joy and delight, (Acts 13:52) "And the disciples were filled with joy and with the Holy Ghost"--meaning as I suppose that they were filled with spiritual joy.

This is confirmed by the symbol of the Holy Ghost, viz., a dove, which is the emblem of love or a lover, and is so used in Scripture, and especially often so in Solomon's Song, (1:15) "Behold thou art fair; my love, behold thou art fair; thou hast dove's eyes:" i.e. "Eyes of love," and again 4:1, the same words; and 5:12, "His eyes are as the eyes of doves," and 5:2, "My love, my dove," and 2:14 and 6:9; and this I believe to be the reason that the dove alone of all birds (except the sparrow in the single case of the leprosy) was appointed to be offered in sacrifice because of its innocence and because it is the emblem of love, love being the most acceptable sacrifice to God. It was under this similitude that the Holy Ghost descended from the Father on Christ at His baptism, signifying the infinite love of the Father to the Son, Who is the true David, or beloved, as we said before.

The same was signified by what was exhibited to the eye in the appearance there was of the Holy Ghost descending from the Father to the Son in the shape of a dove, as was signified by what was exhibited to the eye in the voice there was at the same time, viz., "This is My well Beloved Son in Whom I am well pleased."

(That God's love or His loving kindness is the same with the Holy Ghost seems to be plain by Psalm 36:7-9, "How excellent (or how precious as 'tis in the Hebrew) is Thy loving-kindness O God, therefore the children of men put their trust under the shadow of Thy wings, they shall be abundantly satisfied (in the Hebrew "watered") with the fatness of Thy house and Thou shalt make them to drink of the river of Thy pleasures; for with Thee is the fountain of life and in Thy light shall we see light."

Doubtless that precious loving-kindness and that fatness of God's house and river of His pleasures and the water of the fountain of life and God's light here spoken [of] are the same thing; by which we learn that the Holy anointing oil that was kept in the House of God, which was a type of the Holy Ghost, represented God's love, and that the "River of water of life" spoken of in the 22nd [chapter] of Revelation, which proceeds out of the throne of God and of the Lamb, which is the same with Ezekiel's vision of Living and life-giving water, which is here [in Ps. 36] called the "Fountain of life and river of God's pleasures," is God's loving-kindness.

But Christ Himself expressly teaches us that by spiritual fountains and rivers of water of life is meant the Holy Ghost. (John 4:14; 7:38,39).That by the river of God's pleasures here is meant the same thing with the pure river of water of life spoken of in Revelation 22:1, will be much confirmed if we compare those verses with Revelation 21:23, 24; 22:1,5. (See the notes on chapters 21, 23, 24) I think if we compare these places and weigh them we cannot doubt but that it is the same happiness that is meant in this Psalm which is spoken of there.)

So this well agrees with the similitudes and metaphors that are used about the Holy Ghost in Scripture, such as water, fire, breath, wind, oil, wine, a spring, a river, a being poured out and shed forth, and a being breathed forth. Can there any spiritual thing be thought, or anything belonging to any spiritual being to which such kind of metaphors so naturally agree, as to the affection of a Spirit. The affection, love or joy, may be said to flow out as water or to be breathed forth as breath or wind. But it would [not] sound so well to say that an idea or judgment flows out or is breathed forth.

It is no way different to say of the affection that it is warm, or to compare love to fire, but it would not seem natural to say the same of perception or reason. It seems natural enough to say that the soul is poured out in affection or that love or delight are shed abroad: (Rom. 5:5) "The love of God is shed abroad in our hearts," but it suits with nothing else belonging to a spiritual being.

This is that "river of water of life" spoken of in the 22nd [chapter] of Revelation, which proceeds from the throne of the Father and the Son, for the rivers of living water or water of life are the Holy Ghost, by the same apostle's own interpretation (John 7:38, 39); and the Holy Ghost being the infinite delight and pleasure of God, the river is called the river of God's pleasures (Ps. 36:8), not God's river of pleasures, which I suppose signifies the same as the fatness of God's House, which they that trust in God shall be watered with, by which fatness of God's House I suppose is signified the same thing which oil typifies.

It is a confirmation that the Holy Ghost is God's love and delight, because the saints communion with God consists in their partaking of the Holy Ghost. The communion of saints is twofold: 'tis their communion with God and communion with one another, (I John 1:3) "That ye also may have fellowship with us, and truly our fellowship is with the Father and with His Son, Jesus Christ." Communion is a common partaking of good, either of excellency or happiness, so that when it is said the saints have communion or fellowship with the Father and with the Son, the meaning of it is that they partake with the Father and the Son of their good, which is either their excellency and glory (II Peter 1:4), "Ye are made partakers of the Divine nature"; Heb. 12:10, "That we might be partakers of His holiness;" John 17:22, 23, "And the glory which Thou hast given Me I have given them, that they may be one, even as we are one, I in them and Thou in Me"); or of their joy and happiness: (John 17:13) "That they might have My joy fulfilled in themselves."

But the Holy Ghost being the love and joy of God is His beauty and happiness, and it is in our partaking of the same Holy Spirit that our communion with God consists: (II Cor. 13:14) "The grace of the Lord Jesus Christ, and the love of God, and the communion of the Holy Ghost, be with you all, Amen." They are not different benefits but the same that the Apostle here wisheth, viz., the Holy Ghost: in partaking of the Holy Ghost, we possess and enjoy the love and grace of the Father and the Son, for the Holy Ghost is that love and grace, and therefore I suppose it is that in that forementioned place, (I John 1:3). We are said to have fellowship with the Son and not with the Holy Ghost, because therein consists our fellowship with the Father and the Son, even in partaking with them of the Holy Ghost.

In this also eminently consists our communion with the Son that we drink into the same Spirit. This is the common excellency and joy and happiness in which they all are united; 'tis the bond of perfectness by which they are one in the Father and the Son as the Father is in the Son.

I can think of no other good account that can be given of the apostle Paul's wishing grace and peace from God the Father and the Lord Jesus Christ in the beginning of his Epistles, without ever mentioning the Holy Ghost, - as we find it thirteen times in his salutations in the beginnings of his Epistles, - but [i.e., except] that the Holy Ghost is Himself love and grace of God the Father and the Lord Jesus Christ; and in his blessing at the end of his second Epistle to the Corinthians where all three Persons are mentioned he wishes grace and love from the Son and the Father [except that] in the communion or the partaking of the Holy Ghost, the blessing is from the Father and the Son in the Holy Ghost. But the blessing from the Holy Ghost is Himself, the communication of Himself. Christ promises that He and the Father will love believers (John 14:21,23), but no mention is made of the Holy Ghost, and the love of Christ and the love of the Father are often distinctly mentioned, but never any mention of the Holy Ghost's love.

(This I suppose to be the reason why we have never any account of the

Holy Ghost's loving either the Father or the Son, or of the Son's or the Father's loving the Holy Ghost, or of the Holy Ghost's loving the saints, tho these things are so often predicated of both the other Persons.)

And this I suppose to be that blessed Trinity that we read of in the Holy Scriptures. The Father is the Deity subsisting in the prime, un-originated and most absolute manner, or the Deity in its direct existence. The Son is the Deity generated by God's understanding, or having an idea of Himself and subsisting in that idea. The Holy Ghost is the Deity subsisting in act, or the Divine essence flowing out and breathed forth in God's Infinite love to and delight in Himself. And I believe the whole Divine essence does truly and distinctly subsist both in the Divine idea and Divine love, and that each of them are properly distinct Persons.

It is a maxim amongst divines that everything that is in God is God which must be understood of real attributes and not of mere modalities. If a man should tell me that the immutability of God is God, or that the omnipresence of God and authority of God is God, I should not be able to think of any rational meaning of what he said. It hardly sounds to me proper to say that God's being without change is God, or that God's being everywhere is God, or that God's having a right of government over creatures is God.

But if it be meant that the real attributes of God, viz., His understanding and love are God, then what we have said may in some measure explain how it is so, for Deity subsists in them distinctly; so they are distinct Divine Persons.

One of the principal objections that I can think of against what has been supposed is concerning the Personality of the Holy Ghost - that this scheme of things does not seem well to consist with [the fact] that a person is that which hath understanding and will. If the three in the Godhead are Persons they doubtless each of them have understanding, but this makes the understanding one distinct person and love another. How therefore can this love be said to have understanding, (Here I would observe that divines have not been wont to suppose that these three had three distinct understandings, but all one and the same understanding.)

In order to clear up this matter let it be considered that the whole Divine office is supposed truly and properly to subsist in each of these three, viz., God and His understanding and love, and that there is such a wonderful union between them that they are, after an ineffable and inconceivable manner, One in Another, so that One hath Another and they have communion in One Another and are as it were predicable One of Another; as Christ said of Himself and the Father "I am in the Father and the Father in Me," so may it be said concerning all the Persons in the Trinity, the Father is in the Son and the Son in the Father, the Holy Ghost is in the Father, and the Father in the Holy Ghost, the Holy Ghost is in the Son, and the Son in the Holy Ghost, and the Father understands because the Son Who is the Divine understanding is in Him, the Father loves because the Holy Ghost is in Him, so the Son loves because the Holy Ghost is in Him and proceeds from Him, so the Holy Ghost or the Divine essence subsisting is Divine, but understands because the Son the Divine Idea is in Him.

Understanding may be predicated of this love because it is the love of the understanding both objectively and subjectively. God loves the understanding and that understanding also flows out in love so that the Divine understanding is in the Deity subsisting in love. It is not a blind love. Even in creatures there is consciousness included in the very nature of the will or act of the soul, and tho perhaps not so that it can so properly be said that it is a seeing or undemanding will, yet it may truly and properly be said so in God by reason of God's infinitely more perfect manner of acting so that the whole Divine essence flows out and subsists in this act, and the Son is in the Holy Spirit tho it does not proceed from Him by reason (of the fact) that the understanding must be considered as prior in the order of nature to the will or love or act, both in creatures and in the Creator. The understanding is so in the Spirit that the Spirit may be said to know, as the Spirit of God is truly and perfectly said to know and to search all things, even the deep things of God.

(All the Three are Persons for they all have understanding and will. There is understanding and will in the Father, as the Son and the Holy Ghost are in Him and proceed from Him. There is understanding and will in the Son, as He is understanding and as the Holy Ghost is in Him and proceeds from Him. There is understanding and will in the Holy Ghost as He is the Divine will and as the Son is in Him.

Nor is it to be looked upon as a strange and unreasonable figment that the Persons should be said to have an understanding or love by another person's being in them, for we have Scripture ground to conclude so concerning the Father's having wisdom and understanding or reason that it is by the Son's being in Him; because we are there informed that He is the wisdom and reason and truth of God, and hereby God is wise by His own wisdom being in Him. Understanding and wisdom is in the Father as the Son is in Him and proceeds from Him. Understanding is in the Holy Ghost because the Son is in Him, not as proceeding from Him but as flowing out in Him.)

But I don't pretend fully to explain how these things are and I am sensible a hundred other objections may be made and puzzling doubts and questions raised that I can't solve. I am far from pretending to explaining the Trinity so as to render it no longer a mystery. I think it to be the highest and deepest of all Divine mysteries still, notwithstanding anything that I have said or conceived about it. I don't intend to explain the Trinity. But Scripture with reason may lead to say something further of it than has been wont to be said, tho there are still left many things pertaining to it incomprehensible.

It seems to me that what I have here supposed concerning the Trinity is exceeding analogous to the Gospel scheme and agreeable to the tenor of the whole New Testament and abundantly illustrative of Gospel doctrines, as might be particularly shown, would it not exceedingly lengthen out this discourse.

I shall only now briefly observe that many things that have been wont to be said by orthodox divines about the Trinity are hereby illustrated. Hereby we see how the Father is the fountain of the Godhead, and why when He is spoken of in Scripture He is so often, without any addition or distinction, called God, which has led some to think that He only was truly and properly God. Hereby we may see why in the economy of the Persons of the Trinity the Father should sustain the dignity of the Deity, that the Father should have it as His office to uphold and maintain the rights of the Godhead and should be God not only by essence, but as it were, by His economical office.

Hereby is illustrated the doctrine of the Holy Ghost. Proceeding [from] both the Father and the Son. Hereby we see how that it is possible for the Son to be begotten by the Father and the Holy Ghost to proceed from the Father and

Son, and yet that all the Persons should be Co-etemal. Hereby we may more clearly understand the equality of the Persons among themselves, and that they are every way equal in the society or family of the three.

They are equal in honor: besides the honor which is common to them all, viz., that they are all God, each has His peculiar honor in the society or family. They are equal not only in essence, but the Father's honor is that He is, as it were, the Author of perfect and Infinite wisdom. The Son's honor is that He is that perfect and Divine wisdom itself the excellency of which is that from whence arises the honor of being the author or Generator of it. The honor of the Father and the Son is that they are infinitely excellent, or that from them infinite excellency proceeds; but the honor of the Holy Ghost is equal for He is that Divine excellency and beauty itself.

'Tis the honor of the Father and the Son that they are infinitely holy and are the fountain of holiness, but the honor of the Holy Ghost is that holiness itself. The honor of the Father and the Son is [that] they are infinitely happy and are the original and fountain of happiness and the honor of the Holy Ghost is equal for He is infinite happiness and joy itself.

The honor of the Father is that He is the fountain of the Deity as He from Whom proceed both the Divine wisdom and also excellency and happiness. The honor of the Son is equal for He is Himself the Divine wisdom and is He from Whom proceeds the Divine excellency and happiness, and the honor of the Holy Ghost is equal for He is the beauty and happiness of both the other Persons.

By this also we may fully understand the equality of each Person's concern in the work of redemption, and the equality of the Redeemed's concern with them and dependence upon them, and the equality and honor and praise due to each of them. Glory belongs to the Father and the Son that they so greatly loved the world: to the Father that He so loved that He gave His Only Begotten Son: to the Son that He so loved the world as to give up Himself.

But there is equal glory due to the Holy Ghost for He is that love of the Father and the Son to the world. Just so much as the two first Persons glorify themselves by showing the astonishing greatness of their love and grace, just so much is that wonderful love and grace glorified Who is the Holy Ghost. It shows the Infinite dignity and excellency of the Father that the Son so delighted and prized His honor and glory that He stooped infinitely low rather than [that] men's salvation should be to the injury of that honor and glory.

It showed the infinite excellency and worth of the Son that the Father so delighted in Him that for His sake He was ready to quit His anger and receive into favor those that had [deserved?] infinitely ill at His Hands, and what was done shows how great the excellency and worth of the Holy Ghost Who is that delight which the Father and the Son have in each other: it shows it to be Infinite. So great as the worth of a thing delighted in is to any one, so great is the worth of that delight and joy itself which he has in it.

Our dependence is equally upon each in this office. The Father appoints and provides the Redeemer, and Himself accepts the price and grants the thing purchased; the Son is the Redeemer by offering Himself and is the price; and the Holy Ghost immediately communicates to us the thing purchased by communicating Himself, and He is the thing purchased. The sum of all that Christ purchased for men was the Holy Ghost: (Gal. 3:13,14) "He was made a curse for us... that we might receive the promise of the Spirit through faith."

What Christ purchased for us was that we have communion with God [which] is His good, which consists in partaking of the Holy Ghost: as we have shown, all the blessedness of the Redeemed consists in their partaking of Christ's fullness, which consists in partaking of that Spirit which is given not by measure unto him: the oil that is poured on the head of the Church runs down to the members of His body and to the skirts of His garment (Ps. 133:2). Christ purchased for us that we should have the favor of God and might enjoy His love, but this love is the Holy Ghost.

Christ purchased for us true spiritual excellency, grace and holiness, the sum of which is love to God, which is [nothing] but the indwelling of the Holy Ghost in the heart. Christ purchased for us spiritual joy and comfort, which is in a participation of God's joy and happiness, which joy and happiness is the Holy Ghost as we have shown. The Holy Ghost is the sum of all good things. Good things and the Holy Spirit are synonymous expressions in Scripture: (Matt. 7:11) "How much more shall your Heavenly Father give the Holy Spirit to them that ask Him." The sum of all spiritual good which the finite have in this world is that spring of living water within them which we read of (John 4:10), and those rivers of living water flowing out of them which we read of (John 7:38,39), which we are there told means the Holy Ghost; and the sum of all happiness in the other world is that river of water of life which proceeds out of the throne of God and the Lamb, which we read of (Rev. 22:1), which is the River of God's pleasures and is the Holy Ghost and therefore the sum of the Gospel invitation to come and take the water of life (verse 17).

The Holy Ghost is the purchased possession and inheritance of the saints, as appears because that little of it which the saints have in this world is said to be the earnest of that purchased inheritance. (Eph. 1:14) Tis an earnest of that which we are to have a fullness of hereafter. (II Cor. 1:22; 5:5) The Holy Ghost is the great subject of all Gospel promises and therefore is called the Spirit of promise. (Eph. 1:13) This is called the promise of the Father (Luke 24:49), and the like in other places. (If the Holy Ghost be a comprehension of all good things promised in the Gospel, we may easily see the force of the Apostle's arguing (Gal. 3:2), "This only would I know, Received ye the Spirit by the works of the law or by the hearing of faith?") So that it is God of Whom our good is purchased and it is God that purchases it and it is God also that is the thing purchased.

Thus all our good things are of God and through God and in God, as we read in Romans 11:36: "For of Him and through Him and to Him (or in Him as eis is rendered, I Cor. 8:6) are all things." "To Whom be glory forever." All our good is of God the Father, it is all through God the Son, and all is in the Holy Ghost as He is Himself all our good. God is Himself the portion and purchased inheritance of His people. Thus God is the Alpha and the Omega in this affair of redemption.

If we suppose no more than used to be supposed about the Holy Ghost, the concern of the Holy Ghost in the work of redemption is not equal with the Father's and the Son's, nor is there an equal part of the glory of this work belonging to Him: merely to apply to us or immediately to give or hand to us the blessing purchased, after it was purchased, as subservient to the other two Persons, is but a little thing [compared] to the purchasing of it by the paying an Infinite price, by Christ offering up Himself in sacrifice to procure it, and it is but a little thing to God the Father's giving His infinitely dear Son to be a sacrifice for us and upon His purchase to afford to us all the blessings of His purchased.

But according to this there is an equality. To be the love of God to the world is as much as for the Father and the Son to do so much from love to the world, and to be the thing purchased was as much as to be the price. The price and the thing bought with that price are equal. And it is as much as to afford the thing purchased, for the glory that belongs to Him that affords the thing purchased arises from the worth of that thing that He affords and therefore it is the same glory and an equal glory; the glory of the thing itself is its worth and that is also the glory of him that affords it.

There are two more eminent and remarkable images of the Trinity among the creatures. The one is in the spiritual creation, the soul of man. There is the mind, and the understanding or idea, and the spirit of the mind as it is called in Scripture, i.e., the disposition, the will or affection. The other is in the visible creation, viz., the Sun. The father is as the substance of the Sun. (By substance I don't mean in a philosophical sense, but the Sun as to its internal constitution.) The Son is as the brightness and glory of the disk of the Sun or that bright and glorious form under which it appears to our eyes. The Holy Ghost is the action of the Sun which is within the Sun in its intestine heat, and, being diffusive, enlightens, warms, enlivens and comforts the world. The Spirit as it is God's Infinite love to Himself and happiness in Himself, is as the internal heat of the Sun, but as it is that by which God communicates Himself, it is as the emanation of the sun's action, or the emitted beams of the sun.

The various sorts of rays of the sun and their beautiful colors do well represent the Spirit. They well represent the love and grace of God and were made use of for this purpose in the rainbow after the flood, and I suppose also in that rainbow that was seen round about the throne by Ezekiel (Ezek. 1:28; Rev. 4:3) and round the head of Christ by John (Rev. 10:1), or the amiable excellency of God and the various beautiful graces and virtues of the Spirit. These beautiful colors of the sunbeams we find made use of in Scripture for this purpose, viz., to represent the graces of the Spirit, as (Ps. 68:13) "Though ye have lien among the pots, yet shall be as the wings of a dove covered with silver, and her feathers with yellow gold," i.e., like the light reflected in various beautiful colors from the feathers of a dove, which colors represent the graces of the Heavenly Dove.

The same I suppose is signified by the various beautiful colors reflected from the precious stones of the breastplate, and that these spiritual ornaments of the Church are what are represented by the various colors of the foundation and gates of the new Jerusalem (Rev. 21; Isaiah 54:11, etc.) and the stones of the Temple (I Chron. 29: 2); and I believe the variety there is in the rays of the Sun and their beautiful colors was designed by the Creator for this very purpose, and indeed that the whole visible creation which is but the shadow of being is so made and ordered by God as to typify and represent spiritual things, for which I could give many reasons. (I don't propose this merely as an hypothesis but as a part of Divine truth sufficiently and fully ascertained by the revelation God has made in the Holy Scriptures.)

I am sensible what kind of objections many will be ready to make against what has been said, what difficulties will be immediately found, How can this be? And how can that be!

I am far from affording this as any explication of this mystery, that unfolds and renews the mysteriousness and incomprehensibleness of it, for I am sensible that however by what has been said some difficulties are lessened, others that are new appear, and the number of those things that appear mysterious, wonderful and incomprehensible, is increased by it. I offer it only as a farther manifestation of what of Divine truth the Word of God exhibits to the view of our minds concerning this great mystery.

I think the Word of God teaches us more things concerning it to be believed by us than have been generally believed, and that it exhibits many things concerning it exceeding [i.e., more] glorious and wonderful than have been taken notice of; yea, that it reveals or exhibits many more wonderful mysteries than those which have been taken notice of; which mysteries that have been overvalued are incomprehensible things and yet have been exhibited in the Word of God tho they are an addition to the number of mysteries that are in it. No wonder that the more things we are told concerning that which is so infinitely above our reach, the number of visible mysteries increases.

When we tell a child a little concerning God he has not an hundredth part so many mysteries in view on the nature and attributes of God and His works of creation and Providence as one that is told much concerning God in a Divinity School; and yet he knows much more about God and has a much clearer understanding of things of Divinity and is able more clearly to explicate some things that were dark and very unintelligible to him; I humbly apprehend that the things that have been observed increase the number of visible mysteries in the Godhead in no other manner than as by them we perceive that God has told us much more about it than was before generally observed.

Under the Old Testament the Church of God was not told near so much about the Trinity as they are now. But what the New Testament has revealed, tho it has more opened to our view the nature of God, yet it has increased the number of visible mysteries and they thus appear to us exceeding wonderful and incomprehensible. And so also it has come to pass in the Church being told [i.e., that the churches are told] more about the incarnation and the satisfaction of Christ and other Gospel doctrines.

It is so not only in Divine things but natural things. He that looks on a plant, or the parts of the bodies of animals, or any other works of nature, at a great distance where he has but an obscure sight-of it, may see something in it wonderful and beyond his comprehension, but he that is near to it and views them narrowly indeed understands more about them, has a clearer and distinct sight of them, and yet the number of things that are wonderful and mysterious in them that appear to him are much more than before, and, if he views them with a microscope, the number of the wonders that he sees will be increased still but yet the microscope gives him more a true knowledge concerning them.

God is never said to love the Holy Ghost nor are any epithets that betoken love anywhere given to Him, tho so many are ascribed to the Son, as God's Elect, The Beloved, He in Whom God's soul delights, He in Whom He is well pleased, etc. Yea such epithets seem to be ascribed to the Son as tho He were the object of love exclusive of all other persons, as tho there were no person whatsoever to share the love of the Father with the Son. To this purpose evidently He is called God's Only Begotten Son, at the time that it is added, "In Whom He is well pleased." There is nothing in Scripture that speaks of any acceptance of the Holy Ghost or any reward or any mutual friendship between the Holy Ghost and either of the other Persons, or any command to love the Holy Ghost or to delight in or have any complacence in [the Holy Ghost], tho such commands are so frequent with respect to the other Persons.

That knowledge or understanding in God which we must conceive of as first is His knowledge of every thing possible. That love which must be this knowledge is what we must conceive of as belonging to the essence of the Godhead in it's first subsistence. Then comes a reflex act of knowledge and His viewing Himself and knowing Himself and so knowing His own knowledge and so the Son is begotten. There is such a thing in God as knowledge of knowledge, an idea of an idea. Which can be nothing else than the idea or knowledge repeated.

The world was made for the Son of God especially. For God made the world for Himself from love to Himself; but God loves Himself only in a reflex act. He views Himself and so loves Himself, so He makes the world for Himself viewed and reflected on, and that is. The same with Himself repeated or begotten in His own idea, and that is His Son. When God considers of making any thing for Himself He presents Himself before Himself and views Himself as His End, and that viewing Himself is the same as reflecting on Himself or having an idea of Himself, and to make the world for the Godhead thus viewed and understood is to make the world for the Godhead begotten and that is to make the world for the Son of God.

The love of God as it flows forth ad extra is wholly determined and directed by Divine wisdom, so that those only are the objects of it that Divine wisdom chooses, so that the creation of the world is to gratify Divine love as that is exercised by Divine wisdom. But Christ is Divine wisdom so that the world is made to gratify Divine love as exercised by Christ or to gratify the love that is in Christ's heart, or to provide a spouse for Christ. Those creatures which wisdom chooses for the object of Divine love as Christ's elect spouse and especially those elect creatures that wisdom chiefly pitches upon and makes the end of the rest of creatures.

A Brief Declaration and Vindication of The Doctrine of the Trinity and also of The Person and Satisfaction of Christ

Accommodated to the Capacity and use of such as may be in Danger to be Seduced; and the Establishment of the Truth.

By John Owen (1616-1683)

"Search the Scriptures." -- John v. 39.

Prefatory note

Few of Owen's treatises have been more extensively circulated and generally useful than his "Brief Declaration and Vindication of the Doctrine of the Trinity," etc. It was published in 1669; and the author of the anonymous memoir of Owen, prefixed to an edition of his Sermons in 1720, informs us "This small piece has met with such an universal acceptance by true Christians of all denominations, that the seventh edition of it was lately published." An edition printed in Glasgow was published in 1798, and professes to be the eighth. A translation of the work appeared in the Dutch language (Vitringa, Doct. Christ., pars vi. p. 6, edit. 1776).

At the time when the treatise was published, the momentous doctrines of the Trinity and the Atonement were violently assailed; but it was not so much for the refutation of opponents as for "the edification and establishment of the plain Christian," that our author composed the following little work. The reader will find in it traces of that deep and familiar acquaintance with opposing views, and with the highest theology involved in the questions which might be expected from Dr Owen on a subject which he seems to have studied with peculiar industry and research. Reference may be made to his "Vindiciæ Evangelicæ" and his "Exposition of the Epistle to the Hebrews," in proof how thoroughly he had mastered the whole controversy in regard to the divinity and satisfaction of Christ, so far as the discussion had extended in his day. His controversy with Biddle, in which he wrote his "Vindiciæ Evangelicæ," took place in 1655; and the first volume of the "Exposition" was published only the year before the "Brief Declaration," etc., appeared. The latter may be regarded, accordingly, as the substance of these important works, condensed and adapted to popular use and comprehension, in all that relates to the proper Godhead of the Son, and the nature of the work which he accomplished in the redemption of his people.

For the special object which he had in view, he adopts the course which has since been generally approved of and pursued, as obviously the wisest and safest in defending and expounding the doctrine of the Trinity. He appeals to the broad mass of Scripture evidence in favour of the doctrine, and after proving the divine unity, together with the divinity of Father, Son, and Holy Ghost respectively, is careful not to enter on any discussion in regard to the unrevealed mysteries involved in the relations of the Trinity, beyond what was necessary for the refutation of those who argue, that whatever in this high doctrine is incomprehensible by reason, must be incompatible with revelation. This little work is farther remarkable for the almost total absence of the tedious digressions, which abound in the other works of Owen. Such logical unity and concentration of thought is the more remarkable, when we find that the treatise was written, as he tells us, "in a few hours." But it was a subject on which his mind was fully stored, and his whole heart was interested. The treatise which follows, therefore, was not the spark struck in some moment of collision, and serving only a temporary purpose, but a steady flame nourished from the beaten oil of the sanctuary. -- Ed.

To the Reader

Christian Reader,

This small treatise has no other design but thy good, and establishment in the truth. And therefore, as laying aside that consideration alone, I could desirously have been excused from the labour of those hours which were spent in its composure; so in the work itself I admitted no one thought, but how the things treated of in it might and ought to be managed unto thy spiritual benefit and advantage. Other designs most men have in writing what is to be exposed to public view, and lawfully may have so; in this I have nothing but merely thy good. I have neither been particularly provoked nor opposed by the adversaries of the truth here pleaded for; nor have any need, from any self-respect, to publish such a small, plain discourse as this. Love alone to the truth, and the welfare of thy soul, has given efficacy to their importunity who pressed me to this small service.

The matters here treated of are on all hands confessed to be of the greatest moment, such as the eternal welfare of the souls of men is immediately and directly concerned in. This all those who believe the sacred truths here proposed and explained do unanimously profess and contend for; nor is it denied by those by whom they are opposed. There is no need, therefore, to give thee any especial reasons to evince thy concernment in these things, nor the greatness of that concernment, thereby to induce thee unto their serious consideration. It were well, indeed, that these great, sacred, and mysterious truths might, without contention or controversies about them, be left unto the faith of believers, as proposed in the Scripture, with that explanation of them which, in the ordinary ministry and dispensation of the gospel, is necessary and required.

Certainly, these tremendous mysteries are not by us willingly to be exposed, or prostituted to the cavils of every perverse querist and disputer; -- those συζητηταὶ τοῦ αἰῶνος τούτου, [1] whose pretended wisdom (indeed ignorance, darkness, and folly) God has designed to confound and destroy in them and by them. For my part, I can assure thee, reader, I have no mind to contend and dispute about these things, which I humbly adore and believe as they are revealed. It is the importunity of adversaries, in their attempts to draw and seduce the souls of men from the truth and simplicity of the gospel in these great fundamentals of it, that alone can justify any to debate upon, or eristically [in the form of controversy] to handle these awful mysteries. This renders it our duty, and that indispensably, inasmuch as we are required to "contend earnestly for the faith once delivered unto the saints." But yet, also, when this necessity is imposed on us, we are by no means discharged from that humble reverence of mind wherewith we ought always to be conversant about them; nor from that regard unto the way and manner of their revelation in the Scripture which may preserve us from all unnecessary intermixture of litigious or exotic phrases and expressions in their assertion and declaration. I know our adversaries could, upon the matter, decry any thing peculiarly mysterious in these things, although they are frequently and emphatically in the Scriptures affirmed so to be. But, whilst they deny the mysteries of the things themselves -- which are such as every way become the glorious being and wisdom of God, -- they are forced to assign such an enigmatical sense unto the words, expressions, and propositions wherein they are revealed and declared in the Scripture, as to turn almost the whole gospel into an allegory, wherein nothing is properly expressed but in some kind of allusion unto what is so elsewhere: which irrational way of proceeding, leaving nothing certain in what is or may be expressed by word or writing, is covered over with a pretence of right reason; which utterly refuses to be so employed. These things the reader will find afterward made manifest, so far as the nature of this brief discourse will bear. And I shall only desire these few things of him that intends its perusal:-- First, That he would not look on the subject here treated of as the matter of an ordinary controversy in religion, --

   -- "Neque enim hic levia aut ludicra petuntur Præmia; lectoris de vita animæque salute Certatur." [2]

They are things which immediately and directly in themselves concern the eternal salvation of the souls of men, and their consideration ought always to be attended with a due sense of their weight and importance. Secondly, Let him bring with him a due reverence of the majesty, and infinite, incomprehensible nature of God, as that which is not to be prostituted to the captious and sophistical scanning of men of corrupt minds, but to be humbly adored, according to the revelation that he has made of himself. Thirdly, That he be willing to submit his soul and conscience to the plain and obvious sense of Scripture propositions and testimonies, without seeking out evasions and pretences for unbelief. These requests I cannot but judge equal, and fear not the success where they are sincerely complied withal.

I have only to add, that in handling the doctrine of the satisfaction of Christ, I have proceeded on that principle which, as it is fully confirmed in the Scripture, so it has been constantly maintained and adhered unto by the most of those who with judgment and success have managed these controversies against the Socinians: and this is, that the essential holiness of God with his justice or righteousness, as the supreme governor of all, did indispensably require that sin should not absolutely go unpunished; and that it should do so, stands in a repugnancy to those holy properties of his nature. This, I say, has been always constantly maintained by far the greatest number of them who have thoroughly understood the controversy in this matter, and have successfully engaged in it. And as their arguments for their assertion are plainly unanswerable, so the neglect of abiding by it is causelessly to forego one of the most fundamental and invincible principles in our cause. He who first laboured in the defence of the doctrine of the satisfaction of Christ, after Socinus had formed his imaginations about the salvation that he wrought, and began to dispute about it, was Covetus, [3] a learned man, who laid the foundation of his whole disputation in the justice of God, necessarily requiring, and indispensably, the punishment of sin. And, indeed, the state of the controversy as it is laid down by Socinus, in his book "De Jesu Christo Servatore," which is an answer to this Covetus, is genuine, and that which ought not to be receded from, as having been the direct ground of all the controversial writings on that subject which have since been published in Europe. And it is in these words laid down by Socinus himself: "Communis et orthodoxa (ut asseris) sententia est, Jesum Christum ideo servatorem nostrum esse, quia divinæ justitiæ per quam peccatores damnari merebamur, pro peccatis nostris plene satisfecerit; quæ satisfactio, per fidem, imputatur nobis ex dono Dei credentibus." This he ascribes to Covetus: "The common and orthodox judgment is, that Jesus Christ is therefore our Saviour, because he has satisfied the justice of God, by which we, being sinners, deserved to be condemned for all our sins" [which satisfaction, through faith, is imputed to us who through the grace of God believe.] In opposition whereunto he thus expresses his own opinion: "Ego vero censeo, et orthodoxam sententiam esse arbitror, Jesum Christum ideo servatorem nostrum esse, quia salutis æternæ viam nobis annuntiaverit, confirmaverit, et in sua ipsius persona, cum vitæ exemplo, tum ex mortuis resurgendo, manifestè ostenderit; vitamque æternam nobis ei fidem habentibus ipse daturus sit. Divinæ autem justitiæ, per quam peccatores damnari meremur, pro peccatis nostris neque illum satisfecisse, neque et satisfaceret, opus fuisse arbitror;" -- "I judge and suppose it to be the orthodox opinion, that Jesus Christ is therefore our Saviour, because he has declared unto us the way of eternal salvation, and confirmed it in his own person; manifestly showing it, both by the example of his life and by rising from the dead; and in that he will give eternal life unto us, believing in him. And I affirm, that he neither made satisfaction to the justice of God, whereby we deserved to be damned for our sins, nor was there any need that he should so do." This is the true state of the question; and the principal subtlety of Crellius, the great defender of this part of the doctrine of Socinus, in his book of the "Causes of the Death of Christ," and the defence of this book, "De Jesu Christo Servatore," consists in speaking almost the same words with those whom he does oppose, but still intending the same things with Socinus himself. This opinion, as was said of Socinus, Covetus opposed and everted on the principle before mentioned.

The same truth was confirmed also by Zarnovitius, who first wrote against Socinus' book; as also by Otto Casmannus, who engaged in the same work; and by Abraham Salinarius. Upon the same foundation do proceed Paræus, Piscator, Lubbertus, Lucius, Camero, Voetius, Amyraldus, Placæus, Rivetus, Walæus, Thysius, Altingius, Maresius, Essenius, Arnoldus, Turretinus, Baxter, with many others. The Lutherans who have managed these controversies, as Tarnovius, Meisnerus, Calovius, Stegmannus, Martinius, Franzius, with all others of their way, have constantly maintained the same great fundamental principle of this doctrine of the satisfaction of Christ; and it has well and solidly been of late asserted among ourselves on the same foundation. And as many of these authors do expressly blame some of the schoolmen, as Aquinas, Durandus, Biel, Tataretus, for granting a possibility of pardon without satisfaction, as opening a way to the Socinian error in this matter; so also they fear not to affirm, that the foregoing of this principle of God's vindictive justice indispensably requiring the punishment of sin, does not only weaken the cause of the truth, but indeed leave it indefensible. However, I suppose men ought to be wary how they censure the authors mentioned, as such who expose the cause they undertook to defend unto contempt; for greater, more able, and learned defenders, this truth has not as yet found, nor does stand in need of.

J. O.

Footnotes:

1. [learned researchers of this century]

2. -- "Nec enim levia aut ludicra petuntur
Præmia, sed Turni de vita et sanguine certant." Virg. Æn. xii. 764.

3. The only notice of this divine we can discover will be found in the Bibliotheca of Kongius (1678). All the information he communicates respecting him is in these words: -- "Covetus (Jacobus)Parisiensis Theologus. An. 1608 obiit. Reliquit Apologiam de Justificatione." Socinus, in a curious preface to his work, mentioned above, "De Jesu Christo Servatore," narrates in what manner Covetus and he first happened to meet. They subsequently exchanged communications on the points in dispute between them. It was in reply to the arguments of Covetus in this correspondence, that Socinus wrote the work to which Dr Owen alludes. It is a matter of regret that so little is known of one whom Dr Owen mentions so respectfully, and who had the honour of supplying the first antidote and check to the heresies of Socinus. -- Ed.

The Preface

The disciples of our Lord Jesus Christ having made that great confession of him, in distinction and opposition unto them, who accounted him only as a prophet, "Thou art the Christ, the Son of the living God," Matt. xvi. 14, 16, he does, on the occasion thereof, give out unto them that great charter of the church's stability and continuance, "Upon this rock I will build my church; and the gates of hell shall not prevail against it," verse 18. He is himself the rock upon which his church is built, -- as God is called the rock of his people, on the account of his eternal power and immutability, Deut. xxxii. 4, 18, 31, Isa. xxvi. 4; and himself the spiritual rock which gave out supplies of mercy and assistance to the people in the wilderness, 1 Cor. x. 4.

The relation of the professing church unto this rock consists in the faith of this confession, that he is "the Christ, the Son of the living God." This our Lord Jesus Christ has promised to secure against all attempts; yet so as plainly to declare, that there should be great and severe opposition made thereunto. For whereas the prevalency of the gates of hell in an enmity unto this confession is denied, a great and vigorous attempt to prevail therein is no less certainly foretold. Neither has it otherwise fallen out. In all ages, from the first solemn foundation of the church of the New Testament, it has, one way or other, been fiercely attempted by the "gates of hell." For some time after the resurrection of Christ from the dead, the principal endeavours of Satan, and men acting under him, or acted by him, were pointed against the very foundation of the church, as laid in the expression before mentioned. Almost all the errors and heresies wherewith for three or four centuries of years it was perplexed, were principally against the person of Christ himself; and, consequently, the nature and being of the holy and blessed Trinity. But being disappointed in his design herein, through the watchful care of the Lord Christ over his promise, in the following ages Satan turned his craft and violence against sundry parts of the superstructure, and, by the assistance of the Papacy, cast them into confusion, -- nothing, as it were, remaining firm, stable, and in order, but only this one confession, which in a particular manner the Lord Christ has taken upon himself to secure.

In these latter ages of the world, the power and care of Jesus Christ reviving towards his church, in the reformation of it, even the ruined heaps of its building have been again reduced into some tolerable order and beauty. The old enemy of its peace and welfare falling hereby under a disappointment, and finding his travail and labour for many generations in a great part frustrate, he is returned again to his old work of attacking the foundation itself; as he is unweary and restless, and can be quiet neither conqueror nor conquered, -- nor will be so, until he is bound and cast into the lake that burns with fire. For no sooner had the reformation of religion firmed itself in some of the European provinces, but immediately, in a proportion of distance not unanswerable unto what fell out from the first foundation of the church, sundry persons, by the instigation of Satan, attempted the disturbance and ruin of it, by the very same errors and heresies about the Trinity, the person of Christ and his offices, the person of the Holy Ghost and his grace, wherewith its first trouble and ruin was endeavoured. And hereof we have of late an instance given among ourselves, and that so notoriously known, through a mixture of imprudence and impudence in the managers of it, that a very brief reflection upon it will suffice unto our present design.

It was always supposed, and known to some, that there are sundry persons in this nation, who, having been themselves seduced into Socinianism, did make it their business, under various pretences, to draw others into a compliance with them in the same way and persuasion. Neither has this, for sundry years, been so secretly carried, but that the design of it has variously discovered itself by overt acts of conferences, disputations, and publishing of books; which last way of late has been sedulously pursued. Unto these three is now a visible accession made, by that sort of people whom men will call Quakers, from their deportment at the first erection of their way (long since deserted by them), until, by some new revolutions of opinions, they cast themselves under a more proper denomination. That there is a conjunction issued between both these sorts of men, in an opposition to the holy Trinity, with the person and grace of Christ, the pamphlets of late published by the one and the other do sufficiently evince. For however they may seem in sundry things as yet to look diverse ways, yet, like Samson's foxes, they are knit together by the tail of consent in these fire-brand opinions, and jointly endeavour to consume the standing corn of the church of God. And their joint management of their business of late has been as though it were their design to give as great a vogue and report to their opinions as by any ways they are able. Hence, besides their attempts to be proclaiming their opinions, under various pretences, in all assemblies whereinto they may intrude themselves (as they know) without trouble, they are exceeding sedulous in scattering and giving away, yea, imposing gratis (and, as to some, ingratiis), their small books which they publish, upon all sorts of persons promiscuously, as they have advantage so to do. By this means their opinions being of late become the talk and discourse of the common sort of Christians, and the exercise of many, -- amongst whom are not a few that, on sundry accounts, which I shall not mention, may possibly be exposed unto disadvantage and prejudice thereby, -- it has been thought meet by some that the sacred truths which these men oppose should be plainly and briefly asserted and confirmed from the scripture; that those of the meanest sort of professors, who are sincere and upright, exercising themselves to keep a good conscience in matters of faith and obedience to God, may have somewhat in a readiness, both to guide them in their farther inquiry into the truth, as also to confirm their faith in what they have already received, when at any time it is shaken or opposed by the "cunning sleight of men that lie in wait to deceive."

And this comprises the design of the ensuing discourse. It may possibly be judged needless by some, as it was in its first proposal by him by whom it is written; and that because this matter at present is, by an especial providence, cast on other hands, who both have, and doubtless, as occasion shall require, will well acquit themselves in the defence of the truths opposed. Not to give any other account of the reasons of this small undertaking it may suffice, that "in publico discrimine omnis homo miles est," -- "every man's concernment lying in a common danger," -- it is free for every one to manage it as he thinks best, and is able, so it be without prejudice to the whole or the particular concerns of others. If a city be on fire, whose bucket that brings water to quench it ought to be refused? The attempt to cast fire into the city of God by the opinions mentioned, is open and plain; and a timely stop being to be put unto it, the more hands that are orderly employed in its quenching, the more speedy and secure is the effect like to be.

Now, because the assertors of the opinions mentioned do seem to set out themselves to be some great ones, above the ordinary rate of men, as having found out, and being able publicly to maintain, such things as never would have entered into the minds of others to have thought on or conceived; and also that they seem with many to be thought worthy of their consideration because they now are new, and such as they have not been acquainted withal; I shall, in this prefatory entrance, briefly manifest that those who have amongst us undertaken the management of these opinions have brought nothing new unto them, but either a little contemptible sophistry and caption of words, on the one hand, or futilous, affected, unintelligible expressions, on the other, -- the opinions themselves being no other but such as the church of God, having been opposed by and troubled with from the beginning, has prevailed against and triumphed over in all generations. And were it not that confidence is the only relief which enraged impotency adheres unto and expects supplies from, I should greatly admire that those amongst us who have undertaken an enforcement of these old exploded errors, whose weakness does so openly discover and proclaim itself in all their endeavours, should judge themselves competent to give a new spirit of life to the dead carcass of these rotten heresies, which the faith of the saints in all ages has triumphed over, and which truth and learning have, under the care and watchfulness of Christ, so often baffled out of the world.

The Jews, in the time of our Saviour's converse on the earth, being fallen greatly from the faith and worship of their forefathers, and ready to sink into their last and utmost apostasy from God, seem, amongst many other truths, to have much lost that of the doctrine of the holy Trinity, and of the person of the Messiah. It was, indeed, suited, in the dispensation of God, unto the work that the Lord Jesus had to fulfil in the world, that, before his passion and resurrection, the knowledge of his divine nature, as unto his individual person, should be concealed from the most of men. For this cause, although he was "in the form of God, and thought it not robbery to be equal with God, yet he made himself of no reputation, by taking on him the form of a servant, and being made in the likeness of men, that being found in the fashion of a man, he might be obedient unto death," Phil. ii. 6-8; whereby his divine glory was veiled for a season, until he was "declared to be the Son of God with power, according to the Spirit of holiness, by the resurrection from the dead," Rom. i. 4; and then "was glorified with that glory which he had with the Father before the world was," John xvii. 5. And as this dispensation was needful unto the accomplishment of the whole work which, as our mediator, he had undertaken, so, in particular, he who was in himself the Lord of hosts, a sanctuary to them that feared him, became hereby "a stone of stumbling and a rock of offence to both the houses of Israel, for a gin and for a snare to the inhabitants of Jerusalem," Isa. viii. 13, 14. See Luke ii. 34; Rom. ix. 33; 1 Pet. ii. 8; Isa. xxviii. 16. But yet, notwithstanding, as occasions required, suitably unto his own holy ends and designs, he forbare not to give plain and open testimony to his own divine nature and eternal pre-existence unto his incarnation. And this was it which, of all other things, most provoked the carnal Jews with whom he had to do; for having, as was said, lost the doctrine of the Trinity and person of the Messiah, in a great measure, whenever he asserted his Deity, they were immediately enraged, and endeavoured to destroy him. So was it, plainly, John viii. 56-59. Says he, "Your father Abraham rejoiced to see my day: and he saw it, and was glad. Then said the Jews unto him, Thou art not yet fifty years old, and hast thou seen Abraham? Jesus said unto them, Verily, verily, I say unto you, Before Abraham was, I am. Then took they up stones to cast at him." So, also, John x. 30-33, "I and my Father are one. Then the Jews took up stones again to stone him. Jesus answered them, Many good works have I showed you from my Father; for which of those works do ye stone me? The Jews answered him, saying, For a good work we stone thee not; but for blasphemy; and because that thou, being a man, makes thyself God." They understood well enough the meaning of those words, "I and my Father are one," -- namely, that they were a plain assertion of his being God. This caused their rage. And this the Jews all abide by to this day, -- namely, that he declared himself to be God, and therefore they slew him. Whereas, therefore, the first discovery of a plurality of persons in the divine essence consists in the revelation of the divine nature and personality of the Son, this being opposed, persecuted, and blasphemed by these Jews, they may be justly looked upon and esteemed as the first assertors of that misbelief which now some seek again so earnestly to promote. The Jews persecuted the Lord Christ, because he, being a man, declared himself also to be God; and others are ready to revile and reproach them who believe and teach what he declared.

After the resurrection and ascension of the Lord Jesus, all things being filled with tokens, evidences, and effects of his divine nature and power (Rom. i. 4), the church that began to be gathered in his name, and according to his doctrine, being, by his especial institution, to be initiated into the express profession of the doctrine of the holy Trinity, as being to be baptized in the name of the Father, and, the Son, and the Holy Ghost, -- which confession comprises the whole of the truth contended for, and by the indispensable placing of it at the first entrance into all obedience unto him, is made the doctrinal foundation of the church, -- it continued for a season in the quiet and undisturbed possession of this sacred treasure.

The first who gave disquietment unto the disciples of Christ, by perverting the doctrine of the Trinity, was Simon Magus, with his followers; -- an account of whose monstrous figments and unintelligible imaginations, with their coincidence with what some men dream in these latter days, shall elsewhere be given. Nor shall I need here to mention the colluvies of Gnostics, Valentians, Marcionites, and Manichees; the foundation of all whose abominations lay in their misapprehensions of the being of God, their unbelief of the Trinity and person of Christ, as do those of some others also.

In especial, there was one Cerinthus, who was more active than others in his opposition to the doctrine of the person of Christ, and therein of the holy Trinity. To put a stop unto his abominations, all authors agree that John, writing his Gospel, prefixed unto it that plain declaration of the eternal Deity of Christ which it is prefaced withal. And the story is well attested by Irenæus, Eusebius, and others, from Polycarpus, who was his disciple, that this Cerinthus coming into the place where the apostle was, he left it, adding, as a reason of his departure, lest the building, through the just judgment of God, should fall upon them. And it was of the holy, wise providence of God to suffer some impious persons to oppose this doctrine before the death of that apostle, that he might, by infallible inspiration, farther reveal, manifest, and declare it, to the establishment of the church in future ages. For what can farther be desired to satisfy the minds of men who in any sense own the Lord Jesus Christ and the Scriptures, than that this controversy about the Trinity and person of Christ (for they stand and fall together) should be so eminently and expressly determined, as it were, immediately from heaven?

But he with whom we have to deal in this matter neither ever did, nor ever will, nor can, acquiesce or rest in the divine determination of any thing which he has stirred up strife and controversy about: for as Cerinthus and the Ebionites persisted in the heresy of the Jews, who would have slain our Saviour for bearing witness to his own Deity, notwithstanding the evidence of that testimony, and the right apprehension which the Jews had of his mind therein; so he excited others to engage and persist in their opposition to the truth, notwithstanding this second particular determination of it from beaten, for their confutation or confusion. For after the more weak and confused oppositions made unto it by Theodotus Coriarius [i.e., the tanner], Artemon, and some others, at length a stout champion appears visibly and expressly engaged against these fundamentals of our faith. This was Paulus Samosatenus, bishop of the church of Antioch, about the year 272; -- a man of most intolerable pride, passion, and folly, -- the greatest that has left a name upon ecclesiastical records. This man openly and avowedly denied the doctrine of the Trinity, and the Deity of Christ in an especial manner. For although he endeavoured for a while to cloud his impious sentiments in ambiguous expressions, as others also have done (Euseb., lib. vii. cap. 27), yet being pressed by the professors of the truth, and supposing his party was somewhat confirmed, he plainly defended his heresy, and was cast out of the church wherein he presided. Some sixty years after, Photinus, bishop of Sirmium, with a pretence of more sobriety in life and conversation, undertook the management of the same design, with the same success.

What ensued afterward among the churches of God in this matter is of too large and diffused a nature to be here reported. These instances I have fixed on only to intimate, unto persons whose condition or occasions afford them not ability or leisure of themselves to inquire into the memorials of times past amongst the professors of the gospel of Christ, that these oppositions which are made at present amongst us unto these fundamental truths, and derived immediately from the late renewed enforcement of them made by Faustus Socinus and his followers, are nothing but old baffled attempts of Satan against the rock of the church and the building thereon, in the confession of the Son of the living God.

Now, as all men who have aught of a due reverence of God or his truth remaining with them, cannot but be wary how they give the least admittance to such opinions as have from the beginning been witnessed against and condemned by Christ himself, his apostles and all that followed them in their faith and ways in all generations; so others whose hearts tremble for the danger they apprehend which these sacred truths may be in of being corrupted or defamed by the present opposition against them, may know that it is no other but what the church and faith of professors has already been exercised with, and, through the power of Him that enables them, have constantly triumphed over. And, for any part, I look upon it as a blessed effect of the holy, wise providence of God, that those who have long harboured these abominations of denying the holy Trinity, and the person and satisfaction of Christ, in their minds, but yet have sheltered themselves from common observation under the shades of dark, obscure, and uncouth expressions, with many other specious pretences, should be given up to join themselves with such persons (and to profess a community of persuasion with them in those opinions, as have rendered themselves infamous from the first foundation of Christianity), and wherein they will assuredly meet with the same success as those have done who have gone before them.

For the other head of opposition, made by these persons unto the truth in reference unto the satisfaction of Christ, and the imputation of his righteousness thereon unto our justification, I have not much to say as to the time past. In general, the doctrine wherein they boast, being first brought forth in a rude misshapen manner by the Pelagian heretics, was afterward improved by one Abelardus, a sophistical scholar in France; but owes its principal form and poison unto the endeavours of Faustus Socinus, and those who have followed him in his subtle attempt to corrupt the whole doctrine of the gospel. Of these men are those amongst us who at this day so busily dispute and write about the Trinity, the Deity of Christ, and his satisfaction. -- the followers and disciples. And it is much more from their masters, who were some of them men learned, diligent, and subtle, than from themselves, that they are judged to be of any great consideration. For I can truly say, that, upon the sedate examination of all that I could ever yet hear or get a sight of, either spoken or written by them, -- that is, any amongst us, -- I never yet observed an undertaking of so great importance managed with a greater evidence of incompetency and inability, to give any tolerable countenance unto it. If any of them shall for the future attempt to give any new countenance or props to their tottering errors, it will doubtless be attended unto by some of those many who cannot but know that it is incumbent on them "to contend earnestly for the faith once delivered unto the saints." This present brief endeavour is only to assist and direct those who are less exercised in the ways of managing controversies in religion, that they may have a brief comprehension of the truths opposed, with the firm foundations whereon they are built, and be in a readiness to shield their faith both against the fiery darts of Satan, and secure their minds against the "cunning sleight of men, who lie in wait to deceive." And wherein this discourse seems in any thing to be too brief or concise, the author is not to be blamed who was confined unto these strait bounds by those whose requests enjoined him this service.

The Doctrine of the Holy Trinity Explained and Vindicated

The doctrine of the blessed Trinity may be considered two ways: First, In respect unto the revelation and proposal of it in the Scripture, to direct us unto the author, object, and end of our faith, in our worship and obedience. Secondly, As it is farther declared and explained, in terms, expressions, and propositions, reduced from the original revelation of it, suited whereunto, and meet to direct and keep the mind from undue apprehensions of the things it believes, and to declare them, unto farther edification.

In the first way, it consists merely in the propositions wherein the revelation of God is expressed in the Scripture; and in this regard two things are required of us. First, To understand the terms of the propositions, as they are enunciations of truth; and, Secondly, To believe the things taught, revealed, and declared in them.

In the first instance, no more, I say, is required of us, but that we assent unto the assertions and testimonies of God concerning himself, according to their natural and genuine sense, as he will be known, believed in, feared, and worshipped by us, as he is our Creator, Lord, and Rewarder; and that because he himself has, by his revelation, not only warranted us so to do, but also made it our duty, necessary and indispensable. Now, the sum of this revelation in this matter is, that God is one; -- that this one God is Father, Son, and Holy Ghost; -- that the Father is the Father of the Son; and the Son, the Son of the Father; and the Holy Ghost, the Spirit of the Father and the Son; and that, in respect of this their mutual relation, they are distinct from each other.

This is the substance of the doctrine of the Trinity, as to the first direct concernment of faith therein. The first intention of the Scripture, in the revelation of God towards us, is, as was said, that we might fear him, believe, worship, obey him, and live unto him, as God. That we may do this in a due manner, and worship the only true God, and not adore the false imaginations of our own minds it declares, as was said, that this God is one, the Father, Son, and Holy Ghost; -- that the Father is this one God; and therefore is to be believed in, worshipped, obeyed, lived unto, and in all things considered by us as the first cause, sovereign Lord, and last end of all; -- that the Son is the one true God; and therefore is to be believed in, worshipped, obeyed, lived unto, and in all things considered by us as the first cause, sovereign Lord, and last end of all; -- and so, also, of the Holy Ghost. This is the whole of faith's concernment in this matter, as it respects the direct revelation of God made by himself in the Scripture, and the first proper general end thereof. Let this be clearly confirmed by direct and positive divine testimonies, containing the declaration and revelation of God concerning himself, and faith is secured as to all it concerns; for it has both its proper formal object, and is sufficiently enabled to be directive of divine worship and obedience.

The explication of this doctrine unto edification, suitable unto the revelation mentioned, is of another consideration; and two things are incumbent on us to take care of therein:-- First, That what is affirmed and taught do directly tend unto the ends of the revelation itself, by informing and enlightening of the mind in the knowledge of the mystery of it, so far as in this life we are, by divine assistance, capable to comprehend it; that is, that faith may be increased, strengthened, and confirmed against temptations and oppositions of Satan, and men of corrupt minds; and that we may be distinctly directed unto, and encouraged in, the obedience unto, and worship of God, that are required of us. Secondly, That nothing be affirmed or taught herein that may beget or occasion any undue apprehensions concerning God, or our obedience unto him, with respect unto the best, highest, securest revelations that we have of him and our duty. These things being done and secured, the end of the declaration of this doctrine concerning God is attained.

In the declaration, then, of this doctrine unto the edification of the church, there is contained a farther explanation of the things before asserted, as proposed directly and in themselves as the object of our faith, -- namely, how God is one, in respect of his nature, substance, essence, Godhead, or divine being; how, being Father, Son, and Holy Ghost, he subsists in these three distinct persons or hypostases; and what are their mutual respects to each other, by which, as their peculiar properties, giving them the manner of their subsistence, they are distinguished one from another; with sundry other things of the like necessary consequence unto the revelation mentioned. And herein, as in the application of all other divine truths and mysteries whatever, yea, of all moral commanded duties, use is to be made of such words and expressions as, it may be, are not literally and formally contained in the Scripture; but only are, unto our conceptions and apprehensions, expository of what is so contained. And to deny the liberty, yea, the necessity hereof, is to deny all interpretation of the Scripture, -- all endeavours to express the sense of the words of it unto the understandings of one another; which is, in a word, to render the Scripture itself altogether useless. For if it be unlawful for me to speak or write what I conceive to be the sense of the words of the Scripture, and the nature of the thing signified and expressed by them, it is unlawful for me, also, to think or conceive in my mind what is the sense of the words or nature of the things; which to say, is to make brutes of ourselves, and to frustrate the whole design of God in giving unto us the great privilege of his word.

Wherefore, in the declaration of the doctrine of the Trinity, we may lawfully, nay, we must necessarily, make use of other words, phrases, and expressions, than what are literally and syllabically contained in the Scripture, but teach no other things.

Moreover, whatever is so revealed in the Scripture is no less true and divine as to whatever necessarily follows thereon, than it is as unto that which is principally revealed and directly expressed. For how far soever the lines be drawn and extended, from truth nothing can follow and ensue but what is true also; and that in the same kind of truth with that which it is derived and deduced from. For if the principal assertion be a truth of divine revelation, so is also whatever is included therein, and which may be rightly from thence collected. Hence it follows, that when the Scripture reveals the Father, Son, and Holy Ghost to be one God, seeing it necessarily and unavoidably follows thereon that they are one in essence (wherein alone it is possible they can be one), and three in their distinct subsistences (wherein alone it is possible they can be three), -- this is no less of divine revelation than the first principle from whence these things follow.

These being the respects which the doctrine of the Trinity falls under, the necessary method of faith and reason, in the believing and declaring of it, is plain and evident:--

First. The revelation of it is to be asserted and vindicated, as it is proposed to be believed, for the ends mentioned. Now, this is, as was declared, that there is one God; that this God is Father, Son, and Holy Ghost; and so, that the Father is God, so is the Son, so is the Holy Ghost.

This being received and admitted by faith, the explication of it is, --

Secondly, To be insisted on, and not taken into consideration until the others be admitted. And herein lies the preposterous course of those who fallaciously and captiously go about to oppose this sacred truth:-- they will always begin their opposition, not unto the revelation of it, but unto the explanation of it; which is used only for farther edification. Their disputes and cavils shall be against the Trinity, essence, substance, persons, personality, respects, properties of the divine persons, with the modes of expressing these things; whilst the plain scriptural revelation of the things themselves from whence they are but explanatory deductions, is not spoken to, nor admitted into confirmation. By this means have they entangled many weak, unstable souls, who, when they have met with things too high, hard, and difficult for them (which in divine mysteries they may quickly do), in the explication of this doctrine, have suffered themselves to be taken off from a due consideration of the full and plain revelation of the thing itself in Scripture; until, their temptations being made strong, and their darkness increased, it was too late for them to return unto it; as bringing along with them the cavils wherewith they were prepossessed, rather than that faith and obedience which is required. But yet all this while these explanations, so excepted against, are indeed not of any original consideration in this matter. Let the direct, express revelations of the doctrine be confirmed, they will follow of themselves, nor will be excepted against by those who believe and receive it. Let that be rejected, and they will fall of themselves, and never be contended for by those who did make use of them. But of these things we shall treat again afterward.

This, therefore, is the way, the only way that we rationally can, and that which in duty we ought to proceed in and by, for the asserting and confirming of the doctrine of the holy Trinity under consideration, -- namely, that we produce divine revelations or testimonies, wherein faith may safely rest and acquiesce, that God is one; that this one God is Father, Son, and Holy Ghost; so that the Father is God, so also is the Son, and the Holy Ghost likewise, and, as such, are to be believed in, obeyed, worshipped, acknowledged, as the first cause and last end of all, -- our Lord and reward. If this be not admitted, if somewhat of it be not, particularly [if it be] denied, we need not, we have no warrant or ground to proceed any farther, or at all to discourse about the unity of the divine essence, or the distinction of the persons.

We have not, therefore, any original contest in this matter with any, but such as deny either God to be one, or the Father to be God, or the Son to be God, or the Holy Ghost so to be. If any deny either of these in particular, we are ready to confirm it by sufficient testimonies of Scripture, or clear and undeniable divine revelation. When this is evinced and vindicated, we shall willingly proceed to manifest that the explications used of this doctrine unto the edification of the church are according to truth, and such as necessarily are required by the nature of the things themselves. And this gives us the method of the ensuing small discourse, with the reasons of it:--

I. The first thing which we affirm to be delivered unto us by divine revelation as the object of our faith, is, that God is one. I know that this may be uncontrollably evinced by the light of reason itself, unto as good and quiet an assurance as the mind of man is capable of in any of its apprehensions whatever; but I speak of it now as it is confirmed unto us by divine revelation. How this assertion of one God respects the nature, essence, or divine being of God, shall be declared afterward. At present it is enough to represent the testimonies that he is one, -- only one. And because we have no difference with our adversaries distinctly about this matter, I shall only name few of them. Deut. vi. 4, "Hear, O Israel; The Lord our God is one Lord." A most pregnant testimony; and yet, notwithstanding, as I shall elsewhere manifest, the Trinity itself, in that one divine essence, is here asserted. Isa. xliv. 6, 8, "Thus saith the Lord the King of Israel, and his Redeemer the Lord of hosts; I am the first, and I am the last; and beside me there is no God. Is there a God beside me? yea, there is no God; I know not any." In which also we may manifest that a plurality of persons is included and expressed. And although there be no more absolute and sacred truth than this, that God is one, yet it may be evinced that it is nowhere mentioned in the Scripture, but that, either in the words themselves or the context of the place, a plurality of persons in that one sense is intimated.

II. Secondly, It is proposed as the object of our faith, that the Father is God. And herein, as is pretended, there is also an agreement between us and those who oppose the doctrine of the Trinity. But there is a mistake in this matter. Their hypothesis, as they call it, or, indeed, presumptuous error, casts all the conceptions that are given us concerning God in the Scripture into disorder and confusion. For the Father, as he whom we worship, is often called so only with reference unto his Son; as the Son is so with reference to the Father.

He is the "only begotten of the Father," John i. 14. But now, if this Son had no pre-existence in his divine nature before he was born of the Virgin, there was no God the Father seventeen hundred years ago, because there was no Son. And on this ground did the Marcionites [4] of old plainly deny the Father (whom, under the New Testament, we worship) to be the God of the Old Testament, who made the world, and was worshipped from the foundation of it. For it seems to follow, that he whom we worship being the Father, and on this supposition that the Son had no pre-existence unto his incarnation, he was not the Father under the Old Testament; he is some other from him that was so revealed. I know the folly of that inference; yet how, on this opinion of the sole existence of the Son in time, men can prove the Father to be God, let others determine. "He that abideth in the doctrine of Christ, he has both the Father and the Son;" but "whosoever transgresseth and abideth not in the doctrine of Christ, has not God," 2 John 9. Whoever denies Christ the Son, as the Son, that is, the eternal Son of God, he loses the Father also, and the true God; he has not God. For that God which is not the Father, and which ever was, and was not the Father, is not the true God. Hence many of the fathers, even of the first writers of the church, were forced unto great pains in the confirmation of this truth, that the Father of Jesus Christ was he who made the world, gave the law, spoke by the prophets, and was the author of the Old Testament; and that against men who professed themselves to be Christians. And this brutish apprehension of theirs arose from no other principle but this, that the Son had only a temporal existence, and was not the eternal Son of God.

But that I may not in this brief discourse digress unto other controversies than what lies directly before us, and seeing the adversaries of the truth we contend for do, in words at least, grant that the Father of our Lord Jesus Christ is the true God, or the only true God, I shall not farther show the inconsistency of their hypothesis with this confession, but take it for granted that to us "there is one God, the Father," 1 Cor. viii. 6; see John xvii. 3. So that he who is not the Father, who was not so from eternity, whose paternity is not equally co-existent unto his Deity, is not God unto us.

III. Thirdly, It is asserted and believed by the church that Jesus Christ is God, the eternal Son of God; -- that is, he is proposed, declared, and revealed unto us in the Scripture to be God, that is to be served, worshipped, believed in, obeyed as God, upon the account of his own divine excellencies. And whereas we believe and know that he was man, that he was born, lived, and died as a man, it is declared that he is God also; and that, as God, he did pre-exist in the form of God before his incarnation, which was effected by voluntary actings of his own, -- which could not be without a pre-existence in another nature. This is proposed unto us to be believed upon divine testimony and by divine revelation. And the sole inquiry in this matter is, whether this be proposed in the Scripture as an object of faith, and that which is indispensably necessary for us to believe? Let us, then, nakedly attend unto what the Scripture asserts in this matter, and that in the order of the books of it, in some particular instances which at present occur to mind; as these that follow:--

Ps. xlv. 6, "Thy throne, O God, is for ever and ever." Applied unto Christ, Heb. i. 8, "But unto the Son he saith, Thy throne, O God, is for ever and ever."

Ps. lxviii. 17, 18, "The chariots of God are twenty thousand, even thousands of angels: the Lord is among them, as in Sinai, in the holy place. Thou hast ascended on high, thou hast led captivity captive: thou hast received gifts for men; yea, for the rebellious also, that the Lord God might dwell among them." Applied unto the Son, Eph. iv. 8-10, "Wherefore he saith, When he ascended up on high, he led captivity captive, and gave gifts unto men. Now that he ascended, what is it but that he also descended first into the lower parts of the earth? He that descended is the same also that ascended up far above all heavens that he might fill all things."

Ps. cx. 1, "The Lord said unto my Lord, Sit thou at my right hand." Applied unto Christ by himself, Matt. xxii. 44.

Ps. cii. 25-27, "Of old hast thou laid the foundation of the earth; and the heavens are the work of thy hands. They shall perish, but thou shalt endure: yea, all of them shall wax old like a garment; as a vesture shalt thou change them, and they shall be changed: but thou art the same, and thy years shall have no end." Declared by the apostle to be meant of the Son, Heb. i. 10-12.

Prov. viii. 22-31, "The Lord possessed me in the beginning of his way, before his works of old. I was set up from everlasting, from the beginning, or ever the earth was. When there were no depths, I was brought forth; when there were no fountains abounding with water. Before the mountains were settled, before the hills was I brought forth: while as yet he had not made the earth, nor the fields, nor the highest part of the dust of the world. When he prepared the heavens, I was there: when he set a compass upon the face of the depth: when he established the clouds above: when he strengthened the fountains of the deep: when he gave to the sea his decree, that the waters should not pass his commandment: when he appointed the foundations of the earth: then I was by him, as one brought up with him: and I was daily his delight, rejoicing always before him; rejoicing in the habitable part of his earth; and my delights were with the sons of men."

Isa. vi. 1-3, "I saw also the Lord sitting upon a throne, high and lifted up, and his train filled the temple. Above it stood the seraphim: each one had six wings; With twain he covered his face, and with twain he covered his feet, and with twain he did fly. And one cried unto another, and said, Holy, holy, holy, is the Lord of hosts: the whole earth is full of his glory." Applied unto the Son, John xii. 41.

Isa. viii. 13, 14, "Sanctify the Lord of hosts himself; and let him be your fear, and let him be your dread. And he shall be for a sanctuary; but for a stone of stumbling and for a rock of offence to both the houses of Israel, for a gin and for a snare to the inhabitants of Jerusalem." Applied unto the Son, Luke ii. 34; Rom. ix. 33; 1 Pet. ii. 8.

Isa. ix. 6, "For unto us a child is born, unto us a son is given; and the government shall be upon his shoulder: and his name shall be called Wonderful, Counsellor, The mighty God, The everlasting Father, The Prince of Peace. Of the increase of his government and peace there shall be no end."

Jer. xxiii. 5, 6, "Behold, the days come, saith the Lord, that I will raise unto David a righteous Branch; and this is his name whereby he shall be called, Jehovah our Righteousness."

ὅς. xii. 3-5, "He took his brother by the heel in the womb, and by his strength he had power with God: yea, he had power over the angel, and prevailed: he wept, and made supplication unto him: he found him in Bethel, and there he spake with us; even the Lord God of hosts; the Lord is his memorial."

Zech. ii. 8, 9, "For thus saith the Lord of hosts, After the glory has he sent me unto the nations which spoiled you: and ye shall know that the Lord of hosts has sent me."

Matt. xvi. 16, "Thou art the Christ, the Son of the living God."

Luke i. 35, "The Holy Ghost shall come upon thee, and the power of the highest shall overshadow thee: therefore also that holy thing which shall be born of thee shall be called the Son of God."

John i. 1-3. "In the beginning was the Word, and the Word was with God, and the Word was God. The same was in the beginning with God. All things were made by him; and without him was not any thing made that was made."

Verse 14, "And we beheld his glory, the glory as of the only begotten of the Father."

John iii. 13, "And no man has ascended up to heaven, but he that came down from heaven, even the Son of man, which is in heaven."

John viii. 57, 58, "Then said the Jews unto him, Thou art not yet fifty years old, and hast thou seen Abraham? Jesus said unto them, Verily, verily, I say unto you, Before Abraham was, I am."

John x. 30, "I and my Father are one."

John xvii. 5, "And now, O Father, glorify thou me with thine own self with the glory which I had with thee before the world was."

John xx. 28, "And Thomas answered and said unto him, My Lord and my God."

Acts xx. 28, "Feed the church of God, which he has purchased with his own blood."

Rom. i. 3, 4, "Concerning his Son Jesus Christ our Lord, which was made of the seed of David according to the flesh; and declared to be the Son of God with power, according to the spirit of holiness, by the resurrection from the dead."

Rom. ix. 5, "Of whom as concerning the flesh Christ came, who is over all, God blessed for ever. Amen."

Rom. xiv. 10-12, "For we shall all stand before the judgment-seat of Christ. For it is written, As I live, saith the Lord, every knee shall bow to me, and every tongue shall confess to God. So then every one of us shall give account of himself to God."

1 Cor. viii. 6, "And one Lord Jesus, by whom are all things, and we by him."

1 Cor. x. 9, "Neither let us tempt Christ, as some of them also tempted, and were destroyed of serpents;" compared with Numb. xxi. 6.

Phil. ii. 5, 6, "Let this mind be in you, which was also in Christ Jesus: who, being in the form of God, thought it not robbery to be equal with God."

Col. i. 15-17, "Who is the image of the invisible God, the firstborn of every creature: for by him were all things created, that are in heaven, and that are in earth, visible and invisible, whether they be thrones, or dominions, or principalities, or powers; all things were created by him, and for him: and he is before all things, and by him all things consist."

1 Tim. iii. 16, "Without controversy great is the mystery of godliness: God was manifest in the flesh."

Tit. ii. 13, 14, "Looking for that blessed hope, and the glorious appearing of the great God and our Saviour Jesus Christ; who gave himself for us."

Heb. i. throughout.

Chap. iii. 4, "For every house is builded by some man; but he that built all things is God."

1 Pet. i. 11, "Searching what, or what manner of time, the Spirit of Christ which was in them did signify."

Chap. iii. 18-20, "For Christ also has once suffered for sins, being put to death in the flesh, but quickened by the Spirit: by which also he went and preached unto the spirits in prison; which sometime were disobedient, when once the long-suffering of God waited in the days of Noah."

1 John iii. 16, "Hereby perceive we the love of God, because he laid down his life for us."

Chap. v. 20, "And we are in him that is true, even in his Son Jesus Christ. This is the true God, and eternal life."

Rev. i. 8, "I am Alpha and Omega, the beginning and the ending, saith the Lord, which is, and which was, and which is to come, the Almighty."

Verses 11-13, "I am Alpha and Omega, the first and the last: and, What thou seest, write in a book.... And I turned to see the voice that spake with me. And, being turned, I saw seven golden candlesticks; and in the midst of the seven candlesticks one like unto the Son of man."

Verse 17, "And when I saw him, I fell at his feet as dead. And he laid his right hand upon me, saying unto me, Fear not; I am the first and the last."

Chap. ii. 23, "I am he which searcheth the reins and hearts: and I will give unto every one of you according to your works."

These are some of the places wherein the truth under consideration is revealed and declared, -- some of the divine testimonies whereby it is confirmed and established, which I have not at present inquired after, but suddenly repeated as they came to mind. Many more of the like nature and importance may be added unto them, and shall be so as occasion does require.

Let, now, any one who owns the Scripture to be the word of God, -- to contain an infallible revelation of the things proposed in it to be believed, -- and who has any conscience exercised towards God for the receiving and submitting unto what he declares and reveals, take a view of these testimonies, and consider whether they do not sufficiently propose this object of our faith. Shall a few poor trifling sophisms, whose terms are scarcely understood by the most that amongst us make use of them, according as they have found them framed by others, be thought meet to be set up in opposition unto these multiplied testimonies of the Holy Ghost, and to cast the truth confirmed by them down from its credit and reputation in the consciences of men? For my part, I do not see in any thing, but that the testimonies given to the Godhead of Christ, the eternal Son of God, are every way as clear and unquestionable as those are which testify to the being of God, or that there is any God at all. Were men acquainted with the Scriptures as they ought to be, and as the most, considering the means and advantages they have had, might have been; did they ponder and believe on what they read, or had they any tenderness in their consciences as to that reverence, obedience, and subjection of soul which God requires unto his word; it were utterly impossible that their faith in this matter should ever in the least be shaken by a few lewd sophisms or loud clamours of men destitute of the truth, and of the spirit of it.

That we may now improve these testimonies unto the end under design, as the nature of this brief discourse will bear, I shall first remove the general answers which the Socinians give unto them, and then manifest farther how uncontrollable they are, by giving an instance in the frivolous exceptions of the same persons to one of them in particular. And we are ready, God assisting, to maintain that there is not any one of them which does not give a sufficient ground for faith to rest on in this matter concerning the Deity of Christ, and that against all the Socinians in the world.

They say, therefore, commonly, that we prove not by these testimonies what is by them denied. For they acknowledge Christ to be God, and that because he is exalted unto that glory and authority that all creatures are put into subjection unto him, and all, both men and angels, are commanded to worship and adore him. So that he is God by office, though he be not God by nature. He is God, but he is not the most high God. And this last expression they have almost continually in their mouths, "He is not the most high God." And commonly, with great contempt and scorn, they are ready to reproach them who have solidly confirmed the doctrine of the Deity of Christ as ignorant of the state of the controversy, in that they have not proved him to be the most high God, in subordination unto whom they acknowledge Christ to be God, and that he ought to be worshipped with divine and religious worship.

But there cannot be any thing more empty and vain than these pretences; and, besides, they accumulate in them their former errors, with the addition of new ones. For, --

First. The name of the most high God is first ascribed unto God in Gen. xiv. 18, 19, 22, denoting his sovereignty and dominion. Now, as other attributes of God, it is not distinctive of the subject, but only descriptive of it. So are all other excellencies of the nature of God. It does not intimate that there are other gods, only he is the most high, or one over them all; but only that the true God is most high, -- that is, endued with sovereign power, dominion, and authority over all. To say, then, that Christ indeed is God, but not the most high God, is all one as to say he is God, but not the most holy God, or not the true God; and so they have brought their Christ into the number of false gods, whilst they deny the true Christ, who, in his divine nature, is "over all, God blessed for ever," Rom. ix. 5; a phrase of speech perfectly expressing this attribute of the most high God.

Secondly. This answer is suited only unto those testimonies which express the name of God with a corresponding power and authority into that name; for in reference unto these alone can it be pleaded, with any pretence of reason, that he is a God by office, -- though that also be done very futilously and impertinently. But most of the testimonies produced speak directly unto his divine excellencies and properties, which belong unto his nature necessarily and absolutely. That he is eternal, omnipotent, immense, omniscient, infinitely wise; and that he is, and works, and produces effects suitable unto all these properties, and such as nothing but they can enable him for; is abundantly proved by the foregoing testimonies. Now, all these concern a divine nature, a natural essence, a Godhead, and not such power or authority as a man may be exalted unto; yea, the ascribing any of them to such a one, implies the highest contradiction expressible.

Thirdly. This God in authority and of office, and not by nature, that should be the object of divine worship, is a new abomination. For they are divine, essential excellencies that are the formal reason and object of worship, religious and divine; and to ascribe it unto any one that is not God by nature, is idolatry. By making, therefore, their Christ such a God as they describe, they bring him under the severe commination of the true God. Jer. x. 11, "The gods that have not made the heavens and the earth, even they shall perish from the earth, and from under these heavens." That Christ they worship they say is a God; but they deny that he is "that God that made the heavens and the earth:" and so leave him exposed to the threatenings of him, who will accomplish it to the uttermost.

Some other general exceptions sometimes they make use of, which the reader may free himself from the entanglement of, if he do but heed these ensuing rules:--

First. Distinction of persons (of which afterwards), it being in an infinite substance, does no way prove a difference of essence between the Father and the Son. Where, therefore, Christ, as the Son, is said to be another from the Father, or God, spoken personally of the Father, it argues not in the least that he is not partaker of the same nature with him. That in one essence there can be but one person, may be true where the substance is finite and limited, but has no place in that which is infinite.

Secondly. Distinction and inequality in respect of office in Christ, does not in the least take away his equality and sameness with the Father in respect of nature and essence, Phil. ii. 7, 8. A son, of the same nature with his father, and therein equal to him, may in office be his inferior, -- his subject.

Thirdly. The advancement and exaltation of Christ as mediator to any dignity whatever, upon or in reference to the work of our redemption and salvation, is not at all inconsistent with the essential honour, dignity, and worth, which he has in himself as God blessed for ever. Though he humbled himself, and was exalted in office, yet in nature he was one and the same; he changed not.

Fourthly. The Scriptures, asserting the humanity of Christ, with the concernments thereof, as his birth, life, and death, do no more thereby deny his Deity than, by asserting his Deity, with the essential properties thereof, they deny his humanity.

Fifthly. God working in and by Christ as he was mediator, denotes the Father's sovereign appointment of the things mentioned to be done, -- not his immediate efficiency in the doing of the things themselves.

These rules are proposed a little before their due place in the method which we pursue. But I thought meet to interpose them here, as containing a sufficient ground for the resolution and answering of all the sophisms and objections which the adversaries use in this cause.

From the cloud of witnesses before produced, every one whereof is singly sufficient to evert the Socinian infidelity, I shall in one of them give an instance, both of the clearness of the evidence and the weakness of the exceptions which are wont to be put in against them, as was promised; and this is John i. 1-3, "In the beginning was the Word, and the Word was with God, and the Word was God. The same was in the beginning with God. All things were made by him; and without him was not any thing made that was made."

By the Word, here, or ὁ Λόγος, on what account soever he be so called, either as being the eternal Word and Wisdom of the Father, or as the great Revealer of the will of God unto us, Jesus Christ the Son of God is intended. This is on all hands acknowledged; and the context will admit of no hesitation about it. For of this Word it is said, that "he came" into the world, verse 10; "was rejected by his own," verse 11; "was made flesh and dwelt among us, whose glory was the glory as of the only begotten Son of the Father," verse 14; called expressly "Jesus Christ," verse 17; "the only begotten Son of the Father," verse 18. The subject, then, treated of, is here agreed upon; and it is no less evident that it is the design of the apostle to declare both who and what he was of whom he treats. Here, then, if any where, we may learn what we are to believe concerning the person of Christ; which also we may certainly do, if our minds are not perverted through prejudice, "whereby the god of this world does blind the minds of them which believe not, lest the light of the glorious gospel of Christ, who is the image of God, should shine unto them," 2 Cor. iv. 4. Of this Word, then, this Son of God, it is affirmed, that he "was in the beginning." And this word, if it does not absolutely and formally express eternity, yet it does a pre-existence unto the whole creation; which amounts to the same: for nothing can pre-exist unto all creatures, but in the nature of God, which is eternal; unless we shall suppose a creature before the creation of any. But what is meant by this expression the Scripture does elsewhere declare. Prov. viii. 23,

"I was set up from everlasting, from the beginning, or ever the earth was." John xvii. 5, "Glorify thou me with thine own self, with the glory which I had with thee before the world was." Both which places, as they explain this phrase, so also do they undeniably testify unto the eternal pre-existence of Christ the Son of God. And in this case we prevail against our adversaries, if we prove any pre-existence of Christ unto his incarnation; which, as they absolutely deny, so to grant it would overthrow their whole heresy in this matter. And therefore they know that the testimony of our Saviour concerning himself, if understood in a proper, intelligible sense, is perfectly destructive of their pretensions, John viii. 58, "Before Abraham was, I am." For although there be no proper sense in the words, but a gross equivocation, if the existence of Christ before Abraham was born be not asserted in them (seeing he spoke in answer to that objection of the Jews, that he was not yet fifty years old, and so could not have seen Abraham, nor Abraham him; and the Jews that were present, understood well enough that he asserted a divine pre-existence unto his being born, so long ago, as that hereon, after their manner, they took up stones to stone him, as supposing him to have blasphemed in asserting his Deity, as others now do in the denying of it); yet they [Socinians], seeing how fatal this pre-existence, though not here absolutely asserted to be eternal, would be to their cause, contend that the meaning of the words is, that "Christ was to be the light of the world before Abraham was made the father of many nations;" -- an interpretation so absurd and sottish, as never any man not infatuated by the god of this world could once admit and give countenance unto.

But "in the beginning," as absolutely used, is the same with "from everlasting," as it is expounded, Prov. viii. 23, and denotes an eternal existence; which is here affirmed of the Word, the Son of God. But let the word "beginning," be restrained unto the subject matter treated of (which is the creation of all things), and the pre-existence of Christ in his divine nature unto the creation of all things is plainly revealed, and inevitably asserted. And indeed, not only the word, but the discourse of these verses, does plainly relate unto, and is expository of, the first verse in the Bible, Gen. i. 1, "In the beginning God created the heaven and the earth." There it is asserted that in the beginning God created all things; here, that the Word was in the beginning, and made all things. This, then, is the least that we have obtained from this first word of our testimony, -- namely, that the Word or Son of God had a personal pre-existence unto the whole creation. In what nature this must be, let these men of reason satisfy themselves, who know that Creator and creatures take up the whole nature of beings. One of them he must be; and it may be well supposed that he was not a creature before the creation of any.

But, secondly, Where, or with whom, was this Word in the beginning? "It was," says the Holy Ghost, "with God." There being no creature then existing, he could be nowhere but with God; that is, the Father, as it is expressed in one of the testimonies before going, Prov. viii. 22, "The Lord possessed me in the beginning of his way, before his works of old;" verse 30, "Then was I by him as one brought up with him, and I was daily his delight, rejoicing always before him;" that is, in the beginning this Word, or Wisdom of God, was with God.

And this is the same which our Lord Jesus asserts concerning himself, John iii. 13, "And no man," says he, "has ascended up to heaven, but he that came down from heaven, even the Son of man which is in heaven." And so in other places he affirms his being in heaven, -- that is, with God, -- at the same time when he was on the earth; whereby he declares the immensity of his nature, and the distinction of his person; and his coming down from heaven before he was incarnate on the earth, declaring his pre-existence; by both manifesting the meaning of this expression, that "in the beginning he was with God." But hereunto they have invented a notable evasion. For although they know not well what to make of the last clause of the words, that says, then he was in heaven when he spoke on earth, -- "The Son of man which is in heaven," answerable to the description of God's immensity, "Do not I fill heaven and earth? saith the Lord," Jer. xxiii. 24, but say that he was there by heavenly meditation, as another man may be; yet they give a very clear answer to what must of necessity be included in his descending from heaven, -- namely, his pre-existence to his incarnation: for they tell us that, before his public ministry, he was in his human nature (which is all they allow unto him) taken up into heaven, and there taught the gospel, as the great impostor Mohammed pretended he was taught his Alkoran. If you ask them who told them so, they cannot tell; but they can tell when it was, -- namely, when he was led by the Spirit into the wilderness for forty days after his baptism. But yet this instance is subject to another misadventure; in that one of the evangelists plainly affirms that he was "those forty days in the wilderness with the wild beasts," Mark i. 13, and so, surely, not in heaven in the same nature, by his bodily presence, with God and his holy angels.

And let me add this, by the way, that the interpretation of this place, John i. 1, to be mentioned afterward, and those of the two places before mentioned, John viii. 58, iii. 13, Faustus Socinus [5] learned out of his uncle Lælius' papers, as he confesses; and does more than intimate that he believed he had them as it were by revelation. And it may be so; they are indeed so forced, absurd, and irrational, that no man could ever fix upon them by any reasonable investigation; but the author of these revelations if we may judge of the parent by the child, could be no other but the spirit of error and darkness. I suppose, therefore, that notwithstanding these exceptions, Christians will believe "that in the beginning the Word was with God;" that is, that the Son was with the Father, as is frequently elsewhere declared.

But who was this Word? Says the apostle, He was God. He was so with God (that is, the Father), as that he himself was God also; -- God, in that notion of God which both nature and the Scripture do represent; not a god by office, one exalted to that dignity (which cannot well be pretended before the creation of the world), but as Thomas confessed him, "Our Lord and our God," John xx. 28; or as Paul expresses it, "Over all, God blessed for ever;" or the most high God; which these men love to deny. Let not the infidelity of men, excited by the craft and malice of Satan, seek for blind occasions, and this matter is determined; if the word and testimony of God be able to umpire a difference amongst the children of men. Here is the sum of our creed in this matter, "In the beginning the Word was God," and so continues unto eternity, being Alpha and Omega, the first and the last, the Lord God Almighty.

And to show that he was so God in the beginning, as that he was one distinct, in something, from God the Father, by whom afterward he was sent into the world, he adds, verse 2, "The same was in the beginning with God." Farther, also, to evince what he has asserted and revealed for us to believe, the Holy Ghost adds, both as a firm declaration of his eternal Deity, and also his immediate care of the world (which how he variously exercised, both in a way of providence and grace, he afterward declares), verse 3, "All things were made by him." He was so in the beginning, before all things, as that he made them all. And that it may not be supposed that the "all" that he is said to make or create was to be limited unto any certain sort of things, he adds, that "without him nothing was made that was made;" which gives the first assertion an absolute universality as to its subject.

And this he farther describes, verse 10, "He was in the world, and the world was made by him." The world that was made, has a usual distribution, in the Scripture, into the "heavens and the earth, and all things contained in them;" -- as Acts iv. 24, "Lord, thou art God, which hast made heaven, and earth, and the sea, and all that in them is;" that is, the world, the making whereof is expressly assigned unto the Son, Heb. i. 10, "Thou, Lord, in the beginning hast laid the foundation of the earth; and the heavens are the works of thine hands." And the apostle Paul, to secure our understandings in this matter, instances in the most noble parts of the creation, and which, if any, might seem to be excepted from being made by him, Col. i. 16, "For by him were all things created, that are in heaven, and that are in earth, visible and invisible, whether they be thrones, or dominions, or principalities, or powers; all things were created by him, and for him." The Socinians say, indeed, that he made angels to be thrones and principalities; that is, he gave them their order, but not their being: which is expressly contrary to the words of the text; so that a man knows not well what to say to these persons, who, at their pleasure, cast off the authority of God in his word: "By him were all things created, that are in heaven, and that are in earth."

What now can be required to secure our faith in this matter? In what words possible could a divine revelation of the eternal power and Godhead of the Son of God be made more plain and clear unto the sons of men? Or how could the truth of any thing more evidently be represented unto their minds? If we understand not the mind of God and intention of the Holy Ghost in this matter, we may utterly despair ever to come to an acquaintance with any thing that God reveals unto us; or, indeed, with any thing else that is expressed or is to be expressed, by words. It is directly said that the Word (that is Christ, as is acknowledged by all) "was with God," distinct from him; and "was God," one with him; that he was so "in the beginning," before the creation, that he "made all things," -- the world, all things in heaven and in earth: and if he be not God, who is? The sum is, -- all the ways whereby we may know God are, his name, his properties, and his works; but they are all here ascribed by the Holy Ghost to the Son, to the Word: and he therefore is God, or we know neither who nor what God is.

But say the Socinians, "These things are quite otherwise, and the words have another sense in them than you imagine." What is it, I pray? We bring none to them, we impose no sense upon them, we strain not any word in them, from, beside, or beyond its native, genuine signification, its constant application in the Scripture, and common use amongst men. What, then, is this latent sense that is intended, and is discoverable only by themselves? Let us hear them coining and stamping this sense of theirs.

First, they say that by "In the beginning," is not meant of thebeginning of all things, or the creation of them, but the beginning of the preaching of the gospel. But why so, I pray? Wherever these words are else used in the Scripture, they denote the beginning of all things, or eternity absolutely, or an existence preceding their creation. "In the beginning God created the heaven and the earth," Gen. i. 1. "I was set up from everlasting, from the beginning, or ever the earth was," Prov. viii. 23. "Thou, Lord, in the beginning hast laid the foundation of the earth," Heb. i. 10. And besides, these words are never used absolutely anywhere for the beginning of the gospel. There is mention made, indeed, of the "beginning of the gospel of Jesus Christ," Mark i. 1, which is referred to the preaching of John Baptist: but "In the beginning," absolutely, is never so used or applied; and they must meet with men of no small inclination unto them, who will, upon their desire, in a matter of so great importance, forego the sense of words which is natural and proper, fixed by its constant use in the Scripture, when applied in the same kind, for that which is forced and strained, and not once exemplified in the whole book of God. But the words, they say, are to be restrained to the subject-matter treated of. Well, what is that subject-matter? "The new creation, by the preaching of the gospel." But this is plainly false; nor will the words allow any such sense, nor the contempt, nor is any thing offered to give evidence unto this corrupt perverting of the words, unless it be a farther perverting of other testimonies no less clear than this.

For what is, according to this interpretation, the meaning of these words, "In the beginning was the Word?" "That is, when John Baptist preached, and said, This is the Lamb of God,' which was signally the beginning of the gospel, -- then he was." That is, he was when he was, -- no doubt of it! And is not this a notable way of interpreting of Scripture which these great pretenders to a dictatorship in reason, indeed hucksters in sophistry, do make use of? But to go on with them in this supposition, How was he then with God, -- "The Word was with God?" "That is," say they, "he was then known only to God, before John Baptist preached him in the beginning." But what shall compel us to admit of this uncouth sense and exposition, -- " He was with God;' that is, he was known to God alone?" What is there singular herein? Concerning how many things may the same be affirmed? Besides, it is absolutely false. He was known to the angel Gabriel, who came to his mother with the message of his incarnations Luke i. 35. He was known to the two angels which appeared to the shepherds upon his birth, Luke ii. 9, -- to all the heavenly host assembled to give praise and glory to God on the account of his nativity, as those who came to worship him, and to pay him the homage due unto him, . He was known to his mother, Luke ii. 10, 13, 14, the blessed Virgin, and to Joseph, and Zacharias, and to Elisabeth, to Simeon and Anna, to John Baptist, and probably to many more to whom Simeon and Anna spoke of him, Luke ii. 38. So that the sense pretended to be wrung out and extorted from these words, against their proper meaning and intendment, is indeed false and frivolous, and belongs not at all unto them.

But let this pass. What shall we say to the next words, "And the Word was God?" Give us leave, without disturbance from you, but to believe this expression, which comprises a revelation of God, proposed to us on purpose that we should believe it, and there will be, as was said, an end of this difference and debate. Yea, but say they, "These words have another sense also." Strange! They seem to be so plain and positive, that it is impossible any other sense should be fixed on them but only this, that the Word was in the beginning, and was God; and therefore is so still, unless he who is once God can cease so to be. "But the meaning is, that afterwards God exalted him, and made him God, as to rule, authority, and power." This making of him God is an expression very offensive to the ears of all sober Christians; and was therefore before exploded. And these things here, as all other figments, hang together like a rope of sand. In the beginning of the gospel he was God, before any knew him but only God; that is, after he had preached the gospel, and died, and rose again, and was exalted at the right hand of God, he was made God, and that not properly, which is absolutely impossible, but in an improper sense! How prove they, then, this perverse nonsense to be the sense of these plain words? They say it must needs be so. Let them believe them who are willing to perish with them.

Thus far, then, we have their sense:-- "In the beginning," that is, about sixteen or seventeen hundred years ago, "the Word," that is, the human nature of Christ before it was made flesh, which it was in its being, "was with God," that is, known to God alone; and "in the beginning," that is afterwards, not in the beginning, was made God! -- which is the sum of their exposition of this place.

But what shall we say to what is affirmed concerning his making of all things, so as that without him, that is, without his making of it, nothing was made that was made; especially seeing that these "all things" are expressly said to be the world, verse 10, and all things therein contained, even in heaven and earth? Col. i. 16. An ordinary man would think that they should now be taken hold of, and that there is no way of escape left unto them; but they have it in a readiness. By the "all things" here, are intended all things of the gospel, -- the preaching of it, the sending of the apostles to preach it, and to declare the will of God; and by the "world," is intended the world to come, or the new state of things under the gospel. This is the substance of what is pleaded by the greatest masters amongst them in this matter, and they are not ashamed thus to plead.

And the reader, in this instance, may easily discern what a desperate cause they are engaged in, and how bold and desperate they are in the management of it. For, --

First, The words are a plain illustration of the divine nature of the Word, by his divine power and works, as the very series of them declares. He was God, and he made all things: "He that built all things is God," Heb. iii. 4.

Secondly, There is no one word spoken concerning the gospel, nor the preaching of it, nor any effects of that preaching; which the apostle expressly insists upon and declares afterward, verse 15, and so onwards.

Thirdly, The making of all things, here ascribed unto the Word, was done in the beginning; but that making of all things which they intend, in erecting the church by the preaching of the word, was not done in the beginning, but afterwards, -- most of it, as themselves confess, after the ascension of Christ into heaven.

Fourthly, In this gloss, what is the meaning of "All things?" "Only some things," say the Socinians. What is the meaning of "Were made?" "That is, were mended." "By him?" "That is, the apostles, principally preaching the gospel." And this "In the beginning?" "After it was past;" -- for so they say expressly, that the principal things here intended were effected by the apostles afterwards.

I think, since the beginning, place it when you will, -- the beginning of the world or the beginning of the gospel, -- there was never such an exposition of the words of God or man contended for.

Fifthly, It is said, "He made the world," and he "came" into it, -- namely, the world which he made; and "the world," or the inhabitants of it "knew him not." But the world they intend did know him: for the church knew him, and acknowledged him to be the Son of God; for that was the foundation that it was built upon.

I have instanced directly in this only testimony, to give the reader a pledge of the full confirmation which may be given unto this great fundamental truth, by a due improvement of those other testimonies, or distinct revelations, which speak no less expressly to the same purpose. And of them there is not any one but we are ready to vindicate it, if called whereunto, from the exceptions of these men; which how bold and sophistical they are we may, in these now considered, also learn and know.

It appears, then, that there is a full, sufficient revelation made in the Scripture of the eternal Deity of the Son of God; and that he is so, as is the Father also. More particular testimonies I shall not at present insist upon, referring the full discussion and vindication of these truths to another season.

IV. Fourthly, We are, therefore, in the next place, to manifest that the one, or the like testimony, is given unto the Deity of the Holy Spirit; that is, that he is revealed and declared in the Scripture as the object of our faith, worship, and obedience, on the account and for the reason of those divine excellencies which are the sole reason of our yielding religious worship unto any, or expecting from any the reward that is promised unto us, or to be brought by them to the end for which we are. And herein lies, as was showed, the concernment of faith. When that knows what it is to believe as on divine revelation, and is enabled thereby to regulate the soul in its present obedience and future expectation, seeing it is its nature to work by love and hope, there it rests. Now, this is done to the utmost satisfaction in the revelation that is made of the divine existence, divine excellencies, and divine operations of the Spirit; as shall be briefly manifested.

But before we proceed, we may, in our way, observe a great congruency of success in those who have denied the Deity of the Son and those who have denied that of the Holy Spirit. For as to the Son, after some men began once to disbelieve the revelation concerning him, and would not acknowledge him to be God and man in one person, they could never settle nor agree, either what or who he was, or who was his Father, or why he was the Son. Some said he was a phantasm or appearance, and that he had no real subsistence in this world; and that all that was done by him was an appearance, he himself being they know not what elsewhere. That proud beast, Paulus Samosatenus, [6] whose flagitious life contended for a pre-eminence in wickedness with his prodigious heresies, was one of the first, after the Jews, that positively contended for his being a man, and no more; who was followed by Photinus and others. The Arians perceiving the folly of this opinion, with the odium of it amongst all that bare the name of Christians, and that they had as good deny the whole Scripture as not grant unto him a pre-existence in a divine nature antecedent to his incarnation, they framed a new Deity, which God should make before the world, in all things like himself, but not the same with him in essence and substance, but to be so like him that, by the writings of some of them, ye can scarce know the one from the other; and that this was the Son of God, also, who was afterward incarnate. Others, in the meantime, had more monstrous imaginations: some, that he was an angel; some, that he was the sun; some, that he was the soul of the world; some, the light within men. Departing from their proper rest, so have they hovered about, and so have they continued to do until this day.

In the same manner it is come to pass with them who have denied the Deity of the Holy Ghost. They could never find where to stand or abide; but one has cried up one thing, another another. At first they observed that such things were everywhere ascribed unto him in the Scripture as uncontrollably evidence him to be an intelligent, voluntary agent. This they found so plain and evident, that they could not deny but that he was a person, or an intelligent subsistence. Wherefore, seeing they were resolved not to assent unto the revelation of his being God, they made him a created spirit, chief and above all others; but still, whatever else he were, he was only a creature. And this course some of late also have steered.

The Socinians, on the other hand, observing that such things are assigned and ascribed unto him, as that, if they acknowledge him to be a person, or a substance, they must, upon necessity, admit him to be God, though they seemed not, at first, at all agreed what to think or say concerning him positively, yet they all concurred peremptorily in denying his personality. Hereon, some of them said he was the gospel, which others of them have confuted; some, that he was Christ. Neither could they agree whether there was one Holy Ghost or more; -- whether the Spirit of God, and the good Spirit of God, and the Holy Spirit, be the same or no. In general, now they conclude that he is "vis Dei" or "virtus Dei," or "efficacia Dei;" -- no substance, but a quality, that may be considered either as being in God, and then they say it is the Spirit of God; or as sanctifying and conforming men unto God, and then they say it is the Holy Ghost. Whether these things do answer the revelation made in the Scripture concerning the eternal Spirit of God, will be immediately manifested. Our Quakers, who have for a long season hovered up and down like a swarm of flies, with a confused noise and humming, begin now to settle in the opinions lately by them declared for. But what their thoughts will fall in to be concerning the Holy Ghost, when they shall be contented to speak intelligibly, and according to the usage of other men, or the pattern of Scripture the great rule of speaking or treating about spiritual things, I know not, and am uncertain whether they do so themselves or no. Whether he may be the light within them, or an infallible afflatus, is uncertain. In the meantime, what is revealed unto us in the Scripture to be believed concerning the Holy Ghost, his Deity and personality, may be seen in the ensuing testimonies.

The sum of this revelation is, -- that the Holy Spirit is an eternally existing divine substance, the author of divine operations, and the object of divine and religious worship; that is, "Over all, God blessed for ever," as the ensuing testimonies evince:--

Gen. i. 2, "The Spirit of God moved upon the face of the waters"

Ps. xxxiii. 6, "By the word of the Lord were the heavens made; and all the host of them by the Spirit of his mouth."

Job xxvi. 13, "By his Spirit he has garnished the heavens."

Job xxxiii. 4, "The Spirit of God has made me."

Ps. civ. 30, "Thou sendest forth thy Spirit, they are created."

Matt. xxviii. 19, "Baptizing them in the name of the Father, and of the Son, and of the Holy Ghost."

Acts i. 16, "That scripture must needs have been fulfilled, which the Holy Ghost by the mouth of David spake."

Acts v. 3, "Peter said, Ananias, why has Satan filled thine heart to lie to the Holy Ghost?" verse 4, "Thou hast not lied unto men, but unto God."

Acts xxviii. 25, 26, "Well spake the Holy Ghost by Esaias the prophet unto our fathers, saying, Go unto this people, and say," etc.

1 Cor. iii. 16, "Know ye not that ye are the temple of God, and that the Spirit of God dwelleth in you?"

1 Cor. xii. 11, "All these worketh that one and the self-same Spirit, dividing to every man severally as he will." Verse 6, "And there are diversities of operations, but it is the same God which worketh all in all."

2 Cor. xiii. 14, "The grace of the Lord Jesus Christ, and the love of God, and the communion of the Holy Ghost, be with you all."

Acts xx. 28, "Take heed to the flock over the which the Holy Ghost has made you overseers."

Matt. xii. 31, "All manner of sin and blasphemy shall be forgiven unto men; but the blasphemy against the Holy Ghost shall not be forgiven unto men."

Ps. cxxxix. 7, "Whither shall I go from thy Spirit?"

John xiv. 26, "But the Comforter, which is the Holy Ghost, whom the Father will send in my name, he shall teach you all things."

Luke xii. 12, "The Holy Ghost shall teach you in the same hour what ye ought to say."

Acts xiii. 2, "As they ministered to the Lord, and fasted, the Holy Ghost said, Separate me Barnabas and Saul for the work whereunto I have called them."

Verse 4, "So they, being sent forth by the Holy Ghost, departed unto Seleucia," etc.

2 Pet. i. 21, "For the prophecy came not in old time by the will of man, but holy men of God spake as they were moved by the Holy Ghost."

It is evident, upon the first consideration, that there is not any thing which we believe concerning the Holy Ghost, but that it is plainly revealed and declared in these testimonies. He is directly affirmed to be, and is called, "God," Acts v. 3, 4; which the Socinians will not say is by virtue of an exaltation unto an office or authority, as they say of the Son. He is an intelligent, voluntary, divine agent; he knows, he works as he will: which things, if, in their frequent repetition, they are not sufficient to evince an intelligent agent, a personal subsistence, that has being, life, and will, we must confess that the Scripture was written on purpose to lead us into mistakes and misapprehensions of what we are under penalty of eternal ruin, rightly to apprehend and believe. It declares, also, that he is the author and worker of all sorts of divine operations, requiring immensity, omnipotence, omniscience, and all other divine excellencies, unto their working and effecting. Moreover, it is revealed that he is peculiarly to be believed in, and may peculiarly be sinned against, [as] the great author of all grace in believers and order in the church. This is the sum of what we believe, of what is revealed in the Scripture concerning the Holy Ghost.

As, in the consideration of the preceding head, we vindicated one testimony in particular from the exceptions of the adversaries of the truth, so on this we may briefly sum up the evidence that is given us in the testimonies before produced, that the reader may the more easily understand their intendment, and what, in particular, they bear witness unto.

The sum is that the Holy Ghost is a divine, distinct person, and neither merely the power or virtue of God, nor any created spirit whatever. This plainly appears, from what is revealed concerning him. For he who is placed in the same series or order with other divine persons, without the least note of difference or distinction from them, as to an interest in personality; who has the names proper to a divine person only, and is frequently and directly called by them; who also has personal properties, and is the voluntary author of personal, divine operations, and the proper object of divine worship, -- he is a distinct divine person. And if these things be not a sufficient evidence and demonstration of a divine, intelligent substance, I shall, as was said before, despair to understand any thing that is expressed and declared by words. But now thus it is with the Holy Ghost, according to the revelation made conceding him in the Scripture. For, --

First. He is placed in the same rank and order, without any note of difference or distinction as to a distinct interest in the divine nature (that is, as we shall see, personality) with the other divine persons. Matt. xxviii. 19, "Baptizing them in the name of the Father, and of the Son, and of the Holy Ghost." 1 John v. 7, "There are three that bear record in heaven, the Father, the Word, and the Holy Ghost; and these three are one." 1 Cor. xii. 3-6, "No man can say that Jesus is the Lord, but by the Holy Ghost. Now, there are diversities of gifts, but the same Spirit. And there are differences of administrations, but the same Lord. And there are diversities of operations, but it is the same God which worketh all in all." Neither does a denial of his divine being and distinct existence leave any tolerable sense unto these expressions. For read the words of the first place from the mind of the Socinians, and see what is it that can be gathered from them, "Baptizing them in the name of the Father, and of the Son, and of the virtue or efficacy of the Father." Can any thing be more absonant from faith and reason than this absurd expression? and yet it is the direct sense, if it be any, that these men put upon the words. To join a quality with acknowledged persons, and that in such things and cases as wherein they are proposed under a personal consideration, is a strange kind of mystery. And the like may be manifested concerning the other places.

Secondly. He also has the names proper to a divine person only; for he is expressly called "God," Acts v. He who is termed the "Holy Ghost," verse 3, and the "Spirit of the Lord," verse 9, is called also "God," verse 4. Now, this is the name of a divine person, on one account or other. The Socinians would not allow Christ to be called God were he not a divine person, though not by nature, yet by office and authority. And I suppose they will not find out an office for the Holy Ghost, whereunto he might be exalted, on the account whereof he might become God, seeing this would acknowledge him to be a person, which they deny. So he is called the "Comforter," John xvi. 7. A personal appellation this is also; and because he is the Comforter of all God's people, it can be the name of none but a divine person. In the same place, also, it is frequently affirmed, that he shall come, that he shall and will do such and such things; all of them declaring him to be a person.

Thirdly. He has personal properties assigned unto him; as a will, 1 Cor. xii. 11, "He divideth to every man severally as he will;" and understanding, 1 Cor. ii. 10, "The Spirit searcheth all things, yea, the deep things of God;" -- as also, all the actings that are ascribed unto him are all of them such as undeniably affirm personal properties in their principal and agent. For, --

Fourthly. He is the voluntary author of divine operations. He of old cherished the creation, Gen. i. 2, "The Spirit of God moved upon the face of the waters." He formed and garnished the heavens. He inspired, acted, and spoke, in and by the prophets, Acts xxviii. 25, "Well spake the Holy Ghost by Esaias the prophet unto our fathers;" 2 Pet. i. 21, "The prophecy came not in old time by the will of man; but holy men of God spake as they were moved by the Holy Ghost." He regenerates, enlightens, sanctifies, comforts, instructs, leads, guides, all the disciples of Christ, as the Scriptures everywhere testify. Now, all these are personal operations, and cannot, with any pretence of sobriety or consistency with reason, be constantly and uniformly assigned unto a quality or virtue. He is, as the Father and Son, God, with the properties of omniscience and omnipotence, of life, understanding, and will; and by these properties, works, acts, and produces effects, according to wisdom, choice, and power.

Fifthly. The same regard is had to him in faith, worship, and obedience, as unto the other persons of the Father and Son. For our being baptized into his name, is our solemn engagement to believe in him, to yield obedience to him, and to worship him, as it puts the same obligation upon us to the Father and the Son. So also, in reference unto the worship of the church, he commands that the ministers of it be separated unto himself; Acts xiii. 2, "The Holy Ghost said, Separate me Barnabas and Saul for the work whereunto I have called them;" verse 4, "So they, being sent forth by the Holy Ghost, departed;" -- which is comprehensive of all the religious worship of the church.

And on the same account is he sinned against, as Acts v. 3, 49; for there is the same reason of sin and obedience. Against whom a man may sin formally and ultimately, him he is bound to obey, worship, and believe in. And this can be no quality, but God himself. For what may be the sense of this expression, "Thou hast lied to the efficacy of God in his operations" or how can we be formally obliged unto obedience to a quality? There must, then, an antecedent obligation unto faith, trust, and religious obedience be supposed, as the ground of rendering a person capable of being guilty of sin towards any; for sin is but a failure in faith, obedience, or worship. These, therefore, are due unto the Holy Ghost; or a man could not sin against him so signally and fatally as some are said to do in the foregoing testimonies.

I say, therefore, unto this part of our cause, as unto the other, that unless we will cast off all reverence of God, and, in a kind of atheism, which, as I suppose, the prevailing wickedness of this age has not yet arrived unto, say that the Scriptures were written on purpose to deceive us, and to lead us into mistakes about, and misapprehensions of, what it proposes unto us, we must acknowledge the Holy Ghost to be a substance, a person, God; yet distinct from the Father and the Son. For to tell us, that he will come unto us, that he will be our comforter, that he will teach us, lead us, guide us; that he spoke of old in and by the prophets, -- that they were moved by him, acted by him; that he "searcheth the deep things of God," works as he will; that he appoints to himself ministers in the church; -- in a word, to declare, in places innumerable, what he has done, what he does, what he will do, what he says and speaks, how he acts and proceeds, what his will is, and to warn us that we grieve him not, sin not against him, with things innumerable of the like nature; and all this while to oblige us to believe that he is not a person, a helper, a comforter, a searcher, a willer, but a quality in some especial operations of God, or his power and virtue in them, were to distract men, not to instruct them, and leave them no certain conclusion but this, that there is nothing certain in the whole book of God. And of no other tendency are these and the like imaginations of our adversaries in this matter.

But let us briefly consider what is objected in general unto the truth we have confirmed:--

They say, then, "The Holy Spirit is said to be given, to be sent, to be bestowed on men, and to be promised unto them: and therefore it cannot be that he should be God; for how can any of these things he spoken of God?"

I answer, First, As the expressions do not prove him to be God (nor did ever any produce them to that purpose), yet they undeniably prove him to be a person, or an intelligent, voluntary agent, concerning whom they are spoken and affirmed. For how can the power of God, or a quality, as they speak, be said to be sent, to be given, to be bestowed on men? So that these very expressions are destructive to their imaginations.

Secondly. He who is God, equal in nature and being with the Father, may be promised, sent, and given, with respect unto the holy dispensation and condescension wherein he has undertaken the office of being our comforter and sanctifier.

Thirdly. The communications, distributions, impartings, divisions of the Spirit, which they mention, as they respect the object of them, or those on whom they were or are bestowed, denote only works, gifts, operations, and effects of the Spirit; the rule whereof is expressed, 1 Cor. xii. 11. He works them in whom he will, and as he will. And whether these and the like exceptions, taken from acting and operations which are plainly interpreted and explained in sundry places of Scripture, and evidently enough in the particular places where they are used, are sufficient to impeach the truth of the revelation before declared, all who have a due reverence of God, his word, and truths, will easily understand and discern.

These things being declared in the Scripture concerning the Father, the Son, and the Holy Ghost, it is, moreover, revealed, "And these three are one;" that is, one God, jointly to be worshipped, feared, adored, believed in, and obeyed, in order unto eternal life. For although this does absolutely and necessarily follow from what is declared and has been spoken concerning the one God, or oneness of the Deity, yet, for the confirmation of our faith, and that we may not, by the distinct consideration of the three be taken off from the one, it is particularly declared that "these three are one;" that one, the one and same God. But whereas, as was said before, this can no otherwise be, the testimonies given whereunto are not so frequently multiplied as they are unto those other heads of this truth, which, through the craft of Satan, and the pride of men, might be more liable to exceptions. But yet they are clear, full, and distinctly sufficient for faith to acquiesce in immediately, without any other expositions, interpretations or arguments, beyond our understanding of the naked importance of the words. Such are they, of the Father [and] the Son, John x. 30,

"I and my Father are one;" -- Father, Son, and Spirit, 1 John v. 7, "There are three that bear record in heaven, the Father, the Word, and the Holy Ghost; and these three are one." Matt. xxviii. 19, "Baptizing them in the name of the Father, and of the Son, and of the Holy Ghost." For if those into whose name we are baptized be not one in nature, we are by our baptism engaged into the service and worship of more gods than one. For, as being baptized, or sacredly initiated, into or in the name of any one, does sacramentally bind us unto a holy and religious obedience unto him, and in all things to the avowing of him as the God whose we are, and whom we serve, as here we are in the name of the Father, Son, and Spirit; so if they are not one God, the blasphemous consequence before mentioned must unavoidably be admitted: which it also must upon the Socinian principle, who, whilst of all others they seem to contend most for one God, are indeed direct polytheists, by owning others with religious respect, due to God alone, which are not so.

Once more: It is revealed, also, that these three are distinct among themselves, by certain peculiar relative properties, if I may yet use thee terms. So that they are distinct, living, divine, intelligent, voluntary principles of operation or working, and that in and by internal acts one towards another, and in acts that outwardly respect the creation and the several parts of it. Now, this distinction originally lies in this, -- that the Father begets the Son, and the Son is begotten of the Father, and the Holy Spirit proceeds from both of them. The manner of these things, so far as they may be expressed unto our edification, shall afterwards be spoken to. At present it suffices, for the satisfaction and confirmation of our faith, that the distinctions named are clearly revealed in the Scripture, and are proposed to be its proper object in this matter:-- Ps. ii. 7, "Thou art my Son, this day have I begotten thee." Matt. xvi. 16, "Thou art the Christ, the Son of the living God." John i. 14, "We beheld his glory, the glory as of the only begotten of the Father." Verse 18, "No man has seen God at any time; the only begotten Son, which is in the bosom of the Father, he has declared him." John v. 26, "For as the Father has life in himself, so has he given to the Son to have life in himself." 1 John v. 20, "The Son of God is come, and has given us an understanding." John xv. 26, "But when the Comforter is come, whom I will send unto you from the Father, even the Spirit of truth, which proceeds from the Father, he shall testify of me."

Now, as the nature of this distinction lies in their mutual relation one to another, so it is the foundation of those distinct actings and operations whereby the distinction itself is clearly manifested and confirmed. And these actings, as was said, are either such as where one of them is the object of another's actings, or such as have the creature for their object. The first sort are testified unto, Ps. cx. 1; John i. 18, v. 20, xvii. 5; 1 Cor. ii. 10, 11; Prov. viii. 22; most of which places have been before recited. They which thus know each other, love each other, delight in each other, must needs be distinct; and so are they represented unto our faith. And for the other sort of actings, the Scripture is full of the expressions of them. See Gen. xix. 24; Zech ii. 8; John v. 17; 1 Cor. xii. 7-11; 2 Cor. viii. 9.

Our conclusion from the whole is, -- that there is nothing more fully expressed in the Scripture than this sacred truth, that there is one God, Father, Son, and Holy Ghost; which are divine, distinct, intelligent, voluntary, omnipotent principles of operation and working: which whosoever thinks himself obliged to believe the Scripture must believe; and concerning others, in this discourse, we are not solicitous.

This is that which was first proposed, -- namely, to manifest what is expressly revealed in the Scripture concerning God the Father, Son, and Holy Ghost; so as that we may duly believe in him, yield obedience unto him, enjoy communion with him, walk in his love and fear, and so come at length to be blessed with him for evermore. Nor does faith, for its security, establishment, and direction, absolutely stand in need of any farther exposition or explanation of these things, or the use of any terms not consecrated to the present service by the Holy Ghost. But whereas it may be variously assaulted by the temptations of Satan, and opposed by the subtle sophisms of men of corrupt minds; and whereas it is the duty of the disciples of Christ to grow in the knowledge of God, and our Lord and Saviour Jesus Christ, by an explicit apprehension of the things they do believe, so far as they are capable of them; this doctrine has in all ages of the church been explained and taught in and by such expressions, terms, and propositions, as farther declare what is necessarily included in it, or consequent unto it; with an exclusion of such things, notions, and apprehensions, as are neither the one nor the other. This I shall briefly manifest, and then vindicate the whole from some exceptions, and so close this dissertation.

[First.] That God is one, was declared and proved. Now this oneness can respect nothing but the nature, being, substance, or essence of God. God is one in this respect. Some of these words, indeed, are not used in the Scripture; but whereas they are of the same importance and signification, and none of them include any thing of imperfection, they are properly used in the declaration of the unity of the Godhead. There is mention in the Scripture of the Godhead of God, Rom. i. 20, "His eternal power and Godhead;" and of his nature, by excluding them from being objects of our worship who are not God by nature, Gal. iv. 8. Now, this natural godhead of God is his substance or essence, with all the holy, divine excellencies which naturally and necessarily appertain whereunto. Such are eternity, immensity, omnipotence, life, infinite holiness, goodness, and the like. This one nature, substance, or essence, being the nature, substance, or essence of God, as God, is the nature, essence, and substance of the Father, Son, and Spirit; one and the same absolutely in and unto each of them: for none can be God, as they are revealed to be, but by virtue of this divine nature or being. Herein consists the unity of the Godhead.

Secondly. The distinction which the Scripture reveals between Father, Son, and Spirit, is that whereby they are three hypostases or persons, distinctly subsisting in the same divine essence or being. Now, a divine person is nothing but the divine essence, upon the account of an especial property, subsisting in an especial manner. As in the person of the Father there is the divine essence and being, with its property of begetting the Son, subsisting in an especial manner as the Father, and because this person has the whole divine nature, all the essential properties of that nature are in that person. The wisdom, the understanding of God, the will of God, the immensity of God, is in that person, not as that person, but as the person is God. The like is to be said of the persons of the Son and of the Holy Ghost. Hereby each person having the understanding, the will, and power of God, becomes a distinct principle of operation; and yet all their actings ad extra being the actings of God, they are undivided, and are all the works of one, of the self-same God. And these things do not only necessarily follow, but are directly included, in the revelation made concerning God and his subsistence in the Scriptures.

[Thirdly.] There are, indeed, very many other things that are taught and disputed about this doctrine of the Trinity; as, the manner of the eternal generation of the Son, -- of the essence of the Father, -- of the procession of the Holy Ghost, and the difference of it from the generation of the Son, -- of the mutual in-being of the persons, by reason of their unity in the same substance or essence, -- the nature of their personal subsistence, with respect unto the properties whereby they are mutually distinguished; -- all which are true and defensible against all the sophisms of the adversaries of this truth. Yet, because the distinct apprehension of them, and their accurate expression, is not necessary unto faith, as it is our guide and principle in and unto religious worship and obedience, they need not here be insisted on. Nor are those brief explications themselves before mentioned so proposed as to be placed immediately in the same rank or order with the original revelations before insisted on, but only are pressed as proper expressions of what is revealed, to increase our light and farther our edification. And although they cannot rationally be opposed or denied, nor ever were by any, but such as deny and oppose the things themselves as revealed, yet they that do so deny or oppose them, are to be required positively, in the first place, to deny or disapprove the oneness of the Deity, or to prove that the Father, or Son, or Holy Ghost, in particular, are not God, before they be allowed to speak one word against the manner of the explication of the truth concerning them. For either they grant the revelation declared and contended for, or they do not. If they do, let that concession be first laid down, namely, -- that the Father, Son, and Spirit, are one God and then let it be debated, whether they are one in substance and three in persons, or how else the matter is to be stated. If they deny it, it is a plain madness to dispute of the manner of any thing, and the way of expressing it, whilst the thing itself is denied to have a being; for of that which is not, there is neither manner, property, adjunct, nor effect. Let, then, such persons as this sort of men are ready to attempt with their sophistry, and to amuse with cavils about persons, substances, subsistence, and the like, desire to know of them what it is that they would be at. What would they deny? what would they disapprove? Is it that God is one? or that the Father is God, or the Son, or the Holy Ghost is so? If they deny or oppose either of these, they have testimonies and instances of divine revelation, or may have, in a readiness, to confound the devil and all his emissaries. If they will not do so, if they refuse it, then let them know that it is most foolish and unreasonable to contend about expressions and explications of any thing, or doctrine, about the manner, respects, or relations of any thing, until the thing itself, or doctrine, be plainly confessed or denied. If this they refuse, as generally they do and will (which I speak upon sufficient experience), and will not be induced to deal openly, properly, and rationally, but will keep to their cavils and sophisms about terms and expressions, all farther debate or conference with them may justly, and ought, both conscientiously and rationally, to be refused and rejected. For these sacred mysteries of God and the gospel are not lightly to be made the subject of men's contests and disputations.

But as we dealt before in particular, so here I shall give instances of the sophistical exceptions that are used against the whole of this doctrine, and that with respect unto some late collections and representations of them; from whence they are taken up and used by many who seem not to understand the words, phrases, and expressions themselves, which they make use of.

The sum of what they say in general is, -- 1. "How can these things be? How can three be one, and one be three? Every person has its own substance; and, therefore, if there be three persons, there must be three substances, and so three Gods."

Answer. Every person has distinctly its own substance, for the one substance of the Deity is the substance of each person, so it is still but one; but each person has not its own distinct substance, because the substance of them all is the same, as has been proved.

2. They say, "That if each person be God, then each person is infinite, and there being three persons, there must be three infinites."

Ans. This follows not in the least; for each person is infinite as he is God. All divine properties, such as to be infinite is, belong not to the persons on the account of their personality, but on the account of their nature, which is one, for they are all natural properties.

3. But they say, "If each person be God, and that God subsist in three persons, then in each person there are three persons or Gods."

Ans. The collusion of this sophism consists in that expression, "be God" and "that God." In the first place the nature of God is intended; in the latter, a singular person. Place the words intelligibly, and they are thus:-- If each person be God, and the nature of God subsists in three persons, then in each person there are three persons; and then the folly of it will be evident.

4. But they farther infer, "That if we deny the persons to be infinite, then an infinite being has a finite mode of subsisting, and so I know not what supposition they make hence; that seeing there are not three infinites, then the Father, Son, and Spirit are three infinites, that make up an infinite."

The pitiful weakness of this cavil is open to all; for finite and infinite are properties and adjuncts of beings, and not of the manner of the subsistence of any thing. The nature of each person is infinite, and so is each person because of that nature. Of the manner of their subsistence, finite and infinite cannot be predicated or spoken, no farther than to say, an infinite being does so subsist.

5. "But you grant," say they, "that the only true God is the Father, and then if Christ be the only true God, he is the Father."

Ans. We say, the only true God is Father, Son, and Holy Ghost. We never say, the Scripture never says, that the Father only is the true God; whence it would follow, that, he that is the true God is the Father. But we grant the Father to be the only true God; and so we say is the Son also. And it does not at all thence follow that the Son is the Father; because, in saying the Father is the true God, we respect not his paternity, or his paternal relation to his Son, but his nature, essence, and being. And the same we affirm concerning the other persons. And to say, that because each person is God, one person must be another, is to crave leave to disbelieve what God has revealed, without giving any reason at all for their so doing.

But this sophism being borrowed from another, namely, Crellius, [7] who insisted much upon it, I shall upon his account, and not on theirs, who, as far as I can apprehend, understand little of the intendment of it, remove it more fully out of the way. It is proposed by him in way of syllogism, thus, "The only true God is the Father; Christ is the only true God: therefore he is the Father." Now, this syllogism is ridiculously sophistical. For, in a categorical syllogism the major proposition is not to be particular, or equipollent to a particular; for, from such a proposition, when any thing communicable to more is the subject of it, and is restrained unto one particular, nothing can be inferred in the conclusion. But such is this proposition here, The only true God is the Father. It is a particular proposition, wherein the subject is restrained unto a singular or individual predicate, though in itself communicable to more. Now, the proposition being so made particular, the terms of the subject or predicate are supposed reciprocal, -- namely, that one God, and the Father, are the same; which is false, unless it be first proved that the name God is communicable to no more, or no other, than is the other term of Father: which to suppose, is to beg the whole question; for the only true God has a larger signification than the term of Father or Son. So that, though the only true God be the Father, yet every one who is true God is not the Father. Seeing, then, that the name of God here supplies the place of a species, though it be singular absolutely, as it respects the divine nature, which is absolutely singular and one, and cannot be multiplied, yet in respect of communication it is otherwise; it is communicated unto more, -- namely, to the Father, Son, and Holy Ghost. And, therefore, if any thing be intended to be concluded from hence, the proposition must be expressed according to what the subject requires, as capable of communication or attribution to more than one, as thus: Whoever is the only true God is the Father; -- which proposition these persons and their masters shall never be able to prove.

I have given, in particular, these strictures thus briefly upon these empty sophisms; partly because they are well removed already, and partly because they are mere exscriptions out of an author not long since translated into English, unto whom an entire answer may ere long be returned.

That which at present shall suffice, is to give a general answer unto all these cavils, with all of the same kind which the men of these principles do usually insist upon.

1. "The things," they say, "which we teach concerning the Trinity, are contrary to reason;" and thereof they endeavour to give sundry instances, wherein the sum of the opposition which they make unto this truth does consist. But first, I ask, What reason is it that they intend? It is their own, the carnal reason of men. By that they will judge of these divine mysteries. The Scripture tells us, indeed, that the "spirit of a man which is in him knows the things of a man," -- a man's spirit, by natural reason, may judge of natural things; -- "but the things of God knoweth no man, but the Spirit of God," 1 Cor. ii. 11. So that what we know of these things, we must receive upon the revelation of the Spirit of God merely, if the apostle may be believed. And it is given unto men to know the mysteries of the kingdom of God, -- to some, and not to others; and unless it be so given them, they cannot know them. In particular, none can know the Father unless the Son reveal him. Nor will, or does, or can, flesh and blood reveal or understand Jesus Christ to be the Son of the living God, unless the Father reveal him, and instruct us in the truth of it, Matt. xvi. 17. The way to come to the acknowledgment of these things, is that described by the apostle, Eph. iii. 14-19, "For this cause I bow my knees unto the Father of our Lord Jesus Christ, of whom the whole family in heaven and earth is named, that he would grant you, according to the riches of his glory, to be strengthened with might by his Spirit in the inner man; that Christ may dwell in your hearts by

faith; that ye, being rooted and grounded in love, may be able to comprehend with all saints," etc. As also, Col. ii. 2, 3, That ye might come "unto all riches of the full assurance of understanding, to the acknowledgment of the mystery of God, and of the Father, and of Christ, in whom are hid all the treasures of wisdom and knowledge." It is by faith and prayer, and through the revelation of God, that we may come to the acknowledgment of these things, and not by the carnal reasonings of men of corrupt minds.

2. What reason do they intend? If reason absolutely, the reason of things, we grant that nothing contrary unto it is to be admitted. But reason as it is in this or that man, particularly in themselves, we know to be weak, maimed, and imperfect; and that they are, and all other men, extremely remote from a just and full comprehension of the whole reason of things. Are they in such an estate as that their apprehension shall pass for the measure of the nature of all things? We know they are far from it. So that though we will not admit of any thing that is contrary to reason, yet the least intimation of a truth by divine revelation will make me embrace it, although it should be contrary to the reason of all the Socinians in the world. Reason in the abstract, or the just measure of the answering of one thing unto another, is of great moment: but reason -- that is, what is pretended to be so, or appears to be so unto this or that man, especially in and about things of divine revelation -- is of very small importance (of none at all) where it rises up against the express testimonies of Scripture, and these multiplied, to their mutual confirmation and explanation.

3. Many things are above reason, -- that is, as considered in this or that subject, as men, -- which are not at all against it. It is an easy thing to compel the most curious inquirers of these days to a ready confession hereof, by multitudes of instances in things finite and temporary; and shall any dare to deny but it may be so in things heavenly, divine, and spiritual? Nay, there is no concernment of the being of God, or his properties, but is absolutely above the comprehension of our reason. We cannot by searching find out God, we cannot find out the Almighty to perfection.

4. The very foundation of all their objections and cavils against this truth, is destructive of as fundamental principles of reason as are in the world. They are all, at best, reduced to this: It cannot be thus in things finite; the same being cannot in one respect be one, in another three, and the like: and therefore it is so in things infinite. All these reasonings are built upon this supposition, that that which is finite can perfectly comprehend that which is infinite, -- an assertion absurd, foolish, and contradictory unto itself. Again; it is the highest reason in things of pure revelation to captivate our understandings to the authority of the Revealer; which here is rejected. So that by a loud, specious, pretence of reason, these men, by a little captious sophistry, endeavour not only to countenance their unbelief, but to evert the greatest principles of reason itself.

5. The objections these men principally insist upon, are merely against the explanations we use of this doctrine, -- not against the primitive revelation of it, which is the principal object of our faith; which, how preposterous and irrational a course of proceeding it is, has been declared.

6. It is a rule among philosophers, that if a man, on just grounds and reasons, have embraced any opinion or persuasion, he is not to desert it merely because he cannot answer every objection against it. For if the objections wherewith we may be entangled be not of the same weight and importance with

the reason on which we embraced the opinion, it is a madness to forego it on the account thereof. And much more must this hold amongst the common sort of Christians, in things spiritual and divine. If they will let go and part with their faith in any truth, because they are not able to answer distinctly some objections that may be made against it, they may quickly find themselves disputed into atheism.

7. There is so great an intimation made of such an expression and resemblance of a Trinity in unity in the very works of the creation, as learned men have manifested by various instances, that it is most unreasonable to suppose that to be contrary to reason which many objects of rational consideration do more or less present unto our minds.

8. To add no more considerations of this nature, let any of the adversaries produce any one argument or grounds of reason, or those pretended to be such, against that that has been asserted, that has not already been baffled a thousand times, and it shall receive an answer; or a public acknowledgment, that it is indissoluble.

Footnotes:

4. Marcion was a native of Pontus, and a celebrated heretic, who lived and propagated his errors in the middle of the second century. He seems to have been engaged in teaching his heretical views at Rome in a.d. 139. He held two original and seminal principles, -- the invisible and nameless one, "the Good;" and the visible God, "the Creator." Epiphanius ascribes to him a third, -- "the Devil." The second, according to his system was the God of the Old Testament, the author of evil; and Christ was the Son of the first, sent by him to overthrow the dominion of God the Creator. He held that there was an irreconcilable opposition between God the Creator revealed in the Old Testament Scriptures, and the Christian God revealed in the New. One ground on which he maintained this preposterous notion is mentioned and explained by Dr Owen. Tertullian devotes five books to the errors of Marcion. -- Ed.

5. The two Sozzini were descended from an honourable family, and were both born at

Siena, -- Lælius, the uncle in 1525, and his nephew, Faustus, in 1539. The former became addicted to the careful study of the Scriptures, forsaking the legal profession, for which he had undergone some training; and acquiring, in furtherance of his favourite pursuit, the Greek, Hebrew, and Arabic languages. He is said to have been one of the forty individuals who held meetings for conference on religious topics, chiefly at Vicenza, and who sought to establish a purer creed, by rejection of certain doctrines on which all the divines of the Reformation strenuously insisted. To these Vicentine "colleges," as the meetings were termed, Socinians have been accustomed to trace the origin of their particular tenets. Dr M'Crie, in his "History of the Reformation in Italy" (p. 154), assigns strong reasons for discarding this account of the origin of Socinianism as unworthy of credit. Lælius never committed himself during his life to a direct avowal of his sentiments, and was on terms of intercourse and correspondence with the leading Reformers;

intimating, however, his scruples and doubts to such an extent, that his soundness in the faith was questioned, and he received an admonition from Calvin. He left Italy in 1547, travelled extensively, and at length settled in Zürich, where he died in 1562, leaving behind him some manuscripts, to which Dr Owen alludes, and of which his nephew availed himself, in reducing the errors held in common by uncle and nephew to the form of a theological system. The nephew, Faustus, had rather a chequered life. Tainted at an early age with the heresy of his uncle, he was under the necessity of quitting Siena; and after having held for twelve years some honourable offices in the court of the Duke of Tuscany, he repaired to Basle, and for three years devoted himself to theological study. The doubts of the uncle rose to the importance of convictions in the mind of the nephew. In consequence of divisions among the reformers of Transylvania, who had become Antitrinitarians, he was sent for by Blandrata, one of their leaders, to reason Francis David out of some views he held regarding the adoration due to Christ. The result was, that David was cast into prison, where he died, -- Socinus using no influence to restrain the Prince of Transylvania from such cruel intolerance; a fact too often forgotten by some who delight in reproaching Calvin for the death of Servetus. He visited Poland in 1579; but before his visit, the Antitrinitarians of that country had, by resolutions of their synods in 1563 and 1565, withdrawn from the communion of other churches, and published a Bible and a Catechism, -- commonly known, from Rakau, the town in which it was first published, as the "Racovian Catechism." Faustus Socinus was not at first well received by his Polish brethren; but he overcame their aversion to him, which at one time was so strong that he was nearly torn to pieces by a mob. He acquired considerable influence amongst them; managed to compose their differences, and became so popular, that his co-religionists adopted the name of Socinians, in preference to their old name of Unitarians. He died in 1604. His tracts were collected into two folio volumes of the "Bibliotheca Fratrum Polonorum." Starting with mistaken views of private judgment, he inferred, from competency of reason to determine the credibility of doctrine; but his views differed from modern Rationalism, inasmuch as he adhered more to historical Christianity as the basis of his principles, and was by no means so free in impugning the authenticity of Scripture, when it bore against his system. His heresies assumed a shape more positive and definite than is generally fancied, and affected the doctrines of the Trinity, the divinity of Christ (on which his views were somewhat akin to Arianism), the necessity of an atonement, the nature of repentance, the efficacy of grace, the sacraments, and the eternity of future punishments. -- Ed.

6. A heresiarch of the third century, elevated to the bishopric of Antioch about a.d. 260. He is said to have indulged in haughty pomp and licentious practices, and was deposed by a council held in 269, chiefly for his heretical doctrines; -- amongst which he held, that while the Father, Son,

and Holy Ghost are one God, they are not respectively distinct persons, and that the Son in particular had no distinct personality, but existed in God, and came to dwell in the man Jesus. -- Ed.

7. John Crell is not to be confounded with Samuel Crell, also a Socinian writer, who lived about a century later, and who seems to have been converted to the faith of our Lord's divinity. The former was born in Franconia in 1590. He was rector of the University of Rakau in 1616. He had a controversy with Grotius, and was recognised as a leader among the Socinians. He died 1633, leaving behind him works that occupy four volumes in the "Bibliotheca Fratrum Polonorum." -- Ed.

Of the Person of Christ

The next head of opposition made by the men of this conspiracy against this sacred truth, is against the head of all truth, the person of our Lord Jesus Christ. The Socinians, indeed, would willingly put a better face or colour upon their error about the person of Christ than it will bear or endure to lie on it. For in their catechism, unto this question, "Is the Lord Jesus Christ purus homo, a mere man?" they answer, "By no means." "How then? Has he a divine nature also?" Which is their next question. To this they say, "By no means; for this is contrary to right reason." How, then, will these pretended masters of reason reconcile these things? For to us it seems, that if Christ has no other nature but that of man, he is as to his nature purus homo, a mere man, and no more. Why, they answer, that "he is not a mere man, because he was born of a virgin." Strange! that that should be an argument to prove him more than a man, which the Scripture, and all men in their right wits, grant to be an invincible reason to prove him to be a man, and, as he was born of her, no more. Rom. i. 3, "Concerning his Son Jesus Christ our Lord, which was made of the seed of David according to the flesh" Rom. ix. 5, "Whose are the fathers, and of whom, as concerning the flesh, Christ came." Gal. iv. 4, "God sent forth his Son, made of a woman, made under the law." But, say they, "He was endowed with the Spirit, wrought miracles, was raised from the dead, had all power given [him] in heaven and earth; for by these degrees he became to be God." But all men see that the inquiry is about the nature of Christ, and this answer is about his state and condition. Now this changes not his nature on the one hand, no more than his being humbled, poor, and dying, did on the other. This is the right reason we have to deal withal in these men! If a man should have inquired of some of them of old, whether Melchizedek were purus homo, a mere man, some of them would have said, "No, because he was the Holy Ghost;" some, "No, because he was the Son of God himself;" and some, "No, because he was an angel;" -- for such foolish opinions have men fallen into. But how sottish soever their conceptions were, their answer to that inquiry would have been regular, because the question and answer respect the same subject in the same respect; but never any was so stupid as to answer, "He was not a mere man, (that is, by nature,) because he was a priest of the high God," -- which respects his office and condition. Yet, such is the pretence of these men about the person of Christ, to incrustate and give some colour unto their foul misbelief; as supposing that it would be much to their disadvantage to own Christ only as a mere man, -- though the most part of their disputes that they have troubled the Christian world withal have had no other design nor aim but to prove him so to be, and nothing else. I shall briefly, according to the method insisted on, first lay down what is the direct revelation which is the object of our faith in this matter, then express the revelation itself in the Scripture testimonies wherein it is recorded; and having vindicated some one or other of them from their exceptions, manifest how the doctrine hereof is farther explained, unto the edification of them that believe.

73

That there is a second person, the Son of God, in the holy trin-unity of the Godhead, we have proved before. That this person did, of his infinite love and grace, take upon him our nature, -- human nature, -- so as that the divine and human nature should become one person, one Christ, God and man in one, so that whatever he does in and about our salvation, it is done by that one person, God and man, is revealed unto us in the Scripture as the object of our faith: and this is that which we believe concerning the person of Christ. Whatever acts are ascribed unto him, however immediately performed, in or by the human nature, or in and by his divine nature, they are all the acts of that one person, in whom are both these natures. That this Christ, God and man, is, because he is God, and on the account of what he has done for us as man, to be believed in, worshipped with worship religious and divine, to be trusted and obeyed, this also is asserted in the Scripture. And these things are, as it were, the common notions of Christian religion, -- the common principles of our profession, which the Scriptures also abundantly testify unto.

Isa. vii. 14, "Behold, a virgin shall conceive, and bear a son, and shall call his name Emmanuel;" that is, he shall be God with us, or God in our nature. Not that that should be his name whereby he should be called in this world; but that this should be the condition of his person, -- he should be "God with us," God in our nature. So are the words expounded, Matt. i. 20-23, "That which is conceived in her is of the Holy Ghost. And she shall bring forth a son, and thou shalt call his name Jesus; for he shall save his people from their sins. Now all this was done, that it might be fulfilled which was spoken of the Lord by the prophet, saying, Behold, a virgin shall be with child, and shall bring forth a son, and they shall call his name Emmanuel; which, being interpreted, is, God with us." his name whereby he was to be called, was Jesus; that is, a Saviour. And thereby was accomplished the prediction of the prophet, that he should be Emmanuel; which, being interpreted, is, "God with us." Now, a child born to be "God with us," is God in that child taking our nature upon him; and no otherwise can the words be understood.

Isa. ix. 6, "Unto us a child is born, unto us a son is given: and his name shall be called The mighty God." The child that is born, the son that is given, is the mighty God; and as the mighty God, and a child born, or son given, he is the Prince of Peace, as he is there called, or our Saviour.

John i. 14, "The Word was made flesh." That the Word was God, who made all things, he had before declared. Now, he affirms that this Word was made flesh. How? converted into flesh, into a man, so that he who was God ceased so to be, and was turned or changed into flesh, -- that is, a man? Besides that this is utterly impossible, it is not affirmed. For the Word continued the Word still, although he was "made flesh," or "made of a woman," as it is elsewhere expressed, -- or made of the seed of David, -- or took our flesh or nature to be his own. Himself continuing God, as he was, became man also, which before he was not. "The Word was made flesh;" this is that which we believe and assert in this matter.

See John iii. 13, vi. 62, xvi. 28. All which places assert the person of Christ to have descended from heaven in the assumption of human nature, and ascended into heaven therein [in that nature] being assumed; and to have been in heaven as to his divine nature, when he was on the earth in the flesh that he had assumed.

Acts xx. 28, "Feed the church of God, [8] which he has purchased with his own blood." The person spoken of is said to be God absolutely, -- "the church of God." And this God is said to have blood of his own; -- the blood of Jesus Christ, being the blood of him that was God, though not the blood of him as God; for God is a spirit. And this undeniably testifies to the unity of his person as God and man.

Rom. i. 3, 4, "Concerning his Son Jesus Christ our Lord, who was made of the seed of David according to the flesh; and declared to be the Son of God with power, according to the spirit of holiness, by the resurrection from the dead." Rom. ix. 5, "Whose are the fathers, and of whom, as concerning the flesh, Christ came, who is over all, God blessed for ever. Amen." This is all we desire that we may believe without disturbance from the clamours of these men, -- namely, that the same Christ, as concerning the flesh, came of the fathers, of David, and, in himself, is over all, God blessed for ever. This the Scripture asserts plainly; and why we should not believe it firmly, let these men give a reason when they are able.

Gal. iv. 4, "God sent forth his Son made of a woman." He was his Son, and was made of a woman, according as he expresses it, Heb. x. 5, "A body hast thou prepared me;" as also, Rom. viii. 3.

Phil. ii. 5-7, "Let this mind be in you, which was also in Christ Jesus: who, being in the form of God, thought it not robbery to be equal with God: but made himself of no reputation, and took upon him the form of a servant, and was made in the likeness of men." It is the same Christ that is spoken of. And it is here affirmed of him, that he was "in the form of God, and thought it not robbery to be equal with God." But is this all? Is this Jesus Christ God only? Does he subsist only in the form or nature of God? No; says the apostle, "He took upon him the form of a servant, was made in the likeness of men, and was found in fashion as a man." That his being truly a man is expressed in these words our adversaries deny not; and we therefore believe that the same Jesus Christ is God also, because that is no less plainly expressed.

1 Tim. iii. 16, "And without controversy, great is the mystery of godliness: God [9] was manifest in the flesh, justified in the Spirit, seen of angels." It is a mystery, indeed; under which name it is despised now and reproached; nor are we allowed so to call it, but are reflected on as flying to mysteries for our defence. But we must take leave to speak in this matter according to His directions without whom we cannot speak at all. A mystery it is, and that a great mystery; and that confessedly so, by all that do believe. And this is, that "God was manifested in the flesh." That it is the Lord Christ who is spoken of, every one of the ensuing expressions do evince: "Justified in the Spirit, seen of angels, preached unto the Gentiles, believed on in the world, received up into glory." And this, also, is the substance of what we believe in this matter, -- namely, that Christ is God manifest in the flesh; which we acknowledge, own, and believe to be true, but a great mystery, -- yet no less great and sacred a truth notwithstanding.

Heb. ii. 14, "Forasmuch then as the children are partakers of flesh and blood, he also himself likewise took part of the same." Verse 16, "For verily he took not on him the nature of angels; but he took on him the seed of Abraham." And this plainly affirms his pre-existence unto that assumption of our nature, and the unity of his person in it being so assumed.

1 John iii. 16, "Hereby perceive we the love of God, because he laid down

his life for us." He who was God laid down for a season and parted with that life which was his own, in that nature of ours which he had assumed. And that taking of our nature is called his "coming in the flesh;" which whose denies, is "not of God, but is the spirit of Antichrist," chap. iv. 3.

These are some of the places wherein the person of Christ is revealed unto our faith, that we may believe in the Son of God, and have eternal life.

The method formerly proposed would require that I should take off the general objections of the adversaries against this divine revelation, as also vindicate some peculiar testimonies from their exceptions; but because a particular opposition unto this truth has not, as yet, publicly and directly been maintained and managed by any that I know of among ourselves, though the denial of it be expressly included in what they do affirm, I shall leave the farther confirmation thereof unto some other occasion, if it be offered, and it be judged necessary.

And this is that which the faith of believers rests in, as that which is plainly revealed unto them, -- namely, that Jesus Christ is God and man in one person; and that all his actings in their behalf are the actings of him who is God and man; and that this Son of God, God and man, is to be believed in by them, and obeyed, that they [may] have eternal life.

What is farther added unto these express testimonies, and the full revelation of the truth contained in them in this matter, in way of explication educed from them, and suitable unto them, to the edification of the church, or information of the minds of believers in the right apprehension of this great mystery of God manifested in the flesh, may be reduced to these heads:--

1. That the person of the Son of God did not, in his assuming human nature to be his own, take an individual person of any one into a near conjunction with himself, but preventing the personal subsistence of human nature in that flesh which he assumed, he gave it its subsistence in his own person; whence it has its individuation and distinction from all other persons whatever. This is the personal union. The divine and human nature in Christ have but one personal subsistence; and so are but one Christ, one distinct personal principle of all operations, of all that he did or does as mediator. And this undeniably follows from what is declared in the testimonies mentioned. For the Word could not be made flesh, nor could he take on him the seed of Abraham, nor could the mighty God be a child born and given unto us, nor could God shed his blood for his church, but that the two natures so directly expressed must be united in one person; for otherwise, as they are two natures still, they would be two persons also.

2. Each nature thus united in Christ is entire, and preserves unto itself its own natural properties. For he is no less perfect God for being made man; nor no less a true, perfect man, consisting of soul and body, with all their essential parts, by that nature's being taken into subsistence with the Son of God. His divine nature still continues immense, omniscient, omnipotent, infinite in holiness, etc.; his human nature, finite, limited, and, before its glorification, subject to all infirmities of life and death that the same nature in others, absolutely considered, is obnoxious unto.

3. In each of these natures he acts suitably unto the essential properties and principles of that nature. As God, he made all things, upholds all things by the word of his power, fills heaven and earth, etc.; as man, he lived, hungered, suffered, died, rose, ascended into heaven: yet, by reason of the union of both

these natures in the same person, not only his own person is said to do all these things, but the person expressed by the name which he has on the account of one nature, is said to do that which he did only in the other. So God is said to "redeem his church with his own blood," and to "lay down his life for us," and the Son of man to be in heaven when he was on the earth; all because of the unity of his person, as was declared. And these things do all of them directly and undeniably flow from what is revealed concerning his person, as before is declared.

Footnotes:

8. It involves a critical discussion of long standing, whether Κυρίου or Θεοῦ is the proper reading in this passage. By some recent editors of critical editions of the Greek Testament -- Scholz, for instance -- Θεοῦ is retained. Adhuc sub judice lis est. -- Ed.

9. Since the days of Owen, this reading has been the subject of protracted and sifting discussion. At one time the current opinion had set against Θεός as the reading, and the preference was given to ὅς. The results of later criticism decidedly converge in proof that the text as it stands in the received version is correct. -- Ed.

Of the Satisfaction of Christ

The last thing to be inquired into, upon occasion of the late opposition to the great fundamental truths of the gospel, is the satisfaction of Christ. And the doctrine hereof is such as, I conceive, needs rather to be explained than vindicated. For it being the centre wherein most, if not all, the lines of gospel promises and precepts do meet, and the great medium of all our communion with God in faith and obedience, the great distinction between the religion of Christians and that of all others in the world, it will easily, on a due proposal, be assented unto by all who would he esteemed disciples of Jesus Christ. And whether a parcel of insipid cavils may be thought sufficient to obliterate the revelation of it, men of sober minds will judge and discern.

For the term of satisfaction, we contend not about it. It does, indeed, properly express and connote that great effect of the death of Christ which, in the cause before us, we plead for. But yet, because it belongs rather to the explanation of the truth contended for, than is used expressly in the revelation of it, and because the right understanding of the word itself depends on some notions of law that as yet we need not take into consideration, I shall not, in this entrance of our discourse, insist precisely upon it, but leave it as the natural conclusion of what we shall find expressly declared in the Scripture. Neither do I say this as though I did decline the word, or the right use of it, or what is properly signified by it, but do only cast it into its proper place, answerable unto our method and design in the whole of this brief discourse.

I know some have taken a new way of expressing and declaring the doctrine concerning the mediation of Christ, with the causes and ends of his death, which they think more rational than that usually insisted on: but, as what I have yet heard of or seen in that kind, has been not only unscriptural, but also very irrational, and most remote from that accuracy whereunto they pretend who make use of it; so, if they should publish their conceptions, it is not improbable but that they may meet with a scholastical examination by some hand or other.

Our present work, as has been often declared, is for the establishment of the faith of them who may be attempted, if not brought into danger, to be seducers by the sleights of some who lie in wait to deceive, and the glamours of others who openly drive the same design. What, therefore, the Scripture plainly and clearly reveals in this matter, is the subject of our present inquiry. And either in so doing, as occasion shall be offered, we shall obviate, or, in the close of it remove, those sophisms that the sacred truth now proposed to consideration has been attempted withal.

The sum of what the Scripture reveals about this great truth, commonly called the "satisfaction of Christ," may be reduced unto these ensuing heads:--

First. That Adam, being made upright, sinned against God; and all mankind, all his posterity, in him:-- Gen i. 27, "So God created man in his own image, in the image of God created he him; male and female created he them." Chap. iii. 11, "And he said, Who told thee that thou wast naked? Hast thou

eaten of the tree whereof I commanded thee that thou shouldest not eat?"
Eccles. vii. 29, "Lo, this only have I found, that God made man upright; but
they have sought out many inventions." Rom. v. 12, "Wherefore, as by one man
sin entered into the world, and death by sin; and so death passed upon all men,
for that all have sinned." Verse 18, "Therefore, as by the offence of one
judgment came upon all men to condemnation." Verse 19, "By one man's
disobedience many were made sinners."

Secondly. That, by this sin of our first parents, all men are brought into an
estate of sin and apostasy from God, and of enmity unto him:-- Gen. vi. 5, "God
saw that the wickedness of man was great in the earth, and that every
imagination of the thoughts of his heart was only evil continually." Ps. li. 5,
"Behold, I was shapen in iniquity; and in sin did my mother conceive me."
Rom. iii. 23, "For all have sinned, and come short of the glory of God." Chap.
viii. 7, "The carnal mind is enmity against God: for it is not subject to the law
of God, neither indeed can be." Eph. iv. 18, "Having the understanding
darkened, being alienated from the life of God, through the ignorance that is in
them, because of the blindness of their heart," Chap. ii. 1; Col. ii. 13.

Thirdly. That in this state all men continue in sin against God, nor of
themselves can do otherwise:-- Rom. iii. 10-12, "There is none righteous, no,
not one: there is none that understandeth, there is none that seeketh after God.
They are all gone out of the way, they are together become unprofitable; there
is none that doeth good, no, not one."

Fourthly. That the justice and holiness of God, as he is the supreme
governor and judge of all the world, require that sin be punished:-- Exod.
xxxiv. 7, "That will by no means clear the guilty." Josh. xxiv. 19, "He is a holy
God; he is a jealous God; he will not forgive your transgressions nor your sins."
Ps. v. 4-6, "For thou art not a God that has pleasure in wickedness: neither shall
evil dwell with thee. The foolish shall not stand in thy sight: thou hatest all
workers of iniquity. Thou shalt destroy them that speak leasing." Hab. i. 13,
"Thou art of purer eyes than to behold evil, and canst not look upon iniquity."
Isa. xxxiii. 14, "Who among us shall dwell with the devouring fire? who among
us shall dwell with everlasting burnings?" Rom. i. 32, "Who knowing the
judgment of God, that they which commit such things are worthy of death."
Chap. iii. 5, 6, "Is God unrighteous who taketh vengeance? (I speak as a man)
God forbid: for then how shall God judge the world?" 2 Thess. i. 6, "It is a
righteous thing with God to recompense tribulation to them that trouble you."
Heb. xii. 29, "For our God is a consuming fire;" from Deut. iv. 24.

Fifthly. That God, has also engaged his veracity and faithfulness in the
sanction of the law, not to leave sin unpunished:-- Gen. ii. 17, "In the day thou
eatest thereof thou shalt surely die." Deut. xxvii. 26, "Cursed be he that
confirmeth not all the words of this law to do them." In this state and condition,
mankind, had they been left without divine aid and help, must have perished
eternally.

Sixthly. That God out of his infinite goodness, grace, and love to mankind,
sent his only Son to save and deliver them out of this condition:-- Matt. i. 21,
"Thou shalt call his name Jesus; for he shalt save his people from their sins."
John iii. 16, 17, "God so loved the world, that he gave his only begotten Son,
that whosoever believeth in him should not perish, but have everlasting life. For
God sent not his Son into the world to condemn the world, but that the world

through him might be saved." Rom. v. 8, "God commendeth his love toward us, in that, while we were yet sinners, Christ died for us." 1 John iv. 9, "In this was manifested the love of God toward us, because God sent his only begotten Son into the world, that we might live through him." Verse 10, "Herein is love, not that we loved God, but that he loved us, and sent his Son to be the propitiation for our sins." 1 Thess. i. 10, "Even Jesus, which delivered us from the wrath to come."

Seventhly. That this love was the same in Father and Son, acted distinctly in the manner that shall be afterward declared; so, vain are the pretences of men, who, from the love of the Father in this matter, would argue against the love of the Son, or on the contrary.

Eighthly. That the way, in general, whereby the Son of God, being incarnate, was to save lost sinners, was by a substitution of himself, according to the design and appointment of God, in the room of those whom he was to save:-- 2 Cor. v. 21, "He has made him to be sin for us, who knew no sin; that we might become the righteousness of God in him." Gal. iii. 13, "Christ has redeemed us from the curse of the law, being made a curse for us." Rom. v. 7, 8, "For scarcely for a righteous man will one die; yet peradventure for a good man some would even dare to die. But God commendeth his love toward us, in that, while we were yet sinners, Christ died for us." Chap. viii. 3, "For what the law could not do, in that it was weak through the flesh, God sending his own Son in the likeness of sinful flesh, and for sin, condemned sin in the flesh; that the righteousness of the law might be fulfilled in us." 1 Pet. ii. 24, "Who his own self bare our sins in his own body on the tree." Chap. iii. 18, "For Christ also has once suffered for sins, the just for the unjust, that he might bring us to God." All these expressions undeniably evince a substitution of Christ as to suffering in the stead of them whom he was to save; which, in general, is all that we intend by his satisfaction, -- namely, that he was made "sin for us," a "curse for us," "died for us," that is, in our stead, that we might be saved from the wrath to come. And all these expressions, as to their true, genuine importance, shall be vindicated as occasion shall require.

Ninthly. This way of his saving sinners is, in particular, several ways expressed in the Scriptures. As, --

1. That he offered himself a sacrifice to God, to make atonement for our sins; and that in his death and sufferings:-- Isa liii. 10, "When thou shalt make his soul an offering for sin." John i. 29, "Behold the lamb of God, who taketh away the sin of the world." Eph. v. 2, "Christ hath loved us, and has given himself for us an offering and a sacrifice to God for a sweet-smelling savour." Heb. ii. 17, Was "a merciful high priest in things pertaining to God, to make reconciliation for the sins of the people." Chap. ix. 11-14, "But Christ being come an high priest of good things to come, by a greater and more perfect tabernacle, not made with hands, that is to say, not of this building; neither by the blood of goats and calves, but by his own blood, he entered in once into the holy place, having obtained eternal redemption for us. For if the blood of bulls," etc., "how much more shall the blood of Christ, who through the eternal Spirit offered himself without spot to God, purge your consciences from dead works?"

2. That he redeemed us by paying a price, a ransom, for our redemption:-- Mark x. 45, "The Son of man came to give his life a ransom for many." 1 Cor. vi. 20, vii. 23, "For ye are bought with a price." 1 Tim. ii. 6, "Who gave himself

a ransom for all, to be testified in due time." Tit. ii. 14, "Who gave himself for us, that he might redeem us from all iniquity." 1 Pet. i. 18, 19, "For ye were not redeemed with corruptible things, as silver and gold; but with the precious blood of Christ, as of a lamb without blemish and without spot."

3. That he bare our sins, or the punishment due unto them:-- Isa. liii. 5, 6, "He was wounded for our transgressions, he was bruised for our iniquities; the chastisement of our peace was upon him, and with his stripes we are healed. All we like sheep have gone astray; we have turned every one to his own way; and the Lord has laid on him the iniquity of us all." Verse 11, "For he shall bear their iniquities." 1 Pet. ii. 24, "Who his own self bare our sins in his own body on the tree."

4. That he answered the law and the penalty of it:-- Rom. viii. 3, 4, "God sending his own Son in the likeness of sinful flesh, and for sin, condemned sin in the flesh; that the righteousness of the law might be fulfilled in us." Gal. iii. 13, "Christ has redeemed us from the curse of the law, being made a curse for us." Chap. iv. 4, 5, "God sent forth his Son, made of a woman, made under the law, to redeem them that were under the law."

5. That he died for sin, and sinners, to expiate the one, and in the stead of the other:-- Rom. iv. 25, "He was delivered for our offences." Chap. v. 10, "When we were enemies, we were reconciled to God by the death of his Son." 1 Cor. xv. 3, "Christ died for our sins according to the Scriptures." 2 Cor. v. 14, "For the love of Christ constraineth us; because we thus judge, that if one died for all, then were all dead," 1 Thess. v. 9, 10.

6. Hence, on the part of God it is affirmed, that "he spared him not, but delivered him up for us all," Rom. viii. 32; and caused "all our iniquities to meet upon him," Isa. liii. 6.

7. The effect hereof was, --

(1.) That the righteousness of God was glorified. Rom. iii. 25, 26, "Whom God has set forth to be a propitiation through faith in his blood, to declare his righteousness for the remission of sins." (2.) The law fulfilled and satisfied, as in the places before quoted, chap. viii. 3, 4; Gal. iii. 13, iv. 4, 5. (3.) God reconciled. 2 Cor. v. 18, 19, "God was in Christ reconciling the world unto himself, not imputing their trespasses unto them." Heb. ii. 17, "He made reconciliation for the sins of the people." (4.) Atonement was made for sin. Rom. v. 11, "By whom we have now received the atonement;" and peace was made with God. Eph. ii. 14, 16, "For he is our peace, who has made both one, ... that he might reconcile both unto God in one body by the cross, having slain the enmity thereby." (5.) [He] made an end of sin. Dan. ix. 24, "To finish the transgression, and to make an end of sins, and to make reconciliation for iniquity, and to bring in everlasting righteousness." The glory of God in all these things being exalted, himself was well pleased, righteousness and everlasting redemption, or salvation, purchased for sinners. Heb. ix. 14, For in that "the chastisement of our peace was upon him," and that "by his stripes we are healed," he being punished that we might go free, himself became a captain of salvation unto all that do obey him.

I have fixed on these particulars, to give every ordinary reader an instance how fully and plainly what he is to believe in this matter is revealed in the Scripture. And should I produce all the testimonies which expressly give witness unto these positions, it is known how great a part of the Bible must be transcribed. And these are the things which are indispensably required of us to believe, that we may be able to direct and regulate our obedience according to the mind and will of God. In the explanation of this doctrine unto farther edification, sundry things are usually insisted on, which necessarily and infallibly ensue upon the propositions of Scripture before laid down, and serve to beget in the minds of believers a due apprehension and right understanding of them; as, --

1. That God in this matter is to be considered as the chief, supreme, absolute rector and governor of all, -- as the Lord of the law, and of sinners; but yet so as an offended ruler: not as an offended person, but as an offended ruler, who has right to exact punishment upon transgressions, and whose righteousness of rule requires that he should so do.

2. That because he is righteous and holy, as he is the supreme Judge of all the world, it is necessary that he do right in the punishing of sin; without which the order of the creation cannot be preserved. For sin being the creature's deduction of itself from the order of its dependence upon, and obedience unto, the Creator and supreme Lord of all, without a reduction of it by punishment, confusion would be brought into the whole creation.

3. That whereas the law, and the sanction of it, is the moral or declarative cause of the punishment of sin, and it directly obliges the sinner himself unto punishment; God, as the supreme ruler, dispenses, not with the act of the law, but the immediate object, and substitutes another sufferer in the room of them who are principally liable unto the sentence of it, and are now to be acquitted or freed; -- that so the law may be satisfied, requiring the punishment of sin; justice exalted, whereof the law is an effect; and yet the sinner saved.

4. That the person thus substituted was the Son of God incarnate, who had power so to dispose of himself, with will and readiness for it; and was, upon the account of the dignity of his person, able to answer the penalty which all others had incurred and deserved.

5. That God, upon his voluntary susception of this office, and condescension to this work, did so lay our sins, in and by the sentence of the law, upon him, that he made therein full satisfaction for whatever legally could be charged on them for whom he died or suffered.

6. That the special way, terms, and conditions, whereby and wherein sinners may be interested in this satisfaction made by Christ, are determined by the will of God, and declared in the Scripture.

These, and the like things, are usually insisted on in the explication or declaration of this head of our confession; and there is not any of them but may be sufficiently confirmed by divine testimonies. It may also be farther evinced, that there is nothing asserted in them, but what is excellently suited unto the common notions which mankind has of God and his righteousness; and that in their practice they answer the light of nature and common reason, exemplified in sundry instances among the nations of the world.

I shall therefore take one argument from some of the testimonies before produced in the confirmation of this sacred truth, and proceed to remove the objections that are commonly bandied against it.

If the Lord Christ, according to the will of the Father, and by his own counsel and choice, was substituted, and did substitute himself, as the mediator of the covenant, in the room and in the stead of sinners, that they might be saved, and therein bare their sins, or the punishment due unto their sins, by undergoing the curse and penalty of the law, and therein also, according to the will of God, offered up himself for a propitiatory, expiatory sacrifice, to make atonement for sin, and reconciliation for sinners, that the justice of God being appeased, and the law fulfilled, they might go free, or be delivered from the wrath to come; and if therein, also, he paid a real satisfactory price for their redemption; then he made satisfaction to God for sin: for these are the things that we intend by that expression of satisfaction. But now all these things are openly and fully witnessed unto in the testimonies before produced, as may be observed by suiting some of them unto the several particulars here asserted:--

As, 1. What was done in this matter, was from the will, purpose, and love of God the Father, Ps. xl. 6-8; Heb. x. 5-7; Acts iv. 28; John iii. 16; Rom. viii. 3.

2. It was also done by his own voluntary consent, Phil. ii. 6-8.

3. He was substituted, and did substitute himself, as the mediator of the covenant, in the room and stead of sinners, that they may be saved, Heb. x. 5-7, vii. 22; Rom. iii. 25, v. 7, 8.

4. And he did therein bear their sins, or the punishment due to their sins, Isa. liii. 6, 11; 1 Pet. ii. 24. And this, --

5. By undergoing the curse and penalty of the law, Gal. iii. 13; or the punishment of sin required by the law, 2 Cor. v. 21; Rom. viii. 3.

6. Herein, also, according to the will of God, he offered up himself a propitiatory and expiatory sacrifice, to make atonement for sin and reconciliation for sinners, Eph v. 6; Rom. v. 6; Heb. ix. 11-14; -- which he did, that the justice of God being satisfied, and the law fulfilled, sinners might be freed from the wrath to come, Rom. iii. 25; 1 Thess. i. 10.

7. And hereby also he paid a real price of redemption for sin and sinners, 1 Pet. i. 18, 19; 1 Cor. vi. 20. These are the things which we are to believe concerning the satisfaction of Christ. And our explication of this doctrine we are ready to defend when called whereunto.

The consideration of the objections which are raised against this great fundamental truth shall close this discourse. And they are of two sorts:-- First, In general, to the whole doctrine, as declared, or some of the more signal heads or parts of it. Secondly, Particular instances in this or that supposal, as consequences of the doctrine asserted. And, in general, --

First, they say "This is contrary to, and inconsistent with, the love, grace, mercy, and goodness of God, which are so celebrated in the Scripture as the principal properties of his nature and acts of his will wherein he will be glorified; -- especially contrary to the freedom of forgiveness, which we are encouraged to expect, and commanded to believe." And this exception they endeavour to firm by testimonies that the Lord is good and gracious and that he does freely forgive us our sins and trespasses.

Ans. 1. I readily grant that whatever is really contrary to the grace, goodness, and mercy of God, whatever is inconsistent with the free forgiveness of sin, is not to be admitted; for these things are fully revealed in the Scripture, and must have a consistency with whatever else is therein revealed of God or his will.

2. As God is good, and gracious, and merciful, so also he is holy, righteous, true, and faithful. And these things are no less revealed concerning him than the others; and are no less essential properties of his nature than his

goodness and grace. And as they are all essentially the same in him, and considered only under a different habitude or respect, as they are exerted by acts of his will; so it belongs to his infinite wisdom, that the effects of them, though divers, and produced by divers ways and means, may no way be contrary one to the other, but that mercy be exercised without the prejudice of justice or holiness, and justice be preserved entire, without any obstruction to the exercise of mercy.

3. The grace and love of God, that in this matter the Scripture reveals to be exercised in order unto the forgiveness of sinners, consists principally in two things:-- (1.) In his holy eternal purpose of providing a relief for lost sinners. He has done it, "to the praise of the glory of his grace," Eph. i. 6. (2.) In the sending his Son in the pursuit and for the accomplishment of the holy purpose of his will and grace. Herein most eminently does the Scripture celebrate the love, goodness, and kindness of God, as that whereby, in infinite and for ever to be adored wisdom and grace, he made way for the forgiveness of our sins. John iii. 16, "God so loved the world, that he gave his only begotten Son." Rom. iii. 25, "Whom God has set forth to be a propitiation through faith in his blood." Rom. v. 8, "God commendeth his love toward us, in that, while we were yet sinners, Christ died for us." Tit. iii. 4; 1 John iv. 9, 10. Herein consists that ever to be adored love, goodness, grace, mercy, and condescension of God. Add hereunto, that, in the act of causing our iniquities to meet on Christ, wherein he immediately intended the declaration of his justice, Rom. iii. 25, -- "not sparing him, in delivering him up to death for us all," Rom. viii. 32, -- there was a blessed harmony in the highest Justice and most excellent grace and mercy. This grace, this goodness, this love of God towards mankind, towards sinners, our adversaries in this matter neither know nor understand; and so, indeed, what lies in them, remove the foundation of the whole gospel, and of all that faith and obedience which God requires at our hands.

4. Forgiveness, or the actual condonation of sinners, the pardon and forgiveness of sins, is free; but yet so as it is everywhere restrained unto a respect unto Christ, unto his death and blood-shedding. Eph. i. 7, "We have redemption through his blood, the forgiveness of sins." Chap. iv. 32. "God for Christ's sake has forgiven you." Rom. iii. 25, 26, "God has set him forth to be a propitiation through faith in his blood, to declare his righteousness for the remission of sins." It is absolutely free in respect of all immediate transactions between God and sinners.

(1.) Free on the part of God.

[1.] In the eternal purpose of it, when he might justly have suffered all men to have perished under the guilt of their sins. [2.] Free in the means that he used to effect it, unto his glory. 1st In the sending of his Son; and, 2dly In laying the punishment of our sin upon him. 3dly In his covenant with him, that it should be accepted on our behalf. 4^thly In his tender and proposal of it by the gospel unto sinners, to be received without money or without price. 5^thly In the actual condonation and pardon of them that do believe.

(2.) It is free on the part of the persons that are forgiven; in that, [1.] It is given and granted to them, without any satisfaction made by them for their former transgressions. [2.] Without any merit to purchase or procure it. [3.] Without any penal, satisfactory suffering here, or in a purgatory hereafter. [4.] Without any expectation of future recompense; or that, being pardoned, they should then make or give any satisfaction for what they had done before. And as any of these things would, so nothing else can, impeach the freedom of pardon and forgiveness. Whether, then, we respect the pardoner or the pardoned, pardon is every way free, -- namely, on the part of God who forgives, and on the part of sinners that are forgiven. If God now has, besides all this, provided himself a lamb for a sacrifice; if he has, in infinite wisdom and grace, found out a way thus freely to forgive us our sins, to the praise and glory of his own holiness, righteousness, and severity against sin, as well as unto the unspeakable advancement of that grace, goodness, and bounty which he immediately exercises in the pardon of sin; are these men's eyes evil, because he is good? Will they not be contented to be pardoned, unless they may have it at the rate of despoiling God of his holiness, truth, righteousness, and faithfulness? And as this is certainly done by that way of pardon which these men propose, no reserve in the least being made for the glory of God in those holy properties of his nature which are immediately injured and opposed by sin; so that pardon itself, which they pretend so to magnify, having nothing to influence it but a mere arbitrary act of God's will, is utterly debased from its own proper worth and excellency. And I shall willingly undertake to manifest that they derogate no less from grace and mercy in pardon, than they do from the righteousness and holiness of God, by the forgiveness which they have feigned; and that in it both of them are perverted and despoiled of all their glory.

But they yet say, "If God can freely pardon sin, why does he not do it without satisfaction? If he cannot, he is weaker and more imperfect than man, who can do so."

Ans. 1. God cannot do many things that men can do, -- not that he is more imperfect than they, but he cannot do them on the account of his perfection. He cannot lie, he cannot deny himself, he cannot change; which men can do, and do every day.

2. To pardon sin without satisfaction, in him who is absolutely holy, righteous, true, and faithful, -- the absolute, necessary, supreme Governor of all sinners, -- the author of the law, and sanction of it, wherein punishment is threatened and declared, -- is to deny himself, and to do what one infinitely perfect cannot do.

3. I ask of these men, why God does not pardon sins freely, without requiring faith, repentance, and obedience in them that are pardoned; yea, as the conditions on which they may be pardoned? For, seeing he is so infinitely good and gracious, cannot he pardon men without prescribing such terms and conditions unto them as he knows that men, and that incomparably the greatest number of them, will never come up unto, and so must of necessity perish for ever? Yea, but they say, "This cannot be: neither does this impeach the freedom of pardon; for it is certain that God does prescribe these things, and yet he pardons freely; and it would altogether unbecome the holy God to pardon sinners that continue so to live and die in their sins." But do not these men see that they have hereby given away their cause which they contend for? For, if a prescription of sundry things to the sinner himself, without which he shall not be pardoned, do not at all impeach, as they say, the freedom of pardon, but God may be said freely to pardon sin notwithstanding it; how shall the receiving of satisfaction by another, nothing at all being required of the sinner, have the least appearance of any such thing? If the freedom of forgiveness consists in

such a boundless notion as these men imagine, it is certain that the prescribing of faith and repentance in and unto sinners, antecedently to their participation of it, is much more evidently contrary unto it, than the receiving of satisfaction from another who is not to be pardoned can to any appear to be. Secondly, if it be contrary to the holiness of God to pardon any without requiring faith, repentance, and obedience in them (as it is indeed), let not these persons be offended if we believe him when he so frequently declares it, that it was so to remit sin, without the fulfilling of his law and satisfaction of his justice.

Secondly, they say, "There is no such thing as justice in God requiring the punishment of sin; but that that which in him requires and calls for the punishment of sin is his anger and wrath; which expressions denote free acts of his will, and not any essential properties of his nature." So that God may punish sin or not punish it, at his pleasure; therefore there is no reason that he should require any satisfaction for sin, seeing he may pass it by absolutely as he pleases.

Ans. 1. Is it not strange, that the great Governor, the Judge of all the world, which, on the supposition of the creation of it, God is naturally and necessarily, should not also naturally be so righteous as to do right, in rendering unto every one according to his works?

2. The sanction and penalty of the law, which is the rule of punishment, was, I suppose, an effect of justice, -- of God's natural and essential justice, and not of his anger or wrath. Certainly, never did any man make a law for the government of a people in anger. Draco's laws were not made in wrath, but according to the best apprehension of right and justice that he had, though said to be written in blood; and shall we think otherwise of the law of God?

3. Anger and wrath in God express the effects of justice, and so are not merely free acts of his will. This, therefore, is a tottering cause, that is built on the denial of God's essential righteousness. But it was proved before, and it is so elsewhere.

Thirdly, they say, "That the sacrifice of Christ was only metaphorically so," -- that he was a metaphorical priest, not one properly so called; and, therefore, that his sacrifice did not consist in his death and blood-shedding, but in his appearing in heaven upon his ascension, presenting himself unto God in the most holy place not made with hands as the mediator of the new covenant.

Ans. 1. When once these men come to this evasion, they think themselves safe, and that they may go whither they will without control. For they say it is true, Christ was a priest; but only he was a metaphorical one. He offered sacrifice; but it was a metaphorical one. He redeemed us; but with a metaphorical redemption. And so we are justified thereon; but with a metaphorical justification. And so, for aught I know, they are like to be saved with a metaphorical salvation. This is the substance of their plea in this matter:-- Christ was not really a priest; but did somewhat like a priest. He offered not sacrifice really; but did somewhat that was like a sacrifice. He redeemed us not really; but did somewhat that looked like redemption. And what these things are, wherein their analogy consists, what proportion the things that Christ has done bear to the things that are really so, from whence they receive their denomination, it is meet it should be wholly in the power of these persons to declare. But, --

2. What should hinder the death of Christ to be a sacrifice, a proper sacrifice, and, according to the nature, end, and use of sacrifices, to have made

atonement and satisfaction for sin? (1.) It is expressly called so in the Scripture; wherein he is said to "offer himself, to make his soul an offering, to offer himself a sacrifice," Eph. v. 2; Heb. i. 3, ix. 14, 25, 26, vii. 27. And he is himself directly said to be a "priest," or a sacrificer, Heb. ii. 17. And it is nowhere intimated, much less expressed, that these things are not spoken properly, but metaphorically only. (2.) The legal sacrifices of the old law were instituted on purpose to represent and prepare the way for the bringing in of the sacrifice of the Lamb of God, so to take away the sin of the world; and is it not strange, that true and real sacrifices should be types and representations of that which was not so? On this supposition, all those sacrifices are but so many seductions from the right understanding of things between God and sinners. (3.) Nothing is wanting to render it a proper propitiatory sacrifice. For, -- [1.] There was the person offering, and that was Christ himself, Heb. ix. 14, "He offered himself unto God." "He," that is, the sacrificer, denotes the person of Christ, God and man; and "himself," as the sacrifice, denotes his human nature whence God is said to "purchase his church with his own blood," Acts xx. 28; for he offered himself through the eternal Spirit: so that, -- [2.] There was the matter of the sacrifice, which was the human nature of Christ, soul and body. "His soul was made an offering for sin," Isa. liii. 10; and his body, "The offering of the body of Jesus Christ," Heb. x. 10, -- his blood especially, which is often synecdochically mentioned for the whole. (4.) His death had the nature of a sacrifice: for, -- [1.] Therein were the sins of men laid upon him, and not in his entrance into heaven; for "he bare our sins in his own body on the tree," 1 Pet. ii. 24. God made our sins then "to meet upon him," Isa. liii. 6; which gives the formality unto any sacrifices. "Quod in ejus caput sit," is the formal reason of all propitiatory sacrifices, and ever was so, as is expressly declared, Lev. xvi. 21, 22; and the phrase of "bearing sin," of "bearing iniquity," is constantly used for the undergoing of the punishment due to sin. [2.] It had the end of a proper sacrifice; it made expiation of sin, propitiation and atonement for sin, with reconciliation with God; and so took away that enmity that was between God and sinners, Heb. i. 3; Rom. iii. 25, 26; Heb. ii. 17, 18, v. 10; Rom. viii. 3; 2 Cor. v. 18, 19. And although God himself designed, appointed, and contrived, in wisdom, this way of reconciliation, as he did the means for the atoning of his own anger towards the friends of Job, commanding them to go unto him, and with him offer sacrifices for themselves, which he would accept, chap. xlii. 7, 8; yet, as he was the supreme Governor, the Lord of all, attended with infinite justice and holiness, atonement was made with him, and satisfaction to him thereby.

What has been spoken may suffice to discover the emptiness and weakness of those exceptions which in general these men make against the truth before laid down from the Scripture. A brief examination of some particular instances, wherein they seek not so much to oppose as to reproach the revelation of this mystery of the gospel, shall put a close to this discourse. It is said, then, --

First, "That if this be so, then it will follow that God is gracious to forgive, and yet [it is] impossible for him, unless the debt be fully satisfied."

Ans. 1. I suppose the confused and abrupt expression of things here, in words scarcely affording a tolerable sense, is rather from weakness than captiousness; and so I shall let the manner of the proposal pass. 2. What if this should follow, that God is gracious to forgive sinners, and yet will not, cannot, on the account of his own holiness and righteousness, actually forgive any, without satisfaction and atonement made for sin? The worst that can be hence concluded is, that the Scripture is true, which affirms both these in many places. 3. This sets out the exceeding greatness of the grace of God in forgiveness, that when sin could not be forgiven without satisfaction, and the sinner himself could no way make any such satisfaction, he provided himself a sacrifice of atonement, that the sinner might be discharged and pardoned. 4. Sin is not properly a debt, for then it might be paid in kind, by sin itself; but is called so only because it binds over the sinner to punishment, which is the satisfaction to be made for that which is properly a transgression, and improperly only a debt. It is added, --

Secondly, "Hence it follows, that the finite and impotent creature is more capable of extending mercy and forgiveness than the infinite and omnipotent Creator."

Ans. 1. God being essentially holy and righteous, having engaged his faithfulness in the sanction of the law, and being naturally and necessarily the governor and ruler of the world, the forgiving of sin without satisfaction would be no perfection in him, but an effect of impotency and imperfection, -- a thing which God cannot do, as he cannot lie, nor deny himself. 2. The direct contrary of what is insinuated is asserted by this doctrine; for, on the supposition of the satisfaction and atonement insisted on, not only does God freely forgive, but that in such a way of righteousness and goodness, as no creature is able to conceive or express the glory and excellency of it. And to speak of the poor having pardons of private men, upon particular offences against themselves, who are commanded so to do, and have no right nor authority to require or exact punishment, nor is any due upon the mere account of their own concernment, in comparison with the forgiveness of God, arises out of a deep ignorance of the whole matter under consideration.

Thirdly. It is added by them, that hence it follows, "That God so loved the world, that he gave his only Son to save it; and yet that God stood off in high displeasure, and Christ gave himself as a complete satisfaction to offended justice."

Ans. Something these men would say, if they knew what or how; for, --

1. That God so loved the world as to give his only Son to save it, is the expression of the Scripture, and the foundation of the doctrine whose truth we contend for. 2. That Christ offered himself to make atonement for sinners, and therein made satisfaction to the justice of God, is the doctrine itself which these men oppose, and not any consequent of it. 3. That God stood off in high displeasure, is an expression which neither the Scripture uses, nor those who declare this doctrine from thence, nor is suited unto divine perfections, or the manner of divine operations. That intended seems to be, that the righteousness and law of God required the punishment due to sin to be undergone, and thereby satisfaction to be made unto God; which is no consequent of the doctrine, but the doctrine itself.

Fourthly. It is yet farther objected, "That if Christ made satisfaction for sin, then he did it either as God or as man, or as God and man."

Ans. 1. As God and man. Acts xx. 28, "God redeemed his church with his own blood." 1 John iii. 16, "Hereby perceive we the love of God, because he laid down his life for us." Heb. ix. 14. 2. This dilemma is proposed, as that which proceeds on a supposition of our own principles, that Christ is God and man in one person: which, indeed, makes the pretended difficulty to be vain, and a mere effect of ignorance; for all the mediatory acts of Christ being the acts of his person, must of necessity be the acts of him as God and man. 3. There is yet another mistake in this inquiry; for satisfaction is in it looked on as a real act or operation of one or the other nature in Christ, when it is the apotelesma or effect of the actings, the doing and suffering of Christ -- the dignity of what he did in reference unto the end for which he did it. For the two natures are so united in Christ as not to have a third compound principle of physical acts and operations thence arising; but each nature acts distinctly according to its own being and properties, yet so as what is the immediate act of either nature is the act of him who is one in both; from whence it has its dignity. 4. The sum is, that in all the mediatory actions of Christ we are to consider, -- (1.) The agent; and that is the person of Christ. (2.) The immediate principle by which and from which the agent works; and that is the natures in the person. (3.) The actions; which are the effectual operations of either nature. (4.) The effect or work with respect to God and us; and this relates unto the person of the agent, the Lord Christ, God and man. A blending of the natures into one common principle of operation, as the compounding of mediums unto one end, is ridiculously supposed in this matter.

But yet, again; it is pretended that sundry consequences, irreligious and irrational, do ensue upon a supposition of the satisfaction pleaded for. What, then, are they?

First. "That it is unlawful and impossible for God Almighty to be gracious and merciful, or to pardon transgressors."

Ans. The miserable, confused misapprehension of things which the proposal of this and the like consequences does evidence, manifests sufficiently how unfit the makers of them are to manage controversies of this nature. For, -- 1. It is supposed that for God to be gracious and merciful, or to pardon sinners, are the same; which is to confound the essential properties of his nature with the free acts of his will. 2. Lawful or unlawful, are terms that can with no tolerable sense be used concerning any properties of God, all which are natural and necessary unto his being; as goodness, grace, and mercy, in particular, are. 3. That it is impossible for God to pardon transgressors, according to this doctrine, is a fond imagination; for it is only a declaration of the manner how he does it. 4. As God is gracious and merciful, so also he is holy, and righteous, and true; and it became him, or was every way meet for him, in his way of exercising grace and mercy towards sinners, to order all things so, as that it might be done without the impeachment of his holiness, righteousness, and truth. It is said, again, --

Secondly, "That God was inevitably compelled to this way of saving men; -- the highest affront to his uncontrollable nature."

Ans. 1. Were the authors of these exceptions put to declare what they mean by God's "uncontrollable nature," they would hardly disentangle themselves with common sense; such masters of reason are they, indeed, whatever they would fain pretend to be. Controllable or uncontrollable, respects acting and operations, not beings or natures. 2. That, upon the principle opposed by these men, God was inevitably compelled to this way of saving men, is a fond and childish imagination. The whole business of the salvation of men, according unto this doctrine, depends on a mere free, sovereign act of God's will, exerting itself in a way of infinite wisdom, holiness, and grace. 3. The meaning of this objection (if it has either sense or meaning in it) is, that God, freely purposing to save lost sinners, did it in a way becoming his holy nature and righteous law. What other course Infinite Wisdom could have taken for the satisfaction of his justice we know not; -- that justice was to be satisfied, and that this way it is done we know and believe.

Thirdly. They say it hence follows, "That it is unworthy of God to pardon, but not to inflict punishment on the innocent, or require a satisfaction where there was nothing due."

Ans. 1. What is worthy or unworthy of God, himself alone knows, and of men not any, but according to what he is pleased to declare and reveal; but, certainly, it is unworthy any person, pretending to the least interest in ingenuity or use of reason, to use such frivolous instances in any case of importance, which have not the least pretence of argument in them, but what arises from a gross misapprehension or misrepresentation of a doctrine designed to opposition. 2. To pardon sinners, is a thing becoming the goodness and grace of God; to do it by Christ, that which becomes them, and his holiness and righteousness also, Eph. i. 6, 7; Rom. iii. 25. 3. The Lord Christ was personally innocent; but "he who knew no sin was made sin for us," 2 Cor. v. 21. And as the mediator and surety of the covenant, he was to answer for the sins of them whom he undertook to save from the wrath to come, by giving himself a ransom for them, and making his soul an offering for their sin. 4. That nothing is due to the justice of God for sin, -- that is, that sin does not in the justice of God deserve punishment, -- is a good, comfortable doctrine for men that are resolved to continue in their sins whilst they live in this world. The Scripture tells us that Christ paid what he took not; that all our iniquities were caused to meet upon him; that he bare them in his own body on the tree; that his soul was made an offering for sin, and thereby made reconciliation or atonement for the sins of the people. If these persons be otherwise minded, we cannot help it.

Fourthly. It is added, that "This doctrine does not only disadvantage the true virtue and real intent of Christ's life and death, but entirely deprives God of that praise which is owing to his greatest love and goodness."

Ans. 1. I suppose that this is the first time that this doctrine fell under this imputation; nor could it possibly be liable unto this charge from any who did either understand it or the grounds on which it is commonly opposed. For there is no end of the life or death of Christ which the Socinians themselves admit of, but it is also allowed and asserted in the doctrine now called in question. Do they say, that he taught the truth, or revealed the whole mind and will of God concerning his worship and our obedience? We say the same. Do they say, that by his death he bare testimony unto and confirmed the truth which he had taught? It is also owned by us. Do they say, that in what he did and suffered he set us an example that we should labour after conformity unto? It is what we acknowledge and teach: only, we say that all these things belong principally to his prophetical office. But we, moreover, affirm and believe, that as a priest, or in the discharge of his sacerdotal office, he did, in his death and sufferings, offer himself a sacrifice to God, to make atonement for our sins, -- which they deny; and that he died for us, or in our stead, that we might go free: without the faith and acknowledgment whereof no part of the gospel can be rightly understood. All the ends, then, which they themselves assign of the life and death of Christ are by us granted; and the principal one, which gives life and efficacy to the rest, is by them denied. Neither, -- 2. Does it fall under any possible imagination, that the praise due unto God should be eclipsed hereby. The love and kindness of God towards us is in the Scripture fixed principally and fundamentally on his "sending of his only begotten Son to die for us." And, certainly, the greater the work was that he had to do, the greater ought our acknowledgment of his love and kindness to be. But it is said, --

Fifthly, "That it represents the Son as more kind and compassionate than the Father; whereas if both be the same God, then either the Father is as loving as the Son, or the Son as angry as the Father."

Ans. 1. The Scripture refers the love of the Father unto two heads:-- (1.) The sending of his Son to die for us, John iii. 16; Rom. v. 8; 1 John iv. 9, 10. (2.) In choosing sinners unto a participation of the fruits of his love, Eph. i. 3-6. The love of the Son is fixed signally on his actual giving himself to die for us, Gal. ii. 20; Eph. v. 25; Rev. i. 5. What balances these persons have got to weigh these loves in, and to conclude which is the greatest or most weighty, I know not. 2. Although only the actual discharge of his office be directly assigned to the love of Christ, yet his condescension in taking our nature upon him, -- expressed by his mind, Phil. ii. 5-8, and the readiness of his will, Ps. xl. 8, -- does eminently comprise love in it so. 3. The love of the Father in sending of the Son was an act of his will; which being a natural and essential property of God, it was so far the act of the Son also, as he is partaker of the same nature, though eminently, and in respect of order, it was peculiarly the act of the Father. 4. The anger of God against sin is an effect of his essential righteousness and holiness, which belong to him as God; which yet hinders not but that both Father, and Son, and Spirit, acted love towards sinners. They say again, --

Sixthly, "It robs God of the gift of his Son for our redemption, which the Scriptures attribute to the unmerited love he had for the world, in affirming the Son purchased that redemption from the Father, by the gift of himself to God as our complete satisfaction."

Ans. 1. It were endless to consider the improper and absurd expressions which are made use of in these exceptions, as here; the last words have no tolerable sense in them, according to any principles whatever. 2. If the Son's purchasing redemption for us, procuring, obtaining it, do rob God of the gift of his Son for our redemption, the Holy Ghost must answer for it; for, having "obtained" for us, or procured, or purchased, "eternal redemption," is the word used by himself, Heb. ix. 12; and to deny that he has laid down his life a "ransom" for us, and has "bought us with a price," is openly to deny the gospel. 3. In a word, the great gift of God consisted in giving his Son to obtain redemption for us. 4. Herein he "offered himself unto God," and "gave himself for us;" and if these persons are offended herewithal, what are we, that we should withstand God? They say, --

Seventhly, "Since Christ could not pay what was not his own, it follows, that in the payment of his own the case still remains equally grievous; since the debt is not hereby absolved or forgiven, but transferred only; and, by consequence, we are no better provided for salvation than before, owing that now to the Son which was once owing to the Father."

Ans. The looseness and dubiousness of the expressions here used makes an appearance that there is something in them, when indeed there is not. There is an allusion in them to a debt and a payment, which is the most improper expression that is used in this matter; and the interpretation thereof is to be regulated by other proper expressions of the same thing. But to keep to the allusion:-- 1. Christ paid his own, but not for himself, Dan. ix. 26. 2. Paying it for us, the debt is discharged; and our actual discharge is to be given out according to the ways and means, and upon the conditions, appointed and constituted by the Father and Son. 3. When a debt is so transferred as that one is accepted in the room and obliged to payment in the stead of another, and that payment is made and accepted accordingly, all law and reason require that the original debtor be discharged. 4. What on this account we owe to the Son, is praise, thankfulness, and obedience, and not the debt which he took upon himself and discharged for us, when we were nonsolvent, by his love. So that this matter is plain enough, and not to be involved by such cloudy expressions and incoherent discourse, following the metaphor of a debt. For if God be considered as the creditor, we all as debtors, and being insolvent, Christ undertook, out of his love, to pay the debt for us, and did so accordingly, which was accepted with God; it follows that we are to be discharged upon God's terms, and under a new obligation unto his love who has made this satisfaction for us: which we shall eternally acknowledge. It is said, --

Eighthly, "It no way renders men beholden or in the least obliged to God, since by their doctrine he would not have abated us, nor did he Christ, the least farthing; so that the acknowledgments are peculiarly the Son's: which destroys the whole current of Scripture testimony for his goodwill towards men. O the infamous portraiture this doctrine draws of the infinite goodness! Is this your retribution, O injurious satisfactionists?"

Ans. This is but a bold repetition of what, in other words, was mentioned before over and over. Wherein the love of God in this matter consisted, and what is the obligation on us unto thankfulness and obedience, has been before also declared; and we are not to be moved in fundamental truths by vain exclamations of weak and unstable men. It is said, --

Ninthly, "That God's justice is satisfied for sins past, present, and to come, whereby God and Christ have lost both their power of enjoining godliness and prerogative of punishing disobedience; for what is once paid, is not revocable, and if punishment should arrest any for their debts, it argues a breach on God or Christ's part, or else that it has not been sufficiently solved, and the penalty complete sustained by another."

Ans. The intention of this pretended consequence of our doctrine is that, upon a supposition of satisfaction made by Christ, there is no solid foundation remaining for the prescription of faith, repentance, and obedience, on the one hand; or of punishing them who refuse so to obey, believe, or repent, on the other. The reason of this inference insinuated seems to be this, -- that sin being satisfied for, cannot be called again to an account. For the former part of the pretended consequence, -- namely, that on this supposition there is no foundation left for the prescription of godliness, -- I cannot discern any thing in the least looking towards the confirmation of it in the words of the objection laid down. But these things are quite otherwise; as is manifest unto them that read and obey the gospel. For, -- 1. Christ's satisfaction for sins acquits not the creature of that dependence on God, and duty which he owes to God, which (notwithstanding that) God may justly, and does prescribe unto him, suitable to his own nature, holiness, and will. The whole of our regard unto God does not lie in an acquitment from sin. It is, moreover, required of us, as a necessary and indispensable consequence of the relation wherein we stand unto him, that we live to him and obey him, whether sin be satisfied for or no. The manner and measure hereof are to be regulated by his prescriptions, which are suited to his own wisdom and our condition; and they are now referred to the heads mentioned, of faith, repentance, and new obedience. 2. The satisfaction made for sin being not made by the sinner himself, there must of necessity be a rule, order, and law-constitution, how the sinner may come to be interested in it, and made partaker of it. For the consequent of the freedom of one by the suffering of another is not natural or necessary, but must proceed and arise from a law-constitution, compact, and agreement. Now, the way constituted and appointed is that of faith, or believing, as explained in the Scripture. If men believe not, they are no less liable to the punishment due to their sins than if no satisfaction at all were made for sinners. And whereas it is added, "Forgetting that every one must appear before the judgement-seat of Christ, to receive according to the things done in the body, yea, and every one must give an account of himself to God;" closing all with this, "But many more are the gross absurdities and blasphemies that are the genuine fruits of this so confidently-believed doctrine of satisfaction:" I say it is, -- 3. Certain that we must all appear before the judgment-seat of Christ, to receive according to the things done in the body; and therefore, woe will be unto them at the great day who are not able to plead the atonement made for their sins by the blood of Christ, and an evidence of their interest therein by their faith and obedience, or the things done and wrought in them and by them whilst they were in the body here in this world. And this it would better become these persons to betake themselves unto the consideration of, than to exercise themselves unto an unparalleled confidence in reproaching those with absurdities and blasphemies who believe the Deity and satisfaction of Jesus Christ, the Son of the living God, who died for us; which is the ground and bottom of all our expectation of a blessed life and immortality to come.

The removal of these objections against the truth, scattered of late up and down in the hands of all sorts of men, may suffice for our present purpose. If any amongst these men judge that they have an ability to manage the opposition against the truth as declared by us, with such pleas, arguments, and exceptions, as may pretend an interest in appearing reason, they shall, God assisting, be attended unto. With men given up to a spirit of railing or reviling, -- though it be no small honour to be reproached by them who reject with scorn the eternal Deity of the Son of God, and the satisfactory atonement that he made for the sins of men, -- no person of sobriety will contend. And I shall farther only desire the reader to take notice, that though these few sheets were written in a few hours, upon the desire and for the satisfaction of some private friends, and therefore contain merely an expression of present thoughts, without the least design or diversion of mind towards accuracy or ornament; yet the author is so far confident that the truth, and nothing else, is proposed and confirmed in them, that he fears not but that an opposition to what is here declared will be removed, and the truth reinforced in such a way and manner as may not be to its disadvantage.

An Appendix

The preceding discourse, as has been declared, was written for the use of ordinary Christians, or such as might be in danger to be seduced, or any way entangled in their minds, by the late attempts against the truths pleaded for: for those to whom the dispensation of the gospel is committed, are "debtors both to the Greeks and to the Barbarians; both to the wise and to the unwise," Rom. i. 14. It was therefore thought meet to insist only on things necessary, and such as their faith is immediately concerned in; and not to immix therewithal any such arguments or considerations as might not, by reason of the terms wherein they are expressed, be obvious to their capacity and understanding. Unto plainness and perspicuity, brevity was also required, by such as judged this work necessary. That design, we hope, is answered, and now discharged in some useful measure. But yet, because many of our arguments on the head of the satisfaction of Christ depend upon the genuine signification and notion of the words and terms wherein the doctrine of it is delivered, -- which, for the reasons before mentioned, could not conveniently be discussed in the foregoing discourse, -- I shall here, in some few instances, give an account of what farther confirmation the truth might receive by a due explanation of them. And I shall mention here but few of them, because a large dissertation concerning them all is intended [10] in another way.

First. For the term of satisfaction itself, it is granted that in this matter it is not found in the Scripture, -- that is, it is not so ῥητῶς, or syllabically, -- but it is κατὰ τὸ πρᾶγμα ἀναντιρρήτως; the thing itself intended is asserted in it, beyond all modest contradiction. Neither, indeed, is there in the Hebrew language any word that does adequately answer unto it; no, nor yet in the Greek. As it is used in this cause, ἐγγύη, which is properly "sponsio," or "fide-jussio," in its actual discharge, makes the nearest approach unto it: ἱκανον ποιεῖν is used to the same purpose. But there are words and phrases, both in the Old Testament and in the New, that are equipollent unto it, and express the matter or thing intended by it: as in the Old are, פִּדְיוֹן פָּדָה [Ps. xlix. 9], and כֹּפֶר. This last word we render "satisfaction," Numb. xxxv. 32, 33, where God denies that any compensation, sacred or civil, shall be received to free a murderer from the punishment due unto him; which properly expresses what we intend: "Thou shalt admit of no satisfaction for the life of a murderer."

In the New Testament: Λύτρον, ἀντίλυτρον, ἀπολύτρωσις, τιμή, ἱλασμός and the verbs, λυτροῦν, ἀπολυτροῦν, ἐξαγοράζειν, ἱλάσκεσθαι, are of the same importance, and some of them accommodated to express the thing intended, beyond that which has obtained in vulgar use. For that which we intended hereby is, the voluntary obedience unto death, and the passion or suffering, of our Lord Jesus Christ, God and man, whereby and wherein he offered himself through the eternal Spirit, for a propitiatory sacrifice, that he might fulfil the law, or answer all its universal postulata; and as our sponsor, undertaking our cause, when we were under the sentence of condemnation, underwent the punishment due to us from the justice of God, being transferred on him;

whereby having made a perfect and absolute propitiation or atonement for our sins, he procured for us deliverance from death and the curse, and a right unto life everlasting. Now, this is more properly expressed by some of the words before mentioned than by that of satisfaction; which yet, nevertheless, as usually explained, is comprehensive, and no way unsuited to the matter intended by it.

In general, men by this word understand either "reparationem offensæ" or "solutionem debiti," -- either "reparation made for offence given unto any," or "the payment of a debt." "Debitum" is either "criminale" or "pecuniarium;" that is, either the obnoxiousness of a man to punishment for crimes or the guilt of them, in answer to that justice and law which he is necessarily liable and subject unto; or unto a payment or compensation by and of money, or what is valued by it; -- which last consideration, neither in itself nor in any seasonings from an analogy unto it, can in this matter have any proper place. Satisfaction is the effect of the doing or suffering what is required for the answering of his charge against faults or sins, who has right, authority, and power to require, exact, and inflict punishment for them. Some of the schoolmen define it by "Voluntaria redditio æquivalentis indebiti;" of which more elsewhere. The true meaning of, "to satisfy, or make satisfaction," is "tantum facere aut pati, quantum satis sit justè irato ad vindictam." This satisfaction is impleaded as inconsistent with free remission of sins, -- how causelessly we have seen. It is so far from it, that it is necessary to make way for it, in case of a righteous law transgressed, and the public order of the universal Governor and government of all disturbed. And this God directs unto, Lev. iv. 31, "The priest shall make an atonement for him, and it shall be forgiven him." This atonement was a legal satisfaction, and it is by God himself premised to remission or pardon. And Paul prays Philemon to forgive Onesimus, though he took upon himself to make satisfaction for all the wrong or damage that he had sustained, Epist. verses 18, 19. And when God was displeased with the friends of Job, he prescribes a way to them, or what they shall do, and what they shall get done for them, that they might be accepted and pardoned, Job xlii. 7, 8, "The Lord said unto Eliphaz, My wrath is kindled against thee, and against thy two friends: therefore take unto you now seven bullocks and seven rams, and go to my servant Job, and offer up for yourselves a burnt-offering; and my servant Job shall pray for you: for him will I accept: lest I deal with you after your folly." He plainly enjoins an atonement, that he might freely pardon them. And both these, -- namely, satisfaction and pardon, with their order and consistency, -- were solemnly represented by the great institution of the sacrifice of the scape-goat. For after all the sins of the people were put upon him, or the punishment of them transferred unto him in a type and representation, with "Quod in ejus caput sit," the formal reason of all sacrifices propitiatory, he was sent away with them; denoting the oblation or forgiveness of sin, after a translation made of its punishment, Lev. xvi. 21, 22. And whereas it is not expressly said that that goat suffered, or was slain, but was either עֲזָאזֵל, "hircus," ἀποπομπαῖος, "a goat sent away," or was sent to a rock called Azazel, in the wilderness, as Vatablus [11] and Oleaster, [12] with some others, think (which is not probable, seeing, though it might then be done whilst the people were in the wilderness of Sinai, yet could not, by reason of its distance, when the people were settled in Canaan, be annually observed), it was from the poverty of the types, whereof no one could fully represent that grace which it had particular respect unto. What, therefore, was wanting in that goat was supplied in the other, which was slain as a sin-offering, verses 15, 16.

Neither does it follow, that, on the supposition of the satisfaction pleaded for, the freedom, pardon, or acquitment of the person originally guilty and liable to punishment must immediately and "ipso facto" ensue. It is not of the nature of every solution or satisfaction, that deliverance must "ipso facto" follow. And the reason of it is, because this satisfaction, by a succedaneous substitution of one to undergo punishment for another, must be founded in a voluntary compact and agreement. For there is required unto it a relaxation of the law, though not as unto the punishment to be inflicted, yet as unto the person to be punished. And it is otherwise in personal guilt than in pecuniary debts. In these, the debt itself is solely intended, the person only obliged with reference whereunto. In the other, the person is firstly and principally under the obligation. And therefore, when a pecuniary debt is paid, by whomsoever it be paid, the obligation of the person himself unto payment ceases "ipso facto." But in things criminal, the guilty person himself being firstly, immediately, and intentionally under the obligation unto punishment, when there is introduced by compact a vicarious solution, in the substitution of another to suffer, though he suffer the same absolutely which those should have done for whom he suffers, yet, because of the acceptation of his person to suffer, which might have been refused, and could not be admitted without some relaxation of the law, deliverance of the guilty persons cannot ensue "ipso facto," but by the intervention of the terms fixed on in the covenant or agreement for an admittance of the substitution.

It appears, from what has been spoken, that, in this matter of satisfaction, God is not considered as a creditor, and sin as a debt; and the law as an obligation to the payment of that debt, and the Lord Christ as paying it; -- though these notions may have been used by some for the illustration of the whole matter, and that not without countenance from sundry expressions in the Scripture to the same purpose. But God is considered as the infinitely holy and righteous author of the law, and supreme governor of all mankind, according to the tenor and sanction of it. Man is considered as a sinner, a transgressor of that law, and thereby obnoxious and liable to the punishment constituted in it and by it, -- answerably unto the justice and holiness of its author. The substitution of Christ was merely voluntary on the part of God, and of himself, undertaking to be a sponsor, to answer for the sins of men by undergoing the punishment due unto them. To this end there was a relaxation of the law as to the persons that were to suffer, though not as to what was to be suffered. Without the former, the substitution mentioned could not have been admitted; and on supposition of the latter, the suffering of Christ could not have had the nature of punishment, properly so called: for punishment relates to the justice and righteousness in government of him that exacts it and inflicts it; and this the justice of God does not but by the law. Nor could the law be any way satisfied or fulfilled by the suffering of Christ, if, antecedently thereunto, its obligation, or power of obliging unto the penalty constituted in its sanction unto sin, was relaxed, dissolved, or dispensed withal. Nor was it agreeable to justice, nor would the nature of the things themselves admit of it, that another punishment should be inflicted on Christ than what we had deserved; nor could our sin be the impulsive cause of his death; nor could we have had any benefit thereby.

And this may suffice to be added unto what was spoken before as to the nature of satisfaction, so far as the brevity of the discourse whereunto we are confined will bear, or the use whereunto it is designed does require.

Secondly. The nature of the doctrine contended for being declared and cleared, we may, in one or two instances, manifest how evidently it is revealed, and how fully it may be confirmed or vindicated. It is, then, in the Scripture declared, that "Christ died for us," -- that he "died for our sins;" and that we are thereby delivered. This is the foundation of Christian religion as such. Without the faith and acknowledgment of it, we are not Christians. Neither is it, in these general terms, at all denied by the Socinians. It remains, therefore, that we consider, -- 1. How this is revealed and affirmed in the Scripture; and, 2. What is the true meaning of the expressions and propositions wherein it is revealed and affirmed; -- for in them, as in sundry others, we affirm that the satisfaction pleaded for is contained.

1. Christ is said to die, to give himself, to be delivered, ὑπὲρ ἡμῶν, etc., for us, for his sheep, for the life of the world, for sinners, John vi. 51x. 15; Rom. v. 6; 2 Cor. v. 14, 15; Gal. ii. 20; Heb. ii. 9. Moreover, he is said to die ὑπὲρ ἁμαρτιῶν, for sins, 1 Cor. xv. 3; Gal. i. 4. The end whereof, everywhere expressed in the gospel, is, that we might be freed, delivered, and saved. These things, as was said, are agreed unto and acknowledged.

2. The meaning and importance, we say, of these expressions is, that Christ died in our room, place, or stead, undergoing the death or punishment which we should have undergone in the way and manner before declared. And this is the satisfaction we plead for. It remains, therefore, that from the Scripture, the nature of the things treated of, the proper signification and constant use of the expressions mentioned, the exemplification of them in the customs and usages of the nations of the world, we do evince and manifest that what we have laid down is the true and proper sense of the words wherein this revelation of Christ's dying for us is expressed; so that they who deny Christ to have died for us in this sense do indeed deny that he properly died for us at all, -- whatever benefits they grant that by his death we may obtain.

First. We may consider the use of this expression in the Scripture either indefinitely or in particular instances.

Only we must take this along with us, that dying for sins and transgressions, being added unto dying for sinners or persons, makes the substitution of one in the room and stead of another more evident than when the dying of one for another only is mentioned. For whereas all predicates are regulated by their subjects, and it is ridiculous to say that one dies in the stead of sins, the meaning can be no other but the bearing or answering of the sins of the sinner in whose stead any one dies. And this is, in the Scripture, declared to be the sense of that expression, as we shall see afterward. Let us, therefore, consider some instances:--

John xi. 50, The words of Caiaphas' counsel are, Συμφέρει ἡμῖν, ἵνα εἷς ἄνθρωπος ἀποθάνῃ ὑπὲρ τοῦ λαοῦ, καὶ μὴ ὅλον τὸ ἔθνος ἀπόληται· -- "It is expedient for us, that one man should die for the people, and that the whole nation perish not:" which is expressed again, chap. xviii. 14, ἀπολέσθαι ὑπὲρ τοῦ λαοῦ, "perish for the people." Caiaphas feared that if Christ were spared, the people would be destroyed by the Romans. The way to free them, he thought, was by the destruction of Christ; him, therefore, he devoted to death, in lieu of the people. As he, --

"*Unum pro multi dabitur caput;*" --

"*One head shall be given for many.*"

Not unlike the speech of Otho the emperor in Xiphilin, [13] when he slew himself to preserve his army; for when they would have persuaded him to renew the war after the defeat of some of his forces, and offered to lay down their lives to secure him, he replied, that he would not, adding this reason, Πολὺ γάρ που καὶ κρεῖττον, καὶ δικαιότερόν ἐστιν, ἕνα ὑπὲρ πάντων ἢ πολλοὺς ὑπὲρ ἑνὸς ἀπολέσθαι· -- "It is far better, and more just, that one should perish or die for all, than that many should perish for one;" that is, one in the stead of many, that they may go free; or as another speaks, --

Ἐξὸν πρὸ πατων μίαν ὑπερδοῦναι θανεῖν --

"*Let one be given up to die in the stead of all.*"
      Eurip. Frag. Erech.

John xiii. 37, Τὴν ψυχήν μοῦ ὑπὲρ σοῦ θήσω. They are the words of St. Peter unto Christ, "I will lay down my life for thee;" -- "To free thee, I will expose my own head to danger, my life to death, -- that thou mayest live, and I die." It is plain that he intended the same thing with the celebrated ἀντίψυχοι of old, who exposed their own lives (ψυχὴν ἀντὶ ψυχῆς:) for one another. Such were Damon and Pythias, Orestes and Pylades, Nisus and Euryalus. Whence is that saying of Seneca, "Succurram perituro, sed ut ipse non peream; nisi si futurus ero magni hominis, aut magnæ rei merces;" -- "I will relieve or succour one that is ready to perish; yet so as that I perish not myself, -- unless thereby I be taken in lieu of some great man, or great matter;" -- "For a great man, a man of great worth and usefulness, I could perish or die in his stead, that he might live and go free."

We have a great example, also, of the importance of this expression in these words of David concerning Absalom, 2 Sam. xviii. 33, מִי־יִתֵּן מוּתִי אֲנִי תַחְתֶּיךָ -- "Who will grant me to die, I for thee," or in thy stead, "my son Absalom?" [Literal rendering of the Hebrew.] It was never doubted but that David wished that he had died in the stead of his son, and to have undergone the death which he did, to have preserved him alive. As to the same purpose, though in another sense, Mezentius in Virgil expresses himself, when his son Lausus, interposing between him and danger in battle, was slain by Æneas:--

"*Tantane me tenuit vivendi, nate, voluptas,*
Ut pro me hostili paterer succedere dextræ
Quem genui? tuane hæc genitor per vulnera servor,
Morte tua vivens?"
Æn. x. 846.

"Hast thou, O son, fallen under the enemies' hand in my stead? Am I saved by thy wounds? Do I live by thy death?"

And the word תַּחַת, used by David, does signify, when applied unto persons, either a succession or a substitution; still the coming of one into the place and room of another. When one succeeded to another in government, it is expressed by that word, 2 Sam. x. 1; 1 Kings i. 35, xix. 16. In other cases it denotes a substitution. So Jehu tells his guard, that if any one of them let any of Baal's priests escape, נַפְשׁוֹ תַּחַת נַפְשׁוֹ -- his life should go in the stead of the life that he had suffered to escape.

And this answers unto ἀντὶ in the Greek; which is also used in this matter, and ever denotes either equality, contrariety, or substitution. The two former senses can here have no place; the latter alone has. So it is said, that Archelaus reigned ἀντὶ Ἡρώδου τοῦ πατρὸς αὐτοῦ, Matt. ii. 22, -- "in the room" or stead "of his father Herod." So ὀφθαλμὸς ἀντὶ ὀφθαλμοῦ, ὀδοὺς ἀντὶ ὀδόντος, Matt. v. 38, is "an eye for an eye, and a tooth for a tooth." And this word also is used in expressing the death of Christ for us. He came δοῦναι τὴν ψυχὴν αὐτοῦ λύτρον ἀντὶ πολλῶν, Matt. xx. 28, -- "to give his life a ransom for many;" that is, in their stead to die. So the words are used again, Mark x. 45. And both these notes of a succedaneous substitution are joined together, 1 Tim. ii. 6, Ὁ δοὺς ἑαυτὸν ἀντίλυτρον ὑπὲρ πάντων. And this the Greeks call τῆς ψυχῆς πρίασθαι, -- to buy any thing, to purchase or procure any thing, with the price of one's life. So Tigranes in Xenophon, when Cyrus asked him what he would give or do for the liberty of his wife, whom he had taken prisoner, answered, Κἂν τῆς ψυχῆς πριαίμην ὥστε μήποτε λατρεῦσαι ταύτην· -- "I will purchase her liberty with my life," or "the price of my soul." Whereon the woman being freed, affirmed afterward, that she considered none in the company, but him who said, ὡς τῆς ψυχῆς ἂν πρίαιτο ὥστε μή με δουλεύειν, "that he would purchase my liberty with his own life," [Cyrop. lib. iii.]

And these things are added on the occasion of the instances mentioned in the Scripture; whence it appears, that this expression of "dying for another" has no other sense or meaning, but only dying instead of another, undergoing the death that he should undergo, that he might go free. And in this matter of Christ's dying for us, add that he so died for us as that he also died for our sins; that is, either to bear their punishment or to expiate their guilt (for other sense the words cannot admit); and he that pretends to give any other sense of them than that contended for, which implies the whole of what lies in the doctrine of satisfaction, "erit mihi magnus Apollo," even he who was the author of all ambiguous oracles of old.

And this is the common sense of "mori pro alio," and "pati pro alio," or "pro alio discrimen capitis subire;" a substitution is still denoted by that expression: which suffices us in this whole cause, for we know both into whose room he came, and what they were to suffer. Thus Entellus, killing and sacrificing an ox to Eryx in the stead of Dares, whom he was ready to have slain, when he was taken from him, expresses himself, --

"Hanc tibi, Eryx, meliorem animam pro morte Daretis Persolvo."
Æn. v. 483.

He offered the ox, a better sacrifice, in the stead of Dares, taken from him. So, --

"Fratrem Pollux alterna morte redemit."
    Æn. vi. 121.

And they speak so not only with respect unto death, but wherever any thing of durance or suffering is intended. So the angry master in the comedian:--
"Verberibus cæsum te in pistrinum, Dave, dedam usque ad necem;
Ea lege atque omine, ut, si te inde exemerim, ego pro te molam."
Ter. And., i. 2, 28.
He threatened his servant, to cast him into prison, to be macerated to death with labour; and that with this engagement, that if he ever let him out, he would grind for him; -- that is, in his stead. Wherefore, without offering violence to the common means of understanding things amongst men, another sense cannot be affixed to these words.

The nature of the thing itself will admit of no other exposition than that given unto it; and it has been manifoldly exemplified among the nations of the world. For suppose a man guilty of any crime, and on the account thereof to be exposed unto danger from God or man, in a way of justice, wrath, or vengeance, and when he is ready to be given up unto suffering according unto his demerit, another should tender himself to die for him, that he might be freed; let an appeal be made to the common reason and understandings of all men, whether the intention of this his dying for another be not, that he substitutes himself in his stead, to undergo what he should have done, however the translation of punishment from one to another may be brought about and asserted; for at present we treat not of the right, but of the fact, or the thing itself. And to deny this to be the case as to the sufferings of Christ, is, as far as I can understand, to subvert the whole gospel.

Moreover, as was said, this has been variously exemplified among the nations of the world; whose acting in such cases, because they excellently shadow out the general notion of the death of Christ for others, for sinners, and are appealed unto directly by the apostle to this purpose, Rom. v. 7, 8, I shall in a few instances reflect upon.

Not to insist on the voluntary surrogations of private persons, one into the room of another, mutually to undergo dangers and death for one another, as before mentioned, I shall only remember some public transactions, in reference unto communities, in nations, cities, or armies. Nothing is more celebrated amongst the ancients than this, that when they supposed themselves in danger, from the anger and displeasure of their gods, by reason of any guilt or crimes among them, some one person should either devote himself or be devoted by the people, to die for them; and therein to be made, as it were, an expiatory sacrifice. For where sin is the cause, and God is the object respected; the making of satisfaction by undergoing punishment, and expiating of sin by a propitiatory sacrifice, are but various expressions of the same thing. Now, those who so devoted themselves, as was said, to die in the stead of others, or to expiate their sins, and turn away the anger of God they feared, by their death, designed two things in what they did. First, That the evils which were impendent on the people, and feared, might fall on themselves, so that the people might go free. Secondly, That all good things which themselves desired, might be conferred on the people. Which things have a notable shadow in them of the great expiatory sacrifice, concerning which we treat, and expound the expressions wherein it is declared. The instance of the Decii is known; of whom the poet, --

> *"Plebeiæ Deciorum animæ, plebeian fuerunt*
> *Nomina; pro totis legionibus Hi tamen, et pro*
> *Omnibus auxiliis, atque omni plebe Latina,*
> *Sufficiunt Diis infernis."*

The two Decii, father and son, in imminent dangers of the people, devoted themselves, at several times, unto death and destruction. And says he, "Sufficiunt Diis infernis," -- they satisfied for the whole people; adding the reason whence so it might be:--

> *"Pluris denim Decii quam qui servantur ab illis."*
> Juv., Sat. vii. 254-8.

They were more to be valued than all that were saved by them. And the great historian does excellently describe both the actions and expectations of the one and the other in what they did. The father, when the Roman army, commanded by himself and Titus Manlius, was near a total ruin by the Latins, called for the public priest, and caused him, with the usual solemn ceremonies, to devote him to death for the deliverance and safety of the army; after which, making his requests to his gods, ("dii quorum est potestas nostrorum hostiumque,") "the gods that had power over them and their adversaries," as he supposed, he cast himself into death by the swords of the enemy. "Conspectus ab utrâque acie aliquanto augustior humano visu, sicut coelo missus piaculum omnis deorum iræ, qui pestam ab suis aversam in hostes ferret;" -- "He was looked on by both armies as one more august than a man, as one sent from heaven, to be a piacular sacrifice, to appease the anger of the gods, and to transfer destruction from their own army to the enemies," Liv., Hist. viii. 9. His son, in like manner, in a great and dangerous battle against the Gauls and Samnites, wherein he commanded in chief, devoting himself, as his father had done, added unto the former solemn deprecations:-- "Præ se agere sese formidinem ac fugam, cædemque ac cruorem, coelestium, inferorum iras," lib. x. 28; -- "That he carried away before him, from those for whom he devoted himself, fear and flight, slaughter and blood, the anger of the celestial and infernal gods.' " And as they did, in this devoting of themselves, design "averruncare malum, deûm iras, lustrare populum, aut exercitum, piaculum fieri," or περίψημα, ἀνάθημα, ἀποκάθαρμα, -- "expiare crimina, scelus, reatum," or to remove all evil from others, by taking it on themselves in their stead; so also they thought they might, and intended in what they did, to covenant and contract for the good things they desired. So did these Decii; and so is Menoeceus reported to have done, when he devoted himself for the city of Thebes, in danger to be destroyed by the Argives. So Papinius [Statius] introduces him treating with his gods:--

> *"Armorum superi, tuque ô qui funere tanto*
> *Indulges mihi, Phoebe, mori, date gaudia Thebis,*
> *Quæ pepigi, et toto quæ sanguine prodigus emi."*

[Theb. x. 757.]

He reckoned that he had not only repelled all death and danger from Thebes, by his own, but that he had purchased joy, in peace and liberty, for the people.

And where there was none in public calamities that did voluntarily devote themselves, the people were wont to take some obnoxious person, to make him execrable, and to lay on him, according to their superstition, all the wrath of their gods, and so give him up to destruction. Such the apostle alludes unto, Rom. ix. 3; 1 Cor. iv. 9, 13. So the Massilians were wont to expiate their city by taking a person devoted, imprecating on his head all the evil that the city was obnoxious unto, casting him into the sea with these words, Περίψημα ἡμῶν γένου· -- "Be thou our expiatory sacrifice." To which purpose were the solemn words that many used in their expiatory sacrifices, as Herodotus [lib ii. 39] testifies of the Egyptians, bringing their offerings. Says he, Καταρέονται δὲ, τάδε λέγοντες, τῇσι κεφαλῇσιν εἴ τι μέλλοι ἢ σφισι τοῖσι θύουσι, ἢ Αἰγύπτῳ τῇ συναπάσῃ κακὸν γενέσθαι ἐς κεφαλὴν ταύτην τραπέσθαι· -- "They laid these imprecations on their heads, that if any evil were happening towards the sacrificer, or all Egypt, let it be all turned and laid on this devoted head."

And the persons whom they thus dealt withal, and made execrate, were commonly of the vilest of the people, or such as had rendered themselves detestable by their own crimes; whence was the complaint of the mother of Menoeceus upon her son's devoting himself:--

"Lustralemne feris, ego te puer inclyte Thebis,
Devotumque caput, vilis seu mater alebam?" --
[Statius, Theb. x. 788, 789.]

I have recounted these instances to evince the common intention, sense, and understanding of that expression, of one dying for another, and to manifest by examples what is the sense of mankind about any one's being devoted and substituted in the room of others, to deliver them from death and danger; the consideration whereof, added to the constant use of the words mentioned in the Scripture, is sufficient to found and confirm this conclusion:--

"That whereas it is frequently affirmed in the Scripture, that Christ died for us, and for our sins,' etc., to deny that he died and suffered in our stead, undergoing the death whereunto we were obnoxious, and the punishment due to our sins, is, -- if we respect in what we say or believe the constant use of those words in the Scripture, the nature of the thing itself concerning which they are used, the uncontrolled use of that expression in all sorts of writers in expressing the same thing, with the instances and examples of its meaning and intention among the nations of the world, -- to deny that he died for us at all."

Neither will his dying for our good or advantage only, in what way or sense soever, answer or make good or true the assertion of his dying for us and our sins. And this is evident in the death of the apostles and martyrs. They all died for our good; our advantage and benefit was one end of their sufferings, in the will and appointment of God: and yet it cannot be said that they died for us, or our sins.

And if Christ died only for our good, though in a more effectual manner than they did, yet this alters not the kind of his dying for us; nor can he thence be said, properly, according to the only due sense of that expression, so to do.

I shall, in this brief and hasty discourse, add only one consideration more about the death of Christ, to confirm the truth pleaded for; it and that is, that he is said, in dying for sinners, "to bear their sins." Isa. liii. 11, "He shall bear their iniquities;" verse 12, "He bare the sin of many;" explained, verse 5, "He was wounded for our transgressions, he was bruised for our iniquities; the chastisement of our peace was upon him." 1 Pet. ii. 24, "Who his own self bare our sins in his own body on the tree," etc.

This expression is purely sacred. It occurs not directly in other authors, though the sense of it in other words do frequently. They call it "luere peccata;" that is, "delictorum supplicium ferre," -- "to bear the punishment of sins." The meaning, therefore, of this phrase of speech is to be taken from the Scripture alone, and principally from the Old Testament, where it is originally used; and from whence it is transferred into the New Testament, in the same sense, and no other. Let us consider some of the places:--

Isa. liii. 11, עֲוֹנֹתָם הוּא יִסְבֹּל. The same word, סָבַל, is used verse 4, וּמַכְאֹבֵינוּ סְבָלָם, -- "And our griefs, he has borne them." The word signifies, properly, to bear a weight or a burden, as a man bears it on his shoulders, -- "bajulo, porto." And it is never used with respect unto sin, but openly and plainly it signifies the undergoing of the punishment due unto it. So it occurs directly to our purpose, Lam. v. 7. אֲבֹתֵינוּ חָטְאוּ אֵינָם אֲנַחְנוּ עֲוֹנֹתֵיהֶם סָבָלְנוּ -- "Our fathers have sinned, and are not; and we have borne their iniquities;" the punishment due to their sins. And why a new sense should be forged for these words when they are spoken concerning Christ, who can give a just reason?

Again; נָשָׂא is used to the same purpose, וְהוּא חֵטְא־רַבִּים נָשָׂא, Isa. liii. 12, "And he bare the sin of many." נָשָׂא is often used with respect unto sin; sometimes with reference unto God's acting about it, and sometimes with reference unto men's concerns in it. In the first way, or when it denotes an act of God, it signifies to lift up, to take away or pardon sin; and leaves the word עָוֹן, wherewith it is joined under its first signification, of iniquity, or the guilt of sin, with respect unto punishment ensuing as its consequent; for God pardoning the guilt of sin, the removal of the punishment does necessarily ensue, guilt containing an obligation unto punishment. In the latter way, as it respects men or sinners, it constantly denotes the bearing of the punishment of sin, and gives that sense unto עָוֹן, with respect unto the guilt of sin as its cause. And hence arises the ambiguity of these words of Cain, Gen. iv. 13, גָּדוֹל עֲוֹנִי מִנְּשֹׂא. If נָשָׂא denotes an act of God, if the words be spoken with reference, in the first place, to any acting of his towards Cain, עָוֹן retains the sense of iniquity, and the words are rightly rendered, "My sin is greater than to be forgiven." If it respect Cain himself firstly, עָוֹן assumes the signification of punishment, and the words are to be rendered, "My punishment is greater than I can bear," or "is to be borne by me."

This, I say, is the constant sense of this expression, nor can any instance to the contrary be produced. Some may be mentioned in the confirmation of it. Numb. xix. 33, "Your children shall wander in the wilderness forty years," וְנָשְׂאוּ אֶת־זְנוּתֵיכֶם "and shall bear your whoredoms." Verse 34, תִּשְׂאוּ אֶת־עֲוֹנֹתֵיכֶם אַרְבָּעִים שָׁנָה -- "Ye shall bear your iniquities forty years;" that is, the punishment due to your whoredoms and iniquities, according to God's providential dealings with them at that time. Lev. xix. 8, "He that eateth it עֲוֹנוֹ יִשָּׂא shall bear his iniquity." How? נִכְרְתָה הַנֶּפֶשׁ הַהוּא -- "That soul shall be cut off." To be cut off for sin by the punishment of it, and for its guilt, is to bear iniquity. So chap. xx. 16-18, for a man to bear his iniquity, and to be killed, slain, or put to death for it, are the same.

Ezek. xviii. 20, הַנֶּפֶשׁ הַחֹטֵאת הִיא תָמוּת בֵּן לֹא־יִשָּׂא בַּעֲוֹן הָאָב -- "The soul that sinneth, it shall die. The son shall not bear the sin of the father." To bear sin, and to die for sin, are the same. More instances might be added, all uniformly speaking the same sense of the words.

And as this sense is sufficiently, indeed invincibly, established by the invariable use of that expression in the Scripture so the manner whereby it is affirmed that the Lord Christ bare our iniquities, sets it absolutely free from all danger by opposition. For he bare our iniquities when וַיהוָה הִפְגִּיעַ בּוֹ אֵת עֲוֹן כֻּלָּנוּ -- "the Lord made to meet on him, or laid on him; the iniquity of us all," Isa. liii. 6; which words the LXX. render, Καὶ Κύριος παρέδωκεν αὐτὸν ταῖς ἁμαρτίαις ἡμῶν· -- "The Lord gave him up, or delivered him unto our sins;" that is, to be punished for them, for other sense the words can have none. "He made him in sin for us," 2 Cor. v. 21. So "he bare our sins," Isa. liii. 12. How? "In his own body on the tree," 1 Pet. ii. 24; that when he was, and in his being stricken, smitten, afflicted, wounded bruised, slain, so was the chastisement of our peace upon him.

Wherefore, to deny that the Lord Christ, in his death and suffering for us, underwent the punishment due to our sins, what we had deserved, that we might be delivered, as it everts the great foundation of the gospel, so, by an open perverting of the plain words of the Scripture, because not suited in their sense and importance to the vain imaginations of men, it gives no small countenance to infidelity and atheism.

Footnotes:

10. The "Vindiciæ Evangelicæ" of Owen, in reply to Biddle, had appeared fourteen years before the publication of this treatise. The probability is, therefore, that our author alludes above to the copious and elaborate refutation of Socinian errors in his "Exposition of the Epistle to the Hebrews." -- Ed.

11. A celebrated Hebrew scholar. He was born in Picardy, and died 1547. His Notes on the Old Testament Scriptures, taken by his scholars from his observations, and arranged by Robert Stephens, were published 1557. -- Ed.

12. A Portuguese Dominican and able scholar. He died in 1563, and left behind him Commentaries on the Pentateuch. -- Ed.

13. A monk of Constantinople, who wrote an epitome of Dion Cassius, a.d. 1071-1078. -- Ed.

Of Communion with God the Father, Son and Holy Ghost

each person distinctly, in love, grace, and consolation; or, the saints' fellowship with the Father, Son, and Holy Ghost unfolded.

By John Owen (1616-1683)

"God is love." -- 1 John iv. 8.

"Tell me, O thou whom my soul loveth, where thou feedest." -- Cant. i. 7.

"Make haste, my beloved." -- Cant. viii. 14.

"Grieve not the Holy Spirit of God, whereby ye are sealed unto the day of redemption." -- Eph. iv. 30.

"Now there are diversities of gifts, but the same Spirit. And there are differences of administrations, but the same Lord. And there are diversities of operations, but it is the same God." -- 1 Cor. xii. 4-6.

Prefatory note

The reader may be referred to the Life of Dr Owen (vol. i. p. lxxii.) for a general criticism on the merits of the following treatise. It was published in 1657, shortly after he had ceased to be Vice-Chancellor in the University of Oxford. From the brief preface affixed to it, it appears that, for a period of more than six years, he had been under some engagement to publish the substance of the work. It has been inferred, accordingly, that it is the substance of some discourses which he had preached in Oxford; but, as he became Vice-Chancellor only in September 1652, there is more probability in the supposition that they are the discourses which refreshed and cheered his attached congregation at Coggeshall.

There are two peculiarities which deserve attention in the treatise. The oversight of one of them has created some misconceptions of the author's design, and led some to fancy that he was wandering from it, in various passages which are in strict harmony with his main and original purpose of the work. The term "Communion," as used by Owen, is used in a wider sense than is consistent with that which is now generally attached to it in religious phraseology. It denotes not merely the interchange of feeling between God on his gracious character and a soul in a gracious state, but the gracious relationship upon which this holy interchange is based. On the part of Christ, for example, all his work and its results are described, from the atonement till it takes effect in the actual justification of the sinner.

The grand peculiarity distinguishing the treatise is its fullness of illustration with which he dilates on the communion enjoyed by believers with each person of the Godhead respectively. Fully to comprehend his views on this point, it is needful to bear in mind the meaning under which the word Communion is employed by Owen.

Analysis

Part I. -- The fact of communion with God is asserted, chap. i. Passages in Scripture are quoted to show that special mention is made of communion with all the persons of the Trinity ii. Communion with the Father is described, iii.; and practical inferences deduced from it, iv.

Part II. -- The reality of communion with Christ is proved chap. i.; and the nature of it is subsequently considered, ii. It is shown to consist in grace; and then the grace of Christ is exhibited under three divisions:-- his personal grace, iii.-vi.; and under this branch are two long digressions, designed to unfold the glory and loveliness of Christ; -- purchased grace, vii.-x.; in which the mediatorial work of Christ is fully considered, in reference to our acceptance with God, vii., viii.; sanctification, ix.; and the privileges of the covenant, x.; -- and grace as communicated by the Spirit, and conspicuous in the fruits of personal holiness. This last division is illustrated under sanctification, as contained under the head of purchased grace.

Part III. -- Communion with the Holy Ghost is expounded in the eight following chapters; -- the foundation of it, chap. i.; his gracious and effectual influence in believers, ii.; the elements in which it consists, iii.; the effects in the hearts of believers, iv.; and general inferences and particular directions for communion with the Spirit, v.-viii.

The arrangement of the treatise may seem involved and complicated, and the endless divisions and subdivisions may distract rather than assist the attention of the reader. The warm glow of sanctified emotion, however, and occasionally thoughts of singular power and originality, which are found throughout the treatise, sustain the interest, and more than reward perusal. Few passages in any theological writer are more thrilling than the reference to the spotless humanity of Christ, in terms full of sanctified genius, on page 64.

An account of the strange controversy to which this treatise gave rise, many years after its publication, will be found on page 276. -- Ed.

Preface

Christian Reader,

It is now six years past since I was brought under an engagement of promise for the publishing of some meditations on the subject which thou wilt find handled in the ensuing treatise. The reasons of this delay, being not of public concernment, I shall not need to mention. Those who have been in expectation of this duty from me, have, for the most part, been so far acquainted with my condition and employments, as to be able to satisfy themselves as to the deferring of their desires. That which I have to add at present is only this:-- having had many opportunities, since the time I first delivered any thing in public on this subject (which was the means of bringing me under the engagements mentioned), to re-assume the consideration of what I had first fixed on, I have been enabled to give it that improvement, and to make those additions to the main of the design and matter treated on, that my first debt is come at length to be only the occasion of what is now tendered to the saints of God. I shall speak nothing of the subject here handled; it may, I hope, speak for itself, in that spiritual savour and relish which it will yield to them whose hearts are not so filled with other things as to render the sweet things of the gospel bitter to them. The design of the whole treatise thou wilt find, Christian reader, in the first chapters of the first part; and I shall not detain thee here with the perusal of any thing which in its proper place will offer itself unto thee: know only, that the whole of it hath been recommended to the grace of God in many supplications, for its usefulness unto them that are interested in the good things mentioned therein.

J. O.

Oxon. Ch. Ch. Coll., July 10, 1657.

To the reader

Alphonsus, king of Spain, is said to have found food and physic in reading Livy; and Ferdinand, king of Sicily, in reading Quintus Curtius: but thou hast here nobler entertainments, vastly richer dainties, incomparably more sovereign medicines; -- I had almost said, the very highest of angel's food is here set before thee; and, as Pliny speaks, "permista deliciis auxilia," -- things that minister unto grace and comfort, to holy life and liveliness.

Such is this treatise, -- this, which is the only one extant upon its great and necessary subject, -- this, whose praise hath been long in the churches, and hath gone enamelled with the honourable reproaches of more than one English Bolsec, -- this, whose great author, like the sun, is well known to the world, by eminence of heavenly light and labours, -- this, which, as his many other works, can be no other than manna unto sound Christians, though no better than stone and serpent to Socinians and their fellow-commoners.

Importunity hath drawn me to say thus much more than I could think needful to be said concerning any work of Dr Owen's; -- needful in our day itself, a day wherein "pauci sacras Scripturas, plures nomina rerum, plurimi nomina magistrorum sequuntur;" -- "few do cleave to the holy Scriptures; many do rest in scholastic senseless sounds; and most men do hang their faith upon their rabbi's sleeves."

This only I add:-- of the swarms every day rising, there are few books but do want their readers; yet if I understand aright, there are not many readers but do want this book.

In which censure I think I am no tyrant, which the philosopher names the worst of wild beasts; I am sure I am no flatterer, which he calls justly, the worst of tame beasts, -- Καὶ ταῦτα μὲν δὴ ταῦτα.

Let the simple souls (the "paucissimæ lectionis mancipia") who take the doctrine of distinct communion with the Divine Persons to be a new-fangled one and uncouth, observe the words of the Rev. Samuel Clarke (the annotator on the Bible), in his sermon on 1 John i. 7: "It is to be noted, that there is a distinct fellowship with each of the persons of the blessed Trinity." Let them attend what is said by Mr Lewis Stuckley, in his preface to Mr Polwheil's book of Quenching the Spirit: "It is a most glorious truth, though considered but by a few, that believers have, or may have, distinct communion with the three persons, Father, Son, and Spirit. This is attested by the finger of God, and solemnly owned by the first and best age of Christianity." To name no more, let them read heedfully but the second chapter of this treatise, and it is hoped that then they shall no longer "contra antidotum insanire," -- no longer rage against God's holy medicinal truth, as St Austin saith he did while he was a Manichee; testifying, in so many words, [that] his error was his very god.

Reader, I am Thy servant in Christ Jesus,

Daniel Burgess [1].

Footnotes:

1. See vol. ix., p. 2. [Daniel Burgess was an excellent Nonconformist minister, who was ejected from Collinburn, Wiltshire, under the Bartholomew Act, 1662.] -- Ed.

Part I. Of Communion with each Person distinctly -- Of Communion with the Father

Chapter I - That the saints have communion with God -- 1 John i. 3 considered to that purpose -- Somewhat of the nature of communion in general.

\ na-= */ In the First Epistle of John, chap. i., verse 3, the apostle assures them to whom he wrote that the fellowship of believers "is with the Father, and with his Son Jesus Christ:" [2] and this he doth with such an unusual kind of expression as bears the force of an asseveration; whence we have rendered it, "Truly our fellowship is with the Father, and with his Son Jesus Christ."

The outward appearance and condition of the saints in those days being very mean and contemptible, -- their leaders being accounted as the filth of this world, and as the offscouring of all things, [3] -- the inviting others unto fellowship with them, and a participation of the precious things which they did enjoy, seems to be exposed to many contrary reasonings and objections: "What benefit is there in communion with them? Is it any thing else but to be sharers in troubles, reproaches, scorns, and all manner of evils?" To prevent or remove these and the like exceptions, the apostle gives them to whom he wrote to know (and that with some earnestness of expression), that notwithstanding all the disadvantages their fellowship lay under, unto a carnal view, yet in truth it was, and would be found to be (in reference to some with whom they held it), very honourable, glorious, and desirable. For "truly," saith he, "our fellowship is with the Father, and with his Son Jesus Christ."

This being so earnestly and directly asserted by the apostle, we may boldly follow him with our affirmation, -- namely, "That the saints of God have communion with him." And a holy and spiritual communion it is, as shall be declared. How this is spoken distinctly in reference to the Father and the Son, must afterward be fully opened and carried on.

By nature, since the entrance of sin, no man hath any communion with God. He is light, [4] we darkness; and what communion hath light with darkness? He is life, we are dead, -- he is love, and we are enmity; and what agreement can there be between us? Men in such a condition have neither Christ, [5] nor hope, nor God in the world, Eph. ii. 12; "being alienated from the life of God through the ignorance that is in them," chap. iv. 18. Now, two cannot walk together, unless they be agreed, Amos iii. 3. Whilst there is this distance ;p[between God and man, there is no walking together for them in any fellowship or communion. Our first interest in God was so lost by sin, [6] as that there was left unto us (in ourselves) no possibility of a recovery. As we had deprived ourselves of all power for a returnal, so God had not revealed any way of access unto himself; or that he could, under any consideration, be approached unto by sinners in peace. Not any work that God had made, not any attribute that he had revealed, could give the least light into such a dispensation.

The manifestation of grace and pardoning mercy, which is the only door of entrance into any such communion, is not committed unto any but unto him alone [7] in whom it is, by whom that grace and mercy was purchased, through whom it is dispensed, who reveals it from the bosom of the Father. Hence this communion and fellowship with God is not in express terms mentioned in the Old Testament. The thing itself is found there; but the clear light of it, and the boldness of faith in it, is discovered in the gospel, and by the Spirit administered therein. By that Spirit we have this liberty, 2 Cor. iii. 17, 18. Abraham was the friend of God, Isa. xli. 8; David, a man after his own heart; Enoch walked with him, Gen. v. 22; -- all enjoying this communion and fellowship for the substance of it. But the way into the holiest was not yet made manifest whilst the first tabernacle was standing, Heb. ix. 8. Though they had communion with God, yet they had not παῤῥησίαν, -- a boldness and confidence in that communion. This follows the entrance of our High Priest into the most holy place, Heb. iv. 16, x. 19. The vail also was upon them, that they had not ἐλευθερίαν, freedom and liberty in their access to God, 2 Cor. iii. 15, 16, etc. But now in Christ we have [8] boldness and access with confidence to God, Eph. iii. 12. This boldness and access with confidence the saints of old were not acquainted with. By Jesus Christ alone, then, on all considerations as to being and full manifestation, is this distance taken away. He hath consecrated for us a new and living way (the old being quite shut up), "through the vail, that is to say, his flesh," Heb. x. 20; and "through him we have access by one Spirit unto the Father," Eph. ii. 18. "Ye who sometimes were far off, are made nigh by the blood of Christ, for he is our peace," etc., verses 13, 14. Of this foundation of all our communion with God, more afterward, and at large. Upon this new bottom and foundation, by this new and living way, are sinners admitted into communion with God, and have fellowship with him. And truly, for sinners to have fellowship with God, the infinitely holy God, is an astonishing dispensation. [9] To speak a little of it in general:-- Communion relates to things and persons. A joint participation in any thing whatever, good or evil, [10] duty or enjoyment, nature or actions, gives this denomination to them so partaking of it. A common interest in the same nature gives all men a fellowship or communion therein. Of the elect it is said, Τὰ παιδία κεκοινώνηκε σαρκὸς καὶ αἵματος, Heb. ii. 14, "Those children partook of" (or had fellowship in, with the rest of the world) "flesh and blood," -- the same common nature with the rest of mankind; and, therefore, Christ also came into the same fellowship: Καὶ αὐτὸς παραπλησίως μετέσχε τῶν αὐτῶν. There is also a communion as to state and condition, whether it be good or evil; and this, either in things internal and spiritual, -- such as is the communion of saints among themselves; or in respect of outward things. So was it with Christ and the two thieves, as to one condition, and to one of them in respect of another. They were ἐν τῷ αὐτῷ κρίματι, -- under the same sentence to the cross, Luke xxiii. 40, "ejusdem dolores socii." They had communion as to that evil condition whereunto they were adjudged; and one of them requested (which he also obtained) a participation in that blessed condition whereupon our Saviour was immediately to enter. There is also a communion or fellowship in actions, whether good or evil. In good, is that communion and fellowship in the gospel, or in the performance and celebration of that worship of God which in the gospel is instituted; which the saints do enjoy, Phil. i. 5; which, as to the general kind of it, David so rejoices in, Ps. xlii. 4. In evil, was that wherein Simeon and Levi were brethren, Gen. xlix. 5. They had communion in that cruel act of revenge and murder. Our communion with God is not comprised in any one of these kinds; of some of them it is exclusive. It cannot be natural; it must be voluntary and by consent. It cannot be of state and conditions; but in actions. It cannot be in the same actions upon a third party; but in a return from one to another. The infinite disparity that is between God and man, made the great philosopher conclude that there could be no friendship between them. [11] Some distance in the persons holding friendship he could allow, nor could exactly determine the bounds and extent thereof; but that between God and man, in his apprehension, left no place for it. Another says, indeed, that there is "communitas homini cum Deo," -- a certain fellowship between God and man; but the general intercourse of providence is all he apprehended. Some arose to higher expressions; but they understood nothing whereof they spake. This knowledge is hid in Christ; as will afterward be made to appear. It is too wonderful for nature, as sinful and corrupted. Terror and apprehensions of death at the presence of God is all that it guides unto. But we have, as was said, a new foundation, and a new discovery of this privilege.

Now, communion is the mutual communication of such good things as wherein the persons holding that communion are delighted, bottomed upon some union between them. So it was with Jonathan and David; their souls clave to one another (1 Sam. xx. 17) in love. [12] There was the union of love between them; and then they really communicated all issues of love mutually. [13] In spiritual things this is more eminent: those who enjoy this communion have the most excellent union for the foundation of it; and the issues of that union, which they mutually communicate, are the most precious and eminent.

Of the union which is the foundation of all that communion we have with God I have spoken largely elsewhere, and have nothing farther to add thereunto.

Our communion, then, with God consisteth in his communication of himself unto us, with our returnal unto him of that which he requireth and accepteth, flowing from that union [14] which in Jesus Christ we have with him. And it is twofold:-- 1. Perfect and complete, in the full fruition of his glory and total giving up of ourselves to him, resting in him as our utmost end; which we shall enjoy when we see him as he is; -- and, 2. Initial and incomplete, in the first-fruits and dawnings of that perfection which we have here in grace; which only I shall handle.

It is, then, I say, of that mutual communication [15] in giving and receiving, after a most holy and spiritual manner, which is between God and the saints while they walk together in a covenant of peace, ratified in the blood of Jesus, whereof we are to treat. And this we shall do, if God permit; in the meantime praying the God and Father of our Lord and Saviour Jesus Christ, who hath, of the riches of his grace, recovered us from a state of enmity into a condition of communion and fellowship with himself, that both he that writes, and they that read the words of his mercy, may have such a taste of his sweetness and excellencies therein, as to be stirred up to a farther longing after the fulness of his salvation, and the eternal fruition of him in glory.

Footnotes:

112

2. Καὶ ἡ κοινωνία δὲ ἡ ἡμετέρα, etc.

3. Ὡς περικαθάρματα τοῦ κόσμου. -- 1 Cor. iv. 8-13; Rom. viii. 35-36; Heb. x. 32-34. "Christianos ad leones. Et puto, nos Deus apostolos novissimos elegit veluti bestiarios."--Tert. de Pud., Acts xvii. 18; Gal. vi. 12. "Semper casuris similes, nunquamque cadentes."

4. 1 John i. 5; 2 Cor. vi. 14; Eph. v. 8; John v. 21; Matt. xxii. 32; Eph. ii. 1; 1 John iv. 8; Rom. viii. 7.

5. "Magna hominis miseria est cum illo non esse, sine quo non potest esse."-- August.

6. Eccles. vii. 29; Jer. xiii. 23; Acts iv. 12; Isa. xxxiii. 14.

7. John i. 18; Heb. x. 19-21. "Unus verusque Mediator per sacrificium pacis reconcilians nos Deo; unum cum illo manebat cui offerebat; unum in se fecit, pro quibus offerebat; unus ipse fuit, qui offerabat, et quod offerebat."-- [Slightly changed from] August. de Trinit., iv. c. 14.

8. Παῤῥησίαν καὶ τὴν προσαγωγὴν ἐν πεποιθήσει.

9. 1 John iii. 1. Φίλων μὲν ὄντων, οὐδὲν δεῖ δικαιοσύνης· δίκαιοι δὲ ὄντες προσδέονται φιλίας. -- Arist. Eth., lib. viii. cap. 1.

10. "Quemadmodum enim nobis arrhabonem Spiritus reliquit, ita et a nobis arrhabonem carnis accepit, et vexit in coelum, pignus totius summæ illuc quandoque redigendæ."-- Tertul. De Resur., c. li.

11. Ἀκριβὴς μὲν οὖν ἐν τοιούτοις οὐκ ἔστιν ὁρισμός, ἕως τίνος οἱ φίλον πολλῶν γὰρ ἀφαιρουμένων, ἔτι μένει, πολὺ δὲ χωρισθέντος, οἷον τοῦ Θεοῦ οὐκ ἔτι. -- Aristot. Eth., lib. viii. c. 7; Cicer. de Nat. Deor. lib. i.

12. Πάντα τὰ τῶν φίλων κοινά.

13. Καὶ ἡ παροιμία, κοινὰ τὰ φίλων, ὀρθῶς, ἐν κοινωνίᾳ γὰρ ἡ φιλία. -- Arist. Eth., viii.

14. "Nostra quippe et ipsius conjunctio, nec miscet personas, nec unit substantias, sed affectus consociat, et confoederat voluntates." -- Cyp. de Coen. Domini. [No treatise of Cyprian bears such a title. There is a treatise, "De Coenâ Domini," ascribed to Cyprian, but on grounds so questionable and insufficient that it is sometimes not included among his supposititious works. A statement referring to the union between Christ and his people, as illustrated by the sacramental elements, occurs in his letter to Coecilius, "De Sacramento Dominici Calicis;" but the words of the above quotation are not contained in it.]

15. "Magna etiam illa communitas est, quæ conficitur ex beneficiis ultro citro, datis acceptis." -- Cic. Off., lib. i. c. 17.

Chapter II - That the saints have this communion distinctly with the Father, Son, and Spirit, 1 John v. 7 opened to this purpose; also, 1 Cor. xii. 4-6, Eph. ii. 18 -- Father and Son mentioned jointly in this communion; the Father solely, the Son also, and the Holy Ghost singly -- The saints' respective reward in all worship to each person manifested -- Faith in the Father, John v. 9, 10; and love towards him, 1 John ii. 15, Mal. i. 6 -- So in prayer and praise -- It is so likewise with the Son, John xiv. 1 -- Of our communion with the Holy Ghost -- The truth farther confirmed.

That the saints have communion with God, and what communion in general is, was declared in the first chapter. The manner how this communion is carried on, and the matter wherein it doth consist, comes next under consideration. For the first, in respect of the distinct persons of the Godhead with whom they have this fellowship, it is either distinct and peculiar, or else obtained and exercised jointly and in common. That the saints have distinct communion with the Father, and the Son, and the Holy Spirit (that is, distinctly with the Father, and distinctly with the Son, and distinctly with the Holy Spirit), and in what the peculiar appropriation of this distinct communion unto the several persons doth consist, must, in the first place, be made manifest. [16]

1 John v. 7, the apostle tells us, "There are three that bear record in heaven, the Father, the Word, and the Holy Ghost." In heaven they are, and bear witness to us. And what is it that they bear witness unto? Unto the sonship of Christ, and the salvation of believers in his blood. Of the carrying on of that, both by blood and water, justification and sanctification, is he there treating. Now, how do they bear witness hereunto? even as three, as three distinct witnesses. When God witnesseth concerning our salvation, surely it is incumbent on us to receive his testimony. And as he beareth witness, so are we to receive it. Now this is done distinctly. The Father beareth witness, the Son beareth witness, and the Holy Spirit beareth witness; for they are three distinct witnesses. So, then, are we to receive their several testimonies: and in doing so we have communion with them severally; for in this giving and receiving of testimony consists no small part of our fellowship with God. Wherein their distinct witnessing consists will be afterward declared.

1 Cor. xii. 4-6, the apostle, speaking of the distribution of gifts and graces unto the saints, ascribes them distinctly, in respect of the fountain of their communication, unto the distinct persons. "There are diversities of gifts, but the same Spirit," [17] -- "that one and the self-same Spirit;" that is, the Holy Ghost, verse 11. "And there are differences of administrations, but the same Lord," the same Lord Jesus, verse 5. "And there are diversities of operations, but it is the same God," etc., even the Father, Eph. iv. 6. So graces and gifts are bestowed,

and so are they received.

And not only in the emanation of grace from God, and the illapses of the Spirit on us, but also in all our approaches unto God, is the same distinction observed. [18] "For through Christ we have access by one Spirit unto the Father," Eph. ii. 18. Our access unto God (wherein we have communion with him) is διὰ Χριστοῦ, "through Christ," ἐν Πνεύματι, "in the Spirit," and πρὸς τὸν Πατέρα, "unto the Father;" -- the persons being here considered as engaged distinctly unto the accomplishment of the counsel of the will of God revealed in the gospel.

Sometimes, indeed, there is express mention made only of the Father and the Son, 1 John i. 3, "Our fellowship is with the Father, and with his Son Jesus Christ." The particle "and" is both distinguishing and uniting. Also John xiv. 23, "If a man love me, he will keep my words: and my Father will love him, and we will come unto him, and make our abode with him." It is in this communion wherein Father and Son do make their abode with the soul.

Sometimes the Son only is spoken of, as to this purpose. 1 Cor. i. 9, "God is faithful, by whom ye were called unto the fellowship of his Son Jesus Christ our Lord." And, Rev. iii. 20, "If any man hear my voice, and open the door, I will come in to him, and will sup with him, and he with me;" -- of which place afterward.

Sometimes the Spirit alone is mentioned. 2 Cor. xiii. 14, "The grace of the Lord Jesus Christ, and the love of God, and the communion of the Holy Ghost be with you all." This distinct communion, then, of the saints with the Father, Son, and Spirit, is very plain in the Scripture; but yet it may admit of farther demonstration. Only this caution I must lay in beforehand:-- whatever is affirmed in the pursuit of this truth, it is done with relation to the explanation ensuing, in the beginning of the next chapter.

The way and means, then, on the part of the saints, whereby in Christ they enjoy communion with God, are all the spiritual and holy actings [19] and outgoings of their souls in those graces, and by those ways, wherein both the moral and instituted worship of God doth consist. Faith, love, trust, joy, etc., are the natural or moral worship of God, whereby those in whom they are have communion with him. Now, these are either immediately acted on God, and not tied to any ways or means outwardly manifesting themselves; or else they are farther drawn forth, in solemn prayer and praises, according unto that way which he hath appointed. That the Scripture doth distinctly assign all these unto the Father, Son, and Spirit, -- manifesting that the saints do, in all of them, both as they are purely and nakedly moral, and as farther clothed with instituted worship, respect each person respectively, -- is that which, to give light to the assertion in hand, I shall farther declare by particular instances:--

1. For the Father. Faith, love, obedience, etc., are peculiarly and distinctly yielded by the saints unto him; and he is peculiarly manifested in those ways as acting peculiarly towards them: which should draw them forth and stir them up thereunto. He gives testimony unto, and beareth witness of, his Son, 1 John v. 9, "This is the witness of God which he hath testified of his Son." In his bearing witness he is an object of belief. When he gives testimony (which he doth as the Father, because he doth it of the Son) he is to he received in it by faith. And this is affirmed, verse 10, "He that believeth on the Son of God, hath the witness in himself." To believe on the Son of God in this place, is to receive the

Lord Christ as the Son, the Son given unto us, [20] for all the ends of the Father's love, upon the credit of the Father's testimony; and, therefore, therein is faith immediately acted on the Father. So it follows in the next words, "he that believeth not God" (that is, the Father, who bears witness to the Son) "hath made him a liar." "Ye believe in God," saith our Saviour, John xiv. 1; that is, the Father as such, for he adds, "Believe also in me;" or, "Believe you in God; believe also in me." God, as the prima Veritas, upon whose authority is founded, and whereunto all divine faith is ultimately resolved, is not to be considered ὑποστατικῶς, as peculiarly expressive of any person, but οὐδιωδῶς, comprehending the whole Deity; which undividedly is the prime object thereof. But in this particular it is the testimony and authority of the Father (as such) therein, of which we speak, and whereupon faith is distinctly fixed on him; -- which, if it were not so, the Son could not add, "Believe also in me."

The like also is said of love. 1 John ii. 15, "If any man love the world, the love of the Father is not in him;" that is, the love which we bear to him, not that which we receive from him. The Father is here placed as the object of our love, in opposition to the world, which takes up our affections ἡ ἀγάπη τοῦ Πατρός. The Father denotes the matter and object, not the efficient cause, of the love inquired after. And this love of him as a Father is that which he calls his "honour," Mal. i. 6.

Farther: these graces as acted in prayer and praises, and as clothed with instituted worship, are peculiarly directed unto him. "Ye call on the Father," 1 Pet. i. 17. Eph. iii. 14, 15, "For this cause I bow my knees unto the Father of our Lord Jesus Christ, of whom the whole family in heaven and earth is named." Bowing the knee compriseth the whole worship of God, both that which is moral, in the universal obedience he requireth, and those peculiar ways of carrying it on which are by him appointed, Isa. xlv. 23, "Unto me," saith the Lord, "every knee shall bow, every tongue shall swear." Which, verses 24, 25, he declareth to consist in their acknowledging of him for righteousness and strength. Yea, it seems sometimes to comprehend the orderly subjection of the whole creation unto his sovereignty. [21] In this place of the apostle it hath a far more restrained acceptation, and is but a figurative expression of prayer, taken from the most expressive bodily posture to be used in that duty. This he farther manifests, Eph. iii. 16, 17, declaring at large what his aim was, and whereabout his thoughts were exercised, in that bowing of his knees. The workings, then, of the Spirit of grace in that duty are distinctly directed to the Father as such, as the fountain of the Deity, and of all good things in Christ, -- as the "Father of our Lord Jesus Christ." And therefore the same apostle doth, in another place, expressly conjoin, and yet as expressly distinguish, the Father and the Son in directing his supplications, 1 Thess. iii. 11, "God himself even our Father, and our Lord Jesus Christ, direct our way unto you." The like precedent, also, have you of thanksgiving, Eph. i. 3, 4, "Blessed be the God and Father of our Lord Jesus Christ," etc. I shall not add those very many places wherein the several particulars [22] that do concur unto that whole divine worship (not to be communicated unto any, by nature not God, without idolatry) wherein the saints do hold communion with God, are distinctly directed to the person of the Father.

2. It is so also in reference unto the Son. John xiv. 1, "Ye believe in God," saith Christ, "believe also in me;" -- "Believe also, act faith distinctly on me; faith divine, supernatural, -- that faith whereby you believe in God, that is, the

Father. There is a believing of Christ, namely, that he is the Son of God, the Saviour of the world. That is that whose neglect our Saviour so threatened unto the Pharisees, John viii. 24, "If ye believe not that I am he, ye shall die in your sins." In this sense faith is not immediately fixed on the Son, being only an owning of him (that is, the Christ to be the Son), by closing with the testimony of the Father concerning him. But there is also a believing on him, called "Believing on the name of the Son of God," 1 John v. 13; so also John ix. 36; -- yea, the distinct affixing of faith, affiance, and confidence on the Lord Jesus Christ the Son of God, as the Son of God, is most frequently pressed. John iii. 16, "God" (that is, the Father) "so loved the world, ... that whosoever believeth in him" (that is, the Son) "should not perish." The Son, who is given of the Father, is believed on. "He that believeth on him is not condemned," verse 18. "He that believeth on the Son hath everlasting life," verse 36. "This is the work of God, that ye believe on him whom he hath sent," John vi. 29, 40; 1 John v. 10. The foundation of the whole is laid, John v. 23, "That all men should honour the Son, even as they honour the Father. He that honoureth not the Son honoureth not the Father which hath sent him." But of this honour and worship of the Son I have treated at large elsewhere; [23] and shall not in general insist upon it again. For love, I shall only add that solemn apostolical benediction, Eph. vi. 24, "Grace be with all them that love our Lord Jesus Christ in sincerity," -- that is, with divine love, the love of religious worship; which is the only incorrupt love of the Lord Jesus.

Farther: that faith, hope, and love, acting themselves in all manner of obedience and appointed worship, are peculiarly due from the saints, [24] and distinctly directed unto the Son, is abundantly manifest from that solemn doxology, Rev. i. 5, 6, "Unto him that loved us, and washed us from our sins in his own blood, and hath made us kings and priests unto God and his Father; to him be glory and dominion for ever and ever. Amen." Which yet is set forth with more glory, chap. v. 8, "The four living creatures, and the four and twenty elders fell down before the Lamb, having every one of them harps, and golden vials full of odours, which are the prayers of saints:" and verses 13, 14, "Every creature which is in heaven, and on the earth, and under the earth, and such as are in the sea, and all that are in them, heard I saying, blessing, and honour, and glory, and power, be unto him that sitteth upon the throne, and unto the Lamb for ever and ever." The Father and the Son (he that sits upon the throne, and the Lamb) are held out jointly, yet distinctly, as the adequate object of all divine worship and honour, for ever and ever. And therefore Stephen, in his solemn dying invocation, fixeth his faith and hope distinctly on him, Acts vii. 59, 60, "Lord Jesus, receive my spirit;" and, "Lord, lay not this sin to their charge;" -- for he knew that the Son of man had power to forgive sins also. And this worship of the Lord Jesus, the apostle makes the discriminating character of the saints, 1 Cor. i. 2, "With all," saith he, "that in every place call upon the name of Jesus Christ our Lord, both theirs and ours;" that is, with all the saints of God. And invocation generally comprises the whole worship of God. [25] This, then, is the due of our Mediator, though as God, as the Son, -- not as Mediator.

3. Thus also is it in reference unto the Holy Spirit of grace. The closing of the great sin of unbelief [26] is still described as an opposition unto, and a resisting of that Holy Spirit. And you have distinct mention of the love of the Spirit, Rom. xv. 30. The apostle also peculiarly directs his supplication to him

in that solemn benediction, 2 Cor. xiii. 14, "The grace of the Lord Jesus Christ, and the love of God, and the communion of the Holy Ghost, be with you all." And such benedictions are originally supplications. He is likewise entitled unto all instituted worship, from the appointment of the administration of baptism in his name, Matt. xxviii. 19. Of which things more afterward.

Now, of the things which have been delivered this is the sum:-- there is no grace whereby our souls go forth unto God, no act of divine worship yielded unto him, duty or obedience performed, but they are distinctly directed unto Father, Son, and Spirit. Now, by these and such like ways as these, do we hold communion with God; and therefore we have that communion distinctly, as hath been described.

This also may farther appear, if we consider how distinctly the persons of the Deity are revealed to act in the communication of those good things, wherein the saints have communion with God. [27] As all the spiritual ascendings of their souls are assigned unto them respectively, so all their internal receiving of the communications of God unto them are held out in such a distribution as points at distinct rises and fountains (though not of being in themselves, yet) of dispensations unto us. Now this is declared two ways:--

(1.) When the same thing is, at the same time, ascribed jointly and yet distinctly to all the persons in the Deity, and respectively to each of them. So are grace and peace, Rev. i. 4, 5, "Grace be unto you, and peace, from him which is, and which was, and which is to come; and from the seven Spirits which are before his throne; and from Jesus Christ, who is the faithful witness," etc. The seven Spirits before the throne, are the Holy Spirit of God, considered as the perfect fountain of every perfect gift and dispensation. All are here joined together, and yet all mentioned as distinguished in their communication of grace and peace unto the saints. "Grace and peace be unto you, from the Father, and from," etc.

(2.) When the same thing is attributed severally and singly unto each person. There is, indeed, no gracious influence from above, no illapse of light, life, love, or grace upon our hearts, but proceedeth in such a dispensation. I shall give only one instance, which is very comprehensive, and may be thought to comprise all other particulars; and this is teaching. The teaching of God is the real communication of all and every particular emanation from himself unto the saints whereof they are made partakers. That promise, "They shall be all taught of God," inwraps in itself the whole mystery of grace, as to its actual dispensation unto us, so far as we may be made real possessors of it. Now this is assigned, --

[1.] Unto the Father. The accomplishment of that promise is peculiarly referred to him, John vi. 45, "It is written in the prophets, And they shall be all taught of God. Every man therefore that hath heard, and hath learned of the Father, comes unto me." This teaching, whereby we are translated from death unto life, brought unto Christ, unto a participation of life and love in him, -- it is of and from the Father: him we hear, of him we learn, [28] by him are we brought unto union and communion with the Lord Jesus. This is his drawing us, his begetting us anew of his own will, by his Spirit; and in which work he employs the ministers of the gospel, Acts xxvi. 17, 18.

[2.] Unto the Son. The Father proclaims him from heaven to be the great teacher, in that solemn charge to hear him, which came once [and] again from the excellent glory: "This is my beloved Son; hear him." The whole of his prophetical, and no small part of his kingly office, consists in this teaching; herein is he said to draw men unto him, as the Father is said to do in his teaching, John xii. 32; which he doth with such efficacy, that "the dead hear his voice and live." [29] The teaching of the Son is a life-giving, a spirit-breathing teaching; -- an effectual influence of light, whereby he shines into darkness; a communication of life, quickening the dead; an opening of blind eyes, and changing of hard hearts; a pouring out of the Spirit, with all the fruits thereof. Hence he claims it as his privilege to be the sole master, Matt. xxiii. 10, "One is your Master, even Christ."

[3.] To the Spirit. John xiv. 26, "The Comforter, he shall teach you all things." "But the anointing which ye have received," saith the apostle, "abideth in you, and ye need not that any man teach you: but as the same anointing teacheth you of all things, and is truth, and is no lie, and even as it hath taught you, ye shall abide in him," 1 John ii. 27. That teaching unction which is not only true, but truth itself, is only the Holy Spirit of God: so that he teacheth also; being given unto us "that we might know the things that are freely given to us of God," 1 Cor. ii. 12. I have chosen this special instance because, as I told you, it is comprehensive, and comprises in itself most of the particulars that might be annumerated, -- quickening, preserving, etc.

This, then, farther drives on the truth that lies under demonstration; there being such a distinct communication of grace from the several persons of the Deity, the saints must needs have distinct communion with them.

It remaineth only to intimate, in a word, wherein this distinction lies, and what is the ground thereof. Now, this is, that the Father doth it by the way of original authority; the Son by the way of communicating from a purchased treasury; the Holy Spirit by the way of immediate efficacy.

1st. The Father communicates all grace by the way of original authority: He quickeneth whom he will, John v. 21. "Of his own will begat he us," James i. 18. Life-giving power is, in respect of original authority, invested in the Father by the way of eminency; and therefore, in sending of the quickening Spirit, Christ is said to do it from the Father, or the Father himself to do it. "But the Comforter, which is the Holy Ghost, whom the Father will send," John xiv. 26. "But when the Comforter is come, whom I will send unto you from the Father," John xv. 26; -- though he be also said to send him himself, on another account, John xvi. 7.

2dly. The Son, by the way of making out a purchased treasury: "Of his fulness have all we received, and grace for grace," John i. 16. And whence is this fulness? "It pleased the Father that in him should all fulness dwell," Col. i. 19. And upon what account he hath the dispensation of that fulness to him committed you may see, Phil. ii. 8-11. "When thou shalt make his soul an offering for sin, he shall prolong his days, and the pleasure of the Lord shall prosper in his hand. He shall see of the travail of his soul, and shall be satisfied: by his knowledge shall my righteous servant justify many; for he shall bear their iniquities," Isa. liii. 10, 11. And with this fulness he hath also authority for the communication of it, John v. 25-27; Matt. xxviii. 18.

3dly. The Spirit doth it by the way of immediate efficacy, Rom. viii. 11, "But if the Spirit of him that raised up Jesus from the dead dwell in you, he that raised up Christ from the dead shall also quicken your mortal bodies by his Spirit that dwelleth in you." Here are all three comprised, with their distinct concurrence unto our quickening. Here is the Father's authoritative quickening, -- "He raised Christ from the dead, and he shall quicken you;" and the Son's mediatory quickening, -- for it is done in "the death of Christ;" and the Spirit's immediate efficacy, -- "He shall do it by the Spirit that dwelleth in you." He that desires to see this whole matter farther explained, may consult what I have elsewhere written on this subject. And thus is the distinct communion whereof we treat both proved and demonstrated.

Footnotes:

16. "Ecce dico alium esse patrem, et alium filium, non divisione alium, sed distinctione." -- Tertul. adv. Prax.Οὐ φθάνω τὸ ἕν νοῆσαι, καὶ τοῖς τρισὶ περιλάμπομαι, οὐ φθάνω τὰ τρία διελεῖν, καὶ εἰς τὸ ἕν ἀναφέρομαι. -- Greg. Naz.

17. Χαρίσματα, διακονίας, ἐνεργήματα.

18. Πᾶσαν μὲν γὰρ δέησιν καὶ προσευχὴν καὶ ἔντευξιν, καὶ εὐχαριστίαν ἀναπεμπτέον τῷ ἐπὶ πᾶσι Θεῷ, διὰ τοῦ ἐπὶ πάντων ἀγγέλων ἀρχιερέως ἐμψύχου λόγου καὶ Θεοῦ. -- Orig. cont. Cels., lib. v. [c. 4.]

19. Hic tibi præcipuè sit purâ mente colendus.

20. Isa. ix. 6; 1 Cor. i. 30; Matt. v. 16, 45, vi. 1, 4, 6, 8, vii. 21, xii. 50; Luke xxiv. 49; John iv. 23, vi. 45, xii. 26, xiv. 6, 21, 23, xv. 1, xvi. 25, 27, xx. 17; Gal. i. 1, 3; Eph. ii. 18, v. 20; 1 Thess. i. 1; James i. 17; 1 Pet. i. 17; 1 John ii. 13, etc.

21. Rom. xiv. 10, 11; Phil. ii.

10.

22. Jer. x. 10, xvii. 5, 6; Gal. iv. 8.

23. Vind. Evan., cap. x. vol. xii.

24. Ps. ii. 7, 12; Dan. iii. 25; Matt. iii. 17, xvii. 5, xxii. 45; John iii. 36, v. 19-26, viii. 36; 1 Cor. i. 9; Gal. i. 6, iv. 6; 1 John ii. 22-24, v. 10-13; Heb. i. 6; Phil. ii. 10; John v. 23.

25. Isa. lvi. 7; Rom. x. 12-14.

26. Acts vii. 51.

27. "Tametsi omnia unus idemque Deus efficit, ut dicitur, -- opera Trinitatis ad extra sunt indivisa, distinguuntur tamen personæ discrimine in istis operibus."-- Matt. iii. 16; Acts iii. 13: Gen. xix. 24, i. 26; Matt. xxviii. 19; 2 Cor. xiii. 14.

28. Matt. xi. 25; John i. 13; James i. 18.

29. Matt. iii. 17, xvii. 5; 2 Pet. i. 17; Deut. xviii. 15-20, etc.; Acts iii. 22, 23; John v. 25; Isa. lxi. 1-3; Luke iv. 18, 19.

Chapter III - Of the peculiar and distinct communion which the saints have with the Father -- Observations for the clearing of the whole premised -- Our peculiar communion with the Father is in love -- 1 John iv. 7, 8; 2 Cor. xiii. 14; John xvi. 26, 27; Rom. v. 5; John iii. 16, xiv. 23; Tit. iii. 4, opened to this purpose -- What is required of believers to hold communion with the Father in love -- His love received by faith -- Returns of love to him -- God's love to us and ours to him -- Wherein they agree -- Wherein they differ.

Having proved that there is such a distinct communion in respect of Father, Son, and Spirit, as whereof we speak, it remains that it be farther cleared up by an induction of instances, to manifest what [it is], and wherein the saints peculiarly hold this communion with the several persons respectively: which also I shall do, after the premising some observations, necessary to be previously considered, as was promised, for the clearing of what hath been spoken. And they are these that follow:--

1. When I assign any thing as peculiar wherein we distinctly hold communion with any person, I do not exclude the other persons from communion with the soul in the very same thing. Only this, I say, principally, immediately, and by the way of eminency, we have, in such a thing, or in such a way, communion with some one person; and therein with the others secondarily, and by the way of consequence on that foundation; for the person, as the person, of any one of them, is not the prime object of divine worship, but as it is identified with the nature or essence of God. Now, the works that outwardly are of God (called "Trinitatis ad extra"), [30] which are commonly said to be common and undivided, are either wholly so, and in all respects, as all works of common providence; or else, being common in respect of their acts, they are distinguished in respect of that principle, or next and immediate rise in the manner of operation: so creation is appropriated to the Father, redemption to the Son. In which sense we speak of these things.

2. There is a concurrence of the actings and operations of the whole Deity[31] in that dispensation, wherein each person concurs to the work of our salvation, unto every act of our communion with each singular person. Look, by what act soever we hold communion with any person, there is an influence from every person to the putting forth of that act. [32] As, suppose it to be the act of faith:-- It is bestowed on us by the Father: "It is not of yourselves: it is the gift of God," Eph. ii. 8. It is the Father that revealeth the gospel, and Christ therein, Matt. xi. 25. And it is purchased for us by the Son: "Unto you it is given in the behalf of Christ, to believe on him," Phil. i. 29. In him are we "blessed with spiritual blessings," Eph. i. 3. He bestows on us, and increaseth faith in us, Luke xvii. 5.

And it is wrought in us by the Spirit; he administers that "exceeding greatness of his power," which he exerciseth towards them who believe, "according to the working of his mighty power, which he wrought in Christ, when he raised him from the dead," Eph. i. 19, 20; Rom. viii. 11.

3. When I assign any particular thing wherein we hold communion with any person, I do not do it exclusively unto other mediums of communion; but only by the way of inducing a special and eminent instance for the proof and manifestation of the former general assertion: otherwise there is no grace or duty wherein we have not communion with God in the way described. In every thing wherein we are made partakers of the divine nature, there is a communication and receiving between God and us; so near are we unto him in Christ.

4. By asserting this distinct communion, which merely respects that order in the dispensation of grace which God is pleased to hold out in the gospel, I intend not in the least to shut up all communion with God under these precincts (his ways being exceeding broad, containing a perfection whereof there is no end), nor to prejudice that holy fellowship we have with the whole Deity, in our walking before him in covenant-obedience; which also, God assisting, I shall handle hereafter.

These few observations being premised, I come now to declare what it is wherein peculiarly and eminently the saints have communion with the Father; and this is love, -- free, undeserved, and eternal love. This the Father peculiarly fixes upon the saints; this they are immediately to eye in him, to receive of him, and to make such returns thereof as he is delighted withal. This is the great discovery of the gospel: for whereas the Father, as the fountain of the Deity, is not known any other way but as full of wrath, anger, and indignation against sin, nor can the sons of men have any other thoughts of him (Rom. i. 18; Isa. xxxiii. 13, 14; Hab. i. 13; Ps. v. 4-6; Eph. ii. 3), -- here he is now revealed peculiarly as love, as full of it unto us; the manifestation whereof is the peculiar work of the gospel, Tit. iii. 4.

1. 1 John iv. 8, "God is love." That the name of God is here taken personally, [33] and for the person of the Father, not essentially, is evident from verse 9, where he is distinguished from his only begotten Son whom he sends into the world. Now, saith he, "The Father is love;" that is, not only of an infinitely gracious, tender, compassionate, and loving nature, according as he hath proclaimed himself, Exod. xxxiv. 6, 7, but also one that "eminently and peculiarly dispenseth himself unto us in free love." So the apostle sets it forth in the following verses: "This is love," verse 9; -- "This is that which I would have you take notice of in him, that he makes out love unto you, in sending his only begotten Son into the world, that we might live through him.'?" So also, verse 10, "He loved us, and sent his Son to be the propitiation for our sins." And that this is peculiarly to be eyed in him, the Holy Ghost plainly declares, in making it antecedent to the sending of Christ, and all mercies and benefits whatever by him received. This love, I say, in itself, is antecedent to the purchase of Christ, although the whole fruit thereof be made out alone thereby, Eph. i. 4-6.

2. So in that distribution made by the apostle in his solemn parting benediction, 2 Cor. xiii. 14, "The grace of the Lord Jesus Christ, the love of God, and the fellowship of the Holy Ghost, be with you all." Ascribing sundry things unto the distinct persons, it is love that he peculiarly assigns to the Father. And the fellowship of the Spirit is mentioned with the grace of Christ

and the love of God, because it is by the Spirit alone that we have fellowship with Christ in grace, and with the Father in love, although we have also peculiar fellowship with him; as shall be declared.

3. John xvi. 26, 27, saith our Saviour, "I say not unto you, that I will pray the Father for you; for the Father himself loveth you." [34] But how is this, that our Saviour saith, "I say not that I will pray the Father for you," when he saith plainly, chap. xiv. 16, "I will pray the Father for you?" The disciples, with all the gracious words, comfortable and faithful promises of their Master, with most heavenly discoveries of his heart unto them, were even fully convinced of his dear and tender affections towards them; as also of his continued care and kindness, that he would not forget them when bodily he was gone from them, as he was now upon his departure: but now all their thoughts are concerning the Father, how they should be accepted with him, what respect he had towards them. Saith our Saviour, "Take no care of that, nay, impose not that upon me, of procuring the Father's love for you; but know that this is his peculiar respect towards you, and which you are in him: He himself loves you.' It is true, indeed (and as I told you), that I will pray the Father to send you the Spirit, the Comforter, and with him all the gracious fruits of his love; but yet in the point of love itself, free love, eternal love, there is no need of any intercession for that: for eminently the Father himself loves you. Resolve of that, that you may hold communion with him in it, and be no more troubled about it. Yea, as your great trouble is about the Father's love, so you can no way more trouble or burden him, than by your unkindness in not believing of it." So it must needs be where sincere love is questioned.

4. The apostle teaches the same, Rom. v. 5, "The love of God is shed abroad in our hearts by the Holy Ghost, which is given unto us." God, whose love this is, is plainly distinguished from the Holy Ghost, who sheds abroad that love of his; and, verse 8, he is also distinguished from the Son, for it is from that love of his that the Son is sent: and therefore it is the Father of whom the apostle here specially speaketh. And what is it that he ascribes to him? Even love; which also, verse 8, he commendeth to us, -- sets it forth in such a signal and eminent expression, that we may take notice of it, and close with him in it. To carry this business to its height, there is not only most frequent peculiar mention of the love of God, where the Father is eminently intended, and of the love of the Father expressly, but he is also called "The God of love," 2 Cor. xiii. 11, and is said to be "love:" so that whoever will know him, 1 John iv. 8, or dwell in him by fellowship or communion, verse 16, must do it as he is love."

5. Nay, whereas there is a twofold divine love, beneplaciti and amicitiæ, a love of good pleasure and destination, and a love of friendship and approbation, they are both peculiarly assigned to the Father in an eminent manner:--

(1.) John iii. 16, "God so loved the world, that he gave," etc.; that is, with the love of his purpose and good pleasure, his determinate will of doing good. This is distinctly ascribed to him, being laid down as the cause of sending his Son. So Rom. ix. 11, 12; Eph. i. 4, 5; 2 Thess. ii. 13, 14; 1 John iv. 8, 9.

(2.) John xiv. 23, there is [35] mention of that other kind of love whereof we speak. "If a man love me," saith Christ, "he will keep my words: and my Father will love him, and we will come unto him, and make our abode with him." The love of friendship and approbation is here eminently ascribed to him. Says Christ, "We will come," even Father and Son, "to such a one, and dwell with him;" that is, by the Spirit: but yet he would have us take notice, that, in point of love, the Father hath a peculiar prerogative: "My Father will love him."

6. Yea, and as this love is peculiarly to be eyed in him, so it is to be looked on as the fountain of all following gracious dispensations. Christians walk oftentimes with exceedingly troubled hearts, concerning the thoughts of the Father towards them. They are well persuaded of the Lord Christ and his good-will; the difficulty lies in what is their acceptance with the Father, -- what is his heart towards them? [36] "Show us the Father, and it sufficeth us," John xiv. 8. Now, this ought to be so far away, that his love ought to be looked on as the fountain from whence all other sweetnesses flow. Thus the apostle sets it out, Tit. iii. 4, "After that the kindness and love of God our Saviour toward man appeared." It is of the Father of whom he speaks; for, verse 6, he tells us that "he makes out unto us," or "sheds that love upon us abundantly, through Jesus Christ our Saviour." And this love he makes the hinge upon which the great alteration and translation of the saints doth turn; for, saith he, verse 3, "We ourselves also were sometimes foolish, disobedient, deceived, serving divers lusts and pleasures, living in malice and envy, hateful, and hating one another." All naught, all out of order, and vile. Whence, then, is our recovery? The whole rise of it is from this love of God, flowing out by the ways there described. For when the kindness and love of God appeared, -- that is, in the fruits of it, -- then did this alteration ensue. To secure us hereof, there is not any thing that hath a loving and tender nature in the world, and doth act suitably whereunto, which God hath not compared himself unto. Separate all weakness and imperfection which is in them, yet great impressions of love must abide. He is as a father, a mother, a shepherd, a hen over chickens, and the like, Ps. ciii. 13; Isa. lxiii. 16; Matt. vi. 6; Isa. lxvi. 13; Ps. xxiii. 1; Isa. xl. 11; Matt. xxiii. 37.

I shall not need to add any more proofs. This is that which is demonstrated:-- There is love in the person of the Father peculiarly held out unto the saints, as wherein he will and doth hold communion with them.

Now, to complete communion with the Father in love, two things are required of believers:-- (1.) That they receive it of him. (2.) That they make suitable returns unto him.

(1.) That they do receive it. Communion consists in giving and receiving. Until the love of the Father be received, we have no communion with him therein. How, then, is this love of the Father to be received, so as to hold fellowship with him? I answer, By faith. The receiving of it is the believing of it. God hath so fully, so eminently revealed his love, that it may be received by faith. "Ye believe in God," John xiv. 1; that is, the Father. And what is to be believe in him? His love; for he is "love," 1 John iv. 8.

It is true, there is not an immediate acting of faith upon the Father, but by the Son. "He is the way, the truth, and the life: no man cometh unto the Father but by him," John xiv. 6. He is the merciful high priest over the house of God, by whom we have [37] access to the throne of grace: by him is our manuduction unto the Father; by him we believe in God, 1 Pet. i. 21. But this is that I say, -- When by and through Christ we have an access unto the Father, we then behold his glory also, and see his love that he peculiarly bears unto us, and act faith thereon. We are then, I say, to eye it, to believe it, to receive it, as in him; the issues and fruits thereof being made out unto us through Christ alone. Though there be no light for us but in the beams, yet we may by beams see the sun, which is the fountain of it. Though all our refreshment actually lie in the streams, yet by them we are led up unto the fountain. Jesus Christ, in respect of the love of the Father, is but the beam, the stream; wherein though actually all our light, our refreshment lies, yet by him we are led to the fountain, the sun of eternal love itself. Would believers exercise themselves herein, they would find it a matter of no small spiritual improvement in their walking with God.

This is that which is aimed at. Many dark and disturbing thoughts are apt to arise in this thing. Few can carry up their hearts and minds to this height by faith, as to rest their souls in the love of the Father; they live below it, in the troublesome region of hopes and fears, storms and clouds. All here is serene and quiet. But how to attain to this pitch they know not. This is the will of God, that he may always be eyed as benign, kind, tender, loving, and unchangeable therein; and that peculiarly as the Father, as the great fountain and spring of all gracious communications and fruits of love. This is that which Christ came to reveal, -- God as a Father, John i. 18; that name which he declares to those who are given him out of the world, John xvii. 6. And this is that which he effectually leads us to by himself, as he is the only way of going to God as a Father, John xiv. 5, 6; that is, as love: and by doing so, gives us the rest which he promiseth; for the love of the Father is the only rest of the soul. It is true, as was said, we do not this formally in the first instant of believing. We believe in God through Christ, 1 Pet. i. 21; faith seeks out rest for the soul. This is presented to it by Christ, the mediator, as the only procuring cause. Here it abides not, but by Christ it hath an access to the Father, Eph. ii. 18, -- into his love; finds out that he is love, as having a design, a purpose of love, a good pleasure towards us from eternity, -- a delight, a complacency, a good-will in Christ, -- all cause of anger and aversation being taken away. The soul being thus, by faith through Christ, and by him, brought into the bosom of God, into a comfortable persuasion and spiritual perception and sense of his love, there reposes and rests itself. And this is the first thing the saints do, in their communion with the Father; of the due improvement whereof, more afterward.

(2.) For that suitable return which is required, this also (in a main part of it, beyond which I shall not now extend it) consisteth in love. [38] God loves, that he may be beloved. [39] When he comes to command the return of his received love, to complete communion with him, he says, "My son, give me thine heart," Prov. xxiii. 26, -- thy affections, thy love. "Thou shalt love the Lord thy God with all thy heart, and with all thy soul, and with all thy strength, and with all thy mind," Luke x. 27; this is the return that he demandeth. When the soul sees God, in his dispensation of love, to be love, to be infinitely lovely and loving, rests upon and delights in him as such, then hath it communion with him in love. This is love, that God loves us first, and then we love him again. I shall not now go forth into a description of divine love. Generally, love [40] is an affection of union and nearness, with complacency therein. So long as the Father is looked on under any other apprehension, but only as acting love upon the soul, it breeds in the soul a dread and aversation. [41] Hence the flying and hiding of sinners, in the Scriptures. But when he who is the Father is considered as a father, acting love on the soul, this [42] raises it to love again. This is, in faith, the ground of all acceptable obedience, Deut. v. 10; Exod. xx. 6; Deut. x. 12, xi. 1, 13, xiii. 3.

Thus is this whole business stated by the apostle, Eph. i. 4, "According as he hath chosen us in him before the foundation of the world, that we should be holy and without blame before him in love." It begins in the love of God, and ends in our love to him. That is it which the eternal love of God aims at in us, and works us up unto. It is true, our universal obedience falls within the compass of our communion with God; but that is with him as God, our blessed sovereign, lawgiver, and rewarder: as he is the Father, our Father in Christ, as revealed unto us to be love, above and contrary to all the expectations of the natural man; so it is in love that we have this intercourse with him. Nor do I intend only that love which is as the life and form of all moral obedience; but a peculiar delight and acquiescing in the Father, revealed effectually as love unto the soul.

That this communion with the Father in love may be made the more clear and evident, I shall show two things:-- [1.] Wherein this love of God unto us and our love to him do agree, as to some manner of analogy and likeness. [2.] Wherein they differ; [43] which will farther discover the nature of each of them.

[1.] They agree in two things:--

1st. That they are each a love of rest and complacency.

(1st.) The love of God is so. Zeph. iii. 17, "The Lord thy God in the midst of thee is mighty; he will save, he will rejoice over thee with joy, he will rest in his love; he will joy over thee with singing." Both these things are here assigned unto God in his love, -- [44] rest and delight. The words are, יַחֲרִישׁ בְּאַהֲבָתוֹ, -- "He shall be silent because of his love." To rest with contentment is expressed by being silent; that is, without repining, without complaint. This God doth upon the account of his own love, so full, so every way complete and absolute, that it will not allow him to complain of any thing in them whom he loves, but he is silent on the account thereof. Or, "Rest in his love;" that is, he will not remove it, -- he will not seek farther for another object. It shall make its abode upon the soul where it is once fixed, for ever. And complacency or delight: "He rejoiceth with singing;" as one that is fully satisfied in that object he hath fixed his love on. Here are two words used to express the delight and joy that God hath in his love, -- יָשִׂישׂ and יָגִיל. The first denotes the inward affection of the mind, joy of heart; and to set out the intenseness hereof, it is said he shall do it בְּשִׂמְחָה, -- in gladness, or with joy. To have joy of heart in gladness, is the expression of delight in love. The latter word denotes not the inward affection, but the outward [45] demonstration of it: ἀγαλλιᾷν seems to be formed of it. It is to exult in outward demonstration of internal delight and joy; -- "Tripudiare," to leap, as men overcome with some joyful surprisal. And therefore God is said to do this בְּרִנָּה, -- with a joyful sound, or singing. To rejoice with gladness of heart, to exult with singing and praise, argues the greatest delight and complacency possible. When he would express the contrary of this love, he says οὐκ εὐδόκησε, -- "he was not well pleased," 1 Cor. x. 5; he fixed not his delight nor rest on them. And, "If any man draw back, the Lord's soul hath no pleasure in him," Heb. x. 38; Jer. xxii. 28; ὅς. viii. 8; Mal. i. 10. He takes pleasure in those that abide with him. He sings to his church, "A vineyard of red wine: I the Lord do keep it," Isa. xxvii. 2, 3; Ps. cxlvii. 11, cxlix. 4. There is rest and complacency in his love. There is in the Hebrew but a metathesis of a letter between the word that signifies a love of will and desire (אָהַב is so to love), and that which denotes a love of rest and acquiescence (which is, אָבָה); and both are applied to God. He wills good to us, that he may rest in that will. Some say, ἀγαπᾷν, "to love," is from ἄγαν πόθεσθαι, perfectly to acquiesce in the thing loved. And when God calls his

Son ἀγαπητόν, "beloved," Matt. iii. 17, he adds, as an exposition of it, ἐν ᾧ εὐδόκησα, "in whom I rest well pleased."

(2dly.) The return that the saints make unto him, to complete communion with him herein, holds some analogy with his love in this; for it is a love also of rest and delight. "Return unto thy rest, my soul," says David, Ps. cxvi. 7. He makes God his rest; that is, he in whom his soul doth rest, without seeking farther for a more suitable and desirable object. "Whom have I," saith he, "in heaven but thee and there is none upon earth that I desire beside thee," Ps. lxxiii. 25. [47] Thus the soul gathers itself from all its wanderings, from all other beloveds, to rest in God alone, -- to satiate and content itself in him; choosing the Father for his present and eternal rest. And this also with delight. "Thy loving-kindness," saith the psalmist, "is better than life; therefore will I praise thee," Ps. lxiii. 3. "Than life," מֵחַיִּים, -- before lives. I will not deny but life in a single consideration sometimes is so expressed, but always emphatically; so that the whole life, with all the concernments of it, which may render it considerable, are thereby intended. Austin, on this place, reading it [48] "super vitas," extends it to the several courses of life that men engage themselves in. Life, in the whole continuance of it, with all its advantages whatever, is at least intended. Supposing himself in the jaws of death, rolling into the grave through innumerable troubles, yet he found more sweetness in God than in a long life, under its best and most noble considerations, attended with all enjoyments that make it pleasant and comfortable. From both these is that of the church, in ὅς. xiv. 3, "Asshur shall not save us; we will not ride upon horses: neither will we say any more to the work of our hands, Ye are our gods: for in thee the fatherless findeth mercy." They reject the most goodly appearances of rest and contentment, to make up all in God, on whom they cast themselves, as otherwise helpless orphans.

2dly. The mutual love of God and the saints agrees in this, -- that the way of communicating the issues and fruits of these loves is only in Christ. The Father communicates no issue of his love unto us but through Christ; and we make no return of love unto him but through Christ. He is the treasury wherein the Father disposeth all the riches of his grace, taken from the bottomless mine of his eternal love; and he is the priest into whose hand we put all the offerings that we return unto the Father. Thence he is first, and by way of eminency, said to love the Son; not only as his eternal Son, -- as he was the delight of his soul before the foundation of the world, Prov. viii. 30, -- but also as our mediator, and the means of conveying his love to us, Matt. iii. 17; John iii. 35, v. 20, x. 17, xv. 9, xvii. 24. And we are said through him to believe in and to have access to God.

(1st.) The Father loves us, and "chose us before the foundation of the world;" but in the pursuit of that love, he "blesseth us with all spiritual blessings in heavenly places in Christ," Eph. i. 3, 4. From his love, he sheds or pours out the Holy Spirit richly upon us, through Jesus Christ our Saviour, Tit. iii. 6. In the pouring out of his love, there is not one drop falls besides the Lord Christ. The holy anointing oil was all poured on the head of Aaron, Ps. cxxxiii. 2; and thence went down to the skirts of his clothing. Love is first poured out on Christ; and from him it drops as the dew of Hermon upon the souls of his saints. The Father will have him to have "in all things the pre-eminence," Col. i. 18; "it pleased him that in him all fulness should dwell," verse 19; that "of his fulness we might receive, and grace for grace," John i. 16. Though the love of the Father's purpose and good pleasure have its rise and foundation in his mere grace and will, yet the design of its accomplishment is only in Christ. All the fruits of it are first given to him; and it is in him only that they are dispensed to us. So that though the saints may, nay, do, see an infinite ocean of love unto them in the bosom of the Father, yet they are not to look for one drop from him but what comes through Christ. He is the only means of communication. Love in the Father is like honey in the flower; -- it must be in the comb before it be for our use. Christ must extract and prepare this honey for us. He draws this water from the fountain through union and dispensation of fulness; -- we by faith, from the wells of salvation that are in him. This was in part before discovered.

(2dly.) Our returns are all in him, and by him also. And well is it with us that it is so. What lame and blind sacrifices should we otherwise present unto God! He [49] bears the iniquity of our offerings, and he adds incense unto our prayers. Our love is fixed on the Father; but it is conveyed to him through the Son of his love. He is the only way for our graces as well as our persons to go unto God; through him passeth all our desire, our delight, our complacency, our obedience. Of which more afterward.

Now, in these two things there is some resemblance between that mutual love of the Father and the saints wherein they hold communion.

[2.] There are sundry things wherein they differ:--

1st. The love of God is a love of bounty; our love unto him is a love of duty.

(1st.) The love of the Father is a love of bounty, -- a descending love; such a love as carries him out to do good things to us, great things for us. His love lies at the bottom of all dispensations towards us; and we scarce anywhere find any mention of it, but it is held out as the cause and fountain of some free gift flowing from it. He [50] loves us, and sends his Son to die for us; -- he loves us, and blesseth us with all spiritual blessings. Loving is choosing, Rom. ix. 11, 12. He loves us and chastiseth us. [It is] a [51] love like that of the heavens to the earth, when, being full of rain, they pour forth showers to make it fruitful; as the sea communicates its waters to the rivers by the way of bounty, out of its own fulness, -- they return unto it only what they receive from it. It is the love of a spring, of a fountain, -- always communicating; -- [52] a love from whence proceeds every thing that is lovely in its object. It infuseth into, and creates goodness in, the persons beloved. And this answers the description of love given by the philosopher. "To love," saith he, "ἔστι βούλεσθαι τινὶ ἃ οἴεται ἀγαθά καὶ κατὰ δύαμιν πρακτικὸν εἶαι τούων." He that loves works out good to them he loveth, as he is able. God's power and will are commensurate; -- what he willeth he worketh.

(2dly.) Our love unto God is a love of duty, the love of a child. His love descends upon us in bounty and fruitfulness; [53] our love ascends unto him in duty and thankfulness. He adds to us by his love; we nothing to him by ours. Our goodness extends not unto him. Though our love be fixed on him [54] immediately, yet no fruit of our love reacheth him immediately; though he requires our love, he is not benefited by it, Job xxxv. 5-8, Rom. xi. 35, Job xxii. 2, 3. It is indeed made up of these four things:-- 1. Rest; 2. Delight; 3. Reverence; 4. Obedience. By these do we hold communion with the Father in his love. Hence God calls that love which is due to him as a father, "honour,"

128

Mal. i. 6, "If I be a father, where is mine honour?" It is a deserved act of duty.

2dly. They differ in this:-- The love of the Father unto us is an antecedent love; our love unto him is a consequent love.

(1st.) The love of the Father unto us is an antecedent love, and that in two respects:--

[1st.] It is antecedent in respect of our love, 1 John iv. 10, "Herein is love, not that we loved God, but that he loved us." His love goes before ours. The father loves the child, when the child knows not the father, much less loves him. Yea, we are by nature θεοστυγεῖς, Rom. i. 30, -- haters of God. He is in his own nature φιλάνθρωπος, -- a lover of men; and surely all mutual love between him and us must begin on his hand.

[2dly.] In respect of all other causes of love whatever. It goes not only before our love, but also any thing in us that is lovely. [55] Rom. v. 8, "God commendeth his love towards us, in that whilst we were yet sinners Christ died for us." Not only his love, but the eminent fruit thereof, is made out towards us as sinners. Sin holds out all of unloveliness and undesirableness that can be in a creature. The very mention of that removes all causes, all moving occasions of love whatever. Yet, as such, have we the commendation of the Father's love unto us, by a most signal testimony. Not only when we have done no good, but when we are in our blood, doth he love us; -- not because we are better than others, but because himself is infinitely good. His kindness appears when we are foolish and disobedient. Hence he is said to "love the world;" that is, those who have nothing but what is in and of the world, whose whole [portion] lies in evil.

(2dly.) Our love is consequential in both these regards:--

[1st.] In respect of the love of God. Never did creature turn his affections towards God, if the heart of God were not first set upon him.

[2dly.] In respect of sufficient causes of love. God must be revealed unto us as lovely and desirable, as a fit and suitable object unto the soul to set up its rest upon, before we can bear any love unto him. The saints (in this sense) do not love God for nothing, but for that excellency, loveliness, and desirableness that is in him. As the psalmist says, in one particular, Ps. cxvi. 1, "I love the Lord, because!" so may we in general; we love the Lord, because! Or, as David in another case, "What have I now done? is there not a cause?" If any man inquire about our love to God, we may say, "What have we now done? is there not a cause?"

3dly. They differ in this also:-- The love of God is like himself, -- equal, constant, not capable of augmentation or diminution; our love is like ourselves, -- unequal, increasing, waning, growing, declining. His, like the sun, always the same in its light, though a cloud may sometimes interpose; ours, as the moon, hath its enlargements and straitenings.

(1st.) The love of the Father is equal, etc.; [56] whom he loves, he loves unto the end, and he loves them always alike. "The Strength of Israel is not a man, that he should repent." On whom he fixes his love, it is immutable; it doth not grow to eternity, it is not diminished at any time. It is an eternal love, that had no beginning, that shall have no ending; that cannot be heightened by any act of ours, that cannot be lessened by any thing in us. I say, in itself it is thus; otherwise, in a twofold regard, it may admit of change:--

[1st.] In respect of its fruits. It is, as I said, a fruitful love, a love of bounty.

In reference unto those fruits, it may sometimes be greater, sometimes less; its communications are various. Who among the saints finds it not [so]? What life, what light, what strength, sometimes! and again, how dead, how dark, how weak! as God is pleased to let out or to restrain the fruits of his love. All the graces of the Spirit in us, all sanctified enjoyments whatever, are fruits of his love. How variously these are dispensed, how differently at sundry seasons to the same persons, experience will abundantly testify.

[2dly.] In respect of its discoveries and manifestations. He "sheds abroad his love in our hearts by the Holy Ghost," Rom. v. 5, -- gives us a sense of it, manifests it unto us. Now, this is [57] various and changeable, sometimes more, sometimes less; now he shines, anon hides his face, as it may be for our profit. Our Father will not always chide, lest we be cast down; he doth not always smile, lest we be full and neglect him: but yet, still his love in itself is the same. When for a little moment he hides his face, yet he gathers us with everlasting kindness.

Objection. But you will say, "This comes nigh to that blasphemy, that God loves his people in their sinning as well as in their strictest obedience; and, if so, who will care to serve him more, or to walk with him unto well-pleasing?"

Answer. There are few truths of Christ which, from some or other, have not received like entertainment with this. Terms and appellations are at the will of every imposer; things are not at all varied by them. The love of God in itself is the eternal purpose and act of his will. This is no more changeable than God himself: if it were, no flesh could be saved; but it [58] changeth not, and we are not consumed. What then? loves he his people in their sinning? Yes; his people, -- not their sinning. Alters [59] he not his love towards them? Not the purpose of his will, but the dispensations of his grace. He rebukes them, he chastens them, he hides his face from them, he smites them, he fills them with a sense of [his] indignation; but woe, woe would it be to us, should he change in his love, or take away his kindness from us! Those very things which seem to be demonstrations of the change of his affections towards his, do as clearly proceed from love as those which seem to be the most genuine issues thereof. "But will not this encourage to sin?" He never tasted of the love of God that can seriously make this objection. The doctrine of grace may be turned into wantonness; the principle cannot. I shall not wrong the saints by giving another answer to this objection: Detestation of sin in any may well consist with the acceptation of their persons, and their designation to life eternal.

But now our love to God is ebbing and flowing, waning and increasing. We lose our first love, and we grow again in love; [60] -- scarce a day at a stand. What poor creatures are we! How unlike the Lord and his love! "Unstable as water, we cannot excel." Now it is, "Though all men forsake thee, I will not;" anon, "I know not the man." One day, "I shall never be moved, my hill is so strong;" the next, "All men are liars, I shall perish." When ever was the time, where ever was the place, that our love was one day equal towards God?

And thus, these agreements and discrepancies do farther describe that mutual love of the Father and the saints, wherein they hold communion. Other instances as to the person of the Father I shall not give, but endeavour to make some improvement of this in the next chapter.

Footnotes:

30. Opera ad extra sunt indivisa.

31. Πατὴρ σὺν υἱῷ καὶ πανάγνῳ πνεύματι

Τριὰς προσώποις εὐκρινὴς, μονὰς φύσει.

Μήτ' οὖν ἀριθμῷ συγχέῃς ὑποστάσεις,

Μήτ' ἂν θεὸν σὺ προσκυνῶν τιμᾷς φύσιν·

Μία τριὰς γὰρ, εἷς Θεὸς παντοκράτωρ. Greg. Naz. Iamb. Car. iii.

32. Προσκυνῶμεν τὴν μίαν τοῖς πρισὶ θεότητα. -- Idem. Orat., 24. See Thom. 22, q. 84, a. 3, q. 84, a. 1; Alexan. Ales. Sum. Theol., p. 3, q. 30, m. 1, a. 3.

33. Deut. xxxiii. 3; Jer. xxxi. 3; John iii. 16, v. 42, xiv. 21; Rom. v. 5, viii. 39; Eph. ii. 4; 1 John ii. 15, iv. 10, 11; Heb. xii. 6. "Multo ἐμφατικώτερον loquitur quam si Deum diceret summopere, atque adeo infinite nos amare, cum Deum dicit erga nos ipsam charitatem esse, cujus latissimum τεκμήριον profert." -- Beza in loc.

34. "Quomodo igitur negat? negat secundum quid; hoc est, negat se ideo rogaturum patrem, ut patrem illis concilet, et ad illos amandos et exaudiendos flectat; quasi non sit suapte sponte erga illos propensus. Voluit ergo Christus his verbis persuadere apostolis, non solum se, sed etiam ipsum patrem illos complecti amore maximo. Et ita patrem eos amare, ac promptum habere animum illis gratificandi, et benefaciendi, ut nullius, neque ipsius filii opus habeat tali intercessione, qua solent placari, et flecti homines non admodum erga aliquem bene affecti," etc.-- Zanc. de trib. nom. Elo., lib. iv. cap. 9. Vid. Hilar de Trinit., lib. vi. p. 97.,

ed. Eras.

35. "Diligi a patre, recipi in amicitiam summi Dei; a Deo foveri, adeoque Deo esse in deliciis." -- Bucerus in loc.

36. "Te quod attinet non sumus solliciti, -- illud modo desideramus, ut patrem nobis vel semel intueri concedatur." -- Cartwright Har. in John xiv. 8.

37. Eph. ii. 18.

38. Deut. vi. 4, 5.

39. "Amor supernè descendens ad divinam pulchritudinem omnia convocat." -- Proclus lib. de Anima et Dæm.

40. "Unio substantialis est causa amoris sui ipsius; similitudinis, est causa amoris alterius; sed unio realis quam amans quærit de re amata, est effectus amoris." -- Thom. 12, q. 28, 1, 3.

41. Josh. xxii. 5, xxiii. 11; Neh. i. 5.

42. Ps. xviii. 1, xxxi. 23, xcvii. 10, cxvi. 1; 1 Cor. ii. 9; James i. 12; Isa. lvi. 6; Matt. xxii. 37; Rom. viii. 28.

43. Ἀνάλογον δ' ἐν ἁπάσαις ταῖς καθ' ὑπεροχὴν οὔσαις φιλίαις, καὶ τὴν φίλησιν δεῖ γίνεσθαι, etc. -- Arist. Eth., lib. viii. cap. 7.

44. "Effectus amoris quando habetur amatum, est delectatio." -- Thom. 12, q. 25, a. 2, 1. "Amor est complacentia amantis in amato. Amor est motus cordis, delectantis se in aliquo." -- August.

45. "Externum magis gaudii gestum, quam internam animi lætitiam significat, cum velut tripudiis et volutationibus gaudere se quis ostendit." -- Pagnin. גּוּל; lætitiâ gestiit, animi lætitiam gestu corporis expressit, exilivit gaudio." -- Calas.

46. "Fecisti nos ad te, domine,

et irrequietum est cor nostrum donec veniat ad te." -- Aug. Conf.

47. Ps. xxxvii. 7; Isa. xxviii. 12; Heb. iv. 9.

48. "Super vita; quas vitas? Quas sibi homines eligunt; alius elegit sibi vitam negociandi, alius vitam rusticandi; alius vitam foenerandi, alius vitam militandi, alius illam, alius illam. Diversæ sunt vitæ, sed melior est misericordia tua super vitas nostras." -- Aug. Enarrat. in Ps. lxii.

49. Exod. xxviii. 38; Rev. viii. 3; John xiv. 6; Heb. x. 19-22.

50. John iii. 16; Rom. v. 8; Eph. i. 3, 4; 1 John iv. 9, 10; Heb. xii. 6; Rev. iii. 19.

51. Ἐραν δὲ σεμνὸν οὐρανὸν πληρούμενον ὄμβρου, πεσεῖν εἰς γαῖαν. -- Eurip., [as quoted by Aristotle, Eth. viii. 1. The quotation at large is:--

Ἐρᾷ δ' ὁ σεμνὸς οὐρανὸς πληρούμενος

Ὄμβρου, πεσεῖν εἰς γαῖαν

Ἀφροδίτης ὕπο. Eurip. Frag.]

52. "Amor Dei est infundens et creans bonitatem in amatis." -- Thom. p. p. q. 20, a. 2, c.

53. "Amor Dei causat bonitatem in rebus, sed amor noster causatur ab ea."

54. "Dilectio quæ est appetitivæ virtutis actus, etiam in statum viæ tendit in Deum primo et immediate." -- Thom. 22, q. 27, a 4.

55. Ezek. xvi. 1-14, etc.; Rom. ix. 11, 12; Tit. iii. 3-6; Deut. vii. 6-8; Matt. xi. 25, 26; John iii. 16.

56. 1 Sam. xv. 29; Isa. xlvi. 10; Jer. xxxi. 3; Mal. iii. 6; James i. 17; 2 Tim. ii. 19.

57. Ps. xxxi. 16, lxvii. 1, cxix. 135, xiii. 1, xxvii. 9, xxx. 7, lxxxviii. 14; Isa. viii. 17.

58. Mal. iii. 6.

59. Ps. xxxix. 11; Heb. xii. 7, 8; Rev. iii. 19; Isa. viii. 17, lvii. 17; Job vi. 4; Ps. vi. 6, xxxviii. 3-5, etc.

60. Rev. ii. 4, iii. 2; Eph. iii. 16-19.

Chapter IV - Inferences on the former doctrine concerning communion with the Father in love.

Having thus discovered the nature of that distinct communion which we have with the Father, it remaineth that we give some exhortations unto it, directions in it, and take some observations from it:--

1. First, then, this is a duty wherein it is most evident that Christians are but little exercised, -- namely, in holding immediate communion with the Father in love. Unacquaintedness with our mercies, our privileges, is our sin as well as our trouble. We hearken not to the voice of the Spirit [61] which is given unto us, "that we may know the things that are freely bestowed on us of God." This makes us go heavily, when we might rejoice; and to be weak, where we might be strong in the Lord. How few of the saints are experimentally acquainted with this privilege of holding immediate communion with the Father in love! With what anxious, doubtful thoughts do they look upon him! What fears, what questioning are there, of his good-will and kindness! At the best, many think there is no sweetness at all in him towards us, but what is purchased at the high price of the blood of Jesus. It is true, that alone is the way of communication; but the free fountain and spring of all is in the bosom of the Father. [62] "Eternal life was with the Father, and is manifested unto us." Let us, then, --

(1.) Eye the Father as love; look not on him as an always lowering father, but as one most [63] kind and tender. Let us look on him by faith, as one that hath had thoughts of kindness towards us from everlasting. It is misapprehension of God that makes any run from him, who have the least breathing wrought in them after him. "They that know thee will put their trust in thee." Men cannot abide with God in spiritual meditations. He loseth soul's company by their want of this insight into his love. They fix their thoughts only on his terrible majesty, severity, and greatness; and so their spirits are not endeared. Would a soul continually eye his everlasting tenderness and compassion, his thoughts of kindness that have been from of old, his present gracious acceptance, it could not bear an hour's absence from him; whereas now, perhaps, it cannot watch with him one hour. Let, then, this be the saints' first notion of the Father, -- as one full of eternal, free love towards them: let their hearts and thoughts be filled with breaking through all discouragements that lie in the way. To raise them hereunto, let them consider, --

[1.] Whose love it is. It is the love of him who is in himself all sufficient, infinitely satiated with himself and his own glorious excellencies and perfections; who hath no need to go forth with his love unto others, nor to seek an object of it without himself. There might he rest with delight and complacency to eternity. He is sufficient unto his own love. He had his Son, also, his eternal [64] Wisdom, to rejoice and delight himself in from all eternity, Prov. viii. 30. This might take up and satiate the whole delight of the Father;

but he will love his saints also. And it is such a love, as wherein he seeks not his own satisfaction only, but our good therein also; -- the love of a God, the love of a Father, whose proper outgoings are kindness and bounty.

[2.] What kind of love it is. And it is, --

1st. Eternal. It was fixed on us before the [65] foundation of the world. Before we were, or had done the least good, then were his thoughts upon us, -- then was his delight in us; -- then did the Son rejoice in the thoughts of fulfilling his Father's delight in him, Prov. viii. 30. Yea, the delight of the Father in the Son, there mentioned, is not so much his absolute delight in him as the express image of his person and the brightness of his glory, wherein he might behold all his own excellencies and perfections; as with respect unto his love and his delight in the sons of men. So the order of the words require us to understand it: "I was daily his delight," and, "My delights were with the sons of men;" -- that is, in the thoughts of kindness and redemption for them: and in that respect, also, was he his Father's delight. It was from eternity that he laid in his own bosom a design for our happiness. The very thought of this is enough to make all that is within us, like the babe in the womb of Elisabeth, to leap for joy. A sense of it cannot but prostrate our souls to the lowest abasement of a humble, holy reverence, and make us rejoice before him with trembling.

2dly. Free. He [66] loves us because he will; there was, there is, nothing in us for which we should be beloved. Did we deserve his love, it must go less in its valuation. Things of due debt are seldom the matter of thankfulness; but that which is eternally antecedent to our being, must needs be absolutely free in its respects to our well-being. This gives it life and being, is the reason of it, and sets a price upon it, Rom. ix. 11; Eph. i. 3, 4; Titus iii. 5; James i. 18.

3dly. [67] Unchangeable. Though we change every day, yet his love changeth not. Could any kind of provocation turn it away, it had long since ceased. Its unchangeableness is that which carrieth out the Father unto that infiniteness of patience and forbearance (without which we die, we perish), 2 Pet. iii. 9, which he exerciseth towards us. And it is, --

4thly. [68] Distinguishing. He hath not thus loved all the world: "Jacob have I loved, but Esau have I hated." Why should he fix his love on us, and pass by millions from whom we differ not by [69] nature, -- that he should make us sharers in that, and all the fruits of it, which most of the great and [70] wise men of the world are excluded from? I name but the heads of things. Let them enlarge whose hearts are touched.

Let, I say, the soul frequently eye the love of the Father, and that under these considerations, -- they are all soul-conquering and endearing.

(2.) So eye it as to receive it. Unless this be added, all is in vain as to any communion with God. We do not hold communion with him in any thing, until it be received by faith. This, then, is that which I would provoke the saints of God unto, even to [71] believe this love of God for themselves and their own part, -- believe that such is the heart of the Father towards them, -- accept of his witness herein. His love is not ours in the sweetness of it until it be so received. Continually, then, act thoughts of faith on God, as love to thee, -- as embracing thee with the eternal free love before described. When the Lord is, by his word, presented as such unto thee, let thy mind know it, and assent that it is so; and thy will embrace it, in its being so; and all thy affections be filled with it. Set thy whole heart to it; let it be bound with the cords of this love. [72] If the King be bound in the galleries with thy love, shouldst thou not be bound in heaven with his?

(3.) Let it have its proper fruit and efficacy upon thy heart, in return of love to him again. So shall we walk in the light of God's countenance, and hold holy communion with our Father all the day long. Let us not deal unkindly with him, and return him slighting for his good-will. Let there not be such a heart in us as to deal so unthankfully with our God.

2. Now, to further us in this duty, and the daily constant practice of it, I shall add one or two considerations that may be of importance whereunto; as, --

(1.) It is exceeding acceptable unto God, even our Father, that we should thus hold communion with him in his love, -- that he may be received into our souls as one full of love, tenderness, and kindness, towards us. Flesh and blood is apt to have very hard thoughts of him, -- to think he is always angry, yea, implacable; that it is not for poor creatures to draw nigh to him; that nothing in the world is more desirable than never to come into his presence, or, as they say where he hath any thing to do. "Who [73] among us shall dwell with the devouring fire? who among us shall dwell with everlasting burnings?" say the sinners in Zion. [74] And, "I knew thou wast an austere man," saith the evil servant in the gospels. Now, there is not any thing more grievous to the Lord, nor more subservient to the design of Satan upon the soul, than such thoughts as these. Satan claps his hands (if I may so say) when he can take up the soul with such thoughts of God: he hath enough, -- all that he doth desire. This hath been his design and way from the beginning. The [75] first blood that murderer shed was by this means. He leads our first parents into hard thoughts of God: "Hath God said so? hath he threatened you with death? He knows well enough it will be better with you;" -- with this engine did he batter and overthrow all mankind [76] in one; and being mindful of his ancient conquest, he readily useth the same weapons wherewith then he so successfully contended. Now, it is exceeding grievous to the Spirit of God to be so slandered in the hearts of those whom he dearly loves. How doth he expostulate this with Zion! "What iniquity[77] have ye seen in me?" saith he; "have I been a wilderness unto you, or a land of darkness?" [78] "Zion said, The Lord hath forsaken me, and my Lord hath forgotten me. Can a woman," etc. The Lord takes nothing worse at the hands of his, than such hard thoughts of him, knowing full well what fruit this bitter root is like to bear, -- what alienations of heart, -- what drawings back, -- what unbelief and tergiversations in our walking with him. How unwilling is a child to come into the presence of an angry father! Consider, then, this in the first place, -- receiving of the Father as he holds out love to the soul, gives him the honour he aims at, and is exceeding acceptable unto him. He often sets it out in an eminent manner, that it may be so received:-- "He commendeth his love toward us," Rom. v. 8. "Behold, what manner of love the Father hath bestowed upon us!" 1 John iii. 1. Whence, then, is this folly? Men are afraid to have good thoughts of God. They think it a boldness to eye God as good, gracious, tender, kind, loving: I speak of saints; but for the other side, they can judge him hard, austere, severe, almost implacable, and fierce (the very worst affections of the very worst of men, and most hated of him, Rom. i. 31; 2 Tim. iii. 3), and think herein they do well. Is not this soul-deceit from Satan? Was it not his design from the beginning to inject such thoughts of God? Assure thyself, then, there is nothing more acceptable unto the Father, than for us to keep up our hearts unto him as the eternal fountain of all that rich grace which flows out to sinners in the blood of Jesus. And, --

(2.) This will be exceeding effectual to endear thy soul unto God, to cause thee to delight in him, and to make thy abode with him. Many saints have no greater burden in their lives, than that their hearts do not come clearly and fully up, constantly to delight and rejoice in God, -- that there is still an indisposedness of spirit unto close walking with him. What is at the bottom of this distemper? Is it not their unskilfulness in or neglect of this duty, even of holding communion with the Father in love? So much as we see of the love of God, so much shall we delight in him, and no more. Every other discovery of God, without this, will but make the soul fly from Him; but if the heart be once much taken up with this the eminency of the Father's love, it cannot choose but be overpowered, conquered, and endeared unto him. This, if any thing, will work upon us to make our abode with him. If the love of a father will not make a child delight in him, what will? Put, then, this to the venture: exercise your thoughts upon this very thing, the eternal, free, and fruitful love of the Father, and see if your hearts be not wrought upon to delight in him. I dare boldly say, believers will find it as thriving a course as ever they pitched on in their lives. Sit down a little at the fountain, and you will quickly have a farther discovery of the sweetness of the streams. You who have run from him, will not be able, after a while, to keep at a distance for a moment.

Objection 1. But some may say, "Alas! how shall I hold communion with the Father in love? I know not at all whether he loves me or no; and shall I venture to cast myself upon it? How if I should not be accepted? should I not rather perish for my presumption, than find sweetness in his bosom? God seems to me only as a consuming fire and everlasting burnings; so that I dread to look up unto him."

Answer. I know not what may be understood by knowing of the love of God; though it be carried on by spiritual sense and experience, yet it is received purely by believing. Our knowing of it, is our believing of it as revealed. "We have known and believed the love that God hath to us. God is love," 1 John iv. 16. This is the assurance which, at the very entrance of walking with God, thou mayest have of this love. He who is truth hath said it; and whatever thy heart says, or Satan says, unless thou wilt take it up on this account, thou doest thy endeavour to make him a liar who hath spoken it, 1 John v. 10.

Obj. 2. "I can believe that God is love to others, for he hath said he is love; but that he will be so to me, I see no ground of persuasion; there is no cause, no reason in the world, why he should turn one thought of love or kindness towards me: and therefore I dare not cast myself upon it, to hold communion with him in his special love."

Ans. He hath spoken it as particularly to thee as to any one in the world. And for cause of love, he hath as much to fix it on thee as on any of the children of men; that is, none at all without himself. So that I shall make speedy work with this objection. Never any one from the foundation of the world, who believed such love in the Father, and made returns of love to him again, was deceived; neither shall ever any to the world's end be so, in so doing. Thou art, then, in this, upon a most sure bottom. If thou believest and receivest the Father as love, he will infallibly be so to thee, though others may fall under his severity. But, --

Obj. 3. "I cannot find my heart making returns of love unto God. Could I find my soul set upon him, I could then believe his soul delighted in me."

Ans. This is the most preposterous course that possibly thy thoughts can pitch upon, a most ready way to rob God of his glory. "Herein is love," saith the Holy Ghost, "not that we loved God, but that he loved us" first, 1 John iv. 10, 11. Now, thou wouldst invert this order, and say, "Herein is love, not that God loved me, but that I love him first." This is to take the glory of God from him: that, whereas he loves us without a cause that is in ourselves, and we have all cause in the world to love him, thou wouldst have the contrary, namely, that something should be in thee for which God should love thee, even thy love to him; and that thou shouldst love God, before thou knowest any thing lovely in him, -- namely, whether he love thee or no. This is a course of flesh's finding out, that will never bring glory to God, nor peace to thy own soul. Lay down, then, thy reasonings; take up the love of the Father upon a pure act of believing, and that will open thy soul to let it out unto the Lord in the communion of love.

To make yet some farther improvement of this truth so opened and exhorted unto as before; -- it will discover unto us the eminency and privilege of the saints of God. What low thoughts soever the sons of men may have of them, it will appear that they have meat to eat that the world knows not of. They have close communion and fellowship with the Father. They deal with him in the interchange of love. Men are generally esteemed according to the company they keep. It is an honour to stand in the presence of princes, though but as servants. What honour, then, have all the saints, to stand with boldness in the presence of the Father, and there to enjoy his bosom love! What a blessing did the queen of Sheba pronounce on the servants of Solomon, who stood before him, and heard his wisdom! How much more blessed, then, are they who stand continually before the God of Solomon, hearing his wisdom, enjoying his love! Whilst others have their fellowship with Satan and their own lusts, making provision for them, and receiving perishing refreshments from them, ("whose end is destruction, whose god is their belly, and whose glory is in their shame, who mind earthly things,") they have this sweet communion with the Father.

Moreover, what a safe and sweet retreat is here for the saints, in all the scorns, reproaches, scandals, misrepresentations, which they undergo in the world. When [79] a child is abused abroad in the streets by strangers, he runs with speed to the bosom of his father; there he makes his complaint, and is comforted. In all the hard [80] censures and tongue-persecutions which the saints meet withal in the streets of the world, they may run with their moanings unto their Father, and be comforted. "As one whom his mother comforteth, so will I comfort you," saith the Lord, Isa. lxvi. 13. So that the soul may say, "If I have hatred in the world, I will go where I am sure of love. Though all others are hard to me, yet my Father is tender and full of compassion: I will go to him, and satisfy myself in him. Here I am accounted vile, frowned on, and rejected; but I have honour and love with him, whose kindness is better than life itself. There I shall have all things in the fountain, which others have but in the drops. There is in my Father's love every thing desirable: there is the sweetness of all mercies in the abstract itself, and that fully and durably."

Evidently, then, the saints are the most mistaken men in the world. If they say, [81] "Come and have fellowship with us;" are not men ready to say, "Why, what are you? a sorry company of [82] seditious, factious persons. Be it known unto you, that we despise your fellowship. When we intend to leave fellowship with all honest men, and men of worth, then will we come to you." But, alas! how are men mistaken! Truly their fellowship is with the Father: let men think of it as they please, they have close, spiritual, heavenly refreshing, in the mutual communication of love with the Father himself. How they are generally misconceived, the apostle declares, 2 Cor. vi. 8-10, "As deceivers, and yet true; as unknown, and yet well known; as dying, and, behold, we live; as chastened, and not killed; as sorrowful, yet always rejoicing; as poor, yet making many rich; as having nothing, and yet possessing all things." And as it is thus in general, so in no one thing more than this, that they are looked on as poor, low, despicable persons, when indeed they are the only great and noble personages in the world. Consider the company they keep: it is with the Father; -- who so glorious? The merchandise they trade in, it is love; -- what so precious? Doubtless they are the excellent on the earth, Ps. xvi. 3.

Farther; this will discover a main difference between the saints and empty professors:-- As to the performance of duties, and so the enjoyment of outward privileges, fruitless professors often walk hand in hand with them; but now come to their secret retirements, and what a difference is there! There the saints hold communion with God: hypocrites, for the most part, with the world and their own lusts; -- with them they converse and communicate; they hearken what they will say to them, and make provision for them, when the saints are sweetly wrapt up in the bosom of their Father's love. It is oftentimes even almost impossible that believers should, in outward appearance, go beyond them who have very rotten hearts: but this meat they have, which others know not of; this refreshment in the banqueting house, wherein others have no share; -- in the multitude of their thoughts, the comforts of God their Father refresh their souls.

Now, then (to draw towards a close of this discourse), if these things be so, "what manner of men ought we to be, in all manner of holy conversation?" Even "our God is a consuming fire." What communion is there between light and darkness? Shall sin and lust dwell in those thoughts which receive in and carry out love from and unto the Father? Holiness becometh his presence for ever. An unclean spirit cannot draw nigh unto him; -- an unholy heart can make no abode with him. A lewd person will not desire to hold fellowship with a sober man; and will a man of vain and foolish imaginations hold communion and dwell with the most holy God? There is not any consideration of this love but is a powerful motive unto holiness, and leads thereunto. Ephraim says, "What have I to do any more with idols?" when in God he finds salvation. Communion with the Father is wholly inconsistent with loose walking. "If we say that we have fellowship with him, and walk in darkness, we lie, and do not the truth," 1 John i. 6. "He that saith, I know him" (I have communion with him), "and keepeth not his commandments, is a liar, and the truth is not in him," chap. ii. 4. The most specious and glorious pretence made to an acquaintance with the Father, without holiness and obedience to his commandments, serves only to prove the pretenders to be liars. The love of the world and of the Father dwell not together.

And if this be so (to shut up all), how many that go under the name of Christians, come short of the truth of it! How unacquainted are the generality of professors with the mystery of this communion, and the fruits of it! Do not many very evidently hold communion with their lusts and with the world, and yet would be thought to have a portion and inheritance among them that are sanctified? They have neither new name nor white stone, and yet would be called the people of the Most High. May it not be said of many of them, rather, that God is not in all their thoughts, than that they have communion with him? The Lord open the eyes of men, that they may see and know that walking with God is a matter not of form, but power! And so far of peculiar communion with the Father, in the instance of love which we have insisted on. "He is also faithful who hath called us to the fellowship of his Son Jesus Christ our Lord;" -- of which in the next place.

Footnotes:

61. 1 Cor. ii. 12.

62. Ζωὴ ἥτις ἦν πρὸς τὸν Πατέρα, καὶ ἐφανερώθη ἡμῖν. -- 1 John i. 2.

63. Ps. ciii. 9; Mic. vii. 18.

64. שׁעֲשׁועִים יוֹם יוֹם. "Optime in Dei Filium quadrat patris delicias." -- Mer. in loc.

65. Rom. ix. 11, 12; Acts xv. 18; 2 Tim. i. 9, ii. 19; Prov. viii. 31; Jer. xxxi. 3.

66. Matt. xi. 25, 26. "Hoc tanto et ram ineffabili bono, nemo inventus est dignus; sordet natura sine gratia." -- Pros. de lib. Arb. ad Ruff.

67. Mal. iii. 6; James i. 17; ὃς. xi. 9.

68. Rom. ix. 12. "Omnia diligit Deus, quæ fecit; et inter ea magnis diligit creaturas rationales, et de illis eas amplius quæ sunt membra unigeniti sui. Et multo magis ipsum unigenitum." -- August.

69. Eph. ii. 3.

70. Matt. xi. 25, 26; 1 Cor. i. 20.

71. 1 John iv. 16.

72. Cant. vii. 5.

73. Isa. xxxiii. 14.

74. Luke xix. 21.

75. Gen. iii. 5.

76. Ἐφ’ ᾧ πάντες ἥμαρτον, Rom. v. 12.

77. Jer. ii. 5, 21.

78. Isa. xl. 27-29, xlix. 15, 16.

79. Isa. xxvi. 20.

80. Ἐμπαιγμῶν πεῖραν ἔλαβον, Heb. xi. 36. Ὀνειδισμοῖς θεατριζόμενοι, Heb. x. 33.

81. 1 John i. 3.

82. Acts xvii. 6, xxviii. 22.

Part II. Of Communion with the Son Jesus Christ

Chapter I - Of the fellowship which the saints have with Jesus Christ the Son of God -- That they have such a fellowship proved, 1 Cor. i. 9; Rev. iii. 20; Cant. ii. 1-7 opened; also Prov. ix. 1-5.

Of that distinct communion which we have with the person of the Father we have treated in the foregoing chapters; we now proceed to the consideration of that which we have with his Son, Jesus Christ our Lord. Now the fellowship we have with the second person, is with him as Mediator, -- in that office whereunto, by dispensation, he submitted himself for our sakes; being "made of a woman, made under the law, to redeem them that were under the law, that we might receive the adoption of sons," Gal. iv. 4, 5. And herein I shall do these two things:-- I. Declare that we have such fellowship with the Son of God. II. Show wherein that fellowship or communion doth consist:--

I. For the first, I shall only produce some few places of Scripture to confirm it, that it is so:-- 1 Cor. i. 9, "God is faithful, by whom ye were called unto the fellowship of his Son Jesus Christ our Lord." This is that whereunto all the saints are called, and wherein, by the faithfulness of God, they shall be preserved, even fellowship with Jesus Christ our Lord. We are called of God the Father, as the Father, in pursuit of his love, to communion with the Son, as our Lord.

Rev. iii. 20, "Behold, I stand at the door, and knock: if any man hear my voice, and open the door, I will come in to him, and will sup with him, and he with me." [83] Certainly this is fellowship, or I know not what is. Christ will sup with believers: he refreshes himself with his own graces in them, by his Spirit bestowed on them. The Lord Christ is exceedingly delighted in tasting of the sweet fruits of the Spirit in the saints. Hence is that prayer of the spouse that she may have something for his entertainment when he comes to her, Cant. iv. 16, "Awake, O north wind; and come, thou south; blow upon my garden, that the spices thereof may flow out. Let my Beloved come into his garden, and eat his pleasant fruits." The souls of the saints are the garden of Jesus Christ, the good ground, Heb. vi. 7; -- a garden for delight; he rejoices in them; "his delights are with the sons of men," Prov. viii. 31; and he "rejoices over them," Zeph. iii. 17; -- and a garden for fruit, yea, pleasant fruit; so he describes it, Cant. iv. 12-14, "A garden inclosed is my sister, my spouse; a spring shut up, a fountain sealed. Thy plants are an orchard of pomegranates, with pleasant fruits; camphire, with spikenard, spikenard and saffron; calamus and cinnamon, with all trees of frankincense; myrrh and aloes, with all chief spices." Whatever is sweet and delicious for taste, whatever savoury and odoriferous, whatever is useful and medicinal, is in this garden. There is all manner of spiritual refreshments, of all kinds whatever, in the souls of the saints, for the Lord

Jesus. On this account is the spouse so earnest in the prayer mentioned for an increase of these things, that her Beloved may sup with her, as he hath promised. "Awake, O north wind," etc.; -- "O that the breathings and workings of the Spirit of all grace might stir up all his gifts and graces in me, that the Lord Jesus, the beloved of my soul, may have meet and acceptable entertainment from me." God complains of want of fruit in his vineyard, Isa. v. 2; ὅς. x. 1. Want of good food for Christ's entertainment is that the spouse feared, and labours to prevent. A barren heart is not fit to receive him. And the delight he takes in the fruit of the Spirit is unspeakable. This he expresses at large, Cant. v. 1, "I am come," saith he; "I have eaten, I am refreshed." He calls it פְּרִי מְגָדִים, "The fruit of his sweetnesses;" or most pleasant to him. Moreover, as Christ sups with his saints, so he hath promised they shall sup with him, to complete that fellowship they have with him. Christ provides for their entertainment in a most eminent manner. There are beasts killed, and wine is mingled, and a table furnished, Prov. ix. 2. He calls the spiritual dainties that he hath for them a "feast," a "wedding," [84] "a feast of fat things, wine on the lees," etc. The fatted calf is killed for their entertainment. Such is the communion, and such is the mutual entertainment of Christ and his saints in that communion.

Cant. ii. 1-7, "I am the rose of Sharon, and the lily of the valleys. As the lily among thorns, so is my love among the daughters. As the apple-tree among the trees of the wood, so is my Beloved among the sons. I sat down under his shadow with great delight, and his fruit was sweet to my taste," etc.

In the two first verses you have the description that Christ gives, first of himself, then of his church. Of himself, verse 1; that is, what he is to his spouse: "I am the rose of Sharon, and the lily of the valleys." The Lord [85] Christ is, in the Scripture, compared to all things of eminency in the whole creation. He is in the heavens the sun, and the bright morning star: as the lion among the beasts, the lion of the tribe of Judah. Among the flowers of the field, here he is the rose and the lily. The two eminencies of flowers, sweetness of savour and beauty of colour, are divided between these. The rose for sweetness, and the lily for beauty ("Solomon in all his glory was not arrayed like one of these"), have the pre-eminence. Farther, he is "the rose of Sharon," a fruitful plain, where the choicest herds were fed, 1 Chron. xxvii. 29; so eminent, that it is promised to the church that there shall be given unto her the [86] excellency of Sharon, Isa. xxxv. 2. This fruitful place, doubtless, brought forth the most precious roses. Christ, in the savour of his love, and in his righteousness (which is as the garment wherein Jacob received his blessing, giving forth a smell as the smell of a pleasant field, Gen. xxvii. 27), is as this excellent rose, to draw and allure the hearts of his saints unto him. As God smelled a sweet savour from the blood of his atonement, Eph. v. 2; so from the graces wherewith for them he is anointed, his saints receive a refreshing, cherishing savour, Cant. i. 3. A sweet savour expresses that which is acceptable and delightful, Gen. viii. 21. He is also "the lily of the valleys;" that of all flowers is the most eminent in beauty, Matt. vi. 29. Most desirable is he, for the comeliness and perfection of his person; incomparably fairer than the children of men: of which afterward. He, then, being thus unto them (abundantly satiating all their spiritual senses) their refreshment, their ornament, their delight, their glory; in the next verse he tells us what they are to him: "As the lily among thorns, so is my beloved among the daughters." That Christ and his church are likened unto and termed the same thing (as here the lily), is, as from their union by the indwelling of the same Spirit, so from that [87] conformity and likeness that is between them, and whereunto the saints are appointed. Now she is a lily, very beautiful unto Christ; "as the lily among thorns:" -- 1. By the way of eminency; as the lily excelleth the thorns, so do the saints all others whatever, in the eye of Christ. Let comparison be made, so will it be found to be. And, -- 2. By the way of trial; the residue of the world being "pricking briers and grieving thorns to the house of Israel," Ezek. xxviii. 24. "The best of them is as a brier, the most upright is sharper than a thorn hedge," Mic. vii. 4. And thus are they among the daughters, -- even the most eminent collections of the most improved professors, that are no more but so. There cannot be in any greater comparison, a greater exaltation of the excellency of any thing. So, then, is Christ to them indeed, verse 1; so are they in his esteem, and indeed, verse 2. How he is in their esteem and indeed, we have, verse 3.

"As the apple-tree among the trees of the wood, so is my Beloved among the sons. I sat down under his shadow with great delight, and his fruit was sweet to my taste." To carry on this intercourse, the spouse begins to speak her thoughts of, and to show her delight in, the Lord Christ; and as he compares her to the lily among the thorns, so she him to the apple-tree among the trees of the wood. And she adds this reason of it, even because he hath the two eminent things of trees, which the residue of them have not:-- 1. Fruit for food; 2. Shade for refreshment. Of the one she eateth, under the other she resteth; both with great delight. All other sons, either angels, the sons of God by creation, Job i. 6, xxxviii. 7, or the sons of Adam, -- the best of his offspring, the leaders of those companies which, verse 2, are called daughters, or sons of the old creation, the top branches of all its desirable things, -- are to an hungry, weary soul (such alone seek for shade and fruit) but as the fruitless, leafless trees of the forest, which will yield them neither food nor refreshment. "In Christ," saith she, "there is fruit, fruit sweet to the taste; yea, his flesh is meat indeed, and his blood is drink indeed,'?" John vi. 55. "Moreover, he hath brought forth that everlasting righteousness which will abundantly satisfy any hungry soul, after it hath gone to many a barren tree for food, and hath found none. Besides, he aboundeth in precious and pleasant graces, whereof I may [88] eat; yea, he calls me to do so, and that abundantly." These are the fruits that Christ beareth. They speak of a tree that bringeth forth all things needful for life, in food and raiment. Christ is that tree of life, which hath brought forth all things that are needful unto life eternal. In him is that righteousness which we [89] hunger after; -- in him is that water of life, which whoso [90] drinketh of shall thirst no more. Oh, how sweet are the fruits of Christ's mediation to the faith of his saints! He that can find no relief in mercy, pardon, grace, acceptation with God, holiness, sanctification, etc., is an utter stranger to these things ([91] wine on the lees) that are prepared for believers. Also, he hath shades for refreshment and shelter; -- shelter from wrath without, and refreshment because of weariness from within. The first use of the [92] shade is to keep us from the heat of the sun, as did Jonah's gourd. When the heat of wrath is ready to scorch the soul, Christ, interposing, bears it all. Under the shadow of his wings we sit down constantly, quietly, safely, putting our trust in him; and all this with great delight. Yea, who can express the joy of a soul safe shadowed from wrath under the covert of the righteousness of the Lord Jesus! There is also refreshment in a shade from weariness. He is "as the shadow of a great rock in a weary land," Isa. xxxii. 2. From the power of corruptions, trouble of temptations, distress of persecutions, there is in him quiet, rest, and repose, Matt. xi. 27, 28.

Having thus mutually described each other, and so made it manifest that they cannot but be delighted in fellowship and communion, in the next verses that communion of theirs is at large set forth and described. I shall briefly observe four things therein:-- (1.) Sweetness. (2.) Delight. (3.) Safety. (4.) Comfort.

(1.) Sweetness: "He brought me to the banqueting-house," or "house of wine." It is all set forth under expressions of the greatest sweetness and most delicious refreshment, -- flagons, apples, wine, etc. "He entertains me," saith the spouse, "as some great personage." Great personages, at great entertainments, are had into the banqueting-house, -- the house of wine and dainties. These are the preparations of grace and mercy, -- love, kindness, supplies revealed in the gospel, declared in the assemblies of the saints, exhibited by the Spirit. This "love is better than wine," Cant. i. 2; it is "not meat and drink, but righteousness, and [93] peace, and joy in the Holy Ghost." Gospel dainties are sweet refreshments; whether these houses of wine be the Scriptures, the gospel, or the ordinances dispensed in the assemblies of the saints, or any eminent and signal manifestations of special love (as banqueting is not every day's work, nor used at ordinary entertainments), it is all one. Wine, that cheereth the heart of man, that makes him forget his misery, Prov. xxxi. 6, 7, that gives him a cheerful look and countenance, Gen. xlix. 12, is that which is promised. The grace exhibited by Christ in his ordinances is refreshing, strengthening, comforting, and full of sweetness to the souls of the saints. Woe be to such full souls as loathe these honey-combs! But thus Christ makes all his assemblies to be banqueting-houses; and there he gives his saints entertainment.

(2.) Delight. The spouse is quite ravished with the sweetness of this entertainment, finding love, and care, and kindness, bestowed by Christ in the assemblies of the saints. Hence she cries out, verse 5, "Stay me with flagons, comfort me with apples; for I am sick of love." Upon the discovery of the excellency and sweetness of Christ in the banqueting-house, the soul is instantly overpowered, and cries out to be made partaker of the fulness of it. She is "sick of love:" not (as some suppose) fainting for want of a sense of love, under the apprehension of wrath; but made sick and faint, even overcome, with the mighty actings of that divine affection, after she had once tasted of the sweetness of Christ in the banqueting-house. Her desire deferred, makes her heart sick; therefore she cries, "Stay me," etc.; -- "I have seen a glimpse of the King in his beauty,' -- tasted of the fruit of his righteousness; my soul melteth in longing after him. Oh! support and sustain my spirit with his presence in his ordinances, -- those flagons and apples of his banqueting-house,' -- or I shall quite sink and faint! Oh, what hast thou done, blessed Jesus! I have seen thee, and my soul is become as the chariots of Ammi-nadib. Let me have something from thee to support me, or I die." When a person is fainting on any occasion, these two things are to be done:-- strength is to be used to support him, that he sink not to the ground; and comfortable things are to be applied, to refresh his spirits. These two the soul, overpowered and fainting with the force of its own love, (raised by a sense of Christ's,) prayeth for. It would have strengthening grace to support it in that condition, that it may be able to attend its duty; and consolations of the Holy Ghost, to content, revive, and satiate it, until it come to a full enjoyment of Christ. And thus sweetly and with delight is this communion carried on.

(3.) Safety: "His banner over me was love," verse 4. The banner is an emblem of safety and protection, -- a sign of the presence of an host. Persons belonging to an army do encamp under their banner in security. So did the children of Israel in the wilderness; every tribe kept their camps under their own standard. It is also a token of success and victory, Ps. xx. 5. Christ hath a banner for his saints; and that is love. All their protection is from his love; and they shall have all the protection his love can give them. This safeguards them from hell, death, -- all their enemies. Whatever presses on them, it must pass through the banner of the love of the Lord Jesus. They have, then, great spiritual safety; which is another ornament or excellency of their communion with him.

(4.) Supportment and consolation, verse 6, "His left hand is under my head, and his right hand doth embrace me." Christ here hath the posture of a most tender friend towards any one in sickness and sadness. The soul faints with love, -- spiritual longings after the enjoyment of his presence; and Christ comes in with his embraces. He nourisheth and cherisheth his church, Eph. v. 29; Isa. lxiii. 9. Now, "the hand under the head," is supportment, sustaining grace, in pressures and difficulties; and "the hand that doth embrace," the hand upon the heart, is joy and consolation; -- in both, Christ rejoicing, as the "bridegroom rejoiceth over the bride," Isa. lxii. 5. Now, thus to lie in the arms of Christ's love, under a perpetual influence of supportment and refreshment, is certainly to hold communion with him. And hereupon, verse 7, the spouse is most earnest for the continuance of his fellowship, charging all so to demean themselves, that her Beloved be not disquieted, or provoked to depart.

In brief, this whole book is taken up in the description of the communion that is between the Lord Christ and his saints; and therefore, it is very needless to take from thence any more particular instances thereof

I shall only add that of Prov. ix. 1-5, "Wisdom hath builded her house, she hath hewn out her seven pillars; she hath killed her beasts; she hath mingled her wine; she hath also furnished her table. She hath sent forth her maidens: she crieth upon the highest places of the city, Whoso is simple, let him turn in hither: as for him that wanteth understanding, she saith to him, Come, eat of my bread, and drink of the wine which I have mingled."

The Lord Christ, the eternal Wisdom of the Father, and who of God is made unto us wisdom, erects a spiritual house, wherein he makes provision for the entertainment of those guests whom he so freely invites. His church is the house which he hath built on a perfect number of pillars, that it might have a stable foundation: his slain beasts and mingled wine, wherewith his table is furnished, are those spiritual fat things of the gospel, which he hath prepared for those that come in upon his invitation. Surely, to eat of this bread, and drink of this wine, which he hath so graciously prepared, is to hold fellowship with him; for in what ways or things is there nearer communion than in such?

I might farther evince this truth, by a consideration of all the relations wherein Christ and his saints do stand; which necessarily require that there be a communion between them, if we do suppose they are faithful in those relations: but this is commonly treated on, and something will be spoken to it in one signal instance afterward.

Footnotes:

83. John xiv. 23.

84. Isa. xxv. 6; Matt. xxii. 8;
Rev. xix. 7.

85. Mal. iv. 2; Rev. xii. 1;
Luke i. 78; Ἀνατολὴ ἐξ ὕψους·
Numb. xxiv. 17; 2 Pet. i. 19; Rev.
xxii. 16; Gen. xlix. 9; Mic. v. 8;
Rev. v. 5.

86. Isa. xxxiii. 9, lxv. 10.

87. Rom. viii. 29.

88. Cant. v. 1.

89. Matt. v. 6.

90. John iv. 14.

91. Isa. xxv. 6; Prov. ix. 2.

92. Jonah iv. 6; Isa. xxv. 4,
xxxii. 2; 2 Cor. v. 21; Gal. iii. 13;
Mal. iv. 2.

93. Rom. xiv. 17; John vii. 37;
Prov. xxvii. 7.

Chapter II - What it is wherein we have peculiar fellowship with the Lord Christ -- This is in grace -- This proved, John i. 14, 16, 17; 2 Cor. xiii. 14; 2 Thess. iii. 17, 18 -- Grace of various acceptations -- Personal grace in Christ proposed to consideration -- The grace of Christ as Mediator intended, Ps. xlv. 2 -- Cant. v. 10, Christ, how white and ruddy -- His fitness to save, from the grace of union -- His fulness to save -- His suitableness to endear -- These considerations improved.

II. Having manifested that the saints hold peculiar fellowship with the Lord Jesus, it nextly follows that we show wherein it is that they have this peculiar communion with him.

Now, this is in grace. This is everywhere ascribed to him by the way of eminency. John i. 14, "He dwelt among us, full of grace and truth;" -- grace in the truth and substance of it. [94] All that went before was but typical and in representation; in the truth and substance it comes only by Christ. "Grace and truth came by Jesus Christ," verse 17; "and of his fulness have all we received, and grace for grace," verse 16; -- that is, we have communion with him in grace; we receive from him all manner of grace whatever; and therein have we fellowship with him.

So likewise in that apostolical benediction, wherein the communication of spiritual blessings from the several persons unto the saints is so exactly distinguished; it is grace that is ascribed to our Lord Jesus Christ, 2 Cor. xiii. 14, "The grace of the Lord Jesus Christ, and the love of God, and the communion of the Holy Ghost, be with you all."

Yea, Paul is so delighted with this, that he makes it his motto, and the token whereby he would have his epistles known, 2 Thess. iii. 17, 18, "The salutation of Paul with mine own hand, which is the token in every epistle: so I write. The grace of our Lord Jesus Christ be with you all." Yea, he makes these two, "Grace be with you," and, "The Lord Jesus be with you," to be equivalent expressions; for whereas he affirmed the one to be the token in all his epistles, yet sometimes he useth the one only, sometimes the other of these, and sometimes puts them both together. This, then, is that which we are peculiarly to eye in the Lord Jesus, to receive it from him, even grace, gospel-grace, revealed in or exhibited by the gospel. He is the head-stone in the building of the temple of God, to whom "Grace, grace," is to be cried, Zech. iv. 7.

Grace is a word of various acceptations. In its most eminent significations it may be referred unto one of these three heads:--

1. Grace of personal presence and comeliness. [95] So we say, "A graceful

and comely person," either from himself or his ornaments. This in Christ (upon the matter) is the subject of near one-half of the book of Canticles; it is also mentioned, Ps. xlv. 2, "Thou art fairer than the children of men; grace is poured into thy lips." And unto this first head, in respect of Christ, do I refer also that acceptation of grace which, in respect of us, I fix in the third place. Those inconceivable gifts and fruits of the Spirit which were bestowed on him, and brought forth in him, concur to his personal excellency; as will afterward appear.

2. Grace of free favour and acceptance. [96] "By this grace we are saved;" that is, the free favour and gracious acceptation of God in Christ. In this sense is it used in that frequent expression, "If I have found grace in thy sight;" that is, if I be freely and favourably accepted before thee. So he "giveth grace" (that is, favour) "unto the humble," James iv. 6; Gen. xxxix. 21, xli. 37; Acts vii. 10; 1 Sam. ii. 26; 2 Kings xxv. 27, etc.

3. The fruits of the Spirit, sanctifying and renewing our natures, enabling unto good, and preventing from evil, are so termed. Thus the Lord tells Paul, "his grace was sufficient for him;" that is, the assistance against temptation which he afforded him, Col. iii. 16; 2 Cor. viii. 6, 7; Heb. xii. 28.

These two latter, as relating unto Christ in respect of us who receive them, I call purchased grace, being indeed purchased by him for us; and our communion with him therein is termed a "fellowship in his sufferings, and the power of his resurrection," Phil. iii. 10.

1. Let us begin with the first, which I call personal grace; and concerning that do these two things:-- (1.) Show what it is, and wherein it consisteth; I mean the personal grace of Christ. And, -- (2.) Declare how the saints hold immediate communion with him therein.

(1.) To the handling of the first, I shall only premise this observation:-- It is Christ as mediator of whom we speak; and therefore, by the "grace of his person," I understand not, --

[1.] The glorious excellencies of his Deity considered in itself, abstracting from the office which for us, as God and man, he undertook.

[2.] Nor the outward appearance of his human nature, neither when he conversed here on earth, bearing our infirmities (whereof, by reason of the charge that was laid upon him, the prophet gives quite another character, Isa. lii. 14), concerning which some of the ancients were very poetical in their expressions; nor yet as now exalted in glory; -- a vain imagination whereof makes many bear a false, a corrupted respect unto Christ, even upon carnal apprehensions of the mighty exaltation of the human nature; which is but "to know Christ after the flesh," 2 Cor. v. 16, a mischief much improved by the abomination of foolish imagery. But this is that which I intend, -- the graces of the person of Christ as he is vested with the office of mediation, this spiritual eminency, comeliness, and beauty, as appointed and anointed by the Father unto the great work of bringing home all his elect unto his bosom.

Now, in this respect the Scripture describes him as exceeding excellent, comely, and desirable, -- far above comparison with the chiefest, choicest created good, or any endearment imaginable.

Ps. xlv. 2, "Thou art fairer than the children of men: grace is poured into thy lips." [97] He is, beyond comparison, more beautiful and gracious than any here below, יָפְיָפִיתָ, (japhiaphitha); the word is doubled, to increase its significance, and to exalt its subject beyond all comparison. שופרך מלכא משיחא עדיף מבני נשא, says the Chaldee paraphrast: "Thy fairness, O king Messiah, is more excellent than the sons of men." "Pulcher admodum præ filiis hominum;" -- exceeding desirable. Inward beauty and glory is here expressed by that of outward shape, form, and appearance; [98] because that was so much esteemed in those who were to rule or govern. Isa. iv. 2, the prophet, terming of him "The branch of the Lord," and "The fruit of the earth," affirms that he shall be "beautiful and glorious, excellent and comely;" "for in him dwelleth all the fulness of the Godhead bodily," Col. ii. 9.

Cant. v. 9, the spouse is inquired of as to this very thing, even concerning the personal excellencies of the Lord Christ, her beloved: "What is thy Beloved" (say the daughters of Jerusalem) "more than another beloved, O thou fairest among women? what is thy Beloved more than another beloved?" and she returns this answer, verse 10, "My Beloved is white and ruddy, the chiefest among ten thousand;" and so proceedeth to a particular description of him by his excellencies to the end of the chapter, and there concludeth that "he is altogether lovely," verse 16; whereof at large afterward. Particularly, he is here affirmed to be "white and ruddy;" a due mixture of which colours composes the most beautiful complexion.

1st. He is white in the glory of his Deity, and ruddy in the preciousness of his humanity. "His teeth are white with milk, and his eyes are red with wine," Gen. xlix. 12. Whiteness (if I may so say) is the complexion of glory. In that appearance of the Most High, the "Ancient of days," Dan. vii. 9, it is said, "His garment was white as snow, and the hair of his head like the pure wool;" -- and of Christ in his transfiguration, when he had on him a mighty lustre of the Deity, "His face did shine as the sun, and his raiment was white as the light," Matt. xvii. 2; which, in the phrase of another evangelist, is, "White as snow, so as no fuller on earth can white them," Mark ix. 3. It was a divine, heavenly, surpassing glory that was upon him, Rev. i. 14. Hence the angels and glorified saints, that always behold him, and are fully translated into the image of the same glory, are still said to be in white robes. [99] His whiteness is his Deity, and the glory thereof. And on this account the Chaldee paraphrast ascribes this whole passage unto God. "They say," saith he, "to the house of Israel, Who is the God whom thou wilt serve?' etc. Then began the congregation of Israel to declare the praises of the Ruler of the world, and said, I will serve that God who is clothed in a garment white as snow, the splendour of the glory of whose countenance is as fire.'?" He is also ruddy in the beauty of his humanity. Man was called Adam, from the red earth whereof he was made. The word here[100] used points him out as the second Adam, partaker of flesh and blood, because the children also partook of the same, Heb. ii. 14. The beauty and comeliness of the Lord Jesus in the union of both these in one person, shall afterward be declared.

2dly. He is white in the beauty of his innocency and holiness, and ruddy in the blood of his oblation. Whiteness is the badge of innocence and holiness. It is said of the Nazarites, for their typical holiness, "They were purer than snow, they were whiter than milk," Lam. iv. 7. And the prophet shows us that scarlet, red, and crimson, are the colours of sin and guilt; whiteness of innocency, [101] Isa. i. 18. Our Beloved was "a Lamb without blemish and without spot," 1 Pet. i. 19. "He did no sin, neither was guile found in his mouth," 1 Pet. ii. 22. He was "holy, harmless, undefiled, separate from sinners," Heb. vii. 26; as afterward will appear. And yet he who was so white in his innocence, was made ruddy in his own blood; and that two ways:-- Naturally, in the pouring out of his blood, his precious blood, in that agony of his soul when thick drops of blood trickled to the ground, Luke xxii. 44; as also when the whips and thorns, nails and spears, poured it out abundantly: "There came forth blood and water," John xix. 34. He was ruddy by being drenched all over in his own blood. And morally, by the imputation of sin, whose colour is red and crimson. "God made him to be sin for us, who knew no sin," 2 Cor. v. 21. He who was white, became ruddy for our sakes, pouring out his blood an oblation for sin. This also renders him graceful: by his whiteness he fulfilled the law; by his redness he satisfied justice. "This is our Beloved, O ye daughters of Jerusalem."

3dly. His endearing excellency in the administration of his kingdom is hereby also expressed. [102] He is white in love and mercy unto his own; red with justice and revenge towards his enemies, Isa. lxiii. 3; Rev. xix. 13.

There are three things in general wherein this personal excellency and grace of the Lord Christ doth consist:-- (1st.) His fitness to save, from the grace of union, and the proper necessary effects thereof. (2dly.) His fulness to save, from the grace of communion; or the free consequences of the grace of union. (3dly.) His excellency to endear, from his complete suitableness to all the wants of the souls of men:--

(1st.) His fitness to save, -- his being ἱκανός, a fit Saviour, suited to the work; and this, I say, is from his grace of union. The uniting of the natures of God and man in one person made him fit to be a Saviour to the uttermost. He lays his hand upon God, by partaking of his nature, Zech. xiii. 7; and he lays his hand upon us, by being partaker of our nature, Heb. ii. 14, 16: and so becomes a days-man, or umpire between both. By this means he fills up all the distance that was made by sin between God and us; and we who were far off are made nigh in him. Upon this account it was that he had room enough in his breast to receive, and power enough in his spirit to bear, all the wrath that was prepared for us. Sin was infinite only in respect of the object; and punishment was infinite in respect of the subject. This ariseth from his union.

Union is the conjunction of the two natures of God and man in one person, John i. 14; Isa. ix. 6; Rom. i. 3, ix. 5. The necessary consequences whereof are, --

[1st.] The subsistence of the human nature in the person of the Son of God, having no subsistence of its own, Luke i. 35; 1 Tim. iii. 16.

[2dly.] Κοινωνία ἰδιωμάτων, -- that communication of attributes in the person, whereby the properties of either nature are promiscuously spoken of the person of Christ, under what name soever, of God or man, he be spoken of, Acts xx. 28, iii. 21.

[3dly.] The execution of his office of mediation in his single person, in respect of both natures: wherein is considerable, ὁ ἐνεργῶν, -- the agent, Christ himself, God and man. He is the principium quo, ἐνεργητικὸν, -- the principle that gives life and efficacy to the whole work; and then, 2dly, The principium quod, -- that which operates, which is both natures distinctly considered. 3dly. The ἐνέργεια, or δραστικὴ τῆς φύσεως κινησις, -- the effectual working itself of each nature. And, lastly, the ἐνέργημα, or ἀποτέλεσμα, -- the effect produced, which ariseth from all, and relates to them all: so resolving the excellency I speak of into his personal union.

(2dly.) His fulness to save, from the grace of communion or the effects of his union, which are free; and consequences of it, which is all the furniture that he received from the Father by the unction of the Spirit, for the work of our salvation: "He is able also to save them to the uttermost that come unto God by him," Heb. vii. 25; having all fulness unto this end communicated unto him: "for it pleased the Father that in him should all fulness dwell," Col. i. 19; and he received not "the Spirit by measure," John iii. 34. And from this fulness he makes out a suitable supply unto all that are his; "grace for grace," John i. 16. Had it been given to him by measure, we had exhausted it.

(3dly.) His excellency to endear, from his complete suitableness to all the wants of the souls of men. There is no man whatever, that hath any want in reference unto the things of God, but Christ will be unto him that which he wants: I speak of those who are given him of his Father. Is he dead? [103] Christ is life. Is he weak? Christ is the power of God, and the wisdom of God. Hath he the sense of guilt upon him? Christ is complete righteousness, -- "The Lord our Righteousness." Many poor creatures are sensible of their wants, but know not where their remedy lies. Indeed, whether it be life or light, power or joy, all is wrapped up in him.

This, then, for the present, may suffice in general to be spoken of the personal grace of the Lord Christ:-- He hath a fitness to save, having pity and ability, tenderness and power, to carry on that work to the uttermost; and a fulness to save, of redemption and sanctification, of righteousness and the Spirit; and a suitableness to the wants of all our souls: whereby he becomes exceedingly desirable, yea, altogether lovely; as afterward will appear in particular. And as to this, in the first place, the saints have distinct fellowship with the Lord Christ; the manner whereof shall be declared in the ensuing chapter.

Only, from this entrance that hath been made into the description of him with whom the saints have communion, some motives might be taken to stir us up whereunto; as also considerations to lay open the nakedness and insufficiency of all other ways and things unto which men engage their thoughts and desires, something may be now proposed. The daughters of Jerusalem, ordinary, common professors, having heard the spouse describing her Beloved, Cant. v. 10-16, etc., instantly are stirred up to seek him together with her; chap. vi. 1, "Whither is thy Beloved turned aside? that we may seek him with thee." What Paul says of them that crucified him, may be spoken of all that reject him, or refuse communion with him: "Had they known him, they would not have crucified the Lord of glory;" -- Did men know him, were they acquainted in any measure with him, they would not so reject the Lord of glory. Himself calls them "simple ones," "fools," and "scorners," that despise his gracious invitation, Prov. i. 22. There are none who despise Christ, but only they that know him not; whose eyes the god of this world hath blinded, that they should not behold his glory. The souls of men do naturally seek something to rest and repose themselves upon, -- something to satiate and delight themselves withal, with which they [may] hold communion; and there are two ways whereby men proceed in the pursuit of what they so aim at. Some set before them some certain end, -- perhaps pleasure, profit, or, in religion itself, acceptance with God; others seek after some end, but without any certainty, pleasing themselves now with one path, now with another, with various thoughts and ways, like them, Isa. lvii. 10 -- because something comes in by the life of the hand, they give not over though weary. In what condition soever you may be (either in greediness pursuing some certain end, be it secular or religious; or wandering away in your own imaginations, wearying yourselves in the largeness of your ways), compare a little what you aim at, or what you do, with what you have already heard of Jesus Christ: if any thing you design be like to him, if any thing you desire be equal to him, let him be rejected as one that hath neither form nor comeliness in him; but if, indeed, all your ways be but vanity and vexation of spirit, in comparison of him, why do you spend your "money for that which is not bread, and your labour for that which satisfieth not?"

Use 1. You that are yet in the flower of your days, full of health and strength, and, with all the vigour of your spirits, do pursue some one thing, some another, consider, I pray, what are all your beloveds to this Beloved? What have you gotten by them? Let us see the peace, quietness, assurance of everlasting blessedness that they have given you? Their paths are crooked paths, whoever goes in them shall not know peace. Behold here a fit object for your choicest affections, -- one in whom you may find rest to your souls, -- one in whom there is nothing will grieve and trouble you to eternity. Behold, he stands at the door of your souls, and knocks: O reject him not, lest you seek him and find him not! Pray study him a little; you love him not, because you know him not. Why doth one of you spend his time in idleness and folly, and wasting of precious time, perhaps debauchedly? Why doth another associate and assemble himself with them that scoff at religion and the things of God? Merely because you know not our dear Lord Jesus. Oh, when he shall reveal himself to you, and tell you he is Jesus whom you have slighted and refused, how will it break your hearts, and make you mourn like a dove, that you have neglected him! and if you never come to know him, it had been better you had never been. Whilst it is called To-day, then, harden not your hearts.

Use 2. You that are, perhaps, seeking earnestly after a righteousness, and are religious persons, consider a little with yourselves, -- hath Christ his due place in your hearts? is he your all? doth he dwell in your thoughts? do you know him in his excellency and desirableness? do you indeed account all things "loss and dung" for his exceeding excellency? or rather, do you prefer almost any thing in the world before it? But more of these things afterward.

Footnotes:

94. Acts xv. 11; Rom. xvi. 24; 1 Cor. xvi. 23; 2 Cor. xiii. 14; Gal. vi. 18; Eph. vi. 24.

95. Prov. i. 9, iii. 22, 34; Cant. iii. 6-11, v. 9-16, etc.

96. Ezra ix. 8; Acts iv. 33; Luke ii. 40; Esther ii. 17; Ps. lxxxiv. 11; Eph. ii. 6; Acts xv. 40, xviii. 27; Rom. i. 7, iv. 4, 16, v. 2, 20, xi. 5, 6; 2 Thess. ii. 16; Tit. iii. 7; Rev. i. 4, etc.

97. Isa. xi. 1; Jer. xxiii. 5, xxxiii. 15; Zech. iii. 8, vi. 12.

98. Ὅς ἡδὺ καλὸς ὅταν ἔχει νοῦν σώφρονα πρῶτον μὲν εἶδος ἄξιον τυραννίδος. -- Porphyr. in Isag. Inde Suetonius de Domitiano. "Commendari se verecundiâ oris adeo sentiebat, ut apud senatum sic quondam jactaverit; usque adhuc certe animum meum probastis et vultum." -- Sueton. Domit., cap. xviii. "Formæ elegantia in Rege laudatur, non quod per se decor oris magni æstimari debeat, sed quia in ipso vultu sæpe reluceat

generosa indoles." -- Calvin in loc.

99. Rev. iii. 4, 5, vi. 11, vii. 9, 13, xix. 14.

100. דּוֹדִי צַח וְאָדוֹם, Cant. v. 10.

101. "Alii candidum exponunt esse puris et probis, rubrum et cruentum reprobis ad eos puniendos ut Isaia, cap. lxiii.

dicitur, מַדּוּעַ אָדֹם לִלְבוּשֶׁךָ. Cur rubet vestimenta tua? quod nostri minus recte de Christi passione exponunt." -- Mercer. in loc.

102. Rev. vi. 2.

103. Col. iii. 4; 1 Cor. i. 24, 30; Jer. xxiii. 6.

Chapter III - Of the way and manner whereby the saints hold communion with the Lord Christ as to personal grace -- The conjugal relation between Christ and the saints, Cant. ii. 16; Isa. liv. 5, etc.; Cant. iii. 11, opened -- The way of communion in conjugal relation, Hos. iii. 3; Cant. i. 15 -- On the part of Christ -- On the part of the saints.

(2.) The next thing that comes under consideration is, the way whereby we hold communion with the Lord Christ, in respect of that personal grace whereof we have spoken. Now, this the Scripture manifests to be by the way of a conjugal relation. He is married unto us, and we unto him; which spiritual relation is attended with suitable conjugal affections. And this gives us fellowship with him as to his personal excellencies.

This the spouse expresseth, Cant. ii. 16, "My Beloved is mine, and I am his;" -- "He is mine, I possess him, I have interest in him, as my head and my husband; and I am his, possessed of him, owned by him, given up unto him: and that as to my Beloved in a conjugal relation."

So Isa. liv. 5, "Thy Maker is thine husband; the Lord of hosts is his name; and thy Redeemer the Holy One of Israel; The God of the whole earth shall he be called." This is yielded as the reason why the church shall not be ashamed nor confounded, in the midst of her troubles and trials, -- she is married unto her Maker, and her Redeemer is her husband. And Isaiah, chap. lxi. 10, setting out the mutual glory of Christ and his church in their walking together, he saith it is "as a bridegroom decketh himself with ornaments, and as a bride adorneth herself with jewels." Such is their condition, because such is their relation; which he also farther expresseth, chap. lxii. 5, "As the bridegroom rejoiceth over the bride, so shall thy God rejoice over thee." As it is with such persons in the day of their espousals, in the day of the gladness of their hearts, so is it with Christ and his saints in this relation. He is a husband to them, providing that it may be with them according to the state and condition whereinto he hath taken them.

To this purpose we have his faithful engagement, ὅς. ii. 19, 20, "I will," saith he, "betroth thee unto me for ever; yea, I will betroth thee unto me in righteousness, and in judgment, and in loving-kindness, and in mercies. I will even betroth thee unto me in faithfulness." And it is the main design of the ministry of the gospel, to prevail with men to give up themselves unto the Lord Christ, as he reveals his kindness in this engagement. Hence Paul tells the Corinthians, 2 Cor. xi. 2, that he had "espoused them unto one husband, that he might present them as a chaste virgin unto Christ." This he had prevailed upon them for, by the preaching of the gospel, that they should give up themselves as a virgin, unto him who had betrothed them to himself as a husband.

And this is a relation wherein the Lord Jesus is exceedingly delighted, and inviteth others to behold him in this his glory, Cant. iii. 11, "Go forth," saith he, "O ye daughters of Jerusalem, and behold king Solomon with the crown wherewith his mother crowned him in the day of his espousals, and in the day of the gladness of his heart." He calls forth the daughters of Jerusalem (all sorts of professors) to consider him in the condition of betrothing and espousing his church unto himself. Moreover, he tells them that they shall find on him two things eminently upon this account:-- 1. Honour. It is the day of his coronation, and his spouse is the crown wherewith he is crowned. For as Christ is a diadem of beauty and a crown of glory unto Zion, Isa. xxviii. 5; so Zion also is a diadem and a crown unto him, Isa. lxii. 3. Christ makes this relation with his saints to be his glory and his honour. 2. Delight. The day of his espousals, of taking poor sinful souls into his bosom, is the day of the gladness of his heart. John was but the friend of the Bridegroom, that stood and heard his voice, when he was taking his bride unto himself; and he rejoiced greatly, John iii. 29: how much more, then, must be the joy and gladness of the Bridegroom himself! even that which is expressed, Zeph. iii. 17, "he rejoiceth with joy, he joys with singing."

It is the gladness of the heart of Christ, the joy of his soul, to take poor sinners into this relation with himself. He rejoiced in the thoughts of it from eternity, Prov. viii. 31; and always expresseth the greatest willingness to undergo the hard task required thereunto, Ps. xl. 7, 8; Heb. x. 7; yea, he was pained as a woman in travail, until he had accomplished it, Luke xii. 50. Because he loved his church, he gave himself for it, Eph. v. 25, despising the shame, and enduring the cross, Heb. xii. 2, that he might enjoy his bride, -- that he might be for her, and she for him, and not for another, ὅς. iii. 3. This is joy, when he is thus crowned by his mother. It is believers that are mother and brother of this Solomon, Matt. xii. 49, 50. They crown him in the day of his espousals, giving themselves to him, and becoming his glory, 2 Cor. viii. 23.

Thus he sets out his whole communion with his church under this allusion, and that most frequently. The time of his taking the church unto himself is the day of his marriage; and the church is his bride, his wife, Rev. xix. 7, 8. The entertainment he makes for his saints is a wedding supper, Matt. xxii. 3. The graces of his church are the ornaments of his queen, Ps. xlv. 9-14; and the fellowship he hath with his saints is as that which those who are mutually beloved in a conjugal relation do hold, Cant. i. Hence Paul, in describing these two, makes sudden and insensible transitions from one to the other, -- Eph. v., from verse 22 unto verse 32; concluding the whole with an application unto Christ and the church.

It is now to be inquired, in the next place, how it is that we hold communion with the person of Christ in respect of conjugal relations and affections, and wherein this doth consist. Now, herein there are some things that are common unto Christ and the saints, and some things that are peculiar to each of them, as the nature of this relation doth require. The whole may be reduced unto these two heads:-- [1.] A mutual resignation of themselves one to the other; [2.] Mutual, consequential, conjugal affections.

[1.] There is a mutual resignation, or making over of their persons one to another. This is the first act of communion, as to the personal grace of Christ. Christ makes himself over to the soul, to be his, as to all the love, care, and tenderness of a husband; and the soul gives up itself wholly unto the Lord Christ, to be his, as to all loving, tender obedience. And herein is the main of

Christ's and the saints' espousals. This, in the prophet, is set out under a parable of himself and a harlot, ὅϛ. iii. 3, "Thou shalt abide for me," saith he unto her, "thou shalt not be for another, and I will be for thee." -- "Poor harlot," saith the Lord Christ, "I have bought thee unto myself with the price of mine own blood; and now, this is that which we will consent unto, -- I will be for thee, and thou shalt be for me, and not for another."

1st. Christ gives himself to the soul, with all his excellencies, righteousness, preciousness, graces, and eminencies, to be its Saviour, head, and husband, for ever to dwell with it in this holy relation. He looks upon the souls of his saints, likes them well, counts them fair and beautiful, because he hath made them so. Cant. i. 15, "Behold, thou art fair, my companion; behold, thou art fair; thou hast doves' eyes." Let others think what they please, Christ redoubles it, that the souls of his saints are very beautiful, even perfect, through his comeliness, which he puts upon them, Ezek. xvi. 14, -- "Behold, thou art fair, thou art fair:" [104] particularly, that their spiritual light is very excellent and glorious; like the eyes of a dove, tender, discerning, clear, and shining. Therefore he adds that pathetical wish of the enjoyment of this his spouse, Cant. ii. 14, "O my dove," saith he, "that art in the clefts of the rock, in the secret places of the stairs, let me see thy countenance, let me hear thy voice; for sweet is thy voice, and thy countenance is comely;" -- "Do not hide thyself, as one that flies to the clefts of the rocks; be not dejected, as one that hides herself behind the stairs, and is afraid to come forth to the company that inquires for her. Let not thy spirit be cast down at the weakness of thy supplications, let me yet hear thy sighs and groans, thy breathing and partings to me; they are very sweet, very delightful: and thy spiritual countenance, thy appearance in heavenly things, is comely and delightful unto me." Neither doth he leave her thus, but, chap. iv. 8, presseth her hard to a closer [union] with him in this conjugal bond: "Come with me from Lebanon, my spouse, with me from Lebanon: look from the top of Amana, from the top of Shenir and Herman, from the lions' dens, from the mountains of the leopards;" -- "Thou art in a wandering condition (as the Israelites of old), among lions and leopards, sins and troubles; come from thence unto me, and I will give thee refreshment," Matt. xi. 28. Upon this invitation, the spouse boldly concludes, Cant. vii. 10, that the desire of Christ is towards her; that he doth indeed love her, and aim at taking her into this fellowship with himself. So, in carrying on this union, Christ freely bestoweth himself upon the soul. Precious and excellent as he is, he becometh ours. He makes himself to be so; and with him, all his graces. Hence saith the spouse, "?My Beloved is mine;' in all that he is, he is mine." Because he is righteousness, [105] he is "The Lord our Righteousness," Jer. xxiii. 6. Because he is the wisdom of God, and the power of God, he is "made unto us wisdom," etc., 1 Cor. i. 30. Thus, "the branch of the Lord is beautiful and glorious, and the fruit of the earth is excellent and comely for them that are escaped of Israel," Isa. iv. 2. This is the first thing on the part of Christ, -- the free donation and bestowing of himself upon us to be our Christ, our Beloved, as to all the ends and purposes of love, mercy, grace, and glory; whereunto in his mediation he is designed, in a marriage covenant never to be broken. This is the sum of what is intended:-- The Lord Jesus Christ, fitted and prepared, by the accomplishment and furniture of his person as mediator, and the large purchase of grace and glory which he hath made, to be a husband to his saints, his church, tenders himself in the promises of the gospel to them in all his desirableness; convinces them of his good-will towards them, and his all-sufficiency for a supply of their wants; and upon their consent to accept of him, -- which is all he requires or expects at their hands, -- he engageth himself in a marriage covenant to be theirs for ever.

2dly. On the part of the saints, it is their free, willing consent to receive, embrace, and submit unto the Lord Jesus, as their husband, Lord, and Saviour, -- to abide with him, subject their souls unto him, and to be ruled by him for ever.

Now, this in the soul is either initial, or the solemn consent at the first entrance of union; or consequential, in renewed acts of consent all our days. I speak of it especially in this latter sense, wherein it is proper unto communion; not in the former, wherein it primarily intendeth union.

There are two things that complete this self-resignation of the soul:--

(1st.) The liking of Christ, for his excellency, grace, and suitableness, far above all other beloveds whatever, preferring him in the judgment and mind above them all. In the place above mentioned, Cant. v. 9, the spouse being earnestly pressed, by professors at large, to give in her thoughts concerning the excellency of her Beloved in comparison of other endearments, answereth expressly, that he is "the chiefest of ten thousand, yea," verse 16, "altogether lovely," -- infinitely beyond comparison with the choicest created good or endearment imaginable. The soul takes a view of all that is in this world, "the lust of the flesh, the lust of the eyes, and the pride of life," and sees it all to be vanity, -- that "the world passeth away, and the lust thereof," 1 John ii. 16, 17. These beloveds are no way to be compared unto him. It views also legal righteousness, blamelessness before men, uprightness of conversation, duties upon conviction, and concludes of all as Paul doth, Phil. iii. 8, "Doubtless, I count all these things loss for the excellency of the knowledge of Christ Jesus my Lord." So, also, doth the church, ὅς. xiv. 3, reject all appearing assistances whatever, -- as goodly as Asshur, as promising as idols, -- that God alone may be preferred. And this is the soul's entrance into conjugal communion with Jesus Christ as to personal grace, -- the constant preferring him above all pretenders to its affections, counting all loss and dung in comparison of him. Beloved peace, beloved natural relations, beloved wisdom and learning, beloved righteousness, beloved duties, [are] all loss, compared with Christ.

(2dly.) The accepting of Christ by the will, as its only husband, Lord, and Saviour. This is called "receiving" of Christ, John i. 12; and is not intended only for that solemn act whereby at first entrance we close with him, but also for the constant frame of the soul in abiding with him and owning of him as such. When the soul consents to take Christ on his own terms, to save him in his own way, [106] and says, "Lord, I would have had thee and salvation in my way, that it might have been partly of mine endeavours, and as it were by the works of the law; I am now willing to receive thee and to be saved in thy way, -- merely by grace: and though I would have walked according to my own mind, yet now I wholly give up myself to be ruled by thy Spirit: for in thee have I righteousness and strength, [107] in thee am I justified and do glory;" -- then doth it carry on communion with Christ as to the grace of his person. This it is to receive the Lord Jesus in his comeliness and eminency. Let believers exercise their hearts abundantly unto this thing. This is choice communion with the Son Jesus Christ. Let us receive him in all his excellencies, as he bestows himself upon us; -- be frequent in thoughts of faith, comparing him with other beloveds, sin, world, legal righteousness; and preferring him before them, counting them all loss and dung in comparison of him. And let our souls be persuaded of his sincerity and willingness in giving himself, in all that he is, as mediator unto us, to be ours; and let our hearts give up themselves unto him. Let us tell him that we will be for him, and not for another: let him know it from us; he delights to hear it, yea, he says, "Sweet is our voice, and our countenance is comely;" -- and we shall not fail in the issue of sweet refreshment with him.

Digression I - Some excellencies of Christ proposed to consideration, to endear our hearts unto him -- His description, Cant. v., opened.

To strengthen our hearts in the resignation mentioned of ourselves unto the Lord Christ as our husband, as also to make way for the stirring of us up to those consequential conjugal affections of which mention shall afterward be made, I shall turn aside to a more full description of some of the personal excellencies of the Lord Christ, whereby the hearts of his saints are indeed endeared unto him.

In "The Lord our Righteousness," then, may these ensuing things be considered; which are exceeding suitable to prevail upon our hearts to give up themselves to be wholly his:--

1. He is exceeding excellent and desirable in his [108] Deity, and the glory thereof. He is "Jehovah our Righteousness," Jer. xxiii. 6. In the rejoicing of Zion at his coming to her, this is the bottom, "Behold thy God!" Isa. xl. 9. "We have seen his glory," saith the apostle. What glory is that? "The glory of the only-begotten Son of God," John i. 14. The choicest saints have been afraid and amazed at the beauty of an angel; and the stoutest sinners have trembled at the glory of one of those creatures in a low appearance, representing but the back parts of their glory, who yet themselves, in their highest advancement, do cover their faces at the presence of our Beloved, as conscious to themselves of their utter disability to bear the rays of his glory, Isa. vi. 2; John xii. 39-41. He is "the fellow of the Lord of hosts," Zech. xiii. 7. And though he once appeared in the form of a servant, yet then "he thought it not robbery to be equal with God," Phil. ii. 6. In the glory of this majesty he dwells in light inaccessible. We "cannot by searching find out the Almighty unto perfection: it is as high as heaven; what can we do? deeper than hell; what can we know? the measure thereof is longer than the earth, and broader than the sea," Job xi. 7-9. We may all say one to another of this, "Surely we are more brutish than any man, and have not the understanding of a man. We neither learned wisdom, nor have the knowledge of the holy. Who hath ascended up into heaven, or descended? who hath gathered the wind in his fists? who hath bound the waters in a garment? who hath established all the ends of the earth? what is his name, and what is his Son's name, if ye can tell," Prov. xxx. 2-4.

If any one should ask, now, with them in the Canticles, what is in the Lord Jesus, our beloved, more than in other beloveds, that should make him so desirable, and amiable, and worthy of acceptation? what is he more than others? I ask, What is a king more than a beggar? Much every way. Alas! this is nothing; they were born alike, must die alike, and after that is the judgment.

What is an angel more than a worm? A worm is a creature, and an angel is no more; he hath made the one to creep in the earth, -- made also the other to dwell in heaven. There is still a proportion between these, they agree in something; but what are all the nothings of the world to the God infinitely blessed for evermore? Shall the dust of the balance, or the drop of the bucket be laid in the scale against him? This is he of whom the sinners in Zion are afraid, and cry, "Who amongst us shall dwell with the devouring fire, who amongst us shall dwell with everlasting burnings?" I might now give you a glimpse of his excellency in many of those properties and attributes by which he discovers himself to the faith of poor sinners; but as he that goes into a garden where there are innumerable flowers in great variety, gathers not all he sees, but crops here and there one, and another, I shall endeavour to open a door, and give an inlet into the infinite excellency of the graces of the Lord Jesus, as he is "God blessed for evermore," -- presenting the reader with one or two instances, leaving him to gather for his own use what farther he pleaseth. Hence, then, observe, --

The endless, bottomless, boundless grace and compassion that is in him who is thus our husband, as he is the God of Zion. It is not the grace of a creature, nor all the grace that can possibly at once dwell in a created nature, that will serve our turn. We are too indigent to be suited with such a supply. There was a fulness of grace in the human nature of Christ, -- he received not "the Spirit by measure," John iii. 34; a fulness like that of light in the sun, or of water in the sea (I speak not in respect of communication, but sufficiency); a fulness incomparably above the measure of angels: yet it was not properly an infinite fulness, -- it was a created, and therefore a limited fulness. If it could be conceived as separated from the Deity, surely so many thirsty, guilty souls, as every day drink deep and large draughts of grace and mercy from him, would (if I may so speak) sink him to the very bottom; nay, it could afford no supply at all, but only in a moral way. But when the conduit of his humanity is inseparably united to the infinite, inexhaustible fountain of the Deity, who can look into the depths thereof? If, now, there be grace enough for sinners in an all-sufficient God, it is in Christ; and, indeed, in any other there cannot be enough. The Lord gives this reason for the peace and confidence of sinners, Isa. liv. 4, 5, "Thou shalt not be ashamed, neither be thou confounded; for thou shalt not be put to shame." But how shall this be? So much sin, and not ashamed! so much guilt, and not confounded! "Thy Maker," saith he, "is thine husband; the Lord of hosts is his name; and thy Redeemer the Holy One of Israel; The God of the whole earth shall he be called." This is the bottom of all peace, confidence, and consolation, -- the grace and mercy of our Maker, of the God of the whole earth. So are kindness and power tempered in him; he makes us, and mars us, -- he is our God and our Goël, our Redeemer. "Look unto me," saith he, "and be ye saved; for I am God, and none else," Isa. xlv. 22, "Surely, shall one say, In the Lord have I righteousness," verse 24.

And on this ground it is that if all the world should (if I may so say) set themselves to drink free grace, mercy, and pardon, drawing [109] water continually from the wells of salvation; if they should set themselves to draw from one single promise, an angel standing by and crying, "Drink, O my friends, yea, drink abundantly, take so much grace and pardon as shall be abundantly sufficient for the world of sin which is in every one of you;" -- they would not be able to sink the grace of the promise one hair's breadth. There is enough for millions of worlds, if they were; because it flows into it from an infinite, bottomless fountain. "Fear not, O worm Jacob, I am God, and not man," is the bottom of sinners' consolation. This is that "head of gold" mentioned, Cant. v. 11, that most precious fountain of grace and mercy. This infiniteness of grace, in respect of its spring and fountain, will answer all objections that might hinder our souls from drawing nigh to communion with him, and from a free embracing of him. Will not this suit us in all our distresses? What is our finite guilt before it? Show me the sinner that can spread his iniquities to the dimensions (if I may so say) of this grace. Here is mercy enough for the greatest, the oldest, the stubbornest transgressor, -- "Why will ye die, O house of Israel?" Take heed of them who would rob you of the Deity of Christ. If there were no more grace for me than what can be treasured up in a mere man, I should rejoice [if] my portion might be under rocks and mountains.

Consider, hence, his eternal, free, unchangeable love. Were the love of Christ unto us but the love of a mere man, though never so excellent, innocent, and glorious, it must have a beginning, it must have an ending, and perhaps be fruitless. The love of Christ in his human nature towards his is exceeding, intense, tender, precious, compassionate, abundantly heightened by a sense of our miseries, feeling of our wants, experience of our temptations; all flowing from that rich stock of grace, pity, and compassion, which, on purpose for our good and supply, was bestowed on him: but yet this love, as such, cannot be infinite nor eternal, nor from itself absolutely unchangeable. Were it no more, though not to be paralleled nor fathomed, yet our Saviour could not say of it, as he doth, "As the Father hath loved me, so have I loved you," John xv. 9. His love could not be compared with and equalled unto the divine love of the Father, in those properties of eternity, fruitfulness, and unchangeableness, which are the chief anchors of the soul, rolling itself on the bosom of Christ. But now, --

(1.) It is eternal: "Come ye near unto me, hear ye this; I have not," saith he, "spoken in secret from the beginning; from the time that it was, there am I: and now the Lord God, and his Spirit, hath sent me," Isa. xlviii. 16. He himself is "yesterday, today, and for ever," Heb. xiii. 8; and so is his love, being his who is "Alpha and Omega, the first and the last, the beginning and the ending, which is, which was, and which is to come," Rev. i. 11.

(2.) Unchangeable. Our love is like ourselves; as we are, so are all our affections: so is the love of Christ like himself. We love one, one day, and hate him the next. He changeth, and we change also: this day he is our right hand, our right eye; the next day, "Cut him off, pluck him out." [110] Jesus Christ is still the same; and so is his love. "In the beginning he laid the foundation of the earth; and the heavens are the works of his hands; they shall perish, but he remaineth: they all shall wax old as doth a garment; and as a vesture shall he fold them up, and they shall be changed: but he is the same, and his years fail not," Heb. i. 10-12. He is the Lord, and he changeth not; and therefore we are not consumed. Whom he loves, he loves unto the end. [111] His love is such as never had beginning, and never shall have ending.

(3.) It is also fruitful, -- fruitful in all gracious issues and effects. A man may love another as his own soul, yet perhaps that love of his cannot help him. He may thereby pity him in prison, but not relieve him; bemoan him in misery, but not help him; suffer with him in trouble, but not ease him. We cannot love grace into a child, nor mercy into a friend; we cannot love them into heaven, though it may be the great desire of our soul. It was love that made Abraham cry, "O that Ishmael might live before thee!" but it might not be. But now the love of Christ, being the love of God, is effectual and fruitful in producing all the good things which he willeth unto his beloved. He loves life, grace, and holiness into us; he loves us also into covenant, loves us into heaven. Love in him is properly to will good to any one: whatever good Christ by his love wills to any, that willing is operative of that good.

These three qualifications of the love of Christ make it exceedingly eminent, and him exceeding desirable. How many millions of sins, in every one of the elect, every one whereof were enough to condemn them all, hath this love overcome! what mountains of unbelief doth it remove! Look upon the conversation of any one saint, consider the frame of his heart, see the many stains and spots, the defilements and infirmities, wherewith his life is contaminated, and tell me whether the love that bears with all this be not to be admired. And is it not the same towards thousands every day? What streams of grace, purging, pardoning, quickening, assisting, do flow from it every day! This is our Beloved, O ye daughters of Jerusalem.

2. He is desirable and worthy our acceptation, as considered in his humanity; even therein also, in reference to us, he is exceedingly desirable. I shall only, in this, note unto you two things:-- (1.) Its freedom from sin; (2.) Its fulness of grace; -- in both which regards the Scripture sets him out as exceedingly lovely and amiable.

(1.) He was free from sin; -- the [112] Lamb of God, without spot, and without blemish; the male of the flock, to be offered unto God, the curse falling on all other oblations, and them that offer them, Mal. i. 14. The purity of the snow is not to be compared with the whiteness of this lily, of this [113] rose of Sharon, even from the womb: "For such an high priest became us, who is holy, harmless, undefiled, separate from sinners," Heb. vii. 26. Sanctified persons, whose stains are in any measure washed away, are exceeding fair in the eye of Christ himself. "Thou [114] art all fair," saith he, "my love, thou hast no spot in thee." How fair, then, is he who never had the least spot or stain!

It is true, Adam at his creation had this spotless purity; so had the angels: but they came immediately from the [115] hand of God, without concurrence of any secondary cause. Jesus Christ [116] is a plant and root out of a dry ground, a blossom from the stem of Jesse, a bud from the loins of sinful man, -- born of a sinner, after there had been no innocent flesh in the world for four thousand years, every one upon the roll of his genealogy being infected therewithal. To have a flower of wonderful rarity to grow in paradise, a garden of God's own planting, not sullied in the least, is not so strange; but, as the psalmist speaks (in another kind), to hear of it in a wood, to find it in a forest, to have a spotless bud brought forth in the wilderness of corrupted nature, is a thing which angels may desire to look into. Nay, more, this whole nature was not only defiled, but also accursed; not only unclean, but also guilty, -- guilty of Adam's transgression, in whom we have all sinned. That the human nature of Christ should be derived from hence free from guilt, free from pollution, this is to be adored.

Objection. But you will say, "How can this be? who can bring a clean thing from an unclean? How could Christ take our nature, and not the defilements of it, and the guilt of it? If [117] Levi paid tithes in the loins of Abraham, how is it that Christ did not sin in the loins of Adam?"

Answer. There are two things in original sin:--

[1.] Guilt of the first sin, which is imputed to us. We all sinned in him. Ἐφ’ ᾧ πάντες ἥμαρτον, Rom. v. 12, whether we render it relatively "in whom," or illatively, "being all have sinned," all is one: that one sin is the sin of us all, -- "omnes eramus unus ille homo." We were all in covenant with him; he was not only a natural head, but also a federal head unto us. As Christ is to believers, Rom. v. 17; 1 Cor. xv. 22, so was he to us all; and his transgression of that covenant is reckoned to us.

[2.] There is the derivation of a polluted, corrupted nature from him: [118] "Who can bring a clean thing out of an unclean?" "That which is born of the flesh is flesh," and nothing else; whose wisdom and mind is corrupted also: a polluted fountain will have polluted streams. The first person corrupted nature, and that nature corrupts all persons following. Now, from both these was Christ most free:--

1st. He was never federally in Adam, and so not liable to the imputation of his sin on that account. It is true that sin was imputed to him when he was made sin; [119] thereby he took away the sin of the world, John i. 29: but it was imputed to him in the covenant of the Mediator, through his voluntary susception, and not in the covenant of Adam, by a legal imputation. Had it been reckoned to him as a descendant from Adam, he had not been a fit high priest to have offered sacrifices for us, as not being "separate from sinners," Heb. vii. 26. Had Adam stood in his innocence, Christ had not been incarnate, to have been a mediator for sinners; and therefore the counsel of his incarnation, morally, took not place [120] until after the fall. Though he was in Adam in a natural sense from his first creation, in respect of the purpose of God, Luke iii. 23, 38, yet he was not in him in a law sense until after the fall: so that, as to his own person, he had no more to do with the first sin of Adam, than with any personal sin of [any] one whose punishment he voluntarily took upon him; as we are not liable to the guilt of those progenitors who followed Adam, though naturally we were no less in them than in him. Therefore did he, all the days of his flesh, serve God in a covenant of works; and was therein accepted with him, having done nothing that should disannul the virtue of that covenant as to him. This doth not, then, in the least take off from his perfection.

2dly. For the pollution of our nature, it was prevented in him from the instant of conception, Luke i. 35, "The Holy Ghost shall come upon thee, and the power of the Highest shall overshadow thee: therefore also that holy thing that shall be born of thee shall be called the Son of God." He was "made of a woman," Gal. iv. 4; but that portion whereof he was made was sanctified by the Holy Ghost, that what was born thereof should be a holy thing. Not only the conjunction and union of soul and body, whereby a man becomes partaker of his whole nature, and therein of the pollution of sin, being a son of Adam, was prevented by the sanctification of the Holy Ghost, but it also accompanied the very separation of his bodily substance in the womb unto that sacred purpose whereunto it was set apart: so that upon all accounts he is "holy, harmless, undefiled." Add now hereunto, that he "did no sin, neither was guile found in his mouth," 1 Pet. ii. 22; that he "fulfilled all righteousness," Matt. iii. 15; his Father being always "well pleased" with him, verse 17, on the account of his perfect obedience; yea, even in that sense wherein he chargeth his angels with folly, and those inhabitants of heaven are not clean in his sight; and his excellency and desirableness in this regard will lie before us. Such was he, such is he; and yet for our sakes was he contented not only to be esteemed by the vilest of men to be a transgressor, but to undergo from God the punishment due to the vilest sinners. Of which afterward.

(2.) The fulness of grace in Christ's human nature sets forth the amiableness and desirableness thereof. Should I make it my business to consider his perfections, as to this part of his excellency, -- what he had from the womb, Luke i. 35, what received growth and improvement as to exercise in the days of his flesh, Luke ii. 52, with the complement of them all in glory, -- the whole would tend to the purpose in hand. I am but taking a view of these things in transitu. These two things lie in open sight to all at the first consideration:-- all grace was in him, for the kinds thereof; and all degrees of grace, for its perfections; and both of them make up that fulness that was in him. It is created grace that I intend; and therefore I speak of the kinds of it: it is grace inherent in a created nature, not infinite; and therefore I speak of the degrees of it.

For the fountain of grace, the Holy Ghost, he received not him "by measure," John iii. 34; and for the communications of the Spirit, "it pleased the Father that in him should all fulness dwell," Col. i. 19, -- "that in all things he might have the pre-eminence." But these things are commonly spoken unto.

This is the Beloved of our souls, "holy, harmless, undefiled;" "full of grace and truth;" -- [121] full, to a sufficiency for every end of grace, -- full, for practice, to be an example to men and angels as to obedience, -- full, to a certainty of uninterrupted communion with God, -- full, to a readiness of giving supply to others, -- full, to suit him to all the occasions and necessities of the souls of men, -- full, to a glory not unbecoming a subsistence in the person of the Son of God, -- full, to a perfect victory, in trials, over all temptations, -- full, to an exact correspondence to the whole law, every righteous and holy law of God, -- full to the utmost capacity of a limited, created, finite nature, -- full, to the greatest beauty and glory of a living temple of God, -- full, to the full pleasure and delight of the soul of his Father, -- full to an everlasting monument of the glory of God, in giving such inconceivable excellencies to the Son of man.

And this is the second thing considerable for the endearing of our souls to our Beloved.

3. Consider that he is all this in one person. We have not been treating of two, a God and a man; but of [122] one who is God and man. That Word that was with God in the beginning, and was God, John i. 1, is also made flesh, verse 14; -- not by a conversion of itself into flesh; not by appearing in the outward shape and likeness of flesh; but by assuming that holy thing that was born of the virgin, Luke i. 35, into personal union with himself. So "The mighty God," Isa. ix. 6, is a "child given" to us; that holy thing that was born of the virgin is called "The Son of God," Luke i. 35. That which made the man Christ Jesus to be a man, was the union of soul and body; that which made him that man, and without which he was not the man, was the subsistence of both united in the person of the Son of God. As to the proof hereof, I have spoken of it [123] elsewhere at large; I now propose it only in general, to show the amiableness of Christ on this account. Here lies, hence arises, the grace, peace, life, and security of the church, -- of all believers; as by some few considerations may be

clearly evinced:--

(1.) Hence was he fit [124] to suffer and able to bear whatever was due unto us, in that very action wherein the "Son of man gave his life a ransom for many," Matt. xx. 28. "God redeemed his church with his own blood," Acts xx. 28; and therein was the "love of God seen, that he gave his life for us," 1 John iii. 16. On this account was there room, enough in his breast to receive the points of all the [125] swords that were sharpened by the law against us; and strength enough in his shoulders to bear the burden of that curse that was due to us. Thence was he so willing to undertake the work of our redemption, Heb. x. 7, 8, "Lo, I come to do thy will, O God," -- because he knew his ability to go through with it. Had he not been man, he could not have suffered; -- had he not been God, his suffering could not have availed either himself or us, -- he had not satisfied; the suffering of a mere man could not bear any proportion to that which in any respect was infinite. Had the great and righteous God gathered together all the sins that had been committed by his elect from the foundation of the world, and searched the bosoms of all that were to come to the end of the world, and taken them all, from the sin of their nature to the least deviation from the rectitude of his most holy law, and the highest provocation of their regenerate and unregenerate condition, and laid them on a mere holy, innocent, creature; -- O how would they have overwhelmed him, and buried him for ever out of the presence of God's love! Therefore doth the apostle premise that glorious description of him to the purging of our sin: "He hath spoken unto us by his Son, whom he hath appointed heir of all things, by whom also he made the worlds; who being the brightness of his glory, and the express image of his person, and upholding all things by the word of his power," hath "purged our sins." Heb. i. 2, 3. It was he that purged our sins, who was the Son and heir of all things, by whom the world was made, -- the brightness of his Father's glory, and express image of his person; he did it, he alone was able to do it. "God was manifested in the flesh," 1 Tim. iii. 16, for this work. The sword awaked against him that was the fellow of the Lord of hosts, Zech. xiii. 7; and by the wounds of that great shepherd are the sheep healed, 1 Pet. ii. 24, 25.

(2.) Hence doth he become an endless, bottomless fountain of grace to all them that believe. The fulness that it pleased the Father to commit to Christ, to be the great treasury and storehouse of the church, did not, doth not, lie in the human nature, considered in itself; but in the person of the mediator, God and man. Consider wherein his communication of grace doth consist, and this will be evident. The foundation of all is laid in his satisfaction, merit, and purchase; these are the morally procuring cause of all the grace we receive from Christ. Hence all grace becomes to be his; [126] all the things of the new covenant, the promises of God, all the mercy, love, grace, glory promised, became, I say, to be his. Not as though they were all actually invested, or did reside and were in the human nature, and were from thence really communicated to us by a participation of a portion of what did so inhere: but they are morally his, by a [127] compact, to be bestowed by him as he thinks good, as he is mediator, God and man; that is, the only begotten Son made flesh, John i. 14, "from whose fulness we receive, and grace for grace." The real communication of grace is by Christ sending the Holy Ghost to regenerate us, and to create all the habitual grace, with the daily supplies thereof, in our hearts, that we are made partakers of. Now the Holy Ghost is thus sent by Christ as mediator, God and man, as is at large declared, John xiv., xv., xvi.; of which more afterward. This, then, is that which I intend by this fulness of grace that is in Christ, from whence we have both our beginning and all our supplies; which makes him, as he is the Alpha and Omega of his church, the beginner and finisher of our faith, excellent and desirable to our souls: [128] -- Upon the payment of the great price of his blood, and full acquitment on the satisfaction he made, all grace whatever (of which at large afterward) becomes, in a moral sense, his, at his disposal; and he bestows it on, or works it in, the hearts of his by the Holy Ghost, according as, in his infinite wisdom, he sees it needful. How glorious is he to the soul on this consideration! That is most excellent to us which suits us in a wanting condition, -- that which gives bread to the hungry, water to the thirsty, mercy to the perishing. All our reliefs are thus in our Beloved. Here is the life of our souls, the joy of our hearts, our relief against sin and deliverance from the wrath to come.

(3.) Thus is he fitted for a mediator, a days-man, an umpire between God and us, -- being one with him, and one with us, and one in himself in this oneness, in the unity of one person. His ability and universal fitness for his office of mediator are hence usually demonstrated. And herein is he "Christ,[129] the power of God, and the wisdom of God." Herein shines out the infinitely glorious wisdom of God; which we may better admire than express. What soul that hath any acquaintance with these things falls not down with reverence and astonishment? How glorious is he that is the Beloved of our souls! What can be wanting that should encourage us to take up our rest and peace in his bosom? Unless all ways of relief and refreshment be so obstructed by unbelief, that no consideration can reach the heart to yield it the least assistance, it is impossible but that from hence the soul may gather that which will endear it unto him with whom we have to do. Let us dwell on the thoughts of it. This is the hidden mystery; great without controversy; admirable to eternity. What poor, low, perishing things do we spend our contemplations on! Were we to have no advantage by this astonishing dispensation, yet its excellency, glory, beauty, depths, deserve the flower of our inquiries, the vigour of our spirits, the substance of our time; but when, withal, our life, our peace, our joy, our inheritance, our eternity, our all, lies herein, shall not the thoughts of it always dwell in our hearts, always refresh and delight our souls?

(4.) He is excellent and glorious in this, -- in that he is exalted and invested with all authority. When [130] Jacob heard of the exaltation of his son Joseph in Egypt, and saw the chariots that he had sent for him, his spirit fainted and recovered again, through abundance of joy and other overflowing affections. Is our Beloved lost, who for our sakes was upon the earth poor and persecuted, reviled, killed? No! he was dead, but he is alive, and, lo, he lives for ever and ever, and hath the keys of hell and of death. [131] Our Beloved is made a lord and ruler, Acts ii. 36. He is made a king; God sets him his king on his holy hill of Zion, Ps. ii. 6; [132] and he is crowned with honour and dignity, after he had been "made a little lower than the angels for the suffering of death," Heb. ii. 7-9. And what is he made king of? "All things are put in subjection under his feet," verse 8. And what power over them hath our Beloved? "All power in heaven and earth," Matt. xxviii. 18. As for men, he hath power given him "over all flesh," John xvii. 2. And in what glory doth he exercise this power? He gives eternal life to his elect; ruling them in the power of God, Micah v. 4, until he bring them to himself: and for his enemies, his arrows are sharp in their hearts,

Ps. xlv. 5; he dips his vesture in their blood. [133] Oh, how glorious is he in his authority over his enemies! In this world he terrifies, frightens, awes, convinces, bruises their hearts and consciences, -- fills them with fear, terror, disquietment, until they yield him feigned obedience; and sometimes with outward judgments bruises, breaks, turns the wheel upon them, -- stains all his vesture with their blood, -- fills the earth with their carcases: and at last will gather them all together, beast, false prophet, nations, etc., and cast them into that lake that burns with fire and brimstone. [134]

He is gloriously exalted above angels in this his authority, good and bad, Eph. i. 20-22, "far above all principality, and power, and might, and dominion, and every name that is named, not only in this world, but also in that which is to come." They are all under his feet, -- at his command and absolute disposal. He is at the right hand of God, in the highest exaltation possible, and in full possession of a kingdom over the whole creation; having received a "name above every name," etc., Phil. ii. 9. Thus is he glorious in his throne, which is at "the right hand of the [135] Majesty on high;" glorious in his commission, which is "all power in heaven and earth;" glorious in his name, a name above every name, -- "Lord of lords, and King of kings;" glorious in his sceptre, -- "a sceptre of righteousness is the sceptre of his kingdom;" glorious in his attendants, -- "his chariots are twenty thousand, even thousands of angels," among them he rideth on the heavens, and sendeth out the voice of his strength, attended with ten thousand times ten thousand of his holy ones; glorious in his subjects, -- all creatures in heaven and in earth, nothing is left that is not put in subjection to him; glorious in his way of rule, and the administration of his kingdom, -- full of sweetness, efficacy, power, serenity, holiness, righteousness, and grace, in and towards his elect, -- of terror, vengeance, and certain destruction towards the rebellious angels and men; glorious in the issue of his kingdom, when every knee shall bow before him, and all shall stand before his judgment-seat. And what a little portion of his glory is it that we have pointed to! This is the beloved of the church, -- its head, its husband; this is he with whom we have communion: but of the whole exaltation of Jesus Christ I am elsewhere to treat at large.

Having insisted on these generals, for the farther carrying on the motives to communion with Christ, in the relation mentioned, taken from his excellencies and perfections, I shall reflect on the description given of him by the spouse in the Canticles, to this very end and purpose Cant. v. 10-16, "My Beloved is white and ruddy, the chiefest among ten thousand. His head is as the most fine gold, his locks are bushy, and black as a raven. His eyes are as the eyes of doves by the rivers of waters, washed with milk, and fitly set. His cheeks are as a bed of spices, as sweet flowers: his lips like lilies, dropping sweet-smelling myrrh. His hands are as gold rings, set with the beryl: his belly is as bright ivory overlaid with sapphires. His legs are as pillars of marble, set upon sockets of fine gold: his countenance is as Lebanon, excellent as the cedars. His mouth is most sweet: yea, he is altogether lovely. This is my Beloved, and this is my friend, O daughters of Jerusalem."

The general description given of him, verse 10, hath been before considered; the ensuing particulars are instances to make good the assertion that he is "the chiefest among ten thousand."

The spouse begins with his head and face, verses 11-13. In his head, she speaks first in general, unto the substance of it, -- it is "fine gold;" and then in particular, as to its ornaments, -- "his locks are bushy, and black as a raven."

1. "His head is as the most fine gold," or, "His head gold, solid gold;" so some; -- "made of pure gold;" so others; -- χρυσίον κεφαλή, say the LXX., retaining part of both the Hebrew words, "כֶּתֶם פָּז, -- "massa auri." [136]

Two things are eminent in gold, -- splendour or glory, and duration. This is that which the spouse speaks of the head of Christ. His head is his government, authority, and kingdom. Hence it is said, "A crown of pure gold was on his head," Ps. xxi. 3; and his head is here said to be gold, because of the crown of gold that adorns it, -- as the monarchy in Daniel that was most eminent for glory and duration, is termed a "head of gold," Dan. ii. 38. And these two things are eminent in the kingdom and authority of Christ:--

(1.) It is a glorious kingdom; he is full of glory and majesty, and in his majesty he rides "prosperously," Ps. xlv. 3, 4. "His glory is great in the salvation of God: honour and majesty are laid upon him: he is made blessed for ever and ever," Ps. xxi. 5, 6. I might insist on particulars, and show that there is not any thing that may render a kingdom or government glorious, but it is in this of Christ in all its excellencies. It is a heavenly, a spiritual, a universal, and unshaken kingdom; all which render it glorious. But of this, somewhat before.

(2.) It is durable, yea, eternal, -- solid gold. "His throne is for ever and ever," Ps. xlv. 6; "of the increase of his government there shall be no end, upon the throne of David, and upon his kingdom, to order it, and to establish it with judgment and with justice from henceforth even for ever," Isa. ix. 7. "His kingdom is an everlasting kingdom," Dan. vii. 27, -- "a kingdom that shall never be destroyed," chap. ii. 44; for he must reign until all his enemies be subdued. This is that head of gold, -- the splendour and eternity of his government.

And if you take the head in a natural sense, either the glory of his Deity is here attended to, or the fulness and excellency of his wisdom, which the head is the seat of. The allegory is not to be straitened, whilst we keep to the analogy of faith.

2. For the ornaments of his head; his locks, they are said to be "bushy," or curled, "black as a raven." His curled locks are black; "as a raven," is added by way of illustration of the blackness, not with any allusion to the nature of the raven. Take the head spoken of in a political sense: his locks of hair -- said to be curled, as seeming to be entangled, but really falling in perfect order and beauty, as bushy locks -- are his thoughts, and counsels, and ways, in the administration of his kingdom. They are black or dark, because of their depth and unsearchableness, -- as God is said to dwell in thick darkness; and curled or bushy, because of their exact interweavings, from his infinite wisdom. His thoughts are many as the hairs of the head, seeming to be perplexed and entangled, but really set in a comely order, as curled bushy hair; deep and unsearchable, and dreadful to his enemies, and full of beauty and comeliness to his beloved. Such are, I say, the thoughts of his heart, the counsels of his wisdom, in reference to the administrations of his kingdom:-- dark, perplexed, involved, to a carnal eye; in themselves, and to his saints, deep, manifold, ordered in all things, comely, desirable.

In a natural sense, black and curled locks denote comeliness, and vigour of youth. The strength and power of Christ, in the execution of his counsels, in all his ways, appears glorious and lovely.

The next thing described in him is his eyes. Verse 12, "His eyes are as the eyes of doves by the rivers of waters, washed with milk, and fitly set." The reason of this allusion is obvious:-- doves are tender birds, not birds of prey; and of all others they have the most bright, shining, and piercing eye; their delight also in streams of water is known. Their being washed in milk, or clear, white, crystal water, adds to their beauty. And they are here said to be "fitly set;" that is, in due proportion for beauty and lustre, -- as a precious stone in the foil or fulness of a ring, as the word signifies.

Eyes being for sight, discerning, knowledge, and acquaintance with the things that are to be seen; the knowledge, the understanding, the discerning Spirit of Christ Jesus, are here intended. In the allusion used four things are ascribed to them:-- 1. Tenderness; 2. Purity; 3. Discerning; and, 4. Glory:--

1. The tenderness and compassion of Christ towards his church is here intended. He looks on it with the eyes of galless doves; with tenderness and careful compassion; without anger, fury, or thoughts of revenge. So is the eye interpreted, Deut. xi. 12, "The eyes of the Lord thy God are upon that land." Why so? "It is a land that the Lord thy God careth for;" -- careth for it in mercy. So are the eyes of Christ on us, as the eyes of one that in tenderness cares for us; that lays out his wisdom, knowledge, and understanding, in all tender love, in our behalf. He is the stone, that foundation-stone of the church, whereon "are seven eyes," Zech. iii. 9; wherein is a perfection of wisdom, knowledge, care, and kindness, for its guidance.

2. Purity; -- as washed doves' eyes for purity. This may be taken either subjectively, for the excellency and immixed cleanness and purity of his sight and knowledge in himself; or objectively, for his delighting to behold purity in others. "He is of purer eyes than to behold iniquity," Hab. i. 13. "He hath no pleasure in wickedness; the foolish shall not stand in his sight," Ps. v. 4, 5. If the righteous soul of Lot was vexed with seeing the filthy deeds of wicked men, 2 Pet. ii. 8, who yet had eyes of flesh, in which there was a mixture of impurity; how much more do the pure eyes of our dear Lord Jesus abominate all the filthiness of sinners! But herein lies the excellency of his love to us, that he takes care to take away our filth and stains, that he may delight in us; and seeing we are so defiled, that it could no otherwise be done, he will do it by his own blood, Eph. v. 25-27, "Even as Christ also loved the church, and gave himself for it, that he might sanctify and cleanse it, with the washing of water by the word, that he might present it to himself a glorious church, not having spot, or wrinkle, or any such thing; but that it should be holy, and without blemish." The end of this undertaking is, that the church might be thus gloriously presented unto himself, because he is of purer eyes than to behold it with joy and delight in any other condition. He leaves not his spouse until he says of her, "Thou art all fair, my love; there is no spot in thee," Cant. iv. 7. Partly, he takes away our spots and stains, by the "renewing of the Holy Ghost;" [137] and wholly adorns us with his own righteousness: and that because of the purity of his own eyes, which "cannot behold iniquity," -- that he might present us to himself holy.

3. Discerning. He sees as doves, quickly, clearly, thoroughly, -- to the bottom of that which he looks upon. Hence, in another place it is said that his "eyes are as a flame of fire," Rev. i. 14. And why so? That the churches might know that he is he which "searcheth the reins and hearts," Rev. ii. 23. He hath

discerning eyes, nothing is hid from him; all things are open and naked before him with whom we have to do. It is said of him, whilst he was in this world, that "Jesus knew all men, and needed not that any should testify of man; for he knew what was in man," John ii. 24, 25. His piercing eyes look through all the thick coverings of hypocrites, and the snow [show] of pretences that is on them. He sees the inside of all; and what men are there, that they are to him. He sees not as we see, but ponders the hidden man of the heart. No humble, broken, contrite soul, shall lose one sigh or groan after him, and communion with him; no pant of love or desire is hid from him, -- he sees in secret; no glorious performance of the most glorious hypocrite will avail with him, -- his eyes look through all, and the filth of their hearts lies naked before him.

4. Beauty and glory are here intended also. Every thing of Christ is beautiful, for he is "altogether lovely," verse 16, but most glorious [is he] in his sight and wisdom: he is the wisdom of God's eternal wisdom itself; his understanding is infinite. What spots and stains are in all our knowledge! When it is made perfect, yet it will still be finite and limited. His is without spot of darkness, without foil of limitedness.

Thus, then, is he beautiful and glorious:-- his "head is of gold, his eyes are doves' eyes, washed in milk, and fitly set."

The next thing insisted on is his cheeks. Verse 13, "His cheeks are as a bed of spices; as sweet flowers," or "towers of perfumes" [marginal reading], or well-grown flowers. There are three things evidently pointed at in these words:-- 1. A sweet savour, as from spices, and flowers, and towers of perfume; 2. Beauty and order, as spices set in rows or beds, as the words import; 3. Eminency in that word, as sweet or well-grown, great flowers.

These things are in the cheeks of Christ. The Chaldee paraphrast, who applies this whole song to God's dealings with the people of the Jews, makes these cheeks of the church's husband to be the two tables of stone, with the various lines drawn in them; but that allusion is strained, as are most of the conjectures of that scholiast.

The cheeks of a man are the seat of comeliness and manlike courage. The comeliness of Christ, as hath in part been declared, is from his fulness of grace in himself for us. His manly courage respects the administration of his rule and government, from his fulness of authority; as was before declared. This comeliness and courage the spouse, describing Christ as a beautiful, desirable personage, to show that spiritually he is so, calleth his cheeks; so to make up his parts, and proportion. And to them doth she ascribe, --

1. A sweet savour, order, and eminency. A sweet savour; as God is said to smell a sweet savour from the grace and obedience of his servants (Gen. viii. 21, the Lord smelled a savour of rest from the sacrifice of Noah), so do the saints smell a sweet savour from his grace laid up in Christ, Cant. i. 3. It is that which they rest in, which they delight in, which they are refreshed with. As the smell of aromatical spices and flowers pleases the natural sense, refreshes the spirits, and delights the person; so do the graces of Christ to his saints. They please their spiritual sense, they refresh their drooping spirits, and give delight to their souls. If he be nigh them, they smell his raiment, as Isaac the raiment of Jacob. They say, "It is as the smell of a field which the Lord hath blessed," Gen. xxvii. 27; and their souls are refreshed with it.

2. Order and beauty are as spices set in a garden bed. So are the graces of Christ. When spices are set in order, any one may know what is for his use, and take and gather it accordingly. Their answering, also, one to another makes them beautiful. So are the graces of Christ; in the gospel they are distinctly and in order set forth, that sinners by faith may view them, and take from him according to their necessity. They are ordered for the use of saints in the promises of the gospel. There is light in him, and life in him, and power in him, and all consolation in him; -- a constellation of graces, shining with glory and beauty. Believers take a view of them all, see their glory and excellency, but fix especially on that which, in the condition wherein they are, is most useful to them. One takes light and joy; another, life and power. By faith and prayer do they gather these things in this bed of spices. Not any that comes to him goes away unrefreshed. What may they not take, what may they not gather? what is it that the poor soul wants? Behold, it is here provided, set out in order in the promises of the gospel; which are as the beds wherein these spices are set for our use: and on the account hereof is the covenant said to be "ordered in all things," 2 Sam. xxiii. 5.

3. Eminency. His cheeks are "a tower of perfumes" held up, made conspicuous, visible, eminent. So it is with the graces of Christ, when held out and lifted up in the preaching of the gospel. They are a tower of perfumes, -- a sweet savour to God and man.

The next clause of that verse is, "His lips are like lilies, dropping sweet-smelling myrrh." Two perfections in things natural are here alluded unto:-- First, the glory of colour in the lilies, and the sweetness of savour in the myrrh. The glory and beauty of the lilies in those countries was such as that our Saviour tells us that "Solomon, in all his glory, was not arrayed like one of them," Matt. vi. 29; and the savour of myrrh such as, when the Scripture would set forth any thing to be an excellent savour, it compares it thereunto, Ps. xlv. 8; and thereof was the sweet and holy ointment chiefly made, Exod. xxx. 23-25: mention is also made frequently of it in other places, to the same purpose. It is said of Christ, that "grace was poured into his lips," Ps. xlv. 2; whence men wondered or were amazed -- τοῖς λόγοις τῆς χάριτος, [Luke iv. 22] -- at the words of grace that proceeded out of his mouth. So that by the lips of Christ, and their dropping sweet-smelling myrrh, the word of Christ, its savour, excellency, and usefulness, is intended. Herein is he excellent and glorious indeed, surpassing the excellencies of those natural things which yet are most precious in their kind, -- even in the glory, beauty, and usefulness of his word. Hence they that preach his word to the saving of the souls of men, are said to be a "sweet savour unto God," 2 Cor. ii. 15; and the savour of the knowledge of God is said to be manifested by them, verse 14. I might insist on the several properties of myrrh, whereto the word of Christ is here compared, -- its bitterness in taste, its efficacy to preserve from putrefaction, its usefulness in perfumes and unctions, -- and press the allegory in setting out the excellencies of the word in allusions to them; but I only insist on generals. This is that which the Holy Ghost here intends:-- the word of Christ is sweet, savoury, precious unto believers; and they see him to be excellent, desirable, beautiful, in the precepts, promises, exhortations, and the most bitter threats thereof.

The spouse adds, "His hands are as gold rings set with the beryl" [verse 14]. The word "beryl," in the original, is "Tarshish;" [138] which the Septuagint have retained, not restraining it to any peculiar precious stone; the onyx, say some; the chrysolite, say others; -- any precious stone shining with a sea-green colour, for the word signifies the sea also. Gold rings set with precious, glittering stones, are both valuable and desirable, for profit and ornament: so are the hands of Christ; that is, all his works, -- the effects, by the cause. All his works are glorious; they are all fruits of wisdom, love, and bounty. "And his belly is as bright ivory, overlaid with sapphires." The smoothness and brightness of ivory, the preciousness and heavenly colour of the sapphires, are here called in, to give some lustre to the excellency of Christ." To these is his belly, or rather his bowels (which takes in the heart also), compared. It is the inward bowels, and not the outward bulk that is signified. Now, to show that by "bowels" in the Scripture, ascribed either to God or man, affections are intended, is needless. The tender love, unspeakable affections and kindness, of Christ to his church and people, is thus set out. What a beautiful sight is it to the eye, to see pure polished ivory set up and down with heaps of precious sapphires! How much more glorious are the tender affections, mercies, and compassion of the Lord Jesus unto believers!

Verse 15. The strength of his kingdom, the faithfulness and stability of his promises, -- the height and glory of his person in his dominion, -- the sweetness and excellency of communion with him, is set forth in these words: "His legs are as pillars of marble set upon sockets of fine gold; his countenance is as Lebanon, excellent as the cedars: his mouth is most sweet."

When the spouse hath gone thus far in the description of him, she concludes all in this general assertion: "He is wholly desirable, -- altogether to be desired or beloved." As if she should have said, -- "I have thus reckoned up some of the perfections of the creatures (things of most value, price, usefulness, beauty, glory, here below), and compared some of the excellencies of my Beloved unto them. In this way of allegory I can carry things no higher; I find nothing better or more desirable to shadow out and to present his loveliness and desirableness: but, alas! all this comes short of his perfections, beauty, and comeliness; he is all wholly to be desired, to be beloved;'?" --

Lovely in his person, -- in the glorious all-sufficiency of his Deity, gracious purity and holiness of his humanity, authority and majesty, love and power.

Lovely in his birth and incarnation; when he was rich, for our sakes becoming poor, -- taking part of flesh and blood, because we partook of the same; being made of a woman, that for us he might be made under the law, even for our sakes.

Lovely in the whole course of his life, and the more than angelical holiness and obedience which, in the depth of poverty and persecution, he exercised therein; -- doing good, receiving evil; blessing, and being cursed, reviled, reproached, all his days.

Lovely in his death; yea, therein most lovely to sinners; -- never more glorious and desirable than when he came broken, dead, from the cross. Then had he carried all our sins into a land of forgetfulness; then had he made peace and reconciliation for us; then had he procured life and immortality for us.

Lovely in his whole employment, in his great undertaking, -- in his life, death, resurrection, ascension; being a mediator between God and us, to recover the glory of God's justice, and to save our souls, -- to bring us to an enjoyment of God, who were set at such an infinite distance from him by sin.

Lovely in the glory and majesty wherewith he is crowned. Now he is set down at the right hand of the Majesty on high; where, though he be terrible to his enemies, yet he is full of mercy, love, and compassion, towards his beloved ones.

Lovely in all those supplies of grace and consolations, in all the dispensations of his Holy Spirit, whereof his saints are made partakers.

Lovely in all the tender care, power, and wisdom, which he exercises in the protection, safe-guarding, and delivery of his church and people, in the midst of all the oppositions and persecutions whereunto they are exposed.

Lovely in all his ordinances, and the whole of that spiritually glorious worship which he hath appointed to his people, whereby they draw nigh and have communion with him and his Father.

Lovely and glorious in the vengeance he taketh, and will finally execute, upon the stubborn enemies of himself and his people.

Lovely in the pardon he hath purchased and doth dispense, -- in the reconciliation he hath established, -- in the grace he communicates, -- in the consolations he doth administer, -- in the peace and joy he gives his saints, -- in his assured preservation of them unto glory.

What shall I say? there is no end of his excellencies and desirableness; -- "He is altogether lovely. This is our beloved, and this is our friend, O daughters of Jerusalem."

Digression II - All solid wisdom laid up in Christ -- True wisdom, wherein it consists -- Knowledge of God, in Christ only to be obtained -- What of God may be known by his works -- Some properties of God not discovered but in Christ only; love, mercy -- Others not fully but in him; as vindictive justice, patience, wisdom, all-sufficiency -- No property of God savingly known but in Christ -- What is required to a saving knowledge of the properties of God -- No true knowledge of ourselves but in Christ -- Knowledge of ourselves, wherein it consisteth -- Knowledge of sin, how to be had in Christ; also of righteousness and of judgment -- The wisdom of walking with God hid in Christ -- What is required thereunto -- Other pretenders to the title of wisdom examined and rejected -- Christ alone exalted.

A second consideration of the excellencies of Christ, serving to endear the hearts of them who stand with him in the relation insisted on, arises from that which, in the mistaken apprehension of it, is the great darling of men, and in its true notion the great aim of the saints; which is wisdom and knowledge. Let it be evinced that all true and solid knowledge is laid up in, and is only to be attained from and by, the Lord Jesus Christ; and the hearts of men, if they are but true to themselves and their most predominate principles, must needs be engaged to him. This is the great design of all men, taken off from professed slavery to the world, and the pursuit of sensual, licentious courses, -- that they maybe wise: and what ways the generality of men engage in for the compassing of that end shall be afterward considered. To the glory and honour of our dear Lord Jesus Christ, and the establishment of our hearts in communion with him, the design of this digression is to evince that all wisdom is laid up in him, and that from him alone it is to be obtained.

1 Cor. i. 24, the Holy Ghost tells us that "Christ is the power of God, and the wisdom of God:" not the essential Wisdom of God, as he is the eternal Son of the Father (upon which account he is called "Wisdom" in the Proverbs, chap. viii. 22, 23); but as he is crucified, verse 23. As he is crucified, so he is the wisdom of God; that is, all that wisdom which God layeth forth for the discovery and manifestation of himself, and for the saving of sinners, which makes foolish all the wisdom of the world, -- that is all in Christ crucified; held out in him, by him, and to be obtained only from him. And thereby in him do we see the glory of God, 2 Cor. iii. 18. For he is not only said to be "the wisdom of God," but also to be "made unto us wisdom," 1 Cor. i. 30. He is made, not by creation, but ordination and appointment, wisdom unto us; not only by teaching us wisdom (by a metonymy of the effect for the cause), as he is the great prophet of his church, but also because by the knowing of him we become acquainted with the wisdom of God, -- which is our wisdom; which is a metonymy of the adjunct. This, however verily promised, is thus only to be had. The sum of what is contended for is asserted in terms, Col. ii. 3, "In him are hid all the treasures of wisdom and knowledge."

There are two things that might seem to have some colour in claiming a title and interest in this business:-- 1. Civil wisdom and prudence, for the management of affairs; 2. Ability of learning and literature; -- but God rejecteth both these, as of no use at all to the end and intent of true wisdom indeed. There is in the world that which is called "understanding;" but it comes to nothing. There is that which is called "wisdom;" but it is turned into folly, 1 Cor. i. 19, 20, "God brings to nothing the understanding of the prudent, and makes foolish this wisdom of the world." And if there be neither wisdom nor knowledge (as doubtless there is not), without the knowledge of God, Jer. viii. 9, it is all shut up in the Lord Jesus Christ: "No man hath seen God at any time; the only begotten Son, which is in the bosom of the Father, he hath revealed him." He is not seen at another time, John i. 18, nor known upon any other account, but only the revelation of the Son. He hath manifested him from his own bosom; and therefore, verse 9, it is said that he is "the true Light, which lighteth every man that cometh into the world," -- the true Light, which hath it in himself: and none hath any but from him; and all have it who come unto him. He who doth not so, is in darkness.

The sum of all true wisdom and knowledge may be reduced to these three heads:-- I. The knowledge of God, his nature and his properties. II. The knowledge of ourselves in reference to the will of God concerning us. III. Skill to walk in communion with God:--

I. The knowledge of the works of God, and the chief end of all, doth necessarily attend these. 1. In these three is summed up all true wisdom and knowledge; and, 2, -- Not any of them is to any purpose to be obtained, or is manifested, but only in and by the Lord Christ:--

1. God, by the work of the creation, by the creation itself, did reveal himself in many of his properties unto his creatures capable of his knowledge; -- his power, his goodness, his wisdom, his all-sufficiency, are thereby known.

This the apostle asserts, Rom. i. 19-21. Verse 19, he calls it τὸ γνωστὸν τοῦ Θεοῦ, -- verse 20, that is, his eternal power and Godhead; and verse 21, a knowing of God: and [139] all this by the creation. But yet there are some properties of God which all the works of creation cannot in any measure reveal or make known; -- as his patience, long-suffering, and forbearance. For all things being made [140] good, there could be no place for the exercise of any of these properties, or manifestation of them. The whole fabric of heaven and earth considered in itself, as at first created, will not discover any such thing as patience and forbearance in God; [141] which yet are eminent properties of his nature, as himself proclaims and declares, Exod. xxxiv. 6, 7.

Wherefore the Lord goes farther; and by the works of his providence, in preserving and ruling the world which he made, discovers and reveals these properties also. For whereas by cursing the earth, and filling all the elements oftentimes with signs of his anger and indignation, he hath, as the apostle tells us, Rom. i. 18, "revealed from heaven his wrath against all ungodliness and unrighteousness of men;" yet not proceeding immediately to destroy all things, he hath manifested his patience and forbearance to all. This Paul, Acts xiv. 16, 17, tells us: "He suffered all nations to walk in their own ways; yet he left not himself without witness, in that he did good, and gave rain from heaven and fruitful seasons, filling their hearts with food and gladness." A large account of his goodness and wisdom herein the psalmist gives us, Ps. civ. throughout. By these ways he bare witness to his own goodness and patience; and so it is said, "He endures with much long-suffering," etc., Rom. ix. 22. But now, here all the world is at a stand; by all this they have but an obscure glimpse of God, and see not so much as his back parts. Moses saw not that, until he was put into [142] the rock; and that rock was Christ. There are some of the most eminent and glorious properties of God (I mean, in the manifestation whereof he will be most glorious; otherwise his properties are not to be compared) that there is not the least glimpse to be attained of out of the Lord Christ, but only by and in him; and some that comparatively we have no light of but in him; and of all the rest no true light but by him:--

(1.) Of the first sort, whereof not the least guess and imagination can enter into the heart of man but only by Christ, are love and pardoning mercy:--

[1.] Love; I mean love unto sinners. Without this, man is of all creatures most miserable; and there is not the least glimpse of it that can possibly be discovered but in Christ. The Holy Ghost says, 1 John iv. 8, 16, "God is love;" that is, not only of a loving and tender nature, but one that will exercise himself in a dispensation of his love, eternal love, towards us, -- one that hath purposes of love for us from of old, and will fulfil them all towards us in due season. But how is this demonstrated? how may we attain an acquaintance with it? He tells us, verse 9, "In this was manifested the love of God, because that God sent his only begotten Son into the world, that we might live through him." This is the only discovery that God hath made of any such property in his nature, or of any thought of exercising it towards sinners, -- in that he hath sent Jesus Christ into the world, that we might live by him. Where now is the wise, where is the scribe, where is the disputer of this world, with all their wisdom? Their voice must be that of the hypocrites in Zion, Isa. xxxiii. 14, 15. That wisdom which cannot teach me that God is love, shall ever pass for folly. Let men go to the sun, moon, and stars, to showers of rain and fruitful seasons, and answer truly what by them they learn hereof. Let them not think themselves wiser or better than those that went before them, who, to a man, got nothing by them, but being left inexcusable.

[2.] Pardoning mercy, or grace. Without this, even his love would be fruitless. What discovery may be made of this by a sinful man, may be seen in the father of us all; who, when he had sinned, had no reserve for mercy, but hid himself, Gen. iii. 8. He did it לְרוּחַ הַיּוֹם, when the wind did but a little blow at the presence of God; and he did it foolishly, thinking to "hide himself among trees!" Ps. cxxxix. 7, 8. "The law was given by Moses, but grace and truth came by Jesus Christ," John i. 17, -- grace in the truth and substance. Pardoning mercy, that comes by Christ alone; that pardoning mercy which is manifested in the gospel, and wherein God will be glorified to all eternity, Eph. i. 6. I mean not that general mercy, that velleity of acceptance which some put their hopes in: [143] that πάθος (which to ascribe unto God is the greatest dishonour that can be done him) shines not with one ray out of Christ; it is wholly treasured up in him, and revealed by him. Pardoning mercy is God's free, gracious acceptance of a sinner upon satisfaction made to his justice in the blood of Jesus; nor is any discovery of it, but as relating to the satisfaction of justice, consistent with the glory of God. It is a mercy of inconceivable condescension in forgiveness, tempered with exact justice and severity. Rom. iii. 25, God is said "to set forth Christ to be a propitiation through faith in his blood, to declare his righteousness in the remission of sins;" [144] his righteousness is also manifested in the business of forgiveness of sins: and therefore it is everywhere said to be wholly in Christ, Eph. i. 7. So that this gospel grace and pardoning mercy is alone purchased by him, and revealed in him. And this was the main end of all typical institutions, -- to manifest that remission and forgiveness is wholly wrapped up in the Lord Christ, and that out of him there is not the least conjecture to be made of it, nor the least morsel to be tasted. Had not God set forth [145] the Lord Christ, all the angels in heaven and men on earth could not have apprehended that there had been any such thing in the nature of God as this grace of pardoning mercy. The apostle asserts the full manifestation as well as the exercise of this mercy to be in Christ only, Tit. iii. 4, 5, "After that the kindness and love of God our Saviour towards man appeared," -- namely, in the sending of Christ, and the declaration of him in the gospel. Then was this pardoning mercy and salvation not by works discovered.

And these are of those properties of God whereby he will be known, whereof there is not the least glimpse to be obtained but by and in Christ; and whoever knows him not by these, knows him not at all. They know an idol, and not the only true God. He that hath not the Son, the same hath not the Father, 1 John ii. 23; and not to have God as a Father, is not to have him at all; and he is known as a Father only as he is love, and full of pardoning mercy in Christ. How this is to be had the Holy Ghost tells us, 1 John v. 20, "The Son of God is come and hath given us an understanding, that we may know him that is true." By him alone we have our understanding to know him that is true. Now, these properties of God Christ revealeth in his doctrine, in the revelation he makes of God and his will, as the great prophet of the church, John xvii. 6. And on this account the knowledge of them is exposed to all, with an evidence unspeakably surmounting that which is given by the creation to his eternal power and Godhead. But the life of this knowledge lies in an acquaintance with his person, wherein the express image and beams of this glory of his Father do shine forth,

174

Heb. i. 3; of which before.

(2.) There are other properties of God which, though also otherwise discovered, yet are so clearly, eminently, and savingly only in Jesus Christ; as, - - [1.] His vindictive justice in punishing sin; [2.] His patience, forbearance, and long-suffering towards sinners; [3.] His wisdom, in managing things for his own glory; [4.] His all-sufficiency, in himself and unto others. All these, though they may receive some lower and inferior manifestations out of Christ, yet they clearly shine only in him; so as that it may be our wisdom to be acquainted with them.

[1.] His vindictive justice. God hath, indeed, many ways manifested his indignation and anger against sin; so that men cannot but know that it is "the judgment of God, that they which commit such things are worthy of death," Rom. i. 32. He hath in the law threatened to kindle a fire in his anger that shall burn to the very heart of hell. And even in many providential dispensations, "his wrath is revealed from heaven against all the ungodliness of men," Rom. i. 18. So that men must say that he is a God of judgment. And he that shall but consider that the angels for sin were cast from heaven, shut up under chains of everlasting darkness unto the judgment of the great day (the [146] rumour whereof seems to have been spread among the Gentiles, whence the poet makes his Jupiter threaten the inferior rebellious deities with that punishment); and how Sodom and Gomorrah were condemned with an overthrow, and burned into ashes, that they might be "examples unto those that should after live ungodly," 2 Pet. ii. 6; cannot but discover much of God's vindictive justice and his anger against sin. But far more clear doth this shine into us in the Lord Christ:--

1st. In him God hath manifested the naturalness of this righteousness unto him, in that it was impossible that it should be diverted from sinners without the interposing of a propitiation. Those who lay the necessity of satisfaction merely upon the account of a free act and determination of the will of God, leave, to my apprehension, no just and indispensable [147] foundation for the death of Christ, but lay it upon a supposition of that which might have been otherwise. But plainly, God, in that he [148] spared not his only Son, but made his soul an offering for sin, and would admit of no atonement but in his blood, hath abundantly manifested that it is of necessity to him (his holiness and righteousness requiring it) to render indignation, wrath, tribulation, and anguish unto sin. And the knowledge of this naturalness of vindictive justice, with the necessity of its execution on supposition of sin, is the only true and useful knowledge of it. To look upon it as that which God may exercise or forbear, makes his justice not a property of his nature, but a free act of his will; and a will to punish where one may do otherwise without injustice, is rather ill-will than justice.

2dly. In the penalty inflicted on Christ for sin, this justice is far more gloriously manifested than otherwise. To see, indeed, a world, made [149] good and beautiful, wrapped up in wrath and curses, clothed with thorns and briers; to see the whole beautiful creation made subject to vanity, given up to the bondage of corruption; to hear it groan in pain under that burden; to consider legions of angels, most glorious and immortal creatures, cast down into hell, bound with chains of darkness, and reserved for a more dreadful judgment for one sin; to view the ocean of the blood of souls spilt to eternity on this account, -- will give some insight into this thing. But what is all this to that view of it

175

which may be had by a spiritual eye in the Lord Christ? All these things are worms, and of no value in comparison of him. To see him who is the [150] wisdom of God, and the power of God, always [151] beloved of the Father; to see him, I say, fear, [152] and tremble, and bow, and sweat, and pray, and die; to see him lifted up upon the cross, the earth trembling under him, as if unable to bear his weight; and the heavens darkened over him, as if shut against his cry; and himself hanging between both, as if refused by both; and all this because our sins did meet upon him; -- this of all things doth most abundantly manifest the severity of God's vindictive justice. Here, or nowhere, is it to be learned.

[2.] His patience, forbearance, and long-suffering towards sinners. There are many glimpses of the patience of God shining out in the works of his providence; but all exceedingly beneath that discovery of it which we have in Christ, especially in these three things:--

1st. The manner of its discovery. This, indeed, is evident to all, that God doth not ordinarily immediately punish men upon their offences. It may be learned from his constant way in governing the world: notwithstanding all provocations, yet he doth [153] good to men; causing his sun to shine upon them, sending them rain and fruitful seasons, filling their hearts with food and gladness. Hence it was easy for them to conclude that there was in him abundance of goodness and forbearance. But all this is yet in much darkness, being the exurgency of men's reasonings from their observations; yea, the management of it [God's patience] hath been such as that it hath proved a snare almost universally unto them towards whom it hath been exercised, Eccles. viii. 11, as well as a temptation to them who have looked on, Job xxi. 7; Ps. lxxiii. 2-4, etc.; Jer. xii. 1; Hab. i. 13. The discovery of it in Christ is utterly of another nature. In him the very nature of God is discovered to be love and kindness; and that he will exercise the same to sinners, he hath promised, sworn, and solemnly engaged himself by covenant. And that we may not hesitate about the aim which he hath herein, there is a stable bottom and foundation of acting suitably to those gracious properties of his nature held forth, -- namely, the reconciliation and atonement that is made in the blood of Christ. Whatever discovery were made of the patience and lenity of God unto us, yet if it were not withal revealed that the other properties of God, as his justice and revenge for sin, had their actings also assigned to them to the full, there could be little consolation gathered from the former. And therefore, though God may teach men his goodness and forbearance, by sending them rain and fruitful seasons, yet withal at the same time, upon all occasions, "revealing his wrath from heaven against the ungodliness of men," Rom. i. 18, it is impossible that they should do any thing but miserably fluctuate and tremble at the event of these dispensations; and yet this is the best that men can have out of Christ, the utmost they can attain unto. With the present possession of good things administered in this patience, men might, and did for a season, take up their thoughts and satiate themselves; but yet they were not in the least delivered from the [154] bondage they were in by reason of death, and the darkness attending it. The law reveals no patience or forbearance in God; it speaks, as to the issue of transgressions, nothing but sword and fire, had not God interposed by an act of sovereignty. But now, as was said, with that revelation of forbearance which we have in Christ, there is also a discovery of the satisfaction of his justice and wrath against sin; so that we need not fear any actings from them to interfere with the works of his patience, which are so sweet unto us. Hence God is said to be "in Christ, reconciling the world to himself," 2 Cor. v. 19; manifesting himself in him as one that hath now no more to do for the manifestation of all his attributes, -- that is, for the glorifying of himself, -- but only to forbear, reconcile, and pardon sin in him.

2dly. In the nature of it. What is there in that forbearance which out of Christ is revealed? Merely a not immediate punishing upon the [155] offence, and, withal, giving and continuing temporal mercies; such things as men are prone to abuse, and may perish with their bosoms full of them to eternity. That which lies hid in Christ, and is revealed from him, is full of love, sweetness, tenderness, kindness, grace. It is the Lord's waiting to be gracious to sinners; waiting for an advantage to show love and kindness, for the most eminent endearing of a soul unto himself, Isa. xxx. 18, "Therefore will the Lord wait, that he may be gracious unto you; and therefore will he be exalted, that he may have mercy upon you." Neither is there any revelation of God that the soul finds more sweetness in than this. When it [one's soul] is experimentally convinced that God from time to time hath passed by many, innumerable iniquities, he is astonished to think that God should do so; and admires that he did not take the advantage of his provocations to cast him out of his presence. He finds that, with infinite wisdom, in all long-suffering, he hath managed all his dispensations towards him to recover him from the power of the devil, to rebuke and chasten his spirit for sin, to endear him unto himself; -- there is, I say, nothing of greater sweetness to the soul than this: and therefore the apostle says, Rom. iii. 25, that all is "through the forbearance of God." God makes way for complete forgiveness of sins through this his forbearance; which the other doth not.

3dly. They differ in their ends and aims. What is the aim and design of God in the dispensation of that forbearance which is manifested and may be discovered out of Christ? The apostle tells us, Rom. ix. 22, "What if God, willing to show his wrath, and to make his power known, endured with much long-suffering the vessels of wrath fitted for destruction?" It was but to leave them inexcusable, that his power and wrath against sin might be manifested in their destruction. And therefore he calls it "a suffering of them to walk in their own ways," Acts xiv. 16; which elsewhere he holds out as a most dreadful judgment, -- to wit, in respect of that issue whereto it will certainly come; as Ps. lxxxi. 12, "I gave them up unto their own hearts' lusts, and they walked in their own counsels:" which is as dreadful a [156] condition as a creature is capable of falling into in this world. And Acts xvii. 30, he calls it a "winking at the sins of their ignorance;" as it were taking no care nor thought of them in their dark condition, as it appears by the antithesis, "But now he commandeth all men everywhere to repent." He did not take so much notice of them then as to command them to repent, by any clear revelation of his mind and will. And therefore the exhortation of the apostle, Rom. ii. 4, "Despisest thou the riches of his goodness and forbearance and long suffering, not knowing that the goodness of God leadeth thee to repentance?" is spoken to the Jews, who had advantages to learn the natural tendency of that goodness and forbearance which God exercises in Christ; which, indeed, leads to repentance: or else he doth in general intimate that, in very reason, men ought to make another use of those things than usually they do, and which he chargeth them withal, verse 5, "But after thy hardness and impenitent heart," etc. At [157] best, then, the patience of God unto men out of Christ, by reason of their own incorrigible stubbornness, proves but like the waters of the river Phasis, that are sweet at the top and bitter in the bottom; they swim for a while in the sweet and good things of this life, Luke xvi. 25; wherewith being filled, they sink to the depth of all bitterness.

But now, evidently and directly, the end of that patience and forbearance of God which is exercised in Christ, and discovered in him to us, is the saving and bringing into God those towards whom he is pleased to exercise them. And therefore Peter tells you, 2 Pet. iii. 9, that he is "long-suffering to us-ward, not willing that any should perish, but that all should come to repentance;" -- that is, all us towards whom he exercises forbearance; for that is the end of it, that his will concerning our repentance and salvation may be accomplished. And the nature of it, with its end, is well expressed, Isa. liv. 9, "This is as the waters of Noah unto me: for as I have sworn that the waters of Noah should no more go over the earth, so have I sworn that I would not be wroth," etc. It is God's taking a course, in his infinite wisdom and goodness, that we shall not be destroyed notwithstanding our sins; and therefore, Rom. xv. 5, these two things are laid together in God, as coming together from him, "The God of patience and consolation:" his patience is a matter of the greatest consolation. And this is another property of God, which, though it may break forth in some rays, to some ends and purposes, in other things, yet the treasures of it are hid in Christ; and none is acquainted with it, unto any spiritual advantage, that learns it not in him.

[3.] His wisdom, his infinite wisdom, in managing things for his own glory, and the good of them towards whom he hath thoughts of love. The Lord, indeed, hath laid out and manifested infinite wisdom [158] in his works of creation, providence, and governing of his world: in wisdom hath he made all his creatures. "How manifold are his works! in wisdom hath he made them all; the earth is full of his riches," Ps. civ. 24. So in his providence, his supportment and guidance of all things, in order to one another, and his own glory, unto the ends appointed for them; for all these things "come forth from the Lord of hosts, who is wonderful in counsel, and excellent in working," Isa. xxviii. 29. His law also is for ever to be admired, for the excellency of the wisdom therein, Deut. iv. 7, 8. But yet there is that which Paul is astonished at, and wherein God will for ever be exalted, which he calls, "The depth of the riches of the wisdom and knowledge of God," Rom. xi. 33; -- that is only hid in and revealed by Christ. Hence, as he is said to be "the [159] wisdom of God," and to be "made unto us wisdom;" so the design of God, which is carried along in him, and revealed in the gospel, is called "the wisdom of God," and a "mystery; even the hidden wisdom which God ordained before the world was; which none of the princes of this world knew," 1 Cor. ii. 7, 8. Eph. iii. 10, it is called, "The manifold wisdom of God;" and to discover the depth and riches of this wisdom, he tells us in that verse that it is such, that principalities and powers, that very angels themselves, could not in the least measure get any acquaintance with it, until God, by gathering of a church of sinners, did actually discover it. Hence Peter informs us, that they who are so well acquainted with all the works of God, do yet bow down and desire with earnestness to look into these things (the things of the wisdom of God in the gospel), 1 Pet. i. 12. It asks a man much wisdom to make a curious work, fabric, and building; but if one shall come and deface it, to raise up the same building to more beauty and glory than ever, this is excellence of wisdom indeed. God in the beginning made all things good, glorious, and beautiful. When all things had an innocence and beauty, the clear impress [160] of his wisdom and goodness upon them, they were very glorious; especially man, who was made for his special glory. Now, all this beauty was defaced by sin, and the whole [161] creation rolled up in darkness, wrath, curses, confusion, and the great praise of God buried in the heaps of it. Man, especially, was utterly lost, and came short of the glory of God, for which he was created, Rom. iii. 23. Here, now, doth the depth of the riches of the wisdom and knowledge of God open itself. A design in Christ shines out from his bosom, that was lodged there from eternity, to recover things to such an estate as shall be exceedingly to the advantage of his glory, infinitely above what at first appeared, and for the putting of sinners into inconceivably a better condition than they were in before the entrance of sin. He appears now glorious; he is known to be a God [162] pardoning iniquity and sin, and advances the riches of his grace: which was his design, Eph. i. 6. He hath infinitely vindicated his justice also, in the face of men, angels, and devils, in setting forth his Son for a [163] propitiation. It is also to our advantage; we are more fully established in his favour, and are carried on towards a more exceeding [164] weight of glory than formerly was revealed. Hence was that ejaculation of one of the ancients, "O felix culpa, quæ talem meruit redemptorem!" Thus Paul tells us, "Great is the mystery of godliness," 1 Tim. iii. 16, and that "without controversy." We receive "grace for grace;" [165] -- for that grace lost in Adam, better grace in Christ. Confessedly, this is a depth of wisdom indeed. And of the love of Christ to his church, and his union with it, to carry on this business, "This is a great mystery," Eph. v. 32, says the apostle; great wisdom lies herein.

So, then, this also is hid in Christ, -- the great and unspeakable riches of the wisdom of God, in pardoning sin, saving sinners, satisfying justice, fulfilling the law, repairing his own honour, and providing for us a more exceeding weight of glory; and all this out of such a condition as wherein it was impossible that it should enter into the hearts of angels or men how ever the glory of God should be repaired, and one sinning creature delivered from everlasting ruin. Hence it is said, that at the last day God "shall be glorified in his saints, and admired in all them that believe," 2 Thess. i. 10. It shall be an admirable thing, and God shall be for ever glorious in it, even in the bringing of believers to himself. To save sinners through believing, shall be found to be a far more admirable work than to create the world of nothing.

[4.] His all-sufficiency is the last of this sort that I shall name.

God's all-sufficiency in himself is his absolute and universal perfection, whereby nothing is wanting in him, nothing to him: No accession can be made to his fulness, no decrease or wasting can happen thereunto. There is also in him an all-sufficiency for others; which is his power to impart and communicate his goodness and himself so to them as to satisfy and fill them, in their utmost capacity, with whatever is good and desirable to them. For the first of these, -- his all-sufficiency for the communication of his goodness, that is, in the outward effect of it, -- God abundantly manifested in the creation, in that he made all things good, all things perfect; that is, to whom nothing was wanting in their own kind; -- he put a stamp of his own goodness upon them all. But now for the latter, -- his giving himself as an all-sufficient God, to be enjoyed by the creatures, to hold out all that is in him for the satiating and making them blessed, -- that is alone discovered by and in Christ. In him he is a Father, a God in covenant, wherein he hath promised to lay out himself for them; in him hath he promised to give himself into their everlasting fruition, as their exceeding great reward.

And so I have insisted on the second sort of properties in God, whereof, though we have some obscure glimpse in other things, yet the clear knowledge of them, and acquaintance with them, is only to be had in the Lord Christ.

That which remaineth is, briefly to declare that not any of the properties of God whatever can be known, savingly and to consolation, but only in him; and so, consequently, all the wisdom of the knowledge of God is hid in him alone, and from him to be obtained.

2. There is no saving knowledge of any property of God, nor such as brings consolation, but what alone is to be had in Christ Jesus, being laid up in him, and manifested by him. Some eye the justice of God, and know that this is his righteousness, "that they which do such things" (as sin) "are worthy of death," Rom. i. 32. But this is to no other end but to make them cry, "Who amongst us shall dwell with the devouring fire?" Isa. xxxiii. 14. Others fix upon his patience, goodness, mercy, forbearance; but it doth not at all lead them to repentance; but "they despise the riches of his goodness, and after their hardness and impenitent hearts treasure up unto themselves wrath against the day of wrath," Rom. ii. 4, 5. Others, by the very works of creation and providence, come to know "his eternal power and Godhead; but they glorify him not as God, nor are thankful, but become vain in their imagination, and their foolish hearts are darkened," Rom. i. 20. Whatever discovery men have of truth out of Christ, they "hold it captive under unrighteousness," verse 18. Hence Jude tells us, verse 10, that "in what they know naturally, as brute beasts, in those things they corrupt themselves."

That we may have a saving knowledge of the properties of God, attended with consolation, these three things are required:-- (1.) That God hath manifested the glory of them all in a way of doing good unto us. (2.) That he will yet exercise and lay them out to the utmost in our behalf. (3.) That, being so manifested and exercised, they are fit and powerful to bring us to the everlasting fruition of himself; which is our blessedness. Now, all these three lie hid in Christ; and the least glimpse of them out of him is not to be attained.

(1.) This is to be received, that God hath actually manifested the glory of all his attributes in a way of doing us good. What will it avail our souls, what comfort will it bring unto us, what endearment will it put upon our hearts unto God, to know that he is infinitely righteous, just, and holy, unchangeably true and faithful, if we know not how he may preserve the glory of his justice and faithfulness in his comminations and threatenings, but only in our ruin and destruction? if we can from thence only say it is a righteous thing with him to recompense tribulation unto us for our iniquities? What fruit of this consideration had Adam in the garden? Gen. iii. What sweetness, what encouragement, is there in knowing that he is patient and full of forbearance, if the glory of these is to be exalted in enduring the vessels of wrath fitted for destruction? nay, what will it avail us to hear him proclaim himself "The Lord, The Lord God, [166] merciful and gracious, abundant in goodness and truth," yet, withal, that he will "by no means clear the guilty," -- so shutting up the exercise of all his other properties towards us, upon the account of our iniquity? Doubtless, not at all. Under this naked consideration of the properties of God,

justice will make men fly and hide, Gen. iii.; Isa. ii. 21, xxxiii. 15, 16; --
patience, render them obdurate, Eccles. viii. 11. Holiness utterly deters them
from all thoughts of approach unto him, Josh. xxiv. 19. What relief have we
from thoughts of his immensity and omnipresence, if we have cause only to
contrive how to fly from him (Ps. cxxxix. 11, 12), if we have no pledge of his
gracious presence with us? This is that which brings salvation, when we shall
see that God hath glorified all his properties in a way of doing us good. Now,
this he hath done in Jesus Christ. In him hath he made his justice glorious, in
making all our iniquities to [167] meet upon him, causing him to bear them all, as
the scape-goat in the wilderness; not sparing him, but giving him up to death
for us all; -- so exalting his justice and indignation against sin in a way of
freeing us from the condemnation of it, Rom. iii. 25, viii. 33, 34. In him hath he
made his truth glorious, and his faithfulness, in the exact accomplishment of all
his absolute threatenings and promises. That fountain-threat and commination
whence all others flow, Gen. ii. 17, "In the day thou eatest thereof thou shalt die
the death;" seconded with a curse, Deut. xxvii. 26, "Cursed is every one that
continueth not," etc. [Gal. iii. 10] -- is in him accomplished, fulfilled, and the
truth of God in them laid in a way to our good. He, by the grace of God, tasted
death for us, Heb. ii. 9; and so delivered us who were subject to death, verse 15;
and he hath fulfilled the curse, by being made a curse for us, Gal. iii. 13. So that
in his very threatenings his truth is made glorious in a way to our good. And for
his promises, "They are all yea, and in him Amen, unto the glory of God by us,"
2 Cor. i. 20. And for his mercy, goodness, and the riches of his grace, how
eminently are they made glorious in Christ, and advanced for our good! God
hath set him forth to declare his righteousness for the forgiveness of sin; he
hath made way in him for ever to exalt the glory of his pardoning mercy
towards sinners. To manifest this is the great design of the gospel, as Paul
admirably sets it out, Eph. i. 5-8. There must our souls come to an acquaintance
with them, or for ever live in darkness.

Now, this is a saving knowledge, and full of consolation, when we can see
all the properties of God made glorious and exalted in a way of doing us good.
And this wisdom is hid only in Jesus Christ. Hence, when he desired his Father
to glorify his name, John xii. 24, -- to make in him his name (that is, his nature,
his properties, his will) all glorious in that work of redemption he had in hand, -
- he was instantly answered from heaven, "I have both glorified it and will
glorify it again." He will give it its utmost glory in him.

(2.) That God will yet exercise and lay out those properties of his to the
utmost in our behalf. Though he hath made them all glorious in a way that may
tend to our good, yet it doth not absolutely follow that he will use them for our
good; for do we not see innumerable persons perishing everlastingly,
notwithstanding the manifestation of himself which God hath made in Christ.
Wherefore farther, God hath committed all his properties into the hand of
Christ if I may so say, to be managed in our behalf, and for our good. He [168] is
"The power of God, and the wisdom of God;" he is "The Lord our
Righteousness," and is "made unto us of God wisdom, and righteousness,
sanctification, and redemption." Christ having glorified his Father in all his
attributes, he hath now the exercise of them committed to him, that he might be
the captain of salvation to them that do believe; so that if, in the righteousness,
the goodness, the love, the mercy, the all-sufficiency of God, there be any thing

that will do us good, the Lord Jesus is fully interested with the dispensing of it in our behalf. Hence God is said to be "in him, reconciling the world unto himself," 2 Cor. v. 18. Whatever is in him, he layeth it out for the reconciliation of the world, in and by the Lord Christ; and he becomes "The Lord our Righteousness," Isa. xlv. 24, 25. And this is the second thing required.

(3.) There remaineth only, then, that these attributes of God, so manifested and exercised, are powerful and able to bring us to the everlasting fruition of him. To evince this, the Lord wraps up the whole covenant of grace in one promise, signifying no less: "I will be your God." In the covenant, God becomes our God, and we are his people; and thereby all his attributes are ours also. And lest that we should doubt -- when once our eyes are opened to see in any measure the inconceivable difficulty that is in this thing, what unimaginable obstacles on all hands there lie against us -- that all is not enough to deliver and save us, God hath, I say, wrapped it up in this expression, Gen. xvii. 1, "I am," saith he, [169] "God Almighty" (all-sufficient); -- "I am wholly able to perform all my undertakings, and to be thy exceeding great reward. I can remove all difficulties, answer all objections, pardon all sins, conquer all opposition: I am God all-sufficient." Now, you know in whom this covenant and all the promises thereof are ratified, and in whose blood it is confirmed, -- to wit, in the Lord Christ alone; in him only is God an all-sufficient God to any, and an exceeding great reward. And hence Christ himself is said to "save to the uttermost them that come to God by him," Heb. vii. And these three things, I say, are required to be known, that we may have a saving acquaintance, and such as is attended with consolation, with any of the properties of God; and all these being hid only in Christ, from him alone it is to be obtained.

This, then, is the first part of our first demonstration, -- that all true and sound wisdom and knowledge is laid up in the Lord Christ, and from him alone to be obtained; because our wisdom, consisting, in a main part of it, in the knowledge of God, his nature, and his properties, this lies wholly hid in Christ, nor can possibly be obtained but by him.

II. For the knowledge of ourselves, which is the second part of our [170] wisdom, this consists in these three things, which our Saviour sends his Spirit to convince the world of, -- even "sin, righteousness, and judgment," John xvi. 8. To know ourselves in reference unto these three, is a main part of true and sound wisdom; for they all respect the supernatural and immortal end whereunto we are appointed; and there is none of these that we can attain unto but only in Christ.

1. In respect of sin. There is a sense and knowledge of sin left in the consciences of all men by nature. To tell them what is good and evil in many things, to approve and disapprove of what they do, in reference to a judgment to come, they need not go farther than themselves, Rom. ii. 14, 15. But this is obscure, and relates mostly to greater sins, and is in sum that which the apostle gives us, Rom. i. 32, "They know the judgment of God, that they which do such things are worthy of death." This he placeth among the common presumptions and notions that are received by mankind, -- namely, that it is [171] "righteous with God, that they who do such things are worthy of death." And if that be true, which is commonly received, that no nation is so barbarous or rude, but it retaineth some sense of a Deity; then this also is true, that there is no nation but hath a sense of sin, and the displeasure of God for it. For this is the very first [172] notion of God in the world, that he is the rewarder of good and evil. Hence

were all the sacrifices, purgings, expiations, which were so generally spread over the face of the earth. But this was and is but very dark, in respect of that knowledge of sin with its appurtenances, which is to be obtained.

A farther knowledge of sin, upon all accounts whatever, is giver by the law; that law which was "added because of transgressions." This [173] revives doctrinally all that sense of good and evil which was at first implanted in man; and it is a glass, whereinto whosoever is able spiritually to look, may see sin in all its ugliness and deformity. The truth is, look upon the law in its purity, holiness, compass, and perfection; its manner of delivery, [174] with dread, terror, thunder, earthquakes, fire; the sanction of it, in death, curse, wrath; and it makes a wonderful discovery of sin, upon every account: its pollution, guilt, and exceeding sinfulness are seen by it. But yet all this doth not suffice to give a man a true and thorough conviction of sin. Not but that the glass is clear, but of ourselves we have not eyes to look into it; the rule is straight, but we cannot apply it: and therefore Christ sends his Spirit to convince the world of sin, John xvi. 8; who, though, as to some ends and purposes, he makes use of the law, yet the work of conviction, which alone is a useful knowledge of sin, is his peculiar work. And so the discovery of sin may also be said to be by Christ, -- to be part of the wisdom that is hid in him. But yet there is a twofold regard besides this, of his sending his Spirit to convince us, wherein this wisdom appears to be hid in him:-- First, because there are some near concernments of sin, which are more clearly held out in the Lord Christ's being made sin for us, than any other way. Secondly, in that there is no knowledge to be had of sin, so as to give it a spiritual and saving improvement, but only in him.

For the first, there are four things in sin that clearly shine out in the cross of Christ:-- (1.) The desert of it. (2.) Man's impotency by reason of it. (3.) The death of it. (4.) A new end put to it.

(1.) The desert of sin doth clearly shine in the cross of Christ upon a twofold account:-- [1.] Of the person suffering for it. [2.] Of the penalty he underwent.

[1.] Of the person suffering for it. This the Scripture oftentimes very emphatically sets forth, and lays great weight upon: John iii. 16, "God so loved the world, that he gave his only begotten Son." It was his only Son that God sent into the world to suffer for sin, Rom. viii. 32. "He spared not his own Son, but delivered him up for us all." To see a slave beaten and corrected, it argues a fault committed; but yet perhaps the demerit of it was not very great. The correction of a son argues a great provocation; that of an only son, the greatest imaginable. Never was sin seen to be more abominably sinful and full of provocation, than when the burden of it was upon the shoulders of the Son of God. God having made his Son, the Son of his love, his only begotten, full of grace and truth, [175] sin for us, to manifest his indignation against it, and how utterly impossible it is that he should let the least sin go unpunished, he lays[176] hand on him, and spares him not. If [177] sin be imputed to the dear Son of his bosom, as upon his own voluntary assumption of it it was (for he said to his Father, "Lo, I come to do thy will," and all our iniquities did meet on him), [and] he will not spare him any thing of the due desert of it; is it not most clear from hence, even from the blood of the cross of Christ, that such is the demerit of sin, that it is altogether impossible that God should pass by any, the least, unpunished? If he would have done it for any, he would have done it in reference to his only Son; but he spared him not.

Moreover, God is not at all delighted with, nor desirous of, the blood, the tears, the cries, the inexpressible torments and sufferings, of the Son of his love (for he delights not in the anguish of any, -- "he doth not [178] afflict willingly, nor grieve the children of men," much less the Son of his bosom); only he required that his law be fulfilled, his justice satisfied, his wrath atoned for sin; and nothing less than all this would bring it about. If the debt of sin might have been compounded for at a cheaper rate, it had never been held up at the price of the blood of Christ. Here, then, soul, take a view of the desert of sin; behold it far more evident than in all the threatenings and curses of the law. "I thought, indeed," mayest thou say from thence, "that sin, being found on such a poor worm as I am, was worthy of death; but that it should have this effect if charged on the Son of God, -- that I never once imagined."

[2.] Consider also, farther, what he suffered. For though he was so excellent a one, yet perhaps it was but a light affliction and trial that he underwent, especially considering the strength he had to bear it. Why, whatever it were, it made this [179] "fellow of the Lord of hosts," this [180] "lion of the tribe of Judah," this [181] "mighty one," "the [182] wisdom and power of God," to tremble, [183] sweat, cry, pray, wrestle, and that with strong supplications. Some of the popish devotionists tell us that one drop, the least, of the blood of Christ, was abundantly enough to redeem all the world; but they err, not knowing the desert of sin, nor the severity of the justice of God. If one drop less than was shed, one pang less than was laid on, would have done it, those other drops had not been shed, nor those other pangs laid on. God did not cruciate the dearly-beloved of his soul for nought. But there is more than all this:--

It pleased God to [184] bruise him, to put him to grief, to make his soul an offering for sin, and to pour out his life unto death. He [185] hid himself from him, -- was far from the voice of his cry, until he cried out, "My God, my God, why hast thou forsaken me?" He made him [186] sin and a [187] curse for us; executed on him the sentence of the law; brought him into an agony, wherein he sweat thick drops of blood, was grievously troubled, and his soul was heavy unto death. He that was the power of God, and the wisdom of God, went stooping under the burden, until the whole frame of nature seemed astonished at it. Now this, as I said before that it discovered the indignation of God against sin, so it clearly holds out the desert of it. Would you, then, see the true demerit of sin? -- take the measure of it from the mediation of Christ, especially his cross. It brought him who was the Son of God, equal unto God, God blessed for ever, into the form of a [188] servant, who had not where to lay his head. It pursued him all his life with afflictions and persecutions; and lastly brought him under the rod of God; there bruised him and brake him, -- [189] slew the Lord of life. Hence is deep humiliation for it, upon the account of him whom we [190] have pierced. And this is the first spiritual view of sin we have in Christ.

(2.) The wisdom of understanding our impotency, by reason of sin, is wrapped up in him. By our impotency, I understand two things:-- [1.] Our disability to make any atonement with God for sin. [2.] Our disability to answer his mind and will, in all or any of the obedience that he requireth, by reason of sin.

[1.] For the first, that alone is discovered in Christ. Many inquiries have the sons of men made after an atonement, -- many ways have they entered into to accomplish it. After this they inquire, Mic. vi. 6, 7, "Will any manner of sacrifices, though appointed of God, as burnt-offerings, and calves of a year old; though very costly, thousands of rams, and ten thousand rivers of oil; though dreadful and tremendous, offering violence to nature, as to give my children to the fire;" -- will any of these things make an atonement? David doth positively, indeed, determine this business, Ps. xlix. 7, 8, "None of them" (of the best or richest of men) "can by any means redeem his brother, nor give to God a ransom for him; for the redemption of their soul is precious, and it ceaseth for ever." It cannot be done, -- no atonement can be made; yet men would still be doing, still attempting: hence did they heap up [191] sacrifices, some costly, some bloody and inhuman. The Jews, to this day, think that God was atoned for sin by the sacrifices of bulls and goats, and the like. And the Socinians acknowledge no atonement, but what consists in men's repentance and new obedience. In the cross of Christ are the mouths of all stopped as to this thing. For, --

1st. God hath there discovered that no sacrifices for sin, though of his own appointment, could ever make them perfect that offered them, Heb. x. 11. Those sacrifices could never take away sin; [192] -- those services could never make them perfect that performed them, as to the conscience, Heb. ix. 9; as the apostle proves, chap. x. 1. And thence the Lord rejects all sacrifices and offerings whatever, as to any such end and purpose, verses 6-8, Christ, in their stead, saying, "Lo, I come;" and by him we are "justified from all things, from which we could not be justified by the law," Acts xiii. 39: God, I say, in Christ, hath condemned all sacrifices, as wholly insufficient in the least to make an atonement for sin. And how great a thing it was to instruct the sons of men in this wisdom, the event hath manifested.

2dly. He hath also written vanity on all other endeavours whatever, that have been undertaken for that purpose. Rom. iii. 24-26, by setting forth his only Son "to be a propitiation," he leaves no doubt upon the spirits of men that in themselves they could make no atonement; for "if righteousness were by the law, then were Christ dead in vain." To what purpose should he be made a propitiation, were not we ourselves weak and without strength to any such purpose? So the apostle argues, Rom. v. 6, when we had no power, then did he by death make an atonement; as verses 8, 9.

This, wisdom then, is also hid in Christ. Men may see by other helps, perhaps, far enough to fill them with dread and astonishment, as those in Isa. xxxiii. 14; but such a sight and view of it as may lead a soul to any comfortable settlement about it, -- that only is discovered in this treasury of heaven, the Lord Jesus.

[2.] Our disability to answer the mind and will of God, in all or any of the obedience that he requireth, is in him only to be discovered. This, indeed, is a thing that many will not be acquainted with to this day. To teach a man that he cannot do what he ought to do, and for which he condemns himself if he do it not, is no easy task. Man rises up with all his power to plead against a conviction of impotency. Not to mention the proud [193] conceits and expressions of the philosophers, how many that would be called Christians do yet creep, by several degrees, in the persuasion of a power of fulfilling the law! And from whence, indeed, should men have this knowledge that we have not? Nature will not teach it, -- that is [194] proud and conceited; and it is one part of its pride, weakness, and corruption, not to know it at all. The law will not teach it: for though that will show us what we have done amiss, yet it will not discover to us that we could not do better; yea, by requiring exact obedience of us, it takes for granted that such power is in us for that purpose: it takes no notice that we have lost it; nor doth it concern it so to do. This, then, also lies hid in the Lord Jesus. Rom. viii. 2-4, "The law of the Spirit of life in Christ Jesus hath made me free from the law of sin and death. For what the law could not do, in that it was weak through the flesh, God sending his own Son in the likeness of sinful flesh, and for sin, condemned sin in the flesh; that the righteousness of the law might be fulfilled in us." The law can bring forth no righteousness, no obedience; it is weak to any such purpose, by reason of the flesh, and that corruption that is come on us. These two things are done in Christ, and by him:-- First, Sin is condemned as to its guilt, and we set free from that; the righteousness of the law by his obedience is fulfilled in us, who could never do it ourselves. And, secondly, That obedience which is required of us, his Spirit works it in us. So that that perfection of obedience which we have in him is imputed to us; and the sincerity that we have in obedience is from his Spirit bestowed on us. And this is the most excellent glass, wherein we see our impotency; for what need we his perfect obedience to be made ours, but that we have not, can not attain any? what need we his Spirit of life to quicken us, but that we are dead in trespasses and sins?

(3.) The death of sin; -- sin dying in us now, in some measure, whilst we are alive. This is a third concernment of sin which it is our wisdom to be acquainted with; and it is hid only in Christ. There is a twofold dying of sin:-- as to the exercise of it in our mortal members; and as to the root, principle, and power of it in our souls. The first, indeed, may be learned in part out of Christ. Christless men may have sin dying in them, as to the outward exercise of it. Men's bodies may be disabled for the service of their lusts, or the practice of them may not consist with their interest. Sin is never more alive [195] than when it is thus dying. But there is a dying of it as to the root, the principle of it, -- the daily decaying of the strength, power, and life of it; and this is to be had alone in Christ. Sin is a thing that of itself is not apt to die or to decay, but to get ground, and strength, and life, in the subject wherein it is, to eternity; prevent all its actual eruptions, yet its original enmity against God will still grow. In believers it is still dying and decaying, until it be utterly abolished. The opening of this treasury [mystery?] you have, Rom. vi. 3-6, etc. "Know ye not, that so many of us as were baptised into Jesus Christ were baptised into his death? Therefore we are buried with him by baptism into death, that like as Christ was raised from the dead by the glory of the Father, even so we also should walk in newness of life. For if we have been planted together in the likeness of his death, we shall be also in the likeness of his resurrection; knowing this, that our old man is crucified with him, that the body of sin might be destroyed, that henceforth we should not serve sin." This is the design of the apostle in the beginning of that chapter, not only to manifest whence is the principle and rise of our mortification and the death of sin, even from the death and blood of Christ; but also the manner of sin's continuance and dying in us, from the manner of Christ's dying for sin. He was crucified for us, and thereby sin was crucified in us; he died for us, and the body of sin is destroyed, that we should not serve sin; and as he was raised from the dead, that death should not have dominion over him, so also are we raised from sin, that it should not have dominion over us. This wisdom is hid in Christ only. Moses at his dying day had all his strength and vigour; so have sin and the law to all out of Jesus: at their dying day, sin is no way decayed. Now, next to the receiving of the righteousness prepared for us, to know this is the chiefest part of our wisdom. To be truly acquainted with the principle of the dying of sin, to feel virtue and power flowing from the cross of Christ to that purpose, to find sin crucified in us, as Christ was crucified for us, -- this is wisdom indeed, that is in him alone.

(4.) There is a glorious end whereunto sin is appointed and ordained, and discovered in Christ, that others are unacquainted withal. Sin in its own nature tends merely to the dishonour of God, the debasement of his majesty, and the ruin of the creature in whom it is; hell itself is but the filling of wretched creatures with the [196] fruit of their own devices. The comminations and threats of God in the law do manifest one other end of it, even the demonstration of the vindictive justice of God, in measuring out unto it a meet[197] recompense of reward. But here the law stays (and with it all other light) and discovers no other use or end of it at all. In the Lord Jesus there is the manifestation of another and more glorious end; to wit, the praise of God's glorious [198] grace in the pardon and forgiveness of it; -- God having taken order in Christ that that thing which tended merely to his dishonour should be managed to his infinite glory, and that which of all things he desireth to exalt, -- even that he may be known and believed to be a [199] "God pardoning iniquity, transgression and sin." To return, then, to this part of our demonstration:--

In the knowledge of ourselves, in reference to our eternal condition, doth much of our wisdom consist. There is not any thing wherein, in this depraved condition of nature, we are more concerned than sin; without a knowledge of that, we know not ourselves. "Fools make a mock of sin." A true saving knowledge of sin is to be had only in the Lord Christ: in him may we see the desert of our iniquities, and their pollution, which could not be borne or expiated but by his blood; neither is there any wholesome view of these but in Christ. In him and his cross is discovered our universal impotency, either of atoning God's justice or living up to his will. The death of sin is procured by, and discovered in, the death of Christ; as also the manifestation of the riches of God's grace in the pardoning thereof. A real and experimental acquaintance, as to ourselves, with all which, is our wisdom; and it is that which is of more value than all the wisdom of the world.

2. Righteousness is a second thing whereof the Spirit of Christ convinces the world, and the main thing that it is our wisdom to be acquainted withal. This all men are persuaded of, that God is a most righteous God; (that is a natural notion of God which Abraham insisted on, Gen. xviii. 25, "Shall not the Judge of all the earth do right?") they "know that this is the judgment of God, that they who commit such things are worthy of death," Rom. i. 32; that "it is a righteous thing with him to recompense tribulation unto offenders," 2 Thess. i. 6. He is "a God of purer eyes than to behold evil," Hab. i. 13; and therefore, "the ungodly cannot stand in judgment," Ps. i. 5. Hence the great inquiry of every one (who lies in any measure under the power of it), convinced of immortality and the judgment to come, is concerning the righteousness wherewith to appear in the presence of this righteous God. This more or less they are solicitous about all their days; and so, as the apostle speaks, Heb. ii. 15, "through the fear of death they are all their lifetime subject to bondage," -- they are perplexed with fears about the issue of their righteousness, lest it

should end in death and destruction.

(1.) Unto men set upon this inquiry, that which first and naturally presents itself, for their direction and assistance, assuredly promising them a righteousness that will abide the trial of God, provided they will follow its direction, is the law. The law hath many fair pleas to prevail with a soul to close with it for a righteousness before God. It was given out from God himself for that end and purpose; it contains the whole obedience that God requireth of any of the sons of men; it hath the promise of life annexed to it: "Do this, and live," "The doers of the law are justified;" and, "If thou wilt enter into life, keep the commandments;" -- yea, it is most certain that it must be wholly fulfilled, if we ever think to stand with boldness before God. This being some part of the plea of the law, there is no man that seeks after righteousness but doth, one time or another, attend to it, and attempt its direction. Many do it every day, who yet will not own that so they do. This, then, they set themselves about, -- labouring to correct their lives, amend their ways, perform the duties required, and so follow after a righteousness according to the prescript of the law. And in this course do many men continue long with much perplexity; -- sometimes hoping, oftener fearing; sometimes ready to give quite over; sometimes vowing to continue (their consciences being no way satisfied, nor righteousness in any measure attained) all their days. After they have wearied themselves perhaps for a long season, in the largeness of their ways, they come at length, with fear, trembling, and disappointment, to that conclusion of the apostle, "By the works of the law no flesh is justified;" and with dread cry that if God mark what is done amiss, there is no standing before him. That they have this issue, the apostle witnesseth, [200] Rom. ix. 31, 32, "Israel, who followed after the law of righteousness, hath not attained to the law of righteousness. Wherefore? Because they sought it not by faith, but as it were by the works of the law." It was not solely for want of endeavour in themselves that they were disappointed, for they earnestly followed after the law of righteousness; but from the nature of the thing itself, -- it would not bear it. Righteousness was not to be obtained that way; "For," saith the apostle, "if they which are of the law be heirs, faith is made void, and the promise made of none effect; because the law worketh wrath," Rom. iv. 14, 15. The law itself is now such as that it cannot give life, Gal. iii. 21, "If there had been a law given which would have given life, verily righteousness should have been by the law." And he gives the reason in the next verse why it could not give life; because "the Scripture concludes all under sin;" -- that is, it is very true, and the Scripture affirms it, that all men are sinners, and the law speaks not one word to sinners but death and destruction: therefore the apostle tells us plainly, that God himself found fault with this way of attaining righteousness, Heb. viii. 7, 8. [201] He complains of it; that is, he declares it insufficient for that end and purpose.

Now, there are two considerations that discover unto men the vanity and hopelessness of seeking righteousness in this path:--

[1.] That they have already sinned: [202] "For all have sinned, and come short of the glory of God," Rom. iii. 23. This they are sufficiently sensible of, that although they could for the time to come fulfil the whole law, yet there is a score, a reckoning, upon them already, that they know not how to answer for. Do they consult their guide, the [203] law itself, how they may be eased of the account that is past? it hath not one word of direction or consolation; but bids them prepare to die. The sentence is gone forth, and there is no escaping.

[2.] That if all former debts should be blotted out, yet they are no way able for the future to fulfil the law; they can as well move the earth with a finger, as answer the perfection thereof: and therefore, as I said, on this twofold account, they conclude that this labour is lost. [204] "By the works of the law shall no flesh be justified."

(2.) Wherefore, secondly, Being thus disappointed, by the severity and inexorableness of the law, men generally betake themselves to some other way, that may satisfy them as to those considerations which took them off from their former hopes; and this, for the most part, is by fixing themselves upon some ways of atonement to satisfy God, and helping out the rest with hopes of mercy. Not to insist on the ways of atonement and expiation which the Gentiles had pitched on; nor on the many ways and inventions -- by works satisfactory of their own, supererogations of others, indulgences, and purgatory in the close -- that the Papists have found out for this end and purpose; it is, I say, proper to all convinced persons, as above, to seek for a righteousness, partly by an endeavour to satisfy for what is past, and partly by hoping after general mercy. This the apostle calls a seeking for it "as it were by the works of the law," Rom. ix. 32; [205] not directly, "but as it were" by the works of the law, making up one thing with another. And he tells us what issue they have in this business, chap. x. 3, "Being ignorant of God's righteousness, and going about to establish their own righteousness, they have not submitted themselves unto the righteousness of God." They were by it enemies to the righteousness of God. The ground of this going about to establish their own righteousness was, that they were ignorant of the righteousness of God. Had they known the righteousness of God, and what exact conformity to his will he requireth, they had never undertaken such a fruitless business as to have compassed it "as it were by the works of the law." Yet this many will stick on a long time. Something they do, something they hope for; some old faults they will buy off with new obedience. And this pacifies their consciences for a season; but when the Spirit comes to convince them of righteousness, neither will this hold. Wherefore, --

(3.) The matter comes at length to this issue, -- they look upon themselves under this twofold qualification; as, --

[1.] Sinners, obnoxious to the law of God and the curse thereof; so that unless that be satisfied, that nothing from thence shall ever be laid to their charge, it is altogether in vain once to seek after an appearance in the presence of God.

[2.] As creatures made to a supernatural and eternal end; and therefore bound to answer the whole mind and will of God in the obedience required at their hands. Now, it being before discovered to them that both these are beyond the compass of their own endeavours, and the assistance which they have formerly rested on, if their eternal condition be of any concernment to them, their wisdom is, to find out a righteousness that may answer both these to the utmost.

Now, both these are to be had only in the Lord Christ, who is our righteousness. This wisdom, and all the treasures of it, are hid in him.

1st. He expiates former iniquities, he satisfies for sin, and procures remission of it. Rom. iii. 24, 25, "Being justified freely by his grace, through the redemption that is in Christ Jesus: whom God hath set forth to be a propitiation through faith in his blood, to declare his righteousness for the remission of sins that are past, through the forbearance of God." "All we like sheep," etc., Isa. liii. 6. "Through his blood we have redemption, the forgiveness of sins," Eph. i. 7. "God spared not his own Son, but delivered," etc., Rom. viii. 32. This, even this alone, is our righteousness; as to that first part of it which consists in the removal of the whole guilt of sin, whereby we are come short of the glory of God. On this account it is that we are assured that none shall ever lay any thing to our charge, or condemn us, Rom. viii. 33, 34, -- there being "no condemnation to them that are in Christ Jesus," verse 1. We are purged by the sacrifice of Christ, so as to have "no more conscience of sin," Heb. x. 2; that is, troubles in conscience about it. This wisdom is hid only in the Lord Jesus; in him alone is there an atonement discovered: and give me the wisdom which shall cut all scores concerning sin, and let the world take what remains. But, --

2dly. There is yet something more required; it is not enough that we are not guilty, we must also be actually righteous; -- not only all sin is to be answered for, but all righteousness is to be fulfilled. By taking away the guilt of sin, we are as persons innocent; but something more is required to make us to be considered as persons obedient. I know nothing to teach me that an innocent person shall go to heaven, be rewarded, if he be no more but so. Adam was innocent at his first creation, but he was to "do this," to "keep the commandments," before he entered into "life:" he had no title to life by innocence. This, then, moreover, is required, that the whole law be fulfilled, and all the obedience performed that God requires at our hands. This is the soul's second inquiry; and it finds a resolution only in the Lord Christ: "For if, when we were enemies, we were reconciled to God by the death of his Son, much more, being reconciled, we shall be saved by his life," Rom. v. 10. His death reconciled us; then are we saved by his life. The actual obedience which he yielded to the whole law of God, is that righteousness whereby we are saved; if so be we are found in him, not having on our own righteousness which is of the law, but the righteousness which is of God by faith, Phil. iii. 9. This I shall have occasion to handle more at large hereafter.

To return, then: It is not, I suppose, any difficult task to persuade men, convinced of immortality and judgment to come, that the main of their wisdom lies in this, even to find out such a righteousness as will accompany them for ever, and abide the severe trial of God himself. Now, all the wisdom of the world is but folly, as to the discovery of this thing. The utmost that man's wisdom can do, is but to find out most wretched, burdensome, and vexatious ways of perishing eternally. All the treasures of this wisdom are hid in Christ; he "of God is made unto us wisdom and righteousness," 1 Cor. i. 30.

3. Come we to the last thing, which I shall but touch upon; and that is judgment. The true wisdom of this also is hid in the Lord Christ; I mean, in particular, that judgment that is for to come: so at present I take the word in that place, [John xvi. 8.] Of what concernment this is to us to know, I shall not speak; -- it is that whose [206] influence upon the sons of men is the principle of their discriminating themselves from the beasts that perish. Neither shall I insist on the [207] obscure intimations of it which are given by the present proceedings of Providence in governing the world; nor that greater light of it which shines in the threats and promises of the law. The wisdom of it is in two regards hid in the Lord Jesus:-- (1.) As to the truth of it. (2.) As to the manner of it:--

(1.) For the truth of it; and so in and by him it is confirmed, and that two ways:-- [1.] By his death. [2.] By his resurrection:--

[1.] By his death. God, in the death of Christ, punishing and condemning sin in the flesh of his own Son, in the sight of men, angels, and devils, hath given an abundant assurance of a righteous and universal judgment to come; wherefore, or upon what account imaginable, could he be induced to lay such a load on him, but that he will certainly reckon one day with the sons of men for all their works, ways, and walkings before him. The death of Christ is a most solemn exemplar of the last judgment. Those who own him to be the Son of God, will not deny a judgment to come.

[2.] By his resurrection. Acts xvii. 31, Πίστιν παρασχὼν πᾶσιν, -- he hath given faith and assurance of this thing to all, by raising Christ from the dead, having appointed him to be the judge of all; in whom and by whom he will judge the world in righteousness. And then, --

(2.) And, lastly, for the manner of it: that it shall be by him who hath loved us, and given himself for us, -- who is himself the righteousness that he requires of our hands; and on the other side, by him who hath been, in his person, grace, ways, worship, servants, reviled, despised, contemned by the men of the world; -- which holds out unspeakable consolation on the one hand, and terror on the other: so that the wisdom of this also is hid in Christ.

And this is the second part of our first demonstration. Thus the knowledge of ourselves, in reference to our supernatural end, is no small portion of our wisdom. The things of the greatest concernment hereunto are, sin, righteousness, and judgment; the wisdom of all which is alone hid in the Lord Jesus: which was to be proved.

III. The third part of our wisdom is to walk with God. Now, that one may walk with another, six [208] things are required:-- 1. Agreement. 2. Acquaintance. 3. A way. 4. Strength. 5. Boldness. 6. An aiming at the same end. All these, with the wisdom of them, are hid in the Lord Jesus.

1. Agreement. The prophet tells us that two cannot walk together unless they be agreed, Amos iii. 3. Until agreement be made, there is no communion, no walking together. God and man by nature (or whilst man is in the state of nature) are at the greatest enmity. He declares nothing to us but wrath, Rom. i. 18; whence we are said to be children of it; that is, born obnoxious to it, Eph. ii. 3: and whilst we remain in that condition, "the wrath of God abideth on us," John iii. 36. All the discovery that God makes of himself unto us is, that he is inexpressibly provoked; and therefore preparing wrath against the day of wrath, and the revelation of his righteous judgment. The day of his and sinners' meeting, is called "The day of wrath," Rom. ii. 5, 6. Neither do we come short in our enmity against him; yea, we first began it, and we continue longest in it. To express this enmity, the apostle tells us, that our very minds, the best part of us, are "enmity against God," Rom. viii. 7, 8; and that we neither are, nor will, nor can be, subject to him; our enmity manifesting itself by universal rebellion against him: whatever we do that seems otherwise, is but hypocrisy or flattery; yea, it is a part of this enmity to lessen it. In this state the wisdom of walking with God must needs be most remote from the soul. He is [209] "light, and in him is no darkness at all;" we are darkness, and in us there is no light at all. He is life, a "living God;" we are dead, dead sinners, -- dead in trespasses and sin. He is "holiness," and glorious in it; we wholly defiled, -- an abominable thing. He

is "love;" we full of hatred, -- hating and being hated. Surely this is no foundation for agreement, or, upon that, of walking together: nothing can be more remote than this frame from such a condition. The foundation, then, of this, I say, is laid in Christ, hid in Christ. "He," saith the apostle, "is our peace; he hath made peace" for us, Eph. ii. 14, 15. He slew the enmity in his own body on the cross, verse 16.

(1.) He takes out of the way the cause of the enmity that was between God and us, -- sin and the curse of the law. He makes an end of sin, and that by making atonement for iniquity, Dan. ix. 24; and he blotteth out the hand-writing of ordinances, Col. ii. 14, redeeming us from the curse, by "being made a curse for us," Gal. iii. 13.

(2.) He destroys him who would continue the enmity, and make the breach wider, Heb. ii. 14 "Through death he destroyed him that had the power of death, that is, the devil;" and, Col. ii. 15, "spoiled principalities and powers."

(3.) He made "reconciliation for the sins of the people," Heb. ii. 17; he made by his blood an atonement with God, to turn away that wrath which was due to us, so making peace. Hereupon God is said to be "in Christ, reconciling the world unto himself," 2 Cor. v. 19; -- being reconciled himself, verse 18, he lays down the enmity on his part, and proceeds to what remains, -- to slay the enmity on our part, that we also may be reconciled. And this also, --

(4.) He doth; for, Rom. v. 11, "By our Lord Jesus Christ we do receive the atonement," accept of the peace made and tendered, laying down our enmity to God; and so confirming an agreement betwixt us in his blood. So that "through him we have an access unto the Father," Eph. ii. 18. Now, the whole wisdom of this agreement, without which there is no walking with God, is hid in Christ; out of him God on his part is a consuming fire, -- we are as stubble fully dry, yet setting ourselves in battle array against that fire: if we are brought together we are consumed. All our approachings to him out of Christ are but to our detriment; in his blood alone have we this agreement. And let not any of us once suppose that we have taken any step in the paths of God with him, that any one duty is accepted, that all is not lost as to eternity, if we have not done it upon the account hereof.

2. There is required acquaintance, also, to walking together. Two may meet together in the same way, and have no quarrel between them, no enmity; but if they are mere strangers one to another, they pass by without the least communion together. It doth not suffice that the enmity betwixt God and us be taken away; we must also have acquaintance given us with him. Our not knowing of him is a great cause and a great part of our enmity. Our understandings are "darkened," and we are "alienated from the life of God," etc., Eph. iv. 18. This also, then, must be added, if we ever come to walk with God, which is our wisdom. And this also is hid in the Lord Christ, and comes forth from him. It is true there are sundry other means, as his word and his works, that God hath given the sons of men, to make a discovery of himself unto them, and to give them some acquaintance with him, that, as the apostle speaks, Acts xvii. 27, "they should seek the Lord, if haply they might find him;" but yet, as that knowledge of God which we have by his works is but very weak and imperfect, so that which we have by the word, the letter of it, by reason of our blindness, is not saving to us if we have no other help; for though that be light as the sun in the firmament, yet if we have no eyes in our heads, what can it avail us? -- no saving acquaintance with him, that may direct us to walk with

him, can be obtained. This also is hid in the Lord Jesus, and comes forth from him, 1 John v. 20, "He hath given us an understanding, that we should know him that is true;" -- all other light whatever without his giving us an understanding, will not do it. He is the true Light, which lighteth every one that is enlightened, John i. 9. He opens our understandings that we may understand the Scriptures, Luke xxiv. 45; -- none hath known God at any time, "but he hath revealed him," John i. 18. God dwells in that "light which no man can approach unto," 1 Tim. vi. 16. None hath ever had any such acquaintance with him as to be said to have seen him, but by the revelation of Jesus Christ. Hence he tells the Pharisees, that notwithstanding all their great knowledge which they pretended, indeed they had "neither heard the voice of God at any time, nor seen his shape," John v. 37. They had no manner of spiritual acquaintance with God, but he was unto them as a man whom they had never heard nor seen. There is no acquaintance with God, as love, and full of kindness, patience, grace, and pardoning mercy (on which knowledge of him alone we can walk with him), but only in Christ; but of this fully before. This, then, also is hid in him.

3. There must, moreover, be a way wherein we must walk with God. God did at the beginning assign us a path to walk in with him, even the path of innocence and exact holiness, in a covenant of works. This path, by sin, is so filled with thorns and briers, so stopped up by curses and wrath, that no flesh living can take one step in that path; a new way for us to walk in must be found out, if ever we think to hold communion with God. And this also lies upon the former account. It is hid in Christ. All the world cannot, but by and in him, discover a path that a man may walk one step with God in. And therefore the Holy Ghost tells us that Christ hath consecrated, dedicated, and set apart for that purpose, "a new and living way" into the holiest of all, Heb. x. 20; a new one, for the first, old one was useless; a living one, for the other is dead: therefore, saith he, verse 22, "Let us draw near;" having a way to walk in, let us draw near. And this way that he hath prepared is no other but himself, John xiv. 6. In answer to them who would go to the Father, and hold communion with him, he tells them, "I am the way; and no man comes to the Father but by me." He is the medium of all communication between God and us. In him we meet, in him we walk. All influences of love, kindness, mercy, from God to us, are through him; all our returns of love, delight, faith, obedience unto God, are all through him; -- he being that "one way" God so often promiseth his people: and it is a glorious way, Isa. xxxv. 8, -- a high way, a way of holiness, a way that none can err in that once enter it; which is farther set out, Isa. xlii. 16. All other ways, all paths but this, go down to the chambers of death; they all lead to walk contrary to God.

4. But suppose all this, -- that agreement be made, acquaintance given, and a way provided; yet if we have no strength to walk in that way, what will all this avail us? This also, then, must be added; of ourselves we are of no strength, Rom. v. 6, -- poor weaklings, not able to go a step in the ways of God. When we are set in the way, either we throw ourselves down, or temptations cast us down, and we make no progress: and the Lord Jesus tells us plainly, that "without him we can do nothing," John xv. 5; not any thing at all that shall have the least acceptation with God. Neither can all the creatures in heaven and earth yield us the least assistance. Men's contending to do it in their own power,

comes to nothing. This part of this, wisdom also is hid in Christ. All strength to walk with God is from him. "I can do all things through Christ, which strengtheneth me," saith St Paul, Phil. iv. 13, who denies that of ourselves we have any sufficiency, 2 Cor. iii. 5. We that can do nothing in ourselves, we are such weaklings, can do all things in Jesus Christ, as giants; and therefore in him we are, against all oppositions in our way, "more than conquerors," Rom. viii. 37; and that because "from his fulness we receive grace for grace," John i. 16. From him have we the Spirit of life and power, whereby he bears, as on eagles' wings, swiftly, safely, in the paths of walking with God. Any step that is taken in any way, by strength that is not immediately from Christ, is one step towards hell. He first takes us by the arm and teaches us to go, until he leads us on to perfection. He hath milk and strong meat to feed us; he strengthens us with all might, and is with us in our running the race that is set before us. But yet, --

5. Whence should we take this confidence as to walk with God; even our God, who is "a consuming fire?" Heb. xii. 29. Was there not such a dread upon his people of old, that it was taken for granted among them that if they saw God at any time, it was not to be endured, -- they must die? Can any, but with extreme horror, think of that dreadful appearance that he made unto them of old upon mount Sinai; until Moses himself, who was their mediator, said, "I exceedingly fear and quake?" Heb. xii. 21, and all the people said, "Let not God speak with us, lest we die?" Exod. xx. 19. Nay, though men have apprehensions of the goodness and kindness of God, yet upon any discovery, of his glory, how do they tremble, and are filled with dread and astonishment! Hath it not been so with the "choicest of his saints?" Hab. iii. 16; Isa. vi. 5; Job xlii. 5, 6. Whence, then, should we take to ourselves this boldness, to walk with God? This the apostle will inform us in Heb. x. 19; it is "by the blood of Jesus:" so Eph. iii. 12, "In him we have boldness, and access with confidence;" -- not standing afar off, like the people at the giving of the law, but drawing nigh to God with boldness; and that upon this account:-- The dread and terror of God entered by sin; Adam had not the least thought of hiding himself until he had sinned. The guilt of sin being on the conscience, and this being a common notion left in the hearts of all, that God is a most righteous revenger thereof; this fills men with dread and horror at an apprehension of his presence, fearing that he is come to call their sins to remembrance. Now, the Lord Jesus, by the sacrifice and the atonement that he hath made, hath taken away this conscience of sin; that is, a dread of revenge from God upon the account of the guilt thereof. He hath removed the slaying sword of the law, and on that account gives us great boldness with God; discovering him unto us now, no longer as a revenging Judge, but as a tender, merciful, and reconciled Father. Moreover, whereas there is on us by nature a spirit of bondage, filling us with innumerable tormenting fears, he takes it away, and gives us "the Spirit of adoption, whereby we cry Abba, Father," and behave ourselves with confidence and gracious boldness, as children: for "where the Spirit of the Lord is, there is liberty," 2 Cor. iii. 17; that is, a freedom from all that dread and terror which the administration of the law brought with it. Now, as there is no sin that God will more severely revenge than any boldness that man takes with him out of Christ; so there is no grace more acceptable to him than that boldness which he is pleased to afford us in the blood of Jesus. There is, then, --

6. But one thing more to add; and that is, that two cannot walk together unless they have the same design in hand, and aim at the same end. This also, in a word, is given us in the Lord Jesus. The end of God is the advancement of his own glory; none can aim at this end, but only in the Lord Jesus. The sum of all is, that the whole wisdom of our walking with God is hid in Christ, and from him only to be obtained; as hath been manifest by an enumeration of particulars.

And so have I brought my first demonstration of what I intended unto a close, and manifested that all true wisdom and knowledge is laid up in, and laid out by, the Lord Jesus; and this by an induction of the chief particular heads of those things wherein confessedly our wisdom doth consist. I have but one more to add, and therein I shall be brief.

Secondly, [210] then, I say this truth will be farther manifested by the consideration of the insufficiency and vanity of any thing else that may lay claim or pretend to a title to wisdom.

There be two things in the world that do pass under this account:-- 1. The one is learning or literature; skill and knowledge of arts, sciences, tongues, with the knowledge of the things that are past. 2. Prudence and skill for the management of ourselves in reference to others, in civil affairs, for public good; which is much the fairest flower within the border of nature's garden. Now, concerning both these, I shall briefly evince, -- (1.) That they are utterly insufficient for the compassing and obtaining of those particular ends whereunto they are designed. (2.) That both of them in conjunction, with their utmost improvement, cannot reach the true general end of wisdom. Both which considerations will set the crown, in the issue, upon the head of Jesus Christ:--

1. Begin we with the first of these, and that as to the first particular. Learning itself, if it were all in one man, is not able to compass the particular end whereto it is designed; which writes "vanity and vexation" upon the forehead thereof.

The particular end of literature (though not observed by many, men's eyes being fixed on false ends, which compels them in their progress "aberrare a scopo") is none other but to remove some part of that curse which is come upon us by sin. Learning is the product of the soul's struggling with the curse for sin. Adam, at his first creation, was completely furnished with all that knowledge (excepting only things not then in being, neither in themselves nor in any natural causes, as that which we now call tongues, and those things that are the subject of story), as far as it lies in a needful tendency to the utmost end of man, which we now press after. There was no straitness, much less darkness, upon his understanding, that should make him sweat for a way to improve, and make out those general conceptions of things which he had. For his knowledge of nature, it is manifest, from his imposition of suitable names on all the creatures (the particular reasons of the most of which to us are lost); wherein, from the approbation given of his nomination of things in the Scripture, and the significance of what yet remains evident, it is most apparent it was done upon a clear acquaintance with their natures. Hence Plato could observe, [211] that he was most wise that first imposed names on things; yea, had more than human wisdom. Were the wisest man living, yea, a general collection of all the wise men in the world, to make an experiment of their skill and learning, in giving names to all living creatures, suitable to their natures and expressive of their qualities, they would quickly perceive the loss they have incurred. Adam was made perfect, for the whole end of ruling the creatures and living to God, for which he was made; which, without the knowledge of the nature of the one and the will of the other, he could not be. All this being lost by sin, a multiplication of tongues also being brought in, as a curse for an after rebellion, [212] the whole design of learning is but to disentangle the soul from this issue of sin. Ignorance, darkness, and blindness, is come upon the understanding; acquaintance with the works of God, spiritual and natural, is lost; strangeness of communication is given, by multiplication of tongues; tumultuating of passions and affections, with innumerable darkening prejudices, are also come upon us. To remove and take this away -- to disentangle the mind in its reasonings, to recover an acquaintance with the works of God, to subduct the soul from under the effects of the curse of division of tongues -- is the aim and tendency of literature. This is the "aliquid quo tendit;" and he that hath any other aim in it, "Passim sequitur corvum testâque lutoque." [213] Now, not to insist upon that vanity and vexation of spirit, with the innumerable evils wherewith this enterprise is attended, this is that I only say, it is in itself no way sufficient for the attainment of its end, which writes vanity upon its forehead with characters not to be obliterated. To this purpose I desire to observe these two things:--

(1.) That the knowledge aimed at to be recovered was given unto man in order to his walking with God, unto that supernatural end whereunto he was appointed. For after he was furnished with all his endowments, the law of life and death was given to him, that he might know wherefore he received them. Therefore, knowledge in him was spiritualized and sanctified: even that knowledge which he had by nature, in respect of its principle and end, was spiritual.

(2.) That the loss of it is part of that curse which was inflicted on us for sin. Whatever we come short in of the state of the first man in innocence, whether in loss of good or addition of evil, it is all of the curse for sin. Besides, that blindness, ignorance, darkness, deadness, which is everywhere ascribed to us in the state of nature, doth fully comprise that also whereof we speak.

On these two considerations it is most apparent that learning can no way of itself attain the end it aimeth at. For, --

[1.] That light which by it is discovered (which, the Lord knows, is very little, weak, obscure, imperfect, uncertain, conjectural, for a great part only enabling men to quarrel with and oppose one another, to the reproach of reason, yet I say, that which is attained by it) is not in the least measure by it spiritualized, or brought into that order of living to God, and with God, wherein at first it lay. This is wholly beyond its reach. As to this end, the apostle assures us that the utmost issue that men come to, is darkness and folly, Rom. i. 21, 22. Who knows not the profound inquiries, the subtile disputations, the acute reasonings, the admirable discoveries of Socrates, Plato, and Aristotle, and others? What, as to the purpose in hand, did they attain by all their studies and endeavours? Ἐμωράνθησαν, says the apostle, -- "They became fools." He that, by general consent, bears the crown of reputation for wisdom from them all, with whom to have lived was counted an inestimable happiness, [214] died like a fool, sacrificing a cock to Æsculapius. And another [apostle assures us], that Jesus Christ alone is "the true Light," that lighteth us, John i. 9. And there is not any that hath any true light, but what is immediately from him. After all the learning of men, if they have nothing else, they are still natural men, and perceive not the things of God. Their light is still but darkness; and how great is that darkness! It is the Lord Jesus alone who is anointed to open the eyes of the blind. Men cannot spiritualize a notion, nor lay it in any order to the glorifying of God. After all their endeavours, they are still blind and dark, yea, darkness itself, knowing nothing as they should. I know how the men of these attainments are apt to say, "Are we blind also?" with great contempt of others; but God hath blasted all their pride: [215] "Where," saith he, "is the wise? where is the scribe," etc., 1 Cor. i. 20. I shall not add what Paul hath farther cautioned us, to the seeming condemning of philosophy as being fitted to make spoil of souls; nor what [216] Tertullian with some other of the ancients have spoken of it; being very confident that it was the abuse, and not the true use and advantage of it, that they opposed. But, --

[2.] The darkness and ignorance that it strives to remove, being come upon us as a curse, it is not in the least measure, as it is a curse, able to remove it or take it away. He that hath attained to the greatest height of literature, yet if he hath nothing else, -- if he have not Christ, -- is as much under the curse of blindness, ignorance, stupidity, dullness, as the poorest, silliest soul in the world. The curse is only removed in him who was made a curse for us. Every thing that is penal is taken away only by him on whom all our sins did meet in a way of punishment; yea, upon this account. The more abilities the mind is furnished withal, the more it closes with the curse, and strengthens itself to act its enmity against God. All that it receives doth but help it to set up high thoughts and imaginations against the Lord Christ. So that this knowledge comes short of what in particular it is designed unto; and therefore cannot be that solid wisdom we are inquiring after.

There be sundry other things whereby it were easy to blur the countenance of this wisdom; and, from its intricacy, difficulty, uncertainty, unsatisfactoriness, -- betraying its followers into that which they most profess to avoid, blindness and folly, -- to write upon it "vanity and vexation of spirit." I hope I shall not need to add any thing to clear myself for not giving a due esteem and respect unto literature, my intendment being only to cast it down at the feet of Jesus Christ, and to set the crown upon his head.

2. Neither can the second part of the choicest wisdom out of Christ attain the peculiar end whereunto it is appointed; and that is prudence in the management of civil affairs, -- than which no perishing thing is more glorious, -- nothing more useful for the common good of human kind. Now, the immediate end of this prudence is to keep the rational world in bounds and order, to draw circles about the sons of men, and to keep them from passing their allotted bounds and limits, to the mutual disturbance and destruction of each other. All manner of trouble and disturbance ariseth from irregularity: one man breaking in upon the rights, usages, interests, relations of another, sets this world at variance. The sum and aim of all wisdom below is, to cause all things to move in their proper sphere, whereby it would be impossible there should be any more interfering than is in the celestial orbs, notwithstanding all their divers and various motions: to keep all to their own allotments, within the compass of the lines that are fallen unto them, is the special end of this wisdom.

Now, it will be a very easy task, to demonstrate that all civil prudence whatever [217] (besides the vexation of its attainment, and loss being attained) is no way able to compass this end. The present condition of affairs throughout the world, as also that of former ages, will abundantly testify it; but I shall farther discover the vanity of it for this end in some few observations. And the

(1.) First is, That, through the righteous judgment of God lopping off the top flowers of the pride of men, it frequently comes to pass that those who are furnished with the greatest abilities of this kind do lay them out to a direct contrary end unto that which is their natural tendency and aim. From whom, for the most part, are all the commotions in the world, -- the breaking up of bounds, setting the whole frame of nature on fire? is it not from such men as these. Were not men so wise, the world, perhaps, would be more quiet, when the end of wisdom is to keep it in quietness. This seems to be a curse that God hath spread upon the wisdom of the world, in the most in whom it is, that it shall be employed in direct opposition to its proper end.

(2.) That God hath made this a constant path towards the advancement of his own glory, even to leaven the wisdom and the counsels of the wisest of the sons of men with folly and madness, that they shall, in the depth of their policy, [218] advise things for the compassing of the ends they do propose as unsuitable as any thing that could proceed out of the mouth of a child or a fool, and as directly tending to their own disappointment and ruin as any thing that could be invented against them. "He destroys the wisdom of the wise, and brings to nothing the understanding of the prudent," 1 Cor. i. 19. This he largely describes, Isa. xix. 11-14. Drunkenness and staggering is the issue of all their wisdom; and that upon this account, -- the Lord gives them the spirit of giddiness. So also Job v. 12-14. They meet with darkness in the day-time: [219] when all things seem clear about them, and a man would wonder how men should miss their way, then will God make it darkness to such as these. So Ps. xxxiii. 10. Hence God, as it were, sets them at work, and undertakes their disappointment, Isa. viii. 9, 10, "Go about your counsels," saith the Lord, "and I will take order that it shall come to nought." And, Ps. ii. 3, 4, when men are deep at their plots and contrivances, God is said to have them in derision, to laugh them to scorn, seeing the poor worms industriously working out their own ruin. Never was this made more clear than in the days wherein we live. Scarcely have any wise men been brought to destruction, but it hath evidently been through their own folly; neither hath the wisest counsel of most been one jot better than madness.

(3.) That this wisdom, which should tend to universal quietness, hath almost constantly given universal disquietness unto themselves in whom it hath been most eminent. "In much wisdom is much grief," Eccles. i. 18. And in the issue, some of them have made away with themselves, as Ahithophel; and the most of them have been violently dispatched by others. There is, indeed, no end of the folly of this wisdom. [220] The great men of the world carry away the reputation of it; -- really it is found in few of them. They are, for the most part, common events, whereunto they contribute not the least mite, which are ascribed to their care, vigilance, and foresight. Mean men, that have learned to adore what is above them, reverence the meetings and conferences of those who are in greatness and esteem. Their weakness and folly is little known. Where this wisdom hath been most eminent, it hath dwelt so close upon the borders of atheism, been attended with such falseness and injustice, that it hath made its possessors wicked and infamous.

I shall not need to give any more instances to manifest the insufficiency of this wisdom for the attaining of its own peculiar and immediate end. This is the vanity of any thing whatever, -- that it comes short of the mark it is directed unto. It is far, then, from being true and solid wisdom, seeing on the forehead thereof you may read "Disappointment."

And this is the first reason why true wisdom cannot consist in either of these, -- because they come short even of the particular and immediate ends they aim at. But, --

Secondly, Both these in conjunction, with their utmost improvement, are not able to reach the true general end of wisdom. This assertion also falleth under an easy demonstration, and it were a facile thing to discover their disability and unsuitableness for the true end of wisdom; but it is so professedly done by him who had the largest portion of both of any of the sons of men (Solomon in his Preacher), that I shall not any farther insist upon it.

To draw, then, unto a close:-- if true and solid wisdom is not in the least to be found amongst these, if the pearl be not hid in this field, if these two are but vanity and disappointment, it cannot but be to no purpose to seek for it in any thing else below, these being amongst them incomparably the most excellent; and therefore, with one accord, let us set the crown of this wisdom on the head of the Lord Jesus.

Let the reader, then, in a few words, take a view of the tendency of this whole digression. To draw our hearts to the more cheerful entertainment of and delight in the Lord Jesus, is the aim thereof. If all wisdom be laid up in him, and by an interest in him only to be attained, -- if all things beside him and without him that lay claim thereto are folly and vanity, -- let them that would be wise learn where to repose their souls.

Footnotes:

104. "Repetit non citra πάθος, en tu pulchra es." -- Mercer.

105. Isa. xlv. 24, 25.

106. Rom. ix. 31, 32, x. 3, 4.

107. Isa. xlv. 24.

108. Numb. xxi. 5; 1 Cor. x. 9; Ps. lxviii. 18; Eph. iv. 8, 10; Ps. xcvii. 7; Heb. i. 6; Ps. cii. 25; Isa. vii. 14; Luke ii. 34; Rom. ix. 5; 1 Pet. ii. 6; Isa. xl. 3, xliv. 6, xlv. 22, xlviii. 12; Rom. xiv. 10; Rev. i. 11; Mal. iii. 1; Ps. ii. 12; Isa. xxxv. 4, lii. 5, 6, xlv. 14, 15; Zech. ii. 8, 12, iii. 1, xii. 10; Matt. xvi. 16; Luke i. 16, 17; John v. 18, 19, x. 30, i. 1, 3, 10, 14, vi. 62, viii. 23, 58; Col. i. 16; Heb. i. 2, 10-12; John iii. 13, 31, xvi. 28; Mic. v. 2; Prov. viii. 23; John xvii. 5; Jer. xxiii. 6; 1 John v. 20; Rev. i. 18, iv. 8; Acts xx. 28; 1 John iii. 16; Phil. ii. 6-8; 1 Tim. iii. 16; Heb. ii. 16; 1 John iv. 3; Heb. x. 5; John xx. 28; John x. 29-31; Matt. xvi. 16; Rom. viii. 32; John iii. 16, 18; Col. i. 15; John xvii. 10; Isa. ix. 6; Col. ii. 9; 1 Cor. viii. 6, ii. 8; Ps. lxviii. 17.

109. Cant. v. 1; Isa. lv. 1; Rev. xxii. 17; John vii. 37, 38.

110. Gal. iv. 14, 15.

111. Mal. iii. 6; John xiii. 1.

112. 1 Pet. i. 19.

113. Cant. ii. 1.

114. Cant. i. 15, 16, iv. 1, 7, 10.

115. Eccles. vii. 29.

116. Isa. liii. 2.

117. Heb. vii. 9, 10.

118. Job xiv. 4; Φρόνημα τῆς σαρκός, Rom. viii. 7; John iii. 16. Νοὸς τῆς σαρκός, Col. ii. 18.

119. 2 Cor. v. 21.

120. Gen. iii. 15.

121. John i. 14, 16; 1 Cor. xi.

1; Eph. v. 2; 1 Pet. ii. 21; Matt. iii. 17; Heb. ii. 18, vii. 25.

122. "Qui, propter homines liberandos ab æternâ morte, homo factus est, et ita ad susceptionem humilitatis nostræ, sine suæ majestatis diminutione inclinans, ut manens quod erat, assumensque quod non erat; veram servi formam, ei formæ, in qua Deo patri est æqualis, adunaret, ut nec inferiorem absumeret glorificatio, nec superiorem minueret assumptio; salvâ enim proprietate utriusque substantiæ, et in unum coëunte personam, suscipitur a majestate humilitas, a virtute infirmitas, a mortalitate æternitas, et ad rependendum nostræ conditionis debitum, natura inviolabilis naturæ est unita passibili," etc. -- Leo. Serm. i. De Nat.

123. Vind. Evan. c. viii. vol. xii.

124. "Deus versus, et homo verus in unitatem Domini temperatur, ut, quod nostris remediis congruebat, unus atque idem Dei hominumque mediator et mori possit ex uno, et resurgere possit ex altero." -- Leo. ubi sup.

125. Zech. xiii. 7; Ps. lxxxix. 19.

126. John xvi. 14, 15.

127. Isa. liii. 11, 12; John i. 16; Col. i. 19, 20.

128. Heb. xii. 2; Rev. i. 11.

129. 1 Cor. i. 24.

130. Gen. xlv. 26, 27.

131. Rev. i. 18.

132. Gen. xlix. 10; Numb. xxiv. 17, 19; Ps. ii. 1-9, lxxxix. 19-25, cx. 1-3; Isa. xi. 1, 4, xxxii. 1, 2, liii. 12, lxiii. 1-3; Jer. xxiii. 5, 6; Dan. vii. 13, 14; Luke ii. 11, xix. 38; John v. 22, 23; Acts ii. 34-36, v. 31; Phil. ii. 9-11; Eph. i. 20-22; Rev. v. 12-14, xix. 16.

133. Isa. lxiii. 3.

134. Ps. cx. 6; Rev. xix. 20.

135. Heb. i. 3; Eph. i. 22; Matt. xxviii. 18; Phil. ii. 10, 11; Rev. xix. 16; Ps. xv., lxviii.; Dan. vii. 10.

136. So the words are quoted in all editions of this treatise. Fully to develop the meaning of the allusion, it seems necessary that the whole of the Septuagint rendering should be quoted, -- Κεφαλὴ αὐτοῦ χρυσίον κεφαζ. It is the last word in which part of both the Hebrew words is said to be retained. There is some difficulty in fixing the import of פז. Gesenius refers us to Ps. xix. 10, in proof that it means fine, as distinguished from common gold; from פזז, a root not used in Hebrew, but signifying, in the cognate dialect of Arabic, to separate, to purify metals. Some connect the term with Uphaz, a district from which gold was procured, Jer. x. 9. Schultens derives the word from פזז, to leap, to spring up into notice, in allusion to the amount of gold discovered on the surface of the earth, through the previous disintegration of the rock in which it was disseminated, and when a shower has washed it from the soil by which it was covered. There is coincidence between the etymology of the word suggested by the Dutch critic, and the fact that the largest quantities of gold and gold ore have been discovered, not by excavation, but by the washing of detritus in regions of primary and transitory strata where the eruption of igneous rocks has occurred: "As for the earth, ... it hath dust of gold," Job xxviii. 5, 6. -- Ed.

137. Tit. iii. 5.

138. As Ophir is taken for the gold of Ophir, in Job xxii. 24, so Tarshish, the name of a city, of

which the locality is disputed, is used to denote a precious stone which was brought from it. It is translated "beryl" in the authorized version, though םהַשׁ, in Ezek. xxviii. 13, is also rendered by the same term. Some make תַּרְשִׁישׁ, the chrysolite or topaz of the moderns. The word has been thought to denote the sea, in Isa. xxiii. 10, but on slender ground. -- Ed.

139. Ἐπεὶ οὖν τὸ γενόμενον ὁ κόσμος ἐστὶν ὁ ξύμπας, ὁ τοῦτον θεωρῶν τάχα ἂν ἀκοῦσαι παρ' αὐτοῦ, ὡς ἐμὲ πεποίηκεν ὁ Θεός. -- Plotin.

140. Gen. i. 31.

141. "Quamvis speciali cura atque indulgentia Dei, populum Israelitcum constat electum, omnesque alias nationes suas vias ingredi, hoc est, secundum propriam permissæ sunt vivere voluntatem, non ita tamen se æterna Creatoris bonitas ab cationibus admoneret," -- Prosp. De Vocat. Gent. 2, 4. "Coelum et terra, et omnia quæ in eis sunt, ecce undique mihi dicunt ut te amem, nec cessant dicere omnibus, ut sint inexcusabiles." -- August. Confess, lib. x. cap. 6.

142. Exod. xxxiii. 22; 1 Cor. x. 4.

143. Ἔστω δὴ ἔλεος, λύπη τὶς ἐπὶ φαινομένῳ κακῷ φθαρτικῷ καὶ λυπηρῷ τοῦ ἀναξίου τυγχάνειν. -- Arist. 2. Rhet. "Quid autem misericordia, nisi alienæ miseriæ quædam in nostro corde compassio; quâ alicui, si possumus, subvenire compellimur?" -- August. De Civit. Dei, lib. ix. cap. 5.

144. Κατακαυχᾶται ἔλεος κρισεως, James ii. 13.

145. Προέθετο.

146. Ἥ μιν ἑλὼν ῥίψω ἐξ

Τάρταρον ἠερόεντα,

Τῆλε μαλ' ἧχι βαθιστον ὑπὸ χθονός ἐστι βέρεθρον,

Ἔνθα σιδήρειαί τε πύλαι καὶ χάλκεος οὐδός,

Τόσσον ἔνερθ' Ἀΐδεω, ὅσον οὐρανός ἐστ' ἀπὸ γαίης. Homer, Il. θ. 13-16.

147. Vid. Diatrib. De Just. Divin. [A treatise by Owen, which will be found in vol. x. of this edition of his works.]

148. Rom. viii. 32; Isa. liii. 10; Heb. x. 7-9; Rom. i. 32; 2 Thess. i. 5, 6; Ps. v. 5, 6; Hab. i. 13; Ps. cxix. 137.

149. Gen. iii. 17-19, viii. 21; Rom. viii. 21, 22; 2 Pet. ii. 4-6, iii. 6; Jude 6, 7.

150. 1 Cor. i. 30.

151. Matt. iii. 17.

152. Matt. xxvi. 37, 38; Mark xiv. 33; Luke xxii. 43, 44; Heb. v. 7; Matt. xxvii. 51; Mark xv. 33, 34; Isa. liii. 6.

153. Matt. v. 45; Acts xiv. 17, 18.

154. "Animula vagula, blandula,

Hospes comesque corporis,
Quæ nunc abibis in loca
Pallida, rigida, nudula?
Nec ut soles dabias jocos."
Had. Imp.

155. Rom. ii. 4, 5, ix. 22.

156. "Eos, quibus indulgere videtur, quibus parcere, molles venturis malis (Deus) format." -- Seneca, "De Providentiâ," cap. iv. -- "Pro dii immortales! Cur interdum in hominum sceleribus maximis, aut connivetis, aut præsentis fraudis poenas in diem reservatis!" -- Cic. pro Cæl. 24.

157. Κατὰ μὲν τοῦ ἐπιῤῥέοντος βάψαντα, γλυκὺ τὸ ὕδωρ ἀνιμήοασθαι· εἰ δὲ εἰς βάθος τὶς καθῆκεν τὴν κάλπιν, ἁλμυρόν. -- Arrian. περιπ. Εὐξείνου πόντου.

158. "Si amabilis est sapientia cum cognitione rerum conditiarum, quam amabilis est sapientia, quæ condidit omnia ex nihilo!" -- August. Lib. Meditat., c. xviii.

159. 1 Cor. i. 20, 30.

160. Gen. i. 31.

161. Gen. iii. 17, 18; Rom. i. 18.

162. Exod. xxxiii. 18, 19, xxxiv. 6, 7.

163. Rom. iii. 24, 25.

164. 2 Cor. iv. 17.

165. John i. 16.

166. Exod. xxxiv. 6, 7.

167. Isa. liii. 5, 6; Lev. xvi. 21; Rom. viii. 32.

168. 1 Cor. i. 20, 30; Jer. xxiii. 6.

169. "Shaddai, Aquila interpretatur ἄλκιμον, quod nos robustum et ad omnia perpetranda sufficientem possumus dicere." -- Hieron., Epist. cxxxvi.

170. Ἡ σοφία ἐστὶ τῶν τιμιωτάτων. -- Arist.

171. Τὸ δικαίωμα τοῦ Θεοῦ ἐπιγνόντες ὅτι οἱ τὰ τοιαῦτα πράσσοντες ἄξιοι θανάτου εἰσίν. -- Rom. i. 32. "Perfecto demum scelere, magnitudo ejus intellecta est." -- Tacit.

Τί χρῆμα πάσχεις; τίς σ' ἀπόλλυσιν νόσος;

Ἡ σύνεσις, ὅτι σύνοιδα δείν' εἰργασμένος. Eurip. Orest. 395, 396.

172. "Primus est deorum cultus, Deos credere: deinde reddere illis majestatem suam, reddere bonitatem, sine qua nulla majestas est. Scire illos esse qui præsident mundo: qui universa vi sua temperant: qui humani generis tutelam gerunt." -- Senec., Epist. xcvi. "Neque honor ullus deberi potest Deo, si nihil præstat colenti; nec ullus metus, si non irascitur non colenti." -- Lactan.

"Raro antecedentem scelestum

Deseruit pede pæna claudo." Horat., Od. iii. 2, 31, 32.

"Quo fugis Encelade? quascunque accessseris oras,

Sub Jove semper eris," etc.

? "Hos tu

Evasisse putes, quos diri conscia facti

Mens habet attonitos, et surdo verbere cædit!" Juvenal, Sat. xiii. 192.

Οἴει σὺ τοὺς θανόντας, ὦ Νικόστρατε,

Τρυφῆς ἁπάσης μεταλαβόντας ἐν βίῳ,

Πεφευγέναι, τὸ θεῖον ὡς λεληθότας;

Ἔστιν Δίκης ὀφθαλμός, ὃς τὰ πάνθ' ὁρᾷ.

Καὶ γὰρ καθ' ἅδην δύο τρίβους νομίζομεν,

Μίαν δικαίων, ἑτέραν δ' ἀσεθῶν εἶν' ὁδόν.

Κ' εἰ τοὺς δύο καλύψει ἡ γῆ, φασὶ, χρόνῳ

Ἁρπάζ', ἀπελθών, κλέπτ', ἀποστέρει, κύκα.

Μηδὲν πλανηθῇς, ἔσται κἄν ἅδου κρίσις.

Ἥπερ ποιήσει Θεὸς ὁ πάντων δεσπότης,

Οὗ τοὔνομα φοβερὸν οὐδ' ἂν ὀνομάσαιμ' ἐγώ. κ. τ. λ. Philemon, juxta Justin. Martyr. seu Diphil. juxta Clement.

173. Gal. iii. 19; Rom. vii. 13.

174. Exod. xix. 18-20; Deut. iv. 11; Heb. xii. 18-21.

175. 2 Cor. v. 21.

176. Zech. xiii. 7.

177. Heb. x. 7; Isa. liii. 6.

178. Lam. iii. 33.

179. Zech. xiii. 7.

180. Rev. v. 5.

181. Ps. lxxxix. 19.

182. Prov. viii. 22; 1 Cor. i. 24.

183. Matt. xxvi. 37, 38; Mark xiv. 33, 34; Luke xxii. 44; Heb. v. 7.

184. Isa. liii. 5, 6.

185. Ps. xxii. 1.

186. 2 Cor. v. 21.

187. Gal. iii. 13.

188. Phil. ii. 8.

189. 1 Cor. ii. 7.

190. Zech. xii. 10.

191. Vid. Diatr. de Just. Divin. cap. iii. vol. x.

192. Ps. xl. 6, 7.

193. "Quia unusquisque sibi virtutem acquirit; nemo sapientum de ea gratias Deo egit." -- Cicer.

194. "Natura sic apparet vitiata, ut hoc majoris vitii sit non videre." -- Aug.

195. See Treatise on Mortification. [Works., vol. vi.]

196. Prov. i. 31; Jer. xvii. 10.

197. 2 Thess. i. 6.

198. Eph. i. 6.

199. Heb. viii. 6-13.

200. Διώκων νόμον δικαιοσύνης εἰς νόμον δικαιοσύνης οὐκ ἔφθασε.

201. Μεμφόμενο.

202. Πάντες ἥμαρτον, Rom. iii. 23, v. 12.

203. Deut. xxvii. 26; Gal. iii. 10.

204. Gal. iii. 11, 12.

205. Ὡς ἐξ ἔργων νόμου.

206. "Bene et compositè C. Cæsar ... de vita et morte disseruit, falsa, credo, existimans, ea quæ de infernis memorantur; diverso itinere malos a bonis loca tetra, inculta, foeda atque formidolosa habere," -- Cato. apud. Sallust. Bell. Catil. lii. Ἀλλ' ἔστι καὶ τῷ ὄντι τὸ ἀγκβιώσκεσθαι, καὶ ἐκ τῶν τεθνεώτων τοὺς ζῶντας γίγνεσθαι, καὶ τὰς τῶν τεθνεώτων ψυχὰς εἶναι· καὶ ταῖς μὲν ἀγαθαῖς ἄμεινον εἶναι, ταῖς δὲ κακαῖς, κάκιον. -- Plat. in Phæd. 17.

207. "Devenêre locos lætos, et amoena vireta

Fortunatorum nemorum,

sedesque beatas," etc. Virg., Æn. vi. 638.

208. In the previous editions it is stated that five things are required to walk with God, and then five things are immediately enumerated. It will be found, however, that, in the subsequent illustration, six particulars are specified. A particular, the way, (see p. 109,) had been omitted in the division stated above. We have, therefore, altered it in accordance with Owen's real treatment of his subject. -- Ed.

209. 1 John i. 5, Σκοτία ἐν αὐτῷ οὐκ ἔστιν οὐδεμία. John i. 5; Eph. v. 8, ii. 1; Exod. xv. 11; 1 John iv. 8; Tit. iii. 3.

210. The division of which this indicates the second part, is implied, but not expressed, in p. 79, and the first paragraph of p. 80. -- Ed.

211. Οἶμαι μὲν ἐγὼ τὸν ἀληθέστατον λόγον περὶ τούτων εἶναι ᾧ Σώκρατες, μείζω τινὰ δύναμιν εἶναι ἢ ἀνθρωπείαν, τὴν θεμένην τὰ πρῶτα ὀνόματα τοῖς πράγμασιν. -- Plato in Cratylo.

212. Gen. xi. 3.

213. These words are borrowed from Pers., Sat. iii. 60, 61, in allusion to the fruitless pursuit of any object by the use of inadequate means. -- Ed.

214. Εἰ δέ τις τῶν ἀρετῆς ἐφιεμένων ὠφελιμωτέρω τινὶ Σωκράτους συνεγένετο, ἐκεῖνον ἐγὼ τὸν ἄνδρα ἀξιομακαριστότατον νομίζω. -- Xenoph. apol. pro Socrat. ad finem.

215. "O Sapientia superba irridens Christum crucifixum!" -- August. Expos. In Joh. Trac. 2, de cap. 1.

216. "Hæreses a philosophiâ subornantur. Inde Æones, et formæ

nescio quæ, trinitas homines apud Valentinium, Platonicus fuerat; inde Marcionis Deus melior de tranquillitate, a Stoicis venerat. Et ut anima interire dicatur, ab Epicureis observatur, et ut carnis restitutio negetur, de unâ omnium philosophorum scholâ sumitur: ... Quid ergo Athenis et Hierosolymis? quid Academiæ et Ecclesiæ? quid hæreticis et Christianis? Nostra institutio de porticu Salomonis est. Nobis curiositate opus non est post Jesum Christum; nec inquisitione post evangelium. Cum credimus, nihil desideramus ultra credere. Hoc enim priùs credimus, non esse quod ultra credere debeamus." -- Tertul. de Præscript. ad Hæret. [cap. vii.]? Ἐπειδήπερ ἱκανῶς ἐκ τῶν προειρημένων τὰ τῶν φιλοσόφων ὑμῶν ἐλήλεγκατα πάσης ἀγνοίας καὶ ἀπάτης φανέντα πλήρη. κ. τ. λ. -- Just. Mart. ad Græc. Cohort. [c. xi.]

Μοῦνον ἐμοὶ φίλον ἔσκε λόγων κλέος, οὓς συνάγειραν

Ἀντολίη τι, δύσις τε, καὶ Ἑλλάδος εὖχος Ἀθῆναι,

Τοῖς ἔπι πολλ' ἐμόγησα πολὺν χρόνον, ἀλλὰ καὶ αὐτοῦ,

Πρηνέας ἐν δαπέδῳ Χριστοῦ προπάροιθεν ἔθηκα,

Εἴξαντας μεγάλοιο θεοῦ λόγῳ ὅς ῥα καλύπτει

Πάντα φρενὸς βροτέης στρεπτὸν πολυειδέα μῦθον. Greg. Naz. Car. i. de Reb. Suis.

217. Ὦ γῆρας ὡς ἐπαχθὲς ἀνθρώποισιν εἶ, καὶ πανταχῆ λυπηρόν, οὐ καθ' ἓν μόνον, ἐν ᾧ γὰρ οὐδὲν δυνάμεθ' οὐδ ἰσχύομεν, σὺ τηνικαῦθ' ἡμᾶς διδάσκεις εὖ φρονεῖν. -- Excerp. ex Nicostrat.

218. "Isthuc est sapere, non quod ante pedes modò est,

Videre; sed etiam illa quæ futura sunt,

Prospicere." Teren. Adelph. 3, 3, 33.

219. Isa. xxix. 14, xlvii. 10; Jer. xlix. 7; Obad. 8.

220. "Prudens futuri temporis exitum

Caliginosa nocte permit Deus: Ridetque, si mortalis ultra

Fas trepidat." Horat., Od. iii. 29, 29.

Chapter IV - Of communion with Christ in a conjugal relation in respect of consequential affections -- His delight in his saints first insisted on, Isa. lxii. 5; Cant. iii. 11; Prov. viii. 21 -- Instance of Christ's delight in believers -- He reveals his whole heart to them, John xv. 14, 15; himself, John xiv. 21; his kingdom; enables them to communicate their mind to him, giving them assistance, a way, boldness, Rom. viii. 26, 27 -- The saints delight in Christ; this manifested Cant. ii. 7, viii. 6 -- Cant. iii. 1-5, opened -- Their delight in his servants and ordinances of worship for his sake.

[221] The communion begun, as before declared, between Christ and the soul, is in the next place carried on by suitable consequential affections, -- affections suiting such a relation. Christ having given himself to the soul, loves the soul; and the soul having given itself unto Christ, loveth him also. Christ loves his own, yea, "loves them to the end," John xiii. 1; and the saints they love Christ, they "love the Lord Jesus Christ in sincerity," Eph. vi. 24.

Now the love of Christ, wherewith he follows his saints, consists in these four things:-- I. Delight. II. Valuation. III. Pity, or compassion. IV. Bounty. The love, also, of the saints unto Christ may be referred to these four heads:-- Delight; Valuation; Chastity; Duty.

Two of these are of the same kind, and two distinct; as is required in this relation, wherein all things stand not on equal terms.

I. The first thing on the part of Christ is delight. Delight is the flowing of love and joy, -- the [222] rest and complacence of the mind in a suitable, desirable good enjoyed. Now, Christ delights exceedingly in his saints: "As the bridegroom rejoiceth over the bride, so shall thy God rejoice over thee," Isa. lxii. 5. Hence he calleth the day of his espousals, the day of the "gladness of his heart," Cant. iii. 11. It is known that usually this is the most unmixed delight that the sons of men are in their pilgrimage made partakers of. The delight of the bridegroom in the day of his espousals is the height of what an expression of delight can be carried unto. This is in Christ answerable to the relation he takes us into. His heart is glad in us, without sorrow. And every day whilst we live is his wedding-day. It is said of him, Zeph. iii. 17, "The Lord thy God in the midst of thee" (that is, dwelling amongst us, taking our nature, John i. 14) "is mighty; he will save, he will rejoice over thee with joy; he will rest in his love, he will joy over thee with singing;" which is a full description of delight, in all the parts of it, -- joy and exultation, rest and complacence. "I rejoiced," saith he, "in the habitable parts of the earth, and my delights were with the sons of men," Prov. viii. 31. The thoughts of communion with the saints were the joy of his heart from eternity. On the compact and agreement that was between his

Father and him, that he should divide a portion with the strong, and save a remnant for his inheritance, his soul rejoiced in the thoughts of that pleasure and delight which he would take in them, when he should actually take them into communion with himself. Therefore in the preceding verse it is said he was by him as אָמוֹן, say we, "As one brought up with him," "alumnus;" the LXX. render it ἁρμόζουσα· and the Latin, with most other translations, "cuncta componens," or "disponens." The word taken actively, signifies him whom another takes into his care to breed up, and disposeth of things for his advantage. So did Christ take us then into his care, and rejoiced in the thoughts of the execution of his trust. Concerning them he saith, "Here will I dwell, and here will I make my habitation for ever." For them hath he chosen for his temple and his dwelling-place, because he delighteth in them. This makes him take them so nigh himself in every relation. As he is God, they are his temple; as he is a king, they are his subjects, -- he is the king of saints; as he is a head, they are his body, -- he is the head of the church; as he is a first-born, he makes them his brethren, -- "he is not ashamed to call them brethren."

I shall choose out one particular from among many as an instance for the proof of this thing; and that is this:-- Christ reveals his secrets, his mind, unto his saints, and enables them to reveal the secrets of their hearts to him, -- an evident demonstration of great delight. It was Samson's carnal delight in Delilah that prevailed with him to reveal unto her those things which were of greatest concernment unto him; he will not hide his mind from her, though it cost him his life. It is only a bosom friend into whom we will unbosom ourselves. Neither is there, possibly, a greater evidence of delight in close communion than this, that one will reveal his heart unto him whom he takes into society, and not entertain him with things common and vulgarly known. And therefore have I chose this instance, from amongst a thousand that might be given, of this delight of Christ in his saints.

He, then, communicates his mind unto his saints, and unto them only; -- his mind, the counsel of his love, the thoughts of his heart, the purposes of his bosom, for our eternal good, -- his mind, the ways of his grace, the workings of his Spirit, the rule of his sceptre, And the obedience of his gospel. [223] All spiritual revelation is by Christ. He is "the true Light, that lighteth every man that comes into the world," John i. 9. He is the "Day-spring," the "Day-star," and the "Sun;" so that it is impossible any light should be but by him. From him it is that "the secret of the Lord is with them that fear him, and he shows them his covenant," Ps. xxv. 14; as he expresses it at large, John xv. 14, 15, [224] "Ye are my friends, if ye do whatsoever I command you. Henceforth I call you not servants; for the servant knoweth not what his lord doth: but I have called you friends; for [225] all things that I have heard of my Father I have made known unto you." He makes them as his friends, and useth them as friends, -- as bosom friends, in whom he is delighted. He makes known all his mind unto them; every thing that his Father hath committed to him as Mediator to be revealed, Acts xx. 24. And the apostle declares how this is done, 1 Cor. ii. 10, 11, "?God hath revealed these things unto us by his Spirit;' for we have received him, that we might know the things that are freely given us of God.'?" He sends us his Spirits as he promised, to make known his mind unto his saints, and to lead them into all truth. And thence the apostle concludes, "We have known the mind of Christ," verse 16; "for he useth us as friends, and declareth it unto us," John i. 18. There is not any thing in the heart of Christ, wherein these his friends are concerned, that he doth not reveal to them. All his love, his good-will, the secrets of his covenant, the paths of obedience, the mystery of faith, is told them.

And all this is spoken in opposition to unbelievers, with whom he hath no communion. These know nothing of the mind of Christ as they ought: "The natural man receiveth not the things that are of God," 1 Cor. ii. 14. There is a wide difference between understanding the doctrine of the Scripture as in the letter, and a true knowing the mind of Christ. This we have by special unction from Christ, 1 John ii. 27, "We have an unction from the Holy One, and we know all things," 1 John ii. 20.

Now, the things which in this communion Christ reveals to them that he delights in, may be referred to these two heads:-- 1. Himself. 2. His kingdom.

1. Himself. John xiv. 21, "He that loveth me shall be loved of my Father; and I will love him, and will manifest myself unto him;" -- "manifest myself in all my graces, desirableness, and loveliness; he shall know me as I am, and such I will be unto him, -- a Saviour, a Redeemer, the chiefest of ten thousand." He shall be acquainted with the true worth and value of the pearl of price; let others look upon him as having neither form nor comeliness, as no way desirable, he will manifest himself and his excellencies unto them in whom he is delighted, that they shall see him altogether lovely. He will vail himself to all the world; but the saints with open face shall behold his beauty and his glory, and so be translated into the image of the same glory, as by the Spirit of the Lord, 2 Cor. iii. 18.

2. His kingdom. They shall be acquainted with the government of his Spirit in their hearts; as also with his rule and the administration of authority in his word, and among his churches.

(1.) Thus, in the first place, doth he manifest his delight in his saints, -- he communicates his secrets unto them. He gives them to know his person, his excellencies, his grace, his love, his kingdom, his will, the riches of his goodness, and the bowels of his mercy, more and more, when the world shall neither see nor know any such thing.

(2.) He enables his saints to communicate their mind, to reveal their souls, unto him, that so they may walk together as intimate friends. Christ knows the minds of all. He knows what is in man, and needs not that any man testify of him, John ii. 25. He searcheth the hearts and trieth the reins of all, Rev. ii. 23. But all know not how to communicate their mind to Christ. It will not avail a man at all that Christ knows his mind; for so he doth of every one, whether he will or no; -- but that a man can make his heart known unto Christ, this is consolation. Hence the prayers of the saints are [226] incense, odours; and those of others are [227] howling, cutting off a dog's neck, offering of swine's blood, -- an abomination unto the Lord. Now, three things are required to enable a man to communicate his heart unto the Lord Jesus:--

[1.] Assistance for the work; for of ourselves we cannot do it. And this the saints have by the Spirit of Jesus, Rom. viii. 26, 27, "Likewise the Spirit also helpeth our infirmities: for we know not what we should pray for as we ought; but the Spirit itself maketh intercession for us with groanings which cannot be uttered. And he that searcheth the hearts knoweth what is the mind of the Spirit, because he maketh intercession for the saints according to the will of God." All endeavours, all attempts for communion with God, without the supplies of the

Spirit of supplications, without his effectual working in the heart, is of no value, nor to any purpose. And this opening of our hearts and bosoms to the Lord Jesus is that wherein he is exceedingly delighted. Hence is that affectionate call of his unto us, to be treating with him on this account, Cant. ii. 14, "O my dove, that art in the secret places of the stairs, let me see thy countenance, let me hear thy voice; for sweet is thy voice, and thy countenance is comely." When the soul on any account is driven to hide itself, -- in any neglected condition, in the most unlikely place of abode, -- then doth he call for this communication of itself by prayer to him; for which he gives the assistance of the Spirit mentioned.

[2.] A way whereby to approach unto God with our desires. This, also, we have by him provided for us, John xiv. 5, 6, "Thomas saith unto Jesus, Lord, we know not whither thou goest; and how can we know the way? Jesus saith unto him, I am the [228] way; no man cometh unto the Father, but by me." That way which we had of going unto God at our creation is quite shut up by sin. The sword of the law, which hath fire put into it by sin, turns every way, to stop all passages unto communion with God. Jesus Christ hath "consecrated a [229] new and living way" (for the saints) "through the vail, that is to say, his flesh," Heb. x. 20. He hath consecrated and set it apart for believers, and for them alone. Others pretend to go to God with their prayers, but they come not nigh him. How can they possibly come to the end who go not in the way? Christ only is the way to the throne of grace; none comes to God but by him. "By him we have an access in one Spirit unto the Father," Eph. ii. 18. These two things, then, the saints have for the opening of their hearts at the throne of grace, -- assistance and a way. The assistance of the Spirit, without which they are nothing; and the way of Christ's mediation, without which God is not to be approached unto.

[3.] Boldness to go unto God. The voice of sinners in themselves, if once acquainted with the terror of the Lord, is, -- "Who among us shall dwell with the devouring fire? who among us shall dwell with everlasting burnings?" Isa. xxxiii. 14. And no marvel; [230] shame and trembling before God are the proper issues of sin. God will revenge that carnal, atheistical boldness which sinners out of Christ do use towards him. But we have now "boldness to enter into the holiest by the blood of Jesus, by a new and living way, which he hath consecrated for us, through the vail, that is to say, his flesh: and having an high priest over the house of God, we may draw near with a true heart, in full assurance of faith," Heb. x. 19, 20. The truth is, such is the glory and terror of the Lord, such the infinite perfection of his holiness, that, on clear sight of it, it will make the soul conclude that of itself it [231] cannot serve him; nor will it be to any advantage, but add to the fierceness of his destruction, once to draw nigh to him. It is in Christ alone, and on the account alone of his oblation and intercession, that we have any boldness to approach unto him. And these three advantages have the saints of communicating their minds unto the Lord Christ, which he hath provided for them, because he delights in them.

To touch a little by the way, because this is of great importance, I will instance in one of these, as I might in every one, that you may see the difference between a spiritual revealing of our minds unto Christ in this acceptable manner, and that praying upon conviction which others practise; and this shall be from the first, -- namely, the assistance we have by the Spirit.

1st. The Spirit of Christ reveals to us our own wants, that we may reveal them unto him: "We know not what we should pray for as we ought," Rom. viii. 26; no [232] teachings under those of the Spirit of God are able to make our souls acquainted with their own wants, -- its burdens, its temptations. For a soul to know its wants, its infirmities, is a heavenly discovery. He that hath this[233] assistance, his prayer is more than half made before he begins to pray. His conscience is affected with what he hath to do; his mind and spirit contend within him, there especially where he finds himself most straitened. He brings his burden on his shoulders, and unloads himself on the Lord Christ. He finds (not by a perplexing conviction, but a holy sense and weariness of sin) where he is dead, where dull and cold, wherein unbelieving, wherein tempted above all his strength, where the light of God's countenance is wanting. And all these the soul hath a sense of by the Spirit, -- an inexpressible sense and experience. Without this, prayer is not prayer; [234] men's voices may be heard, but they speak not in their hearts. Sense of want is the spring of desire; -- natural, of natural; spiritual, of spiritual. Without this sense given by the Holy Ghost, there is neither desire nor prayer.

2dly. The expressions, or the words of such persons, come exceeding short of the labouring of their hearts; and therefore, in and after their supplications, "the Spirit makes intercession with sighs and groans that cannot be [235] uttered." Some men's words go exceedingly beyond their hearts. Did their spirits come up to their expressions, it were well. He that hath this assistance can provide no clothing that is large and broad enough to set forth the desires of his heart; and therefore, in the close of his best and most fervent supplications, such a person finds a double dissatisfaction in them:-- 1. That they are not a righteousness to be rested on; that if God should [236] mark what is in them amiss, they could not abide the trial. 2. That his heart in them is not poured out, nor delivered in any proportion to the holy desires and labourings that were conceived therein; though he may in Christ have great refreshment by them. The more they [saints] speak, the more they find they have left unspoken.

3dly. The intercession of the saints thus assisted is according to the mind of God; that is, they are guided by the Spirit to make requests for those things unto God which it is his will they should desire, -- which he knows to be good for them, useful and suitable to them, in the condition wherein they are. There are many ways whereby we may know when we make our supplications according to the will of God. I shall instance only in one; that is, when we do it according to the promise: when our prayers are regulated by the promise, we make them according to the will of God. So David, Ps. cxix. 49, "Remember the word upon which thou hast caused me to hope." He prays, and regulates his desire by the word of promise wherein he had trusted. But yet, men may ask that which is in the promise, and yet not have their prayers regulated by the promise. They may pray for what is in the promise, but not as it is in the promise. So James says some "ask and receive not, because they ask amiss, that they may spend it on their lusts," chap. iv. 3. Though the things which God would have us ask be requested, yet if not according as he would have us do it, we ask amiss.

Two things are required, that we may pray for the things in the promise, as they are in the promise:--

(1st.) That we look upon them as promised, and promised in Christ; that is, that all the reason we have whence we hope for attaining the things we ask for, is from the mediation and purchase of Christ, in whom all the promises are yea and amen. This it is to ask the Father in Christ's name, -- God as a father, the fountain; and Christ as the procurer of them.

(2dly.) That we ask for them for the end of the promise, not to spend on our lusts. When we ask pardon for sin, with secret [237] reserves in our hearts to continue in sin, we ask the choicest mercy of the covenant, to spend it on our lusts. The end of the promise the apostle tells us, 2 Cor. vii. 1, "Having these promises, let us cleanse ourselves from all pollution of the flesh and spirit, perfecting holiness in the fear of God." When we ask what is in the promise, as it is in the promise, to this end of the promise, our supplications are according to the will of God. And this is the first conjugal affection that Christ exerciseth towards believers, -- he delights in them; which that he doth is evident, as upon other considerations innumerable, so from the instance given.

In return hereunto, for the carrying on of the communion between them, the saints delight in Christ; he is their joy, their crown, their rejoicing, their life, food, health, strength, desire, righteousness, salvation, blessedness: without him they have nothing; in him they shall find all things. Gal. vi. 14, "God forbid that I should glory, save in the cross of our Lord Jesus Christ." He hath, from the foundation of the world, been the hope, expectation, desire, and delight of all believers. The promise of him was all (and it was enough) that God gave Adam in his inexpressible distress, to relieve and comfort him, Gen. iii. 15. Eve perhaps supposed that the promised seed had been born in her first-born, when she said, "I have gotten a man from [238] the Lord" (so most properly, אֶת denoting the fourth case); and this was the matter of her joy, Gen. iv. 1. Lamech having Noah given to him as a type of Christ and salvation by him, cries out, "This same shall comfort us concerning our work and toil of our hands, because of the ground which the Lord hath cursed," Gen. v. 29; he rejoices in him who was to take away the curse, by being made a curse for us. When Abraham was in the height of his glory, returning from the conquest of the kings of the east, that came against the confederate kings of the vale of Sodom, God appears to him with a glorious promise, Gen. xv. 1, "Fear not, Abram: I am thy shield, and thy exceeding great reward." What now could his soul more desire? Alas! he cries (as Reuben afterward, upon the loss of Joseph), "The child is not, and whither shall I go?" Verse 2, "Lord God, what wilt thou give me, seeing I go childless?" "Thou hast promised that in my seed shall all the earth be blessed; if I have not that seed, ah! what good will all other things do me?" Thence it is said that he "rejoiced to see the day of Christ; he saw it, and was glad," John viii. 56; the thoughts of the coming of Christ, which he looked on at the distance of two thousand years, was the joy and delight of his heart. Jacob, blessing his sons, lifted up his spirit when he comes to Judah, in whom he considered the Shiloh to come, Gen. xlix. 8, 9; and a little after, wearied with the foresight and consideration of the distresses of his posterity, this he diverts to for his relief, as that great delight of his soul: "I have waited for thy Salvation, O God;" -- for him who was to be the salvation of his people. But it would be endless to instance in particulars. Old Simon sums up the whole: Christ is God's salvation, and Israel's glory, Luke ii. 30, 31; and whatever was called the glory of old, it was either himself or a type of him. The glory of man is their delight. Hence, Haggai ii. 7, he is called "The Desire of all nations." Him whom their soul loves and delights in, [they] desire and long after. So is the saints' delight in him made a description of him, by way of eminence, Mal. iii. 1: "The Lord whom ye seek shall suddenly come to his temple, even the messenger of the covenant whom ye delight in." "He whom ye seek, whom ye delight in," is the description of Christ. He is their delight and desirable one, the person of their desire. To fix on something in particular:--

In that pattern of communion with Jesus Christ which we have in the Canticles, this is abundantly insisted on. The spouse tells us that she sits down under his shadow with great delight, Cant. ii. 3. And this delight to be vigorous and active, she manifests several ways; wherein we should labour to find our hearts in like manner towards him:--

1. By her exceeding great care to keep his company and society, when once she had obtained it, chap. ii. 7, "I charge you, O ye daughters of Jerusalem, by the roes, and by the hinds of the field, that ye stir not up, nor awake my love till he please." Having obtained sweet communion with Christ, described in the verses foregoing (of which before), here she expresseth her delight in it and desire of the continuance of it; and therefore, following on the allusion formerly insisted on, she speaks as one would do to her companion, [as one] that had rest with one she loved: "I charge you, by all that is dear to you, -- by the things you most delight in, which among the creatures are most lovely, all the pleasant and desirable things that you can think of, -- that you disturb him not." The sum of her aim and desire is, that nothing may fall out, nothing of sin or provocation happen, that may occasion Christ to depart from her, or to remove from that dispensation wherein he seemed to take that rest in her: "O stir him not up until he please!" that [239] is, never. הָאַהֲבָה, -- love itself in the abstract, to express a πάθος, or earnest affection; for so that word is often used. When once the soul of a believer hath obtained sweet and real communion with Christ, it looks about him, watcheth all temptations, all ways whereby sin might approach, to disturb him in his enjoyment of his dear Lord and Saviour, his rest and desire. How doth it charge itself not to omit any thing, nor to do any thing that may interrupt the communion obtained! And because the common entrance of temptations, which tend to the disturbance of that rest and complacency which Christ takes in the soul, is from delightful diversions from actual communion with him; therefore is desire strong and active that the companions of such a soul, those with whom it doth converse, would not, by their proposals or allurements, divert it into any such frame as Christ cannot delight nor rest in. A believer that hath gotten Christ in his arms, is like one that hath found great spoils, or a pearl of price. He looks about him every way, and fears every thing that may deprive him of it. Riches make men watchful; and the actual sensible possession of him, in whom are all the riches and treasure of God, will make men look about them for the keeping of him. The line of choicest communion, is a line of the greatest spiritual solicitousness: carelessness in the enjoyment of Christ pretended, is a manifest evidence of a false heart.

2. The spouse manifests her delight in him, by the utmost impatience of his absence, with desires still of nearer communion with him. [240] Chap. viii. 6, "Set me as a seal upon thine heart, as a seal upon thine arm: for love is strong as death; jealousy is cruel as the grave: the coals thereof are coals of fire, which hath a most vehement flame." The allusion is doubtless from the high priest of the Jews, in his spiritual representation of the church before God. He had a breastplate which he is said to wear on his heart, Exod. xxviii. 29, wherein the names of the children of Israel were engraven, after the manner of seals or

signets, and he bare them for a memorial before the Lord. He had the like also upon his shoulders, or on his arms, verses 11, 12; both representing the priesthood of Christ, who bears the names of all his before his Father in the "holy of holies," Heb. ix. 24. Now the seal on the heart, is near, inward, tender love and care, which gives an impression and image on the heart of the thing so loved. "Set me," saith the spouse, "as a seal upon thine heart;" -- "Let me be constantly fixed in thy most tender and affectionate love; let me always have a place in thine heart; let me have an engraving, a mighty impression of love, upon thine heart, that shall never be obliterated." The soul is never satisfied with thoughts of Christ's love to it. "O that it were more, that it were more! that I were as a seal on his heart!'?" is its language. The soul knows, indeed, on serious thoughts, that the love of Christ is inconceivable, and cannot be increased; but it would fain work up itself to an apprehension of it: and therefore she adds here, "Set me as a seal upon thine arm." The heart is the fountain, but close and hidden; the arm is manifestation and power. "Let," saith the spouse, "thy love be manifested to me in thy tender and powerful persuasion of me." Two things are evident in this request:-- the continual mindfulness of Christ of the soul, as having its condition still in his eye, engraven on his arm, Isa. xlix. 15, 16, with the exalting of his power for the preservation of it, suitable to the love of his heart unto it; and the manifestation of the hidden love and care of the heart of Christ unto the soul, being made visible on his arm, or evident by the fruit of it. This is that which she would be assured of; and without a sense whereof there is no rest to be obtained.

The reason she gives of this earnestness in her supplications, is that which principally evinces her delight in him: "Love is strong as death, jealousy is cruel as the grave," or "hard as hell." This is the intendment of what is so loftily set out by so many metaphors in this and the following verse:-- "I am not able to bear the workings of my love to thee, unless I may always have society and fellowship with thee. There is no satisfying of my love without it. It is as the [241] grave, that still says Give, give. Death is not satisfied without its prey; if it have not all, it hath nothing: let what will happen, if death hath not its whole desire, it hath nothing at all. Nor can it be withstood in its appointed season; no ransom will be taken. So is my love; if I have thee not wholly, I have nothing. Nor can all the world bribe it to a diversion; it will he no more turned aside than death in its time. Also, I am not able to bear my jealous thoughts: I fear thou dost not love me, that thou hast forsaken me; because I know I deserve not to be beloved. These thoughts are hard as hell; they give no rest to my soul: if I find not myself on thy heart and arm, I am as one that lies down in a bed of coals." This also argues a holy greediness of delight.

3. She farther manifests this by her solicitousness, trouble, and perplexity, in his loss and withdrawings. Men bewail the loss of that whose whole enjoyment they delight in; we easily bear the absence of that whose presence is not delightful. This state of the spouse is discovered, Cant. iii. 1-3, "By [242] night on my bed I sought him whom [243] my soul loveth: I sought him, but I found him not. I will rise now, and go about the city in the streets, and in the broad ways I will seek him whom my soul loveth: I sought him, but I found him not. The watchmen that go about the city found me: to whom I said, Saw ye him whom my soul loveth?" It is night now with the soul, -- a time of darkness and trouble, or affliction. Whenever Christ is absent, it is night with a believer. He is the [244] sun; if he go down upon them, if his beams be eclipsed, if in his light they see

no light, it is all darkness with them. Here, whether the coming of the night of any trouble on her made her discover Christ's absence, or the absence of Christ made it night with her, is not expressed. I rather think the latter; because, setting that aside, all things seem to be well with her. The absence of Christ will indeed make it night, dark as darkness itself, in the midst of all other glowing consolations. But is the spouse contented with this dispensation? She is upon her bed, -- that is, of ease (the bed, indeed, sometimes signifies tribulation, Rev. ii. 22; but in this book, everywhere, rest and contentment: here is not the least intimation of any tribulation but what is in the want of Christ); but in the greatest peace and opportunity of ease and rest, a believer finds none in the absence of Christ: though he be on his bed, having nothing to disquiet him, he rests not, if Christ, his rest, be not there. She "sought him." Seeking of Christ by night, on the bed (that is, alone, in immediate inquest, and in the dark), hath two parts:-- searching of our own souls for the cause of his absence; secondly, searching the promises for his presence.

(1.) The soul finding not Christ present in his wonted manner, warming, cherishing, reviving it with love, nigh to it, supping with it, always filling its thoughts with himself, dropping myrrh and sweet tastes of love into it; but, on the contrary, that other thoughts crowd in and perplex the heart, and Christ is not nigh when inquired after; it presently inquires into the cause of all this,[245] calls itself to an account what it hath done, how it hath behaved itself, that it is not with it as at other times, -- that Christ hath withdrawn himself, and is not nigh to it in the wonted manner. Here it accomplishes a diligent search; it considers the love, tenderness, and kindness of the Lord Jesus, what delight he takes in abiding with his saints, so that his departure is not without cause and provocation. "How," saith it, "have I demeaned myself, that I have lost my Beloved? where have I been wandering after other lovers?" And when the miscarriage is found out, it abounds in revenge and indignation.

(2.) Having driven this to some issue, the soul applieth itself to the promises of the covenant, wherein Christ is most graciously exhibited unto it; considers one, ponders another, to find a taste of him; -- it considers diligently if it can see the delightful countenance and favour of Christ in them or no. But now, if (as it often falls out) the soul finds nothing but the carcase, but the bare letter, in the promise, -- if it come to it as to the grave of Christ, of which it may be said (not in itself, but in respect of the seeking soul), "He is risen, he is not here," -- this amazes the soul, and it knows not what to do. As a man that hath a jewel of great price, having no occasion to use it, lays it aside, as he supposes, in a safe place; in an agony and extremity of want going to seek for his jewel, he finds it not in the place he expected, and is filled with amazement, and knows not what to do; -- so is it with this pearl of the gospel. After a man hath sold all that he hath for it, and enjoyed it for a season, then to have it missing at a time of need, it must needs perplex him. So was it with the spouse here. "I sought him," saith she, "but I found him not;" a thing which not seldom befalls us in our communion with Christ.

But what doth she now do? doth she give over, and search no more? Nay; but says she, verse 2, "?I will arise;' I will not so give over. I must have Christ, or die. I will now arise," (or, "let me arise,") "and go about this business."

[1.] She resolves to put herself upon another course, a more vigorous inquest: "I will arise and make use of other means besides those of private prayer, meditation, self-searching, and inquiring into the promises;" which she had insisted on before. It carries, --

1st. Resolution, and a zealous, violent casting off that frame wherein she had lost her love. "?I [246] will arise;' I will not rest in this frame: I am undone if I do." So, sometimes God calls his church to arise and shake itself out of the dust. Abide not in that condition.

2dly. Diligence. "I will now take another course; I will leave no way unattempted, no means untried, whereby I may possibly recover communion with my Beloved."

This is the condition of a soul that finds not the wonted presence of Christ in its private and more retired inquiries, -- dull in prayer, wandering in meditations, rare in thoughts of him, -- "I will not bear this frame: whatever way God hath appointed, I will, in his strength, vigorously pursue, until this frame be altered, and I find my Beloved."

[2.] Then the way she puts herself upon, is to go about the city. Not to insist upon particulars, nor to strain the parts of the allegory too far, the city here intended is the city of God, the church; and the passing through the broad and narrow streets, is the diligent inquiry that the spouse makes in all the paths and ordinances given unto it. This, then, is the next thing the soul addresses itself unto in the want of Christ:-- when it finds him not in any private endeavours, it makes vigorous application to the ordinances of public worship; in prayer, in preaching, in administration of the seals, doth it look after Christ. Indeed, the great inquiry the souls of believers make, in every ordinance, is after Christ. So much as they find of him, so much sweetness and refreshment have they, and no more. Especially when under any desertion, they rise up to this inquiry: they listen to every word, to every prayer, to find if any thing of Christ, any light from him, any life, any love, appears to them. "Oh, that Christ would at length meet me in this or that sermon, and recover my poor heart to some sight of his love, -- to some taste at kindness!" The solicitousness of a believer in his inquest after Christ, when he finds not his presence, either for grace or consolation, as in former days, is indeed inexpressible. Much of the frame of such a heart is couched in the redoubling of the expression, "I sought him, I sought him;" setting out an inconceivable passion, and suitably industrious desire. Thus, being disappointed at home, the spouse proceeds.

But yet see the event of this also: "She sought him, but found him not." It doth sometimes so fall out, all will not do: "They shall seek him, and not find him;" they shall not come nigh him. Let them that enjoy any thing of the presence of Christ take heed what they do; if they provoke him to depart, if they lose him, it may cost them many a bitter inquiry before they find him again. When a soul prays and meditates, searches the promises in private; when it with earnestness and diligence attends all ordinances in public, and all to get one glimpse of the face of Jesus Christ, and all in vain, it is a sad condition.

What now follows in this estate? Verse 3, "The watchmen found me," etc. That these watchmen of the city of God are the watchmen and officers of the church, is confessed. And it is of sad consideration, that the Holy Ghost doth sometimes in this book take notice of them on no good account. Plainly, chap. v. 7, they turn persecutors. It was Luther's saying, "Nunquam periclitatur religio nisi inter reverendissimos." Here they are of a more gentle temper, and seeing the poor disconsolate soul, they seem to take notice of her condition.

It is the duty, indeed, of faithful watchmen, to take notice of poor, troubled, deserted souls; -- not to keep at a distance, but to be willing to assist. And a truly pressed soul on the account of Christ's absence cannot cover its love, but must be inquiring after him: "Saw ye him whom my soul loveth?" -- "This is my condition: I have had sweet enjoyment of my blessed Jesus, -- he is now withdrawn from me. Can you help me? can you guide me to my consolation. What acquaintance have you with him? when saw you him? how did he manifest himself to you, and wherein?" All these labourings in his absence sufficiently discover the soul's delight in the presence of Christ. Go one step farther, to the discovery that it made of him once again, and it will yet be more evident. Verses 4, 5, "It was but a little that I passed from them, but I found him whom my soul loveth: I held him, and would not let him go, until I had brought him into my mother's house, and into the chamber of her that conceived me. I charge you, O ye daughters of Jerusalem," etc.

First, She tells you how she came to him: "She found him;" -- what ways and by what means is not expressed. It often so falls out in our communion with Christ, when private and public means fail, and the soul hath nothing left but waiting silently and walking humbly, Christ appears; that his so doing may be evidently of grace. Let us not at any time give over in this condition. When all ways are past, the summer and harvest are gone without relief, -- when neither bed nor watchmen can assist, -- let us wait a little, and we shall see the Salvation of God. Christ honours his immediate absolute actings sometimes, though ordinarily he crowns his ordinances. Christ often manifests himself immediately, and out of ordinances, to them that wait for him in them; -- that he will do so to them that despise them, I know not. Though he will meet men unexpectedly in his way, yet he will not meet them at all out of it. Let us wait as he hath appointed; let him appear as he pleaseth. How she deals with him when found is nextly declared: "She held him, and would not let him go," etc. They are all expressions of the greatest joy and delight imaginable. The sum is:-- having at length come once more to an enjoyment of sweet communion with Christ, the soul lays fast hold on him by faith (κρατεῖν, "to hold fast," is an act of faith), refuses to part with him any more, in vehemency of love, -- tries to keep him in ordinances in the house of its mother, the church of God; and so uses all means for the confirming of the mutual love between Christ and her: all the expressions, all the allusions used, evidencing delight to the utmost capacity of the soul. Should I pursue all the instances and testimonies that are given hereunto, in that one book of the Song of Solomon, I must enter upon an exposition of the greatest part of it; which is not my present business. Let the hearts of the saints that are acquainted with these things be allowed to make the close. What is it they long for, they rejoice in? what is it that satisfies them to the utmost, and gives sweet complacency to their spirits in every condition? what is it whose loss they fear, whose absence they cannot bear? Is it not this their Beloved, and he alone?

This, also, they farther manifest by their delight in every thing that peculiarly belongs to Christ, as his, in this world. This is an evidence of delight, when, for his sake whom we delight in, we also delight in every thing that belongs to him. Christ's great interest in this world lies in his people and his ordinances, -- his household and their provision. Now in both these do the saints exceedingly delight, for his sake. Take an instance in both kinds in one man, namely, David, Ps. xvi. 3, "In the saints and the excellent" (or the noble) "of the earth is all my delight; my delight in them." Christ says of his church that she is "Hephzi-bah," Isa. lxii., "My delight in her." Here says David of the same, "Hephzi-bam, -- "My delight in them." As Christ delights in his saints, so do they in one another, on his account. "Here," says David, "is all my delight." Whatever contentment he took in any other persons, it was nothing in comparison of the delight he took in them. Hence, mention is made of "laying down our lives for the brethren," or any common cause wherein the interest of the community of the brethren doth lie.

Secondly, For the ordinances, consider the same person. Ps. xlii., lxxxiv., and xlviii., are such plentiful testimonies throughout, as we need no farther inquiring; nor shall I go forth to a new discourse on this particular.

And this is the first mutual consequential act of conjugal affection, in this communion between Christ and believers:-- he delights in them, and they delight in him. He delights in their prosperity, hath pleasure in it; they delight in his honour and glory, and in his presence with them. For his sake they delight in his servants (though by the world contemned) as the most excellent in the world; and in his ordinances, as the wisdom of God; -- which are foolishness to the world.

Footnotes:

221. The division to which reference is here made will be found on page 56. The figure [2.] should have been inserted at the head of this chapter, to correspond with [1.] on that page. The insertion of it, however, would have required great changes, and rendered the subsequent numeration very obscure. -- Ed.

222. Ἡδονὴ μᾶλλον ἐν ἠρεμίᾳ ἐστίν, ἢ ἐν κινήσει. -- Arist. Eth., lib. vii., cap. 14. Τέλειοι δὲ τὴν ἐνέργειαν ἡ ἡδονή. -- Id. l. 10, c. 4.

223. Mal. iv. 2; Luke i. 78; 2 Pet. i. 19.

224. "Voluntatem Dei nosse quisquam desiderat? fiat amicus Deo, quia si voluntatem hominis nosse vellet, cujus amicus non esset, omnes ejus impudentiam et stultitiam deriderent." -- August, de Gen. Cont. Man., lib. i. cap. 2.

225. "Vox πάντα ex subjecta materia, restrictionem ad doctrinam salutis requirit." -- Tarnov. in loc.

226. Rev. viii. 3;

227. ὅς. vii. 14; Isa. lxvi. 3; Prov. xxviii. 9.

228. "Vera via vitæ." -- Bez.

229. "Via nullius ante trita solo. Πρόσφατον καὶ ζῶσαν, recens interfectam; tamen viventem."

230. Gen. iii. 8, 9;

231. Josh. xxiv. 19; Exod. xx. 19; Deut. v. 25, xviii. 16; Isa. xxxiii. 14; Mic. vi. 6, 7.

232. Isa. xxxviii. 14.

233. "Ὑπερεντυγχάνειν, est advocatorum qui clientibus desideria dictant."

234. 1 Sam. i. 13.

235. Isa. xxxviii. 14; Exod. xiv. 15.

236. Isa. lxiv. 6; Ps. cxxx. 3;

237. Ps. lxxviii. 35-37.

238. According to the view to which Owen refers, the preposition should be dropped from the translation, and את regarded as in apposition with Jehovah, -- "I have gotten a man, Jehovah." The particle את occurs in this sense, as simply demonstrative, forty times in the first four chapters of Genesis. -- Ed.

239. "Æternitatem temporis juxta sensum mysticum in se

includit, ut alias in Scriptura; quia nunquam a tali somno, id est, conjunctione cum sponso, excitari velit." --Mer. in loc.

240. Hag. ii. 23; Jer. xxii. 24.

241. Prov. xxx. 16.

242. Isa. l. 10.

243. "Eleganter periphrasi utitur loco nominis proprii, ut vim amoris sui exprimat." -- Merc. "Ista repetitio assensum indicat et studium quo eum quærebat, et moerorem quo angebatur, quod occurrere non posset." -- Idem.

244. Mal. iv. 2.

245. 2 Cor. xiii. 5.

246. Isa. lii. 2, lx. 1.

Chapter V - Other consequential affections:-- 1. On the part of Christ -- He values his saints -- Evidences of that valuation:-- (1.) His incarnation; (2.) Exinanition, 2 Cor. viii. 9; Phil. ii. 6, 7; (3.) Obedience as a servant; (4.) In his death. His valuation of them in comparison of others. 2. Believers' estimation of Christ:-- (1.) They value him above all other things and persons; (2.) Above their own lives; (3.) All spiritual excellencies. The sum of all on the part of Christ -- The sum on the part of believers. The third conjugal affection -- On the part of Christ, pity or compassion -- Wherein manifested -- Suffering and supply, fruits of compassion -- Several ways whereby Christ relieves the saints under temptations -- His compassion in their afflictions. Chastity, the third conjugal affection in the saints. The fourth -- On the part of Christ, bounty; on the part of the saints, duty.

II. Christ values his saints, values believers (which is the second branch of that conjugal affection he bears towards them), having taken them into the relation whereof we speak. I shall not need to insist long on the demonstration hereof; heaven and earth are full of evidences of it. Some few considerations will give life to the assertion. Consider them, then, -- 1. Absolutely; 2. In respect of others; and you will see what a valuation he puts upon them:--

1. All that ever he did or doth, all that ever he underwent or suffered as mediator, was for their sakes. Now, these things were so great and grievous, that had he not esteemed them above all that can be expressed, he had never engaged to their performance and undergoing. Take a few instances:--

(1.) For their sakes was he "made [247] flesh;" "manifested in the flesh." Heb. ii. 14, "Forasmuch then as the children are partakers of flesh and blood, he also himself likewise took part of the same." And the height of this valuation of them the apostle aggravates. Verse 16, "Verily he took not on him the nature of angels, but he took on him the seed of Abraham;" he had no such esteem of angels. Whether you take ἐπιλαμβάμεσθαι, properly to "take," or to "take hold of," as our translators, and so supply the word "nature," and refer the whole unto Christ's incarnation, who therein took our nature on him, and not the nature of angels; or for ἀναλαμβάνεσθαι, to "help," (he did not help nor succour fallen angels, but he did help and [248] succour the seed of Abraham,) and so consider it as the fruit of Christ's incarnation, -- it is all one, as to our present business: his preferring the seed of Abraham before angels, his valuing them above the other, is plainly expressed. And observe, that he came to help the seed of Abraham, -- that is, [249] believers. His esteem and valuation is of them only.

(2.) For their sakes he was so made flesh, as that there was an emptying, an exinanition of himself, and an eclipsing of his glory, and a becoming poor for them, 2 Cor. viii. 9, "Ye know the grace of our Lord Jesus Christ, that, though he was rich, yet for our sakes he became poor." Being rich in eternal glory with his Father, John xvii. 5, he became poor for believers. The same person that was rich was also poor. That the riches here meant can be none but those of the Deity, is evident, by its opposition to the poverty which as man he undertook. This is also more fully expressed, Phil. ii. 6, 7, "Who being in the form of God, counted it no robbery to be equal to God, but he emptied himself, taking the form of a servant, and being made in the fashion of a man, and found in form as a man," etc. That the "form of God" is here the essence of the Deity, sundry things inevitably evince; as, --

[1.] That he was therein [250] equal to God; that is, his Father. Now, nothing but God is equal to God. Not [251] Christ as he is mediator, in his greatest glory, -- nothing but that which is infinite, is equal to that which is infinite.

[2.] The form of God is opposed to the form of a servant; and that form of a servant is called the "fashion of a man," verse 8, -- that fashion wherein he was found when he gave himself to death, wherein as a man he poured out his blood and died. Μορφὴν δούλου λαβὼν, (he "took the form of a servant"), is expounded in the next words, ἐν ὁμοιώματι ἀνθρώπων γενόμενος, -- an expression used to set out his incarnation, Rom. viii. 3. God sent him ἐν ὁμοιώματι σαρκὸς ἁμαρτίας· in taking true flesh, he was in the "likeness of sinful flesh." Now, in thus doing, it is said ἑαυτὸν ἐκένωσε, -- "he humbled, emptied himself, made himself of no reputation." In the very taking of flesh, there was a condescension, a debasing of the person of the Son of God; it could not be without it. If God humbled himself to "behold the things that are in heaven, and in the earth," Ps. cxiii. 6, then certainly it was an inconceivable condescension and abasement, not only to behold, but take upon him (into personal union) our nature with himself. And though nothing could possibly be taken off from the essential glory of the Deity, yet that person appearing in the fashion of a man, and form of a servant, the glory of it, as to the manifestation, was eclipsed; and he appeared [252] quite another thing than what indeed he was, and had been from eternity. Hence he prays that his Father would "glorify him with the glory he had with him before the world was," John xvii. 5, as to the manifestation of it. And so, though the divine nature was not abased, the person was.

(3.) For their sakes he so humbled and emptied himself, in taking flesh, as to become therein a servant, -- in the eyes of the world of no esteem nor account; and a true and real servant [253] unto the Father. For their sakes he humbled himself, and became obedient. All that he did and suffered in his life comes under this consideration; all which may be referred to these three heads:-- [254] [1.] Fulfilling all righteousness. [2.] Enduring all manner of persecutions and hardships. [3.] Doing all manner of good to men. He took on him, for their sakes, a life and course pointed to, Heb. v. 7, 8, -- a life of prayers, tears, fears, obedience, suffering; and all this with cheerfulness and delight, calling his employment his "meat and drink," and still professing that the law of this obedience was in his [255] heart, -- that he was content to do this will of God. He that will sorely revenge the least opposition that is or shall be made to him by others, was content to undergo any thing, all things, for believers.

(4.) He stays not here, but (for the consummation of all that went before) for their sakes he becomes obedient to death, the death of the cross. So he professeth to his Father, John xvii. 19, "For their sakes I sanctify myself;" -- "I dedicate myself as an offering, as a sacrifice, to be killed and slain." This was his aim in all the former, that he might die; he was born, and [256] lived, that he might die. He valued them above his life. And if we might stay to consider a little what was in this death that he underwent for them, we should perceive what a price indeed he put upon them. The curse [257] of the law was in it, the [258] wrath of God was in it, the loss of God's [259] presence was in it. It was a [260] fearful cup that he tasted of, and drank of, that they might never taste of it. A man would not for ten thousand worlds be willing to undergo that which Christ underwent for us in that one thing of desertion from God, were it attended with no more distress but what a mere creature might possibly emerge from under. And what thoughts we should have of this himself tells us, John xv. 13, "Greater love hath no man than this, that a man lay down his life for his friends." It is impossible there should be any greater demonstration or evidence of love than this. What can any one do more? And yet he tells us in another place, that it hath another aggravation and heightening, Rom. v. 8, "God commendeth his love toward us, in that, while we were yet sinners, Christ died for us." When he did this for us we were sinners, and enemies, whom he might justly have destroyed. What more can be done? -- to die for us when we were sinners! Such a death, in such a manner, with such attendancies of wrath and curse, -- a death accompanied with the worst that God had ever threatened to sinners, -- argues as high a valuation of us as the heart of Christ himself was capable of.

For one to part with his glory, his riches, his ease, his life, his love from God, to undergo loss, shame, wrath, curse, death, for another, is an evidence of a dear valuation; and that it was all on this account, we are informed, Heb. xii. 2. Certainly Christ had a dear esteem of them, that, rather than they should perish, -- that they should not be his, and be made partakers of his glory, -- he would part with all he had for their sakes, Eph. v. 25, 26.

There would be no end, should I go through all the instances of Christ's valuation of believers, in all their deliverances, afflictions, in all conditions of sinning and suffering, -- what he hath done, what he doth in his intercession, what he delivers them from, what he procures for them; all telling out this one thing, -- they are the apple of his eye, his jewel, his diadem, his crown.

2. In comparison of others. All the world is nothing to him in comparison of them. They are his garden; the rest of the world, a wilderness. Cant. iv. 12, "A garden enclosed is my sister, my spouse; a spring shut up, a fountain sealed." They are his inheritance; the rest, his enemies, of no regard with him. So Isa. xliii. 3, 4, "I am the Lord thy God, the Holy One of Israel, thy Saviour: I gave Egypt for thy ransom, Ethiopia and Seba for thee. Since thou wast [261] precious in my sight, thou hast been honourable, and I have loved thee: therefore will I give men for thee, and people for thy life." The reason of this dealing of Christ with his church, in parting with all others for them, is, because he loves her. She is precious and honourable in his sight; thence he puts this great esteem upon her. Indeed, he disposeth of all nations and their interests according as is for the good of believers. Amos ix. 9, in all the siftings of the nations, the eye of God is upon the house of Israel; not a grain of them shall

perish. Look to heaven; angels are appointed to minister for them, Heb. i. 14. Look into the world; the nations in general are either [262] blessed for their sakes, or [263] destroyed on their account, -- preserved to try them, or rejected for their cruelty towards them; and will receive from Christ their [264] final doom according to their deportment towards these despised ones. On this account are the pillars of the earth borne up, and patience is exercised towards the perishing world. In a word, there is not the meanest, the weakest, the poorest believer on the earth, but Christ prizes him more than all the world besides. Were our hearts filled much with thoughts hereof, it would tend much to our consolation.

To answer this, believers also value Jesus Christ; they have an esteem of him above all the world, and all things in the world. You have been in part acquainted with this before, in the account that was given of their delight in him, and inquiry after him. They say of him in their hearts continually, as David, "Whom have I in heaven but thee? and none upon earth I desire beside thee." Ps. lxxiii. 25. Neither heaven nor earth will yield them an object any way comparable to him, that they can delight in.

1. They value him above all other things and persons. "Mallem,", said one,[265] "ruere cum Christo, quam regnare cum Cæsare. Pulchra terra, pulchrum coelum, sed pulcherrimus dominus Jesus;" -- Christ and a dungeon, Christ and a cross, is infinitely sweeter than a crown, a sceptre without him, to their souls. So was it with Moses, Heb. xi. 26, "He esteemed the reproach of Christ greater riches than the treasures in Egypt." The reproach of Christ is the worst consequent that the wickedness of the world or the malice of Satan can bring upon the followers of him. The treasures of Egypt were in those days the greatest in the world; Moses despised the very best of the world, for the worst of the cross of Christ. Indeed, himself hath told believers, that if they love any thing better than him, father or mother, they are not worthy of him. A despising of all things for Christ is the very first lesson of the gospel. "Give away all, take up the cross and follow me," was the way whereby he tried his disciples of old; and if there be not the same mind and heart in us, we are none of his.

2. They value him above their lives. Acts xx. 24, "My life is not dear, that I may perfect my course with joy, and the ministry I have received of the Lord Jesus;" -- "Let life and all go, so that I may serve him; and, when all is done, enjoy him, and be made like to him." It is known what is reported of [266] Ignatius when he was led to martyrdom: "Let what will," said he, "come upon me, only so I may obtain Jesus Christ." Hence they of old rejoiced when whipped, scourged, put to shame, for his sake, Acts v. 41; Heb. xi. All is welcome that comes from him, or for him. The lives they have to live, the death they have to die, is little, is light, upon the thoughts of him who is the stay of their lives and the end of their death. Were it not for the refreshment which daily they receive by thoughts of him, they could not live, -- their lives would be a burden to them; and the thoughts of enjoyment of him made them cry with Paul, "Oh that we were dissolved!" The stories of the martyrs of old and of late, the sufferers in giving witness to him under the dragon and under the false prophet, the neglect of life in women and children on his account, contempt of torments, whilst his name sweetened all, have rendered this truth clear to men and angels.

3. They value him above all spiritual excellencies, and all other righteousness whatever, Phil. iii. 7, 8, "Those things which were advantage to

me, I esteemed loss for the excellency of the knowledge of Christ Jesus my Lord; for whose sake I have lost all things, and do esteem them common, that I may gain Christ, and be found in him." Having recounted the excellencies which he had, and the privileges which he enjoyed, in his Judaism, -- which were all of a spiritual nature, and a participation wherein made the rest of his countrymen despise all the world, and look upon themselves as the only acceptable persons with God, resting on them for righteousness, -- the apostle tells us what is his esteem of them, in comparison of the Lord Jesus. They are "loss and dung," -- things that for his sake he had really suffered the loss of; that is, whereas he had for many years been a zealot of the law, -- seeking after a righteousness as it were by the works of it, Rom. ix. 32, -- instantly serving God day and night, to obtain the promise, Acts xxvi. 7, -- living in all good conscience from his youth, Acts xxiii., -- all the while very zealous for God and his institutions, -- now [he] willingly casts away all these things, looks upon them as loss and dung, and could not only be contented to be without them, but, as for that end for which he sought after them, he abhorred them all. When men have been strongly convinced of their duty, and have laboured many years to keep a [267] good conscience, -- have prayed, and heard, and done good, and denied themselves, and been [268] zealous for God, and laboured with all their might to [269] please him, and so at length to come to enjoy him; they had rather[270] part with all the world, life and all, than with this they have wrought. You know how unwilling we are to part with any thing we have laboured and beaten our heads about? How much more when the things are so excellent, as our duty to God, blamelessness of conversation, hope of heaven, and the like, which we have beaten our hearts about. But now, when once Christ appears to the soul, when he is known in his excellency, all these things, as without him, have their paint washed off, their beauty fades, their desirableness vanisheth, and the soul is not only contented to part with them all, but puts them away as a defiled thing, and cries, "In the Lord Jesus only is my righteousness [271] and glory." Prov. iii. 13-15, among innumerable testimonies, may be admitted to give witness hereunto, "Happy is the man that findeth wisdom, and the man that getteth understanding. For the merchandise of it is better than the merchandise of silver, and the gain thereof than fine gold. She is more precious than rubies: and all the things that thou canst desire are not to be compared unto her." It is of Jesus Christ, the Wisdom of God, the eternal Wisdom of the Father, that the Holy Ghost speaks, as is evident from the description which is given hereof, chap. viii. He and his ways are better than silver and gold, rubies, and all desirable things; as in the gospel he likens himself to the [272] "pearl in the field," which when the merchant man finds, he sells all that he hath, to purchase. All goes for Christ; -- all righteousness without him, all ways of religion, all goes for that one pearl. The glory of his Deity, the excellency of his person, his all-conquering desirableness, ineffable love, wonderful undertaking, unspeakable condescensions, effectual mediation, complete righteousness, lie in their eyes, ravish their hearts, fill their affections, and possess their souls. And this is the second mutual conjugal affection between Christ and believers; all which, on the part of Christ, may be referred unto two heads:--

    1. All that he parted withal, all that he did, all that he suffered, all that he doth as mediator; he parted withal, did, suffered, doth, on the account of his[273] love to and esteem of believers. He parted with the greatest glory, he underwent the greatest misery, he doth the greatest works that ever were, because he loves

his spouse, -- because he values believers. What can more, what can farther be spoken? how little is the depth of that which is spoken fathomed! how unable are we to look into the mysterious recesses of it! He so loves, so values his saints, as that, having from eternity undertaken to bring them to God, he rejoices his soul in the thoughts of it; and pursues his design through heaven and hell, life and death, by suffering and doing, in mercy and with power; and ceaseth not until he bring it to perfection. For, --

2. He doth so value them, as that he will not lose any of them to eternity, though all the world should combine to take them out of his hand. When in the days of his flesh he foresaw what opposition, what danger, what rocks they should meet withal, he cried out, "Holy Father, keep them," John xvii. 11; -- "Let not one of them be lost;" and tells us plainly, John x. 28, that no man shall take his sheep out of his hand. And because he was then in the form of a servant, and it might be supposed that he might not be able to hold them, he tells them true, as to his present condition of carrying on the work of mediation, his "Father was greater than he;" [274] and therefore to him he committed them, and none should take them out of his Father's hand, John x. 29. And whereas the world, afflictions, and persecutions, which are without, may be conquered, and yet no security given but that sin from within, by the assistance of Satan, may prevail against them to their ruin; as he hath provided against Satan, in his promise that the gates of hell shall not prevail against them, so he hath taken care that sin itself shall not destroy them. Herein, indeed, is the depth of his love to be contemplated, that whereas his holy soul hates every sin (it is a burden, an abomination, a new wound to him), and his poor spouse is sinful (believers are full of sins, failings, and infirmities), he hides all, covers all, bears with all, rather than he will lose them; by his power preserving them from such sins as a remedy is not provided for in the covenant of grace. Oh, the world of sinful follies that our dear Lord Jesus bears withal on this account! Are not our own souls astonished with the thoughts of it? Infinite patience, infinite forbearance, infinite love, infinite grace, infinite mercy, are all set on work for this end, to answer this his valuation of us.

On our part it may also be referred to two heads:--

1. That, upon the discovery of him to our souls, they rejoice to [275] part with all things wherein they have delighted or reposed their confidence, for him and his sake, that they may enjoy him. Sin and lust, pleasure and profit, righteousness and duty, in their several conditions, all shall go, so they may have Christ.

2. That they are willing to part with all things rather than with [276] him, when they do enjoy him. To think of parting with peace, health, liberty, relations, wives, children; it is offensive, heavy, and grievous to the best of the saints: but their souls cannot bear the thoughts of parting with Jesus Christ; such a thought is cruel as the grave. The worst thoughts that, in any fear, [277] in desertions, they have of [278] hell, is, that they shall not enjoy Jesus Christ. So they may enjoy him here, hereafter be like him, be ever with him, stand in his presence; they can part with all things freely, cheerfully, be they never so beautiful, in reference to this life or that which is to come.

III. The third conjugal affection on the part of Christ is pity and compassion. As a man "nourisheth and cherisheth his [279] own flesh, so doth the Lord his church," Eph. v. 29. Christ hath a fellow feeling with his saints in all their troubles, as a man hath with his own flesh. This act of the conjugal love of Christ relates to the many trials and pressures of afflictions that his saints meet withal here below. He doth not deal with believers as the Samaritans with the Jews, that fawned on them in their prosperity, but despised them in their trouble; he is as a tender [280] father, who, though perhaps he love all his children alike, yet he will take most pains with, and give most of his presence unto, one that is sick and weak, though therein and thereby he may be made most froward, and, as it should seem, hardest to be borne with. And (which is more than the pity of any father can extend to) he himself suffers with them, and takes share in all their troubles.

Now, all the sufferings of the saints in this world, wherein their head and husband exerciseth pity, tenderness, care, and compassion towards them, are of two sorts, or may be referred to two heads:-- 1. Temptations. 2. Afflictions.

1. Temptations (under which head I comprise sin also, whereto they tend); as in, from, and by their own infirmities; as also from their adversaries without. The frame of the heart of Christ, and his deportment towards them in this condition, you have, Heb. iv. 15, "We have not an high priest which cannot be touched with the feeling of our infirmities." We have not such a one as cannot. The two negations do vehemently affirm that we have such an high priest as can be, or is, touched. The word "touched" comes exceedingly short of expressing the original word; it is [281] συμπαθῆσαι, -- to "suffer together." "We have," saith the apostle, "such an high priest as can, and consequently doth, suffer with us, -- endure our infirmities." And in what respect he suffers with us in regard of our infirmities, or hath a fellow-feeling with us in them, he declares in the next words, "He was tempted like as we are," verse 15. It is as to our [282] infirmities, our temptations, spiritual weakness; therein, in particular, hath he a compassionate sympathy and fellow-feeling with us. Whatever be our infirmities, so far as they are our temptations, he doth suffer with us under them, and compassionates us. Hence at the last [283] day he saith, "I was an hungered," etc. There are two ways of expressing a fellow-feeling and suffering with another:-- (1.) Per benevolam condolentiam, -- a "friendly grieving." (2.) Per gratiosam opitulationem, -- a "gracious supply:" both are eminent in Christ:--

(1.) He [284] grieves and labours with us. Zech. i. 12, "The angel of the Lord answered and said, O Lord of hosts, how long wilt thou not have mercy on Jerusalem?" He speaks as one intimately affected with the state and condition of poor Jerusalem; and therefore he hath bid all the world take notice that what is done to them is done to him, chap. ii. 8, 9; yea, to "the [285] apple of his eye."

(2.) In the second he abounds. Isa. xl. 11, "He shall feed his flock like a shepherd, he shall gather the lambs with his arm, and carry them in his bosom, and gently lead them that are with young." Yea, we have both here together, -- tender compassionateness and assistance. The whole frame wherein he is here described is a [286] frame of the greatest [287] tenderness, compassion, condescension that can be imagined. His people are set forth under many infirmities; some are lambs, some great with young, some very tender, some burdened with temptations, -- nothing in any of them all strong or comely. To them all Christ is [288] a shepherd, that feeds his own sheep, and drives them out to pleasant pasture; where, if he sees a poor weak lamb, [he] doth not thrust him on, but takes him into his bosom, where he both easeth and refresheth him: he leads him gently and tenderly. As did Jacob them that were burdened with[289] young, so doth our dear Lord Jesus with his flock, in the several ways and paths wherein he leads them. When he sees a poor soul, weak, tender, halting, ready to sink and perish, he takes him into his arms, by some gracious promise administered to him, carries him, bears him up when he is not able to go one step forward. Hence is his great quarrel with those shepherds, Ezek. xxxiv. 4, "Woe be to you shepherds! the diseased have ye not strengthened, neither have ye healed that which was sick, neither have ye bound up that which was broken, neither have ye brought again that which was driven away, neither have ye sought that which was lost." This is that which our careful, tender husband would have done.

So mention being made of his compassionateness and fellow-suffering with us, Heb. iv. 15, it is added, verse 16, that he administers χάριν εἰς εὔκαιρον βοήθειαν, -- seasonable grace, grace for help in a time of need. This is an evidence of compassion, when, like the Samaritan, we afford seasonable help. To lament our troubles or miseries, without affording help, is to no purpose. Now, this Christ doth; he gives εὔκαιρον βοήθειαν, -- seasonable help. Help being a thing that regards want, is always excellent; but its coming in season puts a crown upon it. A pardon to a malefactor when he is ready to be executed, is sweet and welcome. Such is the assistance given by Christ. All his saints may take this as a sure rule, both in their temptations and afflictions:-- when they can want them, they shall not want relief; and when they can bear no longer, they shall be relieved, 1 Cor. x. 13.

So it is said emphatically of him, Heb. ii. 18, "In that he himself hath suffered being tempted, he is able to succour them that are tempted." It is true, there is something in all our temptations more than was in the temptation of Christ. There is something in ourselves to take part with every temptation; and there is enough in ourselves to [290] tempt us, though nothing else should appear against us. With Christ it was not so, John xiv. 30. But this is so far from taking off his compassion towards us, that, on all accounts whatever, it doth increase it; for if he will give us succour because we are tempted, the sorer our temptations are, the more ready will he be to succour us. Take some instances of Christ's giving εὔκαιρον βοήθειαν, -- seasonable help in and under temptations unto sin. Now this he doth several ways:--

[1.] By keeping the soul which is liable to temptation and exposed to it, in a strong habitual bent against that sin that he is obnoxious to the assaults of. So it was in the case of Joseph: Christ knew that Joseph's great trial, and that whereon if he had been conquered he had been undone, would lie upon the hand of his mistress tempting him to lewdness; whereupon he kept his heart in a steady frame against that sin, as his answer without the least deliberation argues, Gen. xxxix. 9. In other things, wherein he was not so deeply concerned, Joseph's heart was not so fortified by habitual grace; as it appears by his swearing by the [291] life of Pharaoh. This is one way whereby Christ gives suitable help to his, in tenderness and compassion. The saints, in the course of their lives, by the company, society, business, they are cast upon, are liable and exposed to temptations great and violent, some in one kind, some in another. Herein is Christ exceedingly kind and tender to them, in fortifying their hearts with abundance of grace as to that sin unto temptations whereunto they are most exposed; when perhaps in other things they are very weak, and are often surprised.

[2.] Christ sometimes, by some strong impulse of actual grace, recovers the soul from the very borders of sin. So it was in the case of David, 1 Sam. xxiv. 4-6. "He was almost gone," as he speaks himself; "his feet had well-nigh slipped." The temptation was at the door of prevalence, when a mighty impulse of grace recovers him. To show his saints what they are, their own weakness and infirmity, he sometimes suffers them to go to the very edge and brow of the hill, and then causeth them to hear a word behind them saying, "This is the right way, walk in it," -- and that with power and efficacy; and so recovers them to himself.

[3.] By taking away the temptation itself, when it grows so strong and violent that the poor soul knows not what to do. This is called "delivering the godly out of temptation," 2 Pet. ii. 9, as a man is plucked out of the snare, and the snare left behind to hold another. This have I known to be the case of many, in sundry perplexing temptations. When they have been quite weary, have tried all means of help and assistance, and have not been able to come to a comfortable issue, on a sudden, unexpectedly, the Lord Christ, in his tenderness and compassion, rebukes Satan, that they hear not one word more of him as to their temptation. Christ comes in in the storm, and saith, "Peace, be still."

[4.] By giving in fresh supplies of grace, according as temptations do grow or increase. So was it in the case of Paul, 2 Cor. xii. 9, "My grace is sufficient for thee." The temptation, whatever it were, grew high; Paul was earnest for its removal; and receives only this answer, of the sufficiency of the grace of God for his supportment, notwithstanding all the growth and increase of the temptation.

[5.] By giving them wisdom to make a right, holy, and spiritual improvement of all temptations. James bids us "count it all joy when we fall into divers temptations," James i. 2: which could not be done were there not a holy and spiritual use to be made of them; which also himself manifests in the words following. There are manifold uses of temptations, which experienced Christians, with assistance suitable from Christ, may make of them. This is not the least, that by them we are brought to know ourselves. So Hezekiah was left to be tried, to know what was in him. By temptation, some bosom, hidden corruption is oftentimes discovered, that the soul knew not of before. As it was with[292] Hazael in respect of enormous crimes, so in lesser things with the saints. They would never have believed there had been such lusts and corruptions in them as they have discovered upon their temptations. Yea, divers having been tempted to one sin, have discovered another that they thought not of; as some, being tempted to pride, or worldliness, or looseness of conversation, have been startled by it, and led to a discovery of neglect of many duties and much communion with God, which before they thought not of. And this is from the tender care of Jesus Christ, giving them in suitable help; without which no man can possibly make use of or improve a temptation. And this is a suitable help indeed, whereby a temptation which otherwise, or to other persons, might be a deadly wound, proves the lancing of a festered sore, and the letting out of corruption that otherwise might have endangered the life itself. So, 1 Pet. i. 6, "If need be ye are in heaviness through manifold temptations."

[6.] When the soul is at any time more or less overcome by temptations, Christ in his tenderness relieves it with mercy and pardon; so that his shall not sink utterly under their burden, 1 John ii. 1, 2.

By one, more, or all of these ways, doth the Lord Jesus manifest his conjugal tenderness and compassion towards the saints, in and under their temptations.

2. Christ is compassionate towards them in their afflictions: "In all their affliction he is afflicted," Isa. lxiii. 9; yea, it seems that all our afflictions (at least those of one sort, -- namely, which consist in persecutions) are his in the first place, ours only by participation. Col. i. 24, We [293] "fill up the measure of the afflictions of Christ." Two things evidently manifest this compassionateness in Christ:--

(1.) His interceding with his Father for their relief, Zech. i. 12. Christ intercedeth on our behalf, not only in respect of our sins, but also our sufferings; and when the work of our afflictions is accomplished, we shall have the relief [294] he intercedes for. The Father always hears him; and we have not a deliverance from trouble, a recovering of health, ease of pain, freedom from any evil that ever laid hold upon us, but it is given us on the intercession of Jesus Christ. Believers are unacquainted with their own condition, if they look upon their mercies as dispensed in a way of common providence. And this may, indeed, be a cause why we esteem them no more, are no more thankful for them, nor fruitful in the enjoyment of them:-- we see not how, by what means, nor on what account, they are dispensed to us. The generation of the people of God in the world are at this day alive, undevoured, merely on the account of the intercession of the Lord Jesus. His compassionateness hath been the fountain of their deliverances. Hence oftentimes he rebukes their sufferings and afflictions, that they shall not act to the utmost upon them when they are under them. He is with them when they pass through fire and water, Isa. xliii. 2, 3.

(2.) In that he doth and will, in the winding up of the matter, so sorely revenge the quarrel of their sufferings upon their enemies. He avenges his elect that cry unto him; yea, he doth it speedily. The controversy of Zion leads on the day of his vengeance, Isa. xxxiv. 8. He looks upon them sometimes in distress, and considers what is the state of the world in reference to them. Zech. i. 11, "We have walked to and fro through the earth, and, behold, all the earth sitteth still, and is at rest," say his messengers to him, whom he sent to consider the world and its condition during the affliction of his people. This commonly is the condition of the world in such a season, "They are at rest and quiet, their hearts are abundantly satiated; [295] they drink wine in bowls, and send gifts to one another." Then Christ looks to see who will come in for their succour, Isa. lix. 16, 17; and finding none engaging himself for their relief, by the destruction of their adversaries, himself undertakes it. Now, this vengeance he accomplishes two ways:--

[1.] Temporally, upon persons, kingdoms, nations, and countries; (a type whereof you have, Isa. lxiii. 1-6); as he did it upon the old Roman world, Rev. vi. 15, 16. And this also he doth two ways:--

1st. By calling out here and there an eminent opposer, and making him an example to all the world. So he dealt with Pharaoh: "For this cause have I raised thee up," Exod. ix. 16. So he doth to this day; he lays his hand upon eminent adversaries, -- fills one with fury, another with folly, blasts a third, and makes another wither, or destroys them utterly and terribly. As a provoked lion, he lies not down without his prey.

2dly. In general, in the vials of his wrath which he will in these latter days pour out upon the antichristian world, and all that partake with them in their thoughts of vengeance and persecution. He will miserably destroy them, and make such work with them in the issue, that whosoever hears, both his ears shall tingle.

[2.] In eternal vengeance will he plead with the adversaries of his beloved, Matt. xxv. 41-46; 2 Thess. i. 6; Jude 15. It is hence evident that Christ abounds in pity and compassion towards his beloved. Instances might be multiplied, but these things are obvious, and occur to the thoughts of all.

In answer to this, I place in the saints chastity unto Christ, in every state and condition. That this might be the state of the church of Corinth, the apostle made it his endeavour. 2 Cor. xi. 2, 3, "I have espoused you to one husband, that I may present you as a chaste virgin to Christ. But I fear, lest by any means, as the serpent beguiled Eve through his subtilty, so your minds should be corrupted from the simplicity that is in Christ." And so is it said of the followers of the Lamb, on mount Sion, Rev. xiv. 4, "These are they which were not defiled with women, for they are virgins." What defilement that was they were free from, shall be afterward declared.

Now, there are three things wherein this chastity consists:--

1. The not taking any thing into their affections and esteem for those ends and purposes for which they have received Jesus Christ. Here the Galatians failed in their conjugal affection to Christ; they preserved not themselves chaste to him. They had received Christ for life, and justification, and him only; but being after a while overcome with [296] charms, or bewitched, they took into the same place with him the righteousness of the law. How Paul deals with them hereupon is known. How sorely, how pathetically doth he admonish them, how severely reprove them, how clearly convince them of their madness and folly! This, then, is the first chaste affection believers bear in their heart to Christ:-- having received him for their righteousness and salvation before God, for the fountain, spring, and well-head of all their supplies, they will not now receive any other thing into his room and in his stead. As to instance, in one particular:-- We receive him for our [297] acceptance with God. All that here can stand in competition with him for our affections, must be our own endeavours for a [298] righteousness to commend us to God. Now, this must be either before we receive him, or after. [As] for all duties and endeavours, of what sort soever, for the pleasing of God before our receiving of Christ, you know what was the apostle's frame, Phil. iii. 8-10. All endeavours, all advantages, all privileges, he rejects with indignation, as loss, -- with abomination, as dung; and winds up all his aims and desires in Christ alone and his righteousness, for those ends and purposes. But the works we do after we have received Christ are of another consideration. Indeed, they are acceptable to God; it pleaseth him that we should walk in them. But as to that end for which we receive Christ, they are of no other account than the former, Eph. ii. 8-10. Even the works we do after believing, -- those which we are created unto in Christ Jesus, those that God hath ordained that believers "should walk in them," -- as to justification and acceptance with God, (here called salvation), are excluded. It will one day appear that Christ abhors the janglings of men about the place of their own works and obedience, in the business of their acceptation with God; nor will the saints find any peace in adulterous thoughts of that kind. The chastity we owe

unto him requires another frame. The necessity, usefulness, and excellency of gospel obedience shall be afterward declared. It is marvellous to see how hard it is to keep some professors to any faithfulness with Christ in this thing; -- how many disputes have been managed,[299] how many distinctions invented, how many shifts and evasions studied, to keep up something, in some place or other, to some purpose or other, that they may dally withal. Those that love him indeed are otherwise minded.

Herein, then, of all things, do the saints endeavour to keep their affections chaste and loyal to Jesus Christ. He is made unto them of God "righteousness;" and they will own nothing else to that purpose: yea, sometimes they know not whether they have any interest in him or no, -- he absents and withdraws himself; they still continue solitary, in a state of widowhood, refusing to be comforted, though many things offer themselves to that purpose, because he is not. When Christ is at any time absent from the soul, when it cannot see that it hath any interest in him, many lovers offer themselves to it, many woo its affections, to get it to rest on this or that thing for relief and succour; but though it go mourning never so long, it will have nothing but Christ to lean upon. Whenever the soul is in the wilderness, in the saddest condition, there it will stay until Christ come for to take it up, until it can come forth leaning upon him, Cant. viii. 5. The many instances of this that the book of Canticles affords us, we have in part spoken of before.

This doth he who hath communion with Christ:-- he watcheth diligently over his own heart, that nothing creep into its affections, to give it any peace or establishment before God, but Christ only. Whenever that question is to be answered, "Wherewith shall I come before the Lord, and appear before the high God?" he doth not gather up, "This or that I will do;" or, "Here and there I will watch, and amend my ways;" but instantly he cries, "In the Lord Jesus have I[300] righteousness; all my desire is, to be found in him, not having on my own righteousness."

2. In cherishing that Spirit, that holy Comforter, which Christ sends to us, to abide with us in his room and stead. He tells us that he sends him to that purpose, John xvi. 7. He gives him to us, "vicariam navare operam," saith Tertullian, -- to abide with us for ever, for all those ends and purposes which he hath to fulfil toward us and upon us; he gives him to dwell in us, to keep us, and preserve us blameless for himself. His name is in him, and with him: and it is upon this account that whatever is done to any of Christ's is done to him, because it is done to them in whom he is and dwells by his Spirit. Now, herein do the saints preserve their conjugal affections entire to Christ, that they labour by all means not to grieve his Holy Spirit, which he hath sent in his stead to abide with them. This the apostle puts them in mind of, Eph. iv. 30, "Grieve not the Holy Spirit."

There be two main ends for which Christ sends his Spirit to believers:-- (1.) For their sanctification; (2.) For their consolation: to which two all the particular acts of purging, teaching, anointing, and the rest that are ascribed to him, may be referred. So there be two ways whereby we may grieve him:-- [1]. In respect of sanctification; [2.] In respect of consolation:--

(1.) In respect of sanctification. He is the Spirit of holiness, -- holy in himself, and the author of holiness in us: he works it in us, Tit. iii. 5, and he persuades us to it, by those motions of his which are not to be [301] quenched.

Now, this, in the first place, grieves the Spirit, when he is carrying on in us and for us a work so infinitely for our advantage, and without which we cannot see God, that we should run cross to him, in ways of unholiness, pollution, and defilement. So the connection of the words in the place before mentioned manifests, Eph. iv. 28-31; and thence doth Paul bottom his powerful and most effectual persuasion unto holiness, even from the abode and indwelling of this Holy Spirit with us, 1 Cor. iii. 16, 17. Indeed, what can grieve a loving and tender friend more than to oppose him and slight him when he is most intent about our good, -- and that a good of the greatest consequence to us. In this, then, believers make it their business to keep their hearts loyal and their affections chaste to Jesus Christ. They labour instantly not to grieve the Holy Spirit by loose and foolish, by careless and negligent walking, which he hath sent to dwell and abide with them. Therefore shall no anger, wrath, malice, envy, dwell in their hearts; because they are contrary to the holy, meek Spirit of Christ, which he hath given to dwell with them. They attend to his motions, make use of his assistance, improve his gifts, and nothing lies more upon their spirits, than that they may walk worthy of the presence of this holy substitute of the Lord Jesus Christ.

(2.) As to consolation. This is the second great end for which Christ gives and sends his Spirit to us; who from thence, by the way of eminency, is called "The Comforter." To this end he seals us, anoints us, establishes us, and gives us peace and joy. Of all which I shall afterward speak at large. Now, there be two ways whereby he may be grieved as to this end of his mission, and our chastity to Jesus Christ thereby violated:--

[1.] By placing our comforts and joys in other things, and not being filled with joy in the Holy Ghost. When we make creatures or creature comforts -- any thing whatever but what we receive by the Spirit of Christ -- to be our joy and our delight, we are false with Christ. So was it with Demas, [302] who loved the present world. When the ways of the Spirit of God are grievous and burdensome to us, -- when we say, "When will the Sabbath be past, that we may exact all our labours?" -- when our delight and refreshment lies in earthly things, -- we are unsuitable to Christ. May not his Spirit say, "Why do I still abide with these poor souls? I provide them joys unspeakable and glorious; but they refuse them, for perishing things. I provide them spiritual, eternal, abiding consolations, and it is all rejected for a thing of nought." This Christ cannot bear; wherefore, believers are exceeding careful in this, not to place their joy and consolation in any thing but what is administered by the Spirit. Their daily work is, to get their hearts crucified to the world and the things of it, and the world to their hearts; that they may not have living affections to dying things: they would fain look on the world as a crucified, dead thing, that hath neither form nor beauty; and if at any times they have been entangled with creatures and inferior contentment, and have lost their better joys, they cry out to Christ, "O restore to us the joys of thy Spirit!"

[2.] He is grieved when, through darkness and unbelief, we will not, do not, receive those consolations which he tenders to us, and which he is abundantly willing that we should receive. But of this I shall have occasion to speak afterward, in handling our communion with the Holy Ghost.

3. In [keeping] his institutions, or matter and manner of his worship. Christ marrying his church to himself, taking it to that relation, still expresseth the main of their chaste and choice affections to him to lie in their keeping his

institutions and his worship according to his appointment. The breach of this he calls "adultery" everywhere, and "whoredom." He is a "jealous God;" and he gives himself that title only in respect of his institutions. And the whole apostasy of the Christian church unto false worship is called [303] "fornication;" and the church that leads the others to false worship, the "mother of harlots." On this account, those believers who really attend to communion with Jesus Christ, do labour to keep their hearts chaste to him in his ordinances, institutions, and worship; and that two ways:--

(1.) They will receive nothing, practice nothing, own nothing his worship, but what is of his appointment. They know that from the foundation of the world he never did allow, nor ever will, that in any thing the will of the creatures should be the measure of his honour or the principle of his worship, either as to matter or manner. It was a witty and true sense that one gave of the second commandment: "Non imago, non simulachrum prohibetur; sed non facies tibi;" -- it is a making to ourselves, an inventing, a finding out, ways of worship, or means of honouring God, not by him appointed, that is so severely forbidden. Believers know what entertainment all will-worship finds with God: "Who hath required these things at your hand?" and, "In vain do you worship me, teaching for doctrines the traditions of men," -- is the best it meets with. I shall take leave to say what is upon my heart, and what (the Lord assisting) I shall willingly endeavour to make good against all the world, -- namely, that that principle, that the church hath power to institute and appoint any thing or ceremony belonging to the worship of God, either as to matter or to manner, beyond the orderly observance of such circumstances as necessarily attend such ordinances as Christ himself hath instituted, lies at the bottom of all the horrible superstition and idolatry, of all the confusion, blood, persecution, and wars, that have for so long a season spread themselves over the face of the Christian world; and that it is the design of a great part of the Revelation to make a discovery of this truth. And I doubt not but that the great controversy which God hath had with this nation for so many years, and which he hath pursued with so much anger and indignation, was upon this account:-- that, contrary to that glorious light of the gospel which shone among us, the wills and fancies of men, under the name of order, decency, and the authority of the church (a chimera that none knew what it was, nor wherein the power of it did consist, nor in whom reside), were imposed on men in the ways and worship of God. Neither was all that pretence of glory, beauty, comeliness, and conformity, that then was pleaded, any thing more or less than what God doth so describe in the church of Israel, Ezek. xvi. 25, and forwards. Hence was the Spirit of God in prayer derided; hence was the powerful preaching of the gospel despised; hence was the Sabbath decried; hence was holiness stigmatised and persecuted; -- to what end? That Jesus Christ might be deposed from the sole privilege and power of law-making in his church; that the true husband might be thrust aside, and adulterers of his spouse embraced; that taskmasters might be appointed in and over his house, which he never gave to his church, Eph. iv. 11; that a ceremonious, pompous, outward show worship, drawn from Pagan, Judaical, and Antichristian observations, might be introduced; -- of all which there is not one word, tittle, or iota, in the whole book of God. This, then, they who hold communion with Christ are careful of:-- they will admit of nothing, practice nothing, in the worship of God, private or public, but what they have his warrant for; unless it comes in his name, with "Thus saith the Lord Jesus," they will not hear "an angel from heaven." They know the apostles themselves were to teach the saints only what Christ commanded them, Matt. xxviii. 20. You know how many in this very nation, in the days not long since past, yea, how many thousands, left their native soil, and went into a vast and howling wilderness in the utmost parts of the world, to keep their souls undefiled and chaste to their dear Lord Jesus, as to this of his worship and institutions.

(2.) They readily embrace, receive, and practice every thing that the Lord Christ hath appointed. They inquire diligently into his mind and will, that they may know it. They go to him for directions, and beg of him to lead them in the way they have not known. The 119th Psalm may be a pattern for this. How doth the good, holy soul breathe after instruction in the ways and ordinances, the statutes and judgments, of God! This, I say, they are tender in: whatever is of Christ, they willingly submit unto, accept of, and give up themselves to the constant practice thereof; whatever comes on any other account they refuse.

IV. Christ manifests and evidences his love to his saints in a way of bounty, -- in that rich, plentiful provision he makes for them. It hath "pleased the Father that in him should all fulness dwell," Col. i. 19; and that for this end, that "of his fulness we might all receive, and grace for grace," John i. 16. I shall not insist upon the particulars of that provision which Christ makes for his saints, with all those influences of the Spirit of life and grace that daily they receive from him, -- that bread that he gives them to the full, the refreshment they have from him; I shall only observe this, that the Scripture affirms him to do all things for them in an abundant manner, or to do it richly, in a way of bounty. Whatever he gives us, -- his grace to assist us, his presence to comfort us, -- he doth it abundantly. You have the general assertion of it, Rom. v. 20, "Where sin abounded, grace did much more abound." If grace abound much more in comparison of sin, it is abundant grace indeed; as will easily be granted by any that shall consider how sin hath abounded, and doth, in every soul. Hence he is said to be able, and we are bid to expect that he should do for us "exceeding abundantly above all that we ask or think," Eph. iii. 20. Is it pardoning mercy we receive of him? why, he doth "abundantly pardon," Isa. lv. 7; he will multiply or add to pardon, -- he will add pardon to pardon, that grace and mercy shall abound above all our sins and iniquities. Is it the Spirit he gives us? he sheds him upon us richly or "abundantly," Tit. iii. 6; not only bidding us drink of the water of life freely, but also bestowing him in such a plentiful measure, that rivers of water shall flow from them that receive him, John vii. 38, 39, -- that they shall never thirst any more when have drank of him. Is it grace that we receive of him? he gives that also in a way of bounty; we receive "abundance of grace," Rom. v. 17; he "abounds toward us in all wisdom and prudence," Eph. i. 8. Hence is that invitation, Cant. v. 1. If in any things, then, we are straitened, it is in ourselves; Christ deals bountifully with us. Indeed, the great sin of believers is, that they make not use of Christ's bounty as they ought to do; that we do not every day take of him mercy in abundance. The oil never ceaseth till the vessels cease; supplies from Christ fail not but only when our faith fails in receiving them.

Then our return to Christ is in a way of duty. Unto this two things are required:--

1. That we follow after and practise holiness in the power of it, as it is obedience unto Jesus Christ. Under this formality, as obedience to him, all gospel obedience is called, "whatsoever Christ commands us," Matt. xxviii. 20; and saith he, John xv. 14, "Ye are my friends, if ye do whatsoever I command you;" and it is required of us that we live to him who died for us, 2 Cor. v. 15, -- live to him in all holy obedience, -- live to him as our Lord and King. Not that I suppose there are peculiar precepts and a peculiar law of Jesus Christ, in the observance whereof we are justified, as the Socinians fancy; for surely the gospel requires of us no more, but "to love the Lord our God with all our hearts, and all our souls," -- which the law also required; -- but that, the Lord Jesus having brought us into a condition of acceptance with God, wherein our obedience is well-pleasing to him, and we being to honour him as we honour the Father, that we have a respect and peculiar regard to him in all our obedience. So Tit. ii. 14, he hath purchased us unto himself. And thus believers do in their obedience; they eye Jesus Christ, --

(1.) As the author of their faith and obedience, for whose sake it is "given to them to believe," Phil. i. 29; and who by his Spirit works that obedience in them. So the apostle, Heb. xii. 1, 2; in the course of our obedience we still look to Jesus, "the author of our faith." Faith is here both the grace of faith, and the fruit of it in obedience.

(2.) As him in, for, and by whom we have acceptance with God in our obedience. They know all their duties are weak, imperfect, not able to abide the presence of God; and therefore they look to Christ as him who bears the iniquity of their holy things, who adds incense to their prayers, gathers out all the weeds of their duties, and makes them acceptable to God.

(3.) As one that hath renewed the commands of God unto them, with mighty obligations unto obedience. So the apostle, 2 Cor. v. 14, 15, "The love of Christ constraineth us;" of which afterward.

(4.) They consider him as God, equal with his Father, to whom all honour and obedience is due. So Rev. v. 13. But these things I have, not long since, opened [304] in another treatise, dealing about the worship of Christ as mediator. This, then, the saints do in all their obedience; they have a special regard to their dear Lord Jesus. He is, on all these accounts, and innumerable others, continually in their thoughts. His love to them, his life for them, his death for them, -- all his kindness and mercy constrains them to live to him.

2. By labouring to abound in fruits of holiness. As he deals with us in a way of bounty, and deals out unto us abundantly, so he requires that we abound in all grateful, obediential returns to him. So we are exhorted to "be always abounding in the work of the Lord," 1 Cor. xv. 58. This is that I intend:-- the saints are not satisfied with that measure that at any time they have attained, but are still pressing, that they may be more dutiful, more fruitful to Christ.

And this is a little glimpse of some of that communion which we enjoy with Christ. It is but a little, from him who hath the least experience of it of all the saints of God; who yet hath found that in it which is better than ten thousand worlds; who desires to spend the residue of the few and evil days of his pilgrimage in pursuit hereof, -- in the contemplation of the excellencies, desirableness, love, and grace of our dear Lord Jesus, and in making returns of obedience according to his will: to whose soul, in the midst of the perplexities of this wretched world, and cursed rebellions of his own heart, this is the great relief, that "He that shall come will come, and will not tarry." "The Spirit and the bride say, Come; and let him that readeth say, Come. Even so, come, Lord Jesus."

Footnotes:

247. John i. 14; 1 Tim. iii. 16.
248. Vide Vind. Evan., cap. xiii. vol. xii.
249. Rom. iv. 17; Gal. iii. 7.
250. See Vind. Evan., cap. xiii. vol. xii.
251. John xiv. 28.
252. Isa. liii. 2.
253. Isa. xlii. 1, 19; John xiv. 31.
254. Matt. iii. 15.
255. Heb. x. 7, 8.
256. Heb. ii. 14, 15.
257. Gal. iii. 13.
258. 2 Cor. v. 21.
259. Ps. xxii. 1.
260. Matt. xxvi. 39.
261. "Amorem istum non esse vulgarem ostendit, dum nos pretiosos esse dicit." --Calv. in loc.
262. Gen. xii. 3; Mic. v. 7, 8.
263. Isa. xxxiv. 8, lxi. 2, lxiii. 4.
264. Matt. xxv. 41-46.
265. Luther.
266. Νῦν ἄρχομαι εἶναι μαθητής, οὐδὲν τούτων τῶν ὁρωμένων ἐπιθυμῶ, ἵνα τὸν Ἰησοῦν Χριστὸν εὕρω. Πῦρ, σταυρός, θηρία, σύγκλασις ὀστέων, καὶ τῶν μελῶν διασπασμός, καὶ παντὸς τοῦ σώματος συντριβή, καὶ βάσανοι τοῦ διαβόλου εἰς ἐμὲ ἔλθωσιν, ἵνα Ἰησοῦ Χριστοῦ ἀπολαύσω. -- Vit. Ignat. [Hieronymus, De Viris Illustribus, c. xvi.]
267. Acts xxiii. 1.
268. Rom. x. 2, 3.
269. Acts xxvi. 7.
270. John ix. 40; Rom. ix. 30, 31.
271. Isa. xlv. 24.
272. Matt. xiii. 45, 46. "Principium culmenque omnium

rerum pretii, margaritæ tenent." -- Plin.
273. Gal. ii. 20; John xiii. 34; Rev. i. 5, 6; Eph. v. 25, 26; Heb. x. 9, 10.
274. John xiv. 28.
275. Matt. xiii. 45, 46; Phil. iii. 8.
276. Matt. x. 37.
277. Cant. viii. 6.
278. Καὶ τοῦτό μοι τῶν ἐν ᾅδου κολάσεων βαρύτερον ἂν εἴη. -- Basil.
279. "Fateor insitam esse nobis corporis nostri caritatem." -- Senec. Epist. xiv. "Generi animantium omni est a natura tributum ut se, vitam, corpusque tueatur." -- Cicer. Off. i. [iv.]
280. Ps. ciii. 13.
281. "Hoc quidem certum est, hoc vocabulo, summum illum consensum membrorum et capitis (id est, ecclesiæ et Christi) significari, de quo toties Paulus disserit. Deinde ut cum de Deo loquitur, ita, etiam de Christo glorioso disserens Scriptura, ad nostrum captum se demittit. Gloriosum autem ad dextram patris Christum sedere credimus; ubi dicitur nostris malis affici, quod sibi factum ducat quicquid nobis fit injuriæ, ideo clamans e coelis, Saul cur me presequeris? Altiores speculationes scrutari, nec utile nec tutum existimo." -- Bez. in loc.
282. Rom. viii. 26; 1 Cor. xi. 32; 2 Cor. xi. 30, xii. 9, 10; Gal. iv. 13.
283. Matt. xxv. 35.
284. Acts. ix. 4; Isa. lxiii. 9.
285. Deut. xxxii. 10; Ps. xvii. 8.
286. "? En ipse capellas

Protinus æger ago; hanc etiam vix Tityre duco," etc. Virg. [Ec. i. 12]

287. "Quod frequentur in Scriptura, pastoris nomen Deus usurpat, personamque induit, non vulgare est teneri in nos amoris signum. Nam quum humilis et abjecta sit loquendi forma, singulariter erga nos affectus sit oportet, qui se nostrâ causa ita demittere non gravatur: mirum itaque nisi tam blanda et familiaris invitatio ad eum nos alliciat." -- Calvin in Ps. xxiii. 1.

288. Heb. xiii. 20; 1 Pet. ii. 25, v, 4; Ps. xxiii. 1; Zech. xiii. 7; Isa. xl. 11; Ezek. xxxiv. 23; John x. 11, 14, 16.

289. Gen. xxxiii. 13.

290. James i. 14, 15.

291. Gen. xlii. 15.

292. 2 Kings viii. 13.

293. "Τῶν παθημάτων Christi duo sunt genera: προτερήματα, quæ passus est in corpore suo, et ὑστερήματα, quæ in sanctis." -- Zanc. in loc.

294. Heb. vii. 25.

295. Amos vi. 3-6; Rev. xi. 10.

296. Gal. iii. 1.

297. 1 Cor. i. 30.

298. Rom. x. 4.

299. "Perfice hoc precibus, pretio, ut hæream in parte aliqua tandem," etc.

300. Isa. xlv. 24; Phil. iii. 9; Hab. ii. 1-4.

301. 1 Thess. v. 19.

302. 2 Tim. iv. 10.

303. Rev. xvii. 5.

304. Vindiciæ Evangel., chap. xiii. vol. xii.

Chapter VI - Of communion with Christ in purchased grace -- Purchased grace considered in respect of its rise and fountain -- The first rise of it, in the obedience of Christ -- Obedience properly ascribed to Christ -- Two ways considered: what it was, and wherein it did consist -- Of his obedience to the law in general -- Of the law of the Mediator -- His habitual righteousness, how necessary; as also his obedience to the law of the Mediator -- Of his actual obedience or active righteousness -- All Christ's obedience performed as he was Mediator -- His active obedience for us -- This proved at large, Gal. iv. 4, 5; Rom. v. 19; Phil. iii. 10; Zech. iii. 3-5 -- One objection removed -- Considerations of Christ's active righteousness closed -- Of the death of Christ, and its influence into our acceptation with God -- A price; redemption, what it is -- A sacrifice; atonement made thereby -- A punishment; satisfaction thereby -- The intercession of Christ; with its influence into our acceptation with God.

Our process [305] is now to communion with Christ in purchased grace, as it was before proposed: "That we may know him, and the power of his resurrection, and the fellowship of his sufferings, and be made conformable to his death," Phil. iii. 10.

By purchased grace, I understand all that righteousness and grace which Christ hath procured, or wrought out for us, or doth by any means make us partakers of, or bestows on us for our benefit, by any thing that he hath done or suffered, or by any thing he continueth to do as mediator:-- First, What this purchased grace is, and wherein it doth consist; Secondly, How we hold communion with Christ therein; are the things that now come under consideration.

The First may be considered two ways:-- 1. In respect of the rise and fountain of it; 2. Of its nature, or wherein it consisteth.

1. It hath a threefold rise, spring, or causality in Christ:-- (1.) The obedience of his life. (2.) The suffering of his death. (3.) His continued intercession. All the actions of Christ as mediator, leading to the communication of grace unto us, may be either referred to these heads, or to some things that are subservient to them or consequents of them.

2. For the nature of this grace wherein we have communion with Christ, flowing from these heads and fountains, it may be referred to these three:-- (1.) Grace of justification, or acceptation with God; which makes a relative change in us, as to state and condition. (2.) Grace of sanctification, or holiness before

God; which makes a real change in us, as to principle and operation. (3.) Grace of privilege; which is mixed, as we shall show, if I go forth to the handling thereof.

Now, that we have communion with Christ in this purchased grace, is evident on this single consideration, -- that there is almost nothing that Christ hath done, which is a spring of that grace whereof we speak, but we are said to do it with him. We are "crucified" with him, Gal. ii. 20; we are "dead" with him, 2 Tim. ii. 11; Col. iii. 3; and "buried" with him, Rom. vi. 4; Col. ii. 12; we are "quickened together with him," Col. ii. 13; "risen" with him, Col. iii. 1. "He hath quickened us together with Christ, and hath raised us up together, and made us sit together in heavenly places," Eph. ii. 5, 6. In the actings of Christ, there is, by virtue of the compact between him as mediator, and the Father, such an assured foundation laid of the communication of the fruits of those actings unto those in whose stead he performed them, that they are said, in the participation of those fruits, to have done the same things with him. The life and power of which truth we may have occasion hereafter to inquire into:--

(1.) The first fountain and spring of this grace, wherein we have our communion with Christ, is first to be considered; and that is the obedience of his life: concerning which it must be declared, -- [1.] What it is that is intended thereby, and wherein it consisteth. [2.] What influence it hath into the grace whereof we speak.

To the handling of this I shall only premise this observation, -- namely, that in the order of procurement, the life of Christ (as was necessary) precedeth his death; and therefore we shall handle it in the first place: but in the order of application, the benefits of his death are bestowed on us antecedently, in the nature of the things themselves, unto those of his life; as will appear, and that necessarily, from the state and condition wherein we are.

[1.] By the obedience of the life of Christ, I intend the universal conformity of the Lord Jesus Christ, as he was or is, in his being mediator, to the whole will of God; and his complete actual fulfilling of the whole of every law of God, or doing of all that God in them required. He might have been perfectly holy by obedience to the law of creation, the moral law, as the angels were; neither could any more, as a man walking with God, be required of him: but he submitted himself also to every law or ordinance that was introduced upon the occasion of sin, which, on his own account, he could not be subject to, it becoming him to "fulfil [306] all righteousness," Matt. iii. 15, as he spake in reference to a newly-instituted ceremony.

That obedience is properly ascribed unto Jesus Christ as mediator, the Scripture is witness, both as to name and thing Heb. v. 8, "Though he were a Son, yet learned he obedience," etc.; yea, he was obedient in his sufferings, and it was that which gave life to his death, Phil. ii. 8. He was obedient to death: for therein "he did make his soul an offering for sin," Isa. liii. 10; or, "his soul made an offering for sin," as it is interpreted, verse 12, "he poured out his soul to death," or, "his soul poured out itself unto death." And he not only sanctified himself to be an offering, John xvii. 19, but he also "offered up himself," Heb. ix. 14, an "offering of a sweet savour to God," Eph. v. 2. Hence, as to the whole of his work, he is called the Father's "servant," Isa. xlii. 1, and verse 19: and he professes of himself that he "came into the world to do the will of God, the will of him that sent him;" for which he manifests "his great readiness," Heb. x. 7; --

all which evince his obedience. But I suppose I need not insist on the proof of this, that Christ, in the work of mediation, and as mediator, was obedient, and did what he did willingly and cheerfully, in obedience to God.

Now, this obedience of Christ may be considered two ways:-- 1st. As to the habitual root and fountain of it. 2dly. As to the actual parts or duties of it:--

1st. The habitual righteousness of Christ as mediator in his human nature, was the absolute, complete, exact conformity of the soul of Christ to the will, mind, or law of God; or his perfect habitually inherent righteousness. This he had necessarily from the grace of union; from whence it is that that which was born of the virgin was a "holy thing," Luke i. 35. It was, I say, necessary consequentially, that it should be so; though the effecting of it were by the free operations of the Spirit, Luke ii. 52. He had an all-fulness of grace on all accounts. This the apostle describes, Heb. vii. 26, "Such an high priest became us, holy, harmless, undefiled, separate from sinners." Every way separate and distant from sin and sinners he was to be; whence he is called "The Lamb of God, without spot or blemish," 1 Pet. i. 19. This habitual holiness of Christ was inconceivably above that of the angels. He who " [307] chargeth his angels with folly," Job iv. 18; "who putteth no trust in his saints; and in whose sight the heavens" (or their inhabitants) "are not clean," chap. xv. 15; always embraceth him in his bosom, and is always well pleased with him, Matt. iii. 17. And the reason of this is, because every other creature, though never so holy, hath the Spirit of God by measure; but he was not given to Christ "by measure," John iii. 34; and that because it pleased him that in him "should all fulness dwell," Col. i. 19. This habitual grace of Christ, though not absolutely infinite, yet, in respect of any other creature, it is as the water of the sea to the water of a pond or pool. All other creatures are depressed from perfection by this, -- that they subsist in a created, dependent being; and so have the fountain of what is communicated to them without them. But the human nature of Christ subsists in the person of the Son of God; and so hath the bottom and fountain of its holiness in the strictest unity with itself.

2dly. The actual obedience of Christ, as was said, was his willing, cheerful, obediential performance of every thing, duty, or command, that God, by virtue of any law whereto we were subject and obnoxious, did require; and [his obedience], moreover, to the peculiar law of the mediator. Hereof, then, are two parts:--

(1st.) That whatever was required of us by virtue of any law, -- that he did and fulfilled. Whatever was required of us by the law of nature, in our state of innocence; whatever kind of duty was added by morally positive or ceremonial institutions; whatever is required of us in way of obedience to righteous judicial laws, -- he did it all. Hence he is said to be "made under the law," Gal. iv. 4; subject or obnoxious to it, to all the precepts or commands of it. So, Matt. iii. 15, he said it became him to [308] "fulfil all righteousness," -- πᾶσαν δικαιοσύνην, -- all manner of righteousness whatever; that is, everything that God required, as is evident from the application of that general axiom to the baptism of John. I shall not need, for this, to go to particular instances, in the duties of the law of nature, -- to God and his parents; of morally positive [duties], in the Sabbath, and other acts of worship; of the ceremonial law, in circumcision, and observation of all the rites of the Judaical church; of the judicial, in paying tribute to governors; -- it will suffice, I presume, that on the one hand he "did no sin, neither was guile found in his mouth;" and on the other, that he "fulfilled all righteousness:" and thereupon the Father was always well pleased with him. This was that which he owned of himself, that he came to do the will of God; and he did it.

(2dly.) There was a peculiar law of the mediator, which respected himself merely, and contained all those acts and duties of his which are not for our imitation. So that obedience which he showed in dying was peculiarly to this[309] law, John x. 18, "I have power to lay down my life: this commandment have I received of my Father." As mediator, he received this peculiar command of his Father, that he should lay down his life, and take it again; and he was obedient thereunto. Hence we say, he who is mediator did some things merely as a man, subject to the law of God in general; so he prayed for his persecutors, -- those that put him to death, Luke xxiii. 34; -- some things as mediator; so he prayed for his elect only, John xvii. 9. There were not worse in the world, really and evidently, than many of them that crucified him; yet, as a man, subject to the law, he forgave them, and prayed for them. When he prayed as mediator, his Father always heard him and answered him, John xi. 41; and in the other prayers he was accepted as one exactly performing his duty.

This, then, is the obedience of Christ; which was the first thing proposed to be considered. The next is, --

[2.] That it hath an influence into the grace of which we speak, wherein we hold communion with him, -- namely, our free acceptance with God; what that influence is, must also follow in its order.

1st. For his habitual righteousness, I shall only propose it under these two considerations:--

(1st.) That upon this supposition, that it was needful that we should have a mediator that was God and man in one person, as it could not otherwise be, so it must needs be that he must be holy. For although there be but one primary necessary effect of the hypostatical union (which is the subsistence of the human nature in the person of the Son of God), yet that he that was so united to him should be a "holy thing," completely holy, was necessary also, -- of which before.

(2dly.) That the relation which this righteousness of Christ hath to the grace we receive from him is only this, -- that thereby he was ἱκανός -- fit to do all that he had to do for us. This is the intendment of the apostle, Heb. vii. 26. Such a one "became us;" it was needful he should be such a one, that he might do what he had to do. And the reasons hereof are two:--

[1st.] Had he not been completely furnished with habitual grace, he could never have actually fulfilled the righteousness which was required at his hands. It was therein that he was able to do all that he did. So himself lays down the presence of the Spirit with him as the bottom and foundation of his going forth to his work, Isa. lxi. 1.

[2dly.] He could not have been a complete and perfect sacrifice, nor have answered all the types and figures of him, that were [310] complete and without blemish. But now, Christ having this habitual righteousness, if he had never yielded any continued obedience to the law actively, but had suffered as soon after his incarnation as Adam sinned after his creation, he had been a fit sacrifice and offering; and therefore, doubtless, his following obedience hath another use besides to fit him for an oblation, for which he was most fit without it.

2dly. For Christ's obedience to the law of mediation, wherein it is not coincident with his passive obedience, as they speak (for I know that expression is improper); it was that which was requisite for the discharging of his office, and is not imputed unto us, as though we had done it, though the ἀποτελέσματα and fruits of it are; but is of the nature of his intercession, whereby he provides the good things we stand in need of, at least subserviently to his oblation and intercession; -- of which more afterward.

3dly. About his actual fulfilling of the law, or doing all things that of us are required, there is some doubt and question; and about it there are three several opinions:--

(1st.) That this active obedience of Christ hath no farther influence into our justification and acceptation with God, but as it was preparatory to his blood-shedding and oblation; which is the sole cause of our justification, the whole righteousness which is imputed to us arising from thence.

(2dly.) That it may be considered two ways:-- [1st.] As it is purely obedience; and so it hath no other state but that before mentioned. [2dly.] As it was accomplished with suffering, and joined with it, as it was part of his humiliation, so it is imputed to us, or is part of that upon the account whereof we are justified.

(3dly.) That this obedience of Christ, being done for us, is reckoned graciously of God unto us; and upon the account thereof are we accepted as righteous before him. My intendment is not to handle this difference in the way of a controversy, but to give such an understanding of the whole as may speedily be reduced to the practice of godliness and consolation; and this I shall do in the ensuing observations:--

[1st.] That the obedience that Christ yielded to the law in general, is not only to the peculiar law of the mediator, though he yielded it as mediator. He was incarnate as mediator, Heb. ii. 14; Gal. iv. 4; and all he afterward did, it was as our mediator. For that cause "came he into the world," and did and suffered whatever he did or suffered in this world. So that of this expression, as mediator, there is a twofold sense: for it may be taken strictly, as relating solely to the law of the mediator, and so Christ may be said to do as mediator only what he did in obedience to that law; but in the sense now insisted on, whatever Christ did as a man subject to any law, he did it as mediator, because he did it as part of the duty incumbent on him who undertook so to be.

[2dly.] That whatever Christ did as mediator, he did it for them whose mediator he was, or in whose stead and for whose good he executed the office of a mediator before God. This the Holy Ghost witnesseth, Rom. viii. 3, 4, "What the law could not do, in that it was wreak through the flesh, God sending his own Son in the likeness of sinful flesh, and for sin, condemned sin in the flesh, that the righteousness of the law might be fulfilled in us;" because that we could not in that condition of weakness whereinto we are cast by sin, come to God, and be freed from condemnation by the law, God sent Christ as a mediator, to do and suffer whatever the law required at our hands for that end and purpose, that we might not be condemned, but accepted of God. It was all to this end, -- "That the righteousness of the law might be fulfilled in us;" that is, which the law required of us, consisting in duties of obedience. This Christ performed for us. This expression of the apostle, "God sending his own Son in the likeness of sinful flesh, and for sin, condemned sin in the flesh;" if you will add to it, that of Gal. iv. 4, that he was so sent forth as that he was ὑπὸ νόμον γενόμενος, "made under the law," (that is, obnoxious to it, to yield all the obedience that it doth require), comprises the whole of what Christ did or suffered; and all this, the Holy Ghost tells us, was for us, verse 4.

[3dly.] That the end of this active obedience of Christ cannot be assigned to be, that he might be fitted for his death and oblation. For he answered all types, and was every way ἱκανός (fit to be made an offering for sin), by his union and habitual grace. So that if the obedience Christ performed be not reckoned to us, and done upon our account, there is no just cause to be assigned why he should live here in the world so long as he did, in perfect obedience to all the laws of God. Had he died before, there had been perfect innocence, and perfect holiness, by his habitual grace, and infinite virtue and worth from the dignity of his person; and surely he yielded not that long course of all manner of obedience, but for some great and special purpose in reference to our salvation.

[4thly.] That had not the obedience of Christ been for us (in what sense we shall see instantly), it might in his life have been required of him to yield obedience to the law of nature, the alone law which he could be liable to as a man; for an innocent man in a covenant of works, as he was, needs no other law, nor did God ever give any other law to any such person (the law of creation is all that an innocent creature is liable to, with what symbols of that law God is pleased to add). And yet to this law also was his subjection voluntary; and that not only consequentially, because he was born upon his own choice, not by any natural course, but also because as mediator, God and man, he was not by the institution of that law obliged unto it; being, as it were, exempted and lifted above that law by the hypostatical union: yet, when I say his subjection hereunto was voluntary, I do not intend that it was merely arbitrary and at choice whether he would yield obedience [311] unto it or no, -- but on supposition of his undertaking to be a mediator, it was necessary it should be so, -- but that he voluntarily and willingly submitted unto, and so became really subject to the commands of it. But now, moreover, Jesus Christ yielded perfect obedience to all those laws which came upon us by the occasion of sin, as the ceremonial law; yea, those very institutions that signified the washing away of sin, and repentance from sin, as the baptism of John, which he had no need of himself. This, therefore, must needs be for us.

[5thly.] That the obedience of Christ cannot be reckoned amongst his sufferings, but is clearly distinct from it, as to all formalities. Doing is one thing, suffering another; they are in diverse predicaments, and cannot be coincident.

See, then, briefly what we have obtained by those considerations; and then I shall intimate what is the stream issuing from this first spring or fountain of purchased grace, with what influence it hath thereinto:--

First, By the obedience of the life of Christ you see what is intended, -- his willing submission unto, and perfect, complete fulfilling of, every law of God, that any of the saints of God were obliged unto. It is true, every act almost of Christ's obedience, from the blood of his circumcision to the blood of his cross, was attended with suffering, so that his whole life might, in that regard, be called a death; but yet, looking upon his willingness and obedience in it, it is distinguished from his sufferings peculiarly so called, and termed his [312] active righteousness. This is, then, I say, as was showed, that complete, absolutely perfect accomplishment of the whole law of God by Christ, our mediator; whereby he not only "did no sin, neither was there guile found in his mouth," but also most perfectly fulfilled all righteousness, as he affirmed it became him to do.

Secondly, That this obedience was performed by Christ not for himself, but for us, and in our stead. It is true, it must needs be, that whilst he had his conversation in the flesh he must be most perfectly and absolutely holy; but yet the prime intendment of his accomplishing of holiness, -- which consists in the complete obedience of his whole life to any law of God, -- that was no less for us than his suffering death. That this is so, the apostle tells us, Gal. iv. 4, 5, "God sent forth his Son, made of a woman, made under the law, to redeem them that were under the law." This Scripture, formerly named, must be a little farther insisted on. He was both made of a woman, and made under the law; that is, obedient to it for us. The end here, both of the incarnation and obedience of Christ to the law (for that must needs be understood here by the phrase ὑπὸ νόμον γενόμενος, -- that is, disposed of in such a condition as that he must yield subjection and obedience to the law), was all to redeem us. In these two expressions, "Made of a woman, made under the law," the apostle doth not knit his incarnation and death together, with an exclusion of the obedience of his life. And he was so made under the law, as those were under the law whom he was to redeem. Now, we were under the law, not only as obnoxious to its penalties, but as bound to all the duties of it. That this is our being "under the law," the apostle informs us, Gal. iv. 21, "Tell me, ye that desire to be under the law." It was not the penalty of the law they desired to be under, but to be under it in respect of obedience. Take away, then, the end, and you destroy the means. If Christ were not incarnate nor made under the law for himself, he did not yield obedience for himself; it was all for us, for our good. Let us now look forward, and see what influence this hath into our acceptation.

Thirdly, Then, I say, this perfect, complete obedience of Christ to the law is reckoned unto us. As there is a truth in that, "The day thou eatest thou shalt die," -- death is the reward of sin, and so we cannot be freed from death but by the death of Christ, Heb. ii. 14, 15; so also is that no less true, "Do this, and live," -- that life is not to he obtained unless all be done that the law requires. That is still true, "If thou wilt enter into life, keep the commandments," Matt. xix. 17. They must, then, be kept by us, or our surety. Neither is it of any value which by some is objected, that if Christ yielded perfect obedience to the law for us, then are we no more bound to yield obedience; for by his undergoing death, the penalty of the law, we are freed from it. I answer, How did Christ undergo death? Merely as it was penal. How, then, are we delivered from death? Merely as it is penal. Yet we must die still; yea, as the last conflict with the effects of sin, as a passage to our Father, we must die. Well, then, Christ yielded perfect obedience to the law; but how did he do it? Purely as it stood in that conditional [arrangement], "Do this, and live." He did it in the strength of the grace he had received; he did it as a means of life, to procure life by it, as the tenor of a covenant. Are we, then, freed from this obedience? Yes; but how far? From doing it in our own strength; from doing it for this end, that we may obtain life everlasting. It is vain that some say confidently, that we must yet work for life; it is all one as to say we are yet under the old covenant, "Hoc fac, et vives:" we are not freed from obedience, as a way of walking with God, but we are, as a way of working to come to him: of which at large afterward.

Rom. v. 18, 19, "By the righteousness of one the free gift came upon all men unto justification of life: by the obedience of one shall many be made righteous," saith the Holy Ghost. By his obedience to the law are we made righteous; it is reckoned to us for righteousness. That the passive obedience of Christ is here only intended is false:--

First, It is opposed to the disobedience of Adam, which was active. The δικαίωμα is opposed παραπτώματι, -- the righteousness to the fault. The fault was an active transgression of the law, and the obedience opposed to it must be an active accomplishment of it. Besides, obedience placed singly, in its own nature, denotes an action or actions conformable to the law; and therein came Christ, not to destroy but to fulfil the law, Matt. v. 17, -- that was the design of his coming, and so for us; he came to fulfil the law for us, Isa. ix. 6, and [was] born to us, Luke ii. 11. This also was in that will of the Father which, out of his infinite love, he came to accomplish. Secondly, It cannot clearly be evinced that there is any such thing, in propriety of speech, as passive obedience; obeying is doing, to which passion or suffering cannot belong: I know it is commonly called so, when men obey until they suffer; but properly it is not so.

So also, Phil. iii. 9, "And be found in him, not having my own righteousness, which is of the law, but that which is through the faith of Christ, the righteousness which is of God by faith." The righteousness we receive is opposed to our own obedience to the law; opposed to it, not as something in another kind, but as something in the same kind excluding that from such an end which the other obtains. Now this is the obedience of Christ to the law, -- himself thereby being "made to us righteousness," 1 Cor. i. 30.

Rom. v. 10, the issue of the death of Christ is placed upon reconciliation; that is, a slaying of the enmity and restoring us into that condition of peace and friendship wherein Adam was before his fall. But is there no more to be done? Notwithstanding that there was no wrath due to Adam, yet he was to obey, if he would enjoy eternal life. Something there is, moreover, to be done in respect of us, if, after the slaying of the enmity and reconciliation made, we shall enjoy life: "Being reconciled by his death," we are saved by that perfect obedience which in his life he yielded to the law of God. There is distinct mention made of reconciliation, through a non-imputation of sin, as Ps. xxxii. 1, Luke i. 77, Rom. iii. 25, 2 Cor. v. 19; and justification through an imputation of righteousness, Jer. xxiii. 6, Rom. iv. 5, 1 Cor. i. 30; -- although these things are so far from being separated, that they are reciprocally affirmed of one another: which, as it doth not evince an identity, so it doth an eminent conjunction. And this last we have by the life of Christ.

This is fully expressed in that typical representation of our justification before the Lord, Zech. iii. 3-5. Two things are there expressed to belong to our free acceptation before God:-- 1. The taking away of the guilt of our sin, our filthy robes; this is done by the death of Christ. Remission of sin is the proper fruit thereof; but there is more also required, even a collation of righteousness, and thereby a right to life eternal. This is here called "Change of raiment;" so the Holy Ghost expresses it again, Isa. lxi. 10, where he calls it plainly "The garments of salvation," and "The robe of righteousness." Now this is only made ours by the obedience of Christ, as the other by his death.

Objection. "But if this be so, then are we as righteous as Christ himself, being righteous with his righteousness."

Answer. But first, here is a great difference, -- if it were no more than that this righteousness was inherent in Christ, and properly his own, it is only reckoned or imputed to us, or freely bestowed on us, and we are made righteous with that which is not ours. But, secondly, the truth is, that Christ was not righteous with that righteousness for himself, but for us; so that here can be no comparison: only this we may say, we are righteous with his righteousness which he wrought for us, and that completely.

And this, now, is the rise of the purchased grace whereof we speak, the obedience of Christ; and this is the influence of it into our acceptation with God. Whereas the guilt of sin, and our obnoxiousness to punishment on that account, is removed and taken away (as shall farther be declared) by the death of Christ; and whereas, besides the taking away of sin, we have need of a complete righteousness, upon the account whereof we may be accepted with God; this obedience of Christ, through the free grace of God, is imputed unto us for that end and purpose.

This is all I shall for the present insist on to this purpose. That the passive righteousness of Christ only is imputed to us in the non-imputation of sin, and that on the condition of our faith and new obedience, so exalting them into the room of the righteousness of Christ, is a thing which, in communion with the Lord Jesus, I have as yet no acquaintance withal. What may be said in the way of argument on the one side or other must be elsewhere considered.

(2.) The second spring of our communion with Christ in purchased grace, is his death and oblation. He lived for us, he died for us; he was ours in all he did, in all he suffered. [313] I shall be the more brief in handling of this, because on another design I have [314] elsewhere at large treated of all the concernments of it.

Now, the death of Christ, as it is a spring of that purchased grace wherein we have communion with him, is in the Scripture proposed under a threefold consideration:-- [1.] Of a price. [2.] Of a sacrifice. [3.] Of a penalty.

In the first regard, its proper effect is redemption; in the second, reconciliation or atonement; in the third, satisfaction; which are the great ingredients of that purchased grace whereby, in the first place, we have communion with Christ.

[1.] It is a price. "We are bought with a price," 1 Cor. vi. 20; being "not redeemed with silver and gold, and corruptible things, but with the precious blood of Christ," 1 Pet. i. 18, 19: which therein answers those things in other contracts. [315] He came to "give his life a ransom for many," Matt. xx. 28, -- a price of redemption, 1 Tim. ii. 6. The proper use and energy of this expression in the Scripture, I have elsewhere declared.

Now, the proper effect and issue of the death of Christ as a price or ransom is, as I said, redemption. Now, redemption is the deliverance of any one from bondage or captivity, and the miseries attending that condition, by the intervention or interposition of a price or ransom, paid by the redeemer to him by whose authority the captive was detained:--

1st. In general, it is a deliverance. Hence Christ is called "The Deliverer," Rom. xi. 26; giving himself to "deliver us," Gal. i. 4. He is "Jesus, who delivers us from the wrath to come," 1 Thess. i. 10.

2dly. It is the delivery of one from bondage or captivity. We are, without him, all prisoners and captives, "bound in prison," Isa. lxi. 1; "sitting in darkness, in the prison house," Isa. xlii. 7, xlix. 9; "prisoners in the pit wherein there is no water," Zech. ix. 11; "the captives of the mighty, and the prey of the terrible," Isa. xlix. 25; under a "captivity that must be led captive," Ps. lxviii. 18: this puts us in "bondage," Heb. ii. 15.

3dly. The person committing thus to prison and into bondage, is God himself. To him we owe "our debts," Matt. vi. 12, xviii. 23-27; against him are our offences, Ps. li. 4; he is the judge and lawgiver, James iv. 12. To sin is to rebel against him. He shuts up men under disobedience, Rom. xi. 32; and he shall cast both body and soul of the impenitent into hell-fire, Matt. x. 28. To his wrath are men obnoxious, John iii. 36; and lie under it by the sentence of the law, which is their prison.

4thly. The miseries that attend this condition are innumerable. Bondage to Satan, sin, and the world, comprises the sum of them; from all which we are delivered by the death of Christ, as a price or ransom. "God hath delivered us from the power of darkness, and hath translated us into the kingdom of his dear Son; in whom we have redemption through his blood," Col. i. 13, 14. And he "redeems us from all iniquity," Tit. ii. 14; "from our vain conversation," 1 Pet. i. 18, 19; even from the guilt and power of our sin; purchasing us to himself "a peculiar people, zealous of good works," Tit. ii. 14: so dying for the "redemption of transgressions," Heb. ix. 15; redeeming us also from the world, Gal. iv. 5.

5thly. And all this is by the payment of the price mentioned into the hand of God, by whose supreme authority we are detained captives, under the sentence of the law. The debt is due to the great householder, Matt. xviii. 23, 24; and the penalty, his curse and wrath: from which by it we are delivered, Rev. i. 5.

This the Holy Ghost frequently insists on. Rom. iii. 24, 25, "Being justified freely by his grace, through the redemption that is in Christ Jesus; whom God hath set forth to be a propitiation through faith in his blood, to declare his righteousness for the remission of sins:" so also, 1 Cor. vi. 20; 1 Pet. i. 18; Matt. xx. 28; 1 Tim. ii. 6; Eph. i. 7; Col. i. 13; Gal. iii. 13. And this is the first consideration of the death of Christ, as it hath an influence into the procurement of that grace wherein we hold communion with him.

[2.] It was a sacrifice also. He had a body prepared him, Heb. x. 5; wherein he was to accomplish what by the typical oblations and burnt-offerings of the law was prefigured. And that body he offered, Heb. x. 10; -- that is, his whole human nature; for "his soul" also was made "an offering for sin," Isa. liii. 10: on which account he is said to offer himself, Eph. v. 2; Heb. i. 3, ix. 26. He gave himself a sacrifice to God of a sweet-smelling savour; and this he did willingly,[316] as became him who was to be a sacrifice, -- the law of this obedience being written in his heart, Ps. xl. 8; that is, he had a readiness, willingness, desire for its performance.

Now, the end of sacrifices, such as his was, bloody and for sin, Rom. v. 10; Heb. ii. 17, was atonement and reconciliation. This is everywhere ascribed to them, that they were to make atonement; that is, in a way suitable to their nature. And this is the tendency of the death of Christ, as a sacrifice, atonement, and reconciliation with God. Sin had broken friendship between God and us, Isa. lxiii. 10; whence his wrath was on us, John iii. 36; and we are by nature obnoxious to it, Eph. ii. 3. This is taken away by the death of Christ, as it was a sacrifice, Dan. ix. 24. "When we were enemies, we were reconciled to God by the death of his Son," Rom. v. 10. And thereby do we "receive the atonement," verse 11; for "God was in Christ reconciling the world to himself, not imputing to them their sins and their iniquities," 2 Cor. v. 19-21: so also, Eph. ii. 12-16, and in sundry other places. And this is the second consideration of the death of Christ; which I do but name, having at large insisted on these things elsewhere.

[3.] It was also a punishment, -- a punishment in our stead. "He was wounded for our transgressions, he was bruised for our iniquities: the chastisement of our peace was upon him," Isa. liii. 5. God made all our iniquities (that is, the punishment of them) "to meet upon him," verse 6. "He bare the sins of many," verse 12; "his own self bare our sins in his own body on the tree," 1 Pet. ii. 24; and therein he "who knew no sin, was made sin for us," 2 Cor. v. 21. What it is in the Scripture to bear sin, see Deut. xix. 15, xx. 17; Numb. xiv. 33; Ezek. xviii. 20. The nature, kind, matter, and manner of this punishment I have, as I said before, elsewhere discussed.

Now, bearing of punishment tends directly to the giving satisfaction to him who was offended, and on that account inflicted the punishment. Justice can desire no more than a proportional punishment, due to the offence. And this, on his own voluntary taking of our persons, undertaking to be our mediator, was inflicted on our dear Lord Jesus. His substituting himself in our room being allowed of by the righteous Judge, satisfaction to him doth thence properly ensue.

And this is the threefold consideration of the death of Christ, as it is a principal spring and fountain of that grace wherein we have communion with him; for, as will appear in our process, the single and most eminent part of purchased grace, is nothing but the natural exurgency of the threefold effect of the death of Christ, intimated to flow from it on the account of the threefold consideration insisted on. This, then, is the second rise of purchased grace, which we are to eye, if we will hold communion with Christ in it, -- his death and blood-shedding, under this threefold notion of a price, an offering, and punishment. But, --

(3.) This is not all: the Lord Christ goes farther yet; he doth not leave us so, but follows on the work to the utmost. [317] "He died for our sins, and rose again for our justification." He rose again to carry on the complete work of purchased grace, -- that is, by his intercession; which is the third rise of it. In respect of this, he is said to be "able to save them to the uttermost that come unto God by him, seeing he ever liveth to make intercession for them," Heb. vii. 25.

Now, the intercession of Christ, in respect of its influence into purchased grace, is considered two ways:--

[1.] As a continuance and carrying on of his oblation, for the making out of all the fruits and effects thereof unto us. This is called his "appearing in the presence of God for us," Heb. ix. 24; that is, as the high priest, having offered the great offering for expiation of sin, carried in the blood thereof into the most holy place, where was the representation of the presence of God, so to perfect the atonement he made for himself and the people; so the Lord Christ, having offered himself as a sweet-smelling sacrifice to God, being sprinkled with his own blood, appears in the presence of God, as it were to mind him of the engagement made to him, for the redemption of sinners by his blood, and the making out the good things to them which were procured thereby. And so this appearance of his hath an influence into purchased grace, inasmuch as thereby he puts in his claim for it in our behalf.

[2.] He procureth the Holy Spirit for us, effectually to collate and bestow all this purchased grace upon us. That he would do this, and doth it, for us, we have his engagement, John xiv. 16. This is purchased grace, in respect of its fountain and spring; -- of which I shall not speak farther at present, seeing I must handle it at large in the matter of the communion we have with the Holy Ghost.

Footnotes:

305. [See beginning of chapter ii., for the leading divisions.]

306. "Vox hæc δικαιοσύνη hoc quidem loco latissimè sumitur, ita ut significet non modo τὸ νόμιμον, sed et quicquid ullam æqui atque honesti habet rationem; nam lex Mosis de hoc baptismo nihil præscripserat." -- Grot."Per δικαιοσύνη Christus hic non designat justitiam legalem, sed, ut ita loqui liceat, personalem; τὸ πρέπον personæ, et τὸ καθῆκον muneri." -- Walæ. Ἐβαπτίσθη δὲ καὶ ἐνήστευσεν, οὐκ αὐτὸς ἀπορρύψεως ἢ νηστείας χρείαν ἔχων, ἢ καθάρσεως, ὁ τῇ φύσει καθαρὸς καὶ ἅγιος. -- Clem.

307. "Sensus est de angelis, qui si cum Deo confederantur, aut si eos secum Deus conferat, non habens rationem eorum quæ in illis posuit, et dotium ac donorum quæ in illos contulit, et quibus eos exornavit et illustravit, inveniat eos stolidos. Sanè quicquid habent angeli, a Deo habent." -- Mercer. in loc.

308. "Fuit legis servituti subjectus, ut eam implendo nos ab ea redimeret, et ab ejus servitute." -- Bez.

309. "Proprium objectum obedientiæ est præceptum, tacitum vel expressum, id est, voluntas superioris quocunque modo innotescat." -- Thom. 2, 2, q. 2, 5. Deut. xviii. 18; Acts iii. 22; John xii. 49, xiv. 31, vi. 38, v. 30.

310. Præcipitur, Lev. xxii. 20, ne offeratur pecus in quo sit מום, mum, id est corporis vitium: a מום, efficitur μῶμος culpa:' unde Christus dicitur ἄμωμος, inculpatus:' opponitur autem מום, to תָּמוּם, hoc est integrum.' Ibid., ver. 19, et sic Exod. xii. 5, præcipitur de agno paschali, ut sit תָּמִים, id est integer,' omnis scilicet vitii expers. Idem præcipitur de agnis jugis sacrificii, Numb. xxviii. 3, quibus ipsa nimirum sanctitas Christi tanquam victimæ paræfigurata est." -- Piscat., in 1 Pet. i. 19.

311. "Obedientia importat necessitatem respectu ejus quod præcipitur, et voluntatem respectu impletionis præcepti." -- Thom. 3, q. 47, 2, 2.

312. "In vita passivam habuit actionem; in morte passionem activam sustinuit; dum salutem operatur in medio terræ." -- Bern. Ser. 4.

313. "Tantane me tenuit vivendi, nate, voluptas,

Ut pro me hostili paterer succedere dextræ,

Quem genui? tuane hæc genitor per vulnera servor,

Morte tua vivens?" Virgil, Æneid. x. 846.

314. Vindic. Evan., cap. xx.-xxii. vol. xii.

315. "Nil quidem emitur nisi interveniente pretio; sed hoc tamen additum magnam emphasin habet." -- Bez.

316. "Observatum est a sacrificantibus, ut si hostia quæ ad aras duceretur, fuisset vehementer reluctata, ostendissetque se invitam altaribus admoveri, amoveretur, quia invito Deo eam offerri putabant; quæ vero stetisset oblata, hanc volenti numini dari existimabant." -- Macrob. Saturnal. lib. iii. "Hoc quoque notandum, vitulos ad aras humeris hominum allatos non fere litare; sicut nec claudicante, nec aliena hostia placari deos; neque trahente se ab aris." -- Plin. lib. viii. cap. 45.

317. Rom. iv. 25.

Chapter VII - *The nature of purchased grace; referred to three heads:-- 1. Of our acceptation with God; two parts of it. 2. Of the grace of sanctification; the several parts of it.*

The fountain of that purchased grace wherein the saints have communion with Christ being discovered, in the next place the nature of this grace itself may be considered. As was said, it may be referred unto three heads:-- 1. Grace of acceptation with God. 2. Grace of sanctification from God. 3. Grace of privileges with and before God.

1. Of acceptation with God. Out of Christ, we are in a state of [318] alienation from God, accepted neither in our persons nor our services. Sin makes a separation between God and us:-- that state, with all its consequences and attendancies, [it] is not my business to unfold. The first issue of purchased grace is to restore us into a state of acceptation. And this is done two ways:-- (1.) By a removal of that for which we are refused, -- the cause of the enmity. (2.) By a bestowing of that for which we are accepted.

Not only all causes of quarrel were to be taken away, that so we should not be under displeasure, but also that was to be given unto us that makes us the objects of God's delight and pleasure, on the account of the want whereof we are distanced from God:--

(1.) It gives a removal of that for which we are refused. This is sin in the guilt, and all the attendancies thereof. The first issue of purchased grace tends to the taking away of sin in its guilt, that it shall not bind over the soul to the wages of it, which is death.

How this is accomplished and brought about by Christ, was evidenced in the close of the foregoing chapter. It is the fruit and effect of his death for us. Guilt of sin was the only cause of our separation and distance from God, as hath been said. This made us obnoxious to wrath, punishment, and the whole displeasure of God; on the account hereof were we imprisoned under the curse of the law, and given up to the power of Satan. This is the state of our unacceptation. By his death, Christ -- bearing the curse, undergoing the punishment that was due to us, paying the ransom that was due for us -- delivers us from this condition. And thus far the death of Christ is the sole cause of our acceptation with God, -- that all cause of quarrel and rejection of us is thereby taken away. And to that end are his sufferings reckoned to us; for, being "made sin for us," 2 Cor. v. 21, he is made "righteousness unto us," 1 Cor. i. 30.

But yet farther; this will not complete our acceptation with God. The old quarrel may be laid aside, and yet no new friendship begun; we may be not sinners, and yet not be so far righteous as to have a right to the kingdom of heaven. Adam had no right to life because he was innocent; he must, moreover, "do this," and then he shall "live." He must not only have a negative righteousness, -- he was not guilty of any thing; but also a positive righteousness, -- he must do all things.

(2.) This, then, is required, in the second place, to our complete acceptation, that we have not only the not imputation of sin, but also a reckoning of righteousness. Now, this we have in the obedience of the life of Christ. This also was discovered in the last chapter. The obedience of the life of Christ was for us, is imputed to us, and is our righteousness before God; -- by his obedience are we "made righteous," Rom. v. 19. On what score the obedience of faith takes place, shall be afterward declared.

These two things, then, complete our grace of acceptation. Sin being removed, and righteousness bestowed, we have peace with God, -- are continually accepted before him. There is not any thing to charge us withal: that which was, is taken out of the way by Christ, and nailed to his cross, -- made fast there; yea, publicly and legally cancelled, that it can never be admitted again as an evidence. What court among men would admit of an evidence that hath been publicly cancelled, and nailed up for all to see it? So hath Christ dealt with that which was against us; and not only so, but also he puts that upon us for which we are received into favour. He makes us comely through his beauty; gives us white raiment to stand before the Lord. This is the first part of purchased grace wherein the saints have communion with Jesus Christ. In remission of sin and imputation of righteousness doth it consist; from the death of Christ, as a price, sacrifice, and a punishment, -- from the life of Christ spent in obedience to the law, doth it arise. The great product it is of the Father's righteousness, wisdom, love, and grace; -- the great and astonishable fruit of the love and condescension of the Son; -- the great discovery of the Holy Ghost in the revelation of the mystery of the gospel.

2. The second is grace of sanctification. He makes us not only accepted, but also acceptable. He doth not only purchase love for his saints, but also makes them lovely. He came not by blood only, but by water and blood. He doth not only justify his saints from the guilt of sin, but also sanctify and wash them from the filth of sin. The first is from his life and death as a sacrifice of propitiation; this from his death as a purchase, and his life as an example. So the apostle, Heb. ix. 14; as also Eph. v. 26, 27. Two things are eminent in this issue of purchased grace:-- (1.) The removal of defilement; (2.) The bestowing of cleanness in actual grace.

(1.) For the first, it is also threefold:--

[1.] The habitual cleansing of our nature. We are naturally unclean, defiled, -- habitually so; for "Who can bring a clean thing out of an unclean?" Job xiv. 4; "That which is born of the flesh is flesh," John iii. 6. It is in the pollution of our blood that we are born, Ezek. xvi., -- wholly defiled and polluted. The grace of sanctification, purchased by the blood of Christ, removes this defilement of our nature. 1 Cor. vi. 11, "Such were some of you; but ye are washed, ye are sanctified." So also Tit. iii. 3-5, "He hath saved us by the washing of regeneration, and the renewing of the Holy Ghost." How far this original, habitual pollution is removed, need not be disputed; it is certain the soul is made fair and beautiful in the sight of God. Though the sin that doth defile remains, yet its habitual defilement is taken away. But the handling of this lies not in my aim.

[2.] Taking away the pollutions of all our actual transgressions. There is a defilement attending every actual sin. Our own clothes make us to be abhorred, Job ix. 31. A spot, a stain, rust, wrinkle, filth, blood, attends every sin. Now, 1

John i. 7, "The blood of Jesus Christ cleanseth us from all sin." Besides the defilement of our natures which he purgeth, Tit. iii. 5, he takes away the defilement of our persons by actual follies. "By one offering he perfected for ever them that are sanctified;" by himself he "purged our sins," before he sat down at the right hand of the Majesty on high, Heb. i. 3.

[3.] In our best duties we have defilement, Isa. lxiv. 6. Self, unbelief, form, drop themselves into all that we do. We may be ashamed of our choicest performances. God hath promised that the saints' good works shall follow them. Truly, were they to be measured by the rule as they come from us, and weighed in the balance of the sanctuary, it might be well for us that they might be buried for ever: But the Lord Christ first, as our high priest, bears the iniquity, the guilt, and provocation, which in severe justice doth attend them, Exod. xxviii. 38; and not only so, but he washes away all their filth and defilements. He is as a refiner's fire, to purge both the sons of Levi and their offerings; adding, moreover, sweet incense to them, that they may be accepted. Whatever is of the Spirit, of himself, of grace, -- that remains; whatever is of self, flesh, unbelief (that is, hay and stubble), -- that he consumes, wastes, takes away. So that the saints' good works shall meet them one day with a changed countenance, that they shall scarce know them: that which seemed to them to be black, deformed, defiled, shall appear beautiful and glorious; they shall not be afraid of them, but rejoice to see and follow them.

And this cleansing of our natures, persons, and duties, hath its whole foundation in the death of Christ. Hence our washing and purifying, our cleansing and purging, is ascribed to his blood and the sprinkling thereof meritoriously, this work is done, by the shedding of the blood of Christ; efficiently, by its sprinkling. The sprinkling of the blood of Christ proceedeth from the communication of the Holy Ghost; which he promiseth to us, as purchased by him for us. He is the pure water, wherewith we are sprinkled from all our sins, that spirit of judgment and burning that takes away the filth and blood of the daughters of Zion. And this is the first thing in the grace of sanctification; of which more afterward.

(2.) By bestowing cleanness as to actual grace. The blood of Christ in this purchased grace doth not only take away defilement, but also it gives purity; and that also in a threefold gradation:--

[1.] It gives the Spirit of holiness to dwell in us. "He is made unto us sanctification," 1 Cor. i. 30, by procuring for us the Spirit of sanctification. Our renewing is of the Holy Ghost, who is shed on us through Christ alone, Tit. iii. 6. This the apostle mainly insists on, Rom. viii., -- to wit, that the prime and principal gift of sanctification that we receive from Christ, is the indwelling of the Spirit, and our following after the guidance hereof. But what concerns the Spirit in any kind, must be referred to that which I have to offer concerning our communion with him.

[2.] He gives us habitual grace; -- a principle of grace, opposed to the principle of lust that is in us by nature. This is the grace that dwells in us, makes its abode with us; which, according to the distinct faculties of our souls wherein it is, or the distinct objects about which it is exercised, receiveth various appellations, being indeed all but one new principle of life. In the understanding, it is light; in the will, obedience; in the affections, love; in all, faith. So, also, it is differenced in respect of its operations. When it carries out the soul to rest on Christ, it is faith; when to delight in him, it is love; but still one and the same habit of grace. And this is the second thing.

[3.] Actual influence for the performance of every spiritual duty whatever. After the saints have both the former, yet Christ tells them that without him "they can do nothing," John xv. 5. They are still in dependence upon him for new influences of grace, or supplies of the Spirit. They cannot live and spend upon the old stock; for every new act they must have new grace. He must "work in us to will and to do of his good pleasure," Phil. ii. 13. And in these three, thus briefly named, consists that purchased grace in the point of sanctification, as to the collating of purity and cleanness, wherein we have communion with Christ.

3. This purchased grace consists in privileges to stand before God, and these are of two sorts, -- primary and consequential. Primary, is adoption, -- the Spirit of adoption; consequential, are all the favours of the gospel, which the saints alone have right unto. But of this I shall speak when I come to the last branch, -- of communion with the Holy Ghost.

These are the things wherein we have communion with Christ as to purchased grace in this life. Drive them up to perfection, and you have that which we call everlasting glory. Perfect acceptance, perfect holiness, perfect adoption, or inheritance of sons, -- that is glory.

Our process now, in the next place, is to what I mainly intend, even the manner how we hold communion with Christ in these things; and that in the order laid down; as, --

I. How we hold communion with him in the obedience of his life and merit of his death, as to acceptance with God the Father.

II. How we hold communion with Christ in his blood, as to the Spirit of sanctification, the habits and acts of grace.

III. How we hold communion with him as to the privileges we enjoy. Of which in the ensuing chapters.

Footnotes:

318. John iii. 36; Eph. ii. 12, 13.

Chapter VIII - How the saints hold communion with Christ as to their acceptation with God -- What is required on the part of Christ hereunto; in his intention; in the declaration thereof -- The sum of our acceptation with God, wherein it consists -- What is required on the part of believers to this communion, and how they hold it, with Christ -- Some objections proposed to consideration, why the elect are not accepted immediately on the undertaking and the death of Christ -- In what sense they are so -- Christ a common or public person -- How he came to be so -- The way of our acceptation with God on that account -- The second objection -- The necessity of our obedience stated, Eph. ii. 8-10 -- The grounds, causes, and ends of it manifested -- Its proper place in the new covenant -- How the saints, in particular, hold communion with Christ in this purchased grace -- They approve of this righteousness; the grounds thereof -- Reject their own; the grounds thereof -- The commutation of sin and righteousness between Christ and believers; some objections answered.

I. Communion with Christ in purchased grace, as unto acceptation with God, from the obedience of his life and efficacy of his death, is the first thing we inquire into. The discovery of what on the part of Christ and what on our part is required thereunto (for our mutual actings, even his and ours, are necessary, that we may have fellowship and communion together herein), is that which herein I intend.

First, On the part of Christ there is no more required but these two things:-- (1.) That what he did, he did not for himself, but for us. (2.) What he suffered, he suffered not for himself, but for us. That is, that his intention from eternity, and when he was in the world, was, that all that he did and suffered was and should be for us and our advantage, as to our acceptance with God; that he still continueth making use of what he so did and suffered for that end and purpose, and that only. Now, this is most evident:--

(1.) What he did, he did for us, and not for himself: "He was made under the law, that we might receive the adoption of sons," Gal. iv. 4, 5. He was made under the law; that is, in that condition that he was obnoxious to the will and commands of it. And why was this? to what end? for himself? No; but to redeem us is the aim of all that he did, -- of all his obedience: and that he did. This very intention in what he did he acquaints us with, John xvii. 19, "For their

253

sakes I sanctify myself, that they may be sanctified through the truth." "I sanctify myself, -- dedicate and set myself apart to all that work I have to do. I came not to do my own will; I came to save that which was lost; to minister, not to be ministered unto; and to give my life a ransom;" -- it was the testimony he bare to all he did in the world. This intendment of his is especially to be eyed. From eternity he had thoughts of what he would do for us; and delighted himself therein. And when he was in the world, in all he went about, he had still this thought, "This is for them, and this is for them, -- my beloved." When he went to be baptised, says John, "I have need to be baptised of thee, and comest thou to me?" Matt. iii. 14, 15; as if he had said, "Thou hast no need at all of it." But says Christ, "Suffer it to be so, now; for thus it becometh us to fulfil all righteousness;" -- "I do it for them who have none at all, and stand obliged unto all."

(2.) In what he suffered. This is more clear, Dan. ix. 26, "Messiah shall be cut off, but not for himself." And the apostle lays down this as a main difference between him and the high priests of the Jews, that when they made their solemn offerings, they offered first for themselves, and then for the people; but Jesus Christ offered only for others. He had no sin, and could make no sacrifice for his own sin, which he had not, but only for others. He "tasted death every man," Heb. ii. 9, -- "gave his life a ransom for many," Matt. xx. 28. The "iniquity of us all was made to meet on him," Isa. liii. 6; -- "He bare our sins in his own body on the tree," 1 Pet. ii. 24; -- "loved the church, and gave himself for it," Eph. v. 25; Gal. ii. 20; Rom. iv. 25; Rev. i. 5, 6; Tit. ii. 14; 1 Tim. ii. 6; Isa. liii. 12; John xvii. 19. But this is exceeding clear and confessed, that Christ in his suffering and oblation, had his intention only upon the good of his elect, and their acceptance with God; suffering for us, "the just for the unjust, that he might bring us to God."

Secondly, To complete this communion on the part of Christ, it is required, --

(1.) That there be added to what he hath done, the gospel tenders of that complete righteousness and acceptance with God which ariseth from his perfect obedience and sufferings. Now, they are twofold:--

[1.] Declaratory, in the conditional promises of the gospel. Mark xvi. 15; Matt. xi. 28, "He that believeth shall be saved;" "Come unto me, and I will give you rest;" "As Moses lifted up the serpent," etc.; "Christ is the end of the law for righteousness to every one that believeth," Rom. x. 4; and innumerable others. Now, declaratory tenders are very precious, there is much kindness in them, and if they be rejected, they will be the "savour of death unto death;" but the Lord Christ knows that the outward letter, though never so effectually held out, will not enable any of his for that reception of his righteousness which is necessary to interest them therein; wherefore, --

[2.] In this tender of acceptation with God, on the account of what he hath done and suffered, a law is established, that whosoever receives it shall be so accepted. But Christ knows the condition and state of his in this world. This will not do; if he do not effectually invest them with it, all is lost. Therefore, --

(2.) He sends them his Holy Spirit, to quicken them, John vi. 63, to cause them that are "dead to hear his voice," John v. 25; and to work in them whatever is required of them, to make them partakers of his righteousness and accepted with God.

Thus doth Christ deal with his:-- he lives and dies with an intention to work out and complete righteousness for them; their enjoying of it, to a perfect acceptation before God, is all that in the one and other he aimed at. Then he tenders it unto them, declares the usefulness and preciousness of it to their souls, stirring them up to a desire and valuation of it; and lastly, effectually bestows it upon them, reckons it unto them as theirs, that they should by it, for it, with it, be perfectly accepted with his Father.

Thus, for our acceptation with God, two things are required:--

First, That satisfaction be made for our disobedience, -- for whatever we had done which might damage the justice and honour of God; and that God be atoned towards us: which could no otherwise be, but by undergoing the penalty of the law. This, I have showed abundantly, is done by the death of Christ. God "made him to be sin for us," 2 Cor. v. 21, -- a "curse," Gal. iii. 13. On this account we have our absolution, -- our acquitment from the guilt of sin, the sentence of the law, the wrath of God, Rom. viii. 33, 34. We are justified, acquitted, freed from condemnation, because it was Christ that died; "he bare our sins in his own body on the tree," 1 Pet. ii. 24.

Second, That the righteousness of the law be fulfilled, and the obedience performed that is required at our hands. And this is done by the life of Christ, Rom. v. 18, 19. So that answerable hereunto, according to our state and the condition of our acceptation with God, there are two parts:--

Our absolution from the guilt of sin, that our disobedience be not charged upon us. This we have by the death of Christ; our sins being imputed to him, shall not be imputed to us, 2 Cor. v. 21; Rom. iv. 25; Isa. liii. 12.

Imputation of righteousness, that we may be accounted perfectly righteous before God; and this we have by the life of Christ. His righteousness in yielding obedience to the law is imputed to us. And thus is our acceptation with God completed. Being discharged from the guilt of our disobedience by the death of Christ, and having the righteousness of the life of Christ imputed to us, we have friendship and peace with God. And this is that which I call our grace of acceptation with God, wherein we have communion with Jesus Christ.

That which remains for me to do, is to show how believers hold distinct communion with Christ in this grace of acceptation, and how thereby they keep alive a sense of it, -- the comfort and life of it being to be renewed every day. Without this, life is a hell; no peace, no joy can we be made partakers of, but what hath its rise from hence. Look what grounded persuasion we have of our acceptation with God, that he is at peace with us; whereunto is the revenue of our peace, comfort, joy, yea, and holiness itself, proportioned.

But yet, before I come in particular to handle our practical communion with the Lord Jesus in this thing, I must remove two considerable objections; -- the one of them lying against the first part of our acceptation with God, the other against the latter.

Objection 1. For our absolution by and upon the death of Christ, it may be said, that "if the elect have their absolution, reconciliation, and freedom by the death, blood, and cross of Christ, whence is it, then, that they were not all actually absolved at the death of Christ, or at least so soon as they are born, but that many of them live a long while under the wrath of God in this world, as being unbelievers, under the sentence and condemning power of the law? John iii. 36. Why are they not immediately freed, upon the payment of the price and making reconciliation for them?"

Obj. 2. "If the obedience of the life of Christ be imputed unto us, and that is our righteousness before God, then what need we yield any obedience ourselves? Is not all our praying, labouring, watching, fasting, giving alms, -- are not all fruits of holiness, in purity of heart and usefulness of conversation, all in vain and to no purpose? And who, then, will or need take care to be holy, humble, righteous, meek, temperate, patient, good, peaceable, or to abound in good works in the world?"

1. I shall, God assisting, briefly remove these two objections, and then proceed to carry on the design in hand, about our communion with Christ:--

(1.) Jesus Christ, in his undertaking of the work of our reconciliation with God, -- for which cause he came into the world, -- and the accomplishment of it by his death, was constituted and considered as a common, public person, in the stead of them for whose reconciliation to God he suffered. Hence he is the "mediator between God and man," 1 Tim. ii. 5, -- that is, one who undertook to God for us, as the next words manifest, verse 6, "Who gave himself a ransom for all," -- and the "surety of the better covenant," Heb. vii. 22; undertaking for and on the behalf of them with whom that covenant was made. Hence he is said to be given "for a covenant of the people," Isa. xlii. 6; and a "leader," lv. 4. He was the second Adam, 1 Cor. xv. 45, 47, to all ends and purposes of righteousness, to his spiritual seed, as the first Adam was of sin to his natural seed, Rom. v. 15-19.

(2.) His being thus a common person, arose chiefly from these things:--

[1.] In general, from the covenant entered into by himself with his Father to this purpose. The terms of this covenant are at large insisted on, Isa. liii., summed up, Ps. xl. 7, 8; Heb. x. 8-10. Hence the Father became to be his God; which is a covenant expression, Ps. lxxxix. 26; Heb. i. 5; Ps. xxii. 1, xl. 8, xlv. 7; Rev. iii. 12; Mic. v. 4. So was he by his Father on this account designed to this work, Isa. xlii. 1, 6, xlix. 9; Mal. iii. 1; Zech. xiii. 7; John iii. 16; 1 Tim. i. 15. Thus the "counsel of peace" became to be "between them both," Zech. vi. 13; that is, the Father and Son. And the Son rejoices from eternity in the thought of this undertaking, Prov. viii. 22-30. The command given him to this purpose, the promises made to him thereon, the assistance afforded to him, I have elsewhere handled.

[2.] In the sovereign grant, appointment, and design of the Father, giving and delivering the elect to Jesus Christ in this covenant, to be redeemed and reconciled to himself. John xvii. 6, "Thine they were, and thou gavest them me." They were God's by eternal designation and election, and he gave them to Christ to be redeemed. Hence, before their calling or believing, he calls them his "sheep," John x. 15, 16, laying down his life for them as such; and hence are we said to be "chosen in Christ," Eph. i. 4, or designed to obtain all the fruits of the love of God by Christ, and committed into his hand for that end and purpose.

[3.] In his undertaking to suffer what was due to them, and to do what was to be done by them, that they might be delivered, reconciled, and accepted with God. And he undertakes to give in to the Father, without loss or miscarriage, what he had so received of the Father as above, John xvii. 2, 12, vi. 37, 39; as Jacob did the cattle he received of Laban, Gen. xxxi. 39, 40. Of both these I have treated somewhat at large elsewhere, in handling the covenant between the Father and the Son; so that I shall not need to take it up here again.

[4.] They being given unto him, he undertaking for them to do and suffer what was on their part required, he received, on their behalf and for them, all the promises of all the mercies, grace, good things, and privileges, which they were to receive upon the account of his undertaking for them. On this account eternal life is said to be promised of God "before the world began," Tit. i. 2; that is, to the Son of God for us, on his undertaking on our behalf. And grace, also, is said to be given unto us "before the world began," 2 Tim. i. 9; that is, in Christ, our appointed head, mediator, and representative.

[5.] Christ being thus a common person, a mediator, surety, and representative, of his church, upon his undertaking, as to efficacy and merit, and upon his actual performance, as to solemn declaration, was as such acquitted, absolved, justified, and freed, from all and every thing that, on the behalf of the elect, as due to them, was charged upon him, or could so be; I say, as to all the efficacy and merit of his undertakings, he was immediately absolved upon his faithfulness, in his first engagement: and thereby all the saints of the Old Testament were saved by his blood no less than we. As to solemn declaration, he was so absolved when, the "pains of death being loosed", he was "declared to be the Son of God with power, by the resurrection from the dead;" Rom. i. 4, God saying to him, "Thou art my Son; this day have I begotten thee," Ps. ii. 7. And this his absolution doth Christ express his confidence of, Isa. l. 5-9. And he was "justified," 1 Tim. iii. 16. That which I intend by this absolution of Christ as a public person is this:-- God having made him under the law, for them who were so, Gal. iv. 4; in their stead, obnoxious to the punishment due to sin, made him sin, 2 Cor. v. 21; and so gave justice, and law, and all the consequents of the curse thereof, power against him, Isa. liii. 6; -- upon his undergoing of that which was required of him, verse 12, God looses the pains and power of death, accepts him, and is well pleased with him, as to the performance and discharge of his work, John xvii. 3-6; pronounceth him free from the obligation that was on him, Acts xiii.; and gave him a promise of all good things he aimed at, and which his soul desired. Hereon are all the promises of God made to Christ, and their accomplishment, -- all the encouragements given him to ask and make demand of the things originally engaged for to him, Ps. ii. 8, (which he did accordingly, John xvii.), -- founded and built. And here lies the certain, stable foundation of our absolution, and acceptation with God. Christ in our stead, acting for us as our surety, being acquitted, absolved, solemnly declared to have answered the whole debt that was incumbent on him to pay, and made satisfaction for all the injury we had done, a general pardon is sealed for us all, to be sued out particularly in the way to be appointed. For, --

[6.] Christ as a public person being thus absolved, it became righteous with God, a righteous thing, from the covenant, compact, and convention, that was between him and the Mediator, that those in whose stead he was, should obtain, and have bestowed on them, all the fruits of his death, in reconciliation with God, Rom. v. 8-11; that as Christ received the general acquittance for them all, so they should every one of them enjoy it respectively. This is everywhere manifested in those expressions which express a commutation designed by God in this matter; as 2 Cor. v. 21; Gal. iii. 13; 1 Pet. ii. 21, 24; -- of which afterward.

[7.] Being thus acquitted in the covenant of the Mediator (whence they are said to be circumcised with him, to die with him, to be buried with him, to rise with him, to sit with him in heavenly places, -- namely, in the covenant of the Mediator), and it being righteous that they should be acquitted personally in the covenant of grace, it was determined by Father, Son, and Holy Ghost, that the way of their actual personal deliverance from the sentence and curse of the law should be in and by such a way and dispensation as might lead to the praise of the glorious grace of God, Eph. i. 5-7. The appointment of God is, that we shall have the adoption of children. The means of it, is by Jesus Christ; the peculiar way of bringing it about, is by the redemption that is in his blood; the end, is the praise of his glorious grace. And thence it is, --

[8.] That until the full time of their actual deliverance, determined and appointed to them in their several generations, be accomplished, they are personally under the curse of the law; and, on that account, are legally obnoxious to the wrath of God, from which they shall certainly be delivered; -- I say, they are thus personally obnoxious to the law, and the curse thereof; but not at all with its primitive intention of execution upon them, but as it is a means appointed to help forward their acquaintance with Christ, and acceptance with God, on his account. When this is accomplished, that whole obligation ceases, being continued on them in a design of love; their last condition being such as that they cannot without it be brought to a participation of Christ, to the praise of the glorious grace of God.

[9.] The end of the dispensation of grace being to glorify the whole Trinity, the order fixed on and appointed wherein this is to be done, is, by ascending to the Father's love through the work of the Spirit and blood of the Son. The emanation of divine love to us begins with the Father, is carried on by the Son, and then communicated by the Spirit; the Father designing, the Son purchasing, the Spirit effectually working: which is their order. Our participation is first by the work of the Spirit, to an actual interest in the blood of the Son; whence we have acceptation with the Father.

This, then, is the order whereby we are brought to acceptation with the Father, for the glory of God through Christ:--

1st. That the Spirit may be glorified, he is given unto us, to quicken us, convert us, work faith in us, Rom. viii. 11; Eph. i. 19, 20; according to all the promises of the covenant, Isa. iv. 4, 5; Ezek. xi. 19, xxxvi. 26.

2dly. This being wrought in us, for the glory of the Son, we are actually interested, according to the tenor of the covenant, at the same instant of time, in the blood of Christ, as to the benefits which he hath procured for us thereby; yea, this very work of the Spirit itself is a fruit and part of the purchase of Christ. But we speak of our sense of this thing, whereunto the communication of the Spirit is antecedent. And, --

3dly. To the glory of the Father, we are accepted with him, justified, freed from guilt, pardoned, and have "peace with God," Rom. v. 1. Thus, "through Christ we have access by one Spirit unto the Father," Eph. ii. 17. And thus are both Father and Son and the Holy Spirit glorified in our justification and acceptation with God; the Father in his free love, the Son in his full purchase, and the Holy Spirit in his effectual working.

[10.] All this, in all the parts of it, is no less fully procured for us, nor less freely bestowed on us, for Christ's sake, on his account, as part of his purchase and merits, than if all of us immediately upon his death, had been translated into heaven; only this way of our deliverance and freedom is fixed on, that the whole Trinity may be glorified thereby. And this may suffice in answer to the first objection. Though our reconciliation with God be fully and completely procured by the death of Christ, and all the ways and means whereby it is accomplished; yet we are brought unto an actual enjoyment thereof, by the way and in the order mentioned, for the praise of the glorious grace of God.

2. The second objection is, "That if the righteousness and obedience of Christ to the law be imputed unto us, then what need we yield obedience ourselves?" To this, also, I shall return answer as briefly as I can in the ensuing observations:--

(1.) The placing of our gospel obedience on the right foot of account (that it may neither be exalted into a state, condition, use, or end, not given it of God; nor any reason, cause, motive, end, necessity of it, on the other hand, taken away, weakened, or impaired), is a matter of great importance. Some make our obedience, the works of faith, our works, the matter or cause of our justification; some, the condition of the imputation of the righteousness of Christ; some, the qualification of the person justified, on the one hand; some exclude all the necessity of them, and turn the grace of God into lasciviousness, on the other. To debate these differences is not my present business; only, I say, on this and other accounts, the right stating of our obedience is of great importance as to our walking with God.

(2.) We do by no means assign the same place, condition, state, and use to the obedience of Christ imputed to us, and our obedience performed to God. If we did, they were really inconsistent. And therefore those who affirm that our obedience is the condition or cause of our justification, do all of them deny the imputation of the obedience of Christ unto us. The righteousness of Christ is imputed to us, as that on the account whereof we are accepted and esteemed righteous before God, and are really so, though not inherently. We are as truly righteous with the obedience of Christ imputed to us as Adam was, or could have been, by a complete righteousness of his own performance. So Rom. v. 18, by his obedience we are made righteous, -- made so truly, and so accepted; as by the disobedience of Adam we are truly made trespassers, and so accounted. And this is that which the apostle desires to be found in, in opposition to his own righteousness, Phil. iii. 9. But our own obedience is not the righteousness whereupon we are accepted and justified before God; although it be acceptable to God that we should abound therein. And this distinction the apostle doth evidently deliver and confirm, so as nothing can be more clearly revealed: Eph. ii. 8-10, "For by grace are ye saved through faith: and that not of yourselves: it is the gift of God: not of works, lest any man should boast. For we are his workmanship, created in Christ Jesus unto good works, which God hath prepared that we should walk in them." We are saved, or justified (for that it is whereof the apostle treats), "by grace through faith," which receives Jesus Christ and his obedience; "not of works, lest any man should boast." "But what works are they that the apostle intends?" The works of believers, as in the very beginning of the next words is manifest: "'For we are,' we believers, with our obedience and our works, of whom I speak." "Yea; but what need, then, of works?" Need still there is: "We are his workmanship," etc.

Two things the apostle intimates in these words:--

[1.] A reason why we cannot be saved by works, -- namely, because we do them not in or by our own strength; which is necessary we should do, if we will be saved by them, or justified by them. "But this is not so," saith the apostle;

"for we are the workmanship of God," etc.; -- all our works are wrought in us, by full and effectual undeserved grace.

[2.] An assertion of the necessity of good works, notwithstanding that we are not saved by them; and that is, that God has ordained that we shall walk in them: which is a sufficient ground of our obedience, whatever be the use of it.

If you will say then, "What are the true and proper gospel grounds, reasons, uses, and motives of our obedience; whence the necessity thereof may be demonstrated, and our souls be stirred up to abound and be fruitful therein?" I say, they are so many, and lie so deep in the mystery of the gospel and dispensation of grace, spread themselves so throughout the whole revelation of the will of God unto us, that to handle them fully and distinctly, and to give them their due weight, is a thing that I cannot engage in, lest I should be turned aside from what I principally intend. I shall only give you some brief heads of what might at large be insisted on:--

1st. Our universal obedience and good works are indispensably necessary, from the sovereign appointment and will of God; Father, Son, and Holy Ghost.

In general. "This is the will of God, even your sanctification," or holiness, 1 Thess. iv. 3. This is that which God wills, which he requires of us, -- that we be holy, that we be obedient, that we do his will as the angels do in heaven. The equity, necessity, profit, and advantage of this ground of our obedience might at large be insisted on; and, were there no more, this might suffice alone, -- if it be the will of God, it is our duty:--

(1st.) The Father hath ordained or appointed it. It is the will of the Father, Eph. ii. 10. The Father is spoken of personally, Christ being mentioned as mediator.

(2dly.) The Son hath ordained and appointed it as mediator. John xv. 16, "'?I have ordained you, that ye should bring forth fruit' of obedience, and that it should remain." And, --

(3dly.) The Holy Ghost appoints and ordains believers to works of obedience and holiness, and to work holiness in others. So, in particular, Acts xiii. 2, he appoints and designs men to the great work of obedience in preaching the gospel. And in sinning, men sin against him.

2dly. Our holiness, our obedience, work of righteousness, is one eminent and especial end of the peculiar dispensation of Father, Son, and Spirit, in the business of exalting the glory of God in our salvation, -- of the electing love of the Father, the purchasing love of the Son, and the operative love of the Spirit:--

(1st.) It is a peculiar end of the electing love of the Father, Eph. i. 4, "He hath chosen us, that we should be holy and without blame." So Isa. iv. 3, 4. His aim and design in choosing of us was, that we should be holy and unblamable before him in love. This he is to accomplish, and will bring about in them that are his. "He chooses us to salvation, through sanctification of the Spirit, and belief of the truth," 2 Thess. ii. 13. This the Father designed as the first and immediate end of electing love; and proposes the consideration of that love as a motive to holiness, 1 John iv. 8-10.

(2dly.) It is so also of the exceeding love of the Son; whereof the testimonies are innumerable. I shall give but one or two:-- Tit. ii. 14, "Who gave himself for us, that he might redeem us from all iniquity, and purify unto himself a peculiar people, zealous of good works." This was his aim, his design, in giving himself for us; as Eph. v. 25-27, "Christ loved the church, and gave himself for it; that he might sanctify and cleanse it with the washing of water by the word; that he might present it to himself a glorious church, not having spot, or wrinkle, or any such thing; but that it should be holy, and without blemish." 2 Cor. v. 15; Rom. vi. 11.

(3dly.) It is the very work of the love of the Holy Ghost. His whole work upon us, in us, for us, consists in preparing of us for obedience; enabling of us thereunto, and bringing forth the fruits of it in us. And this he doth in opposition to a righteousness of our own, either before it or to be made up by it, Tit. iii. 5. I need not insist on this. The fruits of the Spirit in us are known, Gal. v. 22, 23.

And thus have we a twofold bottom of the necessity of our obedience and personal holiness:-- God hath appointed it, he requires it; and it is an eminent immediate end of the distinct dispensation of Father, Son, and Holy Ghost, in the work of our salvation. If God's sovereignty over us is to be owned, if his love towards us be to be regarded, if the whole work of the ever-blessed Trinity, for us, in us, be of any moment, our obedience is necessary.

3dly. It is necessary in respect of the end thereof; and that whether you consider God, ourselves, or the world:--

(1st.) The end of our obedience, in respect of God, is, his glory and honour, Mal. i. 6. This is God's honour, -- all that we give him. It is true, he will take his honour from the stoutest and proudest rebel in the world; but all we give him is in our obedience. The glorifying of God by our obedience is all that we are or can be. Particularly, --

[1st.] It is the glory of the Father. Matt. v. 16, "Let your light so shine before men, that they may see your good works, and glorify your Father which is in heaven." By our walking in the light of faith doth glory arise to the Father. The fruits of his love, of his grace, of his kindness, are seen upon us; and God is glorified in our behalf. And, --

[2dly.] The Son is glorified thereby. It is the will of God that as all men honour the Father, so should they honour the Son, John v. 23. And how is this done? By believing in him, John xiv. 1; obeying of him. Hence, John xvii. 10, he says he is glorified in believers; and prays for an increase of grace and union for them, that he may yet be more glorified, and all might know that, as mediator, he was sent of God.

[3dly.] The Spirit is glorified also by it. He is grieved by our disobedience, Eph. iv. 30; and therefore his glory is in our bringing forth fruit. He dwells in us, as in his temple; which is not to be defiled. Holiness becometh his habitation for ever.

Now, if this that hath been said be not sufficient to evince a necessity of our obedience, we must suppose ourselves to speak with a sort of men who regard neither the sovereignty, nor love, nor glory of God, Father, Son, or Holy Ghost. Let men say what they please, though our obedience should be all lost, and never regarded (which is impossible, for God is not unjust, to forget our labour of love), yet here is a sufficient bottom, ground, and reason of yielding more obedience unto God than ever we shall do whilst we live in this world. I speak also only of gospel grounds of obedience, and not of those that are natural and legal, which are indispensable to all mankind.

(2dly.) The end in respect of ourselves immediately is threefold:-- [1st.] Honour. [2dly.] Peace. [3dly.] Usefulness.

[1st.] Honour. It is by holiness that we are made like unto God, and his image is renewed again in us. This was our honour at our creation, this exalted us above all our fellow-creatures here below, -- we were made in the image of God. This we lost by sin, and became like the beasts that perish. To this honour, of conformity to God, of bearing his image, are we exalted again by holiness alone. "Be ye holy," says God, "for I am holy," 1 Pet. i. 16; and, "Be ye perfect" (that is, in doing good), "even as your Father which is in heaven is perfect," Matt. v. 48, -- in a likeness and conformity to him. And herein is the image of God renewed; Eph. iv. 23, 24, therein we "put on the new man, which after God is created in righteousness and holiness of truth." This was that which originally was attended with power and dominion; -- is still all that is beautiful or comely in the world. How it makes men honourable and precious in the sight of God, of angels, of men; how alone it is that which is not despised, which is of price before the Lord; what contempt and scorn he hath of them in whom it is not, -- in what abomination he hath them and all their ways, -- might easily be evinced.

[2dly.] Peace. By it we have communion with God, wherein peace alone is to be enjoyed. "The wicked are like the troubled sea, that cannot rest;" and, "There is no peace" to them, "saith my God," Isa. lvii. 20, 21. There is no peace, rest, or quietness, in a distance, separation, or alienation from God. He is the rest of our souls. In the light of his countenance is life and peace. Now, "if we walk in the light, as he is in the light, we have fellowship one with another," 1 John i. 7; "and truly our fellowship is with the Father, and with his Son Jesus Christ," verse 3. He that walks in the light of new obedience, he hath communion with God, and in his presence is fulness of joy for ever; without it, there is nothing but darkness, and wandering, and confusion.

[3dly.] Usefulness. A man without holiness is good for nothing. "Ephraim," says the prophet, "is an empty vine, that brings forth fruit to itself." And what is such a vine good for? Nothing. Saith another prophet, "A man cannot make so much as a pin of it, to hang a vessel on." A barren tree is good for nothing, but to be cut down for the fire. Notwithstanding the seeming usefulness of men who serve the providence of God in their generations, I could easily manifest that the world and the church might want them, and that, indeed, in themselves they are good for nothing. Only the holy man is *commune bonum.*

(3dly.) The end of it in respect of others in the world is manifold:--

[1st.] It serves to the conviction and stopping the mouths of some of the enemies of God, both here and hereafter:-- 1. Here. 1 Pet. iii. 16, "Having a good conscience; that, wherein they speak evil of you, as of evil-doers, they may be ashamed that falsely accuse your good conversation in Christ." By our keeping of a good conscience men will be made ashamed of their false accusations; that whereas their malice and hatred of the ways of God hath provoked them to speak all manner of evil of the profession of them, by the holiness and righteousness of the saints, they are convinced and made ashamed, as a thief is when he is taken, and be driven to acknowledge that God is amongst them, and that they are wicked themselves, John xvii. 23. 2. Hereafter. It is said that the saints shall judge the world. It is on this, as well as upon other considerations: their good works, their righteousness, their holiness, shall be brought forth, and manifested to all the world; and the righteousness of God's judgments against wicked men be thence evinced. "See," says Christ, "these are they that I own, whom you so despised and abhorred; and see their works following them: this and that they have done, when you wallowed in your abominations," Matt. xxv. 42, 43.

[2dly.] The conversion of others. 1 Pet. ii. 12, "Having your conversation honest among the Gentiles; that, wherein they speak against you as evil-doers, they may, by your good works, which they shall behold, glorify God in the day of visitation," Matt. v. 16. Even revilers, persecutors, evil-speakers, have been overcome by the constant holy walking of professors; and when their day of visitation hath come, have glorified God on that account, 1 Pet. iii. 1, 2.

[3dly.] The benefit of all; partly in keeping off judgments from the residue of men, as ten good men would have preserved Sodom: [319] partly by their real communication of good to them with whom they have to do in their generation. Holiness makes a man a good man, useful to all; and others eat of the fruits of the Spirit that he brings forth continually.

[4thly.] It is necessary in respect of the state and condition of justified persons; and that whether you consider their relative state of acceptation, or their state of sanctification:--

First. They are accepted and received into friendship with a holy God, -- a God of purer eyes than to behold iniquity, -- who hates every unclean thing. And is it not necessary that they should be holy who are admitted into his presence, walk in his sight, -- yea, lie in his bosom? Should they not with all diligence cleanse themselves from all pollution of [320] flesh and spirit, and perfect holiness in the fear of the Lord?

Secondly. In respect of sanctification. We have in us a new creature, 2 Cor. v. 17. This new creature is fed, cherished, nourished, kept alive, by the fruits of holiness. To what end hath God given us new hearts, and new natures? Is it that we should kill them? stifle the creature that is found in us in the womb? that we should give him to the old man to be devoured?

[5thly.] It is necessary in respect of the proper place of holiness in the new covenant; and that is twofold:--

First. Of the means unto the end. God hath appointed that holiness shall be the means, [321] the way to that eternal life, which, as in itself and originally [it] is his gift by Jesus Christ, so, with regard to his constitution of our obedience, as the means of attaining it, [it] is a reward, and God in bestowing of it a rewarder. Though it be neither the cause, matter, nor condition of our justification, yet it is the way appointed of God for us to walk in for the obtaining of salvation. And therefore, he that hath hope of eternal life purifies himself, as he is pure: and none shall ever come to that end who walketh not in that way; for without holiness it is impossible to see God.

Secondly. It is a testimony and pledge of adoption, -- a sign and evidence of grace; that is, of acceptation with God. And, --

Thirdly. The whole expression of our thankfulness.

Now, there is not one of all these causes and reasons of the necessity, the indispensable necessity of our obedience, good works, and personal righteousness, but would require a more large discourse to unfold and explain than I have allotted to the proposal of them all; and innumerable others there are of the same import, that I cannot name. He that upon these accounts doth not think universal holiness and obedience to be of indispensable necessity, unless also it be exalted into the room of the obedience and righteousness of

Christ, let him be filthy still.

These objections being removed, and having, at the entrance of this chapter, declared what is done on the part of Christ, as to our fellowship with him in this purchased grace, as to our acceptation with God, it remains that I now show what also is required and performed on our part for the completing thereof. This, then, consists in the ensuing particulars:--

1. The saints cordially approve of this righteousness, as that alone which is absolutely complete, and able to make them acceptable before God. And this supposeth six things:--

(1.) Their clear and full conviction of the necessity of a righteousness wherewith to appear before God. This is always in their thoughts; this in their whole lives they take for granted. Many men spend their days in obstinacy and hardness, adding drunkenness unto thirst, never once inquiring what their condition shall be when they enter into eternity; others trifle away their time and their souls, sowing the wind of empty hopes, and preparing to reap a whirlwind of wrath; but this lies at the bottom of all the saints' communion with Christ, -- a deep, fixed, resolved persuasion of an absolute and indispensable necessity of a righteousness wherewith to appear before God. The holiness of God's nature, the righteousness of his government, the severity of his law, the terror of his wrath, are always before them. They have been all convinced of sin, and have looked on themselves as ready to sink under the vengeance due to it. They have all cried, "Men and brethren, what shall we do to be saved?" "Wherewith shall we come before God?" and have all concluded, that it is in vain to flatter themselves with hopes of escaping as they are by nature. If God be holy and righteous, and of purer eyes than to behold iniquity, they must have a righteousness to stand before him; and they know what will be the cry one day of those who now bear up themselves, as if they were otherwise minded, Isa. liii. 1-5; Mic. vi. 6, 7.

(2.) They weigh their own righteousness in the balance, and find it wanting; and this two ways:--

[1.] In general, and upon the whole of the matter, at their first setting themselves before God. When men are convinced of the necessity of a righteousness, they catch at every thing that presents itself to them for relief. Like men ready to sink in deep waters, [they] catch at that which is next, to save them from drowning; which sometimes proves a rotten stick, that sinks with them. So did the Jews, Rom. ix. 31, 32; they caught hold of the law, and it would not relieve them; and how they perished with it the apostle declares, chap. x. 1-4. The law put them upon setting up a righteousness of their own. This kept them doing, and in hope; but kept them from submitting to the righteousness of God. Here many perish, and never get one step nearer God all their days. This the saints renounce; they have no confidence in the flesh: they know that all they can do, all that the law can do, which is weak through the flesh, will not avail them. See what judgment Paul makes of all a man's own righteousness, Phil. iii. 8-10. This they bear in their minds daily, this they fill their thoughts withal, that upon the account of what they have done, can do, ever shall do, they cannot be accepted with God, or justified thereby. This keeps their souls humble, full of a sense of their own vileness, all their days.

[2.] In particular. They daily weigh all their particular actions in the balance, and find them wanting, as to any such completeness as, upon their own account, to be accepted with God. "Oh!" says a saint, "if I had nothing to commend me unto God but this prayer, this duty, this conquest of a temptation, wherein I myself see so many failings, so much imperfection, could I appear with any boldness before him? Shall I, then, piece up a garment of righteousness out of my best duties? Ah! it is all as a defiled cloth," Isa. lxiv. 6. These thoughts accompany them in all their duties, in their best and most choice performances:-- "Lord, what am I in my best estate? How little suitableness unto thy holiness is in my best duties! O spare me, in reference to the best thing that ever I did in my life!" Neh. xiii. 22. When a man who lives upon convictions hath got some enlargements in duties, some conquest over a sin or temptation, he hugs himself, like Micah when he had got a Levite to be his priest: now surely it shall be well with him, now God will bless him: his heart is now at ease; he hath peace in what he hath done. But he who hath communion with Christ, when he is highest in duties of sanctification and holiness, is clearest in the apprehension of his own unprofitableness, and rejects every thought that might arise in his heart of setting his peace in them, or upon them. He says to his soul, "Do these things seem something to thee? Alas! thou hast to do with an infinitely righteous God, who looks through and through all that vanity, which thou art but little acquainted withal; and should he deal with thee according to thy best works, thou must perish."

(3.) They approve of, value, and rejoice in, this righteousness, for their acceptation, which the Lord Jesus hath wrought out and provided for them; this being discovered to them, they approve of it with all their hearts, and rest in it. Isa. xlv. 24, "Surely, shall one say, in the Lord have I righteousness and strength." This is their voice and language, when once the righteousness of God in Christ is made known unto them: "Here is righteousness indeed; here have I rest for my soul. Like the merchant man in the gospel (Matt. xiii. 45, 46) that finds the pearl of price, I had been searching up and down; I looked this and that way for help, but it was far away; I spent my strength for that which was not bread: here is that, indeed, which makes me rich for ever!" When first the righteousness of Christ, for acceptation with God, is revealed to a poor labouring soul, that hath fought for rest and hath found none, he is surprised and amazed, and is not able to contain himself: and such a one always in his heart approves this righteousness on a twofold account:--

[1.] As full of infinite wisdom. "Unto them that believe," saith the apostle, "Christ crucified is the wisdom of God,'?" 1 Cor. i. 24. They see infinite wisdom in this way of their acceptation with God. "In what darkness," says such a one, "in what straits, in what entanglements, was my poor soul! How little able was I to look through the clouds and perplexities wherewith I was encompassed! I looked inwards, and there was nothing but sin, horror, fear, tremblings; I looked upwards, and saw nothing but wrath, curses, and vengeance. I knew that God was a holy and righteous God, and that no unclean thing could abide before him; I knew that I was a poor, vile, unclean, and sinful creature; and how to bring these two together in peace, I knew not. But in the righteousness of Christ doth a world of wisdom open itself, dispelling all difficulties and darkness, and manifesting a reconciliation of all this." "O the depth of the riches both of the wisdom and knowledge of God!" Rom. xi. 33; Col. ii. 3. But of this before.

[2.] As full of grace. He knows that sin had shut up the whole way of grace towards him; and whereas God aims at nothing so much as the manifestation of his grace, he was utterly cut short of it. Now, to have a complete righteousness provided, and yet abundance of grace manifested, exceedingly delights the soul; -- to have God's dealing with his person all grace, and dealing with his righteousness all justice, takes up his thoughts. God everywhere assures us that this righteousness is of grace. It is "by grace, and no more of works," Rom. xi. 6, as the apostle at large sets it out, Eph. ii. 7-9. It is from riches of grace and kindness that the provision of this righteousness is made. It is of mere grace that it is bestowed on us, it is not at all of works; though it be in itself a righteousness of works, yet to us it is of mere grace. So Tit. iii. 4-7, "But after that the kindness and love of God our Saviour toward man appeared, not by works of righteousness which we have done, but according to his mercy he saved us, by the washing of regeneration, and renewing of the Holy Ghost, which he shed on us abundantly through Jesus Christ our Saviour, that being justified by his grace, we should be made heirs according to the hope of eternal life." The rise of all this dispensation is kindness and love; that is, grace, verse 4. The way of communication, negatively, is not by works of righteousness that we have done; -- positively, by the communication of the Holy Ghost, verse 5; the means of whose procurement is Jesus Christ, verse 6; -- and the work itself is by grace, verse 7. Here is use made of every word almost, whereby the exceeding rich grace, kindness, mercy, and goodness of God may be expressed, all concurring in this work. As: 1. Χρηστότης, -- his goodness, benignity, readiness to communicate of himself and his good things that may be profitable to us. 2. Φιλανθρωπία, -- mercy, love, and propensity of mind to help, assist, relieve them of whom he speaks, towards whom he is so affected. 3. Ἔλεος, -- mercy forgiveness, compassion, tenderness, to them that suffer; and χάρις, -- free pardoning bounty, undeserved love. And all this is said to be τοῦ Θεοῦ σωτῆρος, -- he exercises all these properties and attributes of his nature towards us that he may save us; and in the bestowing of it, giving us the Holy Ghost, it is said, ἐξέχεεν, -- he poured him out as water out of a vessel, without stop and hesitation; and that not in a small measure, but πλουσίως, -- richly and in abundance: whence, as to the work itself, it is emphatically said, δικαιωθέντες τῇ ἐκείνου χάριτι, -- justified by the grace of him who is such a one. And this do the saints of God, in their communion with Christ, exceedingly rejoice in before him, that the way of their acceptation before God is a way of grace, kindness, and mercy, that they might not boast in themselves, but in the Lord and his goodness, crying, "How great is thy goodness! how great is thy bounty!"

(4.) They approve of it, and rejoice in it, as a way of great peace and security to themselves and their own souls. They remember what was their state and condition whilst they went about to set up a righteousness of their own, and were not subject to the righteousness of Christ, -- how miserably they were tossed up and down with continual fluctuating thoughts. Sometimes they had hope, and sometimes were full of fear; sometimes they thought themselves in some good condition, and anon were at the very brink of hell, their consciences being racked and torn with sin and fear: but now, "being justified by faith, they have peace with God," Rom. v. 1. All is quiet and serene; not only that storm is over, but they are in the haven where they would be. They have abiding peace with God. Hence is that description of Christ to a poor soul, Isa. xxxii. 2, "And a man shall he as a hiding-place from the wind, and a covert from the tempest; as rivers of water in a dry place, as the shadow of a great rock in a weary land." Wind and tempest, and drought and weariness, -- nothing now troubles the soul that is in Christ; he hath a hiding-place, and a covert, and rivers of water, and the shadow of a great rock, for his security. This is the great mystery of faith in this business of our acceptation with God by Christ:-- that whereas the soul of a believer finds enough in him and upon him to rend the very caul of the heart, to fill him with fears, terror, disquietments all his days, yet through Christ he is at perfect peace with God, Isa. xxvi. 3; Ps. iv. 6-8. Hence do the souls of believers exceedingly magnify Jesus Christ, that they can behold the face of God with boldness, confidence, peace, joy, assurance, -- that they can call him Father, bear themselves on his love, walk up and down in quietness, and without fear. How glorious is the Son of God in this grace! They remember the wormwood and gall that they have eaten; -- the vinegar and tears they have drunk; -- the trembling of their souls, like an aspen leaf that is shaken with the wind. Whenever they thought of God, what contrivances have they had to hide, and fly, and escape! To be brought now to settlement and security, must needs greatly affect them.

(5.) They cordially approve of this righteousness, because it is a way and means of exceeding exaltation and honour of the Lord Jesus, whom their souls do love. Being once brought to an acquaintance with Jesus Christ, their hearts desire nothing more than that he may be honoured and glorified to the utmost, and in all things have the pre-eminence. Now, what can more tend to the advancing and honouring of him in our hearts, than to know that he is made of God unto us "wisdom and righteousness?" 1 Cor. i. 30. Not that he is this or that part of our acceptation with God; but he is all, -- he is the whole. They know that on the account of his working out their acceptation with God, he is, --

[1.] Honoured of God his Father. Phil. ii. 7-11, "He made himself of no reputation, and took upon him the form of a servant, and was made in the likeness of men: and being found in fashion as a man, he humbled himself, and became obedient unto death, even the death of the cross. Wherefore God also hath highly exalted him, and given him a name which is above every name: that at the name of Jesus every knee should bow, of things in heaven, and things in earth, and things under the earth; and that every tongue should confess that Jesus Christ is Lord, to the glory of God the Father." Whether that word "wherefore" denotes a connection of causality or only a consequence, this is evident, that on the account of his suffering, and as the end of it, he was [322] honoured and exalted of God to an unspeakable pre-eminence, dignity, and authority; according as God had promised him on the same account, Isa. liii. 11, 12; Acts ii. 36, v. 30, 31. And therefore it is said, that when "he had by himself purged our sins, he sat down at the right hand of the Majesty on high," Heb. i. 3.

[2.] He is on this account honoured of all the angels in heaven, even because of this great work of bringing sinners unto God; for they do not only bow down and desire to look into the mystery of the cross, 1 Pet. i. 12, but worship and praise him always on this account: Rev. v. 11-14, "I heard the voice of many angels round about the throne, and the living creatures and the elders: and the number of them was ten thousand times ten thousand, and thousands of thousands; saying with a loud voice, Worthy is the Lamb that was slain to receive power, and riches, and wisdom, and strength, and honour, and glory, and blessing. And every creature which is in heaven and earth, and under the earth, and such as are in the sea, and all that are in them, heard I saying, Blessing, and honour, and glory, and power, be unto him that sitteth upon the throne, and unto the Lamb for ever and ever. And the living creatures said, Amen. And the four and twenty elders fell down and worshipped him that liveth for ever and ever." The reason given of this glorious and wonderful doxology, this attribution of honour and glory to Jesus Christ by the whole host of heaven, is, because he was the Lamb that was slain; that is, because of the work of our redemption and our bringing unto God. And it is not a little refreshment and rejoicing to the souls of the saints, to know that all the angels of God, the whole host of heaven, which never sinned, do yet continually rejoice and ascribe praise and honour to the Lord Jesus, for his bringing them to peace and favour with God.

[3.] He is honoured by his saints all the world over; and indeed, if they do not, who should? If they honour him not as they honour the Father, they are, of all men, the most unworthy. But see what they do, Rev. i. 5, 6, "Unto him that loved us, and washed us from our sins in his own blood, and hath made us kings and priests unto God and his Father; to him be glory and dominion for ever and ever. Amen." Chap. v. 8-10, "The four living creatures and four and twenty elders fell down before the Lamb, having every one of them harps, and golden vials full of odours, which are the prayers of saints. And they sung a new song, saying, Thou art worthy to take the book, and to open the seals thereof: for thou wast slain, and hast redeemed us to God by thy blood, out of every kindred, and tongue, and people, and nation; and hast made us unto our God kings and priests: and we shall reign on the earth." The great, solemn worship of the Christian church consists in this assignation of honour and glory to the Lord Jesus: therefore do they love him, honour him, delight in him; as Paul, Phil. iii. 8; and so the spouse, Cant. v. 9-16. And this is on this account, --

(6.) They cordially approve of this righteousness, this way of acceptation, as that which brings glory to God as such. When they were labouring under the guilt of sin, that which did most of all perplex their souls was, that their safety was inconsistent with the glory and honour of the great God, -- [323] with his justice, faithfulness, and truth, all which were engaged for the destruction of sin; and how to come off from ruin without the loss of their honour [i. e., the honour of the fore-mentioned attributes] they saw not. But now by the revelation of this righteousness from faith to faith, they plainly see that all the properties of God are exceedingly glorified in the pardon, justification, and acceptance of poor sinners; as before was manifested.

And this is the first way whereby the saints hold daily communion with the Lord Jesus in this purchased grace of acceptation with God: they consider, approve of, and rejoice in, the way, means, and thing itself.

2. They make an actual commutation with the Lord Jesus as to their sins and his righteousness. Of this there are also sundry parts:--

(1.) They continually keep alive upon their hearts a sense of the guilt and evil of sin; even then when they are under some comfortable persuasions of their personal acceptance with God. Sense of pardon takes away the horror and fear, but not a due sense of the guilt of sin. It is the daily exercise of the saints of God, to consider the great provocation that is in sin, -- their sins, the sin of their nature and lives; to render themselves vile in their own hearts and thoughts on that account; to compare it with the terror of the Lord; and to judge themselves continually. This they do in general. "My sin is ever before me," says David. They set sin before them, not to terrify and affright their souls with it, but that a due sense of the evil of it may be kept alive upon their hearts.

(2.) They gather up in their thoughts the sins for which they have not made a particular reckoning with God in Christ; or if they have begun so to do, yet they have not made clear work of it, nor come to a clear and comfortable issue. There is nothing more dreadful than for a man to be able to digest his convictions; -- to have sin look him in the face, and speak perhaps some words of terror to him, and to be able, by any charms of diversions or delays, to put it off, without coming to a full trial as to state and condition in reference thereunto. This the saints do:-- they gather up their sins, lay them in the balance of the law, see and consider their weight and desert; and then, --

(3.) They make this commutation I speak of with Jesus Christ; that is, --

[1.] They seriously consider, and by faith conquer, all objections to the contrary, that Jesus Christ, by the will and appointment of the Father, hath really undergone the punishment that was due to those sins that lie now under his eye and consideration, Isa. liii. 6; 2 Cor. v. 21. He hath as certainly and really answered the justice of God for them as, if he himself (the sinner) should at that instant be cast into hell, he could do.

[2.] They hearken to the voice of Christ calling them to him with their burden, "Come unto me, all ye that are weary and heavy laden;" -- "Come with your burdens; come, thou poor soul, with thy guilt of sin." Why? what to do? "Why, this is mine," saith Christ; "this agreement I made with my Father, that I should come, and take thy sins, and bear them away: they were my lot. Give me thy burden, give me all thy sins. Thou knowest not what to do with them; I know how to dispose of them well enough, so that God shall be glorified, and thy soul delivered." Hereupon, --

[3.] They lay down their sins at the cross of Christ, upon his shoulders. This is faith's great and bold venture upon the grace, faithfulness, and truth of God, to stand by the cross and say, "Ah! he is bruised for my sins, and wounded for my transgressions, and the chastisement of my peace is upon him. He is thus made sin for me. Here I give up my sins to him that is able to bear them, to undergo them. He requires it of my hands, that I should be content that he should undertake for them; and that I heartily consent unto." This is every day's work; I know not how any peace can be maintained with God without it. If it be the work of souls to receive Christ, as made sin for us, we must receive him as one that takes our sins upon him. Not as though he died any more, or suffered any more; but as the faith of the saints of old made that present and done before their eyes [which had] not yet come to pass, Heb. xi. 1, so faith now makes that present which was accomplished and past many generations ago. This it is to know Christ crucified.

[4.] Having thus by faith given up their sins to Christ, and seen God laying them all on him, they draw nigh, and take from him that righteousness which he hath wrought out for them; so fulfilling the whole of that of the apostle, 2 Cor. v. 21, "He was made sin for us, that we might be made the righteousness of God in him." They consider him tendering himself and his righteousness, to be their righteousness before God; they take it, and accept of it, and complete this blessed bartering and exchange of faith. Anger, curse, wrath, death, sin as to its guilt, he took it all and takes it all away. With him we leave whatever of this nature belongs to us; and from him we receive love, life, righteousness, and peace.

Objection. But it may be said, "Surely this course of procedure can never be acceptable to Jesus Christ. What! shall we daily come to him with our filth, our guilt, our sins? May he not, will he not, bid us keep them to ourselves? they are our own. Shall we be always giving sins, and taking righteousness?"

Answer. There is not any thing that Jesus Christ is more delighted with, than that his saints should always hold communion with him as to this business of giving and receiving. For, --

1. This exceedingly honours him, and gives him the glory that is his due. Many, indeed, cry "Lord, Lord," and make mention of him, but honour him not at all. How so? They take his work out of his hands, and ascribe it unto other things; their repentance, their duties, shall bear their iniquities. They do not say so; but they do so. The commutation they make, if they make any, it is with themselves. All their bartering about sin is in and with their own souls. The work that Christ came to do in the world, was to "bear our iniquities," and lay down his life a ransom for our sins. The cup he had to drink of was filled with our sins, as to the punishment due to them. What greater dishonour, then, can be done to the Lord Jesus, than to ascribe this work to any thing else, -- to think to get rid of our sins [by] any other way or means? Herein, then, I say, is Christ honoured indeed, when we go to him with our sins by faith, and say unto him, "Lord, this is thy work; this is that for which thou camest into the world; this is that thou hast undertaken to do. Thou callest for my burden, which is too heavy for me to bear; take it, blessed Redeemer. Thou tenderest thy righteousness; that is my portion." Then is Christ honoured, then is the glory of mediation ascribed to him, when we walk with him in this communion.

2. This exceedingly endears the souls of the saints to him, and constrains them to put a due valuation upon him, his love, his righteousness, and grace. When they find, and have the daily use of it, then they do it. Who would not love him? "I have been with the Lord Jesus," may the poor soul say: "I have left my sins, my burden, with him; and he hath given me his righteousness, wherewith I am going with boldness to God. I was dead, and am alive; for he died for me: I was cursed, and am blessed; for he was made a curse for me: I was troubled, but have peace; for the chastisement of my peace was upon him. I knew not what to do, nor whither to cause my sorrow to go; by him have I received joy unspeakable and glorious. If I do not love him, delight in him, obey him, live to him, die for him, I am worse than the devils in hell." Now the great aim of Christ in the world is, to have a high place and esteem in the hearts of his people; to have there, as he hath in himself, the pre-eminence in all things, -- not to be jostled up and down among other things, -- to be all, and in all. And thus are the saints of God prepared to esteem him, upon the engaging themselves to this communion with him.

Obj. Yea, but you will say, "If this be so, what need we to repent or amend our ways? it is but going to Christ by faith, making this exchange with him: and so we may sin, that grace may abound."

Ans. I judge no man's person; but this I must needs say, that I do not understand how a man that makes this objection in cold blood, not under a temptation or accidental darkness, can have any true or real acquaintance with

Jesus Christ: however, this I am certain of, that this communion in itself produces quite other effects than those supposed. For, --

1. For repentance; it is, I suppose, a gospel repentance that is intended. For a legal, bondage repentance, full of dread, amazement, terror, self-love, astonishment at the presence of God, I confess this communion takes it away, prevents it, casts it out, with its bondage and fear; but for gospel repentance, whose nature consists in godly sorrow for sin, with its relinquishment, proceeding from faith, love, and abhorrence of sin, on accounts of Father, Son, and Spirit, both law and love, -- that this should be hindered by this communion, is not possible. I told you that the foundation of this communion is laid in a deep, serious, daily consideration of sin, its guilt, vileness, and abomination, and our own vileness on that account; that a sense hereof is to be kept alive in and upon the heart of every one that will enjoy this communion with Christ: without it Christ is of no value nor esteem to him. Now, is it possible that a man should daily fill his heart with the thoughts of the vileness of sin, on all considerations whatever, -- of law, love, grace, gospel, life, and death, -- and be filled with self-abhorrency on this account, and yet be a stranger to godly sorrow? Here is the mistake, -- the foundation of this communion is laid in that which they suppose it overthrows.

2. But what shall we say for obedience? "If Christ be so glorified and honoured by taking our sins, the more we bring to him, the more will he be glorified." A man could not suppose that this objection would be made, but that the Holy Ghost, who knows what is in man and his heart, hath made it for them, and in their name, Rom. vi. 1-3. The very same doctrine that I have insisted on being delivered, chap. v. 18-20, the same objection is made to it: and for those who think it may have any weight, I refer them to the answer given in that chapter by the apostle; as also to what was said before to the necessity of our obedience, notwithstanding the imputation of the righteousness of Christ.

But you will say, "How should we address ourselves to the performance of this duty? what path are we to walk in?"

Faith exercises itself in it, especially three ways:--

(1.) In meditation. The heart goes over, in its own thoughts, the part above insisted on, sometimes severally, sometimes jointly, sometimes fixing primarily on one thing, sometimes on another, and sometimes going over the whole. At one time, perhaps, the soul is most upon consideration of its own sinfulness, and filling itself with shame and self-abhorrency on that account; sometimes it is filled with the thoughts of the righteousness of Christ, and with joy unspeakable and glorious on that account. Especially on great occasions, when grieved and burdened by negligence, or eruption of corruption, then the soul goes over the whole work, and so drives things to an issue with God, and takes up the peace that Christ hath wrought out for him.

(2.) In considering and inquiring into the promises of the gospel, which hold out all these things:-- the excellency, fulness, and suitableness of the righteousness of Christ, the rejection of all false righteousness, and the commutation made in the love of God; which was formerly insisted on.

(3.) In prayer. Herein do their souls go through this work day by day; and this communion have all the saints with the Lord Jesus, as to their acceptation with God: which was the first thing proposed to consideration.

Footnotes:

319. Gen. xviii. 32.
320. 2 Cor. vii. 1.
321. Rom. vi. 23; Heb. xi. 6;
Gen. xvii. 1; Ps. xix. 11, lviii. 11;
Matt. v. 12, x. 41; Rom. iv. 4; Col.
ii. 18, iii. 24; Heb. x. 35, xi. 26; 2
Pet. ii. 13.
322. Ps. cx. 1, 5, ii. 8, 9; Zech.
ix. 10; Ps. lxxii. 8; Rom. xiv. 11;
Isa. xlv, 23; Phil. ii. 10.
323. Rom. i. 17, x. 3, 4.

Chapter IX - Of communion with Christ in holiness -- The several acts ascribed unto the Lord Christ herein: 1. His intercession; 2. Sending of the Spirit; 3. Bestows habitual grace -- What that is, and wherein it consists -- This purchased by Christ; bestowed by him -- Of actual grace -- How the saints hold communion with Christ in these things; manifested in sundry particulars.

II. Our communion with the Lord Jesus as to that grace of sanctification and purification whereof we have made mention, in the several distinctions and degrees thereof, formerly, is nextly to be considered. And herein the former method must be observed; and we must show, -- 1. What are the peculiar actings of the Lord Christ as to this communion; and, 2. What is the duty of the saints herein. The sum is, -- How we hold communion with Christ in holiness, as well as in righteousness; and that very briefly:--

1. There are several acts ascribed unto the Lord Jesus in reference to this particular; as, --

(1.) His interceding with the Father, by virtue of his oblation in the behalf of his, that he would bestow the Holy Spirit on them. Here I choose to enter, because of the oblation of Christ itself I have spoken before; otherwise, every thing is to be run up to that head, that source and spring. There lies the foundation of all spiritual mercies whatever; as afterward also shall be manifested. Now the Spirit, as unto us a Spirit of grace, holiness, and consolation, is of the purchase of Christ. It is upon the matter, the great promise of the new covenant, Ezek. xi. 19, "I will put a new spirit within you;" so also, chap. xxxvi. 27; Jer. xxxii. 39, 40; and in sundry other places, whereof afterward. Christ is the mediator and "surety of this new covenant." Heb. vii. 22, "Jesus was made surety of a better testament," or rather covenant; -- a testament needs no surety. He is the undertaker on the part of God and man also: of man, to give satisfaction; of God, to bestow the whole grace of the promise; as chap. ix. 15, "For this cause he is the mediator of the new testament, that by means of death, for the redemption of transgressions that were under the first testament, they which are called might receive the promise of eternal inheritance." He both satisfied for sin and procured the promise. He procures all the love and kindness which are the fruits of the covenant, being himself the original promise thereof, Gen. iii. 15; the whole being so "ordered in all things, and made sure," 2 Sam. xxiii. 5, that the residue of its effects should all be derived from him, depend upon him, and be procured by him, -- "that he in all things might have the pre-eminence," Col. i. 18; according to the compact and agreement made with him, Isa. liii. 12. They are all the purchase of his blood; and therefore the Spirit also, as promised in that covenant, 1 Cor. i. 30. Now, the whole fruit and purchase of his death is made out from the

Father upon his intercession. This (John xiv. 16-18) he promiseth his disciples, that he will pursue the work which he hath in hand in their behalf, and intercede with the Father for the Spirit, as a fruit of his purchase. Therefore he tells them that he will not pray the Father for his love unto them, because the eternal love of the Father is not the fruit but the fountain of his purchase: but the Spirit, that is a fruit; "That," saith he, "I will pray the Father for," etc. And what Christ asketh the Father as mediator to bestow on us, that is part of his purchase, [324] being promised unto him, upon his undertaking to do the will of God. And this is the first thing that is to be considered in the Lord Jesus, as to the communication of the Spirit of sanctification and purification, the first thing to be considered in this our communion with him, -- he intercedes with his Father, that he may be bestowed on us as a fruit of his death and blood shed in our behalf. This is the relation of the Spirit of holiness, as bestowed on us, unto the mediation of Christ. He is the great [325] foundation of the covenant of grace; being himself everlastingly destinated and freely given to make a purchase of all the good things thereof. Receiving, according to promise, the Holy Ghost, Acts ii. 33, he sheds him abroad on his own. This faith considers, fixes on, dwells upon. For, --

(2.) His prayer being granted, as the [326] Father "hears him always," he actually sends his Spirit into the hearts of his saints, there to dwell in his stead, and to do all things for them and in them which he himself hath to do. This, secondly, is the Lord Christ by faith to be eyed in; and that not only in respect of the first enduing of our hearts with his Holy Spirit, but also of the continual supplies of it, drawing forth and exciting more effectual [327] operations and actings of that indwelling Spirit. Hence, though (John xiv. 16) he says the Father will give them the Comforter, because the original and sovereign dispensation is in his hand, and it is by him made out, upon the intercession of Christ; yet, not being bestowed immediately on us, but, as it were, given into the hand of Christ for us, he affirms that (as to actual collation or bestowing) he sends him himself; chap. xv. 26, "I will send the Comforter to you, from the Father." He receives him from his Father, and actually sends him unto his saints. So, chap. xvi. 7, "I will send him." And, verses 14, 15, he manifests how he will send him. He will furnish him with that which is his to bestow upon them: "He shall take of mine (of that which is properly and peculiarly so, -- mine, as mediator, -- the fruit of my life and death unto holiness), and give it unto you." But of these things more afterward. This, then, is the second thing that the Lord Christ doth, and which is to be eyed in him:-- He sends his Holy Spirit into our hearts; which is the [328] efficient cause of all holiness and sanctification, -- quickening, enlightening, purifying the souls of his saints. How our union with him, with all the benefit thereon depending, floweth from this his communication of the Spirit unto us, to abide with us, and to dwell in us, I have at large [329] elsewhere declared; where also this whole matter is more fully opened. And this is to be considered in him by faith, in reference to the Spirit itself.

(3.) There is that which we call habitual grace; that is, the fruits of the Spirit, -- the spirit which is born of the Spirit, John iii. 6. That which is born of, or produced by, the Holy Ghost, in the heart or soul of a man when he is regenerate, that which makes him so, is spirit; in opposition to [330] the flesh, or that enmity which is in us by nature against God. It is faith, love, joy, hope, and the rest of the graces of the gospel, in their root or common principle, concerning which these two things are to be observed:--

[1.] That though many particular graces are mentioned, yet there are not different habits or qualities in us, -- not several or distinct principles to answer them; but only the same [331] habit or spiritual principle putting forth itself in various operations or ways of working, according to the variety of the objects which it goes forth unto, is their common principle: so that it is called and distinguished, as above, rather in respect of actual exercise, with relation to its objects, than habitual inherence; it being one root which hath these many branches.

[2.] This is that which I intend by this habit of grace, -- a [332] new, gracious, spiritual [333] life, or principle, [334] created, and [335] bestowed on the soul, whereby it is [336] changed in all its faculties and affections, fitted and enabled to go forth in the way of obedience unto every divine object that is proposed unto it, according to the mind of God. For instance, the mind can discern of [337] spiritual things in a spiritual manner; and therein it is light, illumination. The whole soul closes with Christ, as held forth in the promises of the gospel for righteousness and salvation: that is faith; which being the main and principal work of it, it often gives denomination unto the whole. So when it rests in God, in Christ, with delight, desire, and complacency, it is called love; being, indeed, the principle suiting all the faculties of our souls for spiritual and living operations, according to their natural use. Now it differs, --

1st. From the Spirit dwelling in the saints; for it is a created quality. The Spirit dwells in us as a free agent in a holy habitation. This grace, as a quality, remains in us, as in its own proper subject, that hath not any subsistence but therein, and is capable of being intended [338] or restrained under great variety of degrees.

2dly. From actual grace, which is transient; this making its residence in the soul. [339] Actual grace is an illapse of divine influence and assistance, working in and by the soul any spiritual act or duty whatsoever, without any pre-existence unto that act or continuance after it, "God working in us, both to will and to do." But this habitual grace is always resident in us, causing the soul to be a meet principle for all those holy and spiritual operations which by actual grace are to be performed. And, --

3dly. It is capable of augmentation and diminution, as was said. In some it is more large and more effectual than in others; yea, in some persons, more at one time than another. Hence are those [340] dyings, decays, ruins, recoveries, complaints, and rejoicings, whereof so frequent mention is made in the Scripture.

These things being premised as to the nature of it, let us now consider what we are to eye in the Lord Jesus in reference thereunto, to make an entrance into our communion with him therein, as things by him or on his part performed:--

As I said of the Spirit, so, in the first place, I say of this, it is of the purchase of Christ, and is so to be looked on. "It is given unto us for [341] his sake to believe on him," Phil. i. 29. The Lord, on the behalf of Christ, for his sake, because it is purchased and procured by him for us, bestows faith, and (by same rule) all grace upon us. "We are blessed with all spiritual blessings in heavenly places in him," Eph. i. 3. "In him;" [342] that is, in and through his mediation for us. His oblation and intercession lie at the bottom of this dispensation. Were not grace by them procured, it would never by any one soul be enjoyed. All grace is from this fountain. In our receiving it from Christ, we must still consider what it [343] cost him. Want of this weakens faith in its proper workings. His whole intercession is founded on his oblation, 1 John ii. 1, 2. What he purchased by his death, that -- nor more nor less, as hath been often said -- he intercedeth may be bestowed. And he prays that all his saints may have this grace whereof we speak, John xvii. 17. Did we continually consider all grace as the fruit of the purchase of Christ, it would be an exceeding endearment on our spirits: nor can we without this consideration, according to the tenor of the gospel, ask or expect any grace. It is no prejudice to the free grace of the Father, to look on any thing as the purchase of the Son; it was from that grace that he made that purchase: and in the receiving of grace from God, we have not communion with Christ, who is yet the treasury and storehouse of it, unless we look upon it as his purchase. He hath obtained that we should be[344] sanctified throughout, have life in us, be humble, holy, believing, dividing the spoil with the mighty, by destroying the works of the devil in us.

Secondly. The Lord Christ doth actually communicate this grace unto his saints, and bestows it on them: "Of his fulness have all we received, and grace for grace," John i. 16. For, --

(1st.) The Father actually invests him with all the grace whereof, by compact and agreement, he hath made a purchase (as he received the promise of the Spirit); which is all that is of use for the bringing his many sons to glory. "It pleased the Father that in him should all fulness dwell," Col. i. 19, -- that he should be invested with a fulness of that grace which is needful for his people. This himself calls the "power of giving eternal life to his elect," John xvii. 2; which power is not only his ability to do it, but also his right to do it. Hence this delivering of all things unto him by his Father, he lays as the bottom of his inviting sinners unto him for refreshment: "All things are delivered unto me of my Father," Matt. xi. 27. "Come unto me, all that labour and are heavy laden, and I will give you rest," verse 28. This being the covenant of the Father with him, and his promise unto him, that upon the making "his soul an offering for sin, he should see his seed, and the pleasure of the Lord should prosper in his hand," Isa. liii. 10, in the verses following, the "pouring out of his soul unto death, and bearing the sins of many," is laid as the bottom and procuring cause of these things:-- 1. Of justification: "By his knowledge he shall justify many." 2. Of sanctification; in "destroying the works of the devil," verses 11, 12. Thus comes our merciful high priest to be the great possessor of all grace, that he may give out to us according to his own pleasure, quickening whom he will. He hath it in him really as our head, in that he received not that Spirit by measure (John iii. 34) which is the bond of union between him and us, 1 Cor. vi. 17; whereby holding him, the head, we are filled with his fulness, Eph. i. 22, 23; Col. i. 19. He hath it as a common person, intrusted with it in our behalf, Rom. v. 14-17. "The last Adam is made" unto us "a quickening Spirit," 1 Cor. xv. 45. He is also a treasury of this grace in a moral and law sense: not only as "it pleased the Father that in him should all fulness dwell," Col. i. 19; but also because in his mediation, as hath been declared, is founded the whole dispensation of grace.

(2dly.) Being thus actually vested with this power, and privilege, and fulness, he designs the Spirit to take of this fulness, and to give it unto us: "He shall take of mine, and shall show it unto you," John xvi. 15. The Spirit takes of that fulness that is in Christ, and in the name of the Lord Jesus bestows it actually on them for whose sanctification he is sent. Concerning the manner and almighty efficacy of the Spirit of grace whereby this is done (I mean this actual collation of grace upon his peculiar ones), more will be spoken afterward.

(3dly.) For actual grace, or that influence or power whereby the saints are enabled to perform particular duties according to the mind of God, there is not any need of farther enlargement about it. What concerns our communion with the Lord Christ therein, holds proportion with what was spoken before.

There remaineth only one thing more to be observed concerning those things whereof mention hath been made, and I proceed to the way whereby we carry on communion with the Lord Jesus in all these; and that is, that these things may be considered two ways:-- 1. In respect of their first collation, or bestowing on the soul. 2. In respect of their continuance and increase, as unto the degrees of them.

In the first sense, as to the real communicating of the Spirit of grace unto the soul, so raising it from death unto life, the saints have no kind of communion with Christ therein but only what consists in a passive reception of that life-giving, quickening Spirit and power. They are but as the dead bones in the prophet; the wind blows on them, and they live; -- as Lazarus in the grave; Christ calls, and they come forth, the call being accompanied with life and power. This, then, is not that whereof particularly I speak; but it is the second, in respect of farther efficacy of the Spirit and increase of grace, both habitual and actual, whereby we become more holy, and to be more powerful in walking with God, -- have more fruit in obedience and success against temptations. And in this, --

2. They hold communion with the Lord Christ. And wherein and how they do it, shall now be declared.

They continually eye the Lord Jesus as the great Joseph, that hath the disposal of all the granaries of the kingdom of heaven committed unto him; as one in whom it hath pleased the Father to gather all things unto a head, Eph. i. 10, that from him all things might be dispensed unto them. All treasures, all fulness, the Spirit not by measure, are in him. And this fulness in this Joseph, in reference to their condition, they eye in these three particulars:--

(1.) In the preparation unto the dispensation mentioned, in the expiating, purging, purifying efficacy of his blood. It was a sacrifice not only of atonement, as offered, but also of purification, as poured out. This the apostle eminently sets forth, Heb. ix. 13, 14, "For if the blood of bulls and of goats, and the ashes of an heifer sprinkling the unclean, sanctifieth to the purifying of the flesh: how much more shall the blood of Christ, who through the eternal Spirit offered himself without spot to God, purge your conscience from dead works to serve the living God?" This blood of his is that which answers all typical institutions for carnal purification; and therefore hath a spiritually-purifying, cleansing, sanctifying virtue in itself, as offered and poured out. Hence it is called, "A fountain for sin and for uncleanness," Zech. xiii. 1; that is, for their washing and taking away; -- "A fountain opened;" ready prepared, virtuous, efficacious in itself, before any be put into it; because poured out, instituted, appointed to that purpose. The saints see that in themselves they are still exceedingly defiled; and, indeed, to have a sight of the defilements of sin is a more spiritual discovery than to have only a sense of the guilt of sin. This follows every conviction, and is commensurate unto it; that, usually only such as reveal the purity and holiness of God and all his ways. Hereupon they cry with shame, within themselves, "Unclean, unclean," -- unclean in their natures, unclean in their persons, unclean in their conversations; all rolled in the [345] blood of their defilements; their hearts by nature a very sink, and their lives a dung hill. They know, also, that no unclean thing shall enter into the kingdom of God, or have place in the new Jerusalem; that God is of purer eyes than to behold iniquity. They cannot endure to look on themselves; and how shall they dare to appear in his presence? What remedies shall they now use? "Though they wash themselves with nitre, and take them much soap, yet their iniquity will continue marked," Jer. ii. 22. Wherewith, then, shall they come before the Lord? For the removal of this, I say, they look, in the first place, to the purifying virtue of the blood of Christ, which is able to cleanse them from all their sins, 1 John i. 7; being the spring from whence floweth all the purifying virtue, which in the issue will take away all their spots and stains, "make them holy and without blemish, and in the end present them glorious unto himself," Eph. v. 26, 27. This they dwell upon with thoughts of faith; they roll it in their minds and spirits. Here faith obtains new life, new vigour, when a sense of vileness hath even overwhelmed it. Here is a fountain opened: draw nigh, and see its beauty, purity, and efficacy. Here is a foundation laid of that work whose accomplishment we long for. One moment's communion with Christ by faith herein is more effectual to the purging of the soul, to the increasing of grace, than the utmost self-endeavours of a thousand ages.

(2.) They eye the blood of Christ as the blood of sprinkling. Coming to "Jesus, the mediator of the new covenant," they come to the [346] "blood of sprinkling," Heb. xii. 24. The eyeing of the blood of Christ as shed will not of itself take away pollution. There is not only αἱματεκχυσία, -- a "shedding of blood," without which there is no remission, Heb. ix. 22; but there is also αἵματος ῥαντισμός, -- a "sprinkling of blood," without which there is no actual purification. This the apostle largely describes, Heb. ix. 19, "When Moses," saith he, "had spoken every precept to all the people according to the law, he took the blood of calves and of goats, with water, and scarlet wool, and hyssop, and sprinkled both the book and all the people, saying, This is the blood of the testament which God hath enjoined unto you. Moreover he sprinkled likewise with blood both the tabernacle, and all the vessels of the ministry. And almost all things are by the law purged with blood. It was therefore necessary that the patterns of things in the heavens should be purified with these; but the heavenly things themselves with better sacrifices than these," verses 19-23. He had formerly compared the blood of Christ to the blood of sacrifices, as offered, in respect of the impetration and the purchase it made; now he doth it unto that blood as sprinkled, in respect of its application unto purification and holiness. And he tells us how this sprinkling was performed: it was by dipping hyssop in the blood of the sacrifice, and so dashing it out upon the things and persons to be purified; as the institution also was with the paschal lamb, Exod. xii. 7. Hence, David, in a sense of the pollution of sin, prays that he may be "purged with hyssop," Ps. li. 7. For that this peculiarly respected the uncleanness and defilement of sin, is evident, because there is no mention made, in the institution of any sacrifice (after that of the lamb before mentioned), of sprinkling blood with hyssop, but only in those which respected purification of uncleanness; as in the case of leprosy, Lev. xiv. 6; and all other defilements,

Numb. xix. 18: which latter, indeed, is not of blood, but of the water of separation; this also being eminently typical of the blood of Christ, which is the fountain for separation for uncleanness, Zech. xiii. 1. Now, this bunch of hyssop, wherein the blood of purification was prepared for the sprinkling of the unclean, is (unto us) the free promises of Christ. The cleansing virtue of the blood of Christ lies in the promises, as the blood of sacrifices in the hyssop, ready to pass out unto them that draw nigh thereunto. Therefore the apostle argueth from receiving of the promise unto universal holiness and purity: "Having therefore these promises, dearly beloved, let us cleanse ourselves from all filthiness of the flesh and spirit, perfecting holiness in the fear of God," 2 Cor. vii. 1. This, then, the saints do:-- they eye the blood of Christ as it is in the promise, ready to issue out upon the soul, for the purification thereof; and thence is purging and cleansing virtue to be communicated unto them, and by the blood of Christ are they to be purged from all their sins, 1 John i. 7. Thus far, as it were, this purifying blood, thus prepared and made ready, is at some distance to the soul. Though it be shed to this purpose, that it might purge, cleanse, and sanctify, though it be taken up with the bunch of hyssop in the promises, yet the soul may not partake of it. Wherefore, --

(3.) They look upon him as, in his own Spirit, he is the only dispenser of the Spirit and of all grace of sanctification and holiness. They consider that upon his intercession it is granted to him that he shall make effectual all the fruits of his purchase, to the sanctification, the purifying and making glorious in holiness, of his whole people. They know that this is actually to be accomplished by the Spirit, according to the innumerable promises given to that purpose. He is to sprinkle that blood upon their souls; he is to create the holiness in them that they long after; he is to be himself in them a well of water springing up to everlasting life. In this state they look to Jesus: here faith fixes itself, in expectation of his giving out the Spirit for all these ends and purposes; mixing the promises with faith, and so becoming actual partaker of all this grace. This is their way, this their communion with Christ; this is the life of faith, as to grace and holiness. Blessed is the soul that is exercised therein: "He shall be as a tree planted by the waters, and that spreadeth out her roots by the river, and shall not see when heat cometh, but her leaf shall be green; and shall not be careful in the year of drought, neither shall cease from yielding fruit," Jer. xvii. 8. Convinced persons who know not Christ, nor the fellowship of his sufferings, would spin a holiness out of their own bowels; they would work it out in their own strength. They begin it with [347] trying endeavours; and follow it with vows, duties, resolutions, engagements, sweating at it all the day long. Thus they continue for a season, -- their hypocrisy, for the most part, ending in apostasy. The saints of God do, in the very entrance of their walking with him, reckon upon it that they have a threefold want:-- [1.] Of the Spirit of holiness to dwell in them. [2.] Of a habit of holiness to be infused into them. [3.] Of actual assistance to work all their works for them; and that if these should continue to be wanting, they can never, with all their might, power, and endeavours, perform any one act of holiness before the Lord. They know that of themselves they have no sufficiency, -- that [348] without Christ they can do nothing: therefore they look to him, who is intrusted with a fulness of all these in their behalf; and thereupon by faith derive from him an increase of that whereof they stand in need. Thus, I say, have the saints communion with Christ, as to their sanctification and holiness. From him do they receive the Spirit to dwell in them; from him the new principle of life, which is the root of all their obedience; from him have they actual assistance for every duty they are called unto. In waiting for, expectation and receiving of these blessings, on the accounts before mentioned, do they spend their lives and time with him. In vain is help looked for from other mountains; in vain do men spend their strength in following after righteousness, if this be wanting. Fix thy soul here; thou shalt not tarry until thou be ashamed. This is the way, the only way, to obtain full, effectual manifestations of the Spirit's dwelling in us; to have our hearts purified, our consciences purged, our sins mortified, our graces increased, our souls made humble, holy, zealous, believing, -- like to him; to have our lives fruitful, our deaths comfortable. Let us herein abide, eyeing Christ by faith, to attain that measure of conformity to him which is allotted unto us in this world, that when we shall see him as he is, we may be like unto him.

Footnotes:

324. Ps. ii. 8; Isa. liii. 12; Ps. xl. 8-12.

325. Gen. iii. 15; Isa. xlii. 6, xlix. 8; Dan. ix. 24.

326. John xi. 42.

327. "Vicariam navere operam." -- Tertull., Prov. i. 23.

328. Tit. iii. 5, 6.

329. Saints' Perseverance, chap. viii. vol. xi.

330. Gal. v. 17.

331. 2 Cor. v. 17.

332. 2 Cor. v. 17; Ezek. xi. 19, xviii. 31, xxxvi. 26; Gal. vi. 15; Eph. ii. 15, iv. 14; Col. iii. 10; 1 Pet. ii. 2; John iii. 6.

333. Col. iii. 3, 4; Eph. ii. 1, 5; Rom. viii. 11; John v. 21, vi. 63.

334. Ps. li. 10; Eph. ii. 10, iv. 24; Col. iii. 10; 2 Cor. v. 17.

335. 2 Cor. iii. 5, iv. 6; Acts. v. 31; Luke i. 79; John iv. 14, iii. 27; 1 Cor. ii. 12; Eph. iv. 7; Phil. i. 29.

336. Acts xxvi. 18; Eph. v. 8; 2 Cor. v. 17; John v. 24.

337. 1 Cor. ii. 12; Eph. i. 18; 2 Cor. iii. 18, iv. 6.

338. Intended is here used in a sense now obsolete, -- stretched, increased. -- Ed.

339. 2 Cor. iii. 5; Ps. cxix. 36; Phil. ii. 13.

340. Cant. v. 2; Rev. ii. 5, iii. 2, 3, 17, 19; ὅς. xiv. 4; Ps. li., etc.

341. Ὑπὲρ Χριστοῦ.

342. 1 John ii. 1, 2.

343. Rom. viii. 32.

344. Eph. v. 25-27; Tit. ii. 14; Rom. vi. 4.

345. Ezek. xvi. 4, 6, etc; John iii. 3, 5; Πᾶν κοινοῦν, Rev. xxi. 27; Hab. i. 13.

346. Αἷμα ῥαντισμοῦ.

347. Rom. x. 1-4.

348. John xv. 5.

Chapter X - Of communion with Christ in privileges -- Of adoption; the nature of it, the consequences of it -- Peculiar privileges attending it; liberty, title, boldness, affliction -- Communion with Christ hereby.

III. The third thing wherein we have communion with Christ, is grace of privilege before God; I mean, as the third head of purchased grace. The privileges we enjoy by Christ are great and innumerable; to insist on them in particular were work for a man's whole life, not a design to be wrapped up in a few sheets. I shall take a view of them only in the head, the spring and fountain whence they all arise and flow, -- this is our adoption: "Beloved, now are we the sons of God," 1 John iii. 2. This is our great and fountain privilege. Whence is it that we are so? It is from the love of the Father. Verse 1, "Behold, what manner of love the Father hath bestowed upon us, that we should be called the sons of God!" But by whom immediately do we receive this honour? As many as believe on Christ, he gives them this power, to become the sons of God, John i. 12. Himself was appointed to be the first-born among many brethren, Rom. viii. 29; and his taking us to be brethren, Heb. ii. 11, makes us become the children of God. Now, that God is our Father, by being the Father of Christ, and we his children by being the brethren of Christ, being the head and sum of all the honour, privilege, right, and title we have, let us a little consider the nature of that act whereby we are invested with this state and title, -- namely, our adoption.

Now, adoption is the authoritative translation of a believer, by Jesus Christ, from the family of the world and Satan into the family of God, with his investiture in all the privileges and advantages of that family.

To the complete adoption of any person, these five things are required:--

1. That he be actually, and of his own right, of another family than that whereinto he is adopted. He must be the son of one family or other, in his own right, as all persons are.

2. That there be a family unto which of himself he hath no right, whereinto he is to be grafted. If a man comes into a family upon a personal right, though originally at never so great a distance, that man is not adopted. If a man of a most remote consanguinity do come into the inheritance of any family by the death of the nearer heirs, though his right before were little better than nothing, yet he is a born son of that family, -- he is not adopted. [In adoption] he is not to have the plea of the most remote possibility of succession.

3. That there be an authoritative, legal translation of him, by some that have power thereinto, from one family into another. It was not, by the law of old, in the power of particular persons to adopt when and whom they would. It was to be done by the authority of the sovereign power.

4. That the adopted person be freed from all the obligations that be upon him unto the family from whence he is translated; otherwise he can be no way useful or serviceable unto the family whereinto he is ingrafted. He cannot serve two masters, much less two fathers.

5. That, by virtue of his adoption, he be invested in all the rights, privileges, advantages, and title to the whole inheritance, of the family into which he is adopted, in as full and ample manner as if he had been born a son therein.

Now, all these things and circumstances do concur and are found in the adoption of believers:--

1. They are, by their own original right, of another family than that whereinto they are adopted. They are "by nature the children of wrath," Eph. ii. 3, -- sons of wrath, -- of that family whose inheritance is "wrath," -- called "the power of darkness," Col. i. 13; for from thence doth God "translate them into the kingdom of his dear Son." This is the family of the world and of Satan, of which by nature believers are. Whatever is to be inherited in that family, -- as wrath, curse, death, hell, -- they have a right thereunto. Neither can they of themselves, or by themselves, get free of this family: a strong man armed keeps them in subjection. Their natural estate is a family condition, attended with all the circumstances of a family, -- family duties and services, rights and titles, relations and observances. They are of the black family of sin and Satan.

2. There is another family whereinto they are to be translated, and whereunto of themselves they have neither right nor title. This is that family in heaven and earth which is called after the name of Christ, Eph. iii. 15, -- the great family of God. God hath a [349] house and family for his children; of whom some he maintains on the riches of his grace, and some he entertains with the fulness of his glory. This is that house whereof the Lord Christ is the great dispenser, it having pleased the Father to "gather together in one all things in him, both which are in heaven, and which are on earth, even in him," Eph. i. 10. Herein live all the sons and daughters of God, spending largely on the riches of his grace. Unto this family of themselves they have no right nor title; they are wholly alienated from it, Eph. ii. 12, and can lay no claim to any thing in it. God driving fallen Adam out of the garden, and shutting up all ways of return with a flaming sword, ready to cut him off if he should attempt it, abundantly declares that he, and all in him, had lost all right of approaching unto God in any family relation. Corrupted, cursed nature is not vested with the least right to any thing of God. Therefore, --

3. They have an authoritative translation from one of these families to another. It is not done in a private, underhand way, but in the way of authority. John i. 12, "As many as received him, to them gave he power to become the sons of God," -- power or authority. This investing them with the power, excellency, and right of the sons of God, is a forensic act, and hath a legal proceeding in it. It is called the "making us meet to be partakers of the inheritance of the saints in light," Col. i. 12; -- a judicial exalting us into membership in that family, where God is the Father, Christ the [350] elder brother, all saints and angels brethren and fellow-children, and the inheritance a crown immortal and incorruptible, that fades not away.

Now, this authoritative translation of believers from one family into another consisteth of these two parts:--

(1.) An effectual proclamation and declaration of such a person's immunity from all obligations to the former family, to which by nature he was related. And this declaration hath a threefold object:--

[1.] Angels. It is declared unto them; they are the [351] sons of God. They are the sons of God, and so of the family whereinto the adopted person is to be admitted; and therefore it concerns them to know who are invested with the rights of that family, that they may discharge their duty towards them. Unto them, then, it is declared that believers are freed from the family of sin and hell, to become fellow-sons and servants with them. And this is done two ways:--

1st. Generally, by the doctrine of the gospel. Eph. iii. 10, "Unto the principalities and powers in heavenly places is made known by the church the manifold wisdom of God."

By the church is this wisdom made known to the angels, either as the doctrine of the gospel is delivered unto it, or as it is gathered thereby. And what is this wisdom of God that is thus made known to principalities and powers? It is, that "the Gentiles should be fellow-heirs and of the same body with us," verse 6. The mystery of adopting sinners of the Gentiles, taking them from their slavery in the family of the world, that they might have a right of heirship, becoming sons in the family of God, is this wisdom, thus made known. And how was it primitively made known? It was "revealed by the Spirit unto the prophets and apostles," verse 5.

2dly. In particular, by immediate revelation. When any particular soul is freed from the family of this world, it is revealed to the angels. "There is joy in the presence of the angels of God" (that is, among the angels, and by them) "over one sinner that repenteth," Luke xv. 10. Now, the angels cannot of themselves absolutely know the true repentance of a sinner in itself; it is a work wrought in that cabinet which none hath a key unto but Jesus Christ; by him it is revealed to the angels, when the peculiar care and charge of such a one is committed to them. These things have their transaction before the angels, Luke xii. 8, 9. Christ owns the names of his brethren before the angels, Rev. iii. 5. When he gives them admittance into the family where they are, Heb. xii. 22, he declares to them that they are sons, that they may discharge their duty towards them, Heb. i. 14.

[2.] It is denounced in a judicial way unto Satan, the great master of the family whereunto they were in subjection. When the Lord Christ delivers a soul from under the power of that strong armed one, he binds him, -- ties him from the exercise of that power and dominion which before he had over him. And by this means doth he know that such a one is delivered from his family; and all his future attempts upon him are encroaching upon the possession and inheritance of the Lord Christ.

[3.] Unto the conscience of the person adopted. The Spirit of Christ testifies to the heart and conscience of a believer that he is freed from all engagements unto the family of Satan, and is become the son of God, Rom. viii. 14, 15; and enables him to cry, "Abba, Father," Gal. iv. 6. Of the particulars of this testification of the Spirit, and of its absolving the soul from its old alliance, I shall speak afterward. And herein consists the first thing mentioned.

(2.) There is an authoritative ingrafting of a believer actually into the family of God, and investing him with the whole right of sonship. Now this, as unto us, hath sundry acts:--

[1.] The giving a believer a new name in a white stone, Rev. ii. 17. They that are adopted are to take new names; they change their names they had in their old families, to take the names of the families whereinto they are translated. This new name is, "A child of God." That is the new name given in adoption; and no man knoweth what is in that name, but only he that doth receive it. And this new name is given and written in a white stone; -- that is the tessera of our admission into the house of God. It is a stone of judicial acquitment. Our adoption by the Spirit is bottomed on our absolution in the blood of Jesus; and therefore is the new name in the white stone privilege grounded on discharge. The white stone quits the claim of the old family; the new name gives entrance to the other.

[2.] An enrolling of his name in the catalogue of the household of God, admitting him thereby into fellowship therein. This is called the "writing of the house of Israel," Ezek. xiii. 9; that is, the roll wherein all the names of the Israel, the family of God, are written. God hath a catalogue of his household; Christ knows his sheep by name. When God writeth up the people, he counts that "this man was born in Zion," Ps. lxxxvii. 6. This is an extract of the Lamb's book of life.

[3.] Testifying to his conscience his acceptation with God, enabling him to behave himself as a child, Rom. viii. 15; Gal. iv. 5, 6.

4. The two last things required to adoption are, that the adopted person be freed from all obligations to the family from whence he is translated, and invested with the rights and privileges of that whereinto he is translated. Now, because these two comprise the whole issue of adoption, wherein the saints have communion with Christ, I shall handle them together, referring the concernments of them unto these four heads:-- (1.) Liberty. (2.) Title, or right. (3.) Boldness. (4.) Correction. These are the four things, in reference to the family of the adopted person, that he doth receive by his adoption, wherein he holds communion with the Lord Jesus:--

(1.) Liberty. The Spirit of the Lord, that was upon the Lord Jesus, did anoint him to proclaim liberty to the captives, Isa. lxi. 1; and "where the Spirit of the Lord is" (that is, the Spirit of Christ, given to us by him because we are sons), "there is liberty," 2 Cor. iii. 17. All spiritual liberty is from the Spirit of adoption; whatever else is pretended, is licentiousness. So the apostle argues, Gal. iv. 6, 7, "He hath sent forth his Spirit into their hearts, crying, Abba, Father. Wherefore ye are no more servants," -- no more in bondage, but have the liberty of sons. And this liberty respects, --

[1.] In the first place, the family from whence the adopted person is translated. It is his setting free from all the obligations of that family. Now, in this sense, the liberty which the saints have by adoption is either from that which is real or that which is pretended:--

1st. That which is real respects a twofold issue of law and sin. The moral, unchangeable law of God, and sin, being in conjunction, meeting with reference to any persons, hath, and hath had, a twofold issue:--

(1st.) An economical institution of a new law of ordinances, keeping in bondage those to whom it was given, Col. ii. 14.

(2dly.) A natural (if I may so call it) pressing of those persons with its power and efficacy against sin; whereof there are these parts:--

[1st.] Its rigour and terror in commanding.

[2dly.] Its impossibility for accomplishment, and so insufficiency for its primitively appointed end.

[3dly.] The issues of its transgression; which are referred unto two heads:-- 1. Curse. 2. Death. I shall speak very briefly of these, because they are commonly handled, and granted by all.

2dly. That which is pretended, is the power of any whatever over the conscience, when once made free by Christ:--

(1st.) Believers are freed from the instituted law of ordinances, which, upon the testimony of the apostles, was a yoke which neither we nor our fathers (in the faith) could bear, Acts xv. 10; wherefore Christ "blotted out this hand-writing of ordinances that was against them, which was contrary to them, and took it out of the way, nailing it to his cross," Col. ii. 14: and thereupon the apostle, after a long dispute concerning the liberty that we have from that law, concludes with this instruction: Gal. v. 1, "Stand fast in the liberty wherewith Christ hath made us free."

(2dly.) In reference so the moral law:--

[1st.] The first thing we have liberty from, is its rigour and terror in commanding. Heb. xii. 18-22, "We are not come to the mount that might be touched, and that burned with fire, to the whirlwind, darkness, and tempest, to the sound of the trumpet, and the voice of words, which they that heard besought that they might hear it no more; but we are come to mount Sion," etc. As to that administration of the law wherein it was given out with dread and terror, and so exacted its obedience with rigour, we are freed from it, we are not called to that estate.

[2dly.] Its impossibility of accomplishment, and so insufficiency for its primitive end, by reason of sin; or, we are freed from the law as the instrument of righteousness, since, by the impossibility of its fulfilling as to us, it is become insufficient for any such purpose, Rom. viii. 2, 3; Gal. iii. 21-23. There being an impossibility of obtaining life by the law, we are exempted from it as to any such end, and that by the righteousness of Christ, Rom. viii. 3.

[3dly.] From the issue of its transgression:--

First. Curse. There is a solemn curse inwrapping the whole wrath annexed to the law, with reference to the transgression thereof; and from this are we wholly at liberty. Gal. iii. 13, "Christ hath redeemed us from the curse of the law by being made a curse for us."

Secondly. Death, Heb. ii. 15; and therewith from Satan, Heb. ii. 14, Col. i. 13; and sin, Rom. vi. 14, 1 Pet. i. 18; with the world, Gal. i. 4; with all the attendancies, advantages, and claims of them all, Gal. iv. 3-5, Col. ii. 20; without which we could not live one day.

That which is pretended and claimed by some (wherein in deed and in truth we were never in bondage, but are hereby eminently set free), is the power of binding conscience by any laws and constitutions not from God, Col. ii. 20-22.

[2.] [In the second place,] there is a liberty in the family of God, as well as a liberty from the family of Satan. Sons are free. Their obedience is a free obedience; they have the Spirit of the Lord: and where he is, there is liberty, 2 Cor. iii. 17. As a Spirit of adoption, he is opposed to the spirit of bondage, Rom. viii. 15. Now, this liberty of our Father's family, which we have as sons and children, being adopted by Christ through the Spirit, is a spiritual largeness of heart, whereby the children of God do freely, willingly, genuinely, without fear, terror, bondage, and constraint, go forth unto all holy obedience in Christ.

I say, this is our liberty in our Father's family: what we have liberty from, hath been already declared.

There are Gibeonites outwardly attending the family of God, that do the service of his house as the drudgery of their lives. The principle they yield obedience upon, is a spirit of bondage unto fear, Rom. viii. 15; the rule they do it by, is the law in its dread and rigour, exacting it of them to the utmost, without mercy and mitigation; the end they do it for, is to fly from the wrath to come, to pacify conscience, and seek righteousness as it were by the works of the law. Thus servilely, painfully, fruitlessly, they seek to serve their own conviction all their days.

The saints by adoption have a largeness of heart in all holy obedience. Saith David, "I will walk at liberty, for I seek thy precepts," Ps. cxix. 45; Isa. lxi. 1; Luke iv. 18; Rom. viii. 2, 21; Gal. iv. 7, v. 1, 13; James i. 25; John viii. 32, 33, 36; Rom. vi. 18; 1 Pet. ii. 16. Now, this amplitude, or son-like freedom of the Spirit in obedience, consists in sundry things:--

1st. In the principles of all spiritual service; which are life and love; -- the one respecting the matter of their obedience, giving them power; the other respecting the manner of their obedience, giving them joy and sweetness in it:--

(1st.) It is from life; that gives them power as to the matter of obedience. Rom. viii. 2, "The law of the Spirit of life in Christ Jesus sets them free from the law of sin and death." It frees them, it carries them out to all obedience freely; so that "they walk after the Spirit," verse 1, that being the principle of their workings. Gal. ii. 20, "Christ liveth in me; and the life which I now live in the flesh, I live by the faith of the Son of God;" -- "The life which I now live in the flesh (that is, the obedience which I yield unto God whilst I am in the flesh), it is from a principle of life, Christ living in me. There is, then, power for all living unto God, from Christ in them, the Spirit of life from Christ carrying them out thereto. The fruits of a dead root are but dead excrescences; living acts are from a principle of life.

Hence you may see the difference between the liberty that slaves assume, and the liberty which is due to children:--

[1st.] Slaves take liberty from duty; children have liberty in duty. There is not a greater mistake in the world, than that the liberty of sons in the house of God consists in this, -- they can perform duties, or take the freedom to omit them; they can serve in the family of God (that is, they think they may if they will), and they can choose whether they will or no. This is a liberty stolen by slaves, not a liberty given by the Spirit unto sons.

The liberty of sons is in the inward spiritual freedom of their hearts, naturally and kindly going out in all the ways and worship of God. When they find themselves straitened and shut up in them, they wrestle with God for enlargement, and are never contented with the doing of a duty, unless it be done as in Christ, with free, genuine, and enlarged hearts. The liberty that servants have is from duty; the liberty given to sons is in duty.

[2dly.] The liberty of slaves or servants is from mistaken, deceiving conclusions; the liberty of sons is from the power of the indwelling Spirit of grace. Or, the liberty of servants is from outward, dead conclusions; the liberty of sons, from an inward, living principle.

(2dly.) Love, as to the manner of their obedience, gives them delight and joy. John xiv. 15, "If ye love me," says Christ, "keep my commandments." Love is the bottom of all their duties; hence our Saviour resolves all obedience into the love of God and our neighbour; and Paul, upon the same ground, tells us "that love is the fulfilling of the law," Rom. xiii. 10. Where love is in any duty, it is complete in Christ. How often doth David, even with admiration, express this principle of his walking with God! "O," saith he, "how I love thy commandments! "This gives saints delight, that the commandments of Christ are not grievous to them. Jacob's hard service was not grievous to him, because of his love to Rachel. No duty of a saint is grievous to him, because of his love to Christ. They do from hence all things with delight and complacency. Hence do they long for advantages of walking with God, -- pant after more ability; and this is a great share of their son-like freedom in obedience. It gives them joy in it. 1 John iv. 18, "There is no fear in love; but perfect love casteth out fear." When their soul is acted to obedience by love, it expels that fear which is the issue of bondage upon the spirit. Now, when there is a concurrence of these two (life and love), there is freedom, liberty, largeness of heart, exceedingly distanced from that strait and bondaged frame which many walk in all their days, that know not the adoption of sons.

2dly. The object of their obedience is represented to them as desirable, whereas to others it is terrible. In all their approaches to God, they eye him as a Father; they call him Father, Gal. iv. 6, not in the form of words, but in the spirit of sons. God in Christ is continually before them; not only as one deserving all the honours and obedience which he requires, but also as one exceedingly to be delighted in, as being all-sufficient to satisfy and satiate all the desires of the soul. When others napkin their talents, as having to deal with an austere master, they draw out their strength to the uttermost, as drawing nigh to a gracious rewarder. They go, from the principle of life and love, to the bosom of a living and loving Father; they do but return the strength they do receive unto the fountain, unto the ocean.

3dly. Their motive unto obedience is love, 2 Cor. v. 14. From an apprehension of love, they are effectually carried out by love to give up themselves unto him who is love. What a freedom is this! what a largeness of spirit is in them who walk according to this rule! Darkness, fear, bondage, conviction, hopes of righteousness, accompany others in their ways; the sons, by the Spirit of adoption, have light, love, with complacency, in all their walkings with God. The world is a universal stranger unto the frame of children in their Father's house.

4thly. The manner of their obedience is willingness. "They yield themselves unto God, as those that are alive from the dead," Rom. vi. 13; they yield themselves, -- give up themselves willingly, cheerfully, freely. "With my whole heart," saith David. Rom. xii. 1, "They present themselves a living sacrifice," and a willing sacrifice.

5thly. The rule of their walking with God is the law of liberty, as divested of all its terrifying, threatening, killing, condemning, cursing power; and rendered, in the blood of Jesus, sweet, tender, useful, directing, -- helpful as a rule of walking in the life they have received, not the way of working for the life they have not. I might give more instances. These may suffice to manifest that liberty of obedience in the family of God which his sons and daughters have, that the poor convinced Gibeonites are not acquainted withal.

(2.) The second thing which the children of God have by adoption is title. They have title and right to all the privileges and advantages of the family whereinto they are translated. This is the pre-eminence of the true sons of any family. The ground on which Sarah pleaded the ejection of Ishmael was, that he was the son of the bond woman, Gen. xxi. 10, and so no genuine child of the family; and therefore could have no right of heirship with Isaac. The apostle's arguing is, "We are no more servants, but sons; and if sons, then heirs," Rom. viii. 14-17, -- "then have we right and title: and being not born hereunto (for by nature we are the children of wrath), we have this right by our adoption."

Now, the saints hereby have a double right and title: 1st. Proper and direct, in respect of spirituals. 2dly. Consequential, in respect of temporals:--

[1.] The first, also, or the title, as adopted sons, unto spirituals, is, in respect of the object of it, twofold:-- (1st.) Unto a present place, name, and room, in the house of God, and all the privileges and administrations thereof. (2dly.) To a future fulness of the great inheritance of glory, -- of a kingdom purchased for that whole family whereof they are by Jesus Christ:--

1st. They have a title unto, and an interest in, the whole administration of the family of God here.

The supreme administration of the house of God in the hand of the Lord Christ, as to the institution of ordinances and dispensation of the Spirit, to enliven and make effectual those ordinances for the end of their institution, is the prime notion of this administration. And hereof they are the prime objects; all this is for them, and exercised towards them. God hath given Jesus Christ to be the "head over all things unto the church, which is his body," Eph. i. 22, 23: he hath made him the head over all these spiritual things, committed the authoritative administration of them all unto him, to the use and behoof of the church; that is, the family of God. It is for the benefit and advantage of the many sons whom he will bring unto glory that he doth all these things, Heb. ii. 10; see Eph. iv. 8-13. The aim of the Lord Jesus in establishing gospel administrations, and administrators, is "for the perfecting of the saints, the work of the ministry," etc. All is for then, all is for the family. In that is the faithfulness of Christ exercised; he is faithful in all the house of God, Heb. iii. 2. Hence the apostle tells the Corinthians, 1 Cor. iii. 22, 23, of all these gospel administrations and ordinances, they are all theirs, and all for them. What benefit soever redoundeth to the world by the things of the gospel (as much doth every way), it is engaged for it to the children of this family. This, then, is the aim and intendment of the Lord Christ in the institution of all gospel ordinances and administrations, -- that they may be of use for the house and family of God, and all his children and servants therein.

It is true, the word is preached to all the world, to gather in the children of God's purpose that are scattered up and down in the world, and to leave the rest inexcusable; but the prime end and aim of the Lord Christ thereby is, to gather in those heirs of salvation unto the enjoyment of that feast of fat things which he hath prepared for them in his house.

Again: they, and they only, have right and title to gospel administrations, and the privileges of the family of God, as they are held out in his church according to his mind. The church is the "house of God," 1 Tim. iii. 15; Heb. iii. 6; herein he keeps and maintains his whole family, ordering them according to his mind and will. Now, who shall have any right in the house of God, but only his children? We will not allow a right to any but our own children in our houses: will God, think you, allow any right in his house but to his children? Is it meet, to "take the children's bread and cast it unto the dogs?" We shall see that none but children have any right or title to the privileges and advantages of the house of God, if we consider, --

(1st.) The nature of that house. It is made up of such persons as it is impossible that any but adopted children should have right unto a place in it. It is composed of "living stones," 1 Pet. ii. 5; -- a "chosen generation, a royal priesthood, an holy nation, a peculiar people," verse 9; -- "saints and faithful in Christ Jesus," Eph. i. 1; -- "saints and faithful brethren," Col. i. 2; -- a people that are "all righteous," Isa. lx. 21; and the whole fabric of it is glorious, chap. liv. 11-14, -- the way of the house is "a way of holiness," which the unclean shall not pass through, chap. xxxv. 8; yea, expressly, they are the "sons and daughters of the Lord Almighty," and they only, 2 Cor. vi. 17, 18; all others are excluded, Rev. xxi. 27. It is true that oftentimes, at unawares, other persons creep into the great house of God; and so there become in it "not only vessels of gold and silver, but also of wood and of earth," etc., 2 Tim. ii. 20; but they only creep in, as Jude speaks, verse 4, they have no right nor title to it.

(2dly.) The privileges of the house are such as they will not suit nor profit any other. To what purpose is it to give food to a dead man? Will he grow strong by it? will he increase upon it? The things of the family and house of God are food for living souls. Now, children only are alive, all others are dead in trespasses and sins. What will outward signs avail, if life and power be away? Look upon what particular you please of the saints' enjoyments in the family of God, you shall find them all suited unto believers; and, being bestowed on the world, [they] would be a pearl in the snout of a swine.

It is, then, only the sons of the family that have this right; they have fellowship with one another, and that fellowship with the Father and the Son Jesus Christ; they set forth the Lord's death till he come; they are intrusted with all the ordinances of the house, and the administration of them. And who shall deny them the enjoyment of this right, or keep them from what Christ hath purchased for them? And the Lord will in the end give them hearts everywhere to make use of this title accordingly, and not to wander on the mountains, forgetting their resting-place.

2dly. They have a title to the future fulness of the inheritance that is purchased for this whole family by Jesus Christ. So the apostle argues, Rom. viii. 17, "If children, then heirs," etc. All God's children are "first-born," Heb. xii. 23; and therefore are heirs: hence the whole weight of glory that is prepared for them is called the inheritance, Col. i. 12, "The inheritance of the saints in light." "If ye be Christ's, then are ye Abraham's seed, and heirs according to the promise," Gal. iii. 29. Heirs of the promise; that is, of all things promised unto Abraham in and with Christ.

There are three things that in this regard the children of God are said to be heirs unto:--

(1st.) The promise; as in that place of Gal. iii. 29 and Heb. vi. 17. God shows to "the heirs of the promise the immutability of his counsel;" as Abraham, Isaac, and Jacob, are said to be "heirs of the same promise," Heb. xi. 9. God had from the foundation of the world made a most excellent promise in Christ, containing a deliverance from all evil, and an engagement for the bestowing of all good things upon them. It contains a deliverance from all the evil which the guilt of sin and dominion of Satan had brought upon them, with an investiture of them in all spiritual blessings in heavenly things in Christ Jesus. Hence, Heb. ix. 15, the Holy Ghost calls it a "promise of the eternal inheritance." This, in the first place, are the adopted children of God heirs unto. Look, whatever is in the promise which God made at the beginning to fallen man, and hath since solemnly renewed and confirmed by his oath; they are heirs of it, and are accepted in their claim for their inheritance in the courts of heaven.

(2dly.) They are heirs of righteousness, Heb. xi. 7. Noah was an heir of the righteousness which is by faith; which Peter calls a being "heir of the grace of life," 1 Pet. iii. 7. And James puts both these together, chap. ii. 5, "Heirs of the kingdom which God hath promised;" that is, of the kingdom of grace, and the righteousness thereof. And in this respect it is that the apostle tells us, Eph. i. 11, that "we have obtained an inheritance;" which he also places with the righteousness of faith, Acts xxvi. 18. Now, by this righteousness, grace, and inheritance, is not only intended that righteousness which we are here actually made partakers of, but also the end and accomplishment of that righteousness in glory; which is also assured in the next place, --

(3dly.) They are "heirs of salvation," Heb. i. 14, and "heirs according to the hope of eternal life," Tit. iii. 7; which Peter calls an "inheritance incorruptible," 1 Pet. i. 4; and Paul, the "reward of the inheritance," Col. iii. 24, -- that is, the issue of the inheritance of light and holiness, which they already enjoy. Thus, then, distinguish the full salvation by Christ into the foundation of it, the promises; and the means of it, righteousness and holiness; and the end of it, eternal glory. The sons of God have a right and title to all, in that they are made heirs with Christ.

And this is that which is the main of the saints' title and right, which they have by adoption; which in sum is, that the Lord is their portion and inheritance, and they are the inheritance of the Lord: and a large portion it is that they have; the lines are fallen to them in a goodly place.

[2.] Besides this principal, the adopted sons of God have a second consequential right, -- a right unto the things of this world; that is, unto all the portions of it which God is pleased to intrust them here withal. Christ is the "heir of all things," Heb. i. 2; all right and title to the things of the creation was lost and forfeited by sin. The Lord, by his sovereignty, had made an original grant of all things here below for man's use; he had appointed the residue of the works of his hands, in their several stations, to be serviceable unto his behoof. Sin reversed this whole grant and institution, -- all things were set at liberty from this subjection unto him; yet that liberty, being a taking them off from the end to which they were originally appointed, is a part of their vanity and curse. It is evil to any thing to be laid aside as to the end to which it was primitively appointed. By this means the whole creation is turned loose from any subordinate ruler; and man, having lost the whole title whereby he held his dominion over and possession of the creatures, hath not the least colour of interest in any of them, nor can lay any claim unto them. But now the Lord, intending to take a portion to himself out of the lump of fallen mankind, whom he appointed heirs of salvation, he doth not immediately destroy the works of creation, but reserve them for their use in their pilgrimage. To this end he invests the whole right and title of them in the second Adam, which the first had lost; he appoints him "heir of all things." And thereupon his adopted ones, being "fellow-heirs with Christ," become also to have a right and title unto the things of this creation. To clear up this right, what it is, I must give some few observations:--

1st. The right they have is not as the right that Christ hath; that is, sovereign and supreme, to do what he will with his own; but theirs is subordinate, and such as that they must be accountable for the use of those things whereunto they have a right and title. The right of Christ is the right of the Lord of the house; the right of the saints is the right of servants.

2dly. That the whole number of the children of God have a right unto the whole earth, which is the Lord's, and the fulness thereof, in these two regards:--

(1st.) He who is the sovereign Lord of it doth preserve it merely for their use, and upon their account; all others whatever being malæ fidei possessores, invading a portion of the Lord's territories, without grant or leave from him.

(2dly.) In that Christ hath promised to give them the kingdom and dominion of it, in such a way and manner as in his providence he shall dispose; that is, that the government of the earth shall be exercised to their advantage.

3dly. This right is a spiritual right, which doth not give a civil interest, but only sanctifies the right and interest bestowed. God hath providentially disposed of the civil bounds of the inheritance of men, Acts xvii. 26, suffering the men of the world to enjoy a portion here, and that oftentimes very full and plenteous; and that for his children's sake, that those beasts of the forest, which are made to be destroyed, may not break loose upon the whole possession. Hence, --

4thly. No one particular adopted person hath any right, by virtue thereof, to any portion of earthly things whereunto he hath not right and title upon a civil interest, given him by the providence of God. But, --

5thly. This they have by their adoption; that, --

(1st.) Look, what portion soever God is pleased to give them, they have a right unto it, as it is re-invested in Christ, and not as it lies wholly under the curse and vanity that is come upon the creation by sin; and therefore can never be called unto an account for usurping that which they have no right unto, as shall all the sons of men who violently grasp those things which God hath set at liberty from under their dominion because of sin.

(2dly.) By this their right, they are led unto a sanctified use of what thereby they do enjoy; inasmuch as the things themselves are to them pledges of the Father's love, washed in the blood of Christ, and endearments upon their spirits to live to his praise who gives them all things richly to enjoy.

And this is a second thing we have by our adoption; and hence I dare say of unbelievers, they have no true right unto any thing, of what kind soever, that they do possess.

They have no true, unquestionable right, I say, even unto the temporal things they do possess; it is true they have a civil right in respect of others, but they have not a sanctified right in respect of their own souls. They have a right and title that will hold plea in the courts of men, but not a right that will hold in the court of God, and in their own conscience. It will one day be sad with them, when they shall come to give an account of their enjoyments. They shall not only be reckoned withal for the abuse of that they have possessed, that they have not used and laid it out for the glory of him whose it is; but also, that they have even laid their hands upon the creatures of God, and kept them from them for whose sakes alone they are preserved from destruction. When the God of glory shall come home to any of them, either in their consciences here, or in the judgment that is for to come, and speak with the terror of a revengeful judge, "I have suffered you to enjoy corn, wine, and oil, -- a great portion of my creatures; you have rolled yourselves in wealth and prosperity, when the right heirs of these things lived poor, and low, and mean, at the next doors; -- give in now an answer what and how you have used these things. What have you laid out for the service and advancement of the gospel? What have you given unto them for whom nothing was provided? what contribution have you made for the poor saints? Have you had a ready hand, and willing mind, to lay down all for my sake?" -- when they shall be compelled to answer, as the truth is, "Lord, we had, indeed, a large portion in the world; but we took it to be our own, and thought we might have done what we would with our own. We have ate the fat, and drank the sweet, and left the rest of our substance for our babes: we have spent somewhat upon our lusts, somewhat upon our friends; but the truth is, we cannot say that we made friends of this unrighteous mammon, -- that we used it to the advancement of the gospel, or for ministering unto thy poor saints: and now, behold, we must die," etc.:-- so also, when the Lord shall proceed farther, and question not only the use of these things, but also their title to them, and tell them, "The earth is mine, and the fulness thereof. I did, indeed, make an original grant of these things to man; but that is lost by sin: I have restored it only for my saints. Why have you laid, then, your fingers of prey upon that which was not yours? why have you compelled my creatures to serve you and your lusts, which I had set loose from under your dominion? Give me my flax, my wine, and wool; I will set you naked as in the day of your birth, and revenge upon you your rapine, and unjust possession of that which was not yours:" -- I say, at such a time, what will men do?

(3.) [352] Boldness with God by Christ is another privilege of our adoption. But hereof I have spoken at large before, in treating of the excellency of Christ in respect of our approach to God by him; so that I shall not re-assume the consideration of it.

(4.) Affliction, also, as proceeding from love, as leading to spiritual advantages, as conforming unto Christ, as sweetened with his presence, is the privilege of children, Heb. xii. 3-6; but on these particulars I must not insist.

This, I say, is the head and source of all the privileges which Christ hath purchased for us, wherein also we have fellowship with him: fellowship in name; we are (as he is) sons of God: fellowship in title and right; we are heirs, co-heirs with Christ: fellowship in likeness and conformity; we are predestinated to be like the first-born of the family: fellowship in honour; he is not ashamed to call us brethren: fellowship in sufferings; he learned obedience by what he suffered, and every son is to be scourged that is received: fellowship in his kingdom; we shall reign with him. Of all which I must speak peculiarly in another place, and so shall not here draw out the discourse concerning them any farther.

Footnotes:

292

349. Hab. iii. 6.
350. Rom. viii. 29; Heb. ii. 12.
351. Job. i. 6, xxxviii. 7; Heb.
xii. 22-24; Rev. xxii. 9.
352. See division, p. 211.

Part III. Of Communion with the Holy Ghost.

Chapter I - The foundation of our communion with the Holy Ghost (John xvi. 1-7) opened at large -- Παράκλητος, a Comforter; who he is -- The Holy Ghost; his own will in his coming to us; sent also by Christ -- The Spirit sent as a sanctifier and as a comforter -- The adjuncts of his mission considered -- The foundation of his mission, John xv. 26 -- His procession from the Father twofold; as to personality, or to office -- Things considerable in his procession as to office the manner of his collation -- He is given freely; sent authoritatively -- The sin against the Holy Ghost, whence unpardonable -- How we ask the Spirit of the Father -- To grieve the Spirit, what -- Poured out -- How the Holy Ghost is received; by faith -- Faith's actings in receiving the Holy Ghost -- His abode with us, how declared -- How we may lose our comfort whilst the Comforter abides with us.

The foundation of all our communion with the Holy Ghost consisting in his mission, or sending to be our comforter, by Jesus Christ, the whole matter of that economy or dispensation is firstly to be proposed and considered, that so we may have a right understanding of the truth inquired after. Now, the main promise hereof, and the chief considerations of it, with the good received and evil prevented thereby, being given and declared in the beginning of the 16th chapter of John, I shall take a view of the state of it as there proposed.

Our blessed Saviour being to leave the world, having acquainted his disciples, among other things, what entertainment in general they were like to find in it and meet withal, gives the reason why he now gave them the doleful tidings of it, considering how sad and dispirited they were upon the mention of his departure from them. Verse 1, "These things have I spoken unto you, that ye should not be offended." -- "I have," saith he, "given you an acquaintance with these things (that is, the things which will come upon you, which you are to suffer) beforehand, lest you who, poor souls! have entertained expectations of another state of affairs, should be surprised, so as to be offended at me and my doctrine, and fall away from me. You are now forewarned, and know what you have to look for. Yea," saith he, verse 2, "having acquainted you in general that you shall be persecuted, I tell you plainly that there shall be a combination of all men against you, and all sorts of men will put forth their power for your ruin." -- "They shall cast you out of the synagogues; yea, the time comes that whosoever killeth you will think that he doth God service." -- "The ecclesiastical power shall excommunicate you, -- they shall put you out of their synagogues: and that you may not expect relief from the power of the magistrate against their perversity, they will kill you: and that you may know that they will do it to the purpose, without check or control, they will think that in killing you they do God good service; which will cause them to act rigorously, and to the utmost."

"But this is a shaking trial," might they reply: "is our condition such, that men, in killing us, will think to approve their consciences to God?" "Yea, they will," saith our Saviour; "but yet, that you be not mistaken, nor trouble your consciences about their confidences, know that their blind and desperate ignorance is the cause of their fury and persuasion," verse 3, "These things will they do unto you, because they have not known the Father, nor me."

This, then, was to be the state with the disciples. But why did our Saviour tell it them at this season, to add fear and perplexities to their grief and sorrow? what advantage should they obtain thereby? Saith their blessed Master, verse 4, "There are weighty reasons why I should tell you these things; chiefly, that as you may be provided for them, so, when they do befall you, you may be supported with the consideration of my Deity and omniscience, who told you all these things before they came to pass," verse 4, "But these things have I told you, that when the time shall come, ye may remember that I told you of them." "But if they be so necessary, whence is it that thou hast not acquainted us with it all this while? why not in the beginning, -- at our first calling?" "Even," saith our Saviour, "because there was no need of any such thing; for whilst I was with you, you had protection and direction at hand." -- "'And these things I said not at the beginning, because I was present with you:' but now the state of things is altered; I must leave you," verse 4. "And for your parts, so are you astonished with sorrow, that you do not ask me whither I go;' the consideration whereof would certainly relieve you, seeing I go to take possession of my glory, and to carry on the work of your salvation: but your hearts are filled with sorrow and fears, and you do not so much as inquire after relief," verses 5, 6. Whereupon he adjoins that wonderful assertion, verse 7, "Nevertheless I tell you the truth; It is expedient for you that I go away: for if I go not away, the Comforter will not come unto you; but if I depart, I will send him unto you."

This verse, then, being the peculiar foundation of what shall afterward be declared, must particularly be considered, as to the words of it and their interpretation; and that both with respect to the preface of them and the asseveration in them, with the reason annexed thereunto.

1. The preface to them:--

(1.) The first word, ἀλλά, is an adversative, not excepting to any thing of what himself had spoken before, but to their apprehension: "I know you have sad thoughts of these things; but yet, nevertheless."

(2.) Ἐγὼ τὴν ἀλήθειαν λέγω ὑμῖν, "I tell you the truth." The words are exceedingly emphatical, and denote some great thing to be ushered in by them. First, Ἐγὼ, -- "I tell it you, this that shall now be spoken; I who love you, who take care of you, who am now about to lay down my life for you; they are my dying words, that you may believe me; I who am truth itself, I tell you." And, --

Ἐγὼ τὴν ἀλήθειαν λέγω, -- "I tell you the truth." "You have in your sad, misgiving hearts many misapprehensions of things. You think if I would abide with you, all these evils might be prevented; but, alas! you know not what is good for you, nor what is expedient. I tell you the truth;' this is truth itself; and quiet your hearts in it." There is need of a great deal of evidence of truth, to comfort their souls that are dejected and disconsolate under an apprehension of the absence of Christ from them, be the apprehension true or false.

And this is the first part of the words of our Saviour, the preface to what he was to deliver to them, by way of a weighty, convincing asseveration, to disentangle thereby the thoughts of his disciples from prejudice, and to prepare them for the receiving of that great truth which he was to deliver.

2. The assertion itself follows: Συμφέρει ὑμῖν, ἵνα ἐγὼ ἀπέλθω, -- It is expedient for you that I go away."

There are two things in the words:-- Christ's departure; and the usefulness of it to his disciples:--

For his departure, it is known what is intended by it; -- the withdrawing his bodily presence from the earth after his resurrection, the "heaven being to receive him, until the times of the restitution of all things," Acts iii. 21; for in respect of his Deity, and the exercise of love and care towards them, he promised to be with them to the end of the world, Matt. xxviii. 20. Of this saith he, Συμφέρει ὑμῖν, -- "It conduceth to your good; it is profitable for you; it is for your advantage; it will answer the end that you aim at." That is the sense of the word which we have translated "expedient;" -- "It is for your profit and advantage." This, then, is that which our Saviour asserts, and that with the earnestness before mentioned, desiring to convince his sorrowful followers of the truth of it, -- namely, that his departure, which they so much feared and were troubled to think of, would turn to their profit and advantage.

3. Now, although it might be expected that they should acquiesce in this asseveration of truth itself, yet because they were generally concerned in the ground of the truth of it, he acquaints them with that also; and, that we may confess it to be a great matter, that gives certainty and evidence to that proposition, he expresses it negatively and positively: "If I go not away, he will not come; but if I depart, I will send him." Concerning the going away of Christ I have spoken before; of the Comforter, his coming and sending, I shall now treat, as being the thing aimed at.

ὁ παράκλητος: the word being of sundry significations, many translations have thought fit not to restrain it, but do retain the original word "paracletus;" so the Syriac also: and, as some think, it was a word before in use among the Jews (whence the Chaldee paraphrast makes use of it, Job xvi. 20 [353]); and amongst them it signifies one that so taught others as to delight them also in his teaching, -- that is, to be their comforter. In Scripture it hath two eminent significations, -- an "advocate" and a "comforter;" in the first sense our Saviour is called παράκλητος, 1 John ii. 1. Whether it be better rendered here an advocate or a comforter may be doubted.

Look into the foregoing occasion of the words, which is the disciples' sorrow and trouble, and it seems to require the Comforter: "Sorrow hath filled your hearts; but I will send you the Comforter;" -- look into the next words following, which contain his peculiar work for which he is now promised to be sent, and they require he should be an Advocate, to plead the cause of Christ against the world, verse 8. I shall choose rather to interpret the promise by the occasion of it, which was the sorrow of his disciples, and to retain the name of the Comforter.

Who this Comforter is, our blessed Saviour had before declared, chap. xv. 26. He is Πνεῦμα τῆς ἀληθείας, "the Spirit of truth;" that is, the Holy Ghost, who revealeth all truth to the sons of men. Now, of this Comforter two things are affirmed:-- (1.) That he shall come. (2.) That Christ shall send him.

(1.) That he shall come. The affirmative of his coming on the performance of that condition of it, of Christ going away, is included in the negation of his coming without its accomplishment: "If I go not away, he will not come;" -- "If I do go (ἐλεύσεται), he will come." So that there is not only the mission of Christ, but the will of the Spirit, in his coming: "He will come," -- his own will is in his work.

(2.) Πέμψω αὐτόν, -- "I will send him." The mystery of his sending the Spirit, our Saviour instructs his disciples in by degrees. Chap. xiv. 16, he saith, "I will pray the Father, and he shall give you another Comforter;" in the progress of his discourse he gets one step more upon their faith, verse 26, "But the Comforter, which is the Holy Ghost, whom the Father will send in my name;" but, chap. xv. 26, he saith, "I will send him from the Father;" and here, absolutely, "I will send him." The business of sending the Holy Ghost by Christ -- which argues his personal procession also from him, the Son -- was a deep mystery, which at once they could not bear; and therefore he thus instructs them in it by degrees.

This is the sum:-- the presence of the Holy Ghost with believers as a comforter, sent by Christ for those ends and purposes for which he is promised, is better and more profitable for believers than any corporeal presence of Christ can be, now he hath fulfilled the one sacrifice for sin which he was to offer.

Now, the Holy Spirit is promised under a twofold consideration:-- [1.] As a Spirit of sanctification to the elect, to convert them and make them believers. [2.] As a Spirit of consolation to believers, to give them the privileges of the death and purchase of Christ: it is in the latter sense only wherein he is here spoken of. Now, as to his presence with us in this regard, and the end and purposes for which he is sent, for what is aimed at, observe, -- 1st. The rise and fountain of it; 2dly. The manner of his being given; 3dly. Our manner of receiving him; 4thly. His abiding with us; 5thly. His acting in us; 6thly. What are the effects of his working in us: and then how we hold communion with him will from all these appear.

What the Scripture speaketh to these particulars, shall briefly be considered:--

1st. For the fountain of his coming, it is mentioned, John xv. 26, Παρὰ τοῦ Πατρὸς ἐκπορεύεται, -- "He proceedeth from the Father;" this is the fountain of this dispensation, he proceedeth from the Father. Now there is a twofold ἐκπόρευσις, or "procession" of the Spirit:--

(1st.) Φυσική or ὑποστατική, in respect of substance and personality.

(2dly.) Οἰκονομική or dispensatory, in respect of the work of grace.

Of the first -- in which respect he is the Spirit of the Father and the Son, proceeding from both eternally, so receiving his substance and personality -- I speak not: it is a business of another nature than that I have now in hand. Therein, indeed, lies the first and most remote foundation of all our distinct communion with him and our worship of him; but because abiding in the naked consideration hereof, we can make no other progress than the bare acquiescence of faith in the mystery revealed, with the performance of that which is due to the person solely on the account of his participation of the essence, I shall not at present dwell upon it.

His ἐκπόρευσις or proceeding, mentioned in the place insisted on, is his economical or dispensatory proceeding, for the carrying on of the work of grace. It is spoken of him in reference to his being sent by Christ after his ascension: "I will send him which proceedeth," -- namely, "then when I send him." As God is said to "come out of his place," Isa. xxvi. 21, not in regard of any mutation in him, but of the new work which he would effect; so it follows, the Lord comes out of his place "to punish the inhabitants of the earth." And it is in reference to a peculiar work that he is said to proceed, -- namely, to testify of Christ: which cannot be assigned to him in respect of his eternal procession, but of his actual dispensation; as it is said of Christ, "He came forth from God." The single mention of the Father in this place, and not of the Son, belongs to the gradation before mentioned, whereby our Saviour discovers this mystery to his disciples. He speaks as much concerning himself, John xvi. 7. And this relation ad extra (as they call it) of the Spirit unto the Father and the Son, in respect of operation, proves his relation ad intra, in respect of personal procession; whereof I spake before.

Three things are considerable in the foundation of this dispensation, in reference to our communion with the Holy Ghost:--

[1st.] That the will of the Spirit is in the work: Ἐκπορεύεται, -- "He comes forth himself." Frequent mention is made (as we shall see afterward) of his being sent, his being given, and poured out; [but] that it might not be thus apprehended, either that this Spirit were altogether an inferior, created spirit, a mere servant, as some have blasphemed, nor yet merely and principally, as to his personality, the virtue of God, as some have fancied, he hath ἰδιώματα ὑποστατικά, personal properties, applied to him in this work, arguing his personality and liberty. Ἐκπορεύεται, -- "He, of himself and of his own accord, proceedeth."

[2dly.] The condescension of the Holy Ghost in this order of working, this dispensation, to proceed from the Father and the Son, as to this work; to take upon him this work of a Comforter, as the Son did the work of a Redeemer: of which afterward.

[3dly.] The fountain of the whole is discovered to be the Father, that we may know his works in the pursuit of electing love, which everywhere is ascribed to the Father. This is the order here intimated:-- First, there is the πρόθεσις of the Father, or the purpose of his love, the fountain of all; then the ἐρώτησις, the asking of the Son, John xiv. 16, which takes in his merit and purchase; whereunto follows ἐκπόρευσις, or willing proceeding of the Holy Ghost. And this gives testimony, also, to the foundation of this whole discourse, -- namely, our peculiar communion with the Father in love, the Son in grace, and the Holy Ghost in consolation. This is the door and entrance of that fellowship of the Holy Ghost whereunto we are called. His gracious and blessed will, his infinite and ineffable condescension, being eyed by faith as the foundation of all those effects which he works in us, and privileges whereof by him we are made partakers, our souls are peculiarly conversant with him, and their desires, affections, and thankfulness, terminated on him: of which more afterward. This is the first thing considerable in our communion with the Holy Ghost.

2dly. The manner of his collation or bestowing, or the manner of his communication unto us from this fountain, is herein also considerable; and it is variously expressed, to denote three things:--

(1st.) The freeness of it: thus he is said to be given, John xiv. 16; "He shall give you another Comforter." I need not multiply places to this purpose. The most frequent adjunct of the communication of the Spirit is this, that he is given and received as of gift: "He will give his Holy Spirit to them that ask him." That which is of gift is free. The Spirit of grace is given of grace: and not only the Spirit of sanctification, or the Spirit to sanctify and convert us, is a gift of free grace, but in the sense whereof we speak, in respect of consolation, he is of gift also; he is promised to be given unto believers. [354] Hence the Spirit is said to be received by the gospel, not by the law, Gal. iii. 2; that is, of mere grace, and not of our own procuring. And all his workings are called χαρίσματα, -- "free donations." He is freely bestowed, and freely works; and the different measures wherein he is received, for those ends and purposes of consolation which we shall consider, by believers, which are great, various, and inexpressible, arise from hence, that we have him by donation, or free gift. And this is the tenure whereby we hold and enjoy him, a tenure of free donation. So is he to be eyed, so to be asked, so to be received. And this, also, faith takes in and closes withal, in our communion with the Comforter:-- the conjunction and accord of his will with the gift of Father and Son; the one respecting the distinct operation of the Deity in the person of the Holy Ghost; the other, the economy of the whole Trinity in the work of our salvation by Jesus Christ. Here the soul rejoiceth itself in the Comforter, -- that he is willing to come to him, that he is willing to be given him. And seeing all is will and gift, grace is magnified on this account.

(2dly.) The authority of it. Thence he is said to be sent. Chap. xiv. 26, "The Father will send him in my name;" and, chap. xv. 26, "I will send him unto you from the Father;" and, "Him will I send unto you," chap. xvi. 7. This mission of the Holy Ghost by the Father and the Son, as it answers the order of the persons' subsistence in the blessed Trinity, and his procession from them both, so the order voluntarily engaged in by them for the accomplishment, as was said, of the work of our salvation. There is in it, in a most special manner, the condescension of the Holy Ghost, in his love to us, to the authoritative delegation of Father and Son in this business; which argues not a disparity, dissimilitude, or inequality of essence, but of office, in this work. It is the office of the Holy Ghost to be an advocate for us, and a comforter to us; in which respect, not absolutely, he is thus sent authoritatively by Father and Son. It is a known maxim, that "inæqualitas officii non tollit æqualitatem naturæ." This subjection (if I may so call it), or inequality in respect of office, doth no ways prejudice the equality of nature which he hath with Father and Son; no more than the mission of the Son by the Father doth his. And on this authoritative mission of the Spirit doth the right apprehension of many mysteries in the gospel, and the ordering of our hearts in communion with him, depend.

[1st.] Hence is the sin against the Holy Ghost (what it is I do not now dispute) unpardonable, and hath that adjunct of rebellion put upon it that no other sin hath, -- namely, because he comes not, he acts not, in his own name only, though in his own also, but in the name and authority of the Father and Son, from and by whom he is sent; and therefore, to sin against him is to sin against all the authority of God, all the love of the Trinity, and the utmost condescension of each person to the work of our salvation. It is, I say, from the authoritative mission of the Spirit that the sin against him is peculiarly unpardonable; -- it is a sin against the recapitulation of the love of the Father, Son, and Spirit. And from this consideration, were that our present business, might the true nature of the sin against the Holy Ghost be investigated. Certainly it must consist in the contempt of some operation of his, as acting in the name and authority of the whole Trinity, and that in their ineffable condescension to the work of grace. But this is of another consideration.

[2dly.] On this account we are to pray the Father and the Son to give the Spirit to us. Luke xi. 13, "Your heavenly Father will give the Holy Spirit to them that ask him." Now the Holy Ghost, being God, is no less to be invocated, prayed to, and called on, than the Father and Son; as elsewhere I have proved. How, then, do we ask the Father for him, as we do in all our supplications, seeing that we also pray that he himself would come to us, visit us, and abide with us? In our prayers that are directed to himself, we consider him as essentially God over all, blessed for evermore; we pray for him from the Father and Son, as under this mission and delegation from them. And, indeed, God having most plentifully revealed himself in the order of this dispensation to us, we are (as Christians generally do) in our communion to abound in answerable addresses; that is, not only to the person of the Holy Ghost himself, but properly to the Father and Son for him, which refers to this dispensation.

[3dly.] Hence is that great weight, in particular, laid upon our not grieving the Spirit, Eph. iv. 30, -- because he comes to us in the name, with the love, and upon the condescension, of the whole blessed Trinity. To do that which might grieve him so sent, on such an account, for that end and purpose which shall afterward be mentioned, is a great aggravation of sin. He expects cheerful entertainment with us, and may do so justly, upon his own account, and the account of the work which he comes about; but when this also is added, that he is sent of the Father and the Son, commissioned with their love and grace, to communicate them to their souls, -- this is that which is, or ought to be, of unspeakable esteem with believers. And this is that second thing expressed in the manner of his communication, -- he is sent by authority.

(3dly.) He is said to be poured out or shed on us, Tit. iii. 6, Οὗ ἐξέχεεν ἐφ' ἡμᾶς πλουσίως, -- that Holy Ghost which he hath richly poured out upon us, or shed on us abundantly. And this was the chief expression of his communication under the Old Testament; the mystery of the Father and the Son, and the matter of commission and delegation being then not so clearly discovered. Isa. xxxii. 15, "Until the Spirit be poured upon us from on high, and the wilderness be a fruitful field, and the fruitful field be counted for a forest;" that is, till the Gentiles be called, and the Jews rejected. And chap. xliv. 3, "I will pour my Spirit upon thy seed, and my blessing upon thine offspring." That eminent place of Zech. xii. 10 is always in our thoughts. Now, this expression, as is known, is taken from the allusion of the Spirit unto water; and that in relation to all the uses of water, both natural and typical. A particular relation of them I cannot now insist on; perhaps efficacy and plenty are chiefly intended.

Now, this threefold expression, of giving, sending, and pouring out, of the Spirit, gives us the three great properties of the covenant of grace:-- First, That it is free; he is given. Secondly, That it is orderly, ordered in all things, and sure, from the love of the Father, by the procurement of the Son; and thence is that variety of expression, of the Father's sending him, and the Son's sending him from the Father, he being the gift of the Father's love, and purchase of the blood of the Son. Thirdly. The efficacy of it, as was last observed. And this is the second thing considerable.

3dly. The third, which is our receiving him, I shall speak more briefly of. That which I first proposed of the Spirit, considered as a Spirit of sanctification and a Spirit of consolation, is here to be minded. Our receiving of him as a Spirit of sanctification is a mere passive reception, as a vessel receives water. He comes as the wind on Ezekiel's dead bones, and makes them live; he comes into dead hearts, and quickens them, by an act of his almighty power: but now, as he is the Spirit of consolation, it is otherwise. In this sense our Saviour tells us that the "world cannot receive him," John xiv. 17, "The world receiveth him not, because it seeth him not, neither knoweth him: but ye know him, for he dwelleth with you, and shall be in you." That it is the Spirit of consolation, or the Spirit for consolation, that here is promised, is evident from the close of the verse, where he is said then to be in them when he is promised to them. He was in them as a Spirit of quickening and sanctification when promised to them as a Spirit of comfort and consolation, to abide with them for that purpose. Now, the power that is here denied to be in the world, with the reason of it, that they cannot receive the Spirit, because they know him not, is ascribed to believers; -- they can receive him, because they know him. So that there is an active power to be put forth in his reception for consolation, though not in his reception for regeneration and sanctification. And this is the power of faith. So Gal. iii. 2, they received the Spirit by the hearing of faith; -- the preaching of the gospel, begetting faith in them, enabled them to receive the Spirit. Hence, believing is put as the qualification of all our receiving the Holy Ghost. John vii. 39, "This he spake of the Spirit, which they that believe on him should receive." It is believers that thus receive the Spirit; and they receive him by faith. Now, there are three special acts of faith, whereby it goes forth in the receiving of the Spirit. I shall but name them:--

(1st.) It considers the Spirit, in the economy before described, as promised. It is faith alone that makes profit of the benefit of the promises, Heb. iv. 2. Now he is called the Spirit of that promise, Eph. i. 13, -- the Spirit that in the covenant is promised; and we receive the promise of the Spirit through faith, Gal. iii. 14: so that the receiving of the Spirit through faith, is the receiving of him as promised. Faith eyes the promise of God and of Jesus Christ, of sending the Spirit for all those ends that he is desired; thus it depends, waits, mixing the promise with itself, until it receive him.

(2dly.) By prayer. He is given as a Spirit of supplication, that we may ask him as a Spirit of consolation, Luke xi. 13; and, indeed, this asking of the Spirit of God, in the name of Christ, either directly or immediately, or under the name of some fruit and effect; of him, is the chiefest work of faith in this world.

(3dly.) It cherisheth him, by attending to his motions, improving his actings according to his mind and will; which is all I shall say to this third thing, or our receiving of the Spirit, which is sent of Jesus Christ. We do it by faith, looking on him as purchased by Jesus Christ, and promised of the Father; we seek him at the hands of God, and do receive him.

4thly. The next considerable thing is, his abode with us. Now this is two ways expressed in the Scripture:--

(1st.) In general. As to the thing itself, it is said he shall abide with us.

(2dly.) In particular. As to the manner of its abiding, it is by inhabitation or indwelling. Of the inhabitation of the Spirit I have spoken fully [355] elsewhere, nor shall I now insist on it. Only whereas the Spirit, as hath been observed, is considered as a Spirit of sanctification, or a Spirit of consolation, he is said to dwell in us chiefly, or perhaps solely, as he is a Spirit of sanctification: which is evident from the work he doth, as indwelling, -- he quickeneth and sanctifieth, Rom. viii. 11; and the manner of his indwelling, -- as in a temple, which he makes holy thereby, 1 Cor. vi. 19; and his permanency in his so doing, -- which, as is evident, relates to sanctification only: but yet the general notion of it in abiding is ascribed to him as a comforter, John xiv. 16, "He shall abide with you for ever." Now, all the difficulty of this promise lies in this, that whereas the Spirit of sanctification dwells in us always, and it is therefore impossible that we should lose utterly our holiness, whence is it that, if the Comforter abide with us for ever, we may yet utterly lose our comfort? A little to clear this in our passage:--

[1st.] He is promised to abide with the disciples for ever, in opposition to the abode of Christ. Christ, in the flesh, had been with them for a little while, and now was leaving them, and going to his Father. He had been the comforter immediately himself for a season, but is now upon his departing; wherefore, promising them another comforter, they might fear that he would even but visit them for a little season also, and then their condition would be worse than ever. Nay, but saith our Saviour, "Fear it not: this is the last dispensation; there is to be no alteration. When I am gone, the Comforter is to do all the remaining work: there is not another to be looked for, and I promise you him; nor shall he depart from you, but always abide with you."

[2dly.] The Comforter may always abide with us, though not always comfort us; he who is the Comforter may abide, though he do not always that work. For other ends and purposes he is always with us; as to sanctify and make us holy. So was the case with David, Ps. li. 11, 12, "Take not thy Holy Spirit from me." The Holy Spirit of sanctification was still with David; but saith he, "Restore unto me the joy of thy salvation;" -- that is, the Spirit of consolation, that was lost, when the promise was made good in the abode of the other.

[3dly.] The Comforter may abide as a comforter, when he doth not actually comfort the soul. In truth, as to the essence of holiness, he cannot dwell in us but withal he must make us holy; for the temple of God is holy; -- but as to his comforting, his actings therein are all of his sovereign will; so that he may abide, and yet not actually comfort us.

[4thly.] The Spirit often works for it, and tenders consolation to us, when we do not receive it; the well is nigh, and we see it not, -- we refuse to be comforted. I told you that the Spirit as a sanctifier comes with power, to conquer an unbelieving heart; the Spirit as a comforter comes with sweetness, to be received in a believing heart. He speaks, and we believe not that it is his voice; he tenders the things of consolation, and we receive them not. "My sore ran," saith David, "and my soul refused to be comforted."

[5thly.] I deny that ever the Holy Spirit doth absolutely and universally leave a believing soul without consolation. A man may be darkened, clouded, refuse comfort, -- actually find none, feel none; but radically he hath a foundation of consolation, which in due time will be drawn forth: and therefore, when God promises that he will heal sinners, and restore comfort to them, as

Isa. lvii. 18, it is not that they were without any, but that they had not so much as they needed, that that promise is made. To insist on the several ways whereby men refuse comfort, and come short of the strong consolation which God is willing that we should receive, is not my purpose at present. Thus, then, the Spirit being sent and given, abideth with the souls of believers, -- leaves them not, though he variously manifest himself in his operations: of which in the next place.

Footnotes:

353. מְלִיצַי רֵעָי, rendered in our translation, "My friends scorn me," is in the Targum, to which Owen alludes, פְּרַקְלִיטֵי חַבְרָי, "My advocates are my friends." The word is the Greek παράκλετοι, in Hebrew characters. -- Ed.

354. Neh. ix. 20; John xiv. 16, vii. 39, xx. 22; Acts ii. 28, v. 32, viii. 15, x. 47, xv. 8, xix. 2; Rom. v. 5; 1 Cor. ii. 12, vi. 19, xii. 7; 1 Thess. iv. 8; 1 John iv. 13.

355. Perseverance of the Saints, chap. viii. vol. xi.

Chapter II - Of the actings of the Holy Ghost in us, being bestowed on us -- He worketh effectually, distributeth, giveth.

Having thus declared from whence and how the Holy Ghost is given unto us as a Spirit of consolation, I come, in the next place, --

5thly. To declare what are his actings in us and towards us, being so bestowed on us and received by us. Now, here are two general heads to be considered:-- (1st.) The manner and kind of his actings in us, which are variously expressed; and, (2dly.) The particular products of his actings in our souls, wherein we have communion with him. The first is variously expressed; I shall pass through them briefly:--

(1st.) He is said (ἐνεργεῖν) "to work effectually," 1 Cor. xii. 11, "All these worketh" (or effecteth) "that one and the self-same Spirit." It is spoken there, indeed, in respect of his distribution of gifts; but the way is the same for the communication of graces and privileges. He doth it by working: which, as it evinces his personality, especially as considered with the words following, "Dividing to every man according to his will" (for to work according to will is the inseparable property of a person, and is spoken expressly of God, Eph. i. 11); so in relation to verse 6, foregoing, it makes no less evident his Deity. What he is here said to do as the Spirit bestowed on us and given unto us, there is he said as God himself to do: "There are diversities of operations, but it is the same God which worketh all in all;" which here, in other words, is, "All these worketh that one and the self same Spirit, dividing to every man severally as he will." What we have, then, from him, we have by the way of his energetical working. It is not by proposing this or that argument to us, persuading us by these or those moral motives or inducements alone, leaving us to make use of them as we can; but he works effectually himself, what he communicates of grace or consolation to us.

[2dly.] In the same verse, as to the manner of his operation, he is said διαιρεῖν, -- he divideth or distributeth to every one as he will. This of distribution adds to that of operation, choice, judgment, and freedom. He that distributes variously, doth it with choice, and judgment, and freedom of will. Such are the proceedings of the Spirit in his dispensations: to one, he giveth one thing eminently; to another, another; -- to one, in one degree; to another, in another. Thus are the saints, in his sovereignty, kept in a constant dependence on him. He distributes as he will; -- who should not be content with his portion? what claim can any lay to that which he distributeth as he will? which is farther manifested, --

[3dly.] By his being said to give when and what he bestows. They "spake with other tongues, as the Spirit gave them utterance," Acts ii. 4. He gave them to them; that is, freely: whatever he bestows upon us, is of his gift. And hence it is to be observed, that in the economy of our salvation, the acting of no one person doth prejudice the freedom and liberty of any other: so the love of the Father in sending the Son is free, and his sending doth no ways prejudice the liberty and love of the Son, but that he lays down his life freely also; so the satisfaction and purchase made by the Son doth no way prejudice the freedom of the Father's grace in pardoning and accepting us thereupon; so the Father's and Son's sending of the Spirit doth not derogate from his freedom in his workings, but he gives freely what he gives. And the reason of this is, because the will of the Father, Son, and Holy Ghost, is essentially the same; so that in the acting of one there is the counsel of all and each freely therein.

Thus, in general, is the manner and kind of his working in us and towards us, being bestowed upon us, described. Power, choice, freedom, are evidently denoted in the expressions insisted on. It is not any peculiar work of his towards us that is hereby declared, but the manner how he doth produce the effects that shall be insisted on.

(2dly.) That which remains, in the last place, for the explanation of the things proposed to be explained as the foundation of the communion which we have with the Holy Ghost, is, --

The effects that, being thus sent and thus working, he doth produce; which I shall do, not casting them into any artificial method, but taking them up as I find them lying scattered up and down in the Scripture, only descending from those which are more general to those which are more particular, neither aiming nor desiring to gather all the several, but insisting on those which do most obviously occur.

Only as formerly, so now you must observe, that I speak of the Spirit principally (if not only) as a comforter, and not as a sanctifier; and therefore the great work of the Spirit towards us all our days, in the constant and continual supplies of new light, power, vigour, as to our receiving of grace from him, belonging to that head of sanctification, must be omitted.

Nor shall I insist on those things which the Comforter doth in believers effect towards others, in his testifying to them and convincing of the world, which are promised, John xv. 26, xvi. 8, wherein he is properly their advocate; but only on those which as a comforter he works in and towards them on whom he is bestowed.

Chapter III - Of the things wherein we have communion with the Holy Ghost -- He brings to remembrance the things spoken by Christ, John xiv. 26 -- The manner how he doth it -- The Spirit glorifies Christ in the hearts of believers, John xvi. 14, sheds abroad the love of God in them -- The witness of the Spirit, what it is, Rom. viii. 16 -- The sealing of the Spirit, Eph. i. 13 -- The Spirit, how an earnest; on the part of God, on the part of the saints -- Difference between the earnest of the Spirit and tasting of the powers of the world to come -- Unction by the Spirit, Isa. xi. 2, 3 -- The various teachings of the Holy Ghost -- How the Spirit of adoption and of supplication.

The things which, in the foregoing chapters, I called effects of the Holy Ghost in us, or towards us, are the subject-matter of our communion with him, or the things wherein we hold peculiar fellowship with him as our comforter. These are now proposed to consideration:--

1. The first and most general is that of John xiv. 26, "He shall teach you all things, and bring all things to your remembrance, whatsoever I have said unto you." There are two parts of this promise:-- (1.) Of teaching. (2.) Of bringing to remembrance. Of his teaching I shall speak afterward, when I come to treat of his anointing us.

His bringing the things to remembrance that Christ spake is the first general promise of him as a comforter: Ὑπομνήσει ὑμᾶς πάντα, -- "He shall make you mind all these things." Now, this also may be considered two ways:--

[1.] Merely in respect of the things spoken themselves. So our Saviour here promiseth his apostles that the Holy Ghost should bring to their minds, by an immediate efficacy, the things that he had spoken, that by his inspiration they might be enabled to write and preach them for the good and benefit of his church. So Peter tells us, 2 Epist. i. 21, "Holy men of God spake as they were moved by the Holy Ghost" (that is, in writing the Scripture); ὑπὸ Πνεύματος ἁγίου φερόμενοι, -- borne up by him, carried beyond themselves, to speak his words, and what he indited to them. The apostles forgot much of what Christ had said to them, or might do so; and what they did retain, in a natural way of remembrance, was not a sufficient foundation to them to write what they so remembered for a rule of faith to the church. For the word of prophecy is not ἰδίας ἐπιλύσεως, -- from any man's proper impulse; it comes not from any private conception, understanding, or remembrance. Wherefore, Christ promises that the Holy Ghost shall do this work; that they might infallibly give out what he had delivered to them. Hence that expression in Luke i. 3, Πυρηκολουθηκότι ἄνωθεν, is better rendered, "Having obtained perfect knowledge of things from above," -- noting the rise and spring of his so understanding things as to be able infallibly to give them out in a rule of faith to the church, than the beginning of the things themselves spoken of; which the word itself will not easily allow of.

[2.] In respect of the comfort of what he had spoken, which seems to be a great part of the intendment of this promise. He had been speaking to them things suited for their consolation; giving them precious promises of the supplies they should have from him in this life, -- of the love of the Father, of the glory he was providing for them, the sense and comfort whereof is unspeakable, and the joy arising from them full of glory. But saith he, "I know how unable you are to make use of these things for your own consolation; the Spirit, therefore, shall recover them upon your minds, in their full strength and vigour, for that end for which I speak them." And this is one cause why it was expedient for believers that Christ's bodily absence should be supplied by the presence of the Spirit. Whilst he was with them, how little efficacy on their hearts had any of the heavenly promises he gave them! When the Spirit came, how full of joy did he make all things to them! That which was his peculiar work, which belonged to him by virtue of his office, that he also might be glorified, was reserved for him. And this is his work to the end of the world, -- to bring the promises of Christ to our minds and hearts, to give us the comfort of them, the joy and sweetness of them, much beyond that which the disciples found in them, when Christ in person spake them to them; their gracious influence being then restrained, that, as was said, the dispensation of the Spirit might be glorified. So are the next words to this promise, verse 27, "Peace I leave with you. My peace I give unto you." The Comforter being sent to bring what Christ said to remembrance, the consequent of it is peace, and freedom from trouble of heart; -- whatever peace, relief, comfort, joy, supportment, we have at any time received from any work, promise, or thing done by Christ, it all belongs to this dispensation of the Comforter. In vain should we apply our natural abilities to remember, call to mind, consider, the promises of Christ; without success would it be, -- it is so daily: but when the Comforter doth undertake the work, it is done to the purpose. How we have peculiar communion with him herein, in faith and obedience, in the consolation received in and by the promises of him brought to mind, shall be afterward declared. This, in general, is obtained:-- our Saviour Jesus Christ, leaving the efficacy even of those promises which in person he gave to his apostles in their great distress, as to their consolation, unto the Holy Ghost, we may see the immediate spring of all the spiritual comfort we have in this world, and the fellowship which we have with the Holy Ghost therein.

Only here, as in all the particulars following, the manner of the Spirit's working this thing is always to be borne in mind, and the interest of his power, will, and goodness in his working. He doth this, -- 1st. Powerfully, or effectually; 2dly. Voluntarily; 3dly. Freely.

1st. Powerfully: and therefore doth comfort from the words and promises of Christ sometimes break in through all opposition into the saddest and darkest condition imaginable; it comes and makes men sing in a dungeon, rejoice in flames, glory in tribulation; it will into prisons, racks, through temptations, and the greatest distresses imaginable. Whence is this? Τὸ Πνεῦμα ἐνεργεῖ, -- the Spirit works effectually, his power is in it; he will work, and none shall let him.

If he will bring to our remembrance the promises of Christ for our consolation, neither Satan nor man, sin nor world, nor death, shall interrupt our comfort. This the saints, who have communion with the Holy Ghost, know to their advantage. Sometimes the heavens are black over them, and the earth trembles under them; public, personal calamities and distresses appear so full of horror and darkness, that they are ready to faint with the apprehensions of them; -- hence is their great relief, and the retrievement of their spirits; their consolation or trouble depends not on any outward condition or inward frame of their own hearts, but on the powerful and effectual workings of the Holy Ghost, which by faith they give themselves up unto.

2dly. Voluntarily, -- distributing to every one as he will; and therefore is this work done in so great variety, both as to the same person and divers. For the same person, full of joy sometimes in a great distress, full of consolation, -- every promise brings sweetness when his pressures are great and heavy; another time, in the least trial [he] seeks for comfort, searches the promise, and it is far away. The reason is, Πνεῦμα διαιρεῖ καθὼς βούλεται, -- the Spirit distributes as he will. And so with divers persons: to some each promise is full of life and comfort; others taste little all their days, -- all upon the same account. And this faith especially regards in the whole business of consolation:-- it depends on the sovereign will of the Holy Ghost; and so is not tied unto any rules or course of procedure. Therefore doth it exercise itself in waiting upon him for the seasonable accomplishment of the good pleasure of his will.

3dly. Freely. Much of the variety of the dispensation of consolation by promises depends on this freedom of the Spirit's operation. Hence it is that comfort is given unexpectedly, when the heart hath all the reasons in the world to look for distress and sorrow; thus sometimes it is the first means of recovering a backsliding soul, who might justly expect to be utterly cast off. And these considerations are to be carried on in all the other effects and fruits of the Comforter: of which afterward. And in this first general effect or work of the Holy Ghost towards us have we communion and fellowship with him. The life and soul of all our comforts lie treasured up in the promises of Christ. They are the breasts of all our consolation. Who knows not how powerless they are in the bare letter, even when improved to the uttermost by our considerations of them, and meditation on them? as also how unexpectedly they sometimes break upon the soul with a conquering, endearing life and vigour? Here faith deals peculiarly with the Holy Ghost. It considers the promises themselves; looks up to him, waits for him, considers his appearances in the word depended on, -- owns him in his work and efficacy. No sooner doth the soul begin to feel the life of a promise warming his heart, relieving, cherishing, supporting, delivering from fear, entanglements, or troubles, but it may, it ought, to know that the Holy Ghost is there; which will add to his joy, and lead him into fellowship with him.

2. The next general work seems to be that of John xvi. 14, "The Comforter shall glorify me; for he shall receive of mine, and shall show it unto you." The work of the Spirit is to glorify Christ: whence, by the way, we may see how far that spirit is from being the Comforter who sets up himself in the room of Christ; such a spirit as saith he is all himself: "for as for him that suffered at Jerusalem, it is no matter that we trouble ourselves about him." This spirit is now all. This is not the Comforter. His work is to glorify Christ, -- him that sends him. And this is an evident sign of a false spirit, whatever its pretence be,

if it glorify not that Christ who was now speaking to his apostles; and such are many that are gone abroad into the world. But what shall this Spirit do, that Christ may be glorified? "He shall," saith he, "take of mine," -- ἐκ τοῦ ἐμοῦ λήψεται. What these things are is declared in the next verse: "All things that the Father hath are mine; therefore I said he shall take of mine." It is not of the essence and essential properties of the Father and Son that our Saviour speaks; but of the grace which is communicated to us by them. This Christ calls, "My things," being the fruit of his purchase and mediation: on which account he saith all his Father's things are his; that is, the things that the Father, in his eternal love, hath provided to be dispensed in the blood of his Son, -- all the fruits of election. "These," said he, "the Comforter shall receive; that is, they shall be committed unto him to dispose for your good and advantage, to the end before proposed." So it follows, ἀναγγελεῖ, -- "He shall show, or declare and make them known to you." Thus, then, is he a comforter. He reveals to the souls of sinners the good things of the covenant of grace, which the Father hath provided, and the Son purchased. He shows to us mercy, grace, forgiveness, righteousness, acceptation with God; letteth us know that these are the things of Christ, which he hath procured for us; shows them to us for our comfort and establishment. These things, I say, he effectually declares to the souls of believers; and makes them know them for their own good, -- know them as originally the things of the Father, prepared from eternity in his love and good-will; as purchased for them by Christ, and laid up in store in the covenant of grace for their use. Then is Christ magnified and glorified in their hearts; then they know what a Saviour and Redeemer he is. A soul doth never glorify or honour Christ upon a discovery or sense of the eternal redemption he hath purchased for him, but it is in him a peculiar effect of the Holy Ghost as our comforter. "No man can say that Jesus is the Lord, but by the Holy Ghost," 1 Cor. xii. 3.

3. He "sheds the love of God abroad in our hearts," Rom. v. 5. That it is the love of God to us, not our love to God, which is here intended, the context is so clear as nothing can be added thereunto. Now, the love of God is either of ordination or of acceptation, -- the love of his purpose to do us good, or the love of acceptation and approbation with him. Both these are called the love of God frequently in Scripture, as I have declared. Now, how can these be shed abroad in our hearts? Not in themselves, but in a sense of them, -- in a spiritual apprehension of them. Ἐκκέχυται, is "shed abroad;" the same word that is used concerning the Comforter being given us, Tit. iii. 6. God sheds him abundantly, or pours him on us; so he sheds abroad, or pours out the love of God in our hearts. Not to insist on the expression, which is metaphorical, the business is, that the Comforter gives a sweet and plentiful evidence and persuasion of the love of God to us, such as the soul is taken, delighted, satiated withal. This is his work, and he doth it effectually. To give a poor sinful soul a comfortable persuasion, affecting it throughout, in all its faculties and affections, that God in Jesus Christ loves him, delights in him, is well pleased with him, hath thoughts of tenderness and kindness towards him; to give, I say, a soul an overflowing sense hereof, is an inexpressible mercy.

This we have in a peculiar manner by the Holy Ghost; it is his peculiar work. As all his works are works of love and kindness, so this of communicating a sense of the love of the Father mixes itself with all the particulars of his actings. And as we have herein peculiar communion with himself, so by him we have communion with the Father, even in his love, which is thus shed abroad in our hearts: so not only do we rejoice in, and glorify the Holy Ghost, which doth this work, but in him also whose love it is. Thus is it also in respect of the Son, in his taking of his, and showing of it unto us, as was declared. What we have of heaven in this world lies herein; and the manner of our fellowship with the Holy Ghost on this account falls in with what was spoken before.

4. Another effect we have of his, Rom. viii. 16, "The Spirit itself beareth witness with our spirit, that we are the children of God." You know whose children we are by nature, -- children of Satan and of the curse, or of wrath. By the Spirit we are put into another capacity, and are adopted to be the children of God, inasmuch as by receiving the Spirit of our Father we become the children of our Father. Thence is he called, verse 15, "The Spirit of adoption." Now, sometimes the soul, because it hath somewhat remaining in it of the principle that it had in its old condition, is put to question whether it be a child of God or no; and thereupon, as in a thing of the greatest importance, puts in its claim, with all the evidences that it hath to make good its title. The Spirit comes and bears witness in this case. An allusion it is to judicial proceedings in point of titles and evidences. The judge being set, the person concerned lays his claim, produceth his evidences, and pleads them; his adversaries endeavouring all that in them lies to invalidate them, and disannul his plea, and to cast him in his claim. In the midst of the trial, a person of known and approved integrity comes into the court, and gives testimony fully and directly on the behalf of the claimer; which stops the mouths of all his adversaries, and fills the man that pleaded with joy and satisfaction. So is it in this case. The soul, by the power of its own conscience, is brought before the law of God. There a man puts in his plea, -- that he is a child of God, that he belongs to God's family; and for this end produceth all his evidences, every thing whereby faith gives him an interest in God. Satan, in the meantime, opposeth with all his might; sin and law assist him; many flaws are found in his evidences; the truth of them all is questioned; and the soul hangs in suspense as to the issue. In the midst of the plea and contest the Comforter comes, and, by a word of promise or otherwise, overpowers the heart with a comfortable persuasion (and bears down all objections) that his plea is good, and that he is a child of God. And therefore it is said of him, Συμμαρτυρεῖ τῷ Πνεύματι ἡμῶν. When our spirits are pleading their right and title, he comes in and bears witness on our side; at the same time enabling us to put forth acts of filial obedience, kind and childlike; which is called "crying, Abba, Father," Gal. iv. 6. Remember still the manner of the Spirit's working, before mentioned, -- that he doth it effectually, voluntarily, and freely. Hence sometimes the dispute hangs long, -- the cause is pleading many years. The law seems sometimes to prevail, sin and Satan to rejoice; and the poor soul is filled with dread about its inheritance. Perhaps its own witness, from its faith, sanctification, former experience, keeps up the plea with some life and comfort; but the work is not done, the conquest is not fully obtained, until the Spirit, who worketh freely and effectually, when and how he will, comes in with his testimony also; clothing his power with a word of promise, he makes all parties concerned to attend unto him, and puts an end to the controversy.

Herein he gives us holy communion with himself. The soul knows his voice when he speaks, "Nec hominem sonat." There is something too great in it to be the effect of a created power. When the Lord Jesus Christ at one word stilled the raging of the sea and wind, all that were with him knew there was divine power at hand, Matt. viii. 25-27. And when the Holy Ghost by one word stills the tumults and storms that are raised in the soul, giving it an immediate calm and security, it knows his divine power, and rejoices in his presence.

5. He seals us. "We are sealed by the Holy Spirit of promise, Eph. i. 13; and, "Grieve not the Holy Spirit, whereby ye are sealed unto the day of redemption," chap. iv. 30. I am not very clear in the certain peculiar intendment of this metaphor; what I am persuaded of the mind of God in it I shall briefly impart. In a seal two things are considered:-- (1.) The nature of it. (2.) The use of it.

(1.) The nature of sealing consists in the imparting of the image or character of the seal to the thing sealed. This is to seal a thing, -- to stamp the character of the seal on it. In this sense, the effectual communication of the image of God unto us should be our sealing. The Spirit in believers, really communicating the image of God, in righteousness and true holiness, unto the soul, sealeth us. To have this stamp of the Holy Ghost, so as to be an evidence unto the soul that it is accepted with God, is to be sealed by the Spirit; taking the metaphor from the nature of sealing. [356] And in this sense is our Saviour said to be sealed of God, John vi. 27, even from that impression of the power, wisdom, and majesty of God that he had upon him in the discharge of his office.

(2.) The end of sealing is twofold:--

[1.] To confirm or ratify any grant or conveyance made in writing. In such cases men set their seals to make good and confirm their grants; and when this is done they are irrevocable. Or to confirm the testimony that is given by any one of the truth of any thing. Such was the manner among the Jews:-- when any one had given true witness unto any thing or matter, and it was received by the judges, they instantly set their seals to it, to confirm it in judgment. Hence it is said, that he who receives the testimony of Christ "sets to his seal that God is true," John iii. 33. The promise is the great grant and conveyance of life and salvation in Christ to the souls of believers. That we may have full assurance of the truth and irrevocableness of the promise, God gives us the Spirit to satisfy our hearts of it; and thence is he said to seal us, by assuring our hearts of those promises and their stability. But, though many expositors go this way, I do not see how this can consist with the very meaning of the word. It is not said that the promise is sealed, but that we are sealed; and when we seal a deed or grant to any one, we do not say the man is sealed, but the deed or grant.

[2.] To appropriate, distinguish, or keep safe. This is the end of sealing. Men set their seals on that which they appropriate and desire to keep safe for themselves. So, evidently, in this sense are the servants of God said to be sealed, Rev. vii. 4; that is, marked with God's mark, as his peculiar ones, -- for this sealing answers to the setting of a mark, Ezek. ix. 4. Then are believers sealed, when they are marked for God to be heirs of the purchased inheritance, and to be preserved to the day of redemption. Now, if this be the sealing intended, it denotes not an act of sense in the heart, but of security to the person. The Father gives the elect into the hands of Christ to be redeemed; having redeemed them, in due time they are called by the Spirit, and marked for

God, and so give up themselves to the hands of the Father.

If you ask, now, "Which of these senses is chiefly intended in this expression of our being sealed by the Holy Ghost?" I answer, The first, not excluding the other. We are sealed to the day of redemption, when, from the stamp, image, and character of the Spirit upon our souls, we have a fresh sense of the love of God given to us, with a comfortable persuasion of our acceptation with him. But of this whole matter I have treated at large [357] elsewhere.

Thus, then, the Holy Ghost communicates unto us his own likeness; which is also the image of the Father and the Son. "We are changed into this image by the Lord the Spirit," 2 Cor. iii. 18; and herein he brings us into fellowship with himself. Our likeness to him gives us boldness with him. His work we look for, his fruits we pray for; and when any effect of grace, any discovery of the image of Christ implanted in us, gives us a persuasion of our being separated and set apart for God, we have a communion with him therein.

6. He is an earnest unto us. 2 Cor. i. 22, He hath "given the earnest of the Spirit in our hearts;" chap. v. 5, "Who also hath given unto us the earnest of the Spirit;" as also, Eph. i. 13, 14, "Ye are sealed with that Holy Spirit of promise, which is the earnest of our inheritance." In the two former places we are said to have the earnest of the Spirit; in the latter, the Spirit is said to be our earnest: "of the Spirit," then, in the first place, is, as we say, "genitivus materiæ;" denoting not the cause, but the thing itself; -- not the author of the earnest, but the matter of it. The Spirit is our earnest; as in the last place is expressed. The consideration of what is meant by the "Spirit," here, and what is meant by an "earnest," will give some insight into this privilege, which we receive by the Comforter:--

(1.) What grace, what gift of the Spirit, is intended by this earnest, some have made inquiry; I suppose to no purpose. It is the Spirit himself, personally considered, that is said to be this earnest, 2 Cor. i. 22. It is God hath given the earnest of the Spirit in our hearts: an expression directly answering that of Gal. iv. 6, "God hath sent forth the Spirit of his Son into your hearts;" -- that is, the person of the Spirit; for nothing else can be called the Spirit of his Son: and in Eph. i. 14, he hath given the Spirit (ὅς for ὅ); which is that earnest. The Spirit of promise himself is this earnest. In giving us this Spirit he gives us this earnest.

(2.) An earnest it is, -- ἀῤῥαβών. Neither the Greek nor the Latin hath any word to express directly what is here intended. The Latins have made words for it, from that expressed here in the Greek, "arrha" and "arrabo." The Greek word is but the Hebrew "herabon" [עֵרָבוֹן]; which, as some conceive, came amongst them by the Syrian merchants, being a word of trade. It is by some rendered, in Latin, "pignus," a "pledge;" but this cannot be here intended. A pledge is that property which any one gives or leaves in the custody of another, to assure him that he will give him, or pay him, some other thing; in the nature of that which we call a "pawn." Now, the thing that is here intended, is a part of that which is to come, and but a part of it, according to the trade use of the word, whence the metaphor is taken; it is excellently rendered in our language, an "earnest." An earnest is part of the price of any thing, or part of any grant, given beforehand to assure the person to whom it is given that at the appointed season he shall receive the whole that is promised him.

That a thing be an earnest, it is required, --

[1.] That it be part of the whole, of the same kind and nature with it; as we do give so much money in earnest to pay so much more.

[2.] That it be a confirmation of a promise and appointment; first the whole is promised, then the earnest is given for the good and true performance of that promise.

Thus the Spirit is this earnest. God gives us the promise of eternal life. To confirm this to us, he giveth us his Spirit; which is, as the first part of the promise, to secure us of the whole. Hence he is said to be the earnest of the inheritance that is promised and purchased.

And it may be considered how it may be said to be an earnest on the part of God, who gives him; and on the part of believers, who receive him:--

1st. He is an earnest on the part of God, in that God gives him as a choice part of the inheritance itself, and of the same kind with the whole, as an earnest ought to be. The full inheritance promised, is the fulness of the Spirit in the enjoyment of God. When that Spirit which is given us in this world shall have perfectly taken away all sin and sorrow, and shall have made us able to enjoy the glory of God in his presence, that is the full inheritance promised. So that the Spirit given us for the fitting of us for enjoyment of God in some measure, whilst we are here, is the earnest of the whole.

God doth it to this purpose, to assure us and secure us of the inheritance. Having given us so many [358] securities without us, -- his word, promises, covenant, oath, the revelation and discovery of his faithfulness and immutability in them all, -- he is pleased also graciously to give us one within us, Isa. lix. 21, that we may have all the security we are capable of. What can more be done? He hath given us of the Holy Spirit; -- in him the first-fruits of glory, the utmost pledge of his love, the earnest of all.

2dly. On the part of believers he is an earnest, in that he gives them an acquaintance with, --

(1st.) The love of God. Their acceptation with him makes known to them their favour in his sight, -- that he is their Father, and will deal with them as with children; and consequently, that the inheritance shall be theirs. He sends his Spirit into our hearts, "crying, Abba, Father," Gal. iv. 6. And what is the inference of believers from hence? Verse 7, "Then we are not servants, but sons; and if sons, then heirs of God." The same apostle, again, Rom. viii. 17, "If children, then heirs; heirs of God, and joint heirs with Christ." On that persuasion of the Spirit that we are children, the inference is, "Then heirs, heirs of God, and joint heirs with Christ." We have, then, a right to an inheritance, and an eviction of it. This is the use, then, we have of it, -- even the Spirit persuading us of our sonship and acceptation with God our Father. And what is this inheritance of glory? "If we suffer with him, we shall be glorified together." And that the Spirit is given for this end is attested, 1 John iii. 24, "Hereby we know that he abideth in us, by the Spirit which he hath given us." The apostle is speaking of our union with God, which he expresseth in the words foregoing: "He that keepeth his commandments dwelleth in him, and he in him;" -- of that union elsewhere. Now, this we know from hence, even by the Spirit which he hath given us, -- the Spirit acquaints us with it. Not that we have such an acquaintance, but that the argument is good and conclusive in itself, "We have of the Spirit; therefore he dwells in us, and we in him:" because, indeed, his dwelling in us is by that Spirit, and our interest in him is from thence. A sense of this he giveth as he pleaseth.

(2dly.) The Spirit being given as an earnest, acquaints believers with their inheritance, 1 Cor. ii. 9, 10. As an earnest, being part of the whole, gives knowledge of it, so doth the Spirit; as in sundry particulars might be demonstrated.

So is he in all respects completely an earnest, -- given of God, received by us, as the beginning of our inheritance, and the assurance of it. So much as we have of the Spirit, so much we have of heaven in perfect enjoyment, and so much evidence of its future fulness. Under this apprehension of him in the dispensation of grace do believers receive him and rejoice in him. Every gracious, self-evidencing act of his in their hearts they rejoice in, as a drop from heaven, and long for the ocean of it. Not to drive every effect of grace to this issue, is to neglect the work of the Holy Ghost in us and towards us.

There remains only that a difference be, in a few words, assigned between believers receiving the Spirit as an earnest of the whole inheritance, and hypocrites "tasting of the powers of the world to come," Heb. vi. 5. A taste of the powers of the world to come seems to be the same with the earnest of the inheritance. But, --

[1st.] That by "the powers of the world to come" in that place is intended the joys of heaven, there is, indeed, no ground to imagine. They are nowhere so called; nor doth it suitably express the glory that shall be revealed, which we shall be made partakers of. It is, doubtless, the powerful ministry of the ordinances and dispensations of the times of the gospel (there called to the Hebrews according to their own idiom), the powers or great effectual things of the world to come, that is intended. But, --

[2dly.] Suppose that by "the powers of the world to come" the glory of heaven is intended, there is a wide difference between taking a vanishing taste of it ourselves, and receiving an abiding earnest from God. To take a taste of the things of heaven, and to have them assured of God as from his love, differ greatly. A hypocrite may have his thoughts raised to a great deal of joy and contentment in the consideration of the good things of the kingdom of God for a season, considering the things in themselves; but the Spirit, as he is an earnest, gives us a pledge of them as provided for us in the love of God and purchase of his Son Jesus Christ. This by the way.

7. The Spirit anoints believers. We are "anointed" by the Spirit, 2 Cor. i. 21. We have "an unction from the Holy One, and we know all things," 1 John ii. 20, 27. I cannot intend to run this expression up into its rise and original; also, I have done it elsewhere. The use of unctions in the Judaical church, the meaning and intendment of the types attended therewith, the offices that men were consecrated unto thereby, are at the bottom of this expression; nearer the unction of Jesus Christ (from whence he is called Messiah, and the Christ, the whole performance of his office of mediatorship being called also his anointing, Dan. ix. 24, as to his furnishment for it), concurs hereunto. Christ is said to be "anointed with the oil of gladness above his fellows," Heb. i. 9; which is the same with that of John iii. 34, "God giveth not the Spirit by measure unto him." We, who have the Spirit by measure, are anointed with the "oil of gladness;" Christ hath the fulness of the Spirit, whence our measure is communicated: so he is anointed above us, "that in all things he may have the pre-eminence." How Christ was anointed with the Spirit to his threefold office of king, priest, and prophet; how, by virtue of an unction, with the same Spirit dwelling in him and us, we become to be interested in these offices of his, and

are made also kings, priests, and prophets to God, is known, and would be matter of a long discourse to handle; and my design is only to communicate the things treated of:

I shall only, therefore, fix on one place, where the communications of the Spirit in this unction of Christ are enumerated, -- of which, in our measure, from him and with him, by this unction, we are made partakers, -- and that is, Isa. xi. 2, 3, "The Spirit of the Lord shall rest upon him, the Spirit of wisdom and understanding, the Spirit of counsel and might, the Spirit of knowledge, and of the fear of the Lord," etc. Many of the endowments of Christ, from the Spirit wherewith he was abundantly anointed, are here recounted. Principally those of wisdom, counsel, and understanding, are insisted on; on the account whereof all the treasures of wisdom and knowledge are said to be in him, Col. ii. 3. And though this be but some part of the furniture of Jesus Christ for the discharge of his office, yet it is such, as, where our anointing to the same purpose is mentioned, it is said peculiarly on effecting of such qualifications as these: so 1 John ii. 20, 27, the work of the anointing is to teach us; the Spirit therein is a Spirit of wisdom and understanding, of counsel, knowledge, and quick understanding in the fear of the Lord. So was the great promise of the Comforter, that he should "teach us," John xiv. 26, -- that he should "guide us into all truth," chap. xvi. 13. This of teaching us the mind and will of God, in the manner wherein we are taught it by the Spirit, our comforter, is an eminent part of our unction by him; which only I shall instance in. Give me leave to say, there is a threefold teaching by the Spirit:--

(1.) A teaching by the Spirit of conviction and illumination. So the Spirit teacheth the world (that is, many in it) by the preaching of the word; as he is promised to do, John xvi. 8.

(2.) A teaching by the Spirit of sanctification; opening blind eyes, giving a new understanding, shining into our hearts, to give us a knowledge of the glory of God in the face of Jesus Christ; enabling us to receive spiritual things in a spiritual light, 1 Cor. ii. 13; giving a saving knowledge of the mystery of the gospel: and this in several degrees is common to believers.

(3.) A teaching by the Spirit of consolation; -- making sweet, useful, and joyful to the soul, the discoveries that are made of the mind and will of God in the light of the Spirit of sanctification. Here the oil of the Spirit is called the "oil of gladness," -- that which brings joy and gladness with it; and the name of Christ thereby discovered is a sweet "ointment poured forth," that causeth souls to run after him with joy and delight, Cant. i. 3. We see it by daily experience, that very many have little taste and sweetness and relish in their souls of those truths which yet they savingly know and believe; but when we are taught by this unction, oh, how sweet is every thing we know of God! As we may see in the place of John where mention is made of the teaching of this unction, it respects peculiarly the Spirit teaching of us the love of God in Christ, the shining of his countenance; which, as David speaks, puts gladness into our hearts, Ps. iv. 6, 7.

We have this, then, by the Spirit:-- he teacheth us of the love of God in Christ; he makes every gospel truth as wine well refined to our souls, and the good things of it to be a feast of fat things; -- gives us joy and gladness of heart with all that we know of God; which is the great preservative of the soul to keep it close to truth. The apostle speaks of our teaching by this unction, as the means whereby we are preserved from seduction. Indeed, to know any truth in the power, sweetness, joy, and gladness of it, is that great security of the soul's constancy in the preservation and retaining of it. They will readily change truth for error, who find no more sweetness in the one than in the other. I must crave the reader's pardon for my brief passing over these great things of the gospel; my present design is rather to enumerate than to unfold them. This one work of the Holy Ghost, might it be pursued, would require a fuller discourse than I can allot unto the whole matter in hand. All the privileges we enjoy, all the dignity and honour we are invested withal, our whole dedication unto God, our nobility and royalty, our interest in all church advantages and approaches to God in worship, our separation from the world, the name whereby we are called, the liberty we enjoy, -- all flow from this head, all are branches of this effect of the Holy Ghost. I have mentioned only our teaching by this unction, -- a teaching that brings joy and gladness with it, by giving the heart a sense of the truth wherein we are instructed. When we find any of the good truths of the gospel come home to our souls with life, vigour, and power, giving us gladness of heart, transforming us into the image and likeness of it, -- the Holy Ghost is then at his work, is pouring out of his oil.

8. We have adoption also by the Spirit; hence he is called the "Spirit of adoption;" that is, either he who is given to adopted ones, to secure them of it, to beget in their hearts a sense and persuasion of the Father's adopting love; or else to give them the privilege itself, as is intimated, John i. 12. Neither is that opposite hereunto which we have, Gal. iv. 6; for God may send the Spirit of supplication into our hearts, because we are sons, and yet adopted by his Spirit. But of this elsewhere.

9. He is also called the "Spirit of supplication;" under which notion he is promised, Zech. xii. 10; and how he effects that in us is declared, Rom. viii. 26, 27, Gal. iv. 6; and we are thence said to "pray in the Holy Ghost." Our prayers may be considered two ways:--

(1.) First, as a spiritual duty required of us by God; and so they are wrought in us by the Spirit of sanctification, which helps us to perform all our duties, by exalting all the faculties of the soul for the spiritual discharge of their respective offices in them.

(2.) As a means of retaining communion with God, whereby we sweetly ease our hearts in the bosom of the Father, and receive in refreshing tastes of his love. The soul is never more raised with the love of God than when by the Spirit taken into intimate communion with him in the discharge of this duty; and therein it belongs to the Spirit of consolation, to the Spirit promised as a comforter. And this is the next thing to be considered in our communion with the Holy Ghost, -- namely, what are the peculiar effects which he worketh in us, and towards us, being so bestowed on us as was declared, and working in the way and manner insisted on. Now, these are, -- his bringing the promises of Christ to remembrance, glorifying him in our hearts, shedding abroad the love of God in us, witnessing with us as to our spiritual estate and condition, sealing us to the day of redemption (being the earnest of our inheritance), anointing us with privileges as to their consolation, confirming our adoption, and being present with us in our supplications. Here is the wisdom of faith, -- to find out and meet with the Comforter in all these things; not to lose their sweetness, by lying in the dark [as] to their author, nor coming short of the returns which are required of us.

Footnotes:

356. Rev. vii. 4.
357. Perseverance of the Saints, chap. viii. vol. xi.
358. Heb. vi. 17, 18.

Chapter IV - The general consequences in the hearts of believers of the effects of the Holy Ghost before mentioned -- Consolation; its adjuncts, peace, joy -- How it is wrought immediately, mediately.

Having proceeded thus far in discovering the way of our communion with the Holy Ghost, and insisted on the most noble and known effects that he produceth, it remains that it be declared what general consequences of these effects there are brought forth in the hearts of believers; and so we shall at least have made mention of the main heads of his dispensation and work in the economy of grace. Now, these (as with the former) I shall do little more than name; it being not at all in my design to handle the natures of them, but only to show what respects they bear to the business in hand:--

1. Consolation is the first of these: "The disciples walked in the fear of the Lord, and in the consolation of the Holy Ghost," Acts ix. 31, Τῇ παρακλήσει τοῦ ἁγίου Πνεύματος, He is ὁ παράκλητος, and he gives παράκλησιν: from his work towards us, and in us, we have comfort and consolation. This is the first general consequent of his dispensation and work. Whenever there is mention made of comfort and consolation in the Scripture given to the saints (as there is most frequently), it is the proper consequent of the work of the Holy Ghost towards them. Comfort or consolation in general, is the setting and composing of the soul in rest and contentedness in the midst of or from troubles, by the consideration or presence of some good, wherein it is interested, outweighing the evil, trouble, or perplexity that it hath to wrestle withal. Where mention is made of comfort and consolation, properly so called, there is relation to trouble or perplexity; so the apostle, 2 Cor. i. 5, 6, "As the sufferings of Christ abound in us, so our consolation also aboundeth by Christ." Suffering and consolation are opposed, the latter being a relief against the former; so are all the promises of comfort, and all the expressions of it, in the Old and New Testament still proposed as reliefs against trouble.

And, as I said, consolation ariseth from the presence or consideration of a greater good, that outbalances the evil or perplexity wherewith we are to contend. Now, in the effects or acts of the Holy Ghost before mentioned lie all the springs of our consolation. There is no comfort but from them; and there is no trouble that we may not have comfort in and against by them. That a man may have consolation in any condition, nothing is required but the presence of a good, rendering the evil wherewith he is pressed inconsiderable to him. Suppose a man under the greatest calamity that can possibly befall a child of God, or a confluence of all those evils numbered by Paul, Rom. viii. 35, etc.; let this man have the Holy Ghost performing the works mentioned before towards him, and, in despite of all his evils, his consolations will abound. Suppose him to have a sense of the love of God all the while shed abroad in his heart, a clear witness within that he is a child of God, accepted with him, that he is sealed and marked of God for his own, that he is an heir of all the promises of God, and the like; it is impossible that man should not triumph in all his tribulations.

From this rise of all our consolation are those descriptions which we have of it in the Scripture, from its properties and adjuncts; as, --

(1.) It is abiding. Thence it is called "Everlasting consolation," 2 Thess. ii. 16, "God, even our Father, which hath loved us, and given us everlasting consolation;" -- that is, comfort that vanisheth not; and that because it riseth from everlasting things. There may be some perishing comfort given for a little season by perishing things; but abiding consolation, which we have by the Holy Ghost, is from things everlasting:-- everlasting love, eternal redemption, an everlasting inheritance.

(2.) Strong. Heb. vi. 18, "That the heirs of the promise should receive strong consolation." As strong opposition lies sometimes against us, and trouble, whose bands are strong, so is our consolation strong; it abounds, and is unconquerable, -- ἰσχυρὰ παράκλησις. It is such as will make its way through all opposition; it confirms, corroborates, and strengthens the heart under any evil; it fortifies the soul, and makes it able cheerfully to undergo any thing that it is called unto: and that because it is from him who is strong.

(3.) It is precious. Hence the apostle makes it the great motive unto obedience, which he exhorts the Philippians unto, chap. ii. 1, "If there be any consolation in Christ;" -- "If you set any esteem and valuation upon this precious mercy of consolation in Christ, by those comforts, let it be so with you."

And this is the first general consequent in the hearts of believers of those great effects of the Holy Ghost before mentioned. Now, this is so large and comprehensive, comprising so many of our concernments in our walking with God, that the Holy Ghost receives his denomination, as to the whole work he hath to perform for us, from hence, -- he is the Comforter; as Jesus Christ, from the work of redemption and salvation, is the Redeemer and Saviour of his church. Now, as we have no consolation but from the Holy Ghost, so all his effects towards us have certainly this consequent more or less in us. Yea, I dare say, whatever we have in the kinds of the things before mentioned that brings not consolation with it, in the root at least, if not in the ripe fruit, is not of the Holy Ghost. The way whereby comfort issues out from those works of his, belongs to particular cases. The fellowship we have with him consists, in no small portion of it, in the consolation we receive from him. This gives us a valuation of his love; teacheth whither to make applications in our distress, -- whom to pray for, to pray to, -- whom to wait upon, in perplexities.

2. Peace ariseth hence also. Rom. xv. 13, "The God of hope fill you with all peace in believing, that you may abound in hope through the power of the Holy Ghost." The power of the Holy Ghost is not only extended to hope, but to our peace also in believing. So is it in the connection of those promises, John xiv. 26, 27, "I will give you the Comforter:" and what then? what follows that grant? "Peace," saith he, "I leave with you; my peace I give unto you." Nor doth Christ otherwise leave his peace, or give his peace unto them, but by bestowing the Comforter on them. The peace of Christ consists in the soul's sense of its acceptation with God in friendship. So is Christ said to be "our peace," Eph. ii. 14, by slaying the enmity between God and us, and in taking away the handwriting that was against us. Rom. v. 1, "Being justified by faith, we have

peace with God." A comfortable persuasion of our acceptation with God in Christ is the bottom of this peace; it inwraps deliverance from eternal wrath, hatred, curse, condemnation, -- all sweetly affecting the soul and conscience.

And this is a branch from the same root with that foregoing, -- a consequent of the effects of the Holy Ghost before mentioned. Suppose a man chosen in the eternal love of the Father, redeemed by the blood of the Son, and justified freely by the grace of God, so that he hath a right to all the promises of the gospel; yet this person can by no reasonings nor arguings of his own heart, by no considerations of the promises themselves, nor of the love of God or grace of Christ in them, be brought to any establishment in peace, until it be produced in him as a fruit and consequent of the work of the Holy Ghost in him and towards him. "Peace" is the fruit of the Spirit, Gal. v. 22. The savour of the Spirit is "life and peace," Rom. viii. 6. All we have is from him and by him.

3. Joy, also, is of this number. The Spirit, as was showed, is called "The oil of gladness," Heb. i. 9. His anointing brings gladness with it, Isa. lxi. 3, "The oil of joy for mourning." "The kingdom of God is righteousness, and peace, and joy in the Holy Ghost," Rom. xiv. 17; "Received the word with joy in the Holy Ghost," 1 Thess. i. 6, -- "with joy," as Peter tells believers, "unspeakable and full of glory," 1 Epist. i. 8. To give joy to the hearts of believers is eminently the work of the Comforter; and this he doth by the particulars before instanced in. That "rejoicing in hope of the glory of God," mentioned Rom. v. 2, which carries the soul through any tribulation, even with glorying, hath its rise in the Spirit's "shedding abroad the love of God in our hearts," verse 5. Now, there are two ways whereby the Spirit worketh this joy in the hearts of believers:--

(1.) He doth it immediately by himself; without the consideration of any other acts or works of his, or the interposition of any reasonings, or deductions and conclusions. As in sanctification he is a well of water springing up in the soul, immediately exerting his efficacy and refreshment; so in consolation, he immediately works the soul and minds of men to a joyful, rejoicing, and spiritual frame, filling them with exultation and gladness; -- not that this arises from our reflex consideration of the love of God, but rather gives occasion thereunto. When he so sheds abroad the love of God in our hearts, and so fills them with gladness by an immediate act and operation (as he caused John Baptist to leap for joy in the womb upon the approach of the mother of Jesus), -- then doth the soul, even from hence, raise itself to a consideration of the love of God, whence joy and rejoicing doth also flow. Of this joy there is no account to be given, but that the Spirit worketh it when and how he will. He secretly infuseth and distils it into the soul, prevailing against all fears and sorrows, filling it with gladness, exultations; and sometimes with unspeakable raptures of mind.

(2.) Mediately. By his other works towards us, he gives a sense of the love of God, with our adoption and acceptation with him; and on the consideration thereof enables us to receive it. Let what hath been spoken of his operations towards us be considered, -- what assurance he gives us of the love of God; what life, power, and security; what pledge of our eternal welfare, -- and it will be easily perceived that he lays a sufficient foundation of this joy and gladness. Not that we are able, upon any rational consideration, deduction, or conclusion, that we can make from the things mentioned, to affect our hearts with the joy and gladness intended; it is left no less the proper work of the Spirit to do it from hence, and by the intervenience of these considerations, than to do it immediately without them. This process of producing joy in the heart, we have, Ps. xxiii. 5, 6, "Thou anointest my head with oil." Hence is the conclusion, as in the way of exultation, "Surely goodness and mercy shall follow me." Of this effect of the Comforter, see Isa. xxxv. throughout.

4. Hope, also, is an effect of those workings of the Holy Ghost in us and towards us, Rom. xv. 13. These, I say, are the general consequents of the effects of the Holy Ghost upon the hearts of believers; which, if we might consider them in their offspring, with all the branches that shoot out from them, in exultation, assurance, boldness, confidence, expectation, glorying, and the like, it would appear how far our whole communion with God is influenced by them. But I only name the heads of things, and hasten to what remains. It is the general and particular way of our communion with the Holy Ghost that should nextly ensue, but that some other considerations necessarily do here interpose themselves.

Chapter V - Some observations and inferences from discourses foregoing concerning the Spirit -- The contempt of the whole administration of the Spirit by some -- The vain pretence of the Spirit by others -- The false spirit discovered.

This process being made, I should now show immediately, how we hold the communion proposed with the Holy Ghost, in the things laid down and manifested to contain his peculiar work towards us; but there are some miscarriages in the world in reference unto this dispensation of the Holy Ghost, both on the one hand and the other, in contempt of his true work and pretence of that which is not, that I cannot but remark in my passage: which to do shall be the business of this chapter.

Take a view, then, of the state and condition of them who, professing to believe the gospel of Jesus Christ, do yet contemn and despise his Spirit, as to all its operations, gifts, graces, and dispensations to his churches and saints. Whilst Christ was in the world with his disciples, he made them no greater promise, neither in respect of their own good nor of carrying on the work which he had committed to them, than this of giving them the Holy Ghost. Him he instructeth them to pray for of the Father, as that which is needful for them, as bread for children, Luke xi. 13. Him he promiseth them, as a well of water springing up in them, for their refreshment, strengthening, and consolation unto everlasting life, John vii. 37-39; as also to carry on and accomplish the whole work of the ministry to them committed, John xvi. 8-11; with all those eminent works and privileges before mentioned. And upon his ascension, this is laid as the bottom of that glorious communication of gifts and graces in his plentiful effusion mentioned, Eph. iv. 8, 11, 12, -- namely, that he had received of the Father the promise of the Holy Ghost, Act ii. 33; and that in such an eminent manner as thereby to make the greatest and most glorious difference between the administration of the new covenant and old. Especially doth the whole work of the ministry relate to the Holy Ghost; though that be not my present business to evince. He calls men to that work, and they are separated unto him, Acts xiii. 2; he furnisheth them with gifts and abilities for that employment, 1 Cor. xii. 7-10. So that the whole religion we profess, without this administration of the Spirit, is nothing; nor is there any fruit without it of the resurrection of Christ from the dead.

This being the state of things, -- that in our worship of and obedience to God, in our own consolation, sanctification, and ministerial employment, the Spirit is the principle, the life, soul, the all of the whole; yet so desperate hath been the malice of Satan, and wickedness of men, that their great endeavour hath been to shut him quite out of all gospel administrations.

First, his gifts and graces were not only decried, but almost excluded from the public worship of the church, by the imposition of an operose form of service, to be read by the minister; which to do is neither a peculiar gift of the

Holy Ghost to any, nor of the ministry at all. It is marvellous to consider what pleas and pretences were invented and used by learned men, -- from its antiquity, its composure and approbation by martyrs, the beauty of uniformity in the worship of God, established and pressed thereby, etc., -- for the defence and maintenance of it. But the main argument they insisted on, and the chief field wherein they expatiated and laid out all their eloquence, was the vain babbling repetitions and folly of men praying by the Spirit. When once this was fallen upon, all (at least as they supposed) was carried away before them, and their adversaries rendered sufficiently ridiculous: so great is the cunning of Satan, and so unsearchable are the follies of the hearts of men. The sum of all these reasonings amounts to no more but this, -- "Though the Lord Jesus Christ hath promised the Holy Ghost to be with his church to the end of the world, to fit and furnish men with gifts and abilities for the carrying on of that worship which he requires and accepteth at our hands, yet the work is not done to the purpose; the gifts he bestows are not sufficient to that end, neither as to invocation nor doctrine: and, therefore, we will not only help men by our directions, but exclude them from their exercise." This; I say, was the sum of all, as I could undeniably evidence, were that my present business, what innumerable evils ensue on this principle, in a formal setting apart of men to the ministry who had never once "tasted of the powers of the world to come," nor received any gifts from the Holy Ghost to that purpose; of crying up and growing in an outside pompous worship, wholly foreign to the power and simplicity of the gospel; of silencing, destroying, banishing, men whose ministry was accompanied with the evidence and demonstration of the Spirit, -- I shall not need to declare. This is that I aim at, to point out the public contempt of the Holy Ghost, his gifts and graces, with their administration in the church of God, that hath been found even where the gospel hath been professed.

Again: it is a thing of most sad consideration, once to call to mind the improvement of that principle of contempt of the Spirit in private men and their ways. The name of the Spirit was grown a term of reproach. To plead for, or pretend to pray by, the Spirit, was enough to render a man the object of scorn and reproach from all sorts of men, from the pulpit to the stage. "What! you are full of the Spirit; you will pray by the Spirit; you have the gift: let us hear your nonsense;" -- and yet, perhaps, these men would think themselves wronged not to be accounted Christians. Christians! yea, have not some pretending themselves to be leaders of the flock, -- yea, mounted a storey or two above their brethren, and claiming a rule and government over them, -- made it their business to scoff at and reproach the gifts of the Spirit of God? And if this were the frame of their spirit, what might be expected from others of professed profaneness? It is not imaginable to what height of blasphemy the process in this kind amounted. The Lord grant there be nothing of this cursed leaven still remaining amongst us! Some bleatings of ill importance [359] are sometimes heard. Is this the fellowship of the Holy Ghost that believers are called unto? Is this the due entertainment of him whom our Saviour promised to send for the supply of his bodily absence, so as we might be no losers thereby? Is it not enough that men should be contented with such a stupid blindness, as, being called Christians, to look no farther for their comfort and consolation than moral considerations common to heathens would lead them, when one infinitely holy and blessed person of the Trinity hath taken this office upon him to be our comforter, but they must oppose and despise him also? Nothing more discovers how few there are in the world that have interest in that blessed name whereby we are all called. But this is no place to pursue this discourse. The aim of this discourse is, to evince the folly and madness of men in general, who profess to own the gospel of Christ, and yet contemn and despise his Spirit, in whomsoever he is manifested. Let us be zealous of the gifts of the Spirit, not envious at them.

From what hath been discoursed we may also try the spirits that are gone abroad in the world, and which have been exercising themselves, at several seasons, ever since the ascension of Christ. The iniquity of the generation that is past and passing away lay in open, cursed opposition to the Holy Ghost. God hath been above them, wherein they behaved themselves presumptuously. Satan, whose design, as he is god of this world, is to be uppermost, not to dwell wholly in any form cast down by the providence of God, hath now transformed himself into an angel of light; and he will pretend the Spirit also and only. But there are "seducing spirits," 1 Tim. iv. 1; and we have a "command not to believe every spirit, but try the spirits," 1 John iv. 1; and the reason added is, "Because many false prophets are gone out into the world;" -- that is, men pretending to the revelation of new doctrines by the Spirit; whose deceits in the first church Paul intimateth, 2 Thess. ii. 2; calling on men not to be "shaken in mind by spirit." The truth is, the spirits of these days are so gross, that a man of a very easy discerning may find them out and yet their delusion so strong, that not a few are deceived. This is one thing that lies evident to every eye, -- that, according to his wonted course, Satan, with his delusions, is run into an extreme to his former actings.

Not long since, his great design, as I manifested, was to cry up ordinances without the Spirit, casting all the reproach that he could upon him; -- now, to cry up a spirit without and against ordinances, casting all reproach and contempt possible upon them. Then, he would have a ministry without the Spirit; -- now, a Spirit without a ministry. Then, the reading of the word might suffice, without either preaching or praying by the Spirit, -- now, the Spirit is enough, without reading or studying the word at all. Then, he allowed a literal embracing of what Christ had done in the flesh; -- now, he talks of Christ in the Spirit only, and denies him to be come in the flesh, -- the proper character of the false spirit we are warned of, 1 John iv. 1. Now, because it is most certain that the Spirit which we are to hear and embrace is the Spirit promised by Christ (which is so clear, that him the Montanists' paraclete, yea, and Mohammed, pretended himself to be, and those of our days affirm, who pretend the same), let us briefly try them by some of the effects mentioned, which Christ hath promised to give the Holy Ghost for:--

The first general effect, as was observed, was this, -- that he should bring to remembrance the things that Christ spake, for our guidance and consolation. This was to he the work of the Holy Ghost towards the apostles, who were to be the penmen of the Scriptures: this is to be his work towards believers to the end of the world. Now, the things that Christ hath spoken and done are "written that we might believe, and believing, have life through his name," John xx. 31; they are written in the Scripture. This, then, is the work of the Spirit which Christ hath promised; -- he shall bring to our remembrance, and give us understanding of the words of Christ in the Scripture, for our guidance and consolation. Is this, now, the work of the spirit which is abroad in the world, and perverteth many?

Nothing less. His business is, to decry the things that Christ hath spoken which are written in the word; to pretend new revelations of his own; to lead men from the written word, wherein the whole work of God and all the promises of Christ are recorded.

Again: the work of the Spirit promised by Christ is to glorify him: "He shall glorify me; for he shall receive of mine, and shall show it unto you," John xvi. 14. Him who was to suffer at Jerusalem, who then spake to his disciples, it was to make him glorious, honourable, and of high esteem in the hearts of believers; and that by showing his things (his love, kindness, grace, and purchase) unto them. This is the work of the Spirit. The work of the spirit that is gone abroad, is to glorify itself, to decry and render contemptible Christ that suffered for us, under the name of a Christ without us; which it slights and despiseth, and that professedly. Its own glory, its own honour, is all that it aims at; wholly inverting the order of the divine dispensations. The fountain of all being and lying in the Father's love, the Son came to glorify the Father. He still says, "I seek not mine own glory, but the glory of him that sent me." The Son having carried on the work of redemption, was now to be glorified with the Father. So he prays that it might be, John xvii. 1, "The hour is come, glorify thy Son;" and that with the glory which he had before the world was, when his joint counsel was in the carrying on the Father's love. Wherefore the Holy Ghost is sent, and his work is to glorify the Son. But now, as I said, we have a spirit come forth whose whole business is to glorify himself; whereby we may easily know whence he is.

Furthermore: the Holy Ghost sheds abroad the love of God in our hearts, as was declared, and thence fills them with joy, peace, and hope; quieting and refreshing the hearts of them in whom he dwells; giving them liberty and rest, confidence, and the boldness of children. This spirit whereof men now boast is a spirit of bondage, whose utmost work is to make men quake and tremble; casting them into an un-son-like frame of spirit, driving them up and down with horror and bondage, and drinking up their very natural spirits, and making their whole man wither away. There is scarce any one thing that more evidently manifesteth the spirit whereby some are now acted not to be the Comforter promised by Christ, than this, -- that he is a spirit of bondage and slavery in them in whom he is, and a spirit of cruelty and reproach towards others; in a direct opposition to the Holy Ghost in believers, and all the ends and purposes for which, as a spirit of adoption and consolation, he is bestowed on them.

To give one instance more: the Holy Ghost bestowed on believers is a Spirit of prayer and supplication; as was manifested. The spirit wherewith we have to do, pretends the carrying men above such low and contemptible means of communion with God. In a word, it were a very easy and facile task, to pass through all of the eminent effects of the Holy Ghost in and towards believers, and to manifest that the pretending spirit of our days comes in a direct opposition and contradiction to every one of them. Thus hath Satan passed from one extreme to another, -- from a bitter, wretched opposition to the Spirit of Christ, unto a cursed pretending to the Spirit; still to the same end and purpose.

I might give sundry other instances of the contempt or abuse of the dispensation of the Spirit. Those mentioned are the extremes whereunto all other are or may be reduced; and I will not farther divert from that which lies directly in my aim.

Footnotes:

359. Importance, is an obsolete sense of the word, import or meaning. -- Ed.

Chapter VI - Of particular communion with the Holy Ghost -- Of preparation thereunto -- Valuation of the benefits we receive by him -- What it is he comforts us in and against; wherewith; how.

The way being thus made plain for us, I come to show how we hold particular communion with the Holy Ghost, as he is promised of Christ to be our comforter, and as working out our consolation by the means formerly insisted on. Now, the first thing I shall do herein, is the proposal of that which may be some preparation to the duty under consideration; and this by leading the souls of believers to a due valuation of this work of his towards us, whence he is called our Comforter.

To raise up our hearts to this frame, and fit us for the duty intended, let us consider these three things:--

First, What it is he comforts us against.

Secondly, Wherewith he comforts us.

Thirdly, The principle of all his actings and operations in us for our consolation.

First. There are but three things in the whole course of our pilgrimage that the consolations of the Holy Ghost are useful and necessary in:--

1. In our afflictions. Affliction is part of the provision that God hath made in his house for his children, Heb. xii. 5, 6. The great variety of its causes, means, uses, and effects, is generally known. There is a measure of them appointed for every one. To be wholly without them is a temptation; and so in some measure an affliction. That which I am to speak unto is, that in all our afflictions we need the consolations of the Holy Ghost. It is the nature of man to relieve himself, when he is entangled, by all ways and means. According as men's natural spirits are, so do they manage themselves under pressures. "The spirit of a man will bear his infirmity;" at least, will struggle with it.

There are two great evils, one of which doth generally seize on men under their afflictions, and keep them from a due management of them. The apostle mentioneth them both, Heb. xii. 5, Μὴ ὀλιγώρει παιδείας Κυρίου, μηδὲ ἐκλύου, ὑπ' αὐτοῦ ἐλεγχόμενος, -- "Despise not the chastisement of the Lord; neither faint when thou art reproved." One of these extremes do men usually fall into; either they despise the Lord's correction, or sink under it.

(1.) Men despise it. They account that which befalls them to be a light or common thing; they take no notice of God in it; they can shift with it well enough: they look on instruments, second causes; provide for their own defence and vindication with little regard to God or his hand in their affliction. And the ground of this is, because they take in succours, in their trouble, that God will not mix his grace withal; they fix on other remedies than what he hath appointed, and utterly lose all the benefits and advantage of their affliction. And so shall every man do that relieves himself from any thing but the consolations of the Holy Ghost.

(2.) Men faint and sink under their trials and afflictions; which the apostle farther reproves, verse 12. The first despise the assistance of the Holy Ghost through pride of heart; the latter refuse it through dejectedness of spirit, and sink under the weight of their troubles. And who, almost, is there that offends not on one of these hands? Had we not learned to count light of the chastisements of the Lord, and to take little notice of his dealings with us, we should find the season of our afflictions to comprise no small portion of our pilgrimage.

Now, there is no due management of our souls under any affliction, so that God may have the glory of it, and ourselves any spiritual benefit or improvement thereby, but by the consolations of the Holy Ghost. All that our Saviour promiseth his disciples, when he tells them of the great trials and tribulations they were to undergo, is, "I will send you the Spirit, the Comforter; he shall give you peace in me, when in the world you shall have trouble. He shall guide and direct, and keep you in all your trials." And so, the apostle tells us, it came to pass, 2 Cor. i. 4-6; yea, and this, under the greatest afflictions, will carry the soul to the highest joy, peace, rest, and contentment. So the same apostle, Rom. v. 3, "We glory in tribulations." It is a great expression. He had said before, "We rejoice in hope of the glory of God," verse 2. Yea, but what if manifold afflictions and tribulations befall us? "Why, even in them also we glory," saith he; "we glory in our tribulations." But whence is it that our spirits are so borne up to a due management of afflictions, as to glory in them in the Lord? He tells us, verse 5, it is from the "shedding abroad of the love of God in our hearts by the Holy Ghost." And thence are believers said to "receive the word in much affliction, with joy of the Holy Ghost," 1 Thess. i. 6; and to "take joyfully the spoiling of their goods." This is that I aim at:-- there is no management nor improvement of any affliction, but merely and solely by the consolations of the Holy Ghost. Is it, then, of any esteem or value unto you that you lose not all your trials, temptations, and affliction? -- learn to value that whereby alone they are rendered useful.

2. Sin is the second burden of our lives, and much the greatest. Unto this is this consolation peculiarly suited. So Heb. vi. 17, 18, an allusion is taken from the manslayer under the law, who, having killed a man unawares, and brought the guilt of his blood upon himself, fled with speed for his deliverance to the city of refuge. Our great and only refuge from the guilt of sin is the Lord Jesus Christ; in our flying to him, doth the Spirit administer consolation to us. A sense of sin fills the heart with troubles and disquietness; it is the Holy Ghost which gives us peace in Christ; -- that gives an apprehension of wrath; the Holy Ghost sheds abroad the love of God in our hearts; -- from thence doth Satan and the law accuse us, as objects of God's hatred; the Spirit bears witness with our spirits that we are the children of God. There is not any one engine or instrument that sin useth or sets up against our peace, but one effect or other of the Holy Ghost towards us is suited and fitted to the casting of it down.

3. In the whole course of our obedience are his consolations necessary also, that we may go through with it cheerfully, willingly, patiently to the end. This will afterward be more fully discovered, as to particulars, when I come to give directions for our communion with this blessed Comforter. In a word, in all the concernments of this life, and in our whole expectation of another, we stand in need of the consolations of the Holy Ghost.

Without them, we shall either despise afflictions or faint under them, and God be neglected as to his intendments in them.

Without them, sin will either harden us to a contempt of it, or cast us down to a neglect of the remedies graciously provided against it.

Without them, duties will either puff us up with pride, or leave us without that sweetness which is in new obedience.

Without them, prosperity will make us carnal, sensual, and to take up our contentment in these things, and utterly weaken us for the trials of adversity.

Without them, the comforts of our relations will separate us from God, and the loss of them make our hearts as Nabal's.

Without them, the calamity of the church will overwhelm us, and the prosperity of the church will not concern us.

Without them, we shall have wisdom for no work, peace in no condition, strength for no duty, success in no trial, joy in no state, -- no comfort in life, no light in death.

Now, our afflictions, our sins, and our obedience, with the attendancies of them respectively, are the great concernments of our lives. What we are in reference unto God is comprised in them, and the due management of them, with their contraries, which come under the same rule; through all these doth there run a line of consolation from the Holy Ghost, that gives us a joyful issue throughout. How sad is the condition of poor souls destitute of these consolations. What poor shifts are they forced to betake themselves unto! what giants have they to encounter in their own strength! and whether they are conquered or seem to conquer, they have nothing but the misery of their trials!

The second thing considerable, to teach us to put a due valuation on the consolations of the Holy Ghost, is the matter of them, or that wherewith he comforts us. Now, this may be referred to the two heads that I have formerly treated of, -- the love of the Father, and the grace of the Son. All the consolations of the Holy Ghost consist in his acquainting us with, and communicating unto us, the love of the Father and the grace of the Son; nor is there any thing in the one or the other but he makes it a matter of consolation to us: so that, indeed, we have our communion with the Father in his love, and the Son in his grace, by the operation of the Holy Ghost.

1. He communicates to us, and acquaints us with, the love of the Father. Having informed his disciples with that ground and foundation of their consolation which by the Comforter they should receive, our blessed Saviour (John xvi. 27) shuts up all in this, "The Father himself loveth you." This is that which the Comforter is given to acquaint us withal, -- even that God is the Father, and that he loves us. In particular, that the Father, the first person in the Trinity, considered so distinctly, loves us. On this account is he said so often to come forth from the Father, because he comes in pursuit of his love, and to acquaint the hearts of believers therewith, that they may be comforted and established. By persuading us of the eternal and unchangeable love of the Father, he fills us with consolation. And, indeed, all the effects of the Holy Ghost before mentioned have their tendency this way. Of this love and its transcendent excellency you heard at large before. Whatever is desirable in it is thus communicated to us by the Holy Ghost. A sense of this is able not only to relieve us, but to make us in every condition to rejoice with joy unspeakable and glorious. It is not with an increase of corn, and wine, and oil, but with the

shining of the countenance of God upon us, that he comforts our souls, Ps. iv. 6, 7. "The world hateth me," may such a soul as hath the Spirit say; "but my Father loves me. Men despise me as a hypocrite; but my Father loves me as a child. I am poor in this world; but I have a rich inheritance in the love of my Father. I am straitened in all things; but there is bread enough in my Father's house. I mourn in secret under the power of my lusts and sin, where no eyes see me; but the Father sees me, and is full of compassion. With a sense of his kindness, which is better than life, I rejoice in tribulation, glory in affliction, triumph as a conqueror. Though I am killed all the day long, all my sorrows have a bottom that may be fathomed, -- my trials, bounds that may be compassed; but the breadth, and depth, and height of the love of the Father, who can express?" I might render glorious this way of the Spirit's comforting us with the love of the Father, by comparing it with all other causes and means of joy and consolation whatever; and so discover their emptiness, its fulness, -- their nothingness, its being all; as also by revealing the properties of it before rehearsed.

2. Again: he doth it by communicating to us, and acquainting us with, the grace of Christ, -- all the fruits of his purchase, all the desirableness of his person, as we are interested in him. The grace of Christ, as I formerly discoursed of at large, is referred to two heads, -- the grace of his person, and of his office and work. By both them doth the Holy Ghost administer consolation to us, John xvi. 14. He glorifies Christ by revealing his excellencies and desirableness to believers, as the "chiefest of ten thousand, -- altogether lovely," and then he shows them of the things of Christ, -- his love, grace, all the fruits of his death, suffering, resurrection, and intercession: and with these supports their hearts and souls. And here, whatever is of refreshment in the pardon of sin, deliverance from the curse, and wrath to come, in justification and adoption, with the innumerable privileges attending them in the hope of glory given unto us, comes in on this head of account.

Thirdly. The principle and fountain of all his actings for our consolation comes next under consideration, to the same end; and this leads us a little nearer to the communion intended to be directed in. Now, this is his own great love and infinite condescension. He willingly proceedeth or comes forth from the Father to be our comforter. He knew what we were, and what we could do, and what would be our dealings with him, -- he knew we would grieve him, provoke him, quench his motions, defile his dwelling-place; and yet he would come to be our comforter. Want of a due consideration of this great love of the Holy Ghost weakens all the principles of our obedience. Did this dwell and abide upon our hearts, what a dear valuation must we needs put upon all his operations and actings towards us! Nothing, indeed, is valuable but what comes from love and good-will. This is the way the Scripture takes to raise up our hearts to a right and due estimation of our redemption by Jesus Christ. It tells us that he did it freely; that of his own will he hath laid down his life; that he did it out of love. [360] "In this was manifested the love of God, that he laid down his life for us;" "He loved us, and gave himself for us;" "He loved us, and washed us from our sins in his own blood." Hereunto it adds our state and condition, considered as he undertook for us, -- sinners, enemies, dead, alienated; then he loved us, and died for us, and washed us with his blood. May we not hence, also, have a valuation of the dispensation of the Spirit for our consolation? He proceeds to that end from the Father; he distributes as he will, works as he pleaseth. And what are we, towards whom he carrieth on this work? Froward, perverse, unthankful; grieving, vexing, provoking him. Yet in his love and tenderness doth he continue to do us good. Let us by faith consider this love of the Holy Ghost. It is the head and source of all the communion we have with him in this life. This is, as I said, spoken only to prepare our hearts to the communion proposed; and what a little portion is it of what might be spoken! How might all these considerations be aggravated! what a numberless number might be added! It suffices that, from what is spoken, it appears that the work in hand is amongst the greatest duties and most excellent privileges of the gospel.

Footnotes:

360. 1 John iv. 9, iii. 16; Gal. ii. 20; Rev. i. 5.

Chapter VII - The general ways of the saints' acting in communion with the Holy Ghost.

As in the account given of the actings of the Holy Ghost in us, we manifested first the general adjuncts of his actings, or the manner thereof; so now, in the description of the returns of our souls to him, I shall, in the first place, propose the general actings of faith in reference to this work of the Holy Ghost, and then descend unto particulars. Now, there are three general ways of the soul's deportment in this communion, expressed all negatively in the Scripture, but all including positive duties. Now these are, -- First, Not to grieve him. Secondly, Not to quench his motions. Thirdly, Not to resist him.

There are three things considerable in the Holy Ghost:-- 1. His person, as dwelling in us; 2. His actings by grace, or his motions; 3. His working in the ordinances of the word, and the sacraments; -- all for the same end and purpose.

To these three are the three cautions before suited:-- 1. Not to grieve him, in respect of his person dwelling in us. 2. Not to quench him, in respect of the actings and motions of his grace. 3. Not to resist him, in respect of the ordinances of Christ, and his gifts for their administration. Now, because the whole general duty of believers, in their communion with the Holy Ghost, is comprised in these three things, I shall handle them severally:--

1. The first caution concerns his person immediately, as dwelling in us. It is given, Eph. iv. 30, "Grieve not the Holy Spirit of God." There is a complaint, Isa. lxiii. 10, of them who vexed or grieved the Spirit of God; and from thence doth this caution seem to be taken. That it is the person of the Holy Ghost which is here intended, is evident, --

(1.) From the phrase, or manner of expression, with a double article, Τὸ Πνεῦμα τὸ ἅγιον, -- "That Holy Spirit;" and also, --

(2.) From the work assigned to him in the following words, of "sealing to the day of redemption;" which, as hath been manifested, is the work of the Holy Ghost. Now, whereas this may be understood of the Spirit in others, or in ourselves, it is evident that the apostle intends it in the latter sense, by his addition of that signal and eminent privilege which we ourselves enjoy by him: he seals us to the day of redemption.

Let us see, then, the tendency of this expression, as comprising the first general rule of our communion with the Holy Ghost, -- "Grieve not the Spirit."

The term of "grieving," or affecting with sorrow, may be considered either actively, in respect of the persons grieving; or passively, in respect of the persons grieved. In the latter sense the expression is metaphorical. The Spirit cannot be grieved, or affected with sorrow; which infers alteration, disappointment, weakness, -- all incompatible with his infinite perfections; yet men may actively do that which is fit and able to grieve any one that stands affected towards them as doth the Holy Ghost. If he be not grieved, it is no thanks to us, but to his own unchangeable nature. So that there are two things denoted in this expression:--

First, That the Holy Ghost is affected towards us as one that is loving, careful, tender, concerned in our good and well-doing; and therefore upon our miscarriages is said to be grieved: as a good friend of a kind and loving nature is apt to be on the miscarriage of him whom he doth affect. And this is that we are principally to regard in this caution, as the ground and foundation of it, -- the love, kindness, and tenderness of the Holy Ghost unto us. "Grieve him not."

Secondly, That we may do those things that are proper to grieve him, though he be not passively grieved; our sin being no less therein than if he were grieved as we are. Now, how this is done, how the Spirit is grieved, the apostle declareth in the contexture of that discourse, verses 21-24. He presseth to a progress in sanctification, and all the fruits of regeneration, verses 25-29. He dehorts from sundry particular evils that were contrary thereto, and then gives the general enforcement of the one and the other, "And grieve not the Holy Spirit of God;" that is, by coming short of that universal sanctification which our planting into Christ doth require. The positive duty included in this caution, of not grieving the Holy Spirit, is this, -- that we pursue universal holiness with regard unto, and upon the account of, the love, kindness, and tenderness, of the Holy Ghost. This is the foundation of our communion we have in general. When the soul considers the love, kindness, and tenderness of the Holy Ghost unto him; when he considers all the fruits and acts of his love and good-will towards him; and on that account, and under that consideration, because he is so concerned in our ways and walkings, to abstain from evils, and to walk in all duties of holiness, -- this is to have communion with him. This consideration, that the Holy Ghost, who is our comforter, is delighted with our obedience, grieved at our evils and follies, being made a continual motive to, and reason of, our close walking with God in all holiness, is, I say, the first general way of our communion with him.

Here let us fix a little. We lose both the power and pleasure of our obedience for want of this consideration. We see on what account the Holy Ghost undertakes to be our comforter, by what ways and means he performs that office towards us; what an unworthy thing it is to grieve him, who comes to us on purpose to give us consolation! Let the soul, in the whole course of its obedience, exercise itself by faith to thoughts hereof, and lay due weight upon it: "The Holy Ghost, in his infinite love and kindness towards me, hath condescended to be my comforter; he doth it willingly, freely, powerfully. What have I received from him! in the multitude of my perplexities how hath he refreshed my soul! Can I live one day without his consolations? And shall I be regardless of him in that wherein he is concerned? Shall I grieve him by negligence, sin, and folly? Shall not his love constrain me to walk before him to all well-pleasing?" So have we in general fellowship with him.

2. The second is that of 1 Thess. v. 19, "Quench not the Spirit." There are various thoughts about the sense of these words. "The Spirit in others, that is, their spiritual gifts," say some; but then it falls in with what follows, verse 20, "Despise not prophesying." "The light that God hath set up in our hearts," say others; but where is that called absolutely Τὸ Πνεῦμα, -- "The Spirit?" It is the Holy Ghost himself that is here intended, not immediately, in respect of his person (in which regard he is said to be grieved, which is a personal affection); but in respect of his motions, actings, and operations. The Holy Ghost was typified by the fire that was always kept alive on the altar. He is also called a

"Spirit of burning." The reasons of that allusion are manifold; not now to be insisted on. Now, the opposition that is made to fire in its actings, is by quenching. Hence the opposition made to the actings of the Holy Ghost are called "quenching of the Spirit," as some kind of wet wood will do, when it is cast into the fire. Thence are we said, in pursuance of the same metaphor, ἀναζωπυρεῖν, -- to "stir up with new fire," the gifts that are in us. The Holy Ghost is striving with us, acting in us, moving variously for our growth in grace, and bringing forth fruit meet for the principle he hath endued us withal. "Take heed," saith the apostle, "lest, by the power of your lusts and temptations, you attend not to his workings, but hinder him in his good-will towards you; that is, what in you lieth."

This, then, is the second general rule for our communion with the Holy Ghost. It respects his gracious operations in us and by us. There are several and various ways whereby the Holy Ghost is said to act, exert, and put forth his power in us; partly by moving upon and stirring up the grace we have received; partly by new supplies of grace from Jesus Christ, falling in with occasions for their exercise, raising good motions immediately or occasionally within us; -- all tending to our furtherance in obedience and walking with God. All these are we carefully to observe and take notice of, -- consider the fountain whence they come, and the end which they lead us unto. Hence have we communion with the Holy Ghost, when we can consider him by faith as the immediate author of all supplies, assistance, and the whole relief we have by grace; of all good actings, risings, motions in our hearts; of all strivings and contending against sin. When we consider, I say, all these his actings and workings in their tendency to our consolation, and on that account are careful and watchful to improve them all to the end aimed at, as coming from him who is so loving, and kind, and tender to us, we have communion with him.

This is that which is intended, -- every gracious acting of the blessed Spirit in and towards our souls, is constantly by faith to be considered as coming from him in a peculiar manner; his mind, his goodwill is to be observed therein. Hence, care and diligence for the improvement of every motion of his will arise; thence reverence of his presence with us, with due spiritual regard to his holiness, doth ensue, and our souls are wonted to intercourse with him.

3. The third caution concerns him and his work, in the dispensation of that great ordinance of the word. Stephen tells the Jews, Acts vii. 51, that they "resisted the Holy Ghost." How did they do it? Why, as their fathers did it: "As your fathers did, so do ye." How did their fathers resist the Holy Ghost? Verse 52, "They persecuted the prophets, and slew them;" their opposition to the prophets in preaching the gospel, or their showing of the coming of the Just One, was their resisting of the Holy Ghost. Now, the Holy Ghost is said to be resisted in the contempt of the preaching of the word; because the gift of preaching of it is from him. [361] "The manifestation of the Spirit is given to profit." Hence, when our Saviour promiseth the Spirit to his disciples, to be present with them for the conviction of the world, he tells them he will give them a mouth and wisdom, which their adversaries shall not be able to gainsay nor resist, Luke xxi. 15; concerning which, in the accomplishment of it in Stephen, it is said that they "were not able to resist the Spirit by which he spake," Acts vi. 10. The Holy Ghost then setting up a ministry in the church, separating men thereto, furnishing them with gifts and abilities for the dispensation of the word; the not obeying of that word, opposing of it, not

falling down before it, is called resisting of the Holy Ghost. This, in the examples of the wickedness of others, are we cautioned against. And this inwraps the third general rule of our communion with the Holy Ghost:-- in the dispensation of the word of the gospel, the authority, wisdom, and goodness of the Holy Ghost, in furnishing men with gifts for that end and purpose, and his presence with them, as to the virtue thereof, is to be eyed, and subjection given unto it on that account. On this reason, I say, on this ground, is obedience to be yielded to the word, in the ministerial dispensation thereof, -- because the Holy Ghost, and he alone, doth furnish with gifts to that end and purpose. When this consideration causeth us to fall low before the word, then have we communion with the Holy Ghost in that ordinance. But this is commonly spoken unto.

Footnotes:

361. 1 Cor. xii. 7.

Chapter VIII - Particular directions for communion with the Holy Ghost.

Before I name particular directions for our communion with the Holy Ghost, I must premise some cautions, as far as the directions to be given, concerning his worship.

First. The divine nature is the reason and cause of all worship; so that it is impossible to worship any one person, and not worship the whole Trinity. It is, and that not without ground, denied by the schoolmen, that the formal reason and object of divine worship is in the persons precisely considered; that is, under the formally-constitutive reason of their personality, which is their relation to each other. But this belongs to the divine nature and essence, and to their distinct persons as they are identified with the essence itself. Hence is that way of praying to the Trinity, by the repetition of the same petition to the several persons (as in the Litany), groundless, if not impious. It supposeth that one person is worshipped, and not another, when each person is worshipped as God, and each person is so; -- as though we first should desire one thing of the Father, and be heard and granted by him, then ask the same thing of the Son, and so of the Holy Ghost; and so act as to the same thing three distinct acts of worship, and expect to be heard and have the same thing granted three times distinctly, when all the works of the Trinity, ad extra, are indivisible.

The proper and peculiar object of divine worship and invocation is the essence of God, in its infinite excellency, dignity, majesty, and its causality, as the first sovereign cause of all things. Now, this is common to all the three persons, and is proper to each of them; not formally as a person, but as God blessed for ever. All adoration respects that which is common to all; so that in each act of adoration and worship, all are adored and worshipped. The creatures worship their Creator; and a man, him in whose image he was created, -- namely, him "from whom descendeth every good and perfect gift:" all this describing God as God. Hence, --

Secondly. When we begin our prayers to God the Father, and end them in the name of Jesus Christ, yet the Son is no less invocated and worshipped in the beginning than the Father, though he be peculiarly mentioned as mediator in the close, -- not as Son to himself, but as mediator to the whole Trinity, or God in Trinity. But in the invocation of God the Father we invocate every person; because we invocate the Father as God, every person being so.

Thirdly. In that heavenly directory which we have, Eph. ii. 18, this whole business is declared. Our access in our worship is said to be "to the Father;" and this "through Christ," or his mediation; "by the Spirit," or his assistance. Here is a distinction of the persons, as to their operations, but not at all as to their being the object of our worship. For the Son and the Holy Ghost are no less worshipped in our access to God than the Father himself; only, the grace of the Father, which we obtain by the mediation of the Son and the assistance of the Spirit, is that which we draw nigh to God for. So that when, by the distinct dispensation of the Trinity, and every person, we are led to worship (that is, to act faith on or invocate) any person, we do herein worship the whole Trinity; and every person, by what name soever, of Father, Son, or Holy Ghost, we invocate him. So that this is to be observed in this whole matter, -- that when any work of the Holy Ghost (or any other person), which is appropriated to him (we never exclude the concurrence of other persons), draws us to the worship of him, yet he is not worshipped exclusively, but the whole Godhead is worshipped.

Fourthly. These cautions being premised, I say that we are distinctly to worship the Holy Ghost. As it is in the case of faith in respect of the Father and the Son, John xiv. 1, "Believe in God, believe also in me," -- this extends itself no less to the Holy Ghost. Christ called the disciples for the acting of faith on him, he being upon the accomplishment of the great work of his mediation; and the Holy Ghost, now carrying on the work of his delegation, requireth the same. And to the same purpose are their distinct operations mentioned: "My Father worketh hitherto, and I work." Now, as the formal reason of the worship of the Son is not his mediation, but his being God (his mediation being a powerful motive thereto), so the formal reason of our worshipping the Holy Ghost is not his being our comforter, but his being God; yet his being our comforter is a powerful motive thereunto.

This is the sum of the first direction:-- the grace, actings, love, effects of the Holy Ghost, as he is our comforter, ought to stir us up and provoke us to love, worship, believe in, and invocate him; -- though all this, being directed to him as God, is no less directed, on that account, to the other persons than to him. Only by the fruits of his love towards us are we stirred up unto it.

These things being presupposed, let the saints learn to act faith distinctly on the Holy Ghost, as the immediate efficient cause of all the good things mentioned; -- faith, I say, to believe in him; and faith in all things to believe him and to yield obedience to him; faith, not imagination. The distinction of the persons in the Trinity is not to be fancied, but believed. So, then, the Scripture so fully, frequently, clearly, distinctly ascribing the things we have been speaking of to the immediate efficiency of the Holy Ghost, faith closes with him in the truth revealed, and peculiarly regards him, worships him, serves him, waits for him, prayeth to him, praiseth him; -- all these things, I say, the saints do in faith. The person of the Holy Ghost, revealing itself in these operations and effects, is the peculiar object of our worship. Therefore, when he ought to be peculiarly honoured, and is not, he is peculiarly sinned against. Acts v. 3, Ananias is said to lie to the Holy Ghost, -- not to God; which being taken essentially, would denote the whole Trinity, but peculiarly to the Holy Ghost. Him he was to have honoured peculiarly in that especial gift of his which he made profession of; -- not doing it, he sinned peculiarly against him. But this must be a little farther branched into particulars:--

Let us, then, lay weight on every effect of the Holy Ghost in any of the particulars before mentioned, on this account, that they are acts of his love and power towards us. This faith will do, that takes notice of his kindness in all things. Frequently he performs, in sundry particulars, the office of a comforter towards us, and we are not thoroughly comforted, -- we take no notice at all of what he doth. Then is he grieved. Of those who do receive and own the consolation he tenders and administers, how few are there that consider him as the comforter, and rejoice in him as they ought! Upon every work of consolation that the believer receives, this ought his faith to resolve upon, -- "This is from the Holy Ghost; he is the Comforter, the God of all consolation; I know there is no joy, peace, hope, nor comfort, but what he works, gives, and bestows; and, that he might give me this consolation, he hath willingly condescended to this office of a comforter. His love was in it, and on that account doth he continue it. Also, he is sent by the Father and Son for that end and purpose. By this means come I to be partaker of my joy, -- it is in the Holy Ghost; of consolation, -- he is the Comforter. What price, now, shall I set upon his love! how shall I value the mercy that I have received!"

This, I say, is applicable to every particular effect of the Holy Ghost towards us, and herein have we communion and fellowship with him, as was in part discovered in our handling the particulars. Doth he shed abroad the love of God in our hearts? doth he witness unto our adoption? The soul considers his presence, ponders his love, his condescension, goodness, and kindness; is filled with reverence of him, and cares [takes care] not to grieve him, and labours to preserve his temple, his habitation, pure and holy.

Again: our communion with him causeth in us returning praise, and thanks, and honour, and glory, and blessing to him, on the account of the mercies and privileges which we receive from him; which are many. Herein consists our next direction. So do we with the Son of God on the account of our redemption: "Unto him that loved us, and washed us from our sins in his own blood, to him be glory and dominion for ever and ever," Rev. i. 5, 6. And are not the like praises and blessings due to him by whom the work of redemption is made effectual to us? who with no less infinite love undertook our consolation than the Son our redemption. When we feel our hearts warmed with joy, supported in peace, established in our obedience, let us ascribe to him the praise that is due to him, bless his name, and rejoice in him.

And this glorifying of the Holy Ghost in thanksgivings, on a spiritual sense of his consolations, is no small part of our communion with him. Considering his free engagement in this work, his coming forth from the Father to this purpose, his mission by the Son, and condescension therein, his love and kindness, the soul of a believer is poured out in thankful praises to him, and is sweetly affected with the duty. There is no duty that leaves a more heavenly savour in the soul than this doth.

Also, in our prayers to him for the carrying on the work of our consolation, which he hath undertaken, lies our communion with him. John prays for grace and peace from the seven Spirits that are before the throne, or the Holy Ghost, whose operations are perfect and complete. This part of his worship is expressly mentioned frequently in Scripture; and all others do necessarily attend it. Let the saints consider what need they stand in of these effects of the Holy Ghost before mentioned, with many such others as might be insisted on; weigh all the privileges which we are made partakers of; remember that he distributes them as he will, that he hath the sovereign disposal of them; and they will be prepared for this duty.

How and in what sense it is to be performed hath been already declared: what is the formal reason of this worship, and ultimate object of it, I have also manifested. In the duty itself is put forth no small part of the life, efficacy, and vigour of faith; and we come short of that enlargedness of spirit in dealing with God, and are straitened from walking in the breadth of his ways, which we are called unto, if we learn not ourselves to meet him with his worship in every way he is pleased to communicate himself unto us. In these things he doth so in the person of the Holy Ghost. In that person do we meet him, his love, grace, and authority, by our prayers and supplications.

Again: consider him as he condescends to this delegation of the Father and the Son to be our comforter, and ask him daily of the Father in the name of Jesus Christ. This is the daily work of believers. They look upon, and by faith consider, the Holy Ghost as promised to be sent. In this promise, they know, lies all their grace, peace, mercy, joy, and hope. For by him so promised, and him alone, are these things communicated to them. If, therefore, our life to God, or the joy of that life, be considerable, in this we are to abound, -- to ask him of the Father, as children do of their parents daily bread. And as, in this asking and receiving of the Holy Ghost, we have communion with the Father in his love, whence he is sent; and with the Son in his grace, whereby he is obtained for us; so with himself, on the account of his voluntary condescension to this dispensation. Every request for the Holy Ghost implies our closing with all these. O the riches of the grace of God!

Humbling ourselves for our miscarriages in reference to him is another part of our communion with him. That we have grieved him as to his person, quenched him as to the motion of his grace, or resisted him in his ordinances, is to be mourned for; as hath been declared. Let our souls be humbled before him on this account. This one considerable ingredient of godly sorrow, and the thoughts of it, are as suitable to the affecting of our hearts with humiliation, and indignation against sin, as any other whatever. I might proceed in the like considerations; as also make application of them to the particular effects of the Holy Ghost enumerated; but my design is only to point out the heads of things, and to leave them to the improvement of others.

I shall shut up this whole discourse with some considerations of the sad estate and condition of men not interested in this promise of the Spirit, nor made partakers of his consolation:--

1. They have no true consolation or comfort, be their estate and condition what it will. Are they under affliction or in trouble? -- they must bear their own burden; and how much too weak they are for it, if God be pleased to lay on his hand with more weight than ordinary, is easily known. Men may have stoutness of spirit, and put on great resolutions to wrestle with their troubles; but when this is merely from the natural spirit of a man, --

(1.) For the most part it is but an outside. It is done with respect to others, that they may not appear low-spirited or dejected. Their hearts are eaten up and devoured with troubles and anxiety of mind. Their thoughts are perplexed, and they are still striving, but never come to a conquest. Every new trouble, every little alteration in their trials, puts them to new vexation. It is an ungrounded resolution that bears them up, and they are easily shaken.

(2.) What is the best of their resolves and enduring? It is but a contending with God, who hath entangled them, -- the struggling of a flea under a mountain. Yea, though, on outward considerations and principles, they endeavour after patience and tolerance, yet all is but a contending with God, -- a striving to be quiet under that which God hath sent on purpose to disturb them. God doth not afflict men without the Spirit, to exercise their patience; but to disturb their peace and security. All their arming themselves with patience and resolution, is but to keep the hold that God will cast them out of, or else make them the nearer to ruin. This is the best of their consolation in the time of their trouble.

(3.) If they do promise themselves any thing of the care of God towards them, and relieve themselves thereby, -- as they often do, on one account or another, especially when they are driven from other holds, -- all their relief is but like the dreaming of an hungry man, who supposeth that he eateth and drinketh, and is refreshed; but when he awaketh, he is empty and disappointed. So are they as to all their relief that they promise to receive from God, and the support which they seem to have from him. When they are awaked at the latter day, and see all things clearly, they will find that God was their enemy, laughing at their calamity, and mocking when their fear was on them.

So is it with them in trouble. Is it any better with them in their prosperity? This, indeed, is often great, and is marvellously described in Scripture, as to their lives, and oftentimes quiet, peaceable end. But have they any true consolation all their days? They eat, drink, sleep, and make merry, and perhaps heap up to themselves; but how little do these things make them to differ from the beasts that perish! Solomon's advantage, to have the use and know the utmost of these things, much beyond any of the sons of men of our generation, is commonly taken notice of. The account also that he gives of them is known: "They are all vanity and vexation of spirit." This is their consolation:-- a crackling of thorns under the pot, a sudden flash and blaze, that begins but to perish. So that both adversity and prosperity slayeth them; and whether they are laughing or crying, they are still dying.

2. They have no peace, -- no peace with God, nor in their own souls. I know that many of them, upon false bottoms, grounds, and expectations, do make a shift to keep things in some quietness, neither is it my business at present to discover the falseness and unsoundness of it; but this is their state. True and solid peace being an effect of the Holy Ghost in the hearts of believers (as hath been declared), they who are not made partakers of him have no such peace. They may cry, "Peace, peace," indeed, when sudden destruction is at hand. The principles of their peace (as may be easily evinced) are, darkness or ignorance, treachery of conscience, self-righteousness, and vain hope. To these heads may all the principles of their peace be reduced; and what will these avail them in the day when the Lord shall deal with them?

3. I might say the same concerning their joy and hope; -- they are false and perishing. Let them, then, consider this, who have satisfied themselves with a persuasion of their interest in the good things of the gospel, and yet have despised the Spirit of Christ. I know there are many that may pretend to him, and yet are strangers from his grace; but if they perish who in profession use him kindly, and honour him, if he dwell not in them with power, where shall they appear who oppose and affront him? The Scripture tells us, that unless the Spirit of Christ be in us, we are dead, we are reprobates, -- we are none of Christ's. Without him you can have none of those glorious effects of his towards believers before mentioned; and you are so far from inquiring whether he be in you or no, as that you are ready to deride them in whom he is. Are there none who profess the gospel, who have never once seriously inquired whether they are made partakers of the Holy Ghost or no? You that almost account it a ridiculous thing to be put upon any such question, who look on all men as vain pretenders that talk of the Spirit, the Lord awake such men to a

sight of their condition before it be too late! If the Spirit dwell not in you, if he be not your Comforter, neither is God your Father, nor the Son your Advocate, nor have you any portion in the gospel. O that God would awake some poor soul to the consideration of this thing, before the neglect and contempt of the Holy Ghost come to that despising of him from which there is no recovery! that the Lord would spread before them all the folly of their hearts, that they may be ashamed and confounded, and do no more presumptuously!

A Vindication of some Passages in a Discourse Concerning Communion with God, from the Exceptions of William Sherlock, Rector of St George, Botolph Lane

Prefatory Note.

William Sherlock, father of Dr Thomas Sherlock, an eminent bishop of London, was himself distinguished as an author, and mingled deeply in the controversies of his day. His strictures on Owen's work on Communion with God appeared in 1674, after that work had been seventeen years before the public. It seems to have been Sherlock's first appearance in authorship; and some of his subsequent treatises such as those on Providence and on Death afford a better specimen of his abilities. They are destitute of evangelical principle and feeling, and imbued throughout with a freezing rationalism of tone; but, nevertheless, contain some views of the Divine administration, acutely conceived and ably stated. He became rector of St George, Botolph Lane, received a prebend in St Paul's, and was appointed Master of the Temple about 1684. His conduct at the Revolution was not straightforward, and laid him open to the reproaches of the Jacobites, who blamed him for deserting their party. There was a controversy of some importance between him and Dr South. The latter, on the ground of some expressions in the work by the former on the Trinity (1690), accused him of Tritheism. Sherlock retorted by accusing his critic of Sabellianism. He died in 1707, at the age of sixty-six.

Sherlock's work against Owen was entitled, "A Discourse concerning the Knowledge of Jesus Christ, and on Union and Communion with Him," etc. Owen confines himself, in his reply, to an exposure of the misrepresentations in which Sherlock had indulged. The latter, for example, sought to fix on the Puritan divine the doctrine, that the knowledge of divine things was to be obtained from the person of Christ, apart from the truth as revealed in the Scriptures. Our author successfully vindicates himself from this charge, and repudiates other sentiments equally mystical, and ascribed to him with equal injustice. The views of Sherlock, on the points at issue, have been termed, "a confused mass of Socinianized Arminianism." Owen evinces a strength of feeling, in some parts of his "Vindication," which may be accounted for on the ground that he resented the attack as part of a systematic effort made at this time to destroy his standing and reputation as an author. In the main, there is a dignity in his statements which contrasts well with the wayward petulance of his antagonist; and occasionally the reader will find a vein of quiet and skilful irony, in the way in which he disposes of the crude views of Sherlock.

Such was the beginning of the Communion Controversy, which soon embraced a wider range of topics, and points of more importance, than the merits of Owen's book. Besides the original disputants, others entered the field.

Robert Ferguson in 1675, wrote against Sherlock a volume entitled, "The Interest of Reason in Religion," etc. Edward Polhill followed, in "An Answer to the Discourse of Mr William Sherlock," etc. Vincent Alsop first displayed in this controversy his powers of wit and acumen as an author, in his "Antisozzo, or Sherlocismus Enervatus." Henry Hickman, a man of considerable gifts, and pastor of an English congregation at Leyden, wrote the "Speculum Sherlockianum," etc. Samuel Rollè, a nonconformist, wrote the "Prodromus, or the Character of Mr Sherlock's Book;" and also, in the same controversy, "Justification Justified." Thomas Danson, who had been ejected from Sibton, and author of several works against the Quakers, wrote "The Friendly Debate between Satan and Sherlock," and afterwards he published again in defence of it. Sherlock, in 1675, replied to Owen and Ferguson in his "Defence and Continuation of the Discourse concerning the Knowledge of Jesus Christ." He was supported by Thomas Hotchkis, Rector of Staunton, in a "Discourse concerning the Imputation of Christ's Righteousness," etc. The singular diligence of Mr Orme hath compiled this full list of the works published in this controversy; but he is not quite correct in affirming that it was closed by the replies of Sherlock and Hotchkis in 1675. A second part of the work by Hotchkis appeared in 1678, and Sherlock was the author of two other works, "An Answer to Thomas Danson's scandalous pamphlet, entitled A Friendly Conference,'?" etc., which appeared in 1677, and was followed by a "Vindication of Mr Sherlock against the Cavils of Mr Danson." -- Ed.

A Vindication of some Passages in a Discourse concerning Communion with God.

It is now near twenty years since I wrote and published a Discourse concerning Communion with God. Of what use and advantage it hath been to any, as to their furtherance in the design aimed at therein, is left unto them to judge by whom it hath been perused with any candid diligence; and I do know that multitudes of persons fearing God, and desiring to walk before him in sincerity, are ready, if occasion require, to give testimony unto the benefit which they have received thereby; -- as I can also at any time produce the testimonies of [as] learned and holy persons, it may be, as any I know living, both in England and out of it, who, owning the truth contained in it, have highly avowed its usefulness, and are ready yet so to do. With all other persons, so far as ever I heard, it passed at the rate of a tolerable acceptation with discourses of the same kind and nature. And however any thing or passage in it might not, possibly, suit the apprehensions of some, yet, being wholly practical, designed for popular edification, without any direct engagement into things controversial, I looked for no opposition unto it or exception against it; but that it would at least be suffered to pass at that rate of allowance which is universally granted unto that sort of writings, both of ancient and modern authors. Accordingly it so fell out, and continued for many years; until some persons began to judge it their interest, and to make it their business, to cavil at my writings, and to load my person with reproaches. With what little success, as to their avowed designs, they have laboured therein, -- how openly their endeavours are sunk into contempt with all sorts of persons pretending unto the least sobriety or modesty, -- I suppose they are not themselves altogether insensible. Among the things which this sort of men sought to make an advantage of against me, I found that two or three of them began to reflect on that discourse; though it appeared they had not satisfied themselves what as yet to fix upon, their nibbling cavils being exceedingly ridiculous.

But yet, from those intimations of some men's good-will towards it, -- sufficient to provoke the industry of such as either needed their assistance or valued their favour, -- I was in expectation that one or other would possess that province, and attempt the whole discourse or some parts of it. Nor was I dissatisfied in my apprehensions of that design; for, being earnestly solicited to suffer it to be reprinted, I was very willing to see what either could or would be objected against it before it received another impression. For whereas it was written now near twenty years ago, when there was the deepest peace in the minds of all men about the things treated of therein, and when I had no apprehension of any dissent from the principal design, scope, and parts of it by any called Christians in the world, the Socinians only excepted (whom I had therein no regard unto), I thought it highly probable that some things might have been so expressed as to render a review and amendment to them more than ordinarily necessary. And I reckoned it not improbable, but that from one malevolent adversary I might receive a more instructive information of such escapes of diligence than I could do in so long a time from all the more impartial readers of it; for as unto the substance of the doctrine declared in it, I was sufficiently secure, not only of its truth, but that it would immovably endure the rudest assaults of such oppositions as I did expect. I was therefore very well satisfied when I heard of the publishing of this treatise of Mr Sherlock's, -- which, as I was informed, and since have found true, was principally intended against myself, and that discourse (that is, that book), because I was the author of it, which will at last prove it to be its only guilt and crime; -- for I thought I should be at once now satisfied, both what it was which was so long contriving against it (whereof I could give no conjecture), as also be directed unto any such mistakes as might have befallen me in matter or manner of expression, which I would or might rectify before the book received another edition. But, upon a view and perusal of this discourse, I found myself under a double surprisal. For, first, in reference to my own, I could not find any thing, any doctrine, any expressions, any words reflected on, which the exceptions of this man do give me the least occasion to alter, or to desire that they had been otherwise either expressed or delivered; -- not any thing which now, after near twenty years, I do not still equally approve of, and which I am not yet ready to justify. The other part of my surprisal was somewhat particular, though, in truth, it ought to have been none at all; and this was with respect unto those doctrinal principles which he manageth his oppositions upon. A surprisal they were unto me, because wild, uncouth, extravagant, and contrary to the common faith of Christians, -- being all of them traduced, [362] and some of them transcribed, from the writings of the Socinians; [while] yet [they] ought not to have been so, because I was assured that an opposition unto that discourse could be managed on no other [ground]. But, however, the doctrine maintained by this man, and those opposed or scorned by him, are not my special concernment; for what is it to me what the Rector of etc., preacheth or publisheth, beyond my common interest in the truths of the gospel, with other men as great strangers unto him as myself, who to my knowledge never saw him, nor heard of his name till infamed by his book? Only, I shall take leave to say, that the doctrine here published, and licensed so to be, is either the doctrine of the present church of England, or it is not. If it be so, I shall be forced to declare that I neither have, nor will have, any communion therein; and that, as for other reasons, so in particular, because I will not renounce or depart from that which I know to be the true, ancient, and catholic doctrine of this church. If it be not so, -- as I am assured, with respect unto many bishops and other learned men, that it is not, -- it is certainly the concernment of them who preside therein to take care that such kind of discourses be not countenanced with the stamp of their public authority, lest they and the church be represented unto a great disadvantage with many.

It was some months after the publishing of this discourse, before I entertained any thoughts of taking the least notice of it, -- yea, I was resolved to the contrary, and declared those resolutions as I had occasion; neither was it until very lately that my second thoughts came to a compliance with the desires of some others, to consider my own peculiar concernment therein. And this is all which I now design; for the examination of the opinions which this author hath vented under the countenance of public licence, whatever they may think,

I know to be more the concernment of other men than mine. Nor yet do I enter into the consideration of what is written by this author with the least respect unto myself, or my own reputation, which I have the satisfaction to conceive not to be prejudiced by such pitiful attempts; nor have I the least desire to preserve it in the minds of such persons as wherein it can suffer on this occasion. But the vindication of some sacred truths, petulantly traduced by this author, seems to be cast on me in an especial manner; because he hath opposed them, and endeavoured to expose them to scorn, as declared in my book; whence others, more meet for this work, might think themselves discharged from taking notice of them. Setting aside this consideration, I can freely give this sort of men leave to go on with their revilings and scoffings until they are weary or ashamed; which, as far as I can discern, upon consideration of their ability for such a work, and their confidence therein, is not like to be in haste; -- at least, they can change their course, and when they are out of breath in pursuit of one sort of calumnies, betake themselves unto another. Witness the late malicious, and yet withal ridiculous, reports that they have divulged concerning me, even with respect unto civil affairs, and their industry therein; for although they were such as had not any thing of the least probability or likelihood to give them countenance, yet were they so impetuously divulged, and so readily entertained by many, as made me think there was more than the common artifices of calumny employed in their raising and improvement, especially considering what persons I can justly charge those reports upon. But in this course they may proceed whilst they please and think convenient: I find myself no more concerned in what they write or say of this nature than if it were no more but, --

 ? ἐπεὶ ἤτε κακῷ οὔτ' ἄφρονι φωτὶ ἔοικας. [363]

Οὖλέ τε, καὶ μέγα χαῖρε, Θεοὶ δέ τοι ὄλβια δοῖε. [364]

It is the doctrine traduced only that I am concerned about, and that as it hath been the doctrine of the church of England.

It may be it will be said (for there is no security against confidence and immodesty, backed with secular advantages), that the doctrinal principles asserted in this book are agreeable with the doctrine of the church in former times; and therefore those opposed in it, such as are condemned thereby. Hereabout I shall make no long contest with them who once discover that their minds are by any means emboldened to undertake the defence of such shameless untruths; nor shall I multiply testimonies to prove the contrary, which others are more concerned to do, if they intend not to betray the religion of that church with whose preservation and defence they are intrusted. Only, because there are ancient divines of this church, who, I am persuaded, will be allowed with the most to have known as well the doctrine of it, and as firmly to have adhered thereunto, as this author, who have particularly spoken unto most of the things which he hath opposed, or rather reproached, I shall transcribe the words of one of them, whereby he, and those who employ him, may be minded with whom they have to do in those things. For, as to the writers of the ancient church, there is herein no regard had unto them. He whom I shall name is Mr Hooker, and that in his famous book of "Ecclesiastical Polity;" who, in the fifth book thereof, and 56th paragraph, thus discourseth:--

"We have hitherto spoken of the person and of the presence of Christ. Participation is that mutual inward hold which Christ hath of us, and we of him, in such sort that each possesseth other by way of special interest, property, and inherent copulation." And after the interposition of some things conceding the mutual in-being and love of the Father and the Son, he thus proceedeth:-- "We are by nature the sons of Adam. When God created Adam, he created us; and as many as are descended from Adam have in themselves the root out of which they spring. The sons of God we neither are all nor any one of us, otherwise than only by grace and favour. The sons of God have God's own natural Son as a second Adam from heaven; whose race and progeny they are by spiritual and heavenly birth. God therefore loving eternally his Son, he must needs eternally in him have loved, and preferred before all others, them which are spiritually since descended and sprung out of him. These were in God as in their Saviour, and not as in their Creator only. It was the purpose of his saving goodness, his saving wisdom, and his saving power, which inclined itself towards them. They which thus were in God eternally by their intended admission to life, have, by vocation or adoption, God actually now in them, as the artificer is in the work which his hand doth presently frame. Life, as all other gifts and benefits, groweth originally from the Father, and cometh not to us but by the Son, nor by the Son to any of us in particular, but through the Spirit. For this cause the apostle wisheth to the church of Corinth, the grace of our Lord Jesus Christ, and the love of God, and the fellowship of the Holy Ghost;' which three St Peter comprehendeth in one, -- the participation of the divine nature. We are, therefore, in God through Christ eternally, according to that intent and purpose whereby we are chosen to be made his in this present world before the world itself was made. We are in God through the knowledge which is had of us, and the love which is borne towards us from everlasting; but in God we actually are no longer than only from the time of our actual adoption into the body of his true church, into the fellowship of his children. For his church he knoweth and loveth; so that they which are in the church are thereby known to be in him. Our being in Christ by eternal foreknowledge saveth us not, without our actual and real adoption into the fellowship of his saints in this present world. For in him we actually are by our actual incorporation into that society which hath him for their head, and doth make together with him one body (he and they in that respect having one name); for which cause, by virtue of this mystical conjunction, we are of him, and in him, even as though our very flesh and bones should be made continuate with his. We are in Christ, because he knoweth and loveth us, even as parts of himself. No man is actually in him but they in whom he actually is; for he which hath not the Son of God hath not life. I am the vine, ye are the branches: he that abideth in me, and I in him, the same bringeth forth much fruit;' but the branch severed from the vine withereth. We are, therefore, adopted sons of God to eternal life by participation of the only begotten Son of God, whose life is the well-spring and cause of ours. It is too cold an interpretation, whereby some men expound our being in Christ to import nothing else but only that the self-same nature which maketh us to be men is in him, and maketh him man as we are. For what man in the world is there which hath not so far forth communion with Jesus Christ? It is not this that can sustain the weight of such sentences as speak of the mystery of our coherence with Jesus Christ. The church is in Christ, as Eve was in Adam. Yea, by grace we are every [one] of us in Christ and in his church, as by nature we were in those, our first parents. God made Eve of the rib of Adam; and his church he frameth out of the very flesh, the very wounded and bleeding side, of the Son of man. His body crucified, and his blood shed for the life of the world, are the true elements of that heavenly being which maketh us such as himself is of whom we come. For which cause the words of Adam may be fitly the words of Christ concerning his church, Flesh of my flesh, and bone of my bones;' -- A true nature, extract out of mine own body.' So that in him, even according to his manhood, we, according to our heavenly being, are as branches in that root out of which they grow. To all things he is life, and to men light, as the Son of God; to the church, both life and light eternal, by being made the Son of man for us, and by being in us a Saviour, whether we respect him as God or as man. Adam is in us as an original cause of our nature, and of that corruption of nature which causeth death; Christ as the cause original of restoration to life. The person of Adam is not in us, but his nature, and the corruption of his nature, derived into all men by propagation. Christ having Adam's nature, as we have, but incorrupt, deriveth not nature but incorruption, and that immediately from his own person, into all that belong unto him. As, therefore, we are really partakers of the body of sin and death received from Adam; so, except we be truly partakers of Christ, and as really possessed of his Spirit, all we speak of eternal life is but a dream. That which quickeneth us is the Spirit of the second Adam, and his flesh that wherewith he quickeneth. That which in him made our nature incorrupt was the union of his Deity with our nature. And in that respect the sentence of death and condemnation, which only taketh hold upon sinful flesh, could no way possibly extend unto him. This caused his voluntary death for others to prevail with God, and to have the force of an expiatory sacrifice. The blood of Christ, as the apostle witnesseth, doth, therefore, take away sin; because, Through the eternal Spirit he offered himself unto God without spot.' That which sanctified our nature in Christ, -- that which made it a sacrifice available to take away sin, is the same which quickened it, raised it out of the grave after death, and exalted it unto glory. Seeing, therefore, that Christ is in us a quickening Spirit, the first degree of communion with Christ must needs consist in the participation of his Spirit, which Cyprian in that respect terms germanissimam societatem,' -- the highest and truest society that can be between man and him, which is both God and man in one. These things St Cyril duly considering, reproveth their speeches which taught that only the Deity of Christ is the vine whereupon we by faith do depend as branches, and that neither his flesh nor our bodies are comprised in this resemblance. For doth any man doubt but that even from the flesh of Christ our very bodies do receive that life which shall make them glorious at the latter day; and for which they are already accounted parts of his blessed body? Our corruptible bodies could never live the life they shall live, were it not that here they are joined with his body, which is incorruptible; and that his is in ours as a cause of immortality, -- a cause, by removing, through the death and merit of his own flesh, that which hindered the life of ours. Christ is, therefore, both as God and as man, that true vine whereof we both spiritually and corporally are branches. The mixture of his bodily substance with ours is a thing which the ancient fathers disclaim. Yet the mixture of his flesh with ours they speak of, to signify what our very bodies, through mystical conjunction, receive from that vital efficacy which we know to be in his; and from bodily mixtures they borrow divers similitudes, rather to declare the truth than the manner of coherence between his sacred [body] and the sanctified bodies of saints. Thus much no Christian man will deny, that when Christ sanctified his own flesh, giving as God, and taking as man, the Holy Ghost, he did not this for himself only, but for our sakes, that the grace of sanctification and life, which was first received in him, might pass from him to his whole race, as malediction came from Adam into all mankind. Howbeit, because the work of his Spirit to those effects is in us prevented by sin and death possessing us before, it is of necessity that as well our present sanctification into newness of life, as the future restoration of our bodies, should presuppose a participation of the grace, efficacy, merit, or virtue of his body and blood; -- without which foundation first laid, there is no place for those other operations of the Spirit of Christ to ensue. So that Christ imparteth plainly himself by degrees. It pleaseth him, in mercy, to account himself incomplete and maimed without us. But most assured we are, that we all receive of his fulness, because he is in us as a moving and working cause; from which many blessed effects are really found to ensue, and that in sundry both kinds and degrees, all tending to eternal happiness. It must be confessed, that of Christ working as a creator and a governor of the world, by providence all are partakers; -- not all partakers of that grace whereby he inhabiteth whom he saveth. Again: as he dwelleth not by grace in all, so neither doth he equally work in all them in whom he dwelleth. Whence is it,' saith St Augustine, that some be holier than others are, but because God doth dwell in some more plentifully than in others?' And because the divine substance of Christ is equally in all, his human substance equally distant from all, it appeareth that the participation of Christ, wherein there are many degrees and differences, must needs consist in such effects as, being derived from both natures of Christ really into us, are made our own: and we, by having them in us, are truly said to have him from whom they come; Christ also, more or less, to inhabit and impart himself, as the graces are fewer or more, greater or smaller, which really flow into us from Christ. Christ is whole with the whole church, and whole with every part of the church, as touching his person, which can no way divide itself, or be possessed by degrees and portions. But the participation of Christ importeth, besides the presence of Christ's person, and besides the mystical copulation thereof with the parts and members of his whole church, a true actual influence of grace, whereby the life which we live according to godliness is his; and from him we receive those perfections wherein our eternal happiness consisteth. Thus we participate Christ:-- partly by imputation; as when those things which he did and suffered for us are imputed unto us for righteousness; partly by habitual and real infusion; as when grace is inwardly bestowed while we are on earth; -- and afterward more fully, both our souls and bodies made like unto his in glory. The first thing of his so infused into our hearts in this life is the Spirit of Christ; whereupon, because the rest, of what kind soever, do all both necessarily depend and infallibly also ensue, therefore the apostles term it sometimes the seed of God, sometimes the pledge of our heavenly inheritance, sometimes the hansel or earnest of that which is to come. From whence it is that they which belong to the mystical body of our Saviour Christ, and be in number as the stars of heaven, -- divided successively, by reason of their mortal condition, into many generations, -- are, notwithstanding, coupled every one to Christ their head, and all unto every particular person amongst themselves; inasmuch as the same Spirit which anointed the blessed soul of our Saviour Christ doth so formalise, unite, and actuate his whole race, as if both he and they were so many limbs compacted into one body, by being quickened all with one and the same soul. That wherein we are partakers of Jesus Christ by imputation, agreeth equally unto all what have it; for it consisteth in such acts and deeds of his as could not have longer continuance than while they were in doing, nor at that very time belong unto any other but to him from whom they come: and therefore, how men, either then, or before, or since, should be made partakers of them, there can be no way imagined but only by imputation. Again: a deed must either not be imputed to any, but rest altogether in him whose it is; or, if at all it be imputed, they which have it by imputation must have it such as it is, -- whole. So that degrees being neither in the personal presence of Christ, nor in the participation of those effects which are ours by imputation only, it resteth that we wholly apply them to the participation of Christ's infused grace; although, even in this kind also, the first beginning of life, the seed of God, the first-fruits of Christ's Spirit, be without latitude. For we have hereby only the being of the sons of God: in which number, how far soever one may seem to excel another, yet touching this, that all are sons, they are all equals; some, happily, better sons than the rest are, but none any more a son than another. Thus, therefore, we see how the Father is in the Son, and the Son in the Father; how they both are in all things, and all things in them: what communion Christ hath with his church; how his church, and every member thereof, is in him by original derivation, and he personally in them, by way of mystical association, wrought through the gift of the Holy Ghost; which they that are his receive from him, and, together with the same, what benefit soever the vital force of his body and blood may yield; -- yea, by steps and degrees they receive the complete measure of all such divine grace as doth sanctify and save throughout, till the day of their final exaltation to a state of fellowship in glory with him, whose partakers they are now in those things that tend to glory."

This one testimony ought to be enough unto this sort of men, whilst they are at any consistency with their own reputation: for it is evident that there is nothing concerning personal election, effectual vocation, justification by the imputation of the righteousness of Christ, participation of him, union of believers unto and with his person, derivation of grace from him, etc., which are so reproached by our present author, but they are asserted by this great champion of the church of England, who undoubtedly knew the doctrine which it owned, and in his days approved, and that in such words and expressions, as remote from the sentiments, or at least as unsavoury to the palates, of these men, as any they except against in others.

And what themselves so severely charge on us in point of discipline, that nothing be spoken about it until all is answered that is written by Mr Hooker in its defence, may, I hope, not immodestly be so far returned, as to desire them that in point of doctrine they will grant us truce, until they have moved out of the way what is written to the same purpose by Mr Hooker. Why do not they speak to him to leave fooling, and to speak sense, as they do to others? But let these things be as they are; I have no especial concernment in them, nor shall take any farther notice of them, but only as they influence the exceptions which this author makes unto some passages in that book of mine. And in what I shall do herein, I shall take as little notice as may be of those scurrilous and reproachful expressions, which either his inclination or his circumstances induced him to make use of. If he be pleased with such a course of procedure, I can only assure him, that as to my concernment, I am not displeased; and so he is left unto his full liberty for the future.

The first thing he quarrels about, is my asserting the necessity of acquaintance with the person of Christ; which expression he frequently makes use of afterward in a way of reproach. The use of the word "acquaintance," in this matter, is warranted by our translation of the Scripture, and that properly, where it is required of us to acquaint ourselves with God. And that I intended nothing thereby but the knowledge of Jesus Christ, is evident beyond any pretence to the contrary to be suggested by the most subtle or inventive malice. The crime, therefore, wherewith I am here charged, is my assertion that it is necessary that Christians should know Jesus Christ; which I have afterward increased, by affirming also that they ought to love him: for by Jesus Christ all the world of Christians intend the person of Christ; and the most of them, all of them, -- the Socinians only excepted, -- by his person, "the Word made flesh," or the Son of God incarnate, the mediator between God and man. For because the name Christ is sometimes used metonymically, to conclude thence that Jesus Christ is not Jesus Christ, or that it is not the person of Christ that is firstly and properly intended by that name in the gospel, is a lewd and impious imagination; and we may as well make Christ to be only a light within us, as to be the doctrine of the gospel without us. This knowledge of Jesus Christ I aver to be the only fountain of all saving knowledge: which is farther reflected on by this author; and he adds (no doubt out of respect unto me), "that he will not envy the glory of this discovery unto its author;" and therefore honestly confesseth that he met with it in my book. But what doth he intend? Whither will prejudice and corrupt designs carry and transport the minds of men? Is it possible that he should be ignorant that it is the duty of all Christians to know Jesus Christ, to be acquainted with the person of Christ, and that this is the fountain of all saving knowledge, until he met with it in my book about communion with God; which I dare say he looked not into, but only to find what he might except against? It is the Holy Ghost himself that is the author of this discovery; and it is the great fundamental principle of the gospel. Wherefore, surely, this cannot be the man's intention; and therefore we must look a little farther, to see what it is that he aimeth at. After, then, the repetition of some words of mine, he adds, as his sense upon them, p. 39, "So that it seems the gospel of Christ makes a very imperfect and obscure discovery of the nature, attributes, and the will of God, and the methods of our recovery. We may thoroughly understand whatever is revealed in the gospel, and yet not have a clear and saving knowledge of these things, until we get a more intimate acquaintance with the person of Christ." And again, p. 40: "I shall show you what additions these men make to the gospel of Christ by an acquaintance with his person; and I confess I am very much beholden to this author, for acknowledging whence they fetch all their orthodox and gospel mysteries, for I had almost pored my eyes out with seeking for them in the gospel, but could never find them; but I learn now, that indeed they are not to be found there, unless we be first acquainted with the person of Christ." So far as I can gather up the sense of these loose expressions, it is, that I assert a knowledge of the person of Jesus Christ which is not revealed in the gospel, which is not taught us in the writings of Moses, the prophets, or apostles, but must be had some other way. He tells me afterward, p. 41, that I put in a word fallaciously, which expresseth the contrary; as though I intended another knowledge of Christ than

 the Trinity*

what is declared in the gospel. Now, he either thought that this was not my design or intention, but would make use of a pretence of it for his advantage unto an end aimed at (which what it was I know well enough); or he thought, indeed, that I did assert and maintain such a knowledge of the person of Christ as was not received by Scripture revelation. If it was the first, we have an instance of that new morality which these new doctrines are accompanied withal; if the latter, he discovers how meet a person he is to treat of things of this nature. Wherefore, to prevent such scandalous miscarriages, or futilous imaginations for the future, I here tell him, that if he can find in that book, or any other of my writings, any expression, or word, or syllable, intimating any knowledge of Christ, or any acquaintance with the person of Christ, but what is revealed and declared in the gospel, in the writings of Moses, the prophets, and apostles, and as it is so revealed and declared, and learned from thence, I will publicly burn that book with my own hands, to give him and all the world satisfaction. Nay, I say more: if an angel from heaven pretend to give any other knowledge of the person of Christ, but what is revealed in the gospel, let him be accursed. And here I leave this author to consider with himself, what was the true occasion why he should first thus represent himself unto the world in print, by the avowing of so unworthy and notorious a calumny.

Whereas, therefore, by an acquaintance with the person of Christ, it is undeniably evident that I intended nothing but that knowledge of Christ which it is the duty of every Christian to labour after, -- no other but what is revealed, declared, and delivered in the Scripture, as almost every page of my book doth manifest where I treat of these things; I do here again, with the good leave of this author, assert, that this knowledge of Christ is very necessary unto Christians, and the fountain of all saving knowledge whatever. And as he may, if he please, review the honesty and truth of that passage, p. 38, "So that our acquaintance with Christ's person, in this man's divinity, signifies such a knowledge of what Christ is, hath done, and suffered for us, from whence we may learn those greater, deeper, and more saving mysteries of the gospel, which Christ hath not expressly revealed to us;" so I will not so far suspect the Christianity of them with whom we have to do, as to think it necessary to confirm by texts of Scripture either of these assertions; which whoever denies is an open apostate from the gospel.

Having laid this foundation in an equal mixture of that truth and sobriety wherewith sundry late writings of this nature and to the same purpose have been stuffed, he proceeds to declare what desperate consequences ensue upon the necessity of that knowledge of Jesus Christ which I have asserted, addressing himself thereunto, p. 40.

Many instances of such dealings will make me apt to think that some men, whatever they pretend to the contrary, have but little knowledge of Jesus Christ indeed. But whatever this man thinks of him, an account must one day be given before and unto him of such false calumnies as his lines are stuffed withal. Those who will believe him, that he hath almost "pored out his eyes" in reading the gospel, with a design to find out mysteries that are not in it, are left by me to their liberty; only I cannot but say, that his way of expressing the study of the Scripture, is [not?] such as becometh a man of his wisdom, gravity, and principles. He will, I hope, one day be better acquainted with what belongs unto the due investigation of sacred truth in the Scripture, than to suppose it represented by such childish expressions. What he hath learned from me I know not; but that I have anywhere taught that there are mysteries of religion that are not to be found in the gospel, unless we are first acquainted with the person of Christ, is a frontless and impudent falsehood. I own no other, never taught other knowledge of Christ, or acquaintance with his person, but what is revealed and declared in the gospel; and therefore, no mysteries of religion can be thence known and received, before we are acquainted with the gospel itself. Yet I will mind this author of that, whereof if he be ignorant, he is unfit to be a teacher of others, and which if he deny, he is unworthy the name of a Christian, -- namely, that by the knowledge of the person of Christ, the great mystery of God manifest in the flesh, as revealed and declared in the gospel, we are led into a clear and full understanding of many other mysteries of grace and truth; which are all centred in his person, and without which we can have no true nor sound understanding of them. I shall speak it yet again, that this author, if it be possible, may understand it; or, however, that he and his co-partners in design may know that I neither am nor ever will be ashamed of it:-- that without the knowledge of the person of Christ, which is our acquaintance with him (as we are commanded to acquaint ourselves with God) as he is the eternal Son of God incarnate, the mediator between God and man, with the mystery of the love, grace, and truth of God therein, as revealed and declared in the Scripture, there is no true, useful, saving knowledge of any other mysteries or truths of the gospel to be attained. This being the substance of what is asserted in my discourse, I challenge this man, or any to whose pleasure and favour his endeavours in this kind are sacrificed, to assert and maintain the contrary, if so be they are indeed armed with such a confidence as to impugn the foundations of Christianity.

But to evince his intention, he transcribeth the ensuing passages out of my discourse:-- P. 41, "The sum of all true wisdom and knowledge may be reduced to these three heads:-- 1. The knowledge of God; his nature and properties. 2. The knowledge of ourselves with reference to the will of God concerning us. 3. Skill to walk in communion with God. In these three is summed up all true wisdom and knowledge, and not any of them is to any purpose to be obtained, or is manifested, but only in and by the Lord Christ."

This whole passage I am far from disliking, upon this representation of it, or any expression in it. Those who are not pleased with this distribution of spiritual wisdom, may make use of any such of their own wherewith they are better satisfied. This of mine was sufficient unto my purpose. Hereon this censure is passed by him:-- "Where by is fallaciously added to include the revelations Christ hath made; whereas his first undertaking was, to show how impossible it is to understand these things savingly and clearly, notwithstanding all those revelations God hath made of himself and his will by Moses and the prophets, and by Christ himself, without an acquaintance with his person." The fallacy pretended is merely of his own coining; my words are plain, and suited unto my own purpose, and to declare my mind in what I intend; which he openly corrupting, or not at all understanding, frames an end never thought of by me, and then feigns fallacious means of attaining it. The knowledge I mean is to be learned by Christ; neither is any thing to be learned in him but what is learned by him. I do say, indeed, now, whatever I have said before, that it is impossible to understand any sacred truth savingly and clearly, without the knowledge of the person of Christ; and shall say so still, let this man and his companions say what they will to the contrary: but that in my so saying I exclude the consideration of the revelations which Christ hath made, or that God hath made of himself by Moses and the prophets, and Christ himself, the principal whereof concern his person, and whence alone we come to know him, is an assertion becoming the modesty and ingenuity of this author. But hereon he proceeds, and says, that as to the first head he will take notice of those peculiar discoveries of the nature of God of which the world was ignorant before, and of which revelation is wholly silent, but are now clearly and savingly learned from an acquaintance with Christ's person. But what, in the meantime, is become of modesty, truth, and honesty? Do men reckon that there is no account to be given of such falsifications? Is there any one word or tittle in my discourse of any such knowledge of the nature or properties of God as whereof revelation is wholly silent? What doth this man intend? Doth he either not at all understand what I say; or doth he not care what he says himself? What have I done to him? wherein have I injured him? how have I provoked him, that he should sacrifice his conscience and reputation unto such a revenge? Must he yet hear it again? I never thought, I never owned, I never wrote, that there was any acquaintance to be obtained with any property of the nature of God by the knowledge of the person of Christ, but what is taught and revealed in the gospel; from whence alone all knowledge of Christ, his person, and his doctrine, is to be learned. And yet I will say again, if we learn not thence to know the Lord Christ, -- that is, his person, -- we shall never know any thing of God, ourselves, or our duty, clearly and savingly (I use the words again, notwithstanding the reflections on them, as more proper in this matter than any used by our author in his eloquent discourse), and as we ought to do. From hence he proceeds unto weak and confused discourses about the knowledge of God and his properties without any knowledge of Christ; for he not only tells us "what reason we had to believe such and such things of God, if Christ had never appeared in the world," (take care, I pray, that we be thought as little beholden to him as may be), "but that God's readiness to pardon, and the like, are plainly revealed in the Scripture, without any farther acquaintance with the person of Christ," p. 43. What this farther acquaintance with the person of Christ should mean, I do not well understand: it may be, any more acquaintance with respect unto some that is necessary; -- it may be, without any more ado as to an acquaintance with him. And if this be his intention, -- as it must be, if there be sense in his words, -- that God's readiness to pardon sinners is revealed in the Scripture without respect unto the person of Jesus Christ, it is a piece of dull Socinianism; which, because I have sufficiently confuted else where, I shall not here farther discover the folly of. [As] for a knowledge of God's essential properties by the light of nature, it was never denied by me; yea, I have written and contended for it in another way than can be impeached by such trifling declamations. But yet, with his good leave, I do believe that there is no saving knowledge of, or acquaintance with God or his properties, to be attained, but in and through Jesus Christ, as revealed unto us in the gospel. And this I can confirm with testimonies of the Scripture, fathers, schoolmen, and divines of all sorts, with reasons and arguments, such as I know this author cannot answer. And whatever great apprehensions he may have of his skill and abilities to know God and his properties by the light of nature, now that he neither knows nor is able to distinguish what he learns from thence, and what he hath imbibed in his education from an emanation of divine revelation; yet I believe there were as wise men as himself amongst those ancient philosophers, concerning whom and their inquiries into the nature of God our apostle pronounces those censures, Rom. i.; 1 Cor. i.

But on this goodly foundation he proceeds unto a particular inference, p. 44, saying, "And is not this a confident man, to tell us that the love of God to sinners, and his pardoning mercy, could never have entered into the heart of man but by Christ, when the experience of the whole world confutes him? For, whatever becomes of his new theories, both Jews and heathens, who understood nothing at all of what Christ was to do in order to our recovery, did believe God to be gracious and merciful to sinners, and had reason to do so; because God himself had assured the Jews that he was a gracious and merciful God, pardoning iniquity, transgressions, and sins. And those natural notions heathens had of God, and all those discoveries God had made of himself in the works of creation and providence, did assure them that God is very good: and it is not possible to understand what goodness is, without pardoning grace."

I beg his excuse: truth and good company will give a modest man a little confidence sometimes; and against his experience of the whole world, falsely pretended, I can oppose the testimonies of the Scripture, and all the ancient writers of the church, very few excepted. We can know of God only what he hath, one way or other, revealed of himself, and nothing else; and I say again, that God hath not revealed his love unto sinners, and his pardoning mercy, any other way but in and by Jesus Christ. For what he adds as to the knowledge which the Jews had of these things by God's revelation in the Scripture, when he can prove that all those revelations, or any of them, had not respect unto the promised seed, -- the Son of God, -- to be exhibited in the flesh to destroy the works of the devil, he will speak somewhat unto his purpose. In the meantime, this insertion of the consideration of them who enjoyed that revelation of Christ which God was pleased to build his church upon under the Old Testament, is weak and impertinent. Their apprehensions, I acknowledge, concerning the person of Christ, and the speciality of the work of his mediation, were dark and obscure; but so, also, proportionally was their knowledge of all other sacred truths, which yet with all diligence they inquired into. That which I intended is expressed by the apostle, 1 Cor. ii. 9, 10, "It is written, Eye hath not seen, nor ear heard, neither have entered into the heart of man, the things which God hath prepared for them that love him. But God hath revealed them unto us by his Spirit." What a confident man was this apostle, as to affirm that the things of the grace and mercy of God did never enter into the heart of man to conceive, nor would so have done, had they not been revealed by the Spirit of God in the gospel through Jesus Christ!

But this is only a transient charge. There ensues that which is much more severe, p. 45; as, for instance, "He tells us, that in Christ' (that is, in his death and sufferings for our sins) God hath manifested the naturalness of this righteousness' (that is, vindictive justice in punishing sin), that it was impossible that it should be diverted from sinners without the interposing of a propitiation; that is, that God is so just and righteous, that he cannot pardon sin without satisfaction to his justice.' Now, this indeed is such a notion of justice as is perfectly new, which neither Scripture nor nature acquaints us with; for all mankind have accounted it an act of goodness, without the least suspicion of injustice in it, to remit injuries and offences without exacting any punishment, -

- that he is so far from being just, that he is cruel and savage, who will remit no offence till he hath satisfied his revenge." The reader who is in any measure or degree acquainted with these things, knows full well what is intended by that which I have asserted. It is no more but this, -- that such is the essential holiness and righteousness of the nature of God, that, considering him as the supreme governor and ruler of all mankind, it was inconsistent with the holiness and rectitude of his rule, and the glory of his government, to pass by sin absolutely, or to pardon it without satisfaction, propitiation, or atonement. This, I said, was made evident in the death and sufferings of Christ, wherein God made all our iniquities to meet upon him, and spared him not, that we might obtain mercy and grace. This is here now called out by our author as a very dangerous or foolish passage in my discourse, which he thought he might highly advantage his reputation by reflecting upon. But as the orator said to his adversary, "Equidem vehementer lætor eum esse me, in quem tu cum cuperes, nullam contumeliam jacere potueris, quæ non ad maximam partem civium convenerit," -- so it is here fallen out. If this man knows not that this is the judgment of the generality of the most learned divines of Europe upon the matter, of all who have engaged with any success against the Socinians, one or two only excepted, I can pity him, but not relieve him in his unhappiness, unless he will be pleased to take more pains in reading good books than as yet he appeareth to have done. But for the thing itself, and his reflections upon it, I shall observe yet some few things, and so pass on; -- as first, the opposition that he makes unto my position is nothing but a crude assertion of one of the meanest and most absurd sophisms which the Socinians use in this cause, -- namely, that everyone may remit injuries and offences as he pleaseth, without exacting any punishment: which, as it is true in most cases of injuries and offences against private persons, wherein no others are concerned but themselves, nor are they obliged by any law of the community to pursue their own right; so, with respect unto public rulers of the community, and unto such injuries and offences as are done against supreme rule, tending directly unto the dissolution of the society centring in it, to suppose that such rulers are not obliged to inflict those punishments which justice and the preservation of the community doth require, is a fond and ridiculous imagination, -- destructive, if pursued, unto all human society, and rendering government a useless thing in the world. Therefore, what this author (who seems to understand very little of these things) adds, "that governors may spare or punish as they see reason for it;" if the rule of that reason and judgment be not that justice which respects the good and benefit of the society or community, they do amiss, and sin, in sparing and punishing: which I suppose he will not ascribe unto the government of God. But I have fully debated these things in sundry writings against the Socinians; so that I will not again enlarge upon them without a more important occasion. It is not improbable but he knows where to find those discourses; and he may, when he please, exercise his skill upon them. Again: I cannot but remark upon the consequences that he chargeth this position withal; and yet I cannot do it without begging pardon for repeating such horrid and desperate blasphemies. P. 46, "The account," saith he, "of this is very plain; because the justice of God hath glutted itself with revenge on sin in the death of Christ, and so henceforward we may be sure he will be very kind, as a revengeful man is when his passion is over." P. 47, "The sum of which is, that God is all love and patience when he hath taken his fill of revenge; as others use to say that the devil is very good when he is pleased." P. 59, "The justice and vengeance of God, having their actings assigned them to the full, being glutted and satiated with the blood of Christ, God may," etc. I desire the reader to remember that the supposition whereon all these inferences are built, is only that of the necessity of the satisfaction of Christ with respect unto the holiness and righteousness of God as the author of the law, and the supreme governor of mankind. And is this language becoming a son of the church of England? Might it not be more justly expected from a Jew or a Mohammedan, -- from Servetus or Socinus, from whom it is borrowed, -- than from a son of this church, in a book published by licence and authority? But it is to no purpose to complain: those who are pleased with these things, let them be so. But what if, after all, these impious, blasphemous consequences do follow as much upon this author's opinion as upon mine, and that with a greater show of probability? and what if, forgetting himself, within a few leaves he says the very same thing that I do, and casts himself under his own severest condemnation?

For the first: I presume he owns the satisfaction of Christ, and I will suppose it until he directly denies it; therefore, also, he owns and grants that God would not pardon any sin, but upon a supposition of a previous satisfaction made by Jesus Christ. Here, then, lies all the difference between us; -- that I say God could not, with respect unto his holiness and justice, as the author of the law and governor of the world, pardon sin absolutely without satisfaction: he says, that although he might have done so without the least diminution of his glory, yet he would not, but would have his Son by his death and suffering to make satisfaction for sin. I leave it now, not only to every learned and impartial reader, but to every man in his wits who understands common sense, whether the blasphemous consequences, which I will not again defile ink and paper with the expression of, do not seem to follow more directly upon his opinion than mine. For whereas I say not that God requireth any thing unto the exercise of grace and mercy, but what he grants that he doth so also; -- only I say he doth it because requisite unto his justice; he, because he chose it by a free act of his will and wisdom, when he might have done otherwise, without the least disadvantage unto his righteousness or rule, or the least impeachment to the glory of his holiness. The odious blasphemies mentioned do apparently seem to make a nearer approach unto his assertion than unto mine. I cannot proceed unto a farther declaration of it, because I abhor the rehearsal of such horrid profaneness. The truth is, they follow not in the least (if there be any thing in them but odious satanical exprobrations of the truth of the satisfaction of Christ) on either opinion; though I say this author knows not well how to discharge himself of them.

But what if he be all this while only roving in his discourse about the things that he hath no due comprehension of, merely out of a transporting desire to gratify himself and others, in traducing and making exceptions against my writings? What if, when he comes a little to himself, and expresseth the notions that have been instilled into him, he saith expressly as much as I do, or have done in any place of my writings? It is plain he doth so, p. 49, in these words:-- "As for sin, the gospel assures us that God is an irreconcilable enemy to all wickedness, it being so contrary to his own most holy nature, that if he have any love for himself, and any esteem for his own perfections and works, he must hate sin, which is so unlike himself, and which destroys the beauty and perfection of his workmanship. For this end he sent his Son into the world to destroy the works of the devil," etc. Here is the substance of what at any time on this subject I have pleaded for:-- "God is an irreconcilable enemy to all wickedness," -- that it "is contrary to his holy nature, so that he must hate it; and therefore sends his Son," etc. If sin be contrary to God's holy nature, -- if he must hate it, unless he will not love himself, nor value his own perfections, and therefore sent his Son to make satisfaction, we are absolutely agreed in this matter, and our author hath lost "operam et oleum" in his attempt. But for the matter itself, if he be able to come unto any consistency in his thoughts, or to know what is his own mind therein, I do hereby acquaint him that I have written one entire discourse [365] on that subject, and have lately reinforced the same argument in my Exercitations on the Epistle to the Hebrews, wherein my judgment on this point is declared and maintained. Let him attempt an answer, if he please, unto them, or do it if he can. What he farther discourseth on this subject, pp. 46, 47, consisteth only in odious representations and vile reflections on the principal doctrines of the gospel, not to be mentioned without offence and horror. But as to me, he proceeds to except, after his scoffing manner, against another passage, pp. 47, 48, -- "But, however, sinners have great reasons to rejoice in it, when they consider the nature and end of God's patience and forbearance towards them, -- viz., That it is God's taking a course, in his infinite wisdom and goodness, that we should not be destroyed notwithstanding our sins; that as before, the least sin could not escape without punishment, justice being so natural to God that he cannot forgive without punishing; so the justice of God being now satisfied by the death of Christ, the greatest sins can do us no hurt, but we shall escape with a notwithstanding our sins.' This, it seems, we learn from an acquaintance with Christ's person, though his gospel instructs us otherwise, that without holiness no man shall see God.'?" But he is here again at a loss, and understands not what he is about. That whereof he was discoursing is the necessity of the satisfaction of Christ, and that must be it which he maketh his inference from, but the passage he insists on, he lays down as expressive of the end of God's patience and forbearance towards sinners, which here is of no place nor consideration. But so it falls out, that he is seldom at any agreement with himself in any parts of his discourse; the reason whereof I do somewhat more than guess at. However, for the passage which he cites out of my discourse, I like it so well, as that I shall not trouble myself to inquire whether it be there or no, or on what occasion it is introduced. The words are, -- "That God hath, in his justice, wisdom, and goodness, taken a course that we should not be destroyed, notwithstanding our sins" (that is, to save sinners); "for he that believeth, although he be a sinner, shall be saved; and he that believeth not shall be damned," as one hath assured us, whom I desire to believe and trust unto. If this be not so, what will become of this man and myself, with all our writings? for I know that we are both sinners; and if God will not save us, or deliver us from destruction, notwithstanding our sins, -- that is, pardon them through the bloodshedding of Jesus Christ, wherein we have redemption, even the forgiveness of sins, -- it had been better for us that we had never been born. And I do yet again say, that God doth not, that he will not, pardon the least sin, without respect unto the satisfaction of Christ, according as the apostle declares, 2 Cor. v. 18-21; and the expression which must be set on the other side, on the supposition whereof the greatest sin can do us no harm, is this man's addition, which his usual respect unto truth hath produced. But, withal, I never said, I never wrote, that the only supposition of the satisfaction of Christ is sufficient of itself to free us from destruction by sin.

There is, moreover, required on our part, faith and repentance; without which we can have no advantage by it, or interest in it. But he seems to understand by that expression, "notwithstanding our sins," though we should live and die in our sins without faith, repentance, or new obedience; for he supposeth it sufficient to manifest the folly of this assertion, to mention that declaration of the mind of Christ in the gospel, that "without holiness no man shall see God." I wonder whether he thinks that those who believe the satisfaction of Christ, and the necessity thereof, wherein God "made him to be sin who knew no sin, that we might be made the righteousness of God in him," do believe that the personal holiness of men is [not] indispensably necessary unto the pleasing and enjoyment of God. If he suppose that the satisfaction of Christ and the necessity of our personal holiness are really inconsistent, he must be treated in another manner: if he suppose that although they are consistent, yet those whom he opposeth do so trust to the satisfaction of Christ, as to judge that faith, repentance, and holiness, are not indispensably necessary to salvation, he manifests how well skilled he is in their principles and practices. I have always looked on it as a piece of the highest disingenuity among the Quakers, that when any one pleads for the satisfaction of Christ or the imputation of his righteousness, they will clamorously cry out, and hear nothing to the contrary, "Yea, you are for the saving of polluted, defiled sinners; let men live in their sins and be all foul within, it is no matter, so long as they have a righteousness and a Christ without them." I have, I say, always looked upon it as a most disingenuous procedure in them, seeing no one is catechised amongst us, who knoweth not that we press a necessity of sanctification and holiness, equal with that of justification and righteousness. And yet this very course is here steered by this author, contrary to the constant declaration of the judgments of them with whom he hath to do, -- contrary to the common evidence of their writings, preaching, praying, disputing unto another purpose; and that without relieving or countenancing himself by any one word or expression used or uttered by them. He chargeth [them] as though they made holiness a very indifferent thing, and such as it doth not much concern any man whether he have an interest in or no; and I know not whether is more marvellous unto me, that some men can so far concoct all principles of conscience and modesty as to publish such slanderous untruths, or that others can take contentment and satisfaction therein, who cannot but understand their disingenuity and falsehood.

His proceed in the same page is to except against that revelation of the wisdom of God which I affirm to have been made in the person and sufferings of Christ, which I thought I might have asserted without offence. But this man will have it, that "there is no wisdom therein, if justice be so natural to God, that nothing could satisfy him but the death of his own Son." That any thing else could satisfy divine justice but the sufferings and death of the Son of God, so far as I know, he is the first that found out or discovered, if he hath yet found it out. Some have imagined that God will pardon sin, and doth so, without any satisfaction at all; and some have thought that other ways of the reparation of lost mankind were possible, without this satisfaction of divine justice, which yet God in his wisdom determined on; but that satisfaction could be any otherwise made to divine justice, but by the death of the Son of God incarnate, none have used to say who know what they say in these things. "But wisdom," he saith, "consists in the choice of the best and fittest means to attain an end, when there were more ways than one of doing it; but it requires no great wisdom to choose when there is but one possible way." Yea, this it is to measure God, -- things infinite and divine, by ourselves. Doth this man think that God's ends, as ours, have an existence in themselves out of him, antecedent unto any acts of his divine wisdom? Doth he imagine that he balanceth probable means for the attaining of an end, choosing some and rejecting others? Doth he surmise that the acts of divine wisdom with respect unto the end and means are so really distinct, as the one to have a priority in time before the others? Alas, that men should have the confidence to publish such slight and crude imaginations! Again: the Scripture, which so often expresseth the incarnation of the Son of God, and the whole work of his mediation thereon, as the effect of the infinite wisdom of God, -- as that wherein the stores, riches, and treasures of it are laid forth, -- doth nowhere so speak of it in comparison with other means not so suited unto the same end, but absolutely, and as it is in its own nature; unless it be when it is compared with those typical institutions which, being appointed to resemble it, some did rest in. And lastly, whereas there was but this one way for the redemption of mankind, and the restoration of the honour of God's justice and holiness, as he is the supreme lawgiver and governor of the universe; and whereas this one way was not in the least pervious unto any created understanding, angelical or human, nor could the least of its concerns have ever entered into the hearts of any (nor, it may be, shall they ever know or be able to find it out unto perfection, but it will be left the object of their admiration unto eternity); -- if this author can see no wisdom, or no great wisdom, in the finding out and appointing of this way, who can help it? I wish he would more diligently attend unto their teachings who are able to instruct him better; and from whom, as having no prejudice against them, he may be willing to learn.

But this is the least part of what this worthy censurer of theological discourses rebukes and corrects. For whereas I had said, that we "might learn our disability to answer the mind and will of God in all or any part of the obedience he requireth," -- that is, without Christ or out of him; he adds, "That is, that it is impossible for us to do any thing that is good, but we must be acted, like machines, by an external force, -- by the irresistible power of the grace and Spirit of God. This, I am sure, is a new discovery; we learn no such thing from the gospel, and I do not see how he proves it from an acquaintance with Christ." But if he intends what he speaks, "we can do no good, but must be acted, like machines, by an external force," and chargeth this on me, it is a false accusation, proceeding from malice or ignorance, or a mixture of both. If he intend, that we can of ourselves do any thing that is spiritually good and acceptable before God, without the efficacious work of the Spirit and grace of God in us, which I only deny, he is a Pelagian, and stands anathematised by many councils of the ancient church. And [as] for what is my judgment about the impotency that is in us by nature unto any spiritual good, -- the necessity of the effectual operation of the Spirit of God in and to our conversion, with his aids and assistance of actual grace in our whole course of obedience, which is no other but that of the ancient church, the most learned fathers, and the church of England itself in former days, -- I have now sufficiently declared and confirmed it in another discourse; whither this author is remitted, either to learn to speak honestly of what he opposeth, or to understand it better, or answer it if he can.

He adds, "But still there is a more glorious discovery than this behind; and that is, the glorious end whereunto sin is appointed and ordained (I suppose he means by God) is discovered in Christ, -- namely, for the demonstration of God's vindictive justice, in measuring out to it a meet recompense of reward, and for the praise of God's glorious grace in the pardon and forgiveness of it; -- that is, that it could not be known how just and severe God is, but by punishing sin, nor how good and gracious God is, but by pardoning of it; and, therefore, lest his justice and mercy should never be known to the world, he appoints and ordains sin to this end, -- that is, decrees that men shall sin that he may make some of them the vessels of his wrath, and the examples of his fierce vengeance and displeasure, and others the vessels of his mercy, to the praise and glory of his free grace in Christ. This, indeed, is such a discovery as nature and revelation could not make," p. 51; which, in the next page, he calls God's "truckling and bartering with sin and the devil for his glory."

Although there is nothing in the words here reported as mine which is not capable of a fair defence, seeing it is expressly affirmed that "God set forth his Son to be a propitiation to declare his righteousness," yet I know not how it came to pass that I had a mind to turn unto the passage itself in my discourse, which I had not done before on any occasion, as not supposing that he would falsify my words, with whom it was so easy to pervert my meaning at any time, and to reproach what he could not confute. But, that I may give a specimen of this man's honesty and ingenuity, I shall transcribe the passage which he excepts against, because I confess it gave me some surprisal upon its first perusal. My words are these: "There is a glorious end whereunto sin is appointed and ordained discovered in Christ, that others are unacquainted withal. Sin, in its own nature, tends merely to the dishonour of God, the debasement of his majesty, and the ruin of the creature in whom it is. Hell itself is but the filling of wretched creatures with the fruit of their own devices. The comminations and threats of God in the law do manifest one other end of it, -- even the demonstration of the vindicative justice of God in measuring out unto it a meet recompense of reward. But here the law stays, and with it all other light, and discovers no other use or end of it at all. In the Lord Jesus Christ there is the manifestation of another and more glorious end, to wit, the praise of God's glorious grace in the pardon and forgiveness of it; -- God having taken order in Christ, that that thing which tended merely to his dishonour should be managed to his infinite glory, and that which of all things he desired to exalt, -- even that he may be known and believed to be a God pardoning iniquity, transgressions, and sin." Such was my ignorance, that I did not think that any Christian, unless he were a professed Socinian, would ever have made exceptions against any thing in this discourse; the whole of it being openly proclaimed in the gospel, and confirmed in the particulars by sundry texts of Scripture, quoted in the margin of my book, which this man took no notice of. For the advantage he would make from the expression about the end whereunto sin is appointed and ordained, it is childish and ridiculous; for every one who is not wilfully blind must see, that, by "ordained," I intended, not any ordination as to the futurition of sin, but to the disposal of sin to its proper end being committed, or to ordain it unto its end upon a supposition of its being; which quite spoils this author's ensuing harangue. But my judgment in this matter is better expressed by another than I am able to do it myself, and, therefore, in his words I shall represent it. It is Augustine: saith he, "Saluberrime confitemur quod rectissime credimus, Deum Dominumque rerum omnium qui creavit omnia bona valde, et mala ex bonis exortura esse præscivit, et scivit magis ad suam omnipotentissimam bonitatem pertinere, etiam de malis benefacere, quam mala esse non sinere; sic ordinasse angelorum et hominum vitam, ut in ea prius ostenderet quid posset eorum liberum arbitrium, deinde quid posset suæ gratiæ beneficium, justitiæque judicium."

This, our author would have to be God's "bartering with sin and the devil for his glory;" the bold impiety of which expression, among many others, for whose necessary repetition I crave pardon, manifests with what frame of spirit, with what reverence of God himself and all holy things, this discourse is managed.

But it seems I add, that "the demonstration of God's justice in measuring out unto sin a meet recompense of reward is discovered in Christ, as this author says." Let him read again, "The comminations and threatenings of God in the law," etc. If this man were acquainted with Christ, he could not but learn somewhat more of truth and modesty, unless he be wilfully stupid. But what is the crime of this paragraph? That which it teacheth is, that sin, in its own nature, hath no end but the dishonour of God and the eternal ruin of the sinner; that, by the sentence and curse of the law, God hath manifested that he will glorify his justice in the punishing of it; as also, that, in and through Jesus Christ, he will glorify grace and mercy in its pardon, on the terms of the gospel. What would he be at? If he have a mind to quarrel with the Bible, and to conflict the fundamental principles of Christianity, to what purpose doth he cavil at my obscure discourses, when the proper object of his displeasure lies plainly before him?

Let us proceed yet a little farther with our author, although I confess myself to be already utterly wearied with the perusal of such vain and frivolous imaginations. Yet thus he goes on, p. 53, "Thus much for the knowledge of ourselves with respect to sin, which is hid only in the Lord Christ. But then we learn what our righteousness is, wherewith we must appear before God, from an acquaintance with Christ. We have already learned how unable we are to make atonement for our sins, without which they can never be forgiven, and how unable we are to do any thing that is good; -- and yet nothing can deliver us from the justice and wrath of God, but a full satisfaction for our sins; and nothing can give us a title to a reward, but a perfect and unsinning righteousness. What should we do in this case? How shall we escape hell, or get to heaven, when we can neither expiate for our past sins, nor do any good for the time to come? Why, here we are relieved again by an acquaintance with Christ. His death expiates former iniquities, and removes the whole guilt of sin. But this is not enough, that we are not guilty, we must also be actually righteous; not only all sin is to be answered for, but all righteousness is to be fulfilled. Now, this righteousness we find only in Christ; we are reconciled to God by his death, and saved by his life. That actual obedience he yielded to the whole law of God, is that righteousness whereby we are saved; we are innocent by virtue of his sacrifice and expiation, and righteous with his righteousness."

What is here interposed, -- that we cannot do any good for the time to come, -- must be interpreted of ourselves, without the aid or assistance of the grace of God. And the things here reported by this author, are so expressed and represented, to expose them to reproach and scorn, to have them esteemed not only false, but ridiculous. But whether he be in his wits or no, or what he intends, so to traduce and scoff at the fundamental doctrines of the gospel, I profess I know not. What is it he would deny? what is it he would assert? Are we able to make an atonement for our sins? Can we be forgiven without an atonement? Can we of ourselves do any good without the aid and assistance of grace? Can any thing we do be a full satisfaction for our sins, or deliver us from the wrath of God; that is, the punishment due to our sins? Doth not the death of Christ expiate former iniquities, and remove the whole guilt of sin? Is the contrary to these things the doctrine of the church of England? Is this the religion which is authorized to be preached? and are these the opinions that are licensed to be published unto all the world? But, as I observed before, these things are other men's concernment more than mine, and with them I leave them. But I have said, as he quotes the place, "that we are reconciled to God by the death of Christ, and saved by his life, that actual obedience which he yielded to the whole law of God." As the former part of these words are expressly the apostle's, Rom. v. 10, and so produced by me; so the next words I add are these of the same apostle, "If so be we are found in him, not having on our own righteousness which is of the law, but the righteousness which is of God by faith;" which he may do well to consider, and answer when he can.

Once more, and I shall be beholden to this author for a little respite of severity, whilst he diverts to the magisterial reproof of some other persons. Thus, then, he proceeds, p. 55:-- "The third part of our wisdom is, to walk with God: and to that is required agreement, acquaintance, a way, strength, boldness, and aiming at the same end; and all these, with the wisdom of them, are hid in Jesus Christ." So far are my words, to which he adds: "The sum of which, in short, is this:-- that Christ having expiated our sins, and fulfilled all righteousness for us, though we have no personal righteousness of our own, but are as contrary unto God as darkness is to light, and death to life, and a universal pollution and defilement to a universal and glorious holiness, and hatred to love; yet the righteousness of Christ is a sufficient, nay, the only foundation of our agreement, and, upon that, of our walking with God: though St John tells us, If we say that we have fellowship with him, and walk in darkness, we lie, and do not the truth; but if we walk in the light, as God is in the light, we have fellowship one with another, and the blood of Jesus Christ his Son cleanseth us from all sin,' 1 John i. 6, 7. And our only acquaintance with God and knowledge of him is hid in Christ, which his word and works could not discover, as you heard above. And he is the only way wherein we must walk with God; and we receive all our strength from him; and he makes us bold and confident too, having removed the guilt of sin, so that now we may look justice in the face, and whet our knife at the counter door, all our debts being discharged by Christ, as these bold acquaintances and familiars of Christ use to speak. And in Christ we design the same end that God doth, which is the advancement of his own glory; that is, I suppose, by trusting unto the expiation and righteousness of Christ for salvation, without doing any thing ourselves, we take care that God shall not be wronged of the glory of his free grace, by a competition of any merits and deserts of our own."

What the author affirms to be the sum of my discourse in that place, which, indeed, he doth not transcribe, is, as to his affirmation of it, as contrary to God as darkness is to light, or death to life, or falsehood to the truth; that is, it is flagitiously false. That there is any agreement with God, or walking with God, for any men who have no personal righteousness of their own, but are contrary to God, etc., I never thought, I never wrote, nor any thing that should give the least countenance unto a suspicion to that purpose. The necessity of an habitual and actual personal, inherent righteousness, of sanctification and holiness, of gospel obedience, of fruitfulness in good works, unto all who intend to walk with God, or come to the enjoyment of him, I have asserted and proved, with other manner of arguments than this author is acquainted withal. The remainder of his discourse in this place is composed of immorality and profaneness. To the first I must refer his charge, that "our only acquaintance with God and knowledge of him is hid in Christ, which his word could not discover," as he again expresseth it, pp. 98, 99, "But that the reverend doctor confessed the plain truth, that their religion is wholly owing to an acquaintance with the person of Christ, and could never have been clearly and savingly learned from his gospel had they not first grown acquainted with his person;" which is plainly false. I own no knowledge of God, nor of Christ, but what is revealed in the word, as was before declared. And unto the other head belongs the most of what ensues; for what is the intendment of those reproaches which are cast on my supposed assertions? Christ is the only way wherein or whereby we must walk with God. Yes, so he says, "I am the way;" "There is no coming to God but by me;" he having consecrated for us in himself "a new and living way" of drawing nigh to God. We receive all our strength from him; yes, for he says, "Without me ye can do nothing." He makes us bold and confident also, having removed the guilt of sin. So the apostle tells us, Heb. x. 19-22. What then? what follows upon these plain, positive, divine assertions of the Scripture? Why, then "we may look justice in the face, and whet our knife at the counter door." Goodly son of the church of England! Not that I impute these profane scoffings unto the church itself, -- which I shall never do until it be discovered that the rulers of it do give approbation to such abominations; but I would mind the man of his relation to that church, which, to my knowledge, teacheth better learning and manners.

From p. 57 to the end of his second section, p. 75, he giveth us a scheme of religion, which, in his scoffing language, he says, "men learn from an acquaintance with the person of Christ; and affirms, "that there needs no more to expose it to scorn with considering men than his proposal of it;" which therein he owns to be his design. I know not any peculiar concernment of mine therein, until he comes towards the close of it; which I shall particularly consider. But the substance of the religion which he thus avowedly attempts to expose to scorn, is the doctrine of God's eternal election; -- of his infinite wisdom in sending his Son to declare his righteousness for the forgiveness of sins, or in satisfying his justice, that sin might be pardoned, to the praise of the glory of his grace; -- of the imputation of the righteousness of Christ unto them that do believe; -- of a sense of sin, humiliation for it, looking unto Christ for life and salvation, as the Israelites looked up to the brazen serpent in the wilderness; -- of going to Christ by faith for healing our natures and cleansing our sins; with some other doctrines of the same importance. These are the principles which, according to his ability, he sarcastically traduceth and

364

endeavoureth to reflect scorn upon, by the false representation of some of them, and debasing others with an intermixture of vile and profane expressions. It is not impossible but that some or other may judge it their duty to rebuke this horrible (and yet were it not for the ignorance and profaneness of some men's minds, every way contemptible) petulancy. For my part I have other things to do, and shall only add, that I know no other Christian state in the world wherein such discourses would be allowed to pass under the signature of public authority. Only I wish the author more modesty and sobriety than to attempt, or suppose he shall succeed, in exposing to scorn the avowed doctrine in general of the church wherein he lives; and which hath in the parts of it been asserted and defended by the greatest and most learned prelates thereof in the foregoing ages, such as Jewell, Whitgift, Abbot, Morton, Usher, Hall, Davenant, Prideaux, etc., with the most learned persons of its communion, as Reynolds, Whitaker, Hooker, Sutcliffe, etc., and others innumerable; -- testified unto in the name of this church by the divines, sent by public authority to the synod of Dort; -- taught by the principal practical divines of this nation; and maintained by the most learned at the dignified clergy at this day. He is no doubt at liberty to dissent from the doctrine of the church, and of all the learned men thereof; but for a young man to suppose that, with a few loose, idle words, he shall expose to scorn that doctrine which the persons mentioned, and others innumerable, have not only explained, confirmed, and defended, with pains indefatigable, all kind of learning and skill, ecclesiastical, philosophical, and theological, in books and volumes, which the Christian world as yet knoweth, peruseth, and prizeth, but also lived long in fervent prayers to God for the revelation of his mind and truth unto them, and in the holy practice of obedience suited unto the doctrines they professed, -- is somewhat remote from that Christian humility which he ought not only to exercise in himself, but to give an example of unto others. But if this be the fruit of despising the knowledge of the person of Christ, -- of the necessity of his satisfaction, of the imputation of his righteousness, of union unto his person as our head, -- of a sense of the displeasure of God due to sin, -- of the spirit of bondage and adoption, -- of the corruption of nature, and our disability to do any thing that is spiritually good without the effectual aids of grace; -- if these, I say, and the like issues of appearing pride and elation of mind, be the fruit and consequent of rejecting these principles of the doctrine of the gospel, it manifests that there is, and will be, a proportion between the errors of men's minds and the depravation of their affections. It were a most easy task to go over all the particulars mentioned by him, and to manifest how foully he hath prevaricated in their representation, -- how he hath cast contempt on some duties of religion indispensably necessary unto salvation; and brought in the very words of the Scripture, -- and that in the true proper sense and intendment of them, according to the judgment of all Christians, ancient and modern (as that of looking to Christ, as the Israelites looked to the brazen serpent in the wilderness), -- to bear a share and part in his scorn and contempt: as also, to defend and vindicate, not his odious, disingenuous expressions, but what he invidiously designeth to expose, beyond his ability to gainsay, or with any pretence of sober learning to reply unto. But I give it up into the hands of those who are more concerned in the chastisement of such imaginations. Only, I cannot but tell this author what I have learned by long observation, -- namely, that those who, in opposing others, make it their design to [publish] and place their confidence in false representations, and invidious expressions of their judgments and opinions, waiving a true stating of the things in difference, and weighing of the arguments wherewith they are confirmed, -- whatever pretence they may make of confidence, and contempt of them with whom they have to do, yet this way of writing proceeds from a secret sense of their disability to maintain their own opinions, or to reply to the reasonings of their adversaries in a fair and lawful disputation; or from such depraved affections as are sufficient to deter any sober person from the least communication in those principles which are so pleaded for. And the same I must say of that kind of writing (which in some late authors fills up almost every page in their books) which, beyond a design to load the persons of men with reproaches and calumnies, consists only in the collecting of passages here and there, up and down, out of the writings of others; which, as cut off from the body of their discourses, and design of the places which they belong unto, may, with a little artifice, either of addition or detraction, with some false glosses, whereof we shall have an immediate instance, be represented weak, or untrue, or improper, or some way or other obnoxious to censure. When diligence, modesty, love of truth, sobriety, true use of learning, shall again visit the world in a more plentiful manner; though differences should continue amongst us, yet men will be enabled to manage them honestly, without contracting so much guilt on themselves, or giving such fearful offence and scandal unto others. But I return.

That wherein I am particularly concerned, is the close wherewith he winds up this candid, ingenious discourse, p. 74. He quotes my words, "That the soul consents to take Christ on his own terms, to save him in his own way; and saith, Lord, I would have had thee and salvation in my way, that it might have been partly of mine endeavours, and as it were by the works of the law' (that is, by obeying the laws of the gospel); but I am now willing to receive thee, and to be saved in thy way, merely by grace' (that is, without doing any thing, without obeying thee). The most contented spouse, certainly, that ever was in the world, to submit to such hard conditions as to be saved for nothing. But what a pretty compliment doth the soul make to Christ after all this, when she adds, And though I would have walked according to my own mind, yet now I wholly give up myself to be ruled by thy Spirit.'?"

If the reader will be at the pains to look on the discourse whence these passages are taken, I shall desire no more of his favour but that he profess himself to be a Christian, and then let him freely pronounce whether he find any thing in it obnoxious to censure. Or, I desire that any man, who hath not forfeited all reason and ingenuity unto faction and party, if he differ from me, truly to state wherein, and oppose what I have said with an answer unto the testimonies wherewith it is confirmed, referred unto in the margin of my discourse. But the way of this author's proceeding, if there be no plea to be made for it from his ignorance and unacquaintedness not only with the person of Christ, but with most of the other things he undertakes to write about, is altogether inexcusable. The way whereby I have expressed the consent of the soul in the receiving of Jesus Christ, to be justified, sanctified, saved by him, I still avow, as suited unto the mind of the Holy Ghost, and the experience of them that really believe. And whereas I added, that before believing, the soul did seek for salvation by the works of the law, as it is natural unto all, and as the Holy Ghost affirms of some (whose words alone I used, and expressly

366

quoted that place from whence I took them, -- namely, Rom. ix. 31, 32;) -- this man adds, as an exposition of that expression, "That is, by obeying the laws of the gospel." But he knew that these were the words of the apostle, or he did not; if he did not, nor would take notice of them so to be, although directed to the place from whence they are taken, it is evident how meet he is to debate matters of this nature and concernment, and how far he is yet from being in danger to "pore out his eyes" in reading the Scripture, as he pretends. If he did know them to be his words, why doth he put such a sense upon them as, in his own apprehension, is derogatory to gospel obedience? Whatever he thought of beforehand, it is likely he will now say that it is my sense, and not the apostle's, which he intends. But how will he prove that I intended any other sense than that of the apostle? how should this appear? Let him, if he can, produce any word in my whole discourse intimating any other sense. Nay, it is evident that I had no other intention but only to refer unto that place of the apostle, and the proper sense of it; which is to express the mind and actings of those who, being ignorant of the righteousness of God, go about to establish their own righteousness; as he farther explains himself, Rom. x. 3, 4. That I could not intend obedience unto the laws of the gospel is so evident, that nothing but abominable prejudice or ignorance could hinder any man from discerning it. For that faith which I expressed by the soul's consent to take Christ as a saviour and a ruler, is the very first act of obedience unto the gospel: so that therein or thereon to exclude obedience unto the gospel, is to deny what I assert; which, under the favour of this author, I understand myself better than to do. And as to all other acts of obedience unto the laws of the gospel, following and proceeding from sincere believing, it is openly evident that I could not understand them when I spake only of what was antecedent unto them. And if this man knows not what transactions are in the minds of many before they do come unto the acceptance of Christ on his own terms, or believe in him according to the tenor of the gospel, there is reason to pity the people that are committed unto his care and instruction, what regard soever ought to be had unto himself. And his pitiful trifling in the exposition he adds of this passage, "To be saved without doing any thing, without obeying thee, and the law," doth but increase the guilt of his prevarications; for the words immediately added in my discourse are, -- "And although I have walked according unto mine own mind, yet now I wholly give up myself to be ruled by thy Spirit;" which, unto the understanding of all men who understand any thing in these matters, signify no less than an engagement unto the universal relinquishment of sin, and entire obedience unto Jesus Christ in all things. "But this," saith he, "is a pretty compliment that the soul makes to Christ after all." But why is this to be esteemed only a "pretty compliment?" It is spoken at the same time, and, as it were, with the same breath, there being in the discourse no period between this passage and that before; and why must it be esteemed quite of another nature, so that herein the soul should only compliment, and be real in what is before expressed? What if one should say, it was real only in this latter expression and engagement, that the former was only a "pretty compliment?" May it not, with respect unto my sense and intention (from any thing in my words, or that can be gathered from them, or any circumstances of the place), be spoken with as much regard unto truth and honesty? What religion these men are of I know not. If it be such as teacheth them these practices, and countenanceth them in them, I openly declare that I am not of it, nor would be so for all that this world can afford. I shall have done, when I have desired him to take notice, that I not only believe and maintain the necessity of obedience unto all the laws, precepts, commands, and institutions of the gospel, -- of universal holiness, the mortification of all sin, fruitfulness in good works, in all that intend or design salvation by Jesus Christ; but also have proved and confirmed my persuasion and assertions by better and more cogent arguments than any which, by his writings, he seems as yet to be acquainted withal. And unless he can prove that I have spoken or written any thing to the contrary, or he can disprove the arguments whereby I have confirmed it, I do here declare him a person altogether unfit to be dealt withal about things of this nature, his ignorance or malice being invincible; nor shall I, on any provocation, ever hereafter take notice of him until he hath mended his manners.

His third section, p. 76, consists of three parts:-- First, "That some" (wherein it is apparent that I am chiefly, if not only, intended) "do found a religion upon a pretended acquaintance with Christ's person, without and besides the gospel;" whereunto he opposeth his running title of "No acquaintance with Christ but by revelation." Secondly, A supposition of a scheme of religion drawn from the knowledge of Christ's person; whereunto he opposeth another, which he judgeth better. Thirdly, An essay to draw up the whole plot and design of Christianity, with the method of the recovery of sinners unto God. In the first of these, I suppose that I am, if not solely, yet principally, intended; especially considering what he affirms, pp. 98, 99, namely, that "I plainly confess our religion is wholly owing unto acquaintance with the person of Christ, and could never have been clearly and savingly learned from the gospel, had we not first grown acquainted with his person." Now, herein there is an especial instance of that truth and honesty wherewith my writings are entertained by this sort of men. It is true, I have asserted that it is necessary for Christians to know Jesus Christ, -- to be acquainted with his person that is (as I have fully and largely declared it in the discourse excepted against), the glory of his divine nature, the purity of his human, the infinite condescension of his person in the assumption of our nature, his love and grace, etc., as is at large there declared: and now I add, that he by whom this is denied is no Christian. Secondly, I have taught, that by this knowledge of the person of Christ, or an understanding of the great mystery of godliness, God manifested in the flesh, which we ought to pray for and labour after, we come more fully and clearly to understand sundry other important mysteries of heavenly truth; which without the knowledge of Christ we cannot attain unto. And how impertinent this man's exceptions are against this assertion, we have seen already. But, thirdly, that this knowledge of Christ, or acquaintance with him, is to be attained before we come to know the gospel, or by any other means than the gospel, or is any other but the declaration that is made thereof in and by the gospel, was never thought, spoken, or written by me, and is here falsely supposed by this author, as elsewhere falsely charged on me. And I again challenge him to produce any one letter or tittle out of any of my writings to give countenance unto this frontless calumny. And therefore, although I do not like his expression, p. 77, "Whoever would understand the religion of our Saviour, must learn it from his doctrine, and not from his person," for many reasons I could give; yet I believe no less than he, that the efficacy of Christ's mediation depending on God's appointment can be known only by revelation, and that no man can draw any one conclusion from the person of Christ which the gospel hath not expressly taught; because we can know no more of its excellency, worth, and works, than what is there revealed: whereby he may see how miserably ill-will, malice, or ignorance hath betrayed him into the futilous pains of writing this section upon a contrary supposition falsely imputed unto me. And as for his drawing schemes of religion, I must tell him, and let him disprove it if he be able, I own no religion, no article of faith, but what is taught expressly in the Scripture, mostly confirmed by the ancient general councils of the primitive church, and the writings of the most learned fathers, against all sorts of heretics, especially the Gnostics, Photinians, and Pelagians, consonant to the articles of the church of England, and the doctrine of all the reformed churches of Europe. And if in the exposition of any place of Scripture I dissent from any that, for the substance of it, own the religion I do, I do it not without cogent reasons from the Scripture itself; and where, in any opinions which learned men have (and, it may be, always had) different apprehensions about, which hath not been thought to prejudice the unity of faith amongst them, I hope I do endeavour to manage that dissent with that modesty and sobriety which becometh me. And as for the schemes, plots, or designs of religion or Christianity, given us by this author and owned by him (it being taken pretendedly from the person of Christ, when it is hoped that he may have a better to give us from the gospel, seeing he hath told us we must learn our religion from his doctrine and not from his person); besides that it is liable unto innumerable exceptions in particular, which may easily be given in against it by such as have nothing else to do, whereas it makes no mention of the effectual grace of Christ and the gospel for the conversion and sanctification of sinners, and the necessity thereof unto all acts of holy obedience, -- it is merely Pelagianism, and stands anathematised by sundry councils of the ancient church. I shall not, therefore, concern myself farther in any passages of this section, most of them wherein it reflects on others standing in competition for truth and ingenuity with the foundation and design of the whole; only I shall say, that the passage of pp. 88, 89, -- "This made the divine goodness so restlessly zealous and concerned for the recovery of mankind; various ways he attempted in former ages, but with little success, as I observed before; but at last God sent his Son, our Lord Jesus Christ, into the world," -- without a very cautious explanation and charitable construction, is false, scandalous, and blasphemous. For allow this author, who contends so severely for propriety of expressions, against allusions and metaphors, to say that the divine goodness was "restlessly zealous and concerned" (for, indeed, such is our weakness, that, whether we will or no, we must sometimes learn and teach divine things in such words as are suited to convey an apprehension of them unto our minds, though, in their application unto the divine nature, they are incapable of being understood in the propriety of their signification, though this be as untowardly expressed as any thing I have of late met withal); yet what colour can be put upon, what excuse can be made for, this doctrine, that "God in former ages, by various ways, attempted the recovery of mankind, but with little success," I know not. Various attempts in God for any end without success, do not lead the mind into right notions of his infinite wisdom and omnipotence; and that God, by any way, at any time, attempted the recovery of mankind distinctly and separately from the sending of his Son, is lewdly false.

In the greatest part of his fourth section, entitled, "How men pervert the Scripture to make it comply with their fancy," I am not much concerned; save that the foundation of the whole, and that which animates his discourse from first to last, is laid in an impudent calumny, -- namely, that I declare that "our religion is wholly owing to an acquaintance with the person of Christ, and could never have been clearly and savingly learned from his gospel, had we not first grown acquainted with his person." This shameless falsehood is that alone whence he takes occasion and confidence, to reproach myself and others, to condemn the doctrine of all the reformed churches and openly to traduce and vilify the Scripture itself. I shall only briefly touch on some of the impotent dictates of this great corrector of divinity and religion. His discourse of accommodating Scripture expressions to men's own dreams, pp. 99-101, being such as any man may use concerning any other men on the like occasion, if they have a mind unto it, and intend to have no more regard to their consciences than some others seem to have, may be passed by. P. 102, he falls upon the ways of expounding Scripture among those whom he sets himself against, and positively affirms, "that there are two ways of it in great vogue among them:-- First, By the sound and clink of the words and phrases; which, as he says, is all some men understand by keeping a form of sound words. Secondly, When this will not do, they reason about the sense of them from their own preconceived notions and opinions, and prove that this must be the meaning of Scripture, because otherwise it is not reconcilable to their dreams; which is called expounding Scripture by the analogy of faith."

Thus far he; and yet we shall have the same man not long hence pleading for the necessity of holiness. But I wish, for my part, he would take notice that I despise that holiness, and the principles of it, which will allow men to coin, invent, and publish such notorious untruths against any sort of men whatever. And whereas, by what immediately follows, I seem to be principally intended in this charge, as I know the untruth of it, so I have published some expositions on some parts of the Scripture to the judgment of the Christian world; to which I appeal from the censures of this man and his companions, as also for those which, if I live and God will, I shall yet publish; and do declare, that, for reasons very satisfactory to my mind, I will not come to him nor them to learn how to expound the Scripture.

But he will justify his charge by particular instances, telling us, p. 102, "Thus when men are possessed with a fancy of an acquaintance with Christ's person, then to know Christ can signify nothing else but to know his person and all his personal excellencies, and beauties, fulness, and preciousness, etc. And when Christ is said to be made wisdom to us, this is a plain proof that we must learn all our spiritual wisdom from an acquaintance with his person; though some duller men can understand no more by it than the wisdom of those revelations Christ hath made of God's will to the world." I would beg of this man, that if he hath any regard unto the honour of Christian religion, or care of his own soul, he would be tender in this matter, and not reflect with his usual disdain upon the knowledge of the person of Christ. I must tell him again, what all Christians believe, -- Jesus Christ is Jesus Christ, the eternal Son of God incarnate. The person of Christ is Christ himself, and nothing else; his personal excellencies are the properties of his person, as his two natures are united therein, and as he was thereby made meet to be the mediator between God and man. To know Christ in the language of the Scripture, [of] the whole church of

God ancient and present, in common sense and understanding, is to know the person of Christ as revealed and declared in the gospel, with respect unto the ends for which he is proposed and made known therein. And this knowledge of him, as it is accompanied with, and cannot be without, the knowledge of his mind and will, declared in his precepts, promises, and institutions, is effectual to work and produce, in the souls of them who so know him, that faith in him, and obedience unto him, which he doth require. And what would this man have? He who is otherwise minded hath renounced his Christianity, if ever he had any; and if he be thus persuaded, to what purpose is it to set up and combat the mormos and chimeras of his own imagination? Well, then, I do maintain, that to know Christ according to the gospel, is to know the person of Christ; for Christ and his person are the same. Would he now have me to prove this by testimonies or arguments, or the consent of the ancient church? I must beg his excuse at present; and so for the future, unless I have occasion to deal with Gnostics, Familists, or Quakers. And as for the latter clause, wherein Christ is said to be made wisdom unto us, he says, "Some duller men can understand no more by it than the wisdom of those revelations Christ hath made of God's will to the world," -- who are dull men indeed, and so let them pass.

His ensuing discourses, in pp. 103-105, contain the boldest reflections on, and openest derisions of, the expressions and way of teaching spiritual things warranted in and by the Scripture, that to my knowledge I ever read in a book licensed to be printed by public authority: as, in particular, the expressions of faith in Christ, by "coming unto him," and "receiving of him," -- which are the words of the Holy Ghost, and used by him in his wisdom to instruct us in the nature of this duty, -- are, amongst others, the subjects of his scorn. The first part of it, though I remember not to have given any occasion to be particularly concerned in it, I shall briefly consider. P. 103, "Thus when men have first learned, from an acquaintance with Christ, to place all their hopes of salvation in a personal union with Christ, from whom they receive the free communications of pardon and grace, righteousness and salvation, what more plain proof can any man who is resolved to believe this, desire of it, than 1 John v. 12, He that hath the Son hath life, and he that hath not the Son hath not life?' And what can having the Son signify, but having an interest in him, being made one with him? though some will be so perverse as to understand it of believing, and having his gospel. But the phrase of having the Son,' confutes that dull and moral interpretation, especially when we remember it is called, being in Christ, and abiding in him;' which must signify a very near union between Christ's person and us."

I suppose that expression of "personal union" sprung out of design, and not out of ignorance; for, if I mistake not, he doth somewhere in his book take notice that it is disclaimed, and only a union of believers with or unto the person of Christ asserted; or, if it be his mistake, all comes to the same issue. Personal, or hypostatical union, is that of different natures in the same person, giving them the same singular subsistence. This none pretend unto with Jesus Christ. But it is the union of believers unto the person of Christ which is spiritual and mystical, whereby they are in him and he in them, and so are one with him, their head, as members of his mystical body, which is pleaded for herein, with the free communications of grace, righteousness, and salvation, in the several and distinct ways whereby we are capable to receive them from

him, or be made partakers of them; [in this] we place all hopes of salvation. And we do judge, moreover, that he who is otherwise minded must betake himself unto another gospel; for he completely renounceth that in our Bibles. Is this our crime, -- that which we are thus charged with, and traduced for? Is the contrary hereunto the doctrine that the present church of England approveth and instructs her children in? Or doth any man think that we will be scared from our faith and hope by such weak and frivolous attempts against them? Yea, but it may be it is not so much the thing itself, as the miserable proof which we produce from the Scripture in the confirmation of it; for we do it from that of the apostle, 1 John v. 12. If he think that we prove these things only by this testimony, he is mistaken at his wonted rate. Our faith herein is built upon innumerable express testimonies of the Scripture, -- indeed the whole revelation of the will of God and the way of salvation by Jesus Christ in the gospel. Those who prove it, also, from this text, have sufficient ground and reason for what they plead. And, notwithstanding the pleasant scoffing humour of this author, we yet say that it is perverse folly for any one to say that the having of the Son or Christ expressed in the text, doth intend either the having an interest in him and union with him, or the obeying of his gospel, exclusively to the other, -- these being inseparable, and included in the same expression. And as to what he adds about being in Christ, and abiding in him, -- which are the greatest privileges of believers, and that as expressed in words taught by the Holy Ghost, -- it is of the same strain of profaneness with much of what ensues; which I shall not farther inquire into.

I find not myself concerned in his ensuing talk, but only in one reflection on the words of the Scripture, and the repetition of his old, putid, and shameless calumny, p. 108, until we come to p. 126, where he arraigns an occasional discourse of mine about the necessity of holiness and good works; wherein he hath only filched out of the whole what he thought he could wrest unto his end, and scoffingly descant upon. I shall, therefore, for once, transcribe the whole passage as it lies in my book, and refer it to the judgment of the reader, p. 206:[366] --

"2. The second objection is, That if the righteousness and obedience of Christ to the law be imputed unto us, then what need we yield obedience ourselves?' To this, also, I shall return answer as briefly as I can in the ensuing observations:--

"(1.) The placing of our gospel obedience on the right foot of account (that it may neither be exalted into a state, condition, use, or end, not given it of God; nor any reason, cause, motive, end, necessity of it, on the other hand, taken away, weakened, or impaired), is a matter of great importance. Some make our obedience, the works of faith, our works, the matter or cause of our justification; some, the condition of the imputation of the righteousness of Christ; some, the qualification of the person justified, on the one hand; some exclude all the necessity of them, and turn the grace of God into lasciviousness, on the other. To debate these differences is not my present business; only, I say, on this and other accounts, the right stating of our obedience is of great importance as to our walking with God.

"(2.) We do by no means assign the same place, condition, state, and use to the obedience of Christ imputed to us, and our obedience performed to God. If we did, they were really inconsistent. And therefore those who affirm that our obedience is the condition or cause of our justification, do all of them deny the

imputation of the obedience of Christ unto us. The righteousness of Christ is imputed to us, as that on the account whereof we are accepted and esteemed righteous before God, and are really so, though not inherently. We are as truly righteous with the obedience of Christ imputed to us as Adam was, or could have been, by a complete righteousness of his own performance. So Rom. v. 18, by his obedience we are made righteous, -- made so truly, and so accepted; as by the disobedience of Adam we are truly made trespassers, and so accounted. And this is that which the apostle desires to be found in, in opposition to his own righteousness, Phil. iii. 9. But our own obedience is not the righteousness whereupon we are accepted and justified before God; although it be acceptable to God that we should abound therein. And this distinction the apostle doth evidently deliver and confirm, so as nothing can be more clearly revealed: Eph. ii. 8-10, For by grace are ye saved through faith: and that not of yourselves: it is the gift of God: not of works, lest any man should boast. For we are his workmanship, created in Christ Jesus unto good works, which God hath prepared that we should walk in them.' We are saved, or justified (for that it is whereof the apostle treats), by grace through faith,' which receives Jesus Christ and his obedience; not of works, lest any man should boast.' But what works are they that the apostle intends?' The works of believers, as in the very beginning of the next words is manifest: ?"For we are," we believers, with our obedience and our works, of whom I speak.' Yea; but what need, then, of works?' Need still there is: We are his workmanship,' etc.

"Two things the apostle intimates in these words:--

"[1.] A reason why we cannot be saved by works, -- namely, because we do them not in or by our own strength; which is necessary we should do, if we will be saved by them, or justified by them. But this is not so,' saith the apostle; for we are the workmanship of God,' etc.; -- all our works are wrought in us, by full and effectual undeserved grace.

"[2.] An assertion of the necessity of good works, notwithstanding that we are not saved by them; and that is, that God has ordained that we shall walk in them: which is a sufficient ground of our obedience, whatever be the use of it.

"If you will say then, What are the true and proper gospel grounds, reasons, uses, and motives of our obedience; whence the necessity thereof may be demonstrated, and our souls be stirred up to abound and be fruitful therein?' I say, they are so many, and lie so deep in the mystery of the gospel and dispensation of grace, spread themselves so throughout the whole revelation of the will of God unto us, that to handle them fully and distinctly, and to give them their due weight, is a thing that I cannot engage in, lest I should be turned aside from what I principally intend. I shall only give you some brief heads of what might at large be insisted on:--

"1st. Our universal obedience and good works are indispensably necessary, from the sovereign appointment and will of God; Father, Son, and Holy Ghost.

"In general. This is the will of God, even your sanctification,' or holiness, 1 Thess. iv. 3. This is that which God wills, which he requires of us, -- that we be holy, that we be obedient, that we do his will as the angels do in heaven. The equity, necessity, profit, and advantage of this ground of our obedience might at large be insisted on; and, were there no more, this might suffice alone, -- if it be the will of God, it is our duty:--

"(1st.) The Father hath ordained or appointed it. It is the will of the Father, Eph. ii. 10. The Father is spoken of personally, Christ being mentioned as mediator.

"(2dly.) The Son hath ordained and appointed it as mediator. John xv. 16, ?"I have ordained you, that ye should bring forth fruit" of obedience, and that it should remain.' And, --

"(3dly.) The Holy Ghost appoints and ordains believers to works of obedience and holiness, and to work holiness in others. So, in particular, Acts xiii. 2, he appoints and designs men to the great work of obedience in preaching the gospel. And in sinning, men sin against him.

"2dly. Our holiness, our obedience, work of righteousness, is one eminent and especial end of the peculiar dispensation of Father, Son, and Spirit, in the business of exalting the glory of God in our salvation, -- of the electing love of the Father, the purchasing love of the Son, and the operative love of the Spirit:--

"(1st.) It is a peculiar end of the electing love of the Father, Eph. i. 4, He hath chosen us, that we should be holy and without blame.' So Isa. iv. 3, 4. His aim and design in choosing of us was, that we should be holy and unblamable before him in love. This he is to accomplish, and will bring about in them that are his. He chooses us to salvation, through sanctification of the Spirit, and belief of the truth,' 2 Thess. ii. 13. This the Father designed as the first and immediate end of electing love; and proposes the consideration of that love as a motive to holiness, 1 John iv. 8-10.

"(2dly.) It is so also of the exceeding love of the Son; whereof the testimonies are innumerable. I shall give but one or two:-- Tit. ii. 14, Who gave himself for us, that he might redeem us from all iniquity, and purify unto himself a peculiar people, zealous of good works.' This was his aim, his design, in giving himself for us; as Eph. v. 25-27, Christ loved the church, and gave himself for it; that he might sanctify and cleanse it with the washing of water by the word; that he might present it to himself a glorious church, not having spot, or wrinkle, or any such thing; but that it should be holy, and without blemish.' 2 Cor. v. 15; Rom. vi. 11.

"(3dly.) It is the very work of the love of the Holy Ghost. His whole work upon us, in us, for us, consists in preparing of us for obedience; enabling of us thereunto, and bringing forth the fruits of it in us. And this he doth in opposition to a righteousness of our own, either before it or to be made up by it, Tit. iii. 5. I need not insist on this. The fruits of the Spirit in us are known, Gal. v. 22, 23.

"And thus have we a twofold bottom of the necessity of our obedience and personal holiness:-- God hath appointed it, he requires it; and it is an eminent immediate end of the distinct dispensation of Father, Son, and Holy Ghost, in the work of our salvation. If God's sovereignty over us is to be owned, if his love towards us be to be regarded, if the whole work of the ever-blessed Trinity, for us, in us, be of any moment, our obedience is necessary.

"3dly. It is necessary in respect of the end thereof; and that whether you consider God, ourselves, or the world:--

"(1st.) The end of our obedience, in respect of God, is, his glory and honour, Mal. i. 6. This is God's honour, -- all that we give him. It is true, he will take his honour from the stoutest and proudest rebel in the world; but all we give him is in our obedience. The glorifying of God by our obedience is all that we are or can be. Particularly, --

"[1st.] It is the glory of the Father. Matt. v. 16, Let your light so shine before men, that they may see your good works, and glorify your Father which is in heaven.' By our walking in the light of faith doth glory arise to the Father. The fruits of his love, of his grace, of his kindness, are seen upon us; and God is glorified in our behalf. And, --

"[2dly.] The Son is glorified thereby. It is the will of God that as all men honour the Father, so should they honour the Son, John v. 23. And how is this done? By believing in him, John xiv. 1; obeying of him. Hence, John xvii. 10, he says he is glorified in believers; and prays for an increase of grace and union for them, that he may yet be more glorified, and all might know that, as mediator, he was sent of God.

"[3dly.] The Spirit is glorified also by it. He is grieved by our disobedience, Eph. iv. 30; and therefore his glory is in our bringing forth fruit. He dwells in us, as in his temple; which is not to be defiled. Holiness becometh his habitation for ever.

"Now, if this that hath been said be not sufficient to evince a necessity of our obedience, we must suppose ourselves to speak with a sort of men who regard neither the sovereignty, nor love, nor glory of God, Father, Son, or Holy Ghost. Let men say what they please, though our obedience should be all lost, and never regarded (which is impossible, for God is not unjust, to forget our labour of love), yet here is a sufficient bottom, ground, and reason of yielding more obedience unto God than ever we shall do whilst we live in this world. I speak also only of gospel grounds of obedience, and not of those that are natural and legal, which are indispensable to all mankind.

"(2dly.) The end in respect of ourselves immediately is threefold:-- [1st.] Honour. [2dly.] Peace. [3dly.] Usefulness.

"[1st.] Honour. It is by holiness that we are made like unto God, and his image is renewed again in us. This was our honour at our creation, this exalted us above all our fellow-creatures here below, -- we were made in the image of God. This we lost by sin, and became like the beasts that perish. To this honour, of conformity to God, of bearing his image, are we exalted again by holiness alone. Be ye holy,' says God, for I am holy,' 1 Pet. i. 16; and, Be ye perfect' (that is, in doing good), even as your Father which is in heaven is perfect,' Matt. v. 48, -- in a likeness and conformity to him. And herein is the image of God renewed; Eph. iv. 23, 24, therein we put on the new man, which after God is created in righteousness and holiness of truth.' This was that which originally was attended with power and dominion; -- is still all that is beautiful or comely in the world. How it makes men honourable and precious in the sight of God, of angels, of men; how alone it is that which is not despised, which is of price before the Lord; what contempt and scorn he hath of them in whom it is not, -- in what abomination he hath them and all their ways, -- might easily be evinced.

"[2dly.] Peace. By it we have communion with God, wherein peace alone is to be enjoyed. The wicked are like the troubled sea, that cannot rest;' and, There is no peace' to them, saith my God,' Isa. lvii. 20, 21. There is no peace, rest, or quietness, in a distance, separation, or alienation from God. He is the rest of our souls. In the light of his countenance is life and peace. Now, if we walk in the light, as he is in the light, we have fellowship one with another,' 1

John i. 7; and truly our fellowship is with the Father, and with his Son Jesus Christ,' verse 3. He that walks in the light of new obedience, he hath communion with God, and in his presence is fulness of joy for ever; without it, there is nothing but darkness, and wandering, and confusion.

"[3dly.] Usefulness. A man without holiness is good for nothing. Ephraim,' says the prophet, is an empty vine, that brings forth fruit to itself.' And what is such a vine good for? Nothing. Saith another prophet, A man cannot make so much as a pin of it, to hang a vessel on.' A barren tree is good for nothing, but to be cut down for the fire. Notwithstanding the seeming usefulness of men who serve the providence of God in their generations, I could easily manifest that the world and the church might want them, and that, indeed, in themselves they are good for nothing. Only the holy man is commune bonum.

"(3dly.) The end of it in respect of others in the world is manifold:--

"[1st.] It serves to the conviction and stopping the mouths of some of the enemies of God, both here and hereafter:-- 1. Here. 1 Pet. iii. 16, Having a good conscience; that, wherein they speak evil of you, as of evil-doers, they may be ashamed that falsely accuse your good conversation in Christ.' By our keeping of a good conscience men will be made ashamed of their false accusations; that whereas their malice and hatred of the ways of God hath provoked them to speak all manner of evil of the profession of them, by the holiness and righteousness of the saints, they are convinced and made ashamed, as a thief is when he is taken, and be driven to acknowledge that God is amongst them, and that they are wicked themselves, John xvii. 23. 2. Hereafter. It is said that the saints shall judge the world. It is on this, as well as upon other considerations: their good works, their righteousness, their holiness, shall be brought forth, and manifested to all the world; and the righteousness of God's judgments against wicked men be thence evinced. See,' says Christ, these are they that I own, whom you so despised and abhorred; and see their works following them: this and that they have done, when you wallowed in your abominations,' Matt. xxv. 42, 43.

"[2dly.] The conversion of others. 1 Pet. ii. 12, Having your conversation honest among the Gentiles; that, wherein they speak against you as evil-doers, they may, by your good works, which they shall behold, glorify God in the day of visitation,' Matt. v. 16. Even revilers, persecutors, evil-speakers, have been overcome by the constant holy walking of professors; and when their day of visitation hath come, have glorified God on that account, 1 Pet. iii. 1, 2.

"[3dly.] The benefit of all; partly in keeping off judgments from the residue of men, as ten good men would have preserved Sodom: [367] partly by their real communication of good to them with whom they have to do in their generation. Holiness makes a man a good man, useful to all; and others eat of the fruits of the Spirit that he brings forth continually.

"[4thly.] It is necessary in respect of the state and condition of justified persons; and that whether you consider their relative state of acceptation, or their state of sanctification:--

"First. They are accepted and received into friendship with a holy God, -- a God of purer eyes than to behold iniquity, -- who hates every unclean thing. And is it not necessary that they should be holy who are admitted into his presence, walk in his sight, -- yea, lie in his bosom? Should they not with all diligence cleanse themselves from all pollution of [368] flesh and spirit, and perfect holiness in the fear of the Lord?

"Secondly. In respect of sanctification. We have in us a new creature, 2 Cor. v. 17. This new creature is fed, cherished, nourished, kept alive, by the fruits of holiness. To what end hath God given us new hearts, and new natures? Is it that we should kill them? stifle the creature that is found in us in the womb? that we should give him to the old man to be devoured?

"[5thly.] It is necessary in respect of the proper place of holiness in the new covenant; and that is twofold:--

"First. Of the means unto the end. God hath appointed that holiness shall be the means, [369] the way to that eternal life, which, as in itself and originally [it] is his gift by Jesus Christ, so, with regard to his constitution of our obedience, as the means of attaining it, [it] is a reward, and God in bestowing of it a rewarder. Though it be neither the cause, matter, nor condition of our justification, yet it is the way appointed of God for us to walk in for the obtaining of salvation. And therefore, he that hath hope of eternal life purifies himself, as he is pure: and none shall ever come to that end who walketh not in that way; for without holiness it is impossible to see God.

"Secondly. It is a testimony and pledge of adoption, -- a sign and evidence of grace; that is, of acceptation with God. And, --

"Thirdly. The whole expression of our thankfulness.

"Now, there is not one of all these causes and reasons of the necessity, the indispensable necessity of our obedience, good works, and personal righteousness, but would require a more large discourse to unfold and explain than I have allotted to the proposal of them all; and innumerable others there are of the same import, that I cannot name. He that upon these accounts doth not think universal holiness and obedience to be of indispensable necessity, unless also it be exalted into the room of the obedience and righteousness of Christ, let him be filthy still."

I confess this whole discourse proceedeth on the supposition of the imputation of the righteousness of Christ unto us for our justification. And herein I have as good company as the prelacy and whole church of England can afford; sundry from among them having written large discourses in its confirmation, and the rest having, till of late, approved of it in others. I wish this man, or any of his companions in design, would undertake the answering of Bishop Downham on this subject. No man ever carried this matter higher than Luther; nor did he, in all his writings, more positively and plainly contend for it than in his comment on the Epistle to the Galatians; -- yet was that book translated into English by the approbation of the then bishop of London, who also prefixed himself a commendatory epistle unto it. The judgment of Hooker we have heard before. But what need I mention in particular any of the rest of those great and learned names who have made famous the profession of the church of England by their writings throughout the world? Had this man, in their days, treated this doctrine with his present scoffing petulancy, he had scarce been rector of St George, Botolph Lane, much less filled with such hopes and expectations of future advancements, as it is not impossible that he is now possessed with, upon his memorable achievements. But, on this supposition, I do, first, appeal to the judgment of the church of England itself as to the truth of the doctrine delivered in my discourse, and the principles which this man proceedeth on in his exceptions against it. 2. Though it be but a part of a popular discourse, and never intended for scholastic accuracy, yet, as to the assertions contained in it, I challenge this author to take and allow the ordinary, usual sense of the words, with the open design of them, and to answer them when he can. And, 3. In the meantime I appeal unto every indifferent reader whether the mere perusal of this whole passage do not cast this man's futilous cavils out of all consideration? So that I shall only content myself with very few remarks upon them:--

1. Upon my asserting the necessity of good works, he adds, "A very suspicious word; which, methinks, these men should be afraid to name." And why so? We do acknowledge that we do not seek for righteousness by the works of the law; we design not our personal justification by them, nor to merit life or salvation; but betake ourselves unto what even Bellarmine himself came to at last as the safest retreat, -- namely, the merits and righteousness of Christ: but for attendance unto them, performance of them, and fruitfulness in them, we are not afraid nor ashamed at any time to enter into judgment with them by whom we are traduced. And as I have nothing to say unto this author, who is known unto me only by that portraiture and character which he hath given of himself in this book; which I could have wished, for his own sake, had been drawn with a mixture of more lines of truth and modesty: so I know there are not a few who, in the course of a vain, worldly conversation, whilst there is scarce a back or belly of a disciple of Christ that blesseth God upon the account of their bounty or charity (the footsteps of levity, vanity, scurrility, and profaneness, being, moreover, left upon all the paths of their haunt), are wont to declaim about holiness, good works, and justification by them; which is a ready way to instruct men to atheism, or the scorn of every thing that is professed in religion. But yet, 2. He shows how impotent and impertinent our arguments are for the proof of the necessity of holiness. And as to the first of them, from the commands of God, he saith, "That if, after all these commands, God hath left it indifferent whether we obey him or no, I hope such commands cannot make obedience necessary." Wonderful divinity! A man must needs be well acquainted with God and himself who can suppose that any of his commands shall leave it indifferent, whether we will obey them or no. Yea, "But will he damn men if they do not obey his commands for holiness?" Yes, yes; no doubt he will do so. Yea, "But we may be, notwithstanding this command, justified and saved without this holiness." False and impertinent: we are neither justified nor saved without them, though we are not justified by them, nor saved for them.

Unto my enforcement of the necessity of holiness from the ends of God in election and redemption, he replies, p. 127, "The Father hath elected us to be holy, and the Son redeemed us to be holy; but will the Father elect and the Son redeem none but those who are holy, and reject and reprobate all others? Doth this election and redemption suppose holiness in us, or is it without any regard to it? For if we be elected and redeemed without any regard unto our own being holy, our election and redemption is secure, whether we be holy or not." Wonderful divinity again! Election and redemption suppose holiness in us! We are elected and redeemed with regard unto our own holiness that is, antecedently unto our election and redemption; for holiness being the effect and fruit of them, is that which he opposeth. Not many pages after this, he falls into a great admiration of the catechism of the church of England, which none blamed that I know of, as to what is contained in it. But it were to be wished that he had been well instructed in some others, that he might not have divulged and obtruded on the world such crude and palpable mistakes. For this respect of redemption, at least, unto an antecedent holiness in us (that is, antecedent unto it), is such a piece of foppery in religion, as a man would wonder how any one could be guilty of, who hath almost "pored out his eyes" in reading the Scripture. All the remaining cavils of this chapter are but the effects of the like fulsome ignorance; for out of some passages, scraped together from several parts of my discourse (and those not only cut off from their proper scope and end, which is not mentioned by him at all, but also mangled in their representation), he would frame the appearance of a contradiction between what I say on the one hand, that there is no peace with God to be obtained by and for sinners but by the atonement that is made for them in the blood of Jesus Christ, with the remission of sin and justification by faith which ensue thereon (which I hope I shall not live to hear denied by the church of England), and the necessity of holiness and fruitfulness in obedience, to maintain in our own souls a sense of that peace with God which we have, being justified by faith. And he who understands not the consistency of those things, hath little reason to despise good catechisms, whatever thoughts he hath had of his own sufficiency.

The whole design of what remains of this section, is to insinuate that there can be no necessity of holiness or obedience unto God, unless we are justified and saved thereby; which I knew not before to have been, nor indeed do yet know it to be, the doctrine of the church of England. But be it whose it will, I am sure it is not that of the Scripture, and I have so disproved it in other discourses, which this man may now see if he please, as that I shall not here again reassume the same argument; and although I am weary of consulting this woeful mixture of disingenuity and ignorance, yet I shall remark somewhat on one or two passages more, and leave him, if he please, unto a due apprehension, that what remains is unanswerable scoffing.

The first is that of p. 131. "But, however, holiness is necessary with respect to sanctification: We have in us a new creature, 2 Cor. v. 17. This new creature is fed, cherished, nourished, and kept alive, by the fruits of holiness. To what end hath God given us new hearts, and new natures? Is it that we should kill them, stifle the creature that is found in us in the womb? that we should give him to the old man to be devoured?' The phrase of this is admirable, and the reasoning unanswerable; for if men be new creatures, they will certainly live new lives, and this makes holiness absolutely necessary, by the same reason that every thing necessarily is what it is: but still we inquire after a necessary obligation to the practice of holiness, and that we cannot yet discover."

The reader will see easily how this is picked out of the whole discourse, as that which he imagined would yield some advantage to reflect upon; for, let him pretend what he please to the contrary, he hath laid this end too open to be denied; and I am no way solicitous what will be his success therein. Had he aimed at the discovery of truth, he ought to have examined the whole of the discourse, and not thus have rent one piece of it from the other. As to the phrase of speech which I use, it is, I acknowledge, metaphorical; but yet, being used only in a popular way of instruction, is sufficiently warranted from the Scripture, which administers occasion and gives countenance unto every expression in it, the whole being full well understood by those who are exercised in the life of God. And for the reasoning of it, it is such as I know this man cannot answer: for the new creature, however he may fancy, is not a new conversation, nor a living holily; but it is the principle, and spiritual ability, produced in believers by the power and grace of the Holy Ghost, enabling them to walk in newness of life and holiness of conversation. And this principle being bestowed on us, wrought in us, for that very end, it is necessary for us, unless we will neglect and despise the grace which we have received, that we walk in holiness, and abound in the fruits of righteousness, whereunto it leads and tends. Let him answer this if he can, and when he hath done so, answer the apostle in like manner; or scoff not only at me, but at him also.

The last passage I shall remark upon in this section is what he gives us as the sum of the whole. P. 135, "The sum of all is, that to know Christ is not to be thus acquainted with his person, but to understand his gospel in its full latitude and extent; it is not the person, but the gospel of Christ which is the way, the truth, and the life, which directs us in the way to life and happiness. And again, this acquaintance with Christ's person, which these men pretend to, is only a work of fancy, and teaches men the arts of hypocrisy," etc.

I do not know that ever I met with any thing thus crudely asserted among the Quakers, in contempt of the person of Christ; for whereas he says of himself expressly, "I am the way, the truth, and the life," to say he is not so (for Jesus Christ is his person, and nothing else), carries in it a bold contradiction, both parts of which cannot be true. When the subject of a proposition is owned, there may be great controversy about the sense of the predicate; as when Christ says he is the vine: there may be so also about the subject of a proposition, when the expression is of a third thing, and dubious; as where Christ says, "This is my body:" but when the person speaking is the subject, and speaks of himself, to deny what he says, is to give him the lie. "I am the way, the truth, and the life," saith Christ; -- "He is not," saith our author, "but the gospel is so." If he had allowed our Lord Jesus Christ to have spoken the truth, but only to have added, "Though he was so, yet he was so no otherwise but by the gospel," there had been somewhat of modesty in the expression; but this saying, that the "person of Christ is not, -- the gospel is so," is intolerable. It is so, however, that this young man, without consulting or despising the exposition of all divines, ancient or modern, and the common sense of all Christians, should dare to obtrude his crude and undigested conceptions upon so great a word of Christ himself, countenanced only by the corrupt and false glosses of some obscure Socinians: which some or other may possibly in due time mind him of; I have other work to do.

But according to his exposition of this heavenly oracle, what shall any one imagine to be the sense of the context, where "I," and "me," spoken of Christ, do so often occur? Suppose that the words of that whole verse, "I am the way, the truth, and the life, no man comes to the Father but by me," have this sense, -- not Christ himself is the way, the truth, and the life, but the gospel; "No man comes to the Father but by me;" that is, not by me, but by "the gospel," -- must not all the expressions of the same nature in the context have the same exposition? as namely, verse 1, "Ye believe in God, believe also in me;" that is, not in me but in "the gospel;" -- "I go to prepare a place for you;" that is, not I do so, but "the gospel;" verse 3, "I will come again and receive you to myself;" that is, not I, but "the gospel" will do so; and so of all other things which Christ in that place seems to speak of himself. If this be his way of interpreting Scripture, I wonder not that he blames others for their defect and miscarriages therein.

When I first considered these two last sections, I did not suspect but that he had at least truly represented my words, which he thought meet to reflect upon and scoff at; as knowing how easy it was for any one whose conscience would give him a dispensation for such an undertaking, to pick out sayings and expressions from the most innocent discourse, and odiously to propose them, as cut off from their proper coherence, and under a concealment of the end and the principal sense designed in them. Wherefore I did not so much as read over the discourse excepted against; only, once or twice observing my words, as quoted by him, not directly to comply with what I knew to be my sense and intention, I turned unto the particular places to discover his prevarication. But having gone through this ungrateful task, I took the pains to read over the whole digression in my book, which his exceptions are levelled against; and, upon my review of it, my admiration of his dealing was not a little increased. I cannot, therefore, but desire of the most partial adherers unto this censurer of other men's labours, judgments, and expressions, but once to read over that discourse, and if they own themselves to be Christians, I shall submit the whole of it, with the consideration of his reflections upon it, unto their judgments. If they refuse so to do, I let them know I despise their censures, and do look on the satisfaction they take in this man's scoffing reflections as the laughter of fools, or the crackling of thorns under a pot. For those who will be at so much pains to undeceive themselves, they will find that that expression of the "person of Christ" is but once or twice used in all that long discourse, and that occasionally; which, by the outcries here made against it, any one would suppose to have filled up almost all the pages of it. He will find, also, that I have owned and declared the revelation that God hath made of himself, the properties of his nature, and his will, in his works of creation and providence, in its full extent and efficacy; and that by the knowledge of God in Christ, which I so much insist upon, I openly, plainly, and declaredly, intend nothing but the declaration that God hath made of himself in Jesus Christ by the gospel: whereof the knowledge of his person, the great mystery of godliness, God manifested in the flesh, with what he did and suffered as the mediator between God and man, is the chiefest instance; in which knowledge consisteth all our wisdom of living unto God. Hereon I have no more to add, but that he by whom these things are denied or derided, doth openly renounce his Christianity. And that I do not lay this unto the charge of this doughty writer, is because I am satisfied that he hath not done it out of any such design, but partly out of ignorance of the things which he undertakes to write about, and partly to satisfy the malevolence of himself and some others against my person: which sort of depraved affections, where men give up themselves unto their prevalence, will blind the eyes and pervert the judgments of persons as wise as he.

In the first section of his fourth chapter I am not particularly concerned; and whilst he only vents his own conceits, be they never so idle or atheological, I shall never trouble myself, either with their examination or confutation. So many as he can persuade to be of his mind, -- that we have no union with Christ but by virtue of union with the church (the contrary whereof is absolutely true); that Christ is so a head of rule and government unto the church, as that he is not a head of influence and supplies of spiritual life (contrary to the faith of the catholic church in all ages); that these assertions of his have any countenance from antiquity, or the least from the passages quoted out of Chrysostom by himself; that his glosses upon many texts of Scripture (which have an admirable coincidence with those of two other persons whom I shall name when occasion requires it) are sufficient to affix upon them the sense which he pleads for, will many other things of an equal falsehood and impertinency wherewith this section is stuffed, -- shall, without any farther trouble from me, be left to follow their own inclinations. But yet, not withstanding all the great pains he hath taken to instruct us in the nature of the union between Christ and believers, I shall take leave to prefer that given by Mr Hooker before it, not only as more true and agreeable unto the Scripture, but also as better expressing the doctrine of the church of England in this matter. And if these things please the present rulers of the church, -- wherein upon the matter Christ is shuffled off, and the whole of our spiritual union is resolved into the doctrine of the gospel, and the rule of the church by bishops and pastors, let it imply what contradiction it will, as it doth the highest, seeing it is by the doctrine of the gospel that we are taught our union will Christ, and his rule of the church by his laws and Spirit, -- I have only the advantage to know somewhat more than I did formerly, though not much to my satisfaction.

But he that shall consider what reflections are cast in this discourse on the necessity of satisfaction to be made unto divine justice, and from whom they are borrowed; the miserable, weak attempt that is made therein to reduce all Christ's mediatory actings unto his kingly office, and, in particular, his intercession; the faint mention that is made of the satisfaction of Christ, clogged with the addition of ignorance of the philosophy of it, as it is called, well enough complying with them who grant that the Lord Christ did what God was satisfied withal, with sundry other things of the like nature; will not be to seek whence these things come, nor whither they are going, nor to whom our author is beholden for most of his rare notions; which it is an easy thing at any time to acquaint him withal.

The second section of this chapter is filled principally with exceptions against my discourse about the personal excellencies of Christ as mediator; if I may not rather say, with the reflections on the glory of Christ himself. [As] for my own discourse upon it, I acknowledge it to be weak, and not only inconceivably beneath the dignity and merit of the subject, but also far short of what is taught and delivered by many ancient writers of the church unto that purpose; and [as] for his exceptions, they are such a composition of ignorance and spite as is hardly to be paralleled. His entrance upon his work is (p. 200) as followeth:-- "Secondly, Let us inquire what they mean by the person of Christ, to which believers must be united. And here they have outdone all the metaphysical subtilties of Suarez, and have found out a person for Christ distinct from his Godhead and manhood; for there can he no other sense made of what Dr Owen tells us, -- that by the graces of his person' he doth not mean the glorious excellencies of his Deity considered in itself, abstracting from the office which for us, as God and man, he undertook; nor the outward appearance of his human nature, when he conversed here on earth, nor yet as now exalted in glory: but the graces of the person of Christ, as he is vested with the office of mediation, -- his spiritual eminency, comeliness, beauty, as appointed and anointed by the Father unto that great work of bringing home all his elect into his bosom.' Now, unless the person of Christ as mediator be distinct from his person as God-man, all this is idle talk; for what personal graces are there in Christ as mediator which do not belong to him either as God or man? There are some things, indeed, which our Saviour did and suffered, which he was not obliged to, either as God or man, but as mediator; but surely he will not call the peculiar duties and actions of an office personal graces."

I have now learned not to trust unto the honesty and ingenuity of our author, as to his quotations out of my book; which I find that he hath here mangled and altered, as in other places, and shall therefore transcribe the whole passage in my own words, p. 51: [370] "It is Christ as mediator of whom we speak; and therefore, by the grace of his person,' I understand not, first, The glorious excellencies of his Deity considered in itself, abstracting from the office which for us, as God and man, he undertook; nor, secondly, The outward appearance of his human nature, neither when he conversed here on earth, bearing our infirmities (whereof, by reason of the charge that was laid upon him, the prophet gives quite another character, Isa. lii. 14), concerning which some of the ancients are very poetical in their expressions; nor yet as now exalted in glory; -- a vain imagination whereof makes many bear a false, a corrupted respect unto Christ, even upon carnal apprehensions of the mighty exaltation of the human nature; which is but to know Christ after the flesh,' -- a mischief much improved by the abomination of foolish imagery. But this is that which I intend, -- the graces of the person of Christ as he is vested with the office of mediation, his spiritual eminency, comeliness, and beauty, etc. Now, in this respect the Scripture describes him as exceeding excellent, comely, and desirable, -- far above comparison with the chiefest, choicest created good, or any endearment imaginable;" which I prove at large from Ps. xlv. 2; Isa. iv. 2; Cant. v. 9, adding an explanation of the whole.

In the digression, some passages whereof he carps at in this section, my design was to declare, as was said, somewhat of the glory of the person of Christ. To this end I considered both the glory of his divine and the many excellencies of his human nature; but that which I principally insisted on was the excellency of his person as God and man in one, whereby he was meet and able to be the mediator between God and man, and to effect all the great and blessed ends of his mediation. That our Lord Jesus Christ was God, and that there were, on that account, in his person the essential excellencies and properties of the divine nature, I suppose he will not deny; nor will he do so that he was truly man, and that his human nature was endowed with many glorious graces and excellencies which are peculiar thereunto. That there is a distinct consideration of his person as both these natures are united therein, is that which he seems to have a mind to except against. And is it meet that any one who hath aught else to do should spend any moments of that time which he knows how better to improve, in the pursuit of a man's impertinencies, who is so bewildered in his own ignorance and confidence, that he knows neither where he is nor what he says? Did not the Son of God, by assuming our human nature, continuing what he was, become what he was not? Was not the person of Christ, by the communication of the properties of each nature in it and to it, a principle of such operations as he could not have wrought either as God or man, separately considered? How else did God "redeem his church with his own blood?" or how is that true which he says, John iii. 13, "And no man hath ascended up to heaven, but he that came down from heaven, even the Son of man, which is in heaven?" Was not the union of the two natures in the same person (which was a property neither of the divine nor human nature, but a distinct ineffable effect of divine condescension, wisdom, and grace, which the ancients unanimously call the "grace of union," whose subject is the person of Christ) that whereby he was fit, meet, and able, for all the works of his mediation? Doth not the Scripture, moreover, propose unto our faith and consolation the glory, power, and grace of the person of Christ as he is "God over all, blessed for ever;" and his love, sympathy, care and compassion as man; yet all acting themselves in the one and self same person of the Son of God? Let him read the first chapter of the Epistle to the Hebrews, and see what account he can give thereof. And are not these such principles of Christian religion as no man ought to be ignorant of, or can deny, without the guilt of the heresies condemned in the first general councils? And they are no other principles which my whole discourse excepted against doth proceed upon. But saith our author, "Unless the person of Christ as mediator be distinct from his person as God-man, all this is idle talk." Very good! and why so? Why, "What personal graces are there in Christ as mediator, which do not belong unto him either as God or man?" But is he not ashamed of this ignorance? Is it not a personal grace and excellency that he is God and man in one person? which belongs not to him either as God or man. And are there not personal operations innumerable depending hereon, which could not have been wrought by him either as God or man; as raising himself from the dead by his own power, and redeeming the church with his blood? Are not most of the descriptions that are given us of Christ in the Scripture, most of the operations which are assigned unto him, such as neither belong unto nor proceed from the divine or human nature, separately considered, but from the person of Christ, as both these natures are united in it? That which seems to have led him into the maze wherein he is bewildered in his ensuing discourse, is, that considering there are but two natures in Christ, the divine and the human, -- and nature is the principle of all operations, -- he supposed that nothing could be said of Christ, nothing ascribed to his person, but what was directly, formally predicated of one of his natures, distinctly considered. But he might have easily inquired of himself, -- that seeing all the properties and acts of the divine nature are absolutely divine, and all those of the human nature absolutely human, whence it came to pass that all the operations and works of Christ, as mediator, are theandrical? [371] Although there be nothing in the person of Christ but his divine and human nature, yet the person of Christ is neither his divine nature nor his human; for the human nature is, and ever was, of itself, ἀνυπόστατος; and the divine, to the complete constitution of the person of the Mediator, in and unto its own hypostasis assumed the human: so that, although every energy or operation be δραστικὴ τῆς φύσεως κίνησις, and so the distinct natures are distinct principles of Christ's operations, yet his person is the principal or only agent; which being God-man, all the actions thereof, by virtue of the communication of the properties of both natures therein, are theandrical. And the excellency of this person of Christ, wherein he was every way fitted for the work of mediation, I call sometimes his personal grace, and will not go to him to learn to speak and express myself in these things. And it is most false which he affirms, p. 203, "That I distinguish the graces of Christ's person as mediator from the graces of his person as God and man." Neither could any man have run into such an imagination who had competently understood the things which he speaks about; and the bare proposal of these things is enough to defeat the design of all his ensuing cavils and exceptions.

And as to what he closeth withal, that "Surely I will not call the peculiar duties and actions of an office personal graces;" I suppose that he knoweth not well what he intends thereby. Whatever he hath fancied about Christ being the name of an office, Jesus Christ, of whom we speak, is a person, and not an office; and there are no such things in rerum natura as the actions of an office. And if by them he intends the actions of a person in the discharge of an office, whatever he calls them, I will call the habits in Christ, from whence all his actions in the performance of his office do proceed, "personal graces," and that whether he will or no. So he is a "merciful, faithful, and compassionate high priest," Heb. ii. 17, iv. 15, v. 2. And all his actions, in the discharge of his office of priesthood, being principled and regulated by those qualifications, I do call them his personal graces, and do hope that, for the future, I may obtain his leave so to do. The like may be said of his other offices.

The discourse which he thus raves against is didactical, and accommodated unto a popular way of instruction; and it hath been hitherto the common ingenuity of all learned men to give an allowance unto such discourses, so as not to exact from them an accuracy and propriety in expressions, such as is required in those that are scholastical or polemical. It is that which, by common consent, is allowed to the tractates of the ancients of that nature, -- especially where nothing is taught but what, for the substance of it, is consonant unto the truth. But this man attempts not only a severity in nibbling at all expressions which he fancieth liable unto his censures, but, with a disingenuous artifice, waiving the tenor and process of the discourse, which I presume he found not himself able to oppose, he takes out, sometimes here, sometimes there, up and down, backward and forward, at his pleasure, what he will, to put, if it be possible, an ill sense upon the whole. And, if he have not hereby given a sufficient discovery of his good-will towards the doing of somewhat to my disadvantage, he hath failed in his whole endeavour; for there is no expression which he hath fixed on as the subject of his reflections, which is truly mine, but that as it is used by me, and with respect unto its end, I will defend it against him and all his co-partners, whilst the Scripture may be allowed to be the rule and measure of our conceptions and expressions about sacred things. And although at present I am utterly wearied with the consideration of such sad triflings, I shall accept from him the kindness of an obligation to so much patience as is necessary unto the perusal of the ensuing leaves, wherein I am concerned.

First, p. 202, he would pick something, if he knew what, out of my quotations of Cant. v. 9, to express or illustrate the excellency of Christ; which first he calls an "excellent proof," by way of scorn. But as it is far from being the only proof produced in the confirmation of the same truth, and is applied rather to illustrate what was spoken, than to prove it, yet, by his favour, I shall make bold to continue my apprehensions of the occasional exposition of the words which I have given in that place, until he is pleased to acquaint me with a better; which, I suppose, will be long enough. For what he adds, -- "But, however, white and ruddy belong to his divine and human nature, and that without regard to his mediatory office; for he had been white in the glory of his Deity, and ruddy with the red earth of his humanity, whether he had been considered as mediator or not," -- it comes from the same spring of skill and benevolence with those afore. For what wise talk is it, of Christ's being God and man, without the consideration of his being mediator! as though he were ever, or ever should have been, God and man, but with respect unto his mediation? His scoff at the red earth of Christ's humanity, represented as my words, is grounded upon a palpable falsification; for my words are, "He was also ruddy in the beauty of his humanity. Man was called Adam, from the red earth whereof he was made. The word here used points him out as the second Adam, partaker of flesh and blood, because the children also partook of the same." And if he be displeased with these expressions, let him take his own time to be pleased again; it is that wherein I am not concerned. But my fault, which so highly deserved his correction, is, that I apply that to the person of Christ which belongs unto his natures. But what if I say no such thing, or had no such design in that place? For although I do maintain a distinct consideration of the excellency of Christ's person, as comprising both his natures united, -- though every real thing in his person belongs formally and radically unto one [or other] of the natures (those other excellencies being the exurgency of their union), whereby his person was fitted and suited unto his mediatory operations, which in neither nature, singly considered, he could have performed, -- and shall continue to maintain it against whosoever dares directly to oppose it; yet in this place I intended it not, which this man knew well enough, -- the very next words unto what he pretends to prove it [by], being, "The beauty and comeliness of the Lord Jesus Christ, in the union of both these in one person, shall afterward be declared." And so we have an equality in judgment and ingenuity throughout this censure.

Hence he leaps to p. 64 of my book, thence backwards to p. 53, and then up and down, I know not how nor whither. He begins with p. 64: [372] -- "And in his first digression concerning the excellency of Christ Jesus, to invite us to communion with him in a conjugal relation, he tells us that Christ is exceeding excellent and desirable in his Deity, and the glory thereof; he is desirable and worthy our acceptation as considered in his humanity, in his freedom from sin, fulness of grace, etc. Now, though this looks very like a contradiction, that by the graces of his person, he meant neither the excellencies of his divine nor human nature; yet he hath a salvo which will deliver him both from contradiction and from nonsense, -- that he doth not consider these excellencies of his Deity or humanity as abstracted from his office of mediator, though he might if he pleased: for he considers those excellencies which are not peculiar to the office of mediation, but which would have belonged unto him as God and man, whether he had been mediator or not. But what becomes of his distinction of the graces of Christ's person as mediator from the graces of his person as God and man, when there are no personal graces in Christ but what belong to his Deity or his humanity?"

I am sufficiently satisfied that he neither knows where he is nor what he doth, or hath no due comprehension of the things he treats about. That which he opposeth, if he intend to oppose any thing by me asserted, is, that whereas Christ is God, the essential properties of his divine nature are to be considered as the formal motive unto, and object of, faith, love, and obedience; and whereas he is man also, his excellencies, in the glorious endowment of his human nature, with his alliance unto us therein, and his furniture of grace for the discharge of his office, are proposed unto our faith and love in the Scripture. And of these things we ought to take a distinct consideration; our faith concerning them being not only taught in the Scripture, but fully confirmed in the confessions and determinations of the primitive church. But the person of Christ, wherein these two natures are united, is of another distinct consideration; and such things are spoken thereof as cannot, under any single enunciation, be ascribed unto either nature, though nothing be so but what formally belongs unto one of them, or is the necessary consequent and exurgency of their union. See Isa. ix. 6; 1 Tim. iii. 16; John i. 14. It is of the "glory of the Word of God made flesh" that I discourse. But this man talks of what would have belonged to Christ as God-man, whether he had been mediator or not; as though the Son of God either was, or was ever designed to be, or can be, considered as God-man, and not as mediator. And thence he would relieve himself by the calumny of assigning a distinction unto me between the graces of Christ's person as mediator, and the graces of his person as God and man (that is, one person); which is a mere figment of his own misunderstanding. Upon the whole, he comes to that accurate thesis of his own, -- that there are no personal graces in Christ but what belong to his Deity or humanity. Personal graces belonging unto the humanity, or human nature of Christ, -- that nature being ἀνυπόστατος, or such as hath no personal subsistence of its own, -- is a notion that those may thank him for who have a mind to do it. And he may do well to consider what his thoughts are of the grace of our Lord Jesus Christ, mentioned Phil. ii. 6-11.

But he will now discover the design of all these things, and afterward make it good by quotations out of my book. The first he doth, p. 203, and onwards: "But whatever becomes of the sense of the distinction, there is a very deep fetch in it, the observing of which will discover the whole mystery of the person of Christ and our union to him. For these men consider that Christ saves us as he is our mediator, and not merely considered as God or man; and they imagine that we receive grace and salvation from Christ's person just as we do water out of a conduit, or a gift and largess from a prince, -- that it flows to us from our union to his person; and therefore they dress up the person of the Mediator with all those personal excellencies and graces which may make him a fit Saviour, that those who are thus united to his person (of which more in the next section) need not fear missing of salvation. Hence they ransack all the boundless perfections of the Deity, and whatever they can find or fancy speaks any comfort to sinners, this is presently a personal grace of the Mediator; -- they consider all the glorious effects of his mediation; and whatever great things are spoken of his gospel, or religion, or intercession for us, these serve as personal graces: so that all our hopes may be built, not on the gospel covenant, but on the person of Christ. So that the dispute now lies between the person of Christ and his gospel, -- which must be the foundation of our hope, -- which is the way to life and happiness."

First, We do consider and believe that Christ saves as a mediator; that is, as God and man in one person, exercising the office of a mediator, and not merely as God or man. This we believe with all the catholic church of Christ, and can with boldness say, He that doth not so, let him be anathema maran-atha. Secondly, We do not imagine, but believe from the Scripture, and with the whole church of God, that we receive grace and salvation from the person of Christ in those distinct ways wherein they are capable of being received; and let him be anathema who believes otherwise. Only, whether his putting of grace and salvation into the same way of reception belong unto his accuracy in expressing his own sentiments, or his ingenuity in the representation of other men's words, I leave undetermined. The similitudes he useth to express our faith in these things, show his good-will towards scoffing and profaneness. We say, there is real communication of grace from the person of Christ, as the head of the church, unto all the members of his mystical body by his Spirit, whereby they are quickened, sanctified, and enabled unto all holy obedience: and, if it be denied by him, he stands anathematised by sundry councils of the ancient church. We say not, that we receive it as "water out of a conduit," which is of a limited, determined capacity; whereas we say, the person of Christ, by reason of his Deity, is an immense, eternal, living spring or fountain of all grace. And when God calls himself a "fountain of living water;" and the Lord Christ calls his Spirit communicated to believers "living water" (under which appellation he was frequently promised in the Old Testament); as also the grace and mercy of the gospel, the "water of life," -- inviting us to receive them, and to drink of them, -- this author may be advised to take heed of profane scoffing at these things. Whether any have said, that we receive grace and salvation from Christ, as "a gift or largess from a prince," I know not; if they have, the sole defect therein is, that the allusion doth no way sufficiently set forth the freedom and bounty of Christ in the communication of them unto sinners; and wherein else it offends, let him soberly declare, if he can. This is the charge upon us in point of faith and judgment; which, in one word, amounts to no more but this, -- that we are Christians: and so, by the grace of God, we intend to continue, let this man deride us whilst he pleaseth. Thirdly, His next charge concerns our practice in the pursuit of these dreadful principles, which, by their repetition, he hath exposed to scorn: "And therefore they dress up," etc. What doth this poor man intend? what is the design of all this profaneness? The declaration of the natures and person of Christ, -- of his grace and work, -- the ascribing unto him what is directly and expressly in terms ascribed unto him in the Scripture, or relating, as we are able, the description it gives of him, -- is here called, "Dressing up the person of the Mediator with all those personal graces that may make him a fit Saviour." The preparation of the person of Christ to be a fit and meet Saviour for sinners, which he profanely compares to the dressing up of ?, is the greatest, most glorious, and admirable effect that ever infinite wisdom, goodness, power, and love wrought and produced, or will do so unto eternity. And those on whom he reflects design nothing, do nothing in this matter, but only endeavour, according to the measure of the gift of Christ which they have received, to declare and explain what is revealed and taught in the Scripture thereof; and those who exceed the bounds of Scripture revelation herein (if any do so) we do abhor. And as for those who are united unto Christ, although we say not that they need not fear missing of salvation, seeing they are to be brought unto it, not only through the exercise of all graces, whereof fear is one, but also through such trials and temptations as will always give them a fear of heed and diligence, and sometimes such a fear of the event of things as shall combat their faith, and shake its firmest resolves; yet we fear not to say, that those who are really united unto Jesus Christ shall be assuredly saved; which I have proved elsewhere beyond the fear of any opposition from this author, or others like minded. Fourthly, He adds "Hence they ransack," etc. But what is the meaning of these expressions? Doth not the Scripture declare that Christ is God as well as man? Doth it not build all our faith, obedience, and salvation on that consideration? Are not the properties of the divine nature everywhere in the Scripture declared and proposed unto us for the ingenerating and establishing faith in us, and to be the object of, and exercise of, all grace and obedience? And is it now become a crime that any should seek to declare and instruct others in these things from the Scripture, and to the same end for which they are therein revealed? Is this, with any evidence of sobriety, to be traduced as a "ransacking the boundless perfections of the divine nature, to dress up the person of the Mediator"? Is he a Christian, or doth he deserve that name, who contemns or despiseth the consideration of the properties of the divine nature in the person of Christ (see Isa. vi. 1-4; John xii. 41; Isa. ix. 6; John i. 14; Phil. ii. 6, etc.), or shall think that the grace or excellencies of his person do not principally consist in them, as the human nature is united thereunto? Fifthly, "They consider all the glorious effects of his mediation." All the effects of Christ's mediation, -- all the things that are spoken of the gospel, etc., do all of them declare the excellency of the person of Christ, as effects declare their cause, and may and ought to be considered unto that end, as occasion doth require; and no otherwise are they considered by those whom he doth oppose. Sixthly, But the end of these strange principles and practices, he tells us, is, "That all our hopes may be built, not on the gospel covenant, but on the person of Christ." But I say again, What is it that this man intends? What is become of a common regard to God and man? Who do so build their hopes on Christ as to reject or despise the gospel covenant, as he calls it? -- though I am afraid, should he come to explain himself, he will be at a loss about the true nature of the gospel covenant, as I find him to be about the person and grace of Christ. He telleth us, indeed, that "Not the person of Christ, but the gospel, is the way." Did we ever say, "Not the covenant of grace, but the person of Christ is all we regard?" But whence comes this causeless fear and jealousy, -- or rather, this evil surmise, that if any endeavour to exalt the person of Christ, immediately the covenant of the gospel (that is, in truth, the covenant which is declared in the gospel) must be discarded? Is there an inconsistency between Christ and the covenant? I never met with any who was so fearful and jealous lest too much should be ascribed in the matter of our salvation to Jesus Christ; and when there is no more so, but what the Scripture doth expressly and in words assign unto him and affirm of him, instantly we have an outcry that the gospel and the covenant are rejected, and that a "dispute lies between the person of Christ and his gospel." But let him not trouble himself; for as he cannot, and as he knows he cannot, produce any one word or one syllable out of any writings of mine, that should derogate any thing from the excellency, nature, necessity, or use of the new covenant; so, though it may be he do not, and doth therefore fancy and dream of disputes between Christ and the gospel, we do know how to respect both the person of Christ and the covenant, -- both Jesus Christ and the gospel, in their proper places. And in particular, we do know, that as it is the person of Christ who is the author of the gospel, and who as mediator in his work of mediation gives life, and efficacy, and establishment unto the covenant of grace; so both the gospel and that covenant do declare the glory and design the exaltation of Jesus Christ himself. Speaking, therefore, comparatively, all our hopes are built on Jesus Christ, who alone fills all things; yet also we have our hopes in God, through the covenant declared in the gospel, as the way designing the rule of our obedience, securing our acceptance and reward. And to deal as gently as I can warrant myself to do with this writer, the dispute he mentions between the person of Christ and the gospel, which shall be the foundation of our hope, is only in his own fond imagination, distempered by disingenuity and malevolence. For, if I should charge what the appearance of his expressions will well bear, what he says seems to be out of a design, influenced by ignorance or heresy, to exclude Jesus Christ, God and man, from being the principal foundation of the church, and which all its hopes are built upon. This being the sum of his charge, I hope he will fully prove it in the quotations from my discourse, which he now sets himself to produce; assuring him that if he do not, but come short therein, setting aside his odious and foppish profane deductions, I do aver them all in plain terms, that he may, on his next occasion of writing, save his labour in searching after what he may oppose. Thus, therefore, he proceeds, p. 205:--

"To make this appear, I shall consider that account which Dr Owen gives us of the personal graces and excellencies of Christ, which in general consist in three things:-- First, His fitness to save, from the grace of union, and the proper and necessary effects thereof. Secondly, His fulness to save, from the grace of communion, or the free consequences of the grace of union. And, thirdly, His excellency to endear, from his complete suitableness to all the wants of the souls of men. First, That he is fit to be a Saviour, from the grace of union. And if you will understand what this strange grace of union is, it is the uniting the nature of God and man in one person, which makes him fit to be a Saviour to the uttermost. He lays his hand upon God, by partaking of his nature; and he lays his hand on us, by partaking of our nature: and so becomes a days-man or umpire between both. Now, though this be a great truth, that the union of the divine and human nature in Christ did excellently qualify him for the office of a mediator, yet this is the unhappiest man in expressing and proving it that I have met with. For what an untoward representation is this of Christ's mediation, that he came to make peace by laying his hands on God and men, as if he came to part a fray or scuffle: and he might as well have named Gen. i. 1, or Matt. i. 1, or any other place of Scripture, for the proof of it, as those he mentions."

To what end it is that he cites these passages out of my discourse is somewhat difficult to divine. Himself confesseth that what is asserted (at least in one of them) is a great truth, only, I am "the unhappiest man in expressing and proving it that ever he met with." It is evident enough to me, that he hath not met with many who have treated of this subject, or hath little understood those he hath met withal; so that there may be yet some behind as unhappy as myself. And seeing he hath so good a leisure from other occasions, as to spend his time in telling the world how unhappy I am in my proving and expressing of what himself acknowledgeth to be true, he may be pleased to take notice, that I am now sensible of my own unhappiness also, in having fallen under a diversion from better employments by such sad and woeful impertinencies. But being at once charged with both these misadventures, -- untowardness in expression, and weakness in the proof of a plain truth, I shall willingly admit of information, to mend my way of writing for the future. And the first reflection he casts on my expressions, is my calling the union of the two natures in Christ in the same person, the "grace of union;" for so he says, "If you would understand what this strange grace of union is." But I crave his pardon in not complying with his directions, for my company's sake. No man, who hath once consulted the writings of the ancients on this subject, can be a stranger unto χάρις ἐνώσεως, and "gratia unionis," they so continually occur in the writings of all sorts of divines, both ancient and modern. Yea but there is yet worse behind; for, "What an untoward representation is this of Christ's mediation, that he came to make peace by laying his hands on God and men, as if he came to part a fray or scuffle." My words are, "The uniting of the natures of God and man in one person, made him fit to be a Saviour to the uttermost. He laid his hand upon God, by partaking of his nature, Zech. xiii. 7; and he lays his hand upon us, by partaking of our nature, Heb. ii. 14, 16: and so becomes a days-man or umpire between both." See what it is to be adventurous. I doubt not but that he thought that I had invented that expression, or at least, that I was the first who ever applied it unto this interposition of Christ between God and man; but as I took the words, and so my warranty for the expression from the Scripture, Job ix. 33, so it hath commonly been applied by divines in the same manner, particularly by Bishop Usher (in his "Emmanuel," pp. 8, 9, as I remember); whose unhappiness in expressing himself in divinity this man needs not much to bewail. But let my expressions be what they will, I shall not escape the unhappiness and weakness of my proofs; for "I might," he says, "as well have quoted Gen. i. 1, and Matt. i. 1, for the proof of the unity of the divine and human nature in the person of Christ, and his fitness thence to be a Saviour, as those I named," -- namely, Zech. xiii. 7; Heb. ii. 14, 16. Say you so? Why, then, I do here undertake to maintain the personal union, and the fitness of Christ from thence to be a Saviour, from these two texts, against this man and all his fraternity in design. And at present I cannot but wonder at his confidence, seeing I am sure he cannot be ignorant that one of these places, at least, -- namely, that of Heb. ii. 16, -- is as much, as frequently, as vehemently pleaded by all sorts of divines, ancient and modern, to prove the assumption of our human nature into personal subsistence with the Son of God, that so he might be ἱκανός (fit and able to save us), as any one testimony in the whole Scripture. And the same truth is as evidently contained and expressed in the former, seeing no man could be the "fellow of the Lord of hosts" but he that was partaker of the same nature with him; and no one could have the sword of God upon him to smite him, which was needful unto our salvation, but he that was partaker of our nature, or man also. And the mere recital of these testimonies was sufficient unto my purpose in that place, where I designed only to declare, and not dispute the truth. If he yet think that I cannot prove what I assert from these testimonies, let him consult my "Vindicæ Evangelicæ," where, according as that work required, I have directly pleaded these scriptures to the same purpose, insisting at large on the vindication of one of them; and let him answer what I have there pleaded, if he be able. And I shall allow him to make his advantage unto that purpose, if he please, of whatever evasions the Socinians have found out to escape the force of that testimony. For there is none of them of any note but have attempted by various artifices to shield their opinion, in denying the assumption of our human nature into personal union with the Son of God, and wherewithal his pre-existence unto his nativity of the blessed Virgin, from the divine evidence given against it in that place of Heb. ii. 16; which yet, if this author may be believed, doth make no more against them than Gen. i. 1. Wherefore, this severe censure, together with the modesty of the expression, wherein Christ making peace between God and man is compared to the parting of a fray or scuffle, may pass at the same rate and value with those which are gone before.

His ensuing pages are taken up, for the most part, with the transcription of passages out of my discourse, raked together from several places at his pleasure. I shall not impose the needless labour on the reader of a third perusal of them: nor shall I take the pains to restore the several passages to their proper place and coherence, which he hath rent them from, to try his skill and strength upon them separately and apart; for I see not that they stand in need of using the least of their own circumstantial evidence in their vindication. I shall therefore only take notice of his exceptions against them. And, p. 207, whereas I had said on some occasion, that on such a supposition we could have supplies of grace only in a moral way, it falls under his derision in his parenthesis; and that is a very pitiful way indeed. But I must yet tell him, by the way, that if he allow of no supplies of grace but in a moral way, he is a Pelagian, and as such, stands condemned by the catholic church. And when his occasions will permit it, I desire he would answer what is written by myself in another discourse, in the refutation of this sole moral operation of grace, and the assertion of another way of the communication of it unto us. Leave fooling, and "the unhappiest man in expressing himself that ever I met with" will not do it; he must betake himself to another course, if he intend to engage into the handling of things of this nature. He adds, whereas I had said, "?The grace of the promises' (of the person of Christ you mean):" I know well enough what I mean; but the truth is, I know not well what he means; nor whether it be out of ignorance that he doth indeed fancy an opposition between Christ and the promises, that what is ascribed unto the one must needs be derogated from the other, when the promise is but the means and instrument of conveying the grace of Christ unto us; or whether it proceeds from a real dislike that the person of Christ -- that is, Jesus Christ himself -- should be esteemed of any use or consideration in religion, that he talks at this rate. But from whence ever it proceeds, this cavilling humour is unworthy of any man of ingenuity or learning. By his following parenthesis ("a world of sin is something") I suppose I have somewhere used that expression, whence it is reflected on; but he quotes not the place, and I cannot find it. I shall therefore only at present tell him, as (if I remember alight) I have done already, that I will not come to him nor any of his companions to learn to express myself in these things; and, moreover, that I despise their censures. The discourses he is carping at in particular in this place are neither doctrinal nor argumentative, but consist in the application of truths before proved unto the minds and affections of men. And, as I said, I will not come to him nor his fraternity to learn how to manage such a subject, much less a logical and argumentative way of reasoning; nor have I any inducement whereunto from any thing that as yet I have seen in their writings. It also troubles him, p. 208, that whereas I know how unsuited the best and most accurate of our expressions are unto the true nature and being of divine things, as they are in themselves, and what need we have to make use of allusions, and sometimes less proper expressions, to convey a sense of them unto the minds and affections of men, I had once or twice used that ἐπανόθωσις, "if I may so say;" which yet if he had not known used in other good authors, treating of things of the same nature, he knew I could take protection against his severity under the example of the apostle, using words to the same purpose upon an alike occasion, Heb. vii. But at length he intends to be serious, and from those words of mine, "Here is mercy enough for the greatest, the oldest, the stubbornest transgressor;" he adds, "Enough, in all reason, this: what a comfort is it to sinners to have such a God for their Saviour, whose grace is boundless and bottomless, and exceeds the largest dimensions of their sins, though there be a world of sin in them. But what, now, if the divine nature itself have not such an endless, boundless, bottomless grace and compassion as the doctor now talks of? For at other times, when it serves his turn better, we can hear nothing from him but the naturalness of God's vindictive justice.' Though God be rich in mercy, he never told us that his mercy was so boundless and bottomless; he had given a great many demonstrations of the severity of his anger against sinners, who could not be much worse than the greatest, the oldest, and the stubbornest transgressors.'?"

Let the reader take notice, that I propose no grace in Christ unto or for such sinners, but only that which may invite all sorts of them, though under the most discouraging qualifications, to come unto him for grace and mercy by faith and repentance. And on supposition that this was my sense, as he cannot deny it to be, I add only, in answer, that this his profane scoffing at it, is that which reflects on Christ and his gospel, and God himself and his word; which must be accounted for. See Isa. lv. 7. Secondly, For the opposition which he childishly frames between God's vindictive justice and his mercy and grace, it is answered already. Thirdly, It is false that God hath not told us that his grace is boundless and bottomless, in the sense wherein I use those words, sufficient to pardon the greatest, the oldest, the stubbornest of sinners, -- namely, that turn unto him by faith and repentance; and he who knows not how this consists with severity and anger against impenitent sinners, is yet to learn his catechism. But yet he adds farther, pp. 208, 209, "Supposing the divine nature were such a bottomless fountain of grace, how comes this to be a personal grace of the Mediator? For a mediator, as mediator, ought not to be considered as the fountain, but as the minister of grace. God the Father certainly ought to come in for a share, at least, in being the fountain of grace, though the doctor is pleased to take no notice of him. But how excellent is the grace of Christ's person above the grace of the gospel; for that is a bounded and limited thing, a strait gate and narrow way, that leadeth unto life. There is no such boundless mercy as all the sins in the world cannot equal its dimensions, as will save the greatest, the oldest, and the stubbornest transgressors."

I beg the reader to believe that I am now so utterly weary with the repetition of these impertinencies, that I can hardly prevail with myself to fill my pen once more with ink about them; and I see no reason now to go on, but only that I have begun; and, on all accounts, I shall be as brief as possible. I say, then, first, I did not consider this boundless grace in Christ as mediator, but considered it as in him who is mediator; and so the divine nature, with all its properties, are greatly to be considered in him, if the gospel be true. But, secondly, It is untrue that Christ, as mediator, is only the minister of grace, and not the fountain of it; for he is mediator as God and man in one person. Thirdly, To suppose an exemption of the person of the Father from being the fountain of grace absolutely, in the order of the divine subsistence of the persons in the Trinity, and of their operations suited thereunto, upon the ascription of it unto the Son, is a fond imagination, which could befall no man who understands any thing of things of this nature. It doth as well follow, that if the Son created the world, the Father did not; if the Son uphold all things by the word of his power, the Father doth not; -- that is, that the Son is not in the Father, nor the Father in the Son. The acts, indeed, of Christ's mediation respect the ministration of grace, being the procuring and communicating causes thereof; but the person of Christ the mediator is the fountain of grace. So they thought who beheld his glory, -- "The glory as of the only begotten of the Father, full of grace and truth." But the especial relation of grace unto the Father, as sending the Son; unto the Son, as sent by him and incarnate; and unto the Holy Spirit, as proceeding from and sent by them both, I have elsewhere fully declared, and shall not in this place (which, indeed, will scarce give admittance unto any thing of so serious a nature) again insist thereon. Fourthly, The opposition which he would again set between Christ and the gospel is impious in itself; and, if he thinks to charge it on me, openly false. I challenge him and all his accomplices to produce any one word out of any writing of mine that, from a plea or pretence of grace in Christ, should give countenance unto any in the neglect of the least precept given or duty required in the gospel. And notwithstanding all that I have said or taught concerning the boundless, bottomless grace and mercy of Christ towards believing, humble, penitent sinners, I do believe the way of gospel obedience, indispensably required to be walked in by all that will come to the enjoyment of God, to be so narrow, that no revilers, nor false accusers, nor scoffers, nor despisers of gospel mysteries, continuing so to be, can walk therein; -- but that there is not grace and mercy declared and tendered in the gospel also unto all sorts of sinners, under any qualifications whatever, who upon its invitation, will come to God through Jesus Christ by faith and repentance, is an impious imagination.

A discourse much of the same nature follows, concerning the love of Christ, after he hath treated his person and grace at his pleasure. And this he takes occasion for from some passages in my book (as formerly), scraped together from several places, so as he thought fit and convenient unto his purpose. P. 209, "Thus the love of Christ is an eternal love, because his divine nature is eternal; and it is an unchangeable love, because his divine nature is unchangeable; and his love is fruitful, for it being the love of God, it must be effectual and fruitful in producing all the things which he willeth unto his beloved. He loves life, grace, holiness into us, loves us into covenant, loves us into heaven. This is an excellent love, indeed, which doth all for us, and leaves nothing for us to do. We owe this discovery to an acquaintance with Christ's person, or rather with his divine nature; for the gospel is very silent in this matter. All that the gospel tells us is, that Christ loveth sinners, so as to die for them; that he loves good men, who believe and obey his gospel, so as to save them; that he continues to love them while they continue to be good, but hates them when they return to their old vices: and therefore, I say, there is great reason for sinners to fetch their comforts not from the gospel, but from the person of Christ, which as far excels the gospel as the gospel excels the law."

I do suppose the expressions mentioned are, for the substance of them, in my book; and shall, therefore, only inquire what it is in them which he excepteth against, and for which I am reproached, as one that hath an acquaintance with Christ's person; which is now grown so common and trite an expression, that were it not condited unto some men's palates by its profaneness, it would argue a great barrenness in this author's invention, that can vary no more in the topic of reviling. It had been well if his licenser had accommodated him with some part of his talent herein. But what is it that is excepted against? Is it that the love of Christ, as he is God, is eternal? or is it that it is unchangeable? or is it that it is fruitful or effective of good things unto the persons beloved? The philosopher tells us, that to [have] love for any one, is, Βούλεσθαί τινι ἃ οἴεται ἀγαθά, καὶ τὸ κατὰ δύναμιν πρακτικὸν εἶναι τούτων. It is this efficacy of the love of Christ which must bear all the present charge. The meaning of my words, therefore, is, that the love of Christ is unto us the cause of life, grace, holiness, and the reward of heaven. And because it is in the nature of love to be effective, according unto the ability of the person loving, of the good which it wills unto the object beloved, I expressed it as I thought meet, by loving these things to us. And I am so far on this occasion, and [on account of] the severe reflection on me for an acquaintance with Christ, from altering my thoughts, that I say still with confidence, he who is otherwise minded is no Christian. And if this man knows not how the love of Christ is the cause of grace and glory, how it is effective of them, and that in a perfect consistency with all other causes and means of them, and the necessity of our obedience, he may do well to abstain a little from writing, until he is better informed. But saith he, "This is an excellent love, indeed, which doth all for us, and leaves us nothing to do." But who told him so? who ever said so? Doth he think that if our life, grace, holiness, glory, be from the love of Christ originally causally, by virtue of his divine, gracious operations in us and towards us, that there is no duty incumbent on them who would be made partakers of them, or use or improve them unto their proper ends? Shall we, then, to please him, say that we have neither life, nor grace, nor holiness, nor glory, from the love of Christ; but whereas most of them are our own duties, we have them wholly from ourselves? Let them do so who have a mind to renounce Christ and his gospel; I shall come into no partnership with them. [As] for what he adds "All that the gospel teaches us," etc., he should have done well to have said, as far as he knows; which is a limitation with a witness. If this be all the gospel which the man knows and preaches, I pity them whom he hath taken under his instruction. Doth Christ in his love do nothing unto the quickening and conversion of men? nothing to the purification and sanctification of believers? nothing as to their consolation and establishment? nothing as to the administration of strength against temptations? nothing as to supplies of grace, in the increase of faith, love, and obedience, etc.? This ignorance or profaneness is greatly to be bewailed, as his ensuing scoff, repeated now usque ad nauseam, about an opposition between Christ and his gospel, is to be despised. And if the Lord Christ hath no other love but what this man will allow, the state of the church in this world depends on a very slender thread. But attempts of this nature will fall short enough of prevailing with sober Christians to forego their faith and persuasion, -- that it is from the love of Christ that believers are preserved in that condition wherein he doth and will approve of them. Yea, to suppose that this is all the grace of the gospel, that whilst men are good Christ loves them, and when they are bad he hates them (both which are true); and farther, that he doth by his grace neither make them good, nor preserve them that are so made, -- is to renounce all that is properly so called.

He yet proceeds, first to evert this love which I asserted, and then to declare his own apprehensions concerning the love of Christ. The first in the ensuing words, p. 210, "But, methinks this is a very odd way of arguing from the divine nature; for if the love of Christ as God be so infinite, eternal, unchangeable, fruitful, I would willingly understand how sin, death, and misery came into the world. For if this love be so eternal and unchangeable, because the divine nature is so, then it was always so; for God always was what he is, and that which is eternal could never be other than it is now: and why could not this eternal, and unchangeable, and fruitful love, as well preserve us from falling into sin, and misery, and death, as love life and holiness into us? For it is a little odd, first to love us into sin and death, that then he may love us into life and holiness: which, indeed, could not be, if this love of God were always so unchangeable and fruitful as this author persuades us it is now; for if this love had always loved life and holiness into us, I cannot conceive how it should happen that we should sin and die."

It is well if he know what it is that he aims at in these words; I am sure what he says doth not in the least impeach the truth which he designs to oppose. The name and nature of God are everywhere in the Scripture proposed unto us as the object of, and encouragement unto, our faith, and his love in particular is therein represented unchangeable, because he himself is so; but it doth not hence follow that God loveth any one naturally, or necessarily. His love is a free act of his will; and therefore, though it be like himself, such as becomes his nature, yet it is not necessarily determined on any object, nor limited as unto the nature, degrees, and effects of it. He loves whom he pleaseth, and as unto what end he pleaseth. Jacob he loved, and Esau he hated; and those effects which, from his love or out of it, he will communicate unto them, are various, according to the counsel of his will. Some he loves only as to temporal and common mercies, some as to spiritual grace and glory; for he hath mercy on whom he will have mercy. Wherefore it is no way contrary unto, and inconsistent with, the eternity, the immutability, and fruitfulness of the love of God, that he suffered sin to enter into the world, or that he doth dispense more grace in Jesus Christ under the New Testament than he did under the Old. God is always the same that he was; love in God is always of the same nature that it was; but the objects, acts, and effects of this love, with the measures and degrees of them, are the issues of the counsel or free purposes of his will. Want of the understanding hereof makes this man imagine, that if God's love in Christ, wherewith he loveth us, be eternal and fruitful, then must God necessarily always -- in or out of Christ, under the old or new covenant -- love all persons, elect or not elect, with the same love as to the effects and fruits of it; which is a wondrous profound apprehension. The reader, therefore, if he please, may take notice, that the love which I intend, and whereunto I ascribe those properties, is the especial love of God in Christ unto the elect. Concerning this himself says, that he loves them with an everlasting love, and therefore "draws them with loving-kindness," Jer. xxxi. 3; which love, I shall be bold to say, is eternal and fruitful. And hence, as he changeth not, whereon the sons of Jacob are not consumed, Mal. iii. 6, there being with him "neither variableness, nor shadow of turning," James i. 17; so accordingly he hath in this matter, by his promise and oath, declared the immutability of his counsel, Heb. vi. 17, 18, -- which seems to intimate that his love is unchangeable. And whereas this eternal love is in Christ Jesus as the way and means of making it certain in all its effects, and with respect unto its whole design, it is fruitful in all grace and glory, Eph. i. 3-5. And if he cannot understand how, notwithstanding all this, sin so entered into the world under the law of creation and the first covenant as to defeat in us all the benefits thereof, at present I cannot help him; for, as I am sure enough he would scorn to learn any thing of me, so I am not at leisure to put it to the trial.

His own account of the love of God succeeds. P. 211, "Not that I deny that the love of God is eternal, unchangeable, fruitful; that is, that God was always good, and always continues good, and manifesteth his love and goodness in such ways as are suitable to his nature, which is the fruitfulness of it: but then, the unchangeableness of God's love doth not consist in being always determined to the same object, but that he always loves for the same reason; that is, that he always loves true virtue and goodness, wherever he sees it, and never ceases to love any person till he ceases to be good: and then the immutability of his love is the reason why he loves no longer; for should he love a wicked man, the reason and nature of his love would change. And the fruitfulness of God's love, with respect to the methods of his grace and providence, doth not consist in procuring what he loves by an omnipotent and irresistible power; for then sin and death could never have entered into the world: but he governs and doth good to his creatures, in such ways as are most suitable to their natures. He governs reasonable creatures by principles of reason, as he doth the material world by the necessary laws of matter, and brute creatures by the instincts and propensities of nature."

This may pass for a system of his divinity, which how he will reconcile unto the doctrine of the church of England in her articles, she and he may do well to consider. But, whatever he means by the love of God always determined unto the same object, it were an easy thing to prove, beyond the reach of his contradiction, that persons are the objects of God's eternal love, as well as things and qualifications are of his approbation; or, that he loves some persons with an everlasting and unchangeable love, so as to preserve them from all ruining evils, and so as they may be always meet objects of his approving love, unto his glory: and whereas these things have been debated and disputed on all hands with much learning and diligence, our author is a very happy man if, with a few such loose expressions as these repeated, he thinks to determine all the controversies about election and effectual grace, with perseverance, on the Pelagian side. The hypothesis here maintained, that because God always and unchangeably approves of what is good in any, or of the obedience of his creatures, and disapproves or hates sin, condemning it in his law, [and] that therefore he may love the same person one day and hate him another, notwithstanding his pretences that he is constant unto the reason of his love, will inevitably fall into one of these conclusions:-- either, that God indeed never loveth any man, be he who he will; or, that he is changeable in his love, upon outward, external reasons, as we are: and let him choose which he will own. In the meantime, such a love of God towards believers as shall always effectually preserve them meet objects of his love and approbation, is not to be baffled by such trifling impertinencies. His next reflection is on the manner of God's operations in the communication of grace and holiness; which, he says, is "not by omnipotent and irresistible power," -- confirming his assertion by that consideration, that then sin and death could never have entered into the world; which is resolved into another sweet supposition, that God must needs act the same power of grace towards all men, at all times, under each covenant, whether he will or no. But this it is to be a happy disputant, -- all things succeed well with such persons which they undertake. And as to the manner of the operation of grace, how far grace itself may be said to be omnipotent, and in its operations irresistible, I have fully declared there; where he may oppose and refute it, if he have any mind thereunto. His present attempt against it in those words, that God "governs reasonable creatures by principles of reason," is so weak in this case, and impertinent, that it deserves no consideration; for all the operations of divine grace are suited unto the rational constitution of our beings, neither was ever man so wild as to fancy any of them such as are inconsistent with, or do offer force unto, the faculties of our souls in their operations. Yea, that which elevates, aids, and assists our rational faculties in their operations on and towards their proper objects, which is the work of efficacious grace, is the principal preservative of their power and liberty, and can be no way to their prejudice. And we do, moreover, acknowledge that those proposals which are made in the gospel unto our reason, are eminently suited to excite and prevail with it unto its proper use and exercise in compliance with them. Hence, although the habit of faith, or power of believing, be wrought in us by the Holy Ghost, yet the word of the gospel is the cause and means of all its acts, and the whole obedience which it produceth. But if by "governing reasonable creatures by principles of reason," he intends that God deals no otherwise by his grace with the souls of men, but only by proposing objective arguments and motives unto a compliance with his will, without internal aids and assistance of grace, it is a gross piece of Pelagianism, destructive of the gospel, sufficiently confuted elsewhere; and he may explain himself as he pleaseth.

His proceed is, to transcribe some other passages, taken out of my book here and there, in whose repetition he inserts some impertinent exceptions; but the design of the whole is to "state a controversy," as he calls it, between us and them, or those whom he calleth "they" and "we," whoever they be. And this, upon the occasion of my mentioning the fulness of grace, life, and righteousness that is in Christ, he doth in these words:-- P. 215, "They say that these are the personal graces of Christ as mediator, which are inherent in him, and must be derived from his person; we say, they signify the perfection and excellency of his religion, as being the most perfect and complete declaration of the will of God, and the most powerful method of the divine wisdom for the reforming of the world, as it prescribes the only righteousness which is acceptable to God, and directs us in the only way to life and immortality."

I shall not absolutely accept of the terms of this controversy, as to the state of it on our part, proposed by him; and yet I shall not much vary from them. We say, therefore, that "Jesus Christ being full of all grace, excellencies, and perfections, he communicates them unto us in that degree as is necessary for us, and in proportion unto his abundant charity and goodness towards us; and we Christians, as his body, or fellow-members of his human nature, receive grace and mercy, flowing from him to us." This state of the controversy on our side I suppose he will not refuse, nor the terms of it; but will own them to be ours, though he will not, it may be, allow some of them to be proper or convenient. And that he may know who his "they" are, who are at this end of the difference, he may be pleased to take notice that these words are the whole and entire paraphrase of Dr Hammond on John i. 16; the first testimony he undertakes to answer. And when this author hath replied to Mr Hooker, Dr Jackson, and him, and such other pillars of the church of England as concur with them, it will be time enough for me to consider how I shall defend myself against him. Or, if he will take the controversy on our part in terms more directly expressive of my mind, it is the person of Christ is the fountain of all grace to the church (as he well observes my judgment to be), and that from him all grace and mercy is derived unto us; and then I do maintain, that the "they" whom he opposeth, are not only the church of England, but the whole catholic church in all ages. Who the "we" are, on the other hand, who reject this assertion, and believe that all the testimonies concerning the fulness of grace in Christ, and the communication thereof unto us, do only declare the excellency of his religion, is not easy to be conjectured; -- for unless it be the people of Racow, I know not who are his associates. And let him but name three divines of any reputation in the church of England since the Reformation, who have given the least countenance unto his assertions, negative or positive, and I will acknowledge that he hath better associates in his profession than as yet I believe he hath. But that Jesus Christ himself, God and man in one person, the mediator between God and man, is not a fountain of grace and mercy to his church; that there is no real internal grace communicated by him, or derived from him unto his mystical body; that the fulness which is in him, or said to be in him, of grace and truth, of unsearchable riches of grace, etc., is nothing but the doctrine which he taught, as the most complete and perfect declaration of the will of God, -- are opinions that cannot be divulged, under pretence of authority, without the most pernicious scandal to the present church of England. And if this be the man's religion, that this is all the fulness we receive from Christ, -- "a perfect revelation of the divine will concerning the salvation of mankind; which contains so many excellent promises that it may well be called grace;' and prescribes such a plain and simple religion, so agreeable to the natural notions of good and evil, that it may well be called truth;'?" -- and complying with its doctrine, or yielding obedience unto its precepts and believing the promises which it gives, in our own strength, without any real aid, assistance, or communication of internal saving grace from the person of Jesus Christ, is our righteousness before God, whereon and for which we are justified, -- I know as well as he whence it came, and perhaps better than he whither it will go.

The remaining discourse of this chapter consisteth of two parts:-- First, An attempt to disprove any communication of real internal grace from the Lord Christ unto believers for their sanctification; Secondly, An endeavour to refute the imputation of his righteousness unto us for our justification. In the first he contends that all the fulness of grace and truth said to be in Christ consists either in the doctrine of the gospel or in the largeness of his church. In the latter, that faith in Christ is nothing but believing the gospel, and the authority of Christ who revealed it; and by yielding obedience thereunto, we are justified before God, on the account of an internal inherent righteousness in ourselves. Now, these are no small undertakings; the first of them being expressly contrary to the sense of the catholic church in all ages (for the Pelagians and the Socinians are by common agreement excluded from an interest therein); and the latter of them, contrary to the plain confessions of all the reformed churches, with the constant doctrine of this church of England: and therefore we may justly expect that they should be managed with much strength of argument, and evident demonstration. But the unhappiness of it is (I will not say his, but ours), that these are not things which our author as yet hath accustomed himself unto; and I cannot but say, that to my knowledge I never read a more weak, loose, and impertinent discourse, upon so weighty subjects, in my whole life before: he must have little to do, who can afford to spend his time in a particular examination of it, unless it be in the exposition of those places which are almost verbatim transcribed out of Schlichtingius. [373] Besides, for the first truth which he opposeth, I have confirmed it in a discourse which I suppose may be made public before this come to view, beyond what I expect any sober reply unto from him. Some texts of Scripture that mention a fulness in Christ he chooseth out, to manifest (to speak a word by the way) that indeed they do not intend any such fulness in Christ himself. And the first is John i. 16; the exposition whereof which he gives is that of Schlichtingius, who yet extends the import of the words beyond what he will allow. The enforcement which he gives unto his exposition, by comparing the 14th and 17th verses with the 16th, is both weak and contradictory of itself; for the words of the 14th verse are, "The Word was made flesh, and dwelt among us (and we beheld his glory, the glory as of the only begotten of the Father), full of grace and truth." It is evident beyond contradiction, that the expression, "full of grace and truth," is exegetical of his glory as the only begotten of the Father, which was the glory of his person, and not the doctrine of the gospel. And for the opposition that is made between the law given by Moses, and the grace and truth which came by Jesus Christ, I shall yet rather adhere to the sense of the ancient church, and the most eminent doctors of it, which, if he knows not it to be concerning the effectual communication of real, renewing, sanctifying grace by Jesus Christ, there are enow who can inform him; rather than that woeful gloss upon them, -- "His doctrine is called grace,' because accompanied with such excellent promises; and may well be called truth,' because so agreeable to the natural notions of good and evil," -- which is the confession of the Pelagian unbelief: but these things are not my present concernment. For the latter part of his discourse, in his opposition unto the imputation of the righteousness of Christ, as he doth not go about once to state or declare the sense wherein it is pleaded for, nor produceth any one of the arguments wherewith it is confirmed, and omitteth the mention of most of the particular testimonies which declare and establish it; so, as unto those few which he takes notice of, he expressly founds his answers unto them on that woeful subterfuge, that if they are capable of another interpretation, or having another sense given unto them, then nothing can be concluded from them to that purpose, -- by which the Socinians seek to shelter themselves from all the testimonies that are given to his Deity and satisfaction. But I have no concernment, as I said, either in his opinions or his way of reasoning; and do know that those who have so, need not desire a better cause nor an easier adversary to deal withal.

In his third section, p. 279, he enters upon his exceptions unto the union of believers unto Jesus Christ, and with great modesty, at the entrance of his discourse, tells us, first, "how these men," with whom he hath to do, "have fitted the person of Christ unto all the wants and necessities of the sinner;" which yet, if he denies God himself to have done, he is openly injurious unto his wisdom and grace. The very first promise that was given concerning him was, that he should save sinners from all their wants, evils, and miseries, that might, did, or could befall them by the entrance of sin. But thus it falls out, when men will be talking of what they do not understand. Again, he adds how he hath "explained the Scripture metaphors whereby the union between Christ and Christians is represented; but that these men, instead of explaining of those metaphors, turn all religion into an allegory." But what if one should now tell him, that his explanation of these metaphors is the most absurd and irrational, and argues the most fulsome ignorance of the mystery of the gospel, that can be imagined; and that, on the other side, those whom he traduceth do explain them unto the understanding and experience of all that believe, and that in a way suited and directed unto by the Holy Ghost himself, to farther their faith, obedience, and consolation? As far as I perceive, he would be at no small loss how to relieve himself under this censure. The first thing he begins withal, and wherein, in the first place, I fall under his displeasure, is about the conjugal relation between Christ and believers, which he treats of, p. 280. "As for example," saith he, "Christ is called a husband, the church his spouse; and now all the invitations of the gospel are Christ's wooing and making love to his spouse; -- and what other men call believing the gospel of Christ, whereby we devote ourselves to his service, these men call that consent and contract, which make up the marriage betwixt Christ and believers. Christ takes us for his spouse, and we take Christ for our husband, and that with all the solemnities of marriage, except the ring, which is left out as an antichristian ceremony; Christ saying thus, This is that we will consent unto, that I will be for thee, and thou shalt be for me, and not for another.' Christ gives himself to the soul with all his excellencies, righteousness, preciousness, graces, and eminencies, to be its saviour, head, and husband, -- to dwell with it in this holy relation; and the soul likes Christ for his excellencies, graces, suitableness, far above all other beloveds whatsoever, and accepts of Christ by the will for its husband, lord, and saviour. And thus the marriage is completed; and this is the day of Christ's espousals, and of the gladness of his heart. And now follow all mutual conjugal affections; which, on Christ's part, consist in delight, valuation, pity, compassion, bounty; on the saints' part, in delight, valuation, chastity, duty. But I have already corrected this fooling with Scripture metaphors and phrases."

It might, perhaps, not unbecome this author to be a little more sparing of his correction, unless his authority were more than it is, and his skill, also, in the management of it; for at present those whom he attempts upon are altogether insensible of any effects of his severity. But whereas he seems much at a loss how to evidence his own wisdom any other way than by calling them fools with whom he hath to do, it is sufficient to plead his excuse. But what is it that he is here so displeased at, as unfit for a man of his wisdom to bear withal, and therefore calls it "fooling?" Is it that there is a conjugal relation between Christ and the church? -- that he is the bridegroom and husband of the church, and that the church is his bride and spouse? -- that he becomes so unto it by a voluntarily, gracious act of his love, and that the church enters into that relation with him by their acceptance of him in that relation, and voluntarily giving up themselves unto him in faith, love, and obedience, suited thereunto? Is it that he loveth his church and cherisheth it as a husband, or that the church gives up itself in chaste and holy obedience unto him as her spouse? or is it my way and manner of expressing these things wherewith he is so provoked? If it be the latter, I desire he would, for his own satisfaction, take notice that I contemn his censures, and appeal to the judgment of those who have more understanding and experience in these things than, for aught I can discern by his writings, he hath yet attained unto. If it be the former, they are all of them so proved and confirmed from the Scripture in that very discourse which he excepteth against, as that he is not able to answer or reply one serious word thereunto. Indeed, to deny it, is to renounce the gospel and the catholic faith. It is, therefore, to no purpose for me here to go over again the nature of this relation between Christ and the church, -- wherein really and truly it doth consist; what it is the Scripture instructeth us in thereby; what is that love, care, and tenderness of Christ, which it would have us thence to learn; and what is our own duty with respect thereunto, together with the consolation thence arising: the whole of this work is already discharged in that discourse which these impertinent cavils are raised against, and that suitably to the sense of the church in all ages, and of all sound expositors of those very many places of Scripture which I have urged and insisted on to that purpose. Let him, if he please, a little lay aside the severity of his corrections and befooling of men, and answer any material passage in the whole discourse, if he be able; or discover any thing in it not agreeable to the analogy of faith, or the sense of the ancient church, if he can. And though he seem, both here and in some of his ensuing pages, to have a particular contempt of what is cited or improved out of the book of Canticles to this purpose; yet, if he either deny that that whole book doth mystically express the conjugal relation that is between Christ and his church, with their mutual affections and delight in each other, or that the places particularly insisted on by me are not duly applied unto their proper intention, I can, at least, confirm them both by the authority of such persons as whose antiquity and learning will exercise the utmost of his confidence in calling them fools for their pains.

From hence for sundry pages he is pleased to give me a little respite, whilst he diverts his severity unto another; unto whose will and choice what to do in it I shall leave his peculiar concern, as knowing full well how easy it is for him to vindicate what he hath written on this subject from his impertinent exceptions, if he please. In the meantime, if this author supposeth to add unto the reputation of his ingenuity and modesty by assaulting with a few pitiful cavils a book written with so much learning, judgment, and moderation, as that is which he excepts against, not daring in the meantime to contend with it in any thing of the expository or the argumentative part of it, but only to discover a malevolent desire to obstruct the use which it hath been of, and may yet farther be, to the church of God, -- I hope he will not find many rivals in such a design. For my part, I do suppose it more becoming Christian modesty and sobriety, where men have laboured according to their ability in the explication of the mysteries of Christian religion, and that with an avowed intention to promote holiness and gospel obedience, to accept of what they have attained, wherein we can come unto a compliance with them; than, passing by whatever we cannot but approve of, or are not able to disprove, to make it our business to cavil at such expressions as either we do not like, or hope to pervert and abuse to their disadvantage.

P. 296, he returns again to my discourse, and fiercely pursues it for sundry leaves, in such a manner as becomes him, and is usual with him. That part of my book which he deals withal, is from p. 176 [374] unto p. 187; and if any person of ingenuity and judgment will be pleased but to peruse it, and to compare it with this man's exceptions, I am secure it will need no farther vindication. But as it is represented in his cavilling way, it is impossible for any man either to conceive what is the true design of my discourse, or what the arguments wherewith what I assert is confirmed; which he doth most unduly pretend to give an account of: for he so chops, and changes, and alters at his pleasure, going backwards and forwards, and that from one thing to another, without any regard unto a scholastic or ingenuous debate of any thing that might be called a controversy, merely to seek out an appearance of advantage to vent his cavilling exceptions, as no judgment can rationally be made of his whole discourse, but only that he had a mind to have cast aspersions on mine, if he had known how. But such stuff as it is, we must now take the measure of it, and consider of what use it may be. And first he quotes those words from my book, "That Christ fulfilled all righteousness as he was mediator; and that whatever he did as mediator, he did it for them whose mediator he was, or in whose stead and for whose good he executed the office of a mediator before God: and hence it is that his complete and perfect obedience to the law is reckoned to us." He adds, "This is well said, if it were as well proved. And because this is a matter of great consequence, I shall first examine those reasons the doctor alleges to prove that Christ fulfilled all righteousness, as he was mediator, in their stead whose mediator he was."

These assertions are gathered up from several places in my discourse, though p. 182 [375] is cited for them all. And if any one find himself concerned in these things, I may demand of him the labour of their perusal in my book itself; and for those who shall refuse a compliance with so reasonable a request, I do not esteem myself obliged to tender them any farther satisfaction. However, I say again, that the Lord Christ fulfilled all righteousness as mediator; and that what he did as mediator, he did it for them whose mediator he was, or in whose stead and for whose good he executed the office of a mediator before God. He says, "It is well said, if it were as well proved." I say, it is all proved in the places where it is asserted, and that with such testimonies and arguments as he dares not touch upon. And although he pretends to examine the reasons that I allege to prove that Christ fulfilled all righteousness, as he was mediator, in their stead whose mediator he was, yet indeed he doth not do so. For, first, I say no such thing as he here feigns me to say, -- namely, that "Christ as mediator fulfilled all righteousness in our stead;" but only, that "Christ being the mediator, in our stead fulfilled all righteousness:" which is another thing, though perhaps he understands not the difference. Nor doth he so much as take notice of that testimony which is immediately subjoined unto the words he cites in the confirmation of them; but he will disprove this assertion or at least manifest that it cannot be proved. And this he enters upon, p. 297, "As for the first, we have some reason to require good proof of this, since the notion of a mediator includes no such thing. A mediator is one who interposeth between two differing parties, to accommodate the difference; but it was never heard of yet, that it was the office of a mediator to perform the terms and conditions himself. Moses was the mediator of the first covenant, Gal. iii. 19; and his office was to receive the law from God, to deliver it to the people, to command them to observe those rites, and sacrifices, and expiations which God had ordained: but he was not to fulfil the righteousness of the law for the whole congregation. Thus Christ is now the mediator of a better covenant; and his office required that he should preach the gospel, which contains the terms of peace and reconciliation between God and men; and since God would not enter into covenant with sinners without the intervention of a sacrifice, he dies too, as a sacrifice and propitiation for the sins of the world."

I yet suppose that he observed not the inconsistencies of this discourse, and therefore shall a little mind him of them, although I am no way concerned in it or them. For, first, He tells us, that "a mediator is one who interposeth between two differing parties, to accommodate the difference;" and then gives us an instance in Moses, who is called a mediator in receiving the law, but did therein no way interpose himself between differing parties, to reconcile them. Secondly, From the nature of the mediation of Moses, he would describe the nature of the mediation of Christ; which Socinian fiction I could direct him to a sufficient confutation of, but that, thirdly, He rejects it himself in his next words, -- that Christ as a mediator was to die as a sacrifice and propitiation for the sins of the world; which renders his mediation utterly of another kind and nature than that of Moses. The mistake of this discourse is, that he supposeth that men do argue from the general nature of the office of a mediator the work of mediation in this matter; when that which they do intend hence to prove, and what he intends to oppose, is the special nature of the mediatory office and work of Christ; which is peculiar, and hath sundry things essentially belonging unto it, that belong not unto any other kind of mediation whatever; whereof himself gives one signal instance.

In his ensuing pages he wonderfully perplexeth himself in gathering up sayings, backward and forward in my discourse, to make some advantage to his purpose, and hopes that he is arrived at no less success than a discovery of I know not what contradictions in what I have asserted. As I said before, so I say again, that I refer the determination and judgment of this whole matter unto any one who will but once read over the discourse excepted against. But for his part, I greatly pity him, as really supposing him at a loss in the sense of what is yet plainly delivered; and I had rather continue to think so, than to be relieved by supposing him guilty of such gross prevarications as he must be if he understands what he treats about. Plainly, I have showed that there was an especial law of mediation, which Christ was subject unto, at the commandment of the Father: that he should be incarnate; that he should be the king, priest, and prophet of his church; that he should bear our iniquities, make his soul an offering for sin, and give his life a ransom for many, were the principal parts of this law. The whole of it I have lately explained, in my exercitations unto the second part of the Exposition of the Epistle to the Hebrews; whereon, if he please, he may exercise and try his skill in a way of opposition. This law our Lord Jesus Christ did not yield obedience to in our stead, as though we had been obliged originally unto the duties of it, which we neither were nor could be; although what he suffered penally in any of them was in our stead; without which consideration he could not have righteously suffered in any kind. And the following trivial exception of this author, about the obligation on us to lay down our lives for the brethren, is meet for him to put in, seeing we are not obliged so to die for any one as Christ died for us. Was Paul crucified for you? But, secondly, Christ our mediator, and as mediator, was obliged unto all that obedience unto the moral, and all other laws of God, that the church was obliged unto; and that which I have asserted hereon is, that the effects of the former obedience of Christ are communicated unto us, but the latter obedience itself is imputed unto us; and [I] have proved it by those arguments which this man doth not touch upon. All this is more fully, clearly, and plainly declared in the discourse itself; and I have only represented so much of it here again, that it might be evident unto all how frivolous are his exceptions. It is therefore to no purpose for me to transcribe again the quotations out of my book which he fills up his pages with, seeing it is but little in them which he excepteth against; and whoever pleaseth, may consult them at large in the places from whence they are taken; or, because it is not easy to find them out singly, they are so picked up and down, backwards and forwards, curtailed and added to at pleasure, any one may, in a very little space of time, read over the whole unto his full satisfaction. I shall, therefore, only consider his exceptions, and haste unto an end of this fruitless trouble, wherein I am most unwillingly engaged by this man's unsuspected disingenuity and ignorance.

After the citation of some passages, he adds, p. 301, "This, methinks, is very strange, that what he did as mediator is not imputed unto us; but what he did, not as our mediator, but as a man subject to the law, that is imputed to us, and reckoned as if we had done it, by reason of his being our mediator. And it is as strange to the full, that Christ should do whatever was required of us by virtue of any law, when he was neither husband, nor wife, nor father, merchant nor tradesman, seaman nor soldier, captain nor lieutenant, much less a temporal prince and monarch. And how he should discharge the duties of these relations for us, which are required of us by certain laws, when he never was in any of these relations, and could not possibly be in all, is an argument which may exercise the subtilty of schoolmen, and to them I leave it."

It were greatly to be desired that he would be a little more heedful, and with attention read the writings of other men, that he might understand them before he comes to make such a bluster in his opposition to them: for I had told him plainly, that though there was a peculiar law of mediation, whose acts and duties we had no obligation unto, yet the Lord Christ, even as mediator, was obliged unto, and did personally perform, all the duties of obedience unto the law of God whereunto we were subject and obliged, p. 181, [376] sec. 14. And it is strange to apprehend how he came to imagine that I said he did it not as our mediator, but as a private man. That which, possibly, might cast his thoughts into this disorder was, that he knew not that Christ was made a private man as mediator; which yet the Scripture is sufficiently express in. [As] for the following objections, that the Lord Christ was neither "husband nor wife, father nor tradesman," etc. (wherein yet possibly he is out in his account), I have frequently smiled at it when I have met with it in the Socinians, who are perking with it at every turn; but here it ought to be admired. But yet, without troubling those bugbears the schoolmen, he may be pleased to take notice, that the grace of duty and obedience in all relations is the same, -- the relations administering only an external occasion unto its peculiar exercise; and what our Lord Jesus Christ did in the fulfilling of all righteousness in the circumstances and relations wherein he stood, may be imputed to us for our righteousness in all our relations, every act of duty and sin in them respecting the same law and principle. And hereon all his following exceptions for sundry pages, wherein he seems much to have pleased himself, do fall to nothing, as being resolved into his own mistakes, if he doth not prevaricate against his science and conscience; for the sum of them all he gives us in these words, p. 204, "That Christ did those things as mediator which did not belong to the laws of his mediation;" which, in what sense he did so, is fully explained in my discourse. And I am apt to guess, that either he is deceived or doth design to deceive, in expressing it by the "laws of his mediation;" which may comprise all the laws which as mediator he was subject unto. And so it is most true, that he did nothing as mediator but what belonged unto the laws of his mediation; but most false, that I have affirmed that he did: for I did distinguish between that peculiar law which required the public acts of his mediation, and those other laws which, as mediator, he was made subject unto. And if he neither doth nor will understand these things when he is told them, and they are proved unto him beyond what he can contradict, I know no reason why I should trouble myself with one that contends with his own mormos, though he never so lewdly or loudly call my name upon them. And whereas I know myself sufficiently subject unto mistakes and slips, so when I actually fall into them, as I shall not desire this man's forgiveness, but leave him to exercise the utmost of his severity, so I despise his ridiculous attempts to represent contradictions in my discourse, p. 306; all pretences whereunto are taken from his own ignorance, or feigned in his imagination. Of the like nature are all his ensuing cavils. I desire no more of any reader, but to peruse the places in my discourse which he carps at, and if he be a person of ordinary understanding in these things, I declare that I will stand to his censure and judgment, without giving him the least farther intimation of the sense and intendment of what I have written, or vindication of its truth. Thus, whereas I had plainly declared that the way whereby the Lord Christ, in his own person, became obnoxious and subject unto the law of creation, was by his own voluntary antecedent choice, otherwise than it is with those who are inevitably subject unto it by natural generation under it; as also, that the hypostatical union, in the first instant whereof the human nature was fitted for glory, might have exempted him from the obligation of any outward law whatever, -- whence it appears that his consequential obedience, though necessary to himself, when he had submitted himself unto the law (as, "Lo, I come to do thy will, O God"), was designedly for us; -- he miserably perplexeth himself to abuse his credulous readers with an apprehension that I had talked, like himself, at such a rate of nonsense as any one in his wits must needs despise. The meaning and sum of my discourse he would have to be this, p. 308, "That Christ had not been bound to live like a man, had he not been a man," with I know not what futilous cavils of the like nature; when all that I insisted on was the reason why Christ would be a man, and live like a man; which was, that we might receive the benefit and profit of his obedience, as he was our mediator. So in the close of the same wise harangue, from my saying, "That the Lord Christ, by virtue of the hypostatical union, might be exempted, as it were, and lifted above the law, which yet he willingly submitted unto, and in the same instant wherein he was made of a woman, was made also under the law, whence obedience unto it became necessary unto him," -- the man feigns I know not what contradictions in his fancy, whereof there is not the least appearance in the words unto any one who understands the matter expressed in them. And that the assumption of the human nature into union with the Son of God, with submission unto the law thereon to be performed in that nature, are distinct parts of the humiliation of Christ, I shall prove when more serious occasion is administered unto me.

In like manner he proceeds to put in his exceptions unto what I discoursed about the laws that an innocent man is liable unto. For I said, that God never gave any other law to an innocent person, but only the law of his creation, with such symbolical precepts as might be instances of his obedience thereunto. Something he would find fault with, but knows not well what; and therefore turmoils himself to give countenance unto a putid cavil. He tells us, "That it is a great favour that I acknowledge, p. 310, that God might add what symbols he pleased unto the law of creation." But the childishness of these impertinencies is shameful. To whom, I pray, is it a favour, or what doth the man intend by such a senseless scoff? Is there any word in my whole discourse intimating that God might not in a state of innocence give what positive laws he pleased unto innocent persons, as means and ways to express that obedience which they owed into the law of creation? The task wherein I am engaged is so fruitless, so barren of any good use, in contending with such impertinent effects of malice and ignorance, that I am weary of every word I am forced to add in the pursuit of it; but he will yet have it, that "an innocent person, such as Christ was absolutely, may be obliged for his own sake to the observation of such laws and institutions as were introduced by the occasion of sin, and respected all of them the personal sins of them that were obliged by them;" which if he can believe, he is at liberty, for me, to persuade as many as he can to be of his mind, whilst I may be left unto my own liberty and choice, yea, to the necessity of my mind, in not believing contradictions. And for what he adds, that I "know those who conceit themselves above all forms of external worship," I must say to him that at present personally I know none that do so, but fear that some such there are; as also others who, despising not only the ways of external worship appointed by God himself, but also the laws of internal faith and grace, do satisfy themselves in a customary observance of forms of worship of their own devising.

In his next attempt he had been singular, and had spoken something which had looked like an answer to an argument, had he well laid the foundation of his procedure: for that position which he designeth the confutation of is thus laid down by him as mine, "There can be no reason assigned of Christ's obedience unto the law, but only this, that he did it in our stead;" whereas my words are, "That the end of the active obedience of Christ cannot be assigned to be that he might be fit for his death and oblation." And hereon what is afterward said against this particular end, he interprets as spoken against all other ends whatever, instancing in such as are every way consistent with the imputation of his obedience unto us; which could not be, had the only end of it been for himself, to fit him for his death and oblation. And this wilful mistake is sufficient to give occasion to combat his own imaginations for two or three pages together. P. 314, he pretends unto the recital of an argument of mine for the imputation of the righteousness of Christ, with the like pretence of attempting an answer unto it; but his design is not to manage any controversy with me, or against me, but, as he phraseth it, to expose my mistakes. I cannot, therefore, justly expect from him so much as common honesty will require, in case the real handling of a controversy in religion had been intended. But his way of procedure, so far as I know and understand, may be best suited unto his design. In this place, he doth neither fairly nor truly report my words, nor take the least notice of the confirmation of my argument by the removal of objections whereunto it seemed liable, nor of the reasons and testimonies whereby it is farther proved; but, taking out of my discourse what expressions he pleaseth, putting them together with the same rule, he thinks he hath sufficiently exposed my mistakes, -- the thing he aimed at. I have no more concernment in this matter but to refer both him and the reader to the places in my discourse reflected on; -- him, truly to report and answer my arguments, if he be able; and the reader, to judge as he pleaseth between us. And I would for this once desire of him, that if he indeed be concerned in these things, he would peruse my discourse here raved at, and determine in his own mind whether I confidently affirm what is in dispute, (that is, what I had then in dispute; for who could divine so long ago what a doughty disputant this author would by this time sprout up into?) and that this goes for an argument, or that he impudently affirms me so to do, contrary unto his science and conscience, if he had not quite "pored out his eyes" before he came to the end of a page or two in my book. And for the state of the question here proposed by him, let none expect that upon so slight an occasion I shall divert unto the discussion of it. When this author, or any of his consorts in design, shall soberly and candidly, without scoffing or railing, in a way of argument or reasoning, becoming divines and men of learning, answer any of those many writings which are extant against that Socinian justification which he here approves and contends for, or those written by the divines of the church of England on the same subject, in the proof of what he denies, and confutation of what he affirms, they may deserve to be taken notice of in the same rank and order with those with whom they associate themselves. And yet I will not say but that these cavilling exceptions, giving a sufficient intimation of what some men would be at, if ability and opportunity did occur, may give occasion also unto a renewed vindication of the truths opposed by them, in a way suited unto the use and edification of the church, in due time and season.

From p. 185 [377] of my book he retires, upon his new triumph, unto p. 176,[378] as hoping to hook something from thence that might contribute unto the furtherance of his ingenious design, although my discourse in that place have no concernment in what he treateth about. But let him be heard to what purpose he pleaseth. Thus, therefore, he proceeds, p. 315, "The doctor makes a great flourish with some Scripture phrases, that there is almost nothing that Christ hath done but what we are said to do it with him; we are crucified with him, we are dead with him, buried with him, quickened together with him. In the actings of Christ there is, by virtue of the compact between him, as mediator, and the Father, such an assured foundation laid, that by communication of the fruit of these actings unto those in whose stead he performed them, they are said, in the participation of these fruits, to have done the same things with him. But he is quite out in the reason of these expressions, which is not that we are accounted to do the same things which Christ did, -- for the things here mentioned belong to the peculiar office of his mediation, which he told us before were not reckoned as done by us, -- but because we do some things like them. Our dying to sin is a conformity to the death of Christ; and our walking in newness of life is our conformity to his resurrection: and the consideration of the death and resurrection of Christ is very powerful to engage us to die to sin, and to rise unto a new life. And this is the true reason of these phrases."

Any man may perceive, from what he is pleased here himself to report of my words, that I was not treating about the imputation of the righteousness of Christ, which he is now inveighing against; and it will be much more evident unto every one that shall cast an eye on that discourse. But the design of this confused rambling I have been forced now frequently to give an account of, and shall, if it be possible, trouble the reader with it no more. The present difference between us, which he was ambitious to represent, is only this, that whereas it seems he will allow that those expressions of our being "crucified with Christ, dead with him, buried with him, quickened with him," do intend nothing but only our doing of something like unto that which Christ did; I do add, moreover, that we do those things by the virtue and efficacy of the grace which is communicated unto us from what the Lord Christ so did and acted for us, as the mediator of the new covenant, whereby alone we partake of their power, communicate in their virtue, and are conformed unto him as our head; wherein I know I have, as the testimony of the Scripture, so the judgment of the catholic church of Christ on my side, and am very little concerned in the censure of this person, that I am "quite out in the reason of these expressions."

For what remains of his discourse, so far as I am concerned in it, it is made up of such expositions of some texts of Scripture as issue, for the most part, in a direct contradiction to the text itself, or some express passages of the context. So doth that of Gal. iv. 4, 5, which he first undertakes to speak unto, giving us nothing but what was first invented by Crellius, in his book against Grotius, and is almost translated verbatim out of the comment of Schlichtingius upon the place; the remainder of them corruptly Socinianizing against the sense of the church of God. Hereunto are added such pitiful mistakes, with reflections on me for distinguishing between obeying and suffering (which conceit he most profoundly disproves by showing that one may obey in suffering, and that Christ did so, against him who hath written more about the obedience of Christ in dying, or laying down his life for us, than he seems to have read on the same subject, as also concerning the ends and uses of his death; which I challenge him and all his companions to answer and disprove, if they can), as I cannot satisfy myself in the farther consideration of; no, not with that speed and haste of writing now used: which nothing could give countenance unto but the meanness of the occasion, and unprofitableness of the argument in hand. Wherefore, this being the manner of the man, I am not able to give an account unto myself or the reader of the misspense of more time in the review of such impertinencies. I shall add a few things, and conclude.

First. I desire to know whether this author will abide by what he asserts, as his own judgment, in opposition unto what he puts in his exception against in my discourse:-- P. 320, "All the influence which the sacrifice of Christ's death, and the righteousness of his life have, that I can find in the Scripture, is, that to this we owe the covenant of grace;" that is, as he afterward explains himself, "That God would for the sake of Christ enter into a new covenant with mankind, wherein he promiseth pardon of sin and eternal life to them that believe and obey the gospel." I leave him herein to his second thoughts; for as he hath now expressed himself, there is no reconciliation of his assertion to common sense, or the fundamental principles of Christian religion. That God entered into the new covenant originally only for the sake of those things whereby that covenant was ratified and confirmed, and that Christ was so the mediator of the new covenant, that he died not for the redemption of transgressions under the first covenant, whereby the whole consideration of his satisfaction and of redemption, properly so called, is excluded; that there is no consideration to be had of his purchase of the inheritance of grace and glory, with many other things of the same importance; and that the gospel, or the doctrine of the gospel, is the new covenant (which is only a perspicuous declaration of it), are things that may become these new sons of the church of England, which the elder church would not have borne withal.

Secondly. The reader may take notice, that in some other discourses of mine now [379] published, which were all of them finished before I had the advantage to peruse the friendly and judicious animadversions of this author, he will find most of the matters which he excepts against both cleared, proved, and vindicated, and that those principles which he directs his opposition against are so established, as that I neither expect nor fear any such assault upon them, from this sort of men, as becometh a serious debate on things of this nature.

Thirdly. That I have confined myself, in the consideration of this author's discourse, unto what I was personally concerned in, without looking at or accepting of the advantages which offered themselves of reflecting upon him, either as unto the matter of his discourse, or unto the manner of expressing himself in its delivery. For, besides that I have no mind, and that for many reasons, to enter voluntarily into any contest with this man, the mistakes which he hath apparently been led into by ignorance or prejudice, his fulsome errors against the Scripture, the doctrine of the ancient church, and the church of England, are so multiplied and scattered throughout the whole, that a discovery and confutation of them will scarce deserve the expense of time that must be wasted therein, until a more plausible countenance or strenuous defence be given unto them. And as for what he aimeth at, I know well enough where to find the whole of it, handled with more civility and appearance of reason; and therefore, when I am free, or resolved to treat concerning them, I shall do so in the consideration of what is taught by his authors and masters, and not of what he hath borrowed from them.

Fourthly. I shall assure the reader, that as a thousand of such trifling cavillers or revilers, as I have had some to deal withal, shall neither discourage nor hinder me in the remaining service which I may have yet to fulfil, in the patience of God, for the church of Christ and truth of the gospel; nor, it may be, occasion me any more to divert in the least unto the consideration of what they whisper or clamour, unless they are able to betake themselves unto a more sober and Christian way of handling things in controversy: so if they will not, or dare not, forego this supposed advantage of reproaching the doctrine of nonconformists (under which pretence they openly, and as yet securely, scorn and deride them, when they are all of them the avowed doctrines of all the reformed churches, and of this of England in particular); and if they think it not meet to oppose themselves and endeavours unto those writings which have been composed and published professedly in the declaration and defence of the truth scoffed at and impugned by them, but choose rather to exercise their skill and anger on passages rent out of practical discourses, accommodated in the manner of their delivery unto the capacity of the community of believers, as it is fit they should be; I do suppose that, at one time or other, from one hand or another, they may meet with some such discourse, concerning justification and the imputation of the righteousness of Christ, as may give them occasion to be quiet, or to exercise the best of their skill and industry in an opposition unto it, -- as many such there are already extant, which they wisely take no notice of, but only rave against occasional passages in discourses of another nature, -- unless they resolve on no occasion to forego the shelter they have betaken themselves unto.

Footnotes:

410

362. [Brought over, borrowed.]

363. Od. z. 187.

364. Od. o. 401.

365. Owen, in all probability, alludes to his "Diatriba de Justitiâ Divinâ." See vol. x. of his Works. -- Ed.

366. In the present edition of Owen's Works, the passage will be found in page 180 of this volume.

367. Gen. xviii. 32.

368. 2 Cor. vii. 1.

369. Rom. vi. 23; Heb. xi. 6; Gen. xvii. 1; Ps. xix. 11, lviii. 11; Matt. v. 12, x. 41; Rom. iv. 4; Col. ii. 18, iii. 24; Heb. x. 35, xi. 26; 2 Pet. ii. 13.

370. Page 48 of this volume.

371. Proceeding from the divine and human natures in personal union. -- Ed.

372. Page 59 of the present volume.

373. Jonas Schlichtingius was a Socinian author. He wrote "A Confession of Christian Faith, published in the name of the Churches which in Poland acknowledge one God, and his only begotten Son Jesus Christ, and the Holy Spirit." It appeared in the year 1642. -- Ed.

374. From page 154 to page 164 of this volume.

375. Pages 162, 163 of this volume.

376. Page 159 of this volume.

377. Page 162 of this volume.

378. Page 154 of this volume.

379. In the course of the same year in which this reply to Sherlock appeared, Owen's "Discourse on the Holy Spirit," and the second volume of his "Exposition of the Epistle to the Hebrews" were published. There is much in both of them on the points at issue between Owen and Sherlock. -- Ed.